The Tomes of Delphi™ Algorithms and Data Structures

Julian Bucknall

Wordware Publishing, Inc.

Library of Congress Cataloging-in-Publication Data

Bucknall, Julian
Tomes of Delphi: algorithms and data structures / by Julian Bucknall.
p. cm.
Includes bibliographical references and index.
ISBN 1-55622-736-1 (pbk. : alk. paper)
1. Computer software—Development. 2. Delphi (Computer file). 3. Computer algorithms. 4. Data structures (Computer science) I. Title.

QA76.76.D47 .B825 2001 2001033258
005.1--dc21 CIP

2320 Los Rios Boulevard
Plano, Texas 75074

Printed in the United States of America

ISBN 1-55622-736-1
10 9 8 7 6 5 4 3 2 1
0105

All inquiries for volume purchases of this book should be addressed to Wordware Publishing, Inc., at the above address. Telephone inquiries may be made by calling:

(972) 423-0090

For Donna and the Greek cats

Contents

Introduction

You've just picked this book up in the bookshop, or you've bought it, taken it home and opened it, and now you're wondering...

Why a Book on Delphi Algorithms?

Although there are numerous books on algorithms in the bookstores, few of them go beyond the standard Computer Science 101 course to approach algorithms from a practical perspective. The code that is shown in the book is to illustrate the algorithm in question, and generally no consideration is given to real-life, drop-in-and-use application of the technique being discussed. Even worse, from the viewpoint of the commercial programmer, many are textbooks to be used in a college or university course and hence some of the more interesting topics are left as exercises for the reader, with little or no answers.

Of course, the vast majority of them don't use Delphi, Kylix, or Pascal. Some use pseudocode, some C, some C++, some the language *du jour*; and the most celebrated and referenced algorithms book uses an assembly language that doesn't even exist (the MIX assembly language in *The Art of Computer Programming* [11,12,13]—see the references section). Indeed, those books that do have the word "practical" in their titles are for C, C++, or Java. Is that such a problem? After all, an algorithm is an algorithm is an algorithm; surely, it doesn't matter how it's demonstrated, right? Why bother buying and reading one based on Delphi?

Delphi is, I contend, unique amongst the languages and environments used in application development today. Firstly, like Visual Basic, Delphi is an environment for developing applications rapidly, for either 16-bit or 32-bit Windows, or, using Kylix, for Linux. With dexterous use of the mouse, components rain on forms like rice at a wedding. Many double-clicks later, together with a little typing of code, the components are wedded together, intricately and intimately, with event handlers, hopefully producing a halfway decent-looking application.

Secondly, like C++, Delphi can get close to the metal, easily accessing the various operating system APIs. Sometimes, Borland produces units to access APIs and sells them with Delphi itself; sometimes, programmers have to pore over C header files in an effort to translate them into Delphi (witness the Jedi project at *http://www.delphi-jedi.org*). In either case, Delphi can do the job and manipulate the OS subsystems to its own advantage.

Delphi programmers do tend to split themselves into two camps: applications programmers and systems programmers. Sometimes you'll find programmers who can do both jobs. The link between the two camps that both sets of programmers must come into contact with and be aware of is the world of algorithms. If you program for any length of time, you'll come to the point where you absolutely need to code a binary search. Of course, before you reach that point, you'll need a sort routine to get the data in some kind of order for the binary search to work properly. Eventually, you might start using a profiler, identify a problem bottleneck in TStringList, and wonder what other data structure could do the job more efficiently.

Algorithms are the lifeblood of the work we do as programmers. Beginner programmers are often afraid of formal algorithms; I mean, until you are used to it, even the word itself can seem hard to spell! But consider this: a program can be defined as an algorithm for getting information out of the user and producing some kind of output for her.

The standard algorithms have been developed and refined by computer scientists for use in the programming trenches by the likes of you and me. Mastering the basic algorithms gives you a handle on your craft *and* on the language you use. For example, if you know about hash tables, their strengths and weaknesses, what they are used for and why, and have an implementation you could use at a moment's notice, then you will look at the design of the subsystem or application you're currently working on in a new light, and identify places where you could profitably use one. If sorts hold no terrors for you, you understand how they work, and you know when to use a selection sort versus a quicksort, then you'll be more likely to code one in your application, rather than try and twist a standard Delphi component to your needs (for example, a modern horror story: I remember hearing about someone who used a hidden TListBox component, adding a bunch of strings, and then setting the Sorted property to true to get them in order).

"OK," I hear you say, "writing about algorithms is fine, but why bother with Delphi or Kylix?"

By the way, let's set a convention early on; otherwise I shall be writing the phrase "Delphi or Kylix" an awful lot. When I say "Delphi," I really mean either Delphi or Kylix. Kylix was, after all, known for much of its pre-release life as "Delphi" for Linux. In this book, then, "Delphi" means either Delphi for Windows or Kylix for Linux.

So, why Delphi? Well, two reasons: the Object Pascal language and the operating system. Delphi's language has several constructs that are not available in other languages, constructs that make encapsulating efficient algorithms and data structures easier and more natural. Things like properties, for example. Exceptions for when unforeseen errors occur. Although it is perfectly possible to code standard algorithms in Delphi *without* using these Delphi-specific language constructs, it is my contention that we miss out on the beauty and efficiency of the language if we do. We miss out on the ability to learn about the ins and outs of the language. In this book, we shall deliberately be using the breadth of the Object Pascal language in Delphi—I'm not concerned that Java programmers who pick up this book may have difficulty translating the code. The cover says Delphi, and Delphi it will be.

And the next thing to consider is that algorithms, as traditionally taught, are generic, at least as far as CPUs and operating systems are concerned. They can certainly be optimized for the Windows environment, or souped up for Linux. They can be made more efficient for the various varieties of Pentium processor we use, with the different types of memory caches we have, with the virtual memory subsystem in the OS, and so on. This book pays particular attention to these efficiency gains. We won't, however, go as far as coding everything in Assembly language, optimized for the pipelined architecture of modern processors—I have to draw the line somewhere!

So, all in all, the Delphi community does have need for an algorithms book, and one geared for their particular language, operating system, and processor. This is such a book. It was not translated from another book for another language; it was written from scratch by an author who works with Delphi every day of his life, someone who writes library software for a living and knows about the intricacies of developing commercial ready-to-run routines, classes, and tools.

What Should I Know?

This book does not attempt to teach you Delphi programming. You will need to know the basics of programming in Delphi: creating new projects, how to write code, compiling, debugging, and so on. I warn you now: there are no components in this book. You must be familiar with classes, procedure and method references, untyped pointers, the ubiquitous TList, and streams as encapsulated by Delphi's TStream family. You must have some understanding of object-oriented concepts such as encapsulation, inheritance, polymorphism, and delegation. The object model in Delphi shouldn't scare you!

Having said that, a lot of the concepts described in this book are simple in the extreme. A beginner programmer should find much in the book to teach him or her the basics of standard algorithms and data structures. Indeed, looking at the code should teach such a programmer many tips and tricks of the advanced programmer. The more advanced structures can be left for a rainy day, or when you think you might need them.

So, essentially, you need to have been programming in Delphi for a while. Every now and then you need some kind of data structure beyond what TList and its family can give you, but you're not sure what's available, or even how to use it if you found one. Or, you want a simple sort routine, but the only reference book you can find has code written in C++, and to be honest you'd rather watch paint dry than translate it. Or, you want to read an algorithms book where performance and efficiency are just as prominent as the description of the algorithm. This book is for you.

Which Delphi Do I Need?

Are you ready for this? Any version. With the exception of the section discussing dynamic arrays using Delphi 4 or above and Kylix in Chapter 2, and parts of Chapter 12, and little pieces here and there, the code will compile and run with any version of Delphi. Apart from the small amount of the version-specific code I have just mentioned, I have tested all code in this book with all versions of Delphi and with Kylix.

You can therefore assume that all code printed in this book will work with every version of Delphi. Some code listings are version-specific though, and have been so noted.

What Will I Find, and Where?

This book is divided into 12 chapters and a reference section.

Chapter 1 lays out some ground rules. It starts off by discussing performance. We'll look at measurement of the efficiency of algorithms, starting out with the big-Oh notation, continuing with timing of the actual run time of algorithms, and finishing with the use of profilers. We shall discuss data representation efficiency in regard to modern processors and operating systems, especially memory caches, paging, and virtual memory. After that, the chapter will talk about testing and debugging, topics that tend to be glossed over in many books, but that are, in fact, essential to all programmers.

Chapter 2 covers arrays. We'll look at the standard language support for arrays, including dynamic arrays; we'll discuss the TList class; and we'll create a class that encapsulates an array of records. Another specialized array is the string, so we'll take a look at that too.

Chapter 3 introduces linked lists, both the singly and doubly linked varieties. We'll see how to create stacks and queues by implementing them with both singly linked lists and arrays.

Chapter 4 talks about searching algorithms, especially the sequential and the binary search algorithms. We'll see how binary search helps us to insert items into a sorted array or linked list.

Chapter 5 covers sorting algorithms. We will look at various types of sorting methods: bubble, shaker, selection, insertion, Shell sort, quicksort, and merge sort. We'll also sort arrays and linked lists.

Chapter 6 discusses algorithms that create or require random numbers. We'll see pseudorandom number generators (PRNGs) and show a remarkable sorted data structure called a skip list, which uses a PRNG in order to help balance the structure.

Chapter 7 considers hashing and hash tables, why they're used, and what benefits and drawbacks they have. Several standard hashing algorithms are introduced. One problem that occurs with hash tables is collisions; we shall see how to resolve this by using a couple of types of probing and also by chaining.

Chapter 8 presents binary trees, a very important data structure in wide general use. We'll look at how to build and maintain a binary tree and how to traverse the nodes in the tree. We'll also address its unbalanced trees created by inserting data in sorted order. A couple of balancing algorithms will be shown: splay trees and red-black trees.

Chapter 9 deals with priority queues and, in doing so, shows us the heap structure. We'll consider the important heap operations, bubble up and trickle down, and look at how the heap structure gives us a sort algorithm for free: the heapsort.

Chapter 10 provides information about state machines and how they can be used to solve a certain class of problems. After some introductory examples with finite deterministic state machines, the chapter considers regular expressions, how to parse them and compile them to a finite non-deterministic state machine, and then apply the state machine to accept or reject strings.

Chapter 11 squeezes in some data compression techniques. Algorithms such as Shannon-Fano, Huffman, Splay, and LZ77 will be shown.

Chapter 12 includes a variety of advanced topics that may whet your appetite for researching algorithms and structures. Of course, they still will be useful to your programming requirements.

Finally, there is a reference section listing references to help you find out more about the algorithms described in this book; these references not only include other algorithms books but also academic papers and articles.

What Are the Typographical Conventions?

Normal text is written in this font, at this size. Normal text is used for discussions, descriptions, and diversions.

```
Code listings are written in this font, at this size.
```

Emphasized words or phrases, new words about to be defined, and variables will appear in *italic*.

Dotted throughout the text are World Wide Web URLs and e-mail addresses which are italicized and underlined, like this: *http://www.boyet.com/dads*.

> Every now and then there will be a note like this. It's designed to bring out some important point in the narrative, a warning, or a caution.

What Are These Bizarre $IFDEFs in the Code?

The code for this book has been written, with certain noted exceptions, to compile with Delphi 1, 2, 3, 4, 5, and 6, as well as with Kylix 1. (Later compilers will be supported as and when they come out; please see *http://www.boyet.com/dads* for the latest information.) Even with my best efforts, there are sometimes going to be differences in my code between the different versions of Delphi and Kylix.

The answer is, of course, to $IFDEF the code, to have certain blocks compile with certain compilers but not others. Borland supplied us with the official WINDOWS, WIN32, and LINUX compiler defines for the platform, and the VERnnn compiler defined for the compiler version.

To solve this problem, every source file for this book has an include at the top:

```
{$I TDDefine.inc}
```

This include file defines human-legible compiler defines for the various compilers. Here's the list:

DelphiN	define for a particular Delphi version, N = 1,2,3,4,5,6
DelphiNPlus	define for a particular Delphi version or later, N = 1,2,3,4,5,6
KylixN	define for a particular Kylix version, N = 1
KylixNPlus	define for a particular Kylix version or later, N = 1
HasAssert	define if compiler supports Assert

I also make the assumption that every compiler except Delphi 1 has support for long strings.

What about Bugs?

This book is a book of human endeavor, written, checked, and edited by human beings. To quote Alexander Pope in *An Essay on Criticism*, "To err is human, to forgive, divine." This book will contain misstatements of facts, grammatical errors, spelling mistakes, bugs, whatever, no matter how hard I try going over it with *Fowler's Modern English Usage*, a magnifying glass, and a fine-toothed comb. For a technical book like this, which presents hard facts permanently printed on paper, this could be unforgivable.

Hence, I shall be maintaining an errata list on my Web site, together with any bug fixes to the code. Also on the site you'll find other articles that go into greater depth on certain topics than this book. You can always find the latest errata and fixes at *http://www.boyet.com/dads*. If you do find an error, I would be grateful if you would send me the details by e-mail to *julianb@boyet.com*. I can then fix it and update the Web site.

Acknowledgments

There are several people without whom this book would never have been completed. I'd like to present them in what might be termed historical order, the order of their influence on me.

The first two are a couple of gentlemen I've never met or spoken to, and yet who managed to open my eyes to and kindle my enthusiasm for the world of algorithms. If they hadn't, who knows where I might be now and what I might be doing. I'm speaking of Donald Knuth (*http://www-cs-staff.stanford.edu/~knuth/*) and Robert Sedgewick (*http://www.cs.princeton.edu/~rs/*). In fact, it was the latter's *Algorithms* [20] that started me off, it being the first algorithms book I ever bought, back when I was just getting into Turbo Pascal. Donald Knuth needs no real introduction. His masterly *The Art of Computer Programming* [11,12,13] remains at the top of the algorithms tree; I first used it at Kings College, University of London while working toward my B.Sc. Mathematics degree.

Fast forwarding a few years, Kim Kokkonen is the next person I would like to thank. He gave me my job at TurboPower Software (*http://www.turbopower.com*) and gave me the opportunity to learn more computer science than I'd ever dreamt of before. A big thank you, of course, to all TurboPower's employees and those TurboPower customers I've gotten to know over the years. I'd also like to thank Robert DelRossi, our president, for encouraging me in this endeavor.

Next is a small company, now defunct, called Natural Systems. In 1993, they produced a product called Data Structures for Turbo Pascal. I bought it, and, in my opinion, it wasn't very good. Oh, it worked fine, but I just didn't agree with its design or implementation and it just wasn't fast enough. It drove me to write my freeware EZSTRUCS library for Borland Pascal 7, from which I derived EZDSL, my well-known freeware data structures library for Delphi. This effort was the first time I'd really gotten to *understand* data structures, since sometimes it is only through doing that you get to learn.

Thanks also to Chris Frizelle, the editor and owner of *The Delphi Magazine* (*http://www.thedelphimagazine.com*). He had the foresight to allow me to pontificate on various algorithms in his inestimable magazine, finally succumbing to giving me my own monthly column: *Algorithms Alfresco*. Without him and his support, this book *might* have been written, but it certainly wouldn't have been as good. I certainly recommend a subscription to *The Delphi Magazine*, as it remains, in my view, the most in-depth, intelligent reference for Delphi programmers. Thanks to all my readers, as well, for their suggestions and comments on the column.

Next to last, thanks to all the people at Wordware (*http://www.wordware.com*), including my editors, publisher Jim Hill, and developmental editor Wes Beckwith. Jim was a bit dubious at first when I proposed publishing a book on algorithms, but he soon came round to my way of thinking and has been very supportive during its gestation. I'd also like to give my warmest thanks to my tech editors: Steve Teixeira, the co-author of the tome on how to get the best out of Delphi, *Delphi n Developer's Guide* (where, at the time of writing, n = 5), and my friend Anton Parris.

Finally, my thanks and my love go to my wife, Donna (she chivvied me to write this book in the first place). Without her love, enthusiasm, and encouragement, I'd have given up ages ago. Thank you, sweetheart. Here's to the next one!

Julian M. Bucknall
Colorado Springs, April 1999 to February 2001

Chapter 1

What is an Algorithm?

For a book on algorithms, we have to make sure that we know what we are going to be discussing. As we'll see, one of the main reasons for understanding and researching algorithms is to make our applications faster. Oh, I'll agree that sometimes we need algorithms that are more space efficient rather than speed efficient, but in general, it's performance we crave.

Although this book is about algorithms and data structures and how to implement them in code, we should also discuss some of the procedural algorithms as well: how to write our code to help us debug it when it goes wrong, how to test our code, and how to make sure that changes in one place don't break something elsewhere.

What is an Algorithm?

As it happens, we use algorithms all the time in our programming careers, but we just don't tend to think of them as algorithms: "They're not algorithms, it's just the way things are done."

An *algorithm* is a step-by-step recipe for performing some calculation or process. This is a pretty loose definition, but once you understand that algorithms are nothing to be afraid of per se, you'll recognize and use them without further thought.

Go back to your elementary school days, when you were learning addition. The teacher would write on the board a sum like this:

```
 45
 17 +
 ----
```

and then ask you to add them up. You had been taught how to do this: start with the units column and add the 5 and the 7 to make 12, put the 2 under the units column, and then carry 1 above the 4.

```
 1
 45
 17 +
 ----
  2
```

You'd then add the carried 1, the 4 and the other 1 to make 6, which you'd then write underneath the tens column. And, you'd have arrived at the concentrated answer: 62.

Notice that what you had been taught was an *algorithm* to perform this and any similar addition. You were *not* taught how to add 45 and 17 specifically but were instead taught a general way of adding two numbers. Indeed, pretty soon, you could add many numbers, with lots of digits, by applying the same algorithm. Of course, in those days, you weren't told that this was an algorithm; it was just how you added up numbers.

In the programming world we tend to think of algorithms as being complex methods to perform some calculation. For example, if we have an array of customer records and we want to find a particular one (say, John Smith), we might read through the entire array, element by element, until we either found the John Smith one or reached the end of the array. This seems an obvious way of doing it and we don't think of it being an algorithm, but it is—it's known as a *sequential search*.

There might be other ways of finding "John Smith" in our hypothetical array. For example, if the array were sorted by last name, we could use the *binary search* algorithm to find John Smith. We look at the middle element in the array. Is it John Smith? If so, we're done. If it is less than John Smith (by "less than," I mean earlier in alphabetic sequence), then we can assume that John Smith is in the first half of the array. If greater than, it's in the latter half of the array. We can then do the same thing again, that is, look at the middle item and select the portion of the array that should have John Smith, slicing and dicing the array into smaller and smaller parts, until we either find it or the bit of the array we have left is empty.

Well, that algorithm certainly seems much more complicated than our original sequential search. The sequential search could be done with a nice simple For loop with a call to Break at the right moment; the code for the binary search would need a lot more calculations and local variables. So it might seem that sequential search is faster, just because it's simpler to code.

Enter the world of algorithm analysis where we do experiments and try and formulate laws about how different algorithms actually work.

Analysis of Algorithms

Let's look at the two possible searches for "John Smith" in an array: the sequential search and the binary search. We'll implement both algorithms and then play with them in order to ascertain their performance attributes. Listing 1.1 is the simple sequential search.

Listing 1.1: Sequential search for a name in an array

```
function SeqSearch(aStrs : PStringArray; aCount : integer;
          const aName : string5) : integer;
var
  i : integer;
begin
  for i := 0 to pred(aCount) do
    if CompareText(aStrs^[i], aName) = 0 then begin
      Result := i;
      Exit;
    end;
  Result := -1;
end;
```

Listing 1.2 shows the more complex binary search. (At the present time we won't go into what is happening in this routine—we discuss the binary search algorithm in detail in Chapter 4.)

Listing 1.2: Binary search for a name in an array

```
function BinarySearch(aStrs : PStringArray; aCount : integer;
             const aName : string5) : integer;
var
  L, R, M : integer;
  CompareResult : integer;
begin
  L := 0;
  R := pred(aCount);
  while (L <= R) do begin
    M := (L + R) div 2;
    CompareResult := CompareText(aStrs^[M], aName);
    if (CompareResult = 0) then begin
      Result := M;
      Exit;
    end
    else if (CompareResult < 0) then
      L := M + 1
    else
```

```
      R := M - 1;
  end;
  Result := -1;
end;
```

Just by looking at both routines it's very hard to make a judgment about performance. In fact, this is a philosophy that we should embrace wholeheartedly: it can be very hard to tell how speed efficient some code is just by looking at it. The *only* way we can truly find out how fast code is, is to run it. Nothing else will do. Whenever we have a choice between algorithms, as we do here, we should *test* and *time* the code under different environments, with different inputs, in order to ascertain which algorithm is better for our needs.

The traditional way to do this timing is with a *profiler*. The profiler program loads up our test application and then accurately times the various routines we're interested in. My advice is to use a profiler as a matter of course in all your programming projects. It is only with a profiler that you can truly determine where your application spends most of its time, and hence which routines are worth your spending time on optimization tasks.

The company I work for, TurboPower Software Company, has a professional profiler in its Sleuth QA Suite product. I've tested all of the code in this book under both StopWatch (the name of the profiling program in Sleuth QA Suite) and under CodeWatch (the resource and memory leak debugger in the suite). However, even if you do not have a profiler, you can still experiment and time routines; it's just a little more awkward, since you have to embed calls to time routines in your code. Any profiler worth buying does not alter your code; it does its magic by modifying the executable in memory at run time.

For this experiment with searching algorithms, I wrote the test program to do its own timing. Essentially, the code grabs the system time at the start of the code being timed and gets it again at the end. From these two values it can calculate the time taken to perform the task. Actually, with modern faster machines and the low resolution of the PC clock, it's usually beneficial to time several hundred calls to the routine, from which we can work out an average. (By the way, this program was written for 32-bit Delphi and will not compile with Delphi 1 since it allocates arrays on the heap that are greater than Delphi 1's 64 KB limit.)

I ran the performance experiments in several different forms. First, I timed how long it took to find "Smith" in arrays containing 100, 1,000, 10,000, and 100,000 elements, using both algorithms and making sure that a "Smith" element was present. For the next series of tests, I timed how long it took to find

"Smith" in the same set of arrays with both algorithms, but this time I ensured that "Smith" was not present. Table 1.1 shows the results of my tests.

Table 1.1: Timing sequential and binary searches

	Fail	Success
Sequential		
100	0.14	0.10
1,000	1.44	1.05
10,000	15.28	10.84
100,000	149.42	106.35
Binary		
100	0.01	0.01
1,000	0.01	0.01
10,000	0.02	0.02
100,000	0.03	0.02

As you can see, the timings make for some very interesting reading. The time taken to perform a sequential search is proportional to the number of elements in the array. We say that the execution characteristics of sequential search are linear.

However, the binary search statistics are somewhat more difficult to characterize. Indeed, it even seems as if we're falling into a timing resolution problem because the algorithm is so fast. The relationship between the time taken and the number of elements in the array is no longer a simple linear one. It seems to be something much less than this, and something that is not brought out by these tests.

I reran the tests and scaled the binary timings by a factor of 100.

Table 1.2: Retiming binary searches

	Fail	Success
100	0.89	0.57
1,000	1.47	1.46
10,000	2.06	2.06
100,000	2.50	2.41

Here we get a much more impressive set of data. You can see that increasing the number of elements tenfold results in a run time that's increased the time by a constant amount (roughly half a unit). This is a logarithmic relationship: the time taken to do a binary search is proportional to the logarithm of the number of elements in the array.

(This can be a little hard to see for a non-mathematician. Recall from your school days that one way to multiply two numbers is to calculate their logarithms, add them, and then calculate the anti-logarithm to give the answer. Since we are multiplying by a factor of 10 in these profiling tests, it would be equivalent to adding a constant when viewed logarithmically. Exactly the case we see in the test results: we're adding half a unit every time.)

So, what have we learned as a result of this experiment? As a first lesson, we have learned that the only way to understand the performance characteristics of an algorithm is to actually time it.

> In general, the only way to see the efficiency of a piece of code is to time it. That applies to everything you write, whether you're using a well-known algorithm or you've devised one to suit the current situation. Don't guess, measure.

As a lesser lesson, we have also seen that sequential search is linear in nature, whereas binary search is logarithmic. If we were mathematically inclined, we could then take these statistical results and prove them as theorems. In this book, however, I do not want to overburden the text with a lot of mathematics; there are plenty of college textbooks that could do it much better than I.

The Big-Oh Notation

We need a compact notation to express the performance characteristics we measure, rather than having to say things like "the performance of algorithm X is proportional to the number of items cubed," or something equally verbose. Computer science already has such a scheme; it's called the *big-Oh notation.*

For this notation, we work out the mathematical function of n, the number of items, to which the algorithm's performance is proportional, and say that the algorithm is a $O(f(n))$ algorithm, where $f(n)$ is some function of n. We read this as "big-Oh of $f(n)$", or, less rigorously, as "proportional to $f(n)$."

For example, our experiments showed us that sequential search is a $O(n)$ algorithm. Binary search, on the other hand, is a $O(\log(n))$ algorithm. Since $\log(n) < n$, for all positive n we could say that binary search is always faster than sequential search; however, in a moment, I will give you a couple of warnings about taking conclusions from the big-Oh notation too far.

The big-Oh notation is succinct and compact. Suppose that by experimentation we work out that algorithm X is $O(n^2 + n)$; in other words, its performance is proportional to $n^2 + n$. By "proportional to" we mean that we can find a constant k such that the following equation holds true:

$$\text{Performance} = k * (n^2 + n)$$

Because of this equation, and others derived from the big-Oh notation, we can see firstly that multiplying the mathematical function inside the big-Oh parentheses by a constant value has no effect. For example, $O(3 * f(n))$ is equal to $O(f(n))$; we can just take the "3" out of the notation and multiply it into the outside proportionality constant, the one we can conveniently ignore.

If the value of n is large enough when we test algorithm X, we can safely say that the effects of the "$+ n$" term are going to be swallowed up by the n^2 term. In other words, provided n is large enough, $O(n^2 + n)$ is equal to $O(n^2)$. And that goes for any additional term in n: we can safely ignore it if, for a sufficiently large n, its effects are swallowed by another term in n. So, for example, a term in n^2 will be swallowed up by a term in n^3; a term in $\log(n)$ will be swallowed up by a term in n; and so on.

This shows that arithmetic with the big-Oh notation is very easy. Let's, for argument's sake, suppose that we have an algorithm that performs several different tasks. The first task, taken on its own, is $O(n)$, the second is $O(n^2)$, the third is $O(\log(n))$. What is the overall big-Oh value for the performance of the algorithm? The answer is $O(n^2)$, since that is the dominant part of the algorithm, by far.

Herein lies the warning I was about to give you before about drawing conclusions from big-Oh values. Big-Oh values are representative of what happens with *large* values of n. For *small* values of n, the notation breaks down completely; other factors start to come into play and swamp the general results. For example, suppose we time two algorithms in an experiment. We manage to work out these two performance functions from our statistics:

$$\text{Performance of first} = k1 * (n + 100000)$$
$$\text{Performance of second} = k2 * n^2$$

The two constants $k1$ and $k2$ are of the same magnitude. Which algorithm would you use? If we went with the big-Oh notation, we'd always choose the first algorithm because it's $O(n)$. However, if we actually found that in our applications n was never greater than 100, it would make more sense for us to use the second algorithm.

So, when you need to select an algorithm for some purpose, you must take into account not only the big-Oh value of the algorithm, but also its characteristics for the average number of items (or, if you like, the environment) for which you will be using the algorithm. Again, the only way you'll ever know you've selected the right algorithm is by measuring its speed in *your* application, for *your* data, with a profiler. Don't take anything on trust from an author (like me, for example); measure, time, and test.

Best, Average, and Worst Cases

There's another issue we need to consider as well. The big-Oh notation generally refers to an *average-case* scenario. In our search experiment, if "Smith" were always the first item in the array, we'd find that sequential search would always be faster than binary search; we would succeed in finding the element we wanted after only one test. This is known as a *best-case* scenario and is O(1). (Big-Oh of 1 means that it takes a constant time, no matter how many items there are.)

If "Smith" were always the last item in the array, the sequential search would be pretty slow. This is a *worst-case* scenario and would be $O(n)$, just like the average case.

Although binary search has a similar best-case scenario (the item we want is in the middle of the array), its worst-case scenario is still much better than that for sequential search. The performance statistics we gathered for the case where the element was not to be found in the array are all worst-case values.

In general, we should look at the big-Oh value for an algorithm's average and worst cases. Best cases are usually not too interesting: we are generally more concerned with what happens "at the limit," since that is how our applications will be judged.

To conclude this particular section, we have seen that the big-Oh notation is a valuable tool for us to characterize various algorithms that do similar jobs. We have also discussed that the big-Oh notation is generally valid only for large n; for small n we are advised to take each algorithm and time it. Also, the only way for us to truly know how an algorithm will perform in our application is to time it. Don't guess; use a profiler.

Algorithms and the Platform

In all of this discussion about algorithms we didn't concern ourselves with the operating system or the actual hardware on which the implementation of the algorithm was running. Indeed, the big-Oh notation could be said to only be valid for a fantasy machine, one where we can't have any hardware or operating system bottlenecks, for example. Unfortunately, we live and work in the real world and our applications and algorithms will run on real physical machines, so we have to take these factors into account.

Virtual Memory and Paging

The first performance bottleneck we should understand is virtual memory paging. This is easier to understand with 32-bit applications, and, although 16-bit applications suffer from the same problems, the mechanics are slightly different. Note that I will only be talking in layman's terms in this section: my intent is not to provide a complete discussion of the paging system used by your operating system, but just to provide enough information so that you conceptually understand what's going on.

When we start an application on a modern 32-bit operating system, the system provides the application with a 4 GB virtual memory block for both code and data. It obviously doesn't *physically* give the application 4 GB of RAM to use (I don't know about you, but I certainly do not have 4 GB of spare RAM for each application I simultaneously run); rather it provides a logical address space that, in theory, has 4 GB of memory behind it. This is virtual memory. It's not really there, but, provided that we do things right, the operating system will provide us with physical chunks of it that we can use when we need it.

The virtual memory is divided up into *pages*. On Win32 systems, using Pentium processors, the page size is 4 KB. Essentially, Win32 divides up the 4 GB virtual memory block into 4 KB pages and for each page it maintains a small amount of information about that page. (Linux' memory system works in roughly the same manner.) The first piece of information is whether the page has been *committed*. A committed page is one where the application has stored some information, be it code or actual data. If a page is not committed, it is not there at all; any attempt to reference it will produce an access violation.

The next piece of information is a mapping to a page translation table. In a typical system of 256 MB of memory (I'm very aware of how ridiculous that phrase will seem in only a few years' time), there are only 65,536 physical pages available. The page translation table provides a mapping from a particular virtual memory page as viewed by the application to an actual page available as RAM. So when we access a memory address in our application, some effort is going on behind the scenes to translate that address into a physical RAM address.

Now, with many applications simultaneously running on our Win32 system, there will inevitably be a time when all of the physical RAM pages are being used and one of our applications wants to commit a new page. It can't, since there's no free RAM left. When this happens, the operating system writes a physical page out to disk (this is called *swapping*) and marks that part of the translation table as being swapped out. The physical page is then remapped to provide a committed page for the requesting application.

This is all well and good until the application that owns the swapped out page actually tries to access it. The CPU notices that the physical page is no longer available and triggers a *page fault*. The operating system takes over, swaps another page to disk to free up a physical page, maps the requested page to the physical page, and then allows the application to continue. The application is totally unaware that this process has just happened; it just wanted to read the first byte of the page, for example, and that's what (eventually) happened.

All this magic occurs constantly as you use your 32-bit operating system. Physical pages are being swapped to and from disk and page mappings are being reset all the time. In general you wouldn't notice it; however, in one particular situation, you will. That situation is known as *thrashing*.

Thrashing

When thrashing occurs, it can be deadly to your application, turning it from a highly tuned optimized program to a veritable sloth. Suppose you have an application that requires a lot of memory, say at least half the physical memory in your machine. It creates a large array of large blocks, allocating them on the heap. This allocation will cause new pages to be committed, and, in all likelihood, for other pages to be swapped to disk. The program then reads the data in these large blocks in order from the beginning of the array to the end. The system has no problem swapping in required pages when necessary.

Suppose, now, that the application randomly looks at the blocks in the array. Say it refers to an address in block 56, followed by somewhere in block 123, followed by block 12, followed by block 234, and so on. In this scenario, it gets more and more likely that page faults will occur, causing more and more pages to be swapped to and from disk. Your disk drive light seems to blink very rapidly on and off and the program slows to a crawl. This is thrashing: the continual swapping of pages to disk to satisfy random requests from an application.

In general, there is little we can do about thrashing. The majority of the time we allocate our memory blocks from the Delphi heap manager. We have no control over where the memory blocks come from. It could be, for example, that related memory allocations all come from different pages. (By *related* I mean that the memory blocks are likely to be accessed at the same time because they contain data that is related.) One way we can attempt to alleviate thrashing is to use separate heaps for different structures and data in our application. This kind of algorithm is beyond the level of this book.

An example should make this clear. Suppose we have allocated a TList to contain some objects. Each of these objects contains at least one string allocated on the heap (for example, we're in 32-bit Delphi and the object uses long strings). Imagine now that the application has been running for a while and objects have been added and deleted from this TList. It's not inconceivable that the TList instance, its objects, and the objects' strings are spread out across many, many memory pages. If we then read the TList sequentially from start to finish, and access each object and its string(s), we will be touching each of these many pages, possibly resulting in many page swaps. If the number of objects is fairly small, we probably would have most of the pages physically in memory anyway. But, if there were millions of objects in the TList, we might suffer from thrashing as we read through the list.

Locality of Reference

This brings up another concept: *locality of reference*. This principle is a way of thinking about our applications that helps us to minimize the possibility of thrashing. All this phrase means is that related pieces of information should be as close to each other in virtual memory as possible. If we have locality of reference, then when we access one item of data we should find other related items nearby in memory.

For example, an array of some record type has a high locality of reference. The element at index 1 is right next door in memory to the item at index 2, and so on. If we are sequentially accessing all the records in the array, we shall have an admirable locality of reference. Page swapping will be kept to a minimum. A TList instance containing pointers to the same record type—although it is still an array and can be said to have the same contents as the array of records—has low locality of reference. As we saw earlier, each of the items might be found on different pages, so sequentially accessing each item in the TList could presumably cause page swapping to occur. Linked lists (see Chapter 3) suffer from the same problems.

There are techniques to increase the locality of reference for various data structures and algorithms and we will touch on a few in this book. Unfortunately for us, the Delphi heap manager is designed to be as generic as possible; we have no way to tell the heap manager to manage a series of allocations from the same memory page. The fact that all objects are instances allocated from the heap is even worse; it would be nice to be able to allocate certain objects from separate memory pages. (In fact, this is possible by overriding the NewInstance class method, but we would have to do it with every class for which we need this capability.)

We have been talking about locality of reference in a spatial sense ("this object is close in memory to that object"), but we can also consider locality of reference in a temporal sense. This means that if an item has been referenced recently it will be referenced again soon, or that item X is always referenced at the same time as item Y. The embodiment of this temporal locality of reference is a cache. A *cache* is a small block of memory for some process that contains items that have recently been accessed. Every time an item is accessed the cache makes a copy of it in its own memory area. Once the memory area becomes full, the cache uses a *least recently used* (LRU) algorithm to discard an item that hasn't been referred to in a while to replace it with the most recently used item. That way the cache is maintaining a list of spatially local items that are also temporally local.

Normally, caches are used to store items that are held on slower devices, the classic example being a disk cache. However, in theory, a memory cache could work equally as well, especially in an application that uses a lot of memory and has the possibility to be run on a machine with not much RAM.

The CPU Cache

Indeed, the hardware on which we all program and run applications uses a memory cache. The machine on which I'm writing this chapter uses a 512 KB high-speed cache between the CPU and its registers and main memory (of which this machine has 192 MB). This high-speed cache acts as a buffer: when the CPU wants to read some memory, the cache will check to see if it has the memory already present and, if not, will go ahead and read it. Memory that is frequently accessed—that is, has temporal locality of reference—will tend to stay in the cache.

Data Alignment

Another aspect of the hardware that we must take into account is that of data alignment. Current CPU hardware is built to always access data from the cache in 32-bit chunks. Not only that, but the chunks it requests are always *aligned* on a 32-bit boundary. This means that the memory addresses passed to the cache from the CPU are always evenly divisible by four (4 bytes being 32 bits). It's equivalent to the lower two bits of the address being clear. When 64-bit or larger CPUs become more prevalent, we'll be used to the CPU accessing 64 bits at a time (or 128 bits), aligned on the appropriate boundary.

So what does this have to do with our applications? Well, we have to make sure that our longint and pointer variables are also aligned on a 4-byte or 32-bit boundary. If they are not and they straddle a 4-byte boundary, the CPU has to issue *two* reads to the cache, the first read to get the first part of the variable and the second read to get the second part. The CPU then stitches together the value from these two parts, throwing away the bytes it doesn't need. (On other processors, the CPU actually enforces a rule that 32-bit entities must be aligned on 32-bit boundaries. If not, you'll get an access violation. We're lucky that Intel processors don't enforce this rule, but then again, by not doing so it allows us to be sloppy.)

Always ensure that 32-bit entities are aligned on 32-bit boundaries and 16-bit entities on 16-bit boundaries. For slightly better efficiency, ensure that 64-bit entities (double variables, for example) are aligned on 64-bit boundaries.

This sounds complicated, but in reality, the Delphi compiler helps us an awful lot, and it is only in record type definitions that we have to be careful. All atomic variables (that is, of some simple type) that are global or local to a routine are automatically aligned properly. If we haven't forced an alignment option with a compiler define, the 32-bit Delphi compiler will also automatically align fields in records properly. To do this it adds filler bytes to pad out the fields so that they align. With the 16-bit version, this automatic alignment in record types does not happen, so beware.

This automatic alignment feature sometimes confuses programmers. If we had the following record type in a 32-bit version of Delphi, what would sizeof(TMyRecord) return?

```
type
  TMyRecord = record
    aByte : byte;
    aLong : longint;
  end;
```

Many people would say 5 bytes without thinking (and in fact this would be true in Delphi 1). The answer, though, is 8 bytes. The compiler will automatically add three bytes in between the aByte field and the aLong field, just so the latter can be forced onto a 4-byte boundary.

If, instead, we had declared the record type as (and notice the keyword packed),

```
type
  TMyRecord = packed record
    aByte : byte;
    aLong : longint;
  end;
```

then the sizeof function would indeed return 5 bytes. However, under this scheme, accessing the aLong field would take much longer than in the previous type definition—it's straddling a 4-byte boundary. So, the rule is, if you are going to use the packed keyword, you must arrange the fields in your record type definition to take account and advantage of alignment. Put all your 4-byte fields first and then add the other fields as required. I've followed this principle in the code in this book. And another rule is: never guess how big a record type is; use sizeof.

By the way, be aware that the Delphi heap manager also helps us out with alignment: all allocations from the heap manager are 4-byte aligned. Every pointer returned by GetMem or New has the lower two bits clear.

In Delphi 5 and above, the compiler goes even further. Not only does it align 4-byte entities on 4-byte boundaries, but it also aligns larger variables on 8-byte boundaries. This is of greatest importance for double variables: the FPU (floating-point unit) works better if double variables, being 8 bytes in size, are aligned on an 8-byte boundary. If your kind of programming is numeric intensive, make sure that your double fields in record structures are 8-byte aligned.

Space Versus Time Tradeoffs

The more we discover, devise, or analyze algorithms, the more we will come across what seems to be a universal computer science law: fast algorithms seem to have more memory requirements. That is, to use a faster algorithm we shall have to use more memory; to economize on memory might result in having to use a slower algorithm.

A simple example will explain the point I am trying to make. Suppose we wanted to devise an algorithm that counted the number of set bits in a byte value. Listing 1.3 is a first stab at an algorithm and hence a routine to do this.

Listing 1.3: Counting bits in a byte, original

```
function CountBits1(B : byte) : byte;
begin
  Result := 0;
  while (B<>0) do begin
    if Odd(B) then
      inc(Result);
    B := B shr 1;
  end;
end;
```

As you can see, this routine uses no ancillary storage at all. It merely counts the set bits by continually dividing the value by two (shifting an integer right by one bit is equal to dividing the integer by two), and counting the number of times an odd result is calculated. The loop stops when the value is zero, since at that point there are obviously no set bits left. The algorithm big-Oh value depends on the number of set bits in the parameter, and in a worst-case scenario the inner loop would have to be cycled through eight times. It is, therefore, a O(*n*) algorithm.

It seems like a pretty obvious routine and apart from some tinkering, such as rewriting it in Assembly language, there doesn't seem to be any way to improve matters.

However, consider the requirement from another angle. The routine takes a 1-byte parameter, and there can be at most 256 different values passed through that parameter. So, why don't we pre-compute all of the possible answers and store that in a static array in the application? Listing 1.4 shows this new algorithm.

Listing 1.4: Counting bits in a byte, improved

```
const
  BitCounts : array [0..255] of byte =
    (0, 1, 1, 2, 1, 2, 2, 3, 1, 2, 2, 3, 2, 3, 3, 4,
     1, 2, 2, 3, 2, 3, 3, 4, 2, 3, 3, 4, 3, 4, 4, 5,
     1, 2, 2, 3, 2, 3, 3, 4, 2, 3, 3, 4, 3, 4, 4, 5,
     2, 3, 3, 4, 3, 4, 4, 5, 3, 4, 4, 5, 4, 5, 5, 6,
     1, 2, 2, 3, 2, 3, 3, 4, 2, 3, 3, 4, 3, 4, 4, 5,
     2, 3, 3, 4, 3, 4, 4, 5, 3, 4, 4, 5, 4, 5, 5, 6,
     2, 3, 3, 4, 3, 4, 4, 5, 3, 4, 4, 5, 4, 5, 5, 6,
     3, 4, 4, 5, 4, 5, 5, 6, 4, 5, 5, 6, 5, 6, 6, 7,
     1, 2, 2, 3, 2, 3, 3, 4, 2, 3, 3, 4, 3, 4, 4, 5,
     2, 3, 3, 4, 3, 4, 4, 5, 3, 4, 4, 5, 4, 5, 5, 6,
     2, 3, 3, 4, 3, 4, 4, 5, 3, 4, 4, 5, 4, 5, 5, 6,
     3, 4, 4, 5, 4, 5, 5, 6, 4, 5, 5, 6, 5, 6, 6, 7,
     2, 3, 3, 4, 3, 4, 4, 5, 3, 4, 4, 5, 4, 5, 5, 6,
     3, 4, 4, 5, 4, 5, 5, 6, 4, 5, 5, 6, 5, 6, 6, 7,
     3, 4, 4, 5, 4, 5, 5, 6, 4, 5, 5, 6, 5, 6, 6, 7,
     4, 5, 5, 6, 5, 6, 6, 7, 5, 6, 6, 7, 6, 7, 7, 8);
function CountBits2(B : byte) : byte;
begin
  Result := BitCounts[B];
end;
```

Here, at the expense of a static 256-byte array of values, we've simplified the algorithm to an extreme extent. Even better, there are no loops in this algorithm; it's a O(1) algorithm, pure and simple. No matter what the input, the algorithm calculates the number of bits in one simple step. (Note that I calculated the static array automatically by writing a simple program using the first routine.)

On my machine, the second algorithm is 10 times faster than the first; you can call it 10 times in the same amount of time that a single call to the first one takes to execute. (Note, though, that I'm talking about the average-case scenario here—in the best-case scenario for the first routine, the parameter is zero and practically no code would be executed.)

So at the expense of a 256-byte array, we have devised an algorithm that is 10 times faster. We can trade speed for space with this particular need; we either have a fast routine and a large static array (which, it must be remembered, gets compiled into the executable program) or a slower routine without the memory extravagance. (There is another alternative: we could calculate the values in the array at run time, the first time the routine was called. This would mean that the array isn't linked into the executable, but that the first call to the routine takes a relatively long time.)

This simple example is a graphic illustration of space versus time tradeoffs. Often we need to pre-calculate results in order to speed up algorithms, but this uses up more memory.

Long Strings

I cannot let a discussion on performance finish without talking a little about long strings. They have their own set of problems when you start talking about efficiency. Long strings were introduced in Delphi 2 and have appeared in all Delphi and Kylix compilers since that time (Delphi 1 programmers need not worry about them, nor this section).

A long string variable of type string is merely a pointer to a specially formatted memory block. In other words, sizeof(stringvar) = sizeof(pointer). If this pointer is nil, the string is taken to be empty. Otherwise, the pointer points directly to the sequence of characters that makes up the string. The long string routines in the run-time library make sure that this sequence is always null terminated, hence you can easily typecast a string variable to a PChar for calls to the system API, for example. It is not generally well known that the memory block pointed to has some other information. The four bytes prior to the sequence of characters is an integer value containing the length of the string (less the null-terminator). The four bytes prior to that is an integer value with the reference count for the string (constant strings have this value set to –1). If the string is allocated on the heap, the four bytes prior to that is an integer value holding the complete size of the string memory block, including all the hidden integer fields, the sequence of characters that make up the string, and the hidden null terminator, rounded up to the nearest four bytes.

The reference count is there so that code like:

```
MyOtherString := MyString;
```

performs extremely quickly. The compiler converts this assignment to two separate steps: first, it increments the reference count for the string that MyString points to, and second it sets the MyOtherString pointer equal to the MyString pointer.

That's about it for the efficiency gains. Everything else you do with strings will require memory allocations of one form or another.

Use const

If you pass a string into a routine and you don't intend to alter it, then declare it with const. In most cases this will avoid the automatic addition of a hidden Try..finally block. If you don't use const, the compiler assumes that you may be altering it and therefore sets up a local hidden string variable to hold the string. The reference count gets incremented at the beginning and will get decremented at the end. To ensure the latter happens, the compiler adds the hidden try..finally block.

Listing 1.5 is a routine to count the number of vowels in a string.

Listing 1.5: Counting the number of vowels in a string

```
function CountVowels(const S : string) : integer;
var
  i : integer;
begin
  Result := 0;
  for i := 1 to length(S) do
    if upcase(S[i]) in ['A', 'E', 'I', 'O', 'U'] then
      inc(Result);
end;
```

If the keyword const is removed from the function statement, the speed of the routine is reduced by about 12 percent, the cost of the hidden Try..finally block.

Be Wary of Automatic Conversions

Many times we mix characters and strings together without worrying too much about it. The compiler takes care of everything, and we don't realize what is really going on. Take the Pos function, for example. As you know, this function returns the position of a substring in a larger string. If you use it for finding a character:

```
PosOfCh := Pos(SomeChar, MyString);
```

you need to be aware that the compiler will convert the character into a long string. It will allocate a long string on the heap, make it length 1 and copy the character into it. It then calls the Pos function. Because there is an automatic hidden string being used, a hidden Try..finally block is included to free the one-character string at the end of the routine. The routine in Listing 1.6 is *five* times faster (yes, five!), despite it being written in Pascal and not assembler.

Listing 1.6: Position of a character in a string

```
function TDPosCh(aCh : AnsiChar; const S : string) : integer;
var
  i : integer;
begin
  Result := 0;
  for i := 1 to length(S) do
    if (S[i] = aCh) then begin
      Result := i;
      Exit;
    end;
end;
```

My recommendation is to check the syntax of routines you are calling with a character to make sure that the parameter concerned is really a character and not a string.

There's another wrinkle to this hint. The string concatentation operator, +, also acts on strings only. If you are appending a character to a string in a loop, try and find another way to do it (say by presetting the length of the string and then making assignments to the individual characters in the string) since again the compiler will be converting all the characters to strings behind your back.

Debugging and Testing

Let's put aside our discussions of algorithmic performance now and talk a little about procedural algorithms—algorithms for performing the development process, not for calculating a result.

No matter how we write our code, at some point we must test it to make sure that it performs in the manner we intended. For a certain set of input values, do we get the expected result? If we click on the OK button, is the record saved to the database? Of course, if a test we perform fails, we need to try and work out why it failed and fix the problem. This is known as debugging—the test revealed a bug and now we need to remove that bug. Testing and debugging are therefore inextricably linked; they are the two faces of the same coin.

Given that we cannot get away with not testing (we like to think of ourselves as infallible and our code as perfect, but unfortunately this isn't so), what can we do to make it easier for ourselves?

The first golden rule is this: *Code we write will always contain bugs.* There is no moral angle to this rule; there is nothing of which to be ashamed. Buggy code is part of our normal daily lives as programmers. Like it or not, we programmers are fallible. No matter how hard we try we'll introduce at least one bug when developing. Indeed, part of the fun of programming, I find, is finding that particularly elusive bug and nailing it.

Rule 1: Code we write will always contain bugs.

Although I said that there is nothing to be embarrassed about if some of your code is discovered to have a bug, there is one situation where it does reflect badly on you—that is when you didn't test adequately.

Assertions

Since the first rule indicates that we will always have to do some debugging, and the corollary states that we don't want to be embarrassed by inadequately tested code, we need to learn to program defensively. The first tool in our defensive arsenal is the *assertion*.

An assertion is a programmatic check in the code to test whether a particular condition is true. If the condition is false, contrary to your expectation, an exception is raised and you get a nice dialog box explaining the problem. This dialog box is a signal warning you that either your supposition was wrong, or the code is being used in a way you hadn't foreseen. The assertion exception should lead you directly to that part of the code that has the bug. Assertions are a key element of defensive programming: when you add an assertion into your code, you are stating unequivocally that something must be true before continuing past that point.

John Robbins [19] states the next rule as "Assert, assert, assert, and assert." According to him, he judges he has enough assertions in his code when co-workers complain that they keep getting assertion checks when they call his code. So I'll state the next rule as: *Assert early, assert often*. Put assertions into your code when you write it, and do so at every opportunity.

Rule 2: Assert early, assert often.

Unfortunately, some Delphi programmers will have a problem with this. Compiler-supported assertions didn't arrive until Delphi 3. From that moment, programmers could use assertions with impunity. We were given a compiler option that either compiled in the assertion checks into the executable or magically ignored them. For testing and debugging, we would compile with assertions enabled. For a production build, we would disable them and they would not appear in the compiled code.

For Delphi 1 and Delphi 2, we therefore have to do something else. There are two solutions. The first is to write a method called Assert whose implementation is empty when we do a production build, and has a check of the condition together with a call to Raise if not. Listing 1.7 shows this simple assertion procedure.

Listing 1.7: The assertion procedure for Delphi 1 and 2

```
procedure Assert(aCondition : boolean; const aFailMsg : string);
begin
  {$IFDEF UseAssert}
  if not aCondition then
    raise Exception.Create(aFailMsg);
  {$ENDIF}
end;
```

As you can see, we use a compiler define to either compile in the assertion check or to remove it. Although this procedure is simple to use and is fairly easy to call from our main code, it does mean that in a production build there is a call to an empty procedure wherever we code an assertion. The alternative is to move the $IFDEF out of this procedure to wherever we call Assert. Statement blocks would then invade our code in the following manner:

```
...
{$IFDEF UseAssert}
Assert(MyPointer<>nil, 'MyPointer should be allocated by now');
{$ENDIF}
MyPointer^.Field := 0;
...
```

The benefit of this organization is that the calls to the Assert procedure disappear completely in a production build, when the UseAssert compiler define is not defined. Since the code for this book is designed to be compiled with all versions of Delphi, I use the Assert procedure shown in Listing 1.7.

There are three ways to use an assertion: pre-conditions, post-conditions, and invariants. A *pre-condition* is an assertion you place at the beginning of a routine. It states unequivocally what should be true about the program environment and the input parameters before the routine executes. For example, suppose you wrote a routine that is passed an object as a parameter. When you wrote the routine, you decided as designer and coder that the object passed in could not be nil. As well as telling everyone in your project about this condition, you should also code an assertion at the beginning of the routine to check that the object is not nil. That way, should you or anyone else forget about this restriction when calling the routine, the assertion will do the check for you.

Post-conditions are the opposite: it's an assertion you place at the end of the routine to check that the routine did its job properly. Personally, I find that this kind of assertion is less useful. After all, in Delphi, we always code as if everything succeeds. If there's a problem somewhere, an exception will be raised and the rest of the routine will be skipped.

The final type of assertion is an *invariant*, and it covers pretty much everything else. It's an assertion that occurs in the middle of the code to ensure that some aspect of the program is still true.

One of the problems about assertions is when to use them in preference to raising a "normal" exception. This is a gray area. I try and divide up the errors being tested for into two piles: programmer errors and input data errors. Let's try and explain the difference.

The classic example for me is the "List index is out of bounds" exception, especially the one where the index being used is –1. This error is caused by the programmer not checking the index of the item prior to getting it from or putting it into a TList. The TList code checks all item indexes passed to it to validate that they are in range, and if not, this exception is raised. There is no way for the user of the application to cause the error (indeed, I'd maintain that it is deeply nonsensical to most users); it occurs simply because the program wasn't tested enough. In my view, this exception should be an assertion.

Alternately, suppose we were writing a routine that decompressed data from a file; for example, a routine to unzip a file. The format of the compressed data is fairly arcane and complex—after all, it is viewed merely as a sequence of bits, and any sequence looks as good as another. If the decompression routine encountered an error in the stream of bits (for example, it exhausted the stream without finishing), is that an assertion or an exception? In my view, this is a simple exception. It is quite likely that the routine will be presented with files that have become corrupted or files that aren't even Zip files. It's not a programmer error; after all, it's entirely due to circumstances outside the program.

So assertions are there to check that the programmer is doing his job properly and to warn him if he doesn't. Exceptions are there to warn about exceptional circumstances due to the environment in which the program is being run.

Comments

This one is simple:

Rule 3: Comment your code. Explain your assumptions (even better, assert them). Describe tricky code. Maintain comments when you maintain the code. Don't let the comments come adrift from what the code is doing.

Logging

The next item in our defensive programming arsenal is *logging*. By logging, I mean adding extra code, protected by a compiler define, that writes or logs the state or values of important variables to a file.

This is a technique from the very early days of Pascal programming, pre-debuggers, when you'd writeln everything and anything hoping that it would help you find a bug. Nowadays, it's more limited in value. I often write DumpToFile type methods for my classes to log their state. This method can be protected by compiler defines, but it can be an invaluable tool later on when something goes haywire. Turn on the compiler define, call the method a few times at strategic points, and you'll get an easy-to-read lifeline for a particular object.

Rule 4: Write logging code and protect it with compiler defines. It'll come in handy one day, probably sooner rather than later.

In the code for this book, you'll find examples of this technique.

Tracing

In the old days, the practice of tracing was closely allied to logging. *Tracing* used to be the technique of adding writeln statements at the beginning and end of the routines in your program. The writeln statements would print out simple statements like "Entering routine X" or "Leaving routine X." By logging these to a file you could discover the flow of control in your application, how routines were interdependent, and how they called each other. Nowadays, there are programs that do that for you. You run your application inside this special program and it automatically identifies all the routines and where they start and end, and generates the trace log for you as you run your application. No source code changes are required.

These days people don't really bother with this technique. It's far easier to run your debugger and then check out the call stack when the error occurs.

Coverage Analysis

This is a modern practice, since to do it properly, you need a specialized application to do it for you automatically. Coverage analysis is simply logging which statements in your application have been "covered," or executed. If your testing doesn't execute a particular line or block of code, that line or block of code may contain a bug. You won't know until you devise a test that targets the code that hasn't been executed yet.

Rule 5: Use a coverage analyzer regularly as part of your testing. Make sure that you devise tests to execute all your lines of code.

Unit Testing

Unit testing is the process of testing parts of your program divorced from the program itself.

One of the new development methodologies being discussed at the time of this writing is extreme programming [3]. This methodology espouses a number of recommendations, some of which are fairly contentious, but at least one of them makes excellent sense. The recommendation is to write a test at the time you write a method of a class. If the method seems to require more than one test, then you do so. Writing tests at the time you code gives you two things: firstly, the code is familiar to you—after all you've just written it; and secondly, you can use the test as part of a test suite later on, to verify that any changes you make don't break the code.

This is different from the way most of us were taught to test, it seems: we write a monolithic chunk of code, and then two or three months down the line, we try and incorporate it into a system with lots of other monolithic chunks of code and test the system.

Unit testing to this level requires a tool to help us collect the tests, maintain them, and run them automatically in a hands-off fashion at regular intervals. Luckily there is an open source library we can use—DUnit. It is a port to Delphi of a Java unit testing tool, written in part by the original author of *Extreme Programming Explained* by Kent Beck. (Note to Delphi 1 and 2 programmers: DUnit is a tool for Delphi 3 and above.)

DUnit is a *test harness* or *test framework*, itself written in Delphi. Using the framework, you write individual tests to exercise and check your code. The tests can be extremely simple (for instance, a test might be creating an object, checking to see whether its properties have the correct default values and destroying it), but, in total, they are supposed to execute all of the code you've written for a class or a unit. (You use a coverage analyzer to verify that this is the case.) The framework is a user interface that enables you to select individual tests to run or to run them all. After the test or tests are run, you can easily see the result: success or failure (DUnit color codes them to make it simple to see at a glance). Of course, there may be a time when a test is no longer valid because the class changes sufficiently that the test must be rewritten. In that case, you should rewrite the test.

Rule 6: Use a test framework to build up a set of unit tests. Rerun them whenever the code changes.

Once you have this completed DUnit framework for the class or unit you wrote, you can use it again and again for *regression testing*. Regression testing is simply testing the entire class or unit after you've made a change to that class or unit. How many times have you tried to fix a bug, only to cause another one somewhere else?

An example might help. In TurboPower's Internet Professional (a Delphi library for implementing Internet protocols like FTP, HTTP, and so on) there's a routine that parses a URL into its various parts. A URL can point to a Web site or an FTP site, it can be a relative path (for example, a graphic on a Web page could be specified to exist on a folder relative to the main Web page), it can be a MAILTO: address, or it can be referring to an item on your hard disk. The format of the URL is extremely complex. The next time you explore a site like eBay or Amazon, watch the URL control in your browser to see the complexity. The parsing is a hard task, and unfortunately is not that well defined.

An easy example, perhaps, is the URL for errata for this book *http://www.boyet.com/dads*. There are three parts to this particular URL. The "http://" part identifies the protocol. The "www.boyet.com" part is the server, and the "/dads" part identifies a folder on the server.

Before we wrote a set of unit tests for the URL, it was a common occurrence for a fix that properly parsed a complex URL to break the parsing of another, and that the new bug was only noticed much later on.

Writing a set of unit tests for the URL parser enabled us to kill several birds with one stone. Firstly, it gave us a way of making sure that minor bug fixes didn't break working parts of the routine. Secondly, it gave us a way of codifying URLs and how they should be parsed. Adding extra URL tests was a breeze. Thirdly, it enabled us to rewrite the internals of the routine in an attempt to simplify the code; the unit tests gave us a strong description of the results the routine should produce.

DUnit is available on the web at *http://www.dunit.org*. All of the code in this book has been tested with unit tests written with DUnit. The various DUnit tests are provided on the book's CD.

Debugging

At some point in our development, we will have to find a bug and fix it. It is not my intent here to have a protracted discussion on how to debug or how to use the debugger, or even a set of common bugs and how to fix them. My viewpoint here is to provide some rules to make your debugging job easier. I've derived them from Robbins [19].

The first rule of debugging seems to come as a surprise to most developers.

Debug rule 1: Get a reproducible test case.

It is impossible for anything but the simplest bugs to identify and fix a bug from a vague description of the problem. In my viewpoint, a test case that duplicates the bug on demand is at least 90 percent of the way toward finding and fixing the bug. Reproducing the bug at will enables you to track it down step by step through the debugger; if you don't have a way of reproducing a bug, you have no hope.

The second rule of debugging is a tough one.

Debug rule 2: To begin with, assume the bug is your fault.

Maybe you are using the operating system API wrongly or the component library you are using assumes a certain sequence of operations. Maybe the routine you are using doesn't accept a nil parameter after all. It is unlikely that there's a problem in the system API or the compiler. It's more likely that there's a bug in your component library; however, you should try and isolate the problem (which gets us back to Debug rule 1) so that you can verify that it is not in your code. Of course, if it's not in your code, your problems are multiplied since you have to reply on the manufacturer of the operating system, compiler, or component library to produce a fix in a timely fashion.

The next rule follows on from our earlier discussion. You can also use the logging facilities you wrote to check the state of various objects.

Debug rule 3: Use the assertions you built into your code to check that everything seems to be working as expected.

What do you mean you don't have any assertions?

Now we get into some actual debugging.

Debug rule 4: Use some automated debugging tools.

Perhaps your bug is due to a memory overwrite, or accessing memory after it was freed, or you're calling an API but not checking the error returned. All of these types of problems can be found with automated debugging tools like TurboPower's Sleuth QA Suite. Buy a debugging application and use it, not only as part of your normal testing but also when finding a bug.

Of course, after this comes the actual physical debugging part, maybe even using the debugger. This is where the science of programming, of which this book forms a small part, turns into an art. Debugging isn't really an algorithm; it's an contest. My only advice is to never assume anything. If you think a particular variable has such-and-such value, check it. Use the debugger's evaluation dialog; use the CPU view to observe a block of memory. Try and predict what values variables will have, and test your predictions as you debug. Don't be afraid to add more assertions to the code to validate your assumptions, and retest.

Summary

This chapter has been fairly intensive and, to be honest, hasn't really been about algorithms and data structures, per se. Instead, we have concentrated a great deal on code performance and procedural techniques.

Sometimes, performance will come from selecting the correct algorithm, or data structure, or both; other times speed improvements will occur if we apply the knowledge gleaned about our hardware and operating system platforms. Above all, realize that the only way to improve the performance of applications is to profile them. Only with the valuable statistics provided by a profiler can we understand where our code spends its time, and only by concentrating on that section or those sections of code can we hope to optimize our applications and improve their performance. I wish to emphasize that just selecting the "right" algorithm or data structure from this book doesn't mean your application will be the fastest it can be. The information in this book can help you understand the alternatives available to speed up a section of code, certainly, but don't put in some quite complex algorithm implementation in code that is not the bottleneck: you are wasting your time.

Also in this chapter we looked at testing and debugging—again not algorithms as they are usually understood to be, but techniques to aid us in ensuring that our code is as bug-free as possible, and, if not, that it contains enough tracks and pointers to help us identify and fix bugs.

Chapter 2

Arrays

Although there are many, many data structures used in standard (and not so standard) programming, a large majority of them are built upon some variant of two fundamental containers: the array and the linked list. Indeed, if you come away from this book understanding how to use and apply these two data structures, I will have done my job. They are important not only because of their simplicity, but also because of their efficiency. We shall look at arrays in this chapter and linked lists in the next. After discussing linked lists, Chapter 3 will then look at some equally simple data structures derived from these two fundamental ones. Chapters 4 and 5 on searching and sorting, respectively, will also focus on these two fundamental data structures, but from a different angle.

Although I present some complete class implementations of these two types of data structures, sometimes you will find it expedient to code them "from scratch" in your applications. So you should be aware of the underlying concepts that this chapter and the next discuss.

Arrays

Arrays are, in many ways, the simplest data structure; anything simpler would be a primitive data type like an integer or a Boolean. An *array* is a sequential list of elements, fixed in number. The elements are all of the same type, usually stored in one memory block, so that each element immediately follows the previous in memory. The elements are said to be *contiguous* in memory. You refer to the elements of an array by their numeric index: the first element is element 0 (or 1, or anything you like, at least in Delphi); the second one is found at the number after that, and so on. In code, the element at index *i* is referred to as *A[i]*, where *A* is the identifier for the array.

Delphi has many array types built into the language itself, and a few other handy array types are defined as classes in the VCL (with, it must be said, some interesting non-class types). In addition, to support classes as arrays, Delphi's designers created the ability to overload the array operator, [], for properties, the only operator apart from the + operator (addition and string concatenation) to be overloaded in Object Pascal.

Array Types in Delphi

There are three main types of language-supported arrays in Delphi. The first type is the standard array, as defined by the array keyword. The second type was introduced in Delphi 4 to mimic something that has been available in Visual Basic for a long time, the dynamic array: an array that can be re-dimensioned at run time.

The final array type is not usually thought of as an array, although Object Pascal provides several variants of it. I am speaking, of course, of strings: length-byte strings (or the shortstring type in 32-bit Delphi), null-terminated strings (or the PChar type), and long strings in 32-bit Delphi (of which there's also a version using wide characters).

Arrays all have the same structure. They consist of one or more repetitions of some other data type, say a character, an integer, or a multi-byte record, and the elements of the array are contiguous in memory. This latter property of standard arrays makes the access of a particular element of the array very fast. It essentially boils down to a simple calculation of an address requiring just a few machine instructions, as we'll see in a moment.

Standard Arrays

I'm sure we all know the standard way to declare an array in Delphi. The following declaration:

```
var
  MyIntArray : array [0..9] of integer;
```

defines a 10-element array of integers. In Object Pascal, we can define the range of elements, in the case just mentioned, 0 to 9, to be anything we like. The following declaration defines another 10-element array of integers; however this time the elements are numbered from 1 to 10:

```
var
  MyIntArray : array [1..10] of integer;
```

Some people find the second declaration to be an easier array to deal with in code (the *first* element is element *one*, after all).

However, I must mention a few things about using arrays whose first element is not element 0. Firstly, in numerous places throughout the Windows and Linux APIs and the Delphi VCL and CLX, it is assumed that the first element of an array is element 0. After all, in C/C++ and Java, the language enforces this convention; *all* arrays start at element 0. Since Windows and Linux are both written in C (or C++), arrays you pass when calling the system API are all assumed to start at element 0.

Secondly, dynamic arrays start at element 0, so if you want to use this extremely flexible addition to the Object Pascal language, you will have to be used to counting from zero.

Thirdly, if you use open arrays as parameters to routines (we'll discuss what an open array is in a moment) then the Low function (which returns the index of the first element in an array) will return 0 inside the routine, no matter how the array is declared externally to the routine. (Note that this is how it works in all versions of Delphi at the time of writing; later versions may include the ability to reference the actual index limits of the array.)

Another thing to realize is that for basic arrays which are contiguous in memory, the address calculation to access element *N* of a zero-based array (i.e., MyArray*[N]* for some array MyArray) is this:

```
AddressOfElementN := AddressOfArray +
                     (N * sizeof(ElementType));
```

If, instead, the array started at element *X*, the address of element *N* would be calculated as:

```
AddressOfElementN := AddressOfArray +
                     ((N - X) * sizeof(ElementType));
```

which is, as you can see, a slightly more complex and, hence, slightly slower calculation. Although each individual calculation may be just slightly slower—indeed, not even enough to really matter—when you add up all of the small reductions in speed due to all of the arrays in the application which do not start at element 0, it may be detectable.

The final reason for using zero-based arrays is that very often the calculations and coding with such an array are simpler. For example, if you access all the elements with a For loop, the compiler may be able to optimize the loop to count down to zero, because a comparison with zero at the end of each iteration would be faster than the alternative. We'll see several examples of this throughout this book. So, all in all, it makes sense to get used to coding zero-based arrays.

So what's so great about arrays as a data structure to hold a set of elements? The first thing to notice is that calculating the address of element *N* is very, very fast; as stated above, it's generally just a multiplication and an addition. When you access element *N* as MyArray*[N]*, the compiler inserts some simple machine code instructions to calculate the address. No matter what value *N* happens to be, the calculation is the same; in other words, accessing the *N*th element is a O(1) operation, and it doesn't matter how many elements there are or how big or small *N* is.

The next thing to take into account is locality of reference. The elements of an array are right next to each other in memory: if you are stepping through the array, accessing each element in turn, you'll find that the operating system has already helped you out, since a bunch of elements would reside on the same memory page and that would have been swapped into main memory.

So, having seen the pros, of which cons should you be aware with arrays, then? The first one is insertion and deletion of elements. If you want to insert a new element at index *n*, for example, what must happen? Well, basically, all of the elements in the array, starting at position *n*, must be moved along one position, to open up a "hole" where you can place the new element. In essence, you will perform the following piece of code:

```
{first make room}
for i := LastElementIndex downto N do
  MyArray[i+1] := MyArray[i];
{insert new element at N}
MyArray[N] := NewElement;
{we have one more element}
inc(LastElementIndex);
```

(In practice, of course, the loop would be replaced with a call to the Move procedure.)

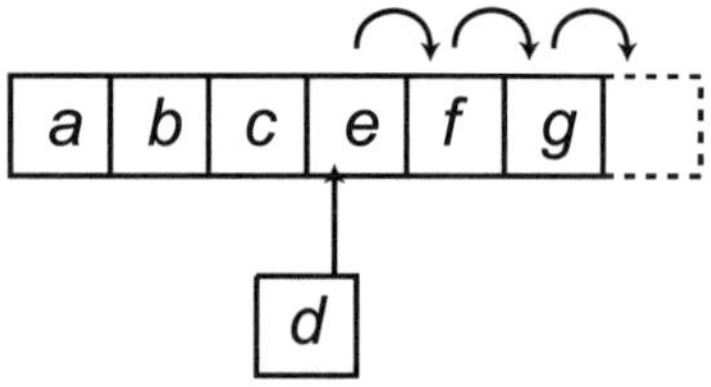

Figure 2.1: Insertion into an array

If you think about it, the amount of memory being moved around would depend on the value of *n* and the number of elements in the array itself. The larger the number of elements to move, the more time it would take. In fact, the time taken by the For loop would be proportional to the number of elements; a O(*n*) operation, in other words.

A similar argument applies to deleting an element. In this case, deleting element n would mean that the elements at positions $n+1$ onwards would have to be shifted back one position to "cover over" the element being deleted. Again, this is a $O(n)$ operation.

```
{delete an element by moving rest over by one}
for i := N+1 to LastElementIndex do
  MyArray[i-1] := MyArray[i];
{we have one less element}
dec(LastElementIndex);
```

(Again, in practice, the loop would be replaced with a call to the Move procedure.)

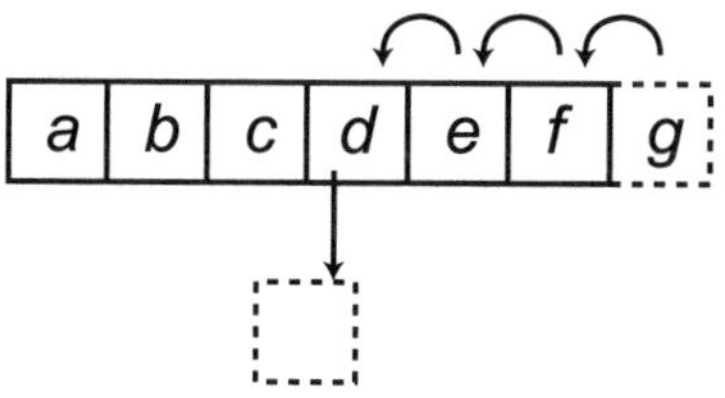

Figure 2.2: Deletion from an array

The point to grasp here is that these two operations will slow down with an increase in number of elements, both of them being $O(n)$ operations.

Of course, there is another consideration to be taken care of with insertion and deletion from an array: we have to maintain a count of active elements, or we have to have a *sentinel* element as the last element of the array to demarcate the end. (Null-terminated strings have the null character, #0, as the sentinel.) An array is usually declared at compile time as fixed size (we'll talk about ways of expanding the size of an array in a moment) and hence we need the ability to know the number of active elements. In the above two examples, I used a variable called LastElementIndex to define the number of active elements. With short or long strings, for example, there is a count of the number of characters in the string. But if we do not intend to use insertion or deletion, we do not need such artifices.

The next problem of which to be aware only affects Delphi 1 programmers. In Delphi 1, the maximum contiguous amount of memory you can allocate and use (at least not without some assembler work on your part) is 64 KB. If the size of your data element were 100 bytes, it would mean that an array of this data would only have a maximum of 655 elements, not very many. This 64 KB limitation may cause you problems and may cause you to use an array of pointers to your data (the famous TList class, for example), rather than an array of the actual data type (with a TList in Delphi 1 you could have an array with a maximum of 16,383 elements instead).

Dynamic Arrays

More often than not, when you are programming some routine that requires an array, you don't know how many elements you want in that array. It may be ten, one hundred, or a thousand, but certainly it's only at run time that you can come up with the answer. Furthermore, because you don't know, it's hard to declare the array as a local variable (declaring the maximum size you may encounter might put strains on the stack, especially in Delphi 1); it certainly makes sense to allocate it on the heap.

This still leaves something to be desired. Suppose you decide that, really, you would never require more than 100 elements. Never say never, because one day the application would require 101 elements, and it would crash with a sudden mysterious memory overwrite or an access violation (unless, of course, you added an assertion in your code to check for that eventuality). And of course, you could also guarantee that *that* would only happen with your best customer.

One technique, which dates from pre-object-oriented Pascal days, is to create an array type with just one element, and a pointer to that array:

```
type
  PMyArray : ^TMyArray;
  TMyArray : array [0..0] of TMyType;
```

When you need an array of TMyType, you allocate the required number of elements:

```
var
  MyArray : PMyArray;
begin
  ...
  GetMem(MyArray, 42*sizeof(TMyType));
  .. use MyArray ..
  FreeMem(MyArray, 42*sizeof(TMyType));
```

> It is only Delphi 1 that requires the size of the allocated block with a call to FreeMem. All 32-bit versions of Delphi and Kylix store the size of an allocated block with the block itself. It appears just before the block you get back from GetMem, and they ignore any size value you pass into FreeMem and use the hidden value instead.

Until you free the memory, MyArray points to an array of 42 TMyType elements. Although this technique is quick and easy, it suffers from some problems of which you must be aware. The first is that you cannot compile your code with range checking enabled ($R+) since the compiler thinks that the array should only have one element and therefore that the only index you can use is 0.

(You can get around this by sizing the upper bound of the the array type to some large number instead. This solution has the opposite problem: any index becomes valid up to the upper limit of the range. An example would be allocating a 42-element array based on a type with 1000 elements: any index from 42 to 999 is valid as far as the compiler's range checking goes.)

The second problem is that the allocated variable has no record of how many elements are in the array. Generally, you have to store this as a variable and keep track of the variable alongside the allocated array. That way you can do your own range checking, possibly with assertions.

Nevertheless, this technique is used a lot in everyday programming tasks. For example, the SysUtils unit has an extremely flexible array type called TByteArray, with the pointer to this type being PByteArray. Using this type (or rather the pointer to it) you can easily typecast an untyped buffer parameter to an array of bytes. There are other array types as well; you should be able to find a longint array type, a word array type, and so on.

The solution to the second problem discussed above shows the way to go. The best idea is to create an array class that would allow you to allocate as many elements as you wanted and that would enable you to access and set individual elements, even grow or shrink the array in size (i.e., increase or decrease the number of elements). Other methods, like the ability to sort the elements, and delete or insert a new element, might come in handy as well. Basically you would create an instance of the array class, declaring the size of each element with the constructor, and let the object deal with memory allocation issues.

Note that I am *not* talking about the TList class here. TList, which we'll discuss in a moment, is an array of pointers. In essence, if you were to use a TList, you'd have to allocate the individual elements on the heap and then manipulate an array of pointers to your elements.

What we will do instead is write a record array class, called TtdRecordList, that mimics a TList in its operations, but which is responsible for allocating the space for the elements themselves. The array class we will discuss has the interface shown in Listing 2.1.

Listing 2.1: Declaration of the TtdRecordList class

```
TtdRecordList = class
  private
    FActElemSize : integer;|
    FArray       : PAnsiChar;
```

```
    FCount       : integer;
    FCapacity    : integer;
    FElementSize : integer;
    FMaxElemCount: integer;
    FName        : TtdNameString;
  protected
    function rlGetItem(aIndex : integer) : pointer;
    procedure rlSetCapacity(aCapacity : integer);
    procedure rlSetCount(aCount : integer);
    procedure rlError(aErrorCode : integer;
                const aMethodName : TtdNameString;
                      aIndex : integer);
    procedure rlExpand;
  public
    constructor Create(aElementSize : integer);
    destructor Destroy; override;
    function Add(aItem : pointer) : integer;
    procedure Clear;
    procedure Delete(aIndex : integer);
    procedure Exchange(aIndex1, aIndex2 : integer);
    function First : pointer;
    function IndexOf(aItem : pointer;
                     aCompare : TtdCompareFunc) : integer;
    procedure Insert(aIndex : integer; aItem : pointer);
    function Last : pointer;
    procedure Move(aCurIndex, aNewIndex : integer);
    function Remove(aItem : pointer;
                    aCompare : TtdCompareFunc) : integer;
    procedure Sort(aCompare : TtdCompareFunc);
    property Capacity : integer read FCapacity write rlSetCapacity;
    property Count : integer read FCount write rlSetCount;
    property ElementSize : integer read FActElemSize;
    property Items[aIndex : integer] : pointer read rlGetItem; default;
    property MaxCount : integer read FMaxElemCount;
    property Name : TtdNameString read FName write FName;
end;
```

If you are familiar with the interface to TList, you'll see that the TtdRecordList class mimics it with similarly named methods and properties. So, for example, Add will append an element onto the end of the list, whereas Insert will add the element at the index given. Both methods will extend the internal structure if necessary and increment the count of elements. The Sort method won't be discussed here; we'll leave this implementation until Chapter 5.

The Create constructor saves the passed element size and also calculates the size of an element, rounded up to the nearest four bytes. This ensures that, for speed reasons, elements always start on a 4-byte boundary. As a final step, the constructor calculates the maximum number of elements the class could hold with the given element size. This is only really required for Delphi 1 since the maximum allocation from the heap is a shade less than 64 KB, and it will be used to check that the array doesn't grow beyond the maximum limit.

Listing 2.2: The constructor for TtdRecordList

```
constructor TtdRecordList.Create(aElementSize : integer);
begin
  inherited Create;
  {save the actual element size}
  FActElemSize := aElementSize;
  {round the actual size to the nearest 4 bytes}
  FElementSize := ((aElementSize + 3) shr 2) shl 2;
  {calculate the maximum number of elements}
  {$IFDEF Delphi1}
  FMaxElemCount := 65535 div FElementSize;
  {$ELSE}
  FMaxElemCount := MaxInt div FElementSize;
  {$ENDIF}
end;
```

Note that the class does not allocate any memory for the elements. This allocation is deferred until an element is actually added; in other words, until the class instance is actually used.

(Listing 2.2 uses a non-standard compiler define, Delphi1. This compiler define is declared in an include file, TDDefine.inc, that is included in all the units for this book. I find it easier to remember a compiler define named Delphi1 than the more official VER80, and this gets easier the more Delphi versions there are. For example, VER100 is for Delphi 3, whereas VER120 is for Delphi 4, but either way it's easier to remember Delphi3 and Delphi4.)

The Destroy destructor is equally simple. We just set the capacity of the instance to zero (we'll discuss what this does in a moment) and the ancestor Destroy destructor is called.

Listing 2.3: The destructor for TtdRecordList

```
destructor TtdRecordList.Destroy;
begin
  Capacity := 0;
  inherited Destroy;
end;
```

Let's see something more interesting: adding or inserting a new element. The Add method is simple; it just calls Insert to insert a new element at the end of the internal array. Insert accepts an index value indicating where to insert the element. The element itself is defined as a pointer (there is another way of defining the element to insert (as a typeless var parameter) but if we stick with pointers, it makes other methods easier to implement and understand, and also provides consistency). When we call the method, we can use Delphi's @ operator to pass the address of our item as the pointer value.

As the new item is a pointer, it could be nil, so the first thing is to make sure that it isn't. Then the method validates the index; it must be between 0 and the current count of elements in the array, inclusive. Now we can do some work. If the number of elements equals the current capacity of the array, the array must be grown with a call to rlExpand. We now move the elements from aIndex to the end of the array along by one element to open up a "hole" for the new element, and then we copy the new element into the hole. We increment the count of elements as the final step.

Listing 2.4: Adding and inserting a new element

```
function TtdRecordList.Add(aItem : pointer) : integer;
begin
  Result := Count;
  Insert(Count, aItem);
end;
procedure TtdRecordList.Insert(aIndex : integer; aItem : pointer);
begin
  if (aItem = nil) then
    rlError(tdeNilItem, 'Insert', aIndex);
  if (aIndex < 0) or (aIndex > Count) then
    rlError(tdeIndexOutOfBounds, 'Insert', aIndex);
  if (Count = Capacity) then
    rlExpand;
  if (aIndex < Count) then
    System.Move((FArray + (aIndex * FElementSize))^,
                (FArray + (succ(aIndex) * FElementSize))^,
                (Count - aIndex) * FElementSize);
  System.Move(aItem^,
              (FArray + (aIndex * FElementSize))^,
              FActElemSize);
  inc(FCount);
end;
```

Having seen Insert, Listing 2.5 shows Delete for deleting an element from the array. Again, we check the index we're given, and if it's acceptable, we move the elements from aIndex to the end of the array over the element we're asked to delete. We have one less element now, so we decrement the count.

Listing 2.5: Deleting an element from the array

```
procedure TtdRecordList.Delete(aIndex : integer);
begin
  if (aIndex < 0) or (aIndex >= Count) then
    rlError(tdeIndexOutOfBounds, 'Delete', aIndex);
  dec(FCount);
  if (aIndex < Count) then
    System.Move((FArray + (succ(aIndex) * FElementSize))^,
                (FArray + (aIndex * FElementSize))^,
                (Count - aIndex) * FElementSize);
end;
```

Allied to Delete is the Remove method where we want to delete a particular element, but we don't necessarily know where it is in the array. We find the item by means of the IndexOf method and a helper comparison routine that we have to write externally to the class. So Remove requires not only the element we wish to delete, but also a routine which will help identify the element that needs removing inside the array. This routine is of type TtdCompareFunc and will be called for every element in the array by the IndexOf method until the routine returns 0 (i.e., equal) for an element. If no element does so, IndexOf returns tdc_ItemNotPresent.

Listing 2.6: Remove and IndexOf methods

```
function TtdRecordList.Remove(aItem    : pointer;
                              aCompare : TtdCompareFunc) : integer;
begin
  Result := IndexOf(aItem, aCompare);
  if (Result<>tdc_ItemNotPresent) then
    Delete(Result);
end;
function TtdRecordList.IndexOf(aItem    : pointer;
                               aCompare : TtdCompareFunc) : integer;
var
  ElementPtr : PAnsiChar;
  i          : integer;
begin
  ElementPtr := FArray;
  for i := 0 to pred(Count) do begin
    if (aCompare(aItem, ElementPtr) = 0) then begin
      Result := i;
      Exit;
    end;
    inc(ElementPtr, FElementSize);
  end;
  Result := tdc_ItemNotPresent;
end;
```

To expand the array (i.e., to allow more elements to be stored in it), you set the Capacity property. Setting Capacity causes the protected rlSetCapacity method to be called. rlSetCapacity looks more complicated than it need be because the Delphi 1 ReAllocMem routine doesn't do everything that the 32-bit version does.

A related method is the protected rlExpand method, which uses a simple algorithm to set the Capacity property based on its current value. rlExpand is called automatically by the Insert method to grow the array, if that method determines that the current array is full (i.e., the capacity of the array is equal to the number of elements in the array).

Listing 2.7: Expanding the array

```
procedure TtdRecordList.rlExpand;
var
  NewCapacity : integer;
begin
  {if current capacity is 0, make new capacity 4 elements}
  if (Capacity = 0) then
    NewCapacity := 4
  {if current capacity is less than 64, increase it by 16 elements}
  else if (Capacity < 64) then
    NewCapacity := Capacity + 16
  {if current capacity is 64 or more, increase it by a quarter}
  else
    NewCapacity := Capacity + (Capacity div 4);
  {make sure we don't grow beyond the array's upper limit}
  if (NewCapacity > FMaxElemCount) then begin
    NewCapacity := FMaxElemCount;
    if (NewCapacity = Capacity) then
      rlError(tdeAtMaxCapacity, 'rlExpand', 0);
  end;
  {set the new capacity}
  Capacity := NewCapacity;
end;
procedure TtdRecordList.rlSetCapacity(aCapacity : integer);
begin
  if (aCapacity<>FCapacity) then begin
    {don't go over the maximum number of elements possible}
    if (aCapacity > FMaxElemCount) then
      rlError(tdeCapacityTooLarge, 'rlSetCapacity', 0);
    {reallocate the array, or free it if the capacity is being reduced
  to zero}
    {$IFDEF Delphi1}
    if (aCapacity = 0) then begin
      FreeMem(FArray, word(FCapacity) * FElementSize);
      FArray := nil;
```

```
      end
      else begin
        if (FCapacity = 0) then
          GetMem(FArray, word(aCapacity) * FElementSize)
        else
          FArray := ReallocMem(FArray,
                                word(FCapacity) * FElementSize,
                                word(aCapacity) * FElementSize);
      end;
      {$ELSE}
      ReallocMem(FArray, aCapacity * FElementSize);
      {$ENDIF}
      {are we shrinking the capacity? if so check the count}
      if (aCapacity < FCapacity) then begin
        if (Count > aCapacity) then
          Count := aCapacity;
      end;
      {save the new capacity}
      FCapacity := aCapacity;
    end;
end;
```

Of course, an array class wouldn't be very useful if we couldn't get at the elements stored in the array. The TtdRecordList class makes use of an array property called Items. The only accessor for this property is the read method: rlGetItem. To avoid excessive copying of the data in an element, the rlGetItem method returns a pointer to the element in the array. This makes it easy to alter a particular element in the array as well, which is why we do not expose a write accessor method for the Items property. Since the Items property is marked with the default keyword it's easy to access individual elements with code like this, MyArray[*i*], rather than MyArray.Items[*i*].

Listing 2.8: Accessing an element in the array

```
function TtdRecordList.rlGetItem(aIndex : integer) : pointer;
begin
  if (aIndex < 0) or (aIndex >= Count) then
    rlError(tdeIndexOutOfBounds, 'rlGetItem', aIndex);
  Result := pointer(FArray + (aIndex * FElementSize));
end;
```

The final method we shall discuss is the one called by setting the Count property: rlSetCount. Setting the Count property makes it easy to preallocate the space for an array and use it in a similar fashion to standard Delphi arrays. Note that the Insert and Delete methods will maintain the count properly when you insert or delete an element. Setting the Count property explicitly will ensure that the Capacity property is properly set as well (Insert takes care of this automatically). If the new value for Count is greater than the current value, the newly accessible elements will automatically be set to binary zeros; if it is less than, the elements at indexes greater than or equal to the new count will no longer be accessible (essentially, you can view them as having been deleted).

Listing 2.9: Setting the number of elements in the array

```
procedure TtdRecordList.rlSetCount(aCount : integer);
begin
  if (aCount<>FCount) then begin
    {if the new count is greater than the capacity, grow the array}
    if (aCount > Capacity) then
      Capacity := aCount;
    {if the new count is greater than the old count, set new elements
     to binary zeros}
    if (aCount > FCount) then
      FillChar((FArray + (FCount * FElementSize))^,
               (aCount - FCount) * FElementSize,
               0);
    {save the new count}
    FCount := aCount;
  end;
end;
```

The code for the TtdRecordList class is on the accompanying CD in the TDRecLst.pas source file. It also includes other standard methods like First, Last, Move, and Exchange.

New-style Dynamic Arrays

In Delphi 4, Borland introduced *dynamic arrays*, an improvement in the language to aid in using arrays whose size is unknown at coding time. The code the compiler adds to your application is similar to that added by long strings. Like these strings, you can set the size of the array by calling the standard SetLength procedure, and dynamic arrays are reference counted. Furthermore, the Copy function has been overloaded so that you can copy parts of arrays. Like normal static arrays, you access individual elements by using the [] operator.

We won't go into any further details on this type of dynamic array in this book. They are limited in that they are only available in Delphi 4 or later and Kylix, and furthermore do not have the richness of functionality provided by TtdRecordList. If you wish to find out more on dynamic arrays, please refer to your Delphi documentation.

TList Class, an Array of Pointers

Ever since the original Delphi 1, there has been another type of array available as standard: the TList class. Unlike the arrays we have been discussing up to now, TList encapsulates an array of pointers.

Overview of the TList Class

The TList class stores pointers in an array format. The pointers can be anything: pointers to records, strings, or objects. Methods are provided to add and delete items, to find items in the list, to rearrange the items in the list, and, in later compiler versions, to sort the items in the list. Like an array a TList object can be used with the [] operator. Since the Items property is marked default you can code MyList[*i*] instead of MyList.Items[*i*] to access pointer number *i* in the list. TList elements are always counted from 0.

Although the TList class is very versatile, people sometimes have problems with it.

One common problem is universal: when you destroy a TList instance, none of the items remaining in it are freed. This is actually a benefit in a way—since you are guaranteed that the TList will never deallocate any of the items in the list, you can add the same item to several lists without worrying that the item will be destroyed without you "knowing" about it. Unfortunately, the tendency when using a TList is to assume it works like components on a form (when a form is destroyed, all of the components on the form are destroyed, too). This is not so, and we must take special care to ensure that items in a list are destroyed when the list itself is destroyed.

There is a subtle bug that a lot of people run into when coding a routine that destroys a lot of items in a list (I'll admit to falling into the same trap on occasion). The item destruction code we tend to write is this:

```
for i := 0 to pred(MyList.Count) do begin
  if SomeConditionApplies(i) then begin
    TObject(MyList[i]).Free;
    MyList.Delete(i);
  end;
end;
```

where SomeConditionApplies is some arbitrary function that decides whether to free the object at *i* or not.

Well, we all tend to think of increasing loop counters and thereby introduce the bug. Suppose the list has three items, so this code will loop three times for indexes 0, 1, and 2. The first time through the loop assume the condition applies: we free the object at index 0 and then delete the item at index 0 from the list. This leaves two items in the list—but they'll now have indexes 0 and 1, rather than 1 and 2. The second time through the loop, again assume the condition is true so we'll free the object at index 1 (which was originally at index 2, remember) and then delete the item at index 1. This leaves us with one item in the list, the one at index 0. The third time through the loop, we attempt to reference the object at index 2 and get a "list index out of bounds" exception.

What we should have done is reverse the loop, starting at the end and working backward to the start, and we'd have avoided this bug.

For freeing all the objects in a list, we'd use the following code rather than calling the Delete method for each item:

```
for i := 0 to pred(MyList.Count) do
  TObject(MyList[i]).Free;
MyList.Clear;
```

The next general problem with using a TList is trying to create a descendant for some purpose. If you try, you'll suddenly run into all sorts of problems with TList methods being static, with private fields being inaccessible, and so on. My advice here is, don't. It is my view that the TList class is *not* a class from which you can descend; it has not been designed to be extensible from the outset like the TStrings class, for example. Instead, create a separate class that uses a TList instance internally to store the data; use *delegation* rather than *inheritance* as your descendence mechanism.

When I originally wrote the above paragraph, I was unaware of what Borland had done to the TList in Delphi 5. In Delphi 5, for some unfathomable reason, Borland changed the operation of a TList in order to better support a new descendant: the TObjectList. This descendant was designed to hold object instances. It can be found in the Contnrs unit, a unit we'll be hearing more of later.

What did they change? Prior to Delphi 5, the TList cleared itself by freeing the internal pointer array, a O(1) operation. Since they wanted the TObjectList to free its held objects under certain circumstances, they changed the fundamental nature of the TList in order to support this type of functionality. In Delphi 5 and above, and Kylix of course, the TList clears itself by calling a new virtual method, Notify, for every item in the list. TList.Notify does nothing. TObjectList.Notify, on the other hand, will free an object when it is being removed from the list.

"So what?" you may ask. Well, this new method of clearing a TList is a O(*n*) operation. The more items in the TList, the longer it takes. Compared with the lean and mean pre-Delphi 5 TList, this is bloated. Every instance and every class that uses a TList suddenly gets to be slower, even if you wanted the previous version's speed. And, remember, the only reason for this drastic change to TList is that someone in Borland R&D didn't want to use delegation to create the new object list class. Far better, in his view, was to alter the standard class to make his job easier.

Even worse from an object-oriented design viewpoint, we have a case where an ancestor is modified to support a descendant. A TList does not ever free its items—a cardinal rule from Delphi 1 days. However, TList was modified to support the ability to do so in its descendants (of which there is only one in Delphi 5's VCL that overrides any of TList's methods: the TObjectList class).

Danny Thorpe, one of the clearest thinkers and designers in Delphi R&D I know, has this to say in his book *Delphi Component Design* [23]:

"TList is a worker drone, not a promiscuous ancestor class. . . . If [a] list is exposed . . . you should create a simple wrapper class (derived from TObject, not TList) that exposes only the property and function equivalents of TList that you need and whose function return types and method parameter types match the type of the data that the list contains. The wrapper class then contains a TList instance internally and uses that for actual storage. Implement the functions and property access methods of this wrapper class with simple one-line calls to the corresponding methods or properties of the internal TList, wrapped in appropriate typecasts."

It is a shame, in my view, that Thorpe's book was not required reading in Borland R&D.

TtdObjectList Class

What we shall do at this juncture is create a new list class that works like TList does, but with two differences. It will store instances of some class (or descendants of it), and it will destroy the objects it contains whenever necessary. In other words, a specialized list that circumvents the two problems mentioned above. This class is the TtdObjectList class. It differs from the TObjectList in Delphi 5 and later versions in that it is typesafe.

This class will not be a descendant of TList. It will certainly interface the same methods as TList does, but the implementation of these methods will be delegated to the same-named methods of an internal TList instance.

The TtdObjectList class has an important new attribute, that of data ownership. The class will either act in the same manner as TList, i.e., the items it contains will not be freed when the list is destroyed (it does not own the data), or it will assume that it has full control of the items it holds and destroy them whenever required (it owns the data). An instance of the TtdObjectList class is marked as a data owner when it is created, and you cannot suddenly decide to make it a data owner when it wasn't before, or vice versa.

The class will also impose *type safety*. When an instance of the class is created, we shall state what kind (or class) of objects it will accept. When we add or insert a new item in this list, the method will verify that the object being added is of the correct class (or is a descendant of that class).

The interface looks a lot like that of TList. I've not bothered implementing the Pack method since only non-nil objects will be added to the list. Again, the Sort method won't be discussed here; we'll leave the implementation until Chapter 5.

Listing 2.10: The TtdObjectList definition

```
TtdObjectList = class
  private
    FClass     : TClass;
    FDataOwner : boolean;
    FList      : TList;
    FName      : TtdNameString;
  protected
    function olGetCapacity : integer;
    function olGetCount : integer;
    function olGetItem(aIndex : integer) : TObject;

    procedure olSetCapacity(aCapacity : integer);
    procedure olSetCount(aCount : integer);
    procedure olSetItem(aIndex : integer;
                        aItem  : TObject);

    procedure olError(aErrorCode  : integer;
                      const aMethodName : TtdNameString;
                            aIndex      : integer);
  public
    constructor Create(aClass : TClass; aDataOwner : boolean);
    destructor Destroy; override;

    function Add(aItem : TObject) : integer;
    procedure Clear;
    procedure Delete(aIndex : integer);
    procedure Exchange(aIndex1, aIndex2 : integer);
    function First : TObject;
    function IndexOf(aItem : TObject) : integer;
    procedure Insert(aIndex : integer; aItem : TObject);
```

```
    function Last : TObject;
    procedure Move(aCurIndex, aNewIndex : integer);
    function Remove(aItem : TObject) : integer;
    procedure Sort(aCompare : TtdCompareFunc);

    property Capacity : integer read olGetCapacity write olSetCapacity;
    property Count : integer read olGetCount write olSetCount;
    property DataOwner : boolean read FDataOwner;
    property Items[Index : integer] : TObject
       read olGetItem write olSetItem; default;
    property List : TList read FList;
    property Name : TtdNameString read FName write FName;
end;
```

A number of the methods in TtdObjectList are simple wrappers around a call to the equivalent method for the internal FList object. For example, here is the TtdObjectList.First method implementation:

Listing 2.11: The TtdObjectList.First method

```
function TtdObjectList.First : TObject;
begin
  Result := TObject(FList.First);
end;
```

Those methods that accept an index parameter validate that parameter prior to calling the equivalent FList method. This is not strictly necessary since FList will validate the index, but the TtdObjectList methods will provide more information in case of an error. Here's a representative example, the Move method:

Listing 2.12: The TtdObjectList.Move method

```
procedure TtdObjectList.Move(aCurIndex, aNewIndex : integer);
begin
  {instead of the list doing it, we'll check the indexes}
  if (aCurIndex < 0) or (aCurIndex >= FList.Count) then
    olError(tdeIndexOutOfBounds, 'Move', aCurIndex);
  if (aNewIndex < 0) or (aNewIndex >= FList.Count) then
    olError(tdeIndexOutOfBounds, 'Move', aNewIndex);
  {move the items}
  FList.Move(aCurIndex, aNewIndex);
end;
```

The constructor for the class accepts the class type for the objects that will be stored in the list (this provides the type safety aspects of the list) and whether the list is going to own the objects within it or not. It then creates the internal TList instance. The destructor clears the list and frees it.

Listing 2.13: The constructor and destructor for TtdObjectList

```
constructor TtdObjectList.Create(aClass     : TClass;
                                 aDataOwner : boolean);
begin
  inherited Create;
  {save the class and the data owner flag}
  FClass := aClass;
  FDataOwner := aDataOwner;
  {create the internal list}
  FList := TList.Create;
end;
destructor TtdObjectList.Destroy;
begin
  {if the list is assigned, clear it and destroy it}
  if (FList<>nil) then begin
    Clear;
    FList.Destroy;
  end;
  inherited Destroy;
end;
```

If you are unsure how to pass a value for the aClass parameter, here is an example using TButton:

```
var
  MyList : TtdObjectList;
begin
. . .
  MyList := TtdObjectList.Create(TButton, false);
```

The Clear method provides the first real change from the standard TList. It checks to see whether the list owns its data or not and, if so, will free all of the objects in the list before clearing the list itself. (Notice that we don't bother using the FList's Delete method for each item; it's far more efficient to clear the list after all items have been freed.)

Listing 2.14: The Clear method for TtdObjectList

```
procedure TtdObjectList.Clear;
var
  i : integer;
begin
  {if we own the items present, free them before clearing the list}
  if DataOwner then
    for i := 0 to pred(FList.Count) do
      TObject(FList[i]).Free;
  FList.Clear;
end;
```

The Delete and Remove methods perform the same kind of checking and will free the object prior to deleting it, if the list is a data owner. Notice that I elected not to call FList.Remove in the Remove method, but instead coded the routine directly. This is referred to as "coding from first principles" and gives us more control and is more efficient.

Listing 2.15: Deleting an item from a TtdObjectList

```
procedure TtdObjectList.Delete(aIndex : integer);
begin
  {instead of the list doing it, we'll check the index}
  if (aIndex < 0) or (aIndex >= FList.Count) then
    olError(tdeIndexOutOfBounds, 'Delete', aIndex);
  {if we own the objects, then free the one we're about to delete}
  if DataOwner then
    TObject(FList[aIndex]).Free;
  {delete the item from the list}
  FList.Delete(aIndex);
end;
function TtdObjectList.Remove(aItem : TObject) : integer;
begin
  {find the item}
  Result := IndexOf(aItem);
  {if we found it...}
  if (Result<>-1) then begin
    {if we own the objects, free the one about to be deleted}
    if DataOwner then
      TObject(FList[Result]).Free;
    {delete the item}
    FList.Delete(Result);
  end;
end;
```

A small "gotcha" can be found in the method that sets or puts an item into the list, olSetItem (the write accessor method for the Items array property). Suppose the programmer using the class writes this:

```
var
  MyObjectList : TtdObjectList;
  SomeObject   : TObject;
begin
  . . .
  MyObjectList[0] := SomeObject;
```

It seems innocuous, but think about what happens if the list is a data owner. The effect of the assignment statement is that the item at index 0 is replaced with the new object, SomeObject. The previous object is lost and can no longer be referenced. We should, in fact, free the object that is about to be replaced by the new one. Of course, we should also check that the new object is of the correct type.

Listing 2.16: Setting an item in a TtdObjectList

```
procedure TtdObjectList.olSetItem(aIndex : integer;
                                  aItem  : TObject);
begin
  {test for item class}
  if (aItem = nil) then
    olError(tdeNilItem, 'olSetItem', aIndex);
  if not (aItem is FClass) then
    olError(tdeInvalidClassType, 'olSetItem', aIndex);
  {instead of the list doing it, we'll check the index}
  if (aIndex < 0) or (aIndex >= FList.Count) then
    olError(tdeIndexOutOfBounds, 'olSetItem', aIndex);
  {if we own the objects and we're about to replace the current object
   at this index with another different one, then free the current one
   first}
  if DataOwner and (aItem<>FList[aIndex]) then
    TObject(FList[aIndex]).Free;
  {set the new item}
  FList[aIndex] := aItem;
end;
```

Finally, let's see the Add and Insert methods. Like Remove, Add is coded from first principles and calls FList.Insert instead of FList.Add.

Listing 2.17: Add and Insert for a TtdObjectList

```
function TtdObjectList.Add(aItem : TObject) : integer;
begin
  {test for item class}
  if (aItem = nil) then
    olError(tdeNilItem, 'Add', FList.Count);
  if not (aItem is FClass) then
    olError(tdeInvalidClassType, 'Add', FList.Count);
  {insert the new item at the end of the list}
  Result := FList.Count;
  FList.Insert(Result, aItem);
end;
procedure TtdObjectList.Insert(aIndex : integer; aItem : TObject);
begin
  {test for item class}
  if (aItem = nil) then
    olError(tdeNilItem, 'Insert', aIndex);
  if not (aItem is FClass) then
    olError(tdeInvalidClassType, 'Insert', aIndex);
  {instead of the list doing it, we'll check the index}
  if (aIndex < 0) or (aIndex > FList.Count) then
```

```
    olError(tdeIndexOutOfBounds, 'Insert', aIndex);
  {insert into the list}
  FList.Insert(aIndex, aItem);
end;
```

The full code for TtdObjectList can be found in the TDObjLst.pas file.

Arrays on Disk

One application of arrays that many books gloss over is arrays on disk, that is, files of fixed length records. This type of array has its own peculiarities that deserve some discussion, after which we will write a class embodying a record file (or data file). With persistent arrays, the array is generally known as a data file, or file of records, and the elements or items in the array are known as records. The index of an item in the array is known as the record number.

Pascal has always provided support for files of some fixed record type, and Delphi follows with that tradition. The standard method of dealing with files of records is as follows:

```
var
  MyRecord : TMyRecord;
  MyFile : file of TMyRecord;
begin
  {open data file}
  System.Assign(MyFile, 'MyData.DAT');
  System.Rewrite(MyFile);
  try

    {write a record to position 0}
    ..set fields of MyRecord..
    System.Write(DF, MyRecord);

    {read the record from position 0}
    System.Seek(DF, 0);
    System.Read(DF, MyRecord);

  finally
    System.Close(DF);
  end;
end;
```

In this snippet of code we open a data file (the Assign and Rewrite procedures), we write a new record to the file (the Write procedure), and we reread that record (the Seek and Read procedures). Notice the requirement to call Seek to position the file pointer to the start of the record we want to read before we read it; otherwise we'd read the second record of the file. This code also includes a Try..finally block to ensure that the file is closed no matter what may happen after the call to Rewrite.

There are a couple of things wrong with this way of accessing records in a data file. The first is subtle, but important. The only way to know the size of each record is to read it from the source code of the program accessing the file. If you are given a file of records, it requires some detective work with a hex viewer to guess at the record length. Once you know the record length, given the file size you can determine the number of records in the file.

Another problem is that the data file stores no information about the makeup of the records; in other words, the different fields and their types in the record. Actually, we can do an awful lot with the records and data file without knowing this information if we store more information in the file.

So what information should we store in the file as well as the records? Well, one item is the record length, as we've discussed. Another is the number of records that are currently present in the file. With these two pieces of information we can determine that the file could be valid (i.e., does the file size equal the number of records multiplied by the record length, plus the size of the header information?).

Let us suppose then that we have a special header block for the file. This header block would contain some essential data about the file, and it would then be followed by some number of equal-sized records. To put it another way, the header block would contain some essential persistent information about the array (element size, number of elements, other items we haven't decided on yet), followed by the array of items.

Using this scheme, we can envisage writing a class that can open a file and then add records to it (which would alter the data in the header block, of course), read records by record number, write or update records by record number, and close the file. But what about deleting records? We certainly don't want to move the records up a slot as we did with the in-memory version—that would take an inordinate amount of time.

There are two possibilities. The first is the simplest and is the one used in dBASE data files. The records in the file are prefixed by a single byte to store a deletion marker. This could be a Boolean value (true/false), or it could be a character field ('Y'/'N', or '*'/blank). When we delete a record, we will set the deletion marker to indicate that the record is deleted. All fine and dandy, but what do we do with these deleted records? Plan A is to just ignore them. The file eventually gets more and more of these deleted, unusable records, and at some point we have to *pack* the file to get rid of them and reduce the data file size. Plan B is to reuse them. When we add a new record to the file we search through the records that are present until we find a deleted one and then reuse that. Plan B, as you can no doubt imagine, is pretty bad. Suppose we have just one deleted record in a data file of 10,000 records; we'd have to read through at least half the file on average—5,000 records—just to find the single deleted record. It is for this reason, the $O(n)$ running time, that Plan B is never implemented.

Yet Plan B does have its attractions, namely the reuse of deleted records, providing we can make it run in O(1) time instead. This leads to the second method of deleting records: the deleted record chain. (For this algorithm we must have a header block, so it's now a given.)

We precede each record by 4 bytes, a longint value. This extra field, a deleted flag, will denote whether the record is deleted or not; the normal value is –1, a value we define to mean the record is active. Any other value will mean that the record is deleted, but we shall impose more information to this value in a moment. Notice that the size of the record grows internally by 4 bytes: the user, on the other hand, still thinks of the record as being the original size. We store, in the header block, another longint value to be the record number of the first deleted record. Normally this value is –2, which we take to mean that there are no more deleted records.

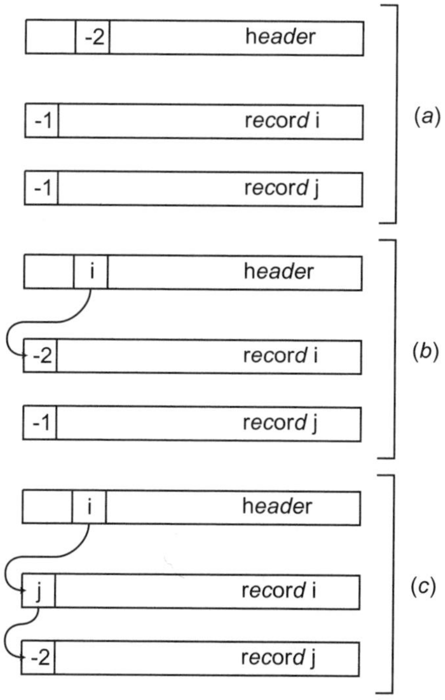

Figure 2.3: Deleting a record

When we first delete a record, we proceed as follows. We set the record's deleted flag equal to the header block's first deleted record value, i.e., -2. This deleted flag is written to disk. We then set the header record's first deleted record number to the number of the record just deleted. There are two results of this behavior: firstly, the deleted record's flag has been set to a value not equal to -1 (in other words, it is marked as deleted); and secondly, the header block's field now points to this deleted record as one that can be reused.

When we delete a second record, we proceed in the same manner. The result this time is that the second record's flag will contain the first deleted record's number (which is not -1, therefore the record is recognizably deleted), and the header block's field will point to the second deleted record.

OK, so what happens when we add a new record? Instead of blindly adding the record to the end of the file as before, we first check the header block's first deleted record field. If it is not equal to –2 we know that it is a record number that we can reuse. If we do reuse it, we will have to set the header field to something else; otherwise, the next time we add a record, we'll reuse the same record, with bizarre and disastrous results. We read the deleted flag for the record we are about to reuse, and set the header field to this value. Notice that when we reuse the final deleted record the header field will be set to –2 again, since the very first record we deleted had this value as its deleted flag.

There is one more consideration before we show the code. It is my belief that it would be foolish of us to limit the persistent array to just a disk file. Although we'd be using a file in a vast majority of cases, there is nothing to stop us from wanting a persistent array in memory, or on some other device. Better would be to create the persistent array class to use a stream. Delphi provides us with a rich variety of stream classes, including a file stream, so if we design the code to use a TStream, it will be usable with all the other TStream descendants.

Here is the interface to the TtdRecordStream class, a class used to persistently store an array of records to a stream.

Listing 2.18: Persistent arrays with a TtdRecordStream class

```
type
  TtdRecordStream = class
    private
      FStream       : TStream;
      FCount        : longint;
      FCapacity     : longint;
      FHeaderRec    : PtdRSHeaderRec;
      FName         : TtdNameString;
      FRecord       : PByteArray;
      FRecordLen    : integer;
      FRecordLen4   : integer;
      FZeroPosition : longint;
    protected
      procedure rsSetCapacity(aCapacity : longint);
      procedure rsError(aErrorCode  : integer;
                  const aMethodName : TtdNameString;
                        aNumValue   : longint);
      function rsCalcRecordOffset(aIndex : longint) : longint;
      procedure rsCreateHeaderRec(aRecordLen : integer);
      procedure rsReadHeaderRec;
```

```
      procedure rsReadStream(var aBuffer; aBufLen : integer);
      procedure rsWriteStream(var aBuffer; aBufLen : integer);
      procedure rsSeekStream(aOffset : longint);
    public
      constructor Create(aStream       : TStream;
                         aRecordLength : integer);
      destructor Destroy; override;
      procedure Flush; virtual;
      function Add(var aRecord) : longint;
      procedure Clear;
      procedure Delete(aIndex : longint);
      procedure Read(aIndex : longint;
                 var aRecord;
                 var aIsDeleted : boolean);
      procedure Write(aIndex : longint;
                  var aRecord);
      property Capacity : longint read FCapacity write rsSetCapacity;
      property Count : longint read FCount;
      property RecordLength : integer read FRecordLen;
      property Name : TtdNameString read FName write FName;
  end;
```

Unfortunately, with these persistent arrays it is hard to get the Delphi overloaded [] operator to work for us efficiently, and so we abandon a possible Items array property for simpler Read and Write methods.

The Create constructor can be called in two modes: either there is a persistent array on the stream or there isn't. The constructor has to determine this and create the header block if the stream is new.

Listing 2.19: The constructor for the TtdRecordStream class

```
constructor TtdRecordStream.Create(aStream       : TStream;
                                   aRecordLength : integer);
begin
  inherited Create;
  {save the stream, and its current position}
  FStream := aStream;
  FZeroPosition := aStream.Position;
  {if the stream size is zero we have to create the header record}
  if (aStream.Size - FZeroPosition = 0) then
    rsCreateHeaderRec(aRecordLength)
  {otherwise, check to see if it has a valid header record, read it
    and set up our fields}
  else
    rsReadHeaderRec;
  {allocate a work record}
  FRecordLen4 := FRecordLen + sizeof(longint);
```

```
  GetMem(FRecord, FRecordLen4);
end;
```

Notice that the very first thing that the constructor does is to mark the current position of the stream and store it in FZeroPosition. This value, usually zero, will be used to mark the position of the header block for the persistent array. This behavior means that you can write your own header information to the stream before calling this Create constructor, and the rest of the class's methods will not touch it. The class does assume, however, that the remainder of the stream from FZeroPosition onwards belongs to the class, to do with as it wishes.

The constructor calls either rsCreateHeaderRec to create a brand new header record for a stream that is empty (i.e., the array needs to be created), or rsReadHeaderRec to read the current header record (this latter routine will also validate the header record).

Finally, Create allocates a work record off the heap (this allocation having enough additional room for the deleted flag). The Destroy destructor frees this work record.

Listing 2.20: The destructor for the TtdRecordStream class

```
destructor TtdRecordStream.Destroy;
begin
  if (FHeaderRec<>nil) then
    FreeMem(FHeaderRec, FHeaderRec^.hrHeaderLen);
  if (FRecord<>nil) then
    FreeMem(FRecord, FRecordLen4);
  inherited Destroy;
end;
```

Let's have a look at the two subsidiary methods that either create a header record or read the one that's already there.

Listing 2.21: Creating or reading the header record

```
procedure TtdRecordStream.rsCreateHeaderRec(aRecordLen : integer);
begin
{allocate a header record}
  if ((aRecordLen + sizeof(longint)) < sizeof(TtdRSHeaderRec)) then begin
    FHeaderRec := AllocMem(sizeof(TtdRSHeaderRec));
    FHeaderRec^.hrHeaderLen := sizeof(TtdRSHeaderRec);
  end
  else begin
    FHeaderRec := AllocMem(aRecordLen + sizeof(longint));
    FHeaderRec^.hrHeaderLen := aRecordLen + sizeof(longint);
  end;
  {set other standard fields}
```

```
  with FHeaderRec^ do begin
    hrSignature := cRSSignature;
    hrVersion := $00010000; {Major=1; Minor=0}
    hrRecordLen := aRecordLen;
    hrCapacity := 0;
    hrCount := 0;
    hr1stDelRec := cEndOfDeletedChain;
  end;
  {now update the header record}
  rsSeekStream(FZeroPosition);
  rsWriteStream(FHeaderRec^, FHeaderRec^.hrHeaderLen);
  {set the record length field}
  FRecordLen := aRecordLen;
end;
procedure TtdRecordStream.rsReadHeaderRec;
var
  StreamSize : longint;
begin
  {if the stream size is not at least the size of the header record,
  it can't be one of ours}
  StreamSize := FStream.Size - FZeroPosition;
  if (StreamSize < sizeof(TtdRSHeaderRec)) then
    rsError(tdeRSNoHeaderRec, 'rsReadHeaderRec', 0);
  {read the header record}
  rsSeekStream(FZeroPosition);
  rsReadStream(TempHeaderRec, sizeof(TtdRSHeaderRec));
  {first sanity check: the signature and count/capacity}
  with TempHeaderRec do begin
    if (hrSignature<>cRSSignature) or
       (hrCount > hrCapacity) then
      rsError(tdeRSBadHeaderRec, 'rsReadHeaderRec', 0);
  end;
  {allocate the true header record, copy the data already read}
  FHeaderRec := AllocMem(TempHeaderRec.hrHeaderLen);
  Move(TempHeaderRec, FHeaderRec^, TempHeaderRec.hrHeaderLen);
  {second sanity check: check the record info}
  with FHeaderRec^ do begin
    FRecordLen4 := hrRecordLen + 4; {for rsCalcRecordOffset}
    if (StreamSize<>rsCalcRecordOffset(hrCapacity)) then
      rsError(tdeRSBadHeaderRec, 'rsReadHeaderRec', 0);
    {set up the class fields}
    FCount := hrCount;
    FCapacity := hrCapacity;
    FRecordLen := hrRecordLen;
  end;
end;
function TtdRecordStream.rsCalcRecordOffset(aIndex : longint) : longint;
begin
```

```
  Result := FZeroPosition + FHeaderRec^.hrHeaderLen +
            (aIndex * FRecordLen4);
end;
```

The method to create a header record is only called if the stream is empty and is very simple itself. We set up the header record in memory and then write it to the stream. If the record length is greater than the nominal size of the header record, we grow the header record to be the same size as the record length. We currently have seven fields in the header: a signature value, which we can use as a check when we read the header record; the version number of this header (this means that we can add more fields to the header later on and still understand older versions of the header); the header record length; the record length; the capacity of the stream, i.e., the number of records, whether active or deleted, the stream currently holds; the count of active records; and finally, the number of the first deleted record (here being set to cEndOfDeletedChain, or –2).

The method to read a header record has to do some validation first to make sure that the header record is really one of ours. We check to see if the signature matches ours, that the count of active records is less than or equal to the capacity, and that there is exactly enough room in the stream for the published record capacity. At that point, we assume the header record is valid and update the class's fields with the values from the stream.

rsCalcRecordOffset merely calculates the offset of the record number passed in as parameter, taking into account the initial position of the stream and the size of the header record.

Now we can look at the Add method for adding records to the persistent array.

Listing 2.22: Adding a new record to the persistent array

```
function TtdRecordStream.Add(var aRecord) : longint;
begin
  {if the deleted record chain is empty, we'll be adding the record
   to the end of the stream}
  if (FHeaderRec^.hr1stDelRec = cEndOfDeletedChain) then begin
    Result := FCapacity;
    inc(FCapacity);
    inc(FHeaderRec^.hrCapacity);
  end
  {otherwise, use the first deleted record, update the header record's
   deleted record chain to start at the next deleted record}
  else begin
    Result := FHeaderRec^.hr1stDelRec;
    rsSeekStream(rsCalcRecordOffset(FHeaderRec^.hr1stDelRec));
    rsReadStream(FHeaderRec^.hr1stDelRec, sizeof(longint));
```

```
  end;
  {seek to the record offset and write the new record}
  rsSeekStream(rsCalcRecordOffset(Result));
  PLongint(FRecord)^ := cActiveRecord;
  Move(aRecord, FRecord^[sizeof(longint)], FRecordLen);
  rsWriteStream(FRecord^, FRecordLen4);
  {we have one more record}
  inc(FCount);
  inc(FHeaderRec^.hrCount);
  {now update the header record}
  rsSeekStream(FZeroPosition);
  rsWriteStream(FHeaderRec^, sizeof(TtdRSHeaderRec));
end;
```

If the deleted record chain is not empty, make a note of the first deleted record (this is the one we will reuse). Read the deleted flag for this record and update the first deleted record number field in the header to its value. Now we seek to the start of the deleted record we're going to reuse, and write out a deleted flag set to cActiveRecord (–1) and, following that, the record we've been passed as parameter.

Reading and writing records must take account of whether the requested record is deleted or not. Records are identified by their record number.

Listing 2.23: Reading and updating a record in the persistent array

```
procedure TtdRecordStream.Read(aIndex : longint;
                           var aRecord;
                           var aIsDeleted : boolean);
begin
  {check the record number to be valid}
  if (aIndex < 0) or (aIndex >= Capacity) then
    rsError(tdeRSOutOfBounds, 'Read', aIndex);
  {seek to the record offset and read the record}
  rsSeekStream(rsCalcRecordOffset(aIndex));
  rsReadStream(FRecord^, FRecordLen4);
  if (PLongint(FRecord)^ = cActiveRecord) then begin
    aIsDeleted := false;
    Move(FRecord^[sizeof(longint)], aRecord, FRecordLen);
  end
  else begin
    aIsDeleted := true;
    FillChar(aRecord, FRecordLen, 0);
  end;
end;
procedure TtdRecordStream.Write(aIndex : longint;
                            var aRecord);
var
  DeletedFlag : longint;
```

```
begin
  {check the record number to be valid}
  if (aIndex < 0) or (aIndex >= Capacity) then
    rsError(tdeIndexOutOfBounds, 'Write', aIndex);
  {check to see that the record is not already deleted}
  rsSeekStream(rsCalcRecordOffset(aIndex));
  rsReadStream(DeletedFlag, sizeof(longint));
  if (DeletedFlag<>cActiveRecord) then
    rsError(tdeRSRecIsDeleted, 'Write', aIndex);
  {write the record}
  rsWriteStream(aRecord, FRecordLen);
end;
```

The Read method will return a flag showing whether the requested record is deleted or not. If it wasn't deleted, the record buffer parameter is filled in with the record from the stream. The code merely reads the entire record and its deleted flag in one go and proceeds according to the latter's value.

The first thing the Write method does is check to see if the requested record is deleted or not. If it is deleted, no changes are allowed to the record and an exception is raised. Otherwise, the new value of the record is written to the stream.

The final record-oriented method is the Delete method.

Listing 2.24: Deleting a record from the persistent array

```
procedure TtdRecordStream.Delete(aIndex : longint);
var
  DeletedFlag : longint;
begin
  {check the record number to be valid}
  if (aIndex < 0) or (aIndex >= Capacity) then
    rsError(tdeRSOutOfBounds, 'Delete', aIndex);
  {check to see that the record is not already deleted}
  rsSeekStream(rsCalcRecordOffset(aIndex));
  rsReadStream(DeletedFlag, sizeof(longint));
  if (DeletedFlag<>cActiveRecord) then
    rsError(tdeRSAlreadyDeleted, 'Delete', aIndex);
  {write the first deleted record number to the first 4
   bytes of the record we're deleting}
  rsSeekStream(rsCalcRecordOffset(aIndex));
  rsWriteStream(FHeaderRec^.hr1stDelRec, sizeof(longint));
  {update the header record's deleted record chain to
   start at the record we're deleting}
  FHeaderRec^.hr1stDelRec := aIndex;
  {we have one less record}
  dec(FCount);
  dec(FHeaderRec^.hrCount);
```

```
  {now update the header record}
  rsSeekStream(FZeroPosition);
  rsWriteStream(FHeaderRec^, sizeof(TtdRSHeaderRec));
end;
```

The first thing we do with Delete is check that the record hasn't already been deleted, as this situation is counted as an error. If everything is fine, the current first deleted record value from the header record is written to the deleted flag for the record we are deleting. We then update the first deleted record value to be the record we are deleting, decrement the number of active records, and update the header record onto the stream.

Closely allied to Delete is Clear, which deletes all active records in the persistent array.

Listing 2.25: Clearing the persistent array

```
procedure TtdRecordStream.Clear;
var
  Inx : longint;
  DeletedFlag : longint;
begin
  {visit all records and join them to the deleted record chain}
  for Inx := 0 to pred(FCapacity) do begin
    rsSeekStream(rsCalcRecordOffset(Inx));
    rsReadStream(DeletedFlag, sizeof(longint));
    if (DeletedFlag = cActiveRecord) then begin
      {write the first deleted record number to the first
       4 bytes of the record we're deleting}
      rsSeekStream(rsCalcRecordOffset(Inx));
      rsWriteStream(FHeaderRec^.hr1stDelRec, sizeof(longint));
      {update the header record's deleted record chain to
       start at the record we're deleting}
      FHeaderRec^.hr1stDelRec := Inx;
    end;
  end;
  {we have no records}
  FCount := 0;
  FHeaderRec^.hrCount := 0;
  {now update the header record}
  rsSeekStream(FZeroPosition);
  rsWriteStream(FHeaderRec^, sizeof(TtdRSHeaderRec));
end;
```

Essentially, the method visits each record, and if it is active, deletes it according to the algorithm used in the Delete method.

The class also enables the capacity of the stream to be increased in one go, rather than a record at a time with the Add method. This helps reserve enough space for the persistent array if you happen to know roughly how many records you wish to store. Capacity is a property whose write access method is rsSetCapacity.

Listing 2.26: Preallocating records for a persistent array

```
procedure TtdRecordStream.rsSetCapacity(aCapacity : longint);
var
  Inx : longint;
begin
  {we only accept increases in capacity}
  if (aCapacity > FCapacity) then begin
    {fill the work record with zeros}
    FillChar(FRecord^, FRecordLen4, 0);
    {seek to the end of the file}
    rsSeekStream(rsCalcRecordOffset(FCapacity));
    {write out the extra records, remembering to add
     them to the deleted record chain}
    for Inx := FCapacity to pred(aCapacity) do begin
      PLongint(FRecord)^ := FHeaderRec^.hr1stDelRec;
      rsWriteStream(FRecord^, FRecordLen4);
      FHeaderRec^.hr1stDelRec := Inx;
    end;
    {save the new capacity}
    FCapacity := aCapacity;
    FHeaderRec^.hrCapacity := aCapacity;
    {now update the header record}
    rsSeekStream(FZeroPosition);
    rsWriteStream(FHeaderRec^, sizeof(TtdRSHeaderRec));
  end;
end;
```

Essentially, the rsSetCapacity method continually adds a blank record to the end of the stream, making sure that all the new deleted records appear in the deleted record chain. Finally, the header record is updated and at this point we have a bunch of deleted records ready for a series of calls to the Add method.

The final methods we shall look at are all very simple. These are the low-level methods that read from, write to, and seek into the stream, with validation of the results.

Listing 2.27: Low-level methods for accessing the stream

```
procedure TtdRecordStream.rsReadStream(var aBuffer; aBufLen : integer);
var
  BytesRead : longint;
begin
  BytesRead := FStream.Read(aBuffer, aBufLen);
  if (BytesRead<>aBufLen) then
```

```
    rsError(tdeRSReadError, 'rsReadStream', aBufLen);
end;
procedure TtdRecordStream.rsSeekStream(aOffset : longint);
var
  NewOffset : longint;
begin
  NewOffset := FStream.Seek(aOffset, soFromBeginning);
  if (NewOffset<>aOffset) then
    rsError(tdeRSSeekError, 'rsSeekStream', aOffset);
end;
procedure TtdRecordStream.rsWriteStream(var aBuffer; aBufLen : integer);
var
  BytesWritten : longint;
begin
  BytesWritten := FStream.Write(aBuffer, aBufLen);
  if (BytesWritten<>aBufLen) then
    rsError(tdeRSWriteError, 'rsWriteStream', aBufLen);
  Flush;
end;
```

As you can see, if the result of the stream access for each operation is not what we want, the routine will raise an exception.

There is one method called in rsWriteStream that we haven't yet come across. This is the Flush method. This is a virtual method called when data has been written to a stream and needs to be flushed to the underlying device (for example, a disk). The implementation at this class level is a do nothing routine because we cannot know how to flush a standard TStream. It is there to be overridden by a descendant that is dealing with a disk-based stream, for example a file stream.

Listing 2.28: Implementation of persistent arrays with a file stream

```
constructor TtdRecordFile.Create(const aFileName : string;
                                       aMode     : word;
                                       aRecordLength : integer);
begin
  FStream := TFileStream.Create(aFileName, aMode);
  inherited Create(FStream, aRecordLength);
  FFileName := aFileName;
  FMode := aMode;
end;
destructor TtdRecordFile.Destroy;
begin
  inherited Destroy;
  FStream.Free;
end;
procedure TtdRecordFile.Flush;
```

```
{$IFDEF Delphi1}
var
  DosError : word;
  Handle   : THandle;
begin
  Handle := FStream.Handle;
  asm
    mov ah, $68
    mov bx, Handle
    call DOS3Call
    jc @@Error
    xor ax, ax
  @@Error:
    mov DosError, ax
  end;
  if (DosError<>0) then
    rsError(tdeRSFlushError, 'Flush', DosError)
end;
{$ENDIF}
{$IFDEF Delphi2Plus}
begin
  if not FlushFileBuffers(FStream.Handle) then
    rsError(tdeRSFlushError, 'Flush', GetLastError)
end;
{$ENDIF}
```

This listing shows the overridden Flush method that flushes the handle associated with the file stream holding the persistent array. We have to have different implementations for Delphi 1 and the 32-bit Delphis because of the different ways to flush a handle.

The code for TtdRecordStream can be found in the TDRecFil.pas file on the CD.

Summary

In this chapter, we have discussed arrays, one of the fundamental data structures. We have seen their strengths (O(1) access to individual elements, locality of reference) and their drawbacks (inserting and deleting an element are O(*n*) operations). An array class, TtdRecordList, was shown. The standard TList was then discussed and a simple derivative class, the TtdObjectList, was introduced.

We also discussed implementing persistent arrays, in the form of a stream of records. We showed how to design a persistent array class, the TtdRecord-Stream, that allows the reading, writing, and deleting of individual records.

Chapter 3
Linked Lists, Stacks, and Queues

Like arrays, linked lists are another ubiquitous, universal data structure that everyone uses at one stage or another. Unlike arrays, linked lists are not part of the Object Pascal language. However, it is extremely easy to create a linked list with Object Pascal—the only language construct really required is the pointer, although classes and objects can be used equally well.

From linked lists we can easily create stacks and queues, two other simple, yet powerful, data structures. Although these structures don't seem to have anything to do with linked lists, it's easy to write them with singly linked lists. And sometimes, as we'll see, it makes better sense to write stacks and queues using an array instead of a linked list.

But before we get ahead of ourselves, let's talk about what a linked list is and what kind of operations we should implement.

Singly Linked Lists

At its most basic level, a *linked list* is a chain of items or objects of some description (usually called nodes), with each item containing a pointer pointing to the next item in the chain. This is known as a singly linked list—every item has a single link or pointer to the next. The list itself is identified by the first node, from which all other nodes can be found (or *visited*) by following the links one by one. Notice the difference in definition from an array, where the next item in line is physically adjacent to the current item. With a linked list, the items may be all over the place, their ordering being maintained by the links.

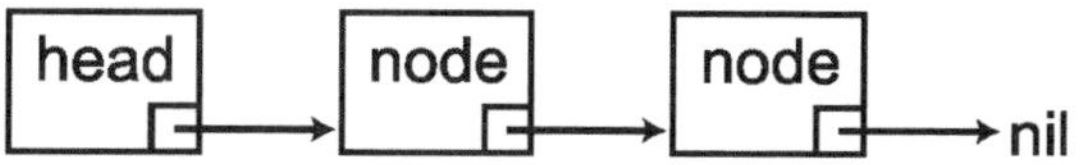

Figure 3.1: A singly linked list

How do we identify the end of the list? The simplest method is to have the last item's link pointer set to nil, indicating that there are no further items in the list. Another method is to allocate a special node, called the tail node, and have the last item's link point to it. Yet another method is to have the last item's link point to the first item, creating what's known as a circular linked list.

So what's so special about this type of layout as compared with an array? The first thing to realize is that the linked list does not have to have a preset size. With an array we have to know exactly how many items we're going to have (so that we can statically preallocate the single chunk of contiguous memory required for them), or we have to have some clever scheme for growing (or shrinking for that matter) the array to accommodate more (or less) items than were expected. With a linked list, each node is a separate entity; in simple cases, they are separately allocated. If we need another item in the list, allocate one and link it in. If we want to get rid of a node, just unlink it from the list and deallocate it.

All right, if this linked list structure is so great, why isn't it used exclusively instead of arrays? What's the downside? The first, albeit minor, downside is that each item in the list requires a pointer to the next item. Each item has to grow by sizeof(pointer) bytes (currently 4), to be inserted into a linked list compared with being inserted into an array.

Worse is that each node is separately allocated. Compare this situation with that for an array. Allocating *n* items for an array is essentially a O(1) operation: all the items have to be contiguous in memory, therefore we allocate them all as one block. (Indeed, be aware that arrays don't have to be allocated on the heap; they can be local variables on the stack, for example.) For a linked list, the nodes are all separately allocated, a O(*n*) operation. Even if we ignore the efficiency problem, this could result in heap fragmentation.

The biggest downside, compared with an array, is how to access the *n*th item. With an array, because it is a single contiguous block of memory, finding the *n*th item reduces to a simple address calculation. With a linked list, on the other hand, finding the *n*th item is done by starting at the beginning of the list, following the links, and counting the items until we reach the *n*th. There is nothing else to do: we have to follow *n* links. (Notice that we could do some clever tricks, such as maintaining a cache item and its position in the list, where we determine whether it would be more expedient to start at the beginning or at the cached node.)

Linked List Nodes

Just before we get to operations on linked lists, let's see how to represent a node in memory. Once we nail this down we can be a little more concrete in describing the basic linked list operations. The basic node structure, without using classes and objects, is as follows:

```
type
  PSimpleNode = ^TSimpleNode;
  TSimpleNode = record
    Next : PSimpleNode;
    Data : SomeDataType;
  end;
```

The PSimpleNode type is a pointer to a TSimpleNode record. The Next field of this record is the link, a pointer to a node just like this one. The Data field is the actual item itself, the data type being left deliberately ambiguous in this declaration. To follow a link we would write code similar to this:

```
var
  NextNode, CurrentNode : PSimpleNode;
begin
  . . .
  NextNode := CurrentNode^.Next;
```

Creating a Singly Linked List

This is trivial. At its most simple, the first node in a linked list defines the linked list. This first node is usually called the *head* node.

```
var
  MyLinkedList : PSimpleNode;
```

If MyLinkedList is nil, there is no linked list, so this value is the initial value of the linked list.

```
{initialize the linked list}
MyLinkedList := nil;
```

Inserting into and Deleting from a Singly Linked List

So, how do we insert a new node into a linked list? And what about deleting an existing node from a list? It turns out that both are simple operations that just require some minor pointer twiddling.

For a singly linked list there's just a single basic possibility: insertion after a given node in the list. We set the Next pointer in our new node to the node after the given node and we set the Next pointer of the given node to our new node. In code:

```
var
  GivenNode, NewNode : PSimpleNode;
begin
  . . .
  New(NewNode);
  ..set the Data field..
  NewNode^.Next := GivenNode^.Next;
  GivenNode^.Next := NewNode;
```

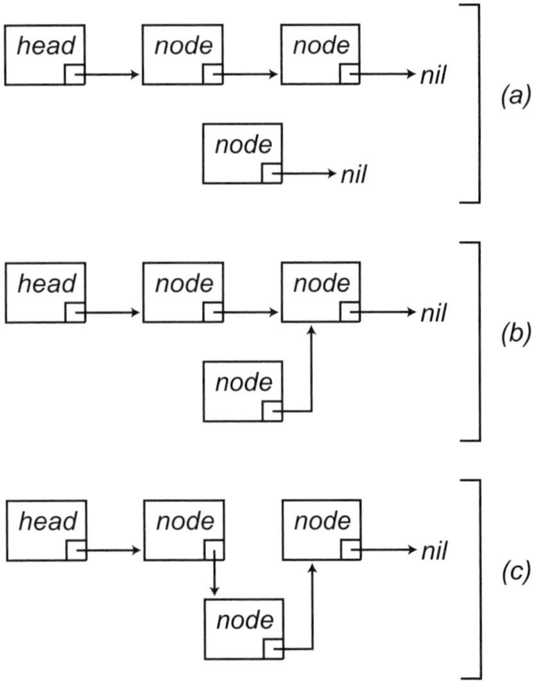

Figure 3.2: Insertion into a singly linked list

Similarly for deletion, the simplest basic possibility is deleting the node after a given node in the list. Here we set the given node's Next pointer to the node after the one we are about to delete; at that point the node to be deleted is unlinked from the list and we can dispose of it. In code:

```
var
  GivenNode, NodeToGo : PSimpleNode;
begin
  . . .
  NodeToGo := GivenNode^.Next;
  GivenNode^.Next := NodeToGo^.Next;
  Dispose(NodeToGo);
```

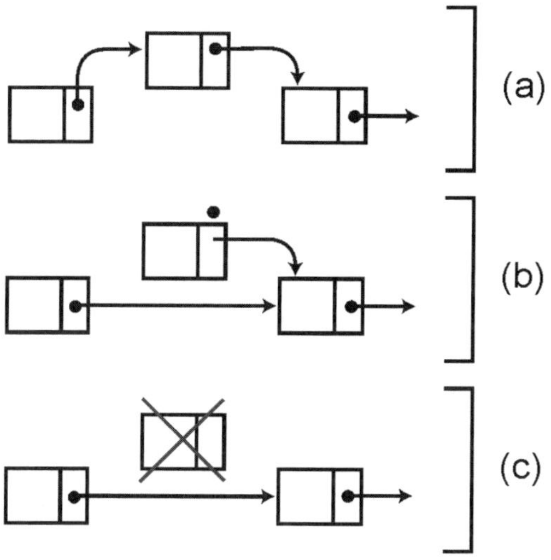

Figure 3.3: Deletion from a singly linked list

However, there is a special case for both these operations: inserting before the first item in the list (so that the new node becomes the first item) and deleting the first item in the list (so that there is a new first item in the list). Since our current discussions have the linked list identified by the first node, we have to write these special cases separately. Inserting before the first node would look like this:

```
var
  MyLinkedList, NewNode : PSimpleNode;
begin
  . . .
  New(NewNode);
  ..set the Data field..
  NewNode^.Next := MyLinkedList;
  MyLinkedList := NewNode;
```

and deletion of the first node would look like this:

```
var
  MyLinkedList, NodeToGo : PSimpleNode;
begin
  . . .
  NodeToGo := MyLinkedList;
  MyLinkedList := NodeToGo^.Next;
  Dispose(NodeToGo);
```

Notice that the special insertion code will work if the linked list was originally empty—that is, nil—and the special deletion code will properly set the linked list to nil on deleting the last node in the list.

Traversing a Linked List

Traversing a linked list is pretty simple as well. We essentially walk the list, going from node to node following the Next pointers, until we reach the nil node that signifies the end of the list.

```
var
  FirstNode, TempNode : PSimpleNode;
begin
  . . .
  TempNode := FirstNode;
  while TempNode <> nil do begin
    Process(TempNode^.Data);
    TempNode := TempNode^.Next;
  end;
```

In this simple loop the Process procedure is defined elsewhere and presumably will do something with the Data field it is passed. Emptying a linked list uses a slight variation of this technique in order make sure we don't refer to the Next field of the node after it is freed (a common mistake).

```
var
  MyLinkedList, TempNode, NodeToGo : PSimpleNode;
begin
  NodeToGo := MyLinkedList;
  while NodeToGo <> nil do begin
    TempNode := NodeToGo^.Next;
    Dispose(NodeToGo);
    NodeToGo := TempNode;
  end;
  MyLinkedList := nil;
```

Now we've seen traversals, let's ask the question you may have asked in your mind a couple of paragraphs back. What if we want to add a node before another? How do we do it? The only way with a singly linked list is to traverse the list, looking for the node before which we want to add our new node. As we traverse the list, we maintain two variables: one that points to the current node and one that points to its prior node (its parent, if you will). Once we find the node we are looking for we'll have the pointer to the previous node and we can just use the "insert after" algorithm on this parent node. In code:

```
var
  FirstNode, GivenNode,
  TempNode, ParentNode : PSimpleNode;
begin
  ParentNode := nil;
  TempNode := FirstNode;
  while TempNode <> GivenNode do begin
    ParentNode := TempNode;
    TempNode := ParentNode^.Next;
  end;
  if TempNode = GivenNode then begin
    if (ParentNode = nil) then begin
      NewNode^.Next := FirstNode;
      FirstNode := NewNode;
    end
    else begin
      NewNode^.Next := ParentNode^.Next;
      ParentNode^.Next := NewNode;
    end;
  end;
```

Notice the special code for the case when you're adding a node before the first node (the parent is nil in this case). This code isn't as fast as the "insert after" algorithm discussed above, because it requires the linked list to be walked beforehand to find the parent of the given node. In general, if there is a possibility of inserting before a node, we'd use a doubly linked list instead, which we'll come to in a moment.

Efficiency Considerations

If that were all there was to say about linked lists, this would be a very short chapter. We'd just present a class encapsulation of a singly linked list and move on. However, there is more to be said before writing a linked list class, especially with regard to efficiency.

Using a Head Node

Look again at the code for insertion and deletion. Doesn't it strike you as messy to have separate cases for both operations? It does me. We have to have this special code in order to cope with processing the first node in the list, something that we might not do all that often. Isn't there a better way? The answer is yes, by using a dummy head node. A dummy head node is a node that is just used as a placeholder; we store no data with this node. The first real node in the list will be the one pointed to by the head node's Next field. The end of the linked list is determined by a Next value equal to nil, as before. We have to properly initialize the list this time by allocating this head node and setting its Next pointer to nil.

```
var
  HeadNode : PSimpleNode;
begin
  . . .
  New(HeadNode);
  HeadNode^.Next := nil;
```

After this minor preparation is done, all insertions and deletions can be done using the "insert after" and "delete after" operations. The "insertion before the first node" operation translates to an insertion after the dummy head node. The "deletion of the first node operation" becomes a deletion of the node after the head node. By the use of a head node, we've managed to remove the special cases.

Of course, in using a head node we've made the case even stronger for using a class implementation: we have a node to preallocate when we create the linked list, and we have to destroy this node when we've finished with the list.

Using a Node Manager

Before we actually write such a class there's yet one more thing to consider. We started off by declaring a node record type (the TSimpleNode type) to hold (1) the data we were interested in and (2) a pointer to the next node in the linked list. The second item is invariant—we must have it to construct a linked list—but the first depends on our particular application, or on the particular use we have at the moment. We could have one field, or two or more; we could have a record structure; we could have an object. It seems hard to write a generic, reusable linked list class when we don't know ahead of time what we are going to store in it.

There are two solutions to this conundrum. The first one is to declare an ancestor node class that just consists of the Next pointer. The items containing your data are then defined as descendants of this class. In this case, you are responsible for allocating and deallocating the nodes—all the linked list class wants are preallocated nodes whose Next pointers it can manipulate. This solution is, at the same time, elegant and inelegant; it seems to encapsulate the object-oriented paradigm, but you are forced to declare descendants of the ancestor node class to store your data (what if the items you wanted to put in the linked list were instances of a class that you had no control over?).

The second solution, and the one I consider to be much better, is to abstract out the data into the form of a typeless pointer. (We have a good precedent for this: it's the way that the standard Delphi TList class works.) When we add an item to the linked list, we just present the linked list class with a pointer value (say a pointer to our data, or an object of ours on the heap) and let the linked list do the rest: allocating a node, setting the data, maintaining the links. This solution is a clean way around the problem since the user of the class doesn't have to know anything about the Next pointers, doesn't have to reserve space for them, doesn't have to create a special descendant of some ancestor class, and so on.

This second solution has a consequence that is even more compelling. The nodes used by the class in this case are *always* 8 bytes in size—a Next pointer and a Data pointer, both 4 bytes.

> Notice that this discussion presupposes that pointers are 4 bytes in size. I presume that later Delphis would be written for 64-bit operating systems, in which case pointers will be 8 bytes in size. Please don't assume that pointers are always 4 bytes in your code; use sizeof(pointer) instead. It'll make the eventual conversion easier. For this discussion, however, we'll assume that pointers are 4 bytes, even though the actual code written for the book uses sizeof(pointer). It just makes the text flow a little easier because I can say things like "8 bytes in size" instead of "twice sizeof(pointer) bytes in size."

What does this constant node size buy us? Well, when the linked list wants to store some data, it has to allocate the node first. To do this it would have to use the highly complex Delphi heap manager to allocate 8 bytes of memory. The heap manager has all sorts of fabulous code to manage chunks of memory and to allocate and free arbitrarily sized blocks for our use, and it manages all this complexity and functionality in an amazingly efficient manner. But we know that we only want 8-byte blocks and we will always want just 8-byte blocks. Can we use this regularity to speed up the allocation and deallocation of our fixed-size nodes? The answer is, of course, yes: we allocate a batch of nodes from the Delphi heap manager inside the linked list object and dole them out whenever required. Of course, we don't allocate a batch of nodes by allocating them one by one; instead we allocate an array of 100 nodes, for example. If we require more nodes, we then allocate another array to give us a further 100 nodes.

But here comes the interesting part. We store the arrays of nodes we allocate in an internal linked list, and the nodes we get from these arrays go into a free list, which is also a linked list. So, our linked list class will rely on arrays and linked lists itself to work more efficiently.

What do I mean by a free list? This is a common construction in programming. What happens is that we have a set of some kind of items that we "allocate" and "free." When an item is freed, it will, in all likelihood, be reused at some stage, so instead of releasing it to the heap manager we keep a hold of it in a *free list*: a list of freed items. Delphi's heap manager, uses a free list of deallocated memory blocks of differing sizes. Many database engines will have a free list of deleted records that can be reused hidden internally in the depths of the engine. The record array we introduced in Chapter 2 uses a deleted record chain, which is nothing but a fancy name for a free list. When we want to allocate an item we go to our free list and reuse one of the items on it.

Let's design a *node allocation manager*. It will contain a free list of nodes, initially set to nil, meaning that it is empty. When we want to allocate a node, the node manager looks to its free list. If there are no nodes present (the free list is nil), the manager allocates a large chunk of memory from Delphi's heap manager—usually called a page. It then splits up this page into node-sized pieces and pushes them all onto the free list. After this process, it can pop a node off the free list and return it to the consumer. When a node is freed, the node allocation manager just pushes it onto the free list. By "push" I mean insert a node at the top of the list, and by "pop" I mean delete the node at the top of the list.

Listing 3.1: The TtdNodeManager class

```
TtdNodeManager = class
  private
    FNodeSize     : cardinal;
    FFreeList     : pointer;
    FNodesPerPage : cardinal;
    FPageHead     : pointer;
    FPageSize     : cardinal;
  protected
    procedure nmAllocNewPage;
  public
    constructor Create(aNodeSize : cardinal);
    destructor Destroy; override;

    function AllocNode : pointer;
    procedure FreeNode(aNode : pointer);
end;
```

As you see, its public interface is not all that complex. We can create and destroy an instance, and we can allocate and free a node. The Create constructor takes a single parameter, the node size, and calculates a couple of values from it: the number of nodes per page and the page size. The class will try to allocate pages of 1,024 bytes in size, unless the node size is so large that only one node would fit, in which case the page is sized to fit the node. For efficiency purposes, the node size is rounded up to the nearest 4 bytes (actually, we round it up to the nearest sizeof(pointer) bytes).

Listing 3.2: The TtdNodeManager.Create constructor

```
constructor TtdNodeManager.Create(aNodeSize : cardinal);
begin
  inherited Create;
  {save the node size rounded to nearest 4 bytes}
  if (aNodeSize <= sizeof(pointer)) then
    aNodeSize := sizeof(pointer)
  else
    aNodeSize := ((aNodeSize + 3) shr 2) shl 2;
  FNodeSize := aNodeSize;
  {calculate the page size (default 1024 bytes) and the number of
    nodes per page; if the default page size is not large enough for
    two or more nodes, force a single node per page}
  FNodesPerPage := (PageSize - sizeof(pointer)) div aNodeSize;
  if (FNodesPerPage > 1) then
    FPageSize := 1024
  else begin
    FNodesPerPage := 1;
    FPagesize := aNodeSize + sizeof(pointer);
  end;
end;
```

The code for AllocNode is very simple. If the free list is empty, the nmAllocNewPage method is called to allocate a new page and add all the nodes to the free list. Once the free list has some nodes, we take the top one from the list (essentially by using the "delete the first node" code).

Listing 3.3: Allocating a node from the TtdNodeManager class

```
function TtdNodeManager.AllocNode : pointer;
begin
 {if the free list is empty, allocate a new page; this'll fill the
  free list}
  if (FFreeList = nil) then
    nmAllocNewPage;
  {return the top of the free list}
  Result := FFreeList;
  FFreeList := PGenericNode(FFreeList)^.gnNext;
end;
```

The PGenericNode type is a pointer to a record type that has one field, the gnNext link. This type, and the typecast in the code, makes it easy to treat the nodes on the free list in a generic way, a bit like the TSimpleNode record type we had earlier. Notice that the constructor makes sure that the nodes being tracked by the node manager are at least 4 bytes long, the size of a pointer.

The FreeNode method is equally simple: the node is just added to the top of the free list (we use the special "insert before first node" code).

Listing 3.4: Freeing a node with the TtdNodeManager class

```
procedure TtdNodeManager.FreeNode(aNode : pointer);
begin
  {add the node (if non-nil) to the top of the free list}
  if (aNode <> nil) then begin
    PGenericNode(aNode)^.gnNext := FFreeList;
    FFreeList := aNode;
  end;
end;
```

The next interesting method is the nmAllocNewPage method. This routine will allocate a new page of size FPageSize, calculated in Create. Each page consists of a single pointer followed by FNodesPerPage nodes. The initial pointer is used to create a linked list of pages (this is the reason for Create taking into account the sizeof(pointer) bytes in its calculations). The nodes in the page are then added to the free list, by the simple expedient of calling FreeNode. Because the NewPage variable is defined as a PAnsiChar, we can perform simple pointer arithmetic without having to type cast to integer types to identify the individual nodes in the page.

Listing 3.5: Allocating a new page with the TtdNodeManager class

```
procedure TtdNodeManager.nmAllocNewPage;
var
  NewPage : PAnsiChar;
  i       : integer;
begin
  {allocate a new page and add it to the front of the page list}
  GetMem(NewPage, FPageSize);
  PGenericNode(NewPage)^.gnNext := FPageHead;
  FPageHead := NewPage;
  {now split up the new page into nodes and push them all onto the
    free list; note that the first 4 bytes of the page is a pointer
    to the next page, so remember to skip over them}
  inc(NewPage, sizeof(pointer));
  for i := pred(FNodesPerPage) downto 0 do begin
    FreeNode(NewPage);
    inc(NewPage, FNodeSize);
  end;
end;
```

Finally, the Destroy destructor will free all the pages in the page list. It doesn't bother with the free list because all of the nodes on it are part of the pages that are getting freed anyway.

Listing 3.6: Destroying a TtdNodeManager instance

```
destructor TtdNodeManager.Destroy;
var
  Temp : pointer;
begin
  {dispose of all the pages, if there are any}
  while (FPageHead <> nil) do begin
    Temp := PGenericNode(FPageHead)^.gnNext;
    FreeMem(FPageHead, FPageSize);
    FPageHead := Temp;
  end;
  inherited Destroy;
end;
```

A note for the future: before very much longer we shall have a version of Windows that uses 64-bit pointers, written for the Intel 64-bit CPUs that are currently being designed. Similarly, I dare say there'll be a version of Linux that does the same. I would imagine that pretty soon thereafter, we should have a version of Delphi or of Kylix that supports these large pointers. The code for this book has been carefully written to assume that a pointer is not necessarily 4 bytes or 32 bits in size; I use sizeof(pointer) throughout. Indeed, nowhere is it assumed that sizeof(pointer) equals sizeof(longint), another clever, common trick that may not be true in future versions of Delphi. The node manager class is an example of this type of coding. *Caveat* programmer.

The entire code for the node manager class is found in the TDNdeMgr.pas file on the CD.

Before we return to the singly linked list that started all this discussion about node managers, it will be instructive to point out a couple of problems with this TtdNodeManager class. The first thing to note is that the FreeNode method makes no attempt to verify that the node being freed actually belongs to the class, i.e., that it appears in a page being managed by the class. This is crucial to the proper operation of the class; if the class has a node that doesn't belong to the class, it may be the wrong size (eventually causing a memory overwrite), or it may belong to another class which then frees the page containing the node, and so on. For debugging purposes, it makes sense to have the class validate any nodes that are freed. The implementation on the CD incorporates this validation code if the unit is compiled to use assertions.

The second problem comes about because it is entirely possible for us to destroy a node manager instance before we destroy any objects that are using its nodes. This would cause unknown and untold bugs. There's not a lot we can do about this, so we'll just have to be careful.

(By the way, just to show that it's worth going to all the trouble of writing this node allocation manager class, my tests have shown that it is three or four times as fast as the Delphi heap manager over a full cycle of allocations and deallocations of millions of nodes.)

The Singly Linked List Class

Before delving into the design of the singly linked list class TtdSingleLinkList, a couple of notes are in order.

First things, first. As I said earlier, it would be nice to be able to use the linked list without having to worry about nodes. Like the TList, we would like to have the class accept untyped pointers. To be able to access items in the linked list, we'd certainly like to use an index (although, as I pointed out this can be slow), but better still would be to borrow some database terminology. It would be advantageous to have a cursor in the linked list, a pointer to the "current" item, if you will. We could then define methods to position the cursor before all items in the list, to move the cursor to the next item, to be able to insert a new item or delete the item at the cursor, and so on. Indeed, because we are writing the linked list as a class, we could also maintain the parent of the current item so that we could efficiently code an Insert method to work in the same way as the TList (i.e., by moving the current item and its successors over by one, and inserting the new item in the hole), and a Delete method to do likewise.

The interface to the TtdSingleLinkList class is as follows:

Listing 3.7: The TtdSingleLinkList class

```
TtdSingleLinkList = class
  private
    FCount   : longint;
    FCursor  : PslNode;
    FCursorIx: longint;
    FDispose : TtdDisposeProc;
    FHead    : PslNode;
    FName    : TtdNameString;
    FParent  : PslNode;
  protected
    function sllGetItem(aIndex : longint) : pointer;
    procedure sllSetItem(aIndex : longint; aItem  : pointer);
    procedure sllError(aErrorCode  : integer;
```

```
                   const aMethodName : TtdNameString);
    class procedure sllGetNodeManager;
    procedure sllPositionAtNth(aIndex : longint);
  public
    constructor Create(aDispose : TtdDisposeProc);
    destructor Destroy; override;
    function Add(aItem : pointer) : longint;
    procedure Clear;
    procedure Delete(aIndex : longint);
    procedure DeleteAtCursor;
    function Examine : pointer;
    function First : pointer;
    function IndexOf(aItem : pointer) : longint;
    procedure Insert(aIndex : longint; aItem : pointer);
    procedure InsertAtCursor(aItem : pointer);
    function IsAfterLast : boolean;
    function IsBeforeFirst : boolean;
    function IsEmpty : boolean;
    function Last : pointer;
    procedure MoveBeforeFirst;
    procedure MoveNext;
    procedure Remove(aItem : pointer);
    procedure Sort(aCompare : TtdCompareFunc);
    property Count : longint read FCount;
    property Items[aIndex : longint] : pointer
       read sllGetItem write sllSetItem; default;
    property Name : TtdNameString read FName write FName;
end;
```

Although the method names follow the TList standard, there are a few new ones. The MoveBeforeFirst method positions the cursor before all of the items in the linked list. IsBeforeFirst and IsAfterLast return true if the cursor is before all of the items in the list or after all of them, respectively. MoveNext moves the cursor one position, following the internal link. The Items property works in the same way as TList's: items are numbered from 0 to Count−1.

The Create constructor makes sure the node manager is instanced and then it allocates itself a node to act as the dummy head node. It then positions the cursor to be before all nodes (since there aren't any, that isn't too hard). The Destroy destructor clears the linked list and then frees the dummy head node Create allocated.

Listing 3.8: The constructor and destructor for TtdSingleLinkList

```
constructor TtdSingleLinkList.Create(aDispose : TtdDisposeProc);
begin
  inherited Create;
  {save the dispose procedure}
```

```
  FDispose := aDispose;
  {get the node manager}
  sllGetNodeManager;
  {allocate a head node}
  FHead := PslNode(SLNodeManager.AllocNode);
  FHead^.slnNext := nil;
  FHead^.slnData := nil;
  {set the cursor}
  MoveBeforeFirst;
end;
destructor TtdSingleLinkList.Destroy;
begin
  {delete all the nodes, including the head node}
  Clear;
  SLNodeManager.FreeNode(FHead);
  inherited Destroy;
end;
```

As a matter of interest, the singly linked list class is coded in such a way that there is just one node manager for all TtdSingleLinkList instances that may be created. They all share the one node manager. I could have coded the class so that every TtdSingleLinkList instance had its own node manager, but that would have meant a lot of overhead per instance, and given that if an application uses one linked list it's likely to use several, I decided to use a class variable. All instances of the class use the same variable. There is one minor flaw in this argument: Delphi does not support class variables. Instead we fake one, by using a global variable declared in the implementation part of the unit. If you look at the TDLnkLst.pas file, you'll see the following declaration in the implementation part of the unit:

```
var
  SLNodeManager : TtdNodeManager;
```

The methods of the singly linked list separate themselves into two varieties: those that act in a sequential type manner (MoveBeforeFirst, InsertAtCursor, etc.) and those that treat the linked list as an array (the Items property, Delete, IndexOf, etc.). The methods in the former set are the easiest to illustrate first, since we've shown how they work in the linked list discussion at the start of this chapter. To make things a lot easier we not only store the cursor in the object (i.e., the pointer to the current node), we also store the parent of that cursor as well (i.e., the pointer to the parent of the current cursor). This methodology makes for more usable insert and delete operations.

Listing 3.9: The standard linked list operations for TtdSingleLinkList

```
procedure TtdSingleLinkList.Clear;
var
  Temp : PslNode;
begin
  {delete all the nodes, except the head node;
    if we can dispose of data, do so}
  Temp := FHead^.slnNext;
  while (Temp <> nil) do begin
    FHead^.slnNext := Temp^.slnNext;
    if Assigned(FDispose) then
      FDispose(Temp^.slnData);
    SLNodeManager.FreeNode(Temp);
    Temp := FHead^.slnNext;
  end;
  FCount := 0;
  MoveBeforeFirst;
end;

procedure TtdSingleLinkList.DeleteAtCursor;
begin
  if (FCursor = nil) or (FCursor = FHead) then
    sllError(tdeListCannotDelete, 'Delete');
  {dispose of its contents}
  if Assigned(FDispose) then
    FDispose(FCursor^.slnData);
  {unlink the node and free it}
  FParent^.slnNext := FCursor^.slnNext;
  SLNodeManager.FreeNode(FCursor);
  FCursor := FParent^.slnNext;
  dec(FCount);
end;

function TtdSingleLinkList.Examine : pointer;
begin
  if (FCursor = nil) or (FCursor = FHead) then
    sllError(tdeListCannotExamine, 'Examine');
  {return the data part of the cursor}
  Result := FCursor^.slnData;
end;

procedure TtdSingleLinkList.InsertAtCursor(aItem : pointer);
var
  NewNode : PslNode;
begin
  {make sure we aren't trying to insert at the before first
    position; if we're there, move forward one position}
```

```
  if (FCursor = FHead) then
    MoveNext;
  {allocate a new node and insert at the cursor}
  NewNode := PslNode(SLNodeManager.AllocNode);
  NewNode^.slnData := aItem;
  NewNode^.slnNext := FCursor;
  FParent^.slnNext := NewNode;
  FCursor := NewNode;
  inc(FCount);
end;

function TtdSingleLinkList.IsAfterLast : boolean;
begin
  Result := FCursor = nil;
end;

function TtdSingleLinkList.IsBeforeFirst : boolean;
begin
  Result := FCursor = FHead;
end;

function TtdSingleLinkList.IsEmpty : boolean;
begin
  Result := (Count = 0);
end;

procedure TtdSingleLinkList.MoveBeforeFirst;
begin
  {set the cursor to the head node}
  FCursor := FHead;
  FParent := nil;
  FCursorIx := -1;
end;

procedure TtdSingleLinkList.MoveNext;
begin
  {advance the cursor to its own next pointer, ignore
    attempts to move beyond the end of the list}
  if (FCursor <> nil) then begin
    FParent := FCursor;
    FCursor := FCursor^.slnNext;
    inc(FCursorIx);
  end;
end;
```

You may have noticed that a couple of these methods make use of a field of the object called FCursorIx. It is this field that enables the index-based method to be as efficient as possible since it stores the index of the cursor (with the first node being at index 0, like TList). This field is used by the method sllPositionAtNth, which optimally moves the cursor to the node with the passed index.

Listing 3.10: The sllPositionAtNth method

```
procedure TtdSingleLinkList.sllPositionAtNth(aIndex : longint);
var
  WorkCursor   : PslNode;
  WorkParent   : PslNode;
  WorkCursorIx : longint;
begin
  {check for a valid index}
  if (aIndex < 0) or (aIndex >= Count) then
    sllError(tdeListInvalidIndex, 'sllPositionAtNth');
  {take care of easy case}
  if (aIndex = FCursorIx) then
    Exit;
  {--now use local variables for speed--}
  {if the index wanted is before the cursor's index,
   move work cursor before all of the nodes}
  if (aIndex < FCursorIx) then begin
    WorkCursor := FHead;
    WorkParent := nil;
    WorkCursorIx := -1;
  end
  {otherwise set work cursor to current cursor}
  else begin
    WorkCursor := FCursor;
    WorkParent := FParent;
    WorkCursorIx := FCursorIx;
  end;
  {while the work cursor index is less than the index required,
   advance the work cursor}
  while (WorkCursorIx < aIndex) do begin
    WorkParent := WorkCursor;
    WorkCursor := WorkCursor^.slnNext;
    inc(WorkCursorIx);
  end;
  {set the real cursor equal to the work cursor}
  FCursor := WorkCursor;
  FParent := WorkParent;
  FCursorIx := WorkCursorIx;
end;
```

The method makes use of local variables for the best speed. It works out whether the required index is greater than the cursor's index (in which case the search for that node can start at the cursor) or less than the cursor's index (in which case the search starts from the beginning of the list). Without the cursor index we would have to start at the beginning of the list every time.

With this method under our belt, the majority of the remaining index-based methods become relatively easy to implement:

Listing 3.11: The index-based methods for TtdSingleLinkList

```
procedure TtdSingleLinkList.Delete(aIndex : longint);
begin
  {position the cursor}
  sllPositionAtNth(aIndex);
  {delete the item at the cursor}
  DeleteAtCursor;
end;
function TtdSingleLinkList.First : pointer;
begin
  {position the cursor}
  sllPositionAtNth(0);
  {return the data}
  Result := FCursor^.slnData;
end;
procedure TtdSingleLinkList.Insert(aIndex : longint; aItem : pointer);
begin
  {position the cursor}
  sllPositionAtNth(aIndex);
  {insert the item at the cursor}
  InsertAtCursor(aItem);
end;
function TtdSingleLinkList.Last : pointer;
begin
  {position the cursor}
  sllPositionAtNth(pred(Count));
  {return the data}
  Result := FCursor^.slnData;
end;
function TtdSingleLinkList.sllGetItem(aIndex : longint) : pointer;
begin
  {position the cursor}
  sllPositionAtNth(aIndex);
  {return the data}
  Result := FCursor^.slnData;
end;
procedure TtdSingleLinkList.sllSetItem(aIndex : longint; aItem  : pointer);
begin
  {position the cursor}
  sllPositionAtNth(aIndex);
  {if we can dispose of the data about to be replaced, do so}
  if Assigned(FDispose) and (aItem <> FCursor^.slnData) then
```

```
    FDispose(FCursor^.slnData);
  {replace the data}
  FCursor^.slnData := aItem;
end;
```

This leaves a couple of methods that, for one reason or another, are coded from first principles. The Add method appends an item to the end of the linked list. Coding the search for the final node is simple and it makes sense to have the code explicitly in the method itself. IndexOf is another such method. Searching for a particular item with this method can only be done by the explicit code for the job. Once IndexOf is written, Remove becomes simple.

Listing 3.12: Add, IndexOf, and Remove

```
function TtdSingleLinkList.Add(aItem : pointer) : longint;
var
  WorkCursor : PslNode;
  WorkParent : PslNode;
begin
  {use work variables for speed}
  WorkCursor := FCursor;
  WorkParent := FParent;
  {move to the very end of the linked list}
  while (WorkCursor <> nil) do begin
    WorkParent := WorkCursor;
    WorkCursor := WorkCursor^.slnNext;
  end;
  {set the real cursor}
  FParent := WorkParent;
  FCursor := nil;
  FCursorIx := Count;
  Result := Count;
  {insert at the cursor}
  InsertAtCursor(aItem);
end;
function TtdSingleLinkList.IndexOf(aItem : pointer) : longint;
var
  WorkCursor   : PslNode;
  WorkParent   : PslNode;
  WorkCursorIx : longint;
begin
  {set the work cursor to the first node (if it exists)}
  WorkParent := FHead;
  WorkCursor := WorkParent^.slnNext;
  WorkCursorIx := 0;
  {walk the linked list looking for the item}
  while (WorkCursor <> nil) do begin
```

```
    if (WorkCursor^.slnData = aItem) then begin
      {we found it; set the result; set the real cursor}
      Result := WorkCursorIx;
      FCursor := WorkCursor;
      FParent := WorkParent;
      FCursorIx := WorkCursorIx;
      Exit;
    end;
    {advance to the next node}
    WorkParent := WorkCursor;
    WorkCursor := WorkCursor^.slnNext;
    inc(WorkCursorIx);
  end;
  {didn't find it}
  Result := -1;
end;
procedure TtdSingleLinkList.Remove(aItem : pointer);
begin
  if (IndexOf(aItem) <> -1) then
    DeleteAtCursor;
end;
```

The code for the singly linked list class, TtdSingleLinkList, is found in the TDLnkLst.pas file on the CD.

The class we have just written is as efficient as we can make it. Nodes are allocated in batches in contiguous memory. Moving from node to node would, in general, be efficient as far as the operating system's virtual memory paging goes, but obviously it all depends on the usage of the linked list. If you have a random mix of deletes and inserts, you can imagine that the nodes from the different pages get shuffled somewhat. Like TList, the data pointed to by each item can be all over memory—there's not a lot we can do about that.

Doubly Linked Lists

Having discussed the singly linked list fairly exhaustively, we now move on to the doubly linked list. Here, we still have a set of nodes linked to each other like the singly linked list, but this time, instead of having just one link to the next node in line, we have an additional link to the previous node.

```
type
  PSimpleNode = ^TSimpleNode;
  TSimpleNode = record
    Next  : PSimpleNode;
    Prior : PSimpleNode;
    Data  : SomeDataType;
  end;
```

Hence, not only can we move forward through the list, node by node, following the Next links, we can now move backward through the list by following the Prior links. This is the doubly linked list.

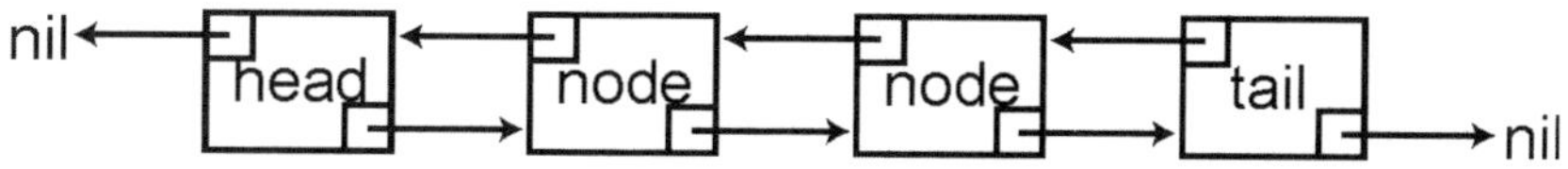

Figure 3.4: A doubly linked list

Inserting and Deleting from a Doubly Linked List

How do we insert a new node into a doubly linked list? For a singly linked list we had to break a single link and then form two new links to insert a node, so for a doubly linked list we have to break two links and form four new ones. We can insert either before or after a node in the list because the Prior pointers make it easy to traverse the list in either direction. Indeed, an "insert before" operation can be coded as a "move back one node, insert after" operation, so we'll just consider the "insert after" operation.

We set the Next pointer in our new node to the node after the given node and we set the Next pointer of the given node to our new node. To set up the backward pointers, we set the Prior pointer in our new node to point to the given node and our just-assigned Next node's Prior pointer to point to our new node. In code:

```
var
  GivenNode, NewNode : PSimpleNode;
begin
  . . .
  New(NewNode);
  ..set the Data field..
  NewNode^.Next := GivenNode^.Next;
  GivenNode^.Next := NewNode;
  NewNode^.Prior := GivenNode;
  NewNode^.Next^.Prior := NewNode;
```

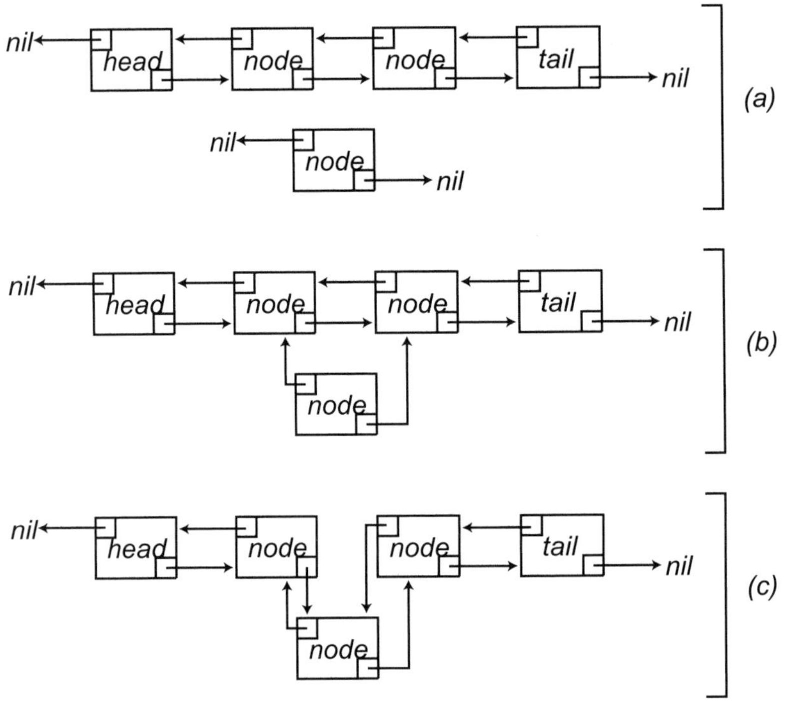

Figure 3.5: Insertion into a doubly linked list

To delete a node, the simplest possibility is deleting the node after a given node in the list. Here we set the given node's Next pointer to the node after the one we are about to delete; we then set the Prior pointer of the node after the one we are deleting to point to the given node. At that point, the node to be deleted is unlinked from the list and we can dispose of it. In code:

```
var
  GivenNode, NodeToGo : PSimpleNode;
begin
  . . .
  NodeToGo := GivenNode^.Next;
  GivenNode^.Next := NodeToGo^.Next;
  NodeToGo^.Next^.Prior := GivenNode;
  Dispose(NodeToGo);
```

Again, there is a special case for both these operations: inserting before the first item in the list (so that the new node becomes the first item) and deleting the first item in the list (so that there is a new first item in the list). Since we identify the list by the first node, we have to write these special cases separately.

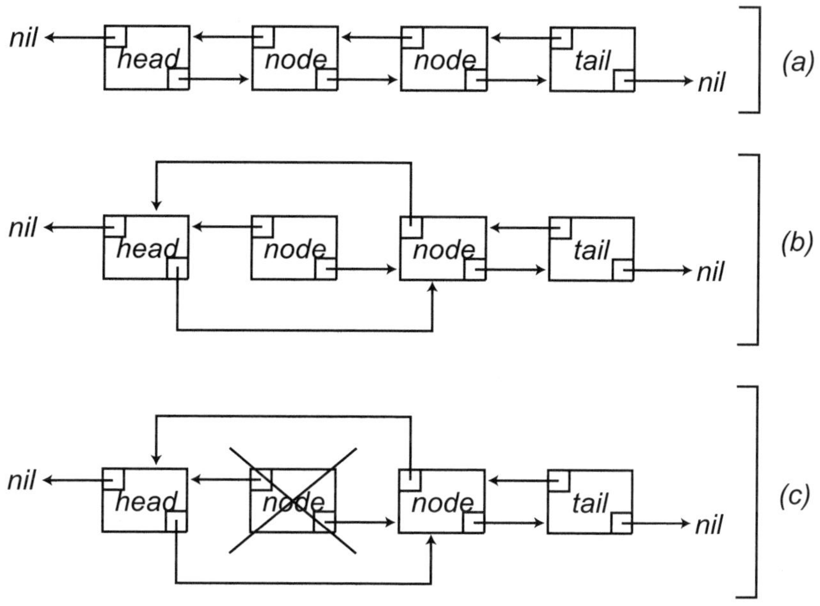

Figure 3.6: Deletion from a doubly linked list

Insert:

```
var
  FirstNode, NewNode : PSimpleNode;
begin
  . . .
  New(NewNode);
  ..set the Data field..
  NewNode^.Next := FirstNode;
  NewNode^.Prior := nil;
  FirstNode^.Prior := NewNode;
  FirstNode := NewNode;
```

Delete:

```
var
  FirstNode, NodeToGo : PSimpleNode;
begin
  . . .
  NodeToGo := FirstNode;
  FirstNode := NodeToGo^.Next;
  FirstNode^.Prior := nil;
  Dispose(NodeToGo);
```

Efficiency Considerations

Like the singly linked list, we can be a little more proactive with regard to efficiency.

Using Head and Tail Nodes

With a singly linked list we saw that having a head node improved matters nicely with regard to insertion and deletion. The corresponding case for doubly linked lists is to have two dummy nodes: the head node and the tail node. With these two placeholder nodes we can easily walk the list from the first node to the last, and also backward from the last node to the first. There are no longer special cases for insertion and deletion.

Using a Node Manager

Again, it makes sense to store data in the form of pointers in the linked list so that we can more easily write a generic doubly linked list class. With a doubly linked list, each node will have a forward pointer, a backward pointer and a data pointer, 12 bytes in all (i.e., 3 * sizeof(pointer) bytes). All nodes are the same, so we can use a node manager with a doubly linked list as well.

The Doubly Linked List Class

The interface to the TtdDoubleLinkList class is as follows:

Listing 3.13: The TtdDoubleLinkList class

```
TtdDoubleLinkList = class
  private
    FCount    : longint;
    FCursor   : PdlNode;
    FCursorIx: longint;
    FDispose  : TtdDisposeProc;
    FHead     : PdlNode;
    FName     : TtdNameString;
    FTail     : PdlNode;
  protected
    function dllGetItem(aIndex : longint) : pointer;
    procedure dllSetItem(aIndex : longint; aItem  : pointer);
    procedure dllError(aErrorCode  : integer;
                 const aMethodName : TtdNameString);
    class procedure dllGetNodeManager;
    procedure dllPositionAtNth(aIndex : longint);
  public
    constructor Create(aDispose : TtdDisposeProc);
    destructor Destroy; override;
```

```
    function Add(aItem : pointer) : longint;
    procedure Clear;
    procedure Delete(aIndex : longint);
    procedure DeleteAtCursor;
    function Examine : pointer;
    function First : pointer;
    function IndexOf(aItem : pointer) : longint;
    procedure Insert(aIndex : longint; aItem : pointer);
    procedure InsertAtCursor(aItem : pointer);
    function IsAfterLast : boolean;
    function IsBeforeFirst : boolean;
    function IsEmpty : boolean;
    function Last : pointer;
    procedure MoveAfterLast;
    procedure MoveBeforeFirst;
    procedure MoveNext;
    procedure MovePrior;
    procedure Remove(aItem : pointer);
    procedure Sort(aCompare : TtdCompareFunc);
    property Count : longint read FCount;
    property Items[aIndex : longint] : pointer
       read dllGetItem write dllSetItem; default;
    property Name : TtdNameString read FName write FName;
end;
```

As you can see, the interface is remarkably similar to the TtdSingleLinkList class. This is as it should be. To the user of the class it should make no difference which class he eventually chooses, it should work in the same way. The choice as to which class to use, the singly linked list or the doubly linked list, depends on the use the programmer wishes to make of it. If the majority of movement of the list cursor is to be forward, with little random access of individual elements, then the singly linked list is the premier choice. If there is likely to be a lot of forward or backward cursor movement, then taking the extra memory hit of the larger node size makes sense and the doubly linked list is the choice. If there is likely to be a lot of random item access, the TList is the choice, despite the slightly longer insert and deletion times.

Because of the backward pointer in the doubly linked list, we find that the implementation of the methods, although similar to their singly linked siblings, is simpler to code; we have the luxury of going in reverse, if need be.

The Create constructor allocates a further dummy node, the FTail node, from the node manager. As discussed in the introduction to doubly linked lists, this node will terminate the list, making certain operations easier and more efficient to code. The head and tail dummy nodes are initially linked together, with the head node's Next pointer pointing to the tail node and the latter's Prior node pointing to the head. The Destroy destructor will, of course, free this extra dummy tail node by returning it with the dummy head node, FHead, to the node manager.

Listing 3.14: Create and Destroy for the TtdDoubleLinkList class

```
constructor TtdDoubleLinkList.Create;
begin
  inherited Create;
  {save the dispose procedure}
  FDispose := aDispose;
  {get the node manager}
  dllGetNodeManager;
  {allocate a head and a tail node and link them together}
  FHead := PdlNode(DLNodeManager.AllocNode);
  FTail := PdlNode(DLNodeManager.AllocNode);
  FHead^.dlnNext := FTail;
  FHead^.dlnPrior := nil;
  FHead^.dlnData := nil;
  FTail^.dlnNext := nil;
  FTail^.dlnPrior := FHead;
  FTail^.dlnData := nil;
  {set the cursor to the head node}
  FCursor := FHead;
  FCursorIx := -1;
end;
destructor TtdDoubleLinkList.Destroy;
begin
    if (Count <> 0) then
    Clear;
  DLNodeManager.FreeNode(FHead);
  DLNodeManager.FreeNode(FTail);
  inherited Destroy;
end;
```

The sequential access methods, that is, the traditional linked list ones, are fairly straightforward to code. We don't have to maintain a parent node, which makes things easier, but insertion and deletion do require four links to be made, compared with two for the singly linked case.

Listing 3.15: The standard linked list operations for TtdDoubleLinkList

```
procedure TtdDoubleLinkList.Clear;
var
  Temp : PdlNode;
begin
  {delete all the nodes, except the head and tail nodes;
    if we can dispose of nodes, do so}
  Temp := FHead^.dlnNext;
  while (Temp <> FTail) do begin
```

```
    FHead^.dlnNext := Temp^.dlnNext;
    if Assigned(FDispose) then
      FDispose(Temp^.dlnData);
    DLNodeManager.FreeNode(Temp);
    Temp := FHead^.dlnNext;
  end;
  {patch up the linked list}
  FTail^.dlnPrior := FHead;
  FCount := 0;
  {set the cursor to the head of the list}
  FCursor := FHead;
  FCursorIx := -1;
end;
procedure TtdDoubleLinkList.DeleteAtCursor;
var
  Temp : PdlNode;
begin
  {let Temp equal the node we are to delete}
  Temp := FCursor;
  if (Temp = FHead) or (Temp = FTail) then
    dllError(tdeListCannotDelete, 'Delete');
  {dispose of its contents}
  if Assigned(FDispose) then
    FDispose(Temp^.dlnData);
  {unlink the node and free it; the cursor moves to the next node}
  Temp^.dlnPrior^.dlnNext := Temp^.dlnNext;
  Temp^.dlnNext^.dlnPrior := Temp^.dlnPrior;
  FCursor := Temp^.dlnNext;
  DLNodeManager.FreeNode(Temp);
  dec(FCount);
end;
function TtdDoubleLinkList.Examine : pointer;
begin
  if (FCursor = nil) or (FCursor = FHead) then
    dllError(tdeListCannotExamine, 'Examine');
  {return the data part of the cursor}
  Result := FCursor^.dlnData;
end;
procedure TtdDoubleLinkList.InsertAtCursor(aItem : pointer);
var
  NewNode : PdlNode;
begin
  {if the cursor is at the head, rather than raise
   an exception, move it forward one node}
  if (FCursor = FHead) then
    MoveNext;
  {allocate a new node and insert before the cursor}
  NewNode := PdlNode(DLNodeManager.AllocNode);
```

```
  NewNode^.dlnData := aItem;
  NewNode^.dlnNext := FCursor;
  NewNode^.dlnPrior := FCursor^.dlnPrior;
  NewNode^.dlnPrior^.dlnNext := NewNode;
  FCursor^.dlnPrior := NewNode;
  FCursor := NewNode;
  inc(FCount);
end;
function TtdDoubleLinkList.IsAfterLast : boolean;
begin
  Result := FCursor = FTail;
end;
function TtdDoubleLinkList.IsBeforeFirst : boolean;
begin
  Result := FCursor = FHead;
end;
function TtdDoubleLinkList.IsEmpty : boolean;
begin
  Result := (Count = 0);
end;
procedure TtdDoubleLinkList.MoveAfterLast;
begin
  {set the cursor to the tail node}
  FCursor := FTail;
  FCursorIx := Count;
end;
procedure TtdDoubleLinkList.MoveBeforeFirst;
begin
  {set the cursor to the head node}
  FCursor := FHead;
  FCursorIx := -1;
end;
procedure TtdDoubleLinkList.MoveNext;
begin
  {advance the cursor to its own next pointer}
  if (FCursor <> FTail) then begin
    FCursor := FCursor^.dlnNext;
    inc(FCursorIx);
  end;
end;
procedure TtdDoubleLinkList.MovePrior;
begin
  {move the cursor back to its own previous pointer}
  if (FCursor <> FHead) then begin
    FCursor := FCursor^.dlnPrior;
    dec(FCursorIx);
  end;
end;
```

If you compare the code just shown with the equivalent singly linked list code (Listing 3.9), you'll get a flavor of the differences the extra link makes in writing these methods. At one extreme, the method is slightly simpler to code; an example of this is the MoveNext method where we don't have an FParent variable to maintain in the doubly linked case. At the other extreme, there's a lot more fiddling around—witness the extra code that goes into maintaining the prior links in both the InsertAtCursor and DeleteAtCursor methods, compared with the singly linked list case.

The index-based methods for the TtdDoubleLinkList class are simpler than the previous class, the only complexity being the dllPositionAtNth method, used for positioning the cursor at the item with the given index. Remember the algorithm for the singly linked list: if the index we wanted was after the cursor, we started at the cursor and followed links, counting as we went. If it was before the cursor, we started at the first node instead. In the doubly linked list, we can also move backward if we want. So the algorithm changes slightly. As before, we work out on which side of the cursor the given index appears. Once we have determined that, we make another calculation: is the given index closer to the cursor, or closer to the relevant end of the list? We start counting from the closer node, moving backward or forward as required.

Listing 3.16: Positioning at the *n*th item with a TtdDoubleLinkList

```
procedure TtdDoubleLinkList.dllPositionAtNth(aIndex : longint);
var
  WorkCursor   : PdlNode;
  WorkCursorIx : longint;
begin
  {check for a valid index}
  if (aIndex < 0) or (aIndex >= Count) then
    dllError(tdeListInvalidIndex, 'dllPositionAtNth');
  {use local variables for speed}
  WorkCursor := FCursor;
  WorkCursorIx := FCursorIx;
  {take care of easy case}
  if (aIndex = WorkCursorIx) then
    Exit;
  {the desired index is either before the current cursor or after it;
    in either case the required index is either closer to the cursor or
   closer to the relevant end; work out the shortest route}
  if (aIndex < WorkCursorIx) then begin
    if ((aIndex - 0) < (WorkCursorIx - aIndex)) then begin
      {start at front and work forwards towards aIndex}
      WorkCursor := FHead;
      WorkCursorIx := -1;
    end;
  end
```

```
  else {aIndex > FCursorIx} begin
    if ((aIndex - WorkCursorIx) < (Count - aIndex)) then begin
      {start at end and work back towards aIndex}
      WorkCursor := FTail;
      WorkCursorIx := Count;
    end;
  end;
  {while the work cursor index is less than the index required,
   advance the work cursor}
  while (WorkCursorIx < aIndex) do begin
    WorkCursor := WorkCursor^.dlnNext;
    inc(WorkCursorIx);
  end;
  {while the work cursor index is greater than the index required,
   move the work cursor backwards}
  while (WorkCursorIx > aIndex) do begin
    WorkCursor := WorkCursor^.dlnPrior;
    dec(WorkCursorIx);
  end;
  {set the real cursor equal to the work cursor}
  FCursor := WorkCursor;
  FCursorIx := WorkCursorIx;
end;
```

Once the cursor positioning is worked out we can go ahead and write the remaining methods: they're all pretty much the same as those in the list's singly linked sibling.

Listing 3.17: Index-based methods for a TtdDoubleLinkList

```
function TtdDoubleLinkList.Add(aItem : pointer) : longint;
begin
  {move to the very end of the linked list}
  FCursor := FTail;
  FCursorIx := Count;
  {return the index of the new node}
  Result := Count;
  {insert at the cursor}
  InsertAtCursor(aItem);
end;
procedure TtdDoubleLinkList.Delete(aIndex : longint);
begin
  {position the cursor}
  dllPositionAtNth(aIndex);
  {delete the item at the cursor}
  DeleteAtCursor;
end;
function TtdDoubleLinkList.dllGetItem(aIndex : longint) : pointer;
begin
```

```
  {position the cursor}
  dllPositionAtNth(aIndex);
  {return the data}
  Result := FCursor^.dlnData;
end;
procedure TtdDoubleLinkList.dllSetItem(aIndex : longint; aItem  : pointer);
begin
  {position the cursor}
  dllPositionAtNth(aIndex);
  {if we can dispose of the data about to be replaced, do so}
  if Assigned(FDispose) and (aItem <> FCursor^.dlnData) then
    FDispose(FCursor^.dlnData);
  {replace the data}
  FCursor^.dlnData := aItem;
end;
function TtdDoubleLinkList.First : pointer;
begin
  {position the cursor}
  dllPositionAtNth(0);
  {return the data}
  Result := FCursor^.dlnData;
end;
function TtdDoubleLinkList.IndexOf(aItem : pointer) : longint;
var
  WorkCursor   : PdlNode;
  WorkCursorIx : longint;
begin
  {set the work cursor to the first node (if it exists)}
  WorkCursor := FHead^.dlnNext;
  WorkCursorIx := 0;
  {walk the linked list looking for the item}
  while (WorkCursor <> FTail) do begin
    if (WorkCursor^.dlnData = aItem) then begin
      {we found it; set the result; set the real cursor}
      Result := WorkCursorIx;
      FCursor := WorkCursor;
      FCursorIx := WorkCursorIx;
      Exit;
    end;
    {advance to the next node}
    WorkCursor := WorkCursor^.dlnNext;
    inc(WorkCursorIx);
  end;
  {didn't find it}
  Result := -1;
end;
procedure TtdDoubleLinkList.Insert(aIndex : longint; aItem : pointer);
begin
```

```
  {position the cursor}
  dllPositionAtNth(aIndex);
  {insert the item at the cursor}
  InsertAtCursor(aItem);
end;
function TtdDoubleLinkList.Last : pointer;
begin
  {position the cursor}
  dllPositionAtNth(pred(Count));
  {return the data}
  Result := FCursor^.dlnData;
end;
procedure TtdDoubleLinkList.Remove(aItem : pointer);
begin
  if (IndexOf(aItem) <> -1) then
    DeleteAtCursor;
end;
```

The code for the doubly linked list class, TtdDoubleLinkList, is found in the TDLnkLst.pas file on the CD.

Benefits and Drawbacks of Linked Lists

Linked lists have one large benefit: insertion and deletion are O(1) operations. It doesn't matter where you are in the linked list or how many items exist in the list, it takes the same amount of time to insert a new item or to delete an existing item.

The one main drawback to linked lists is that accessing an item by index is a O(n) operation. In this case, how many items are in the list matters: to find the nth item, we have to start at some point in the list and follow links, counting as we go. The more items, the more links we have to follow. The tricks we used in our class implementations only help a little bit: the operation is still O(n) overall.

Compared with a TList, linked lists of either variety will take up extra memory. The TList uses a single pointer to reference an item, so a TList uses at least sizeof(pointer) bytes per item. The singly linked list, on the other hand, requires a pointer to reference the item and also needs a Next link for each item. So singly linked lists use at least 2*sizeof(pointer) bytes per item. By a similar argument, doubly linked lists use at least 3*sizeof(pointer) bytes per item.

This is, however, only part of the story. If we use a TList inefficiently (in other words, not using the Capacity property to preset the size of the TList), we shall have allocated several, increasingly larger, blocks of memory and copied much data around in order to get to a populated TList. If we always insert items into the front of a list, the TList becomes much slower. We shall see some implementations of algorithms and data structures in this book in which linked lists provide much better efficiency than TLists, but in general usage we'll find that TList is better, faster, and more efficient than linked lists.

Stacks

Another well-known basic data structure in wide general use is the stack. A stack is a structure with two main operations: push, to add an item to the stack, and pop, to retrieve one. The structure is set up in such a manner that pop always returns the last item that was pushed (the "newest" item in the stack); in other words, popping returns the items in the stack in the reverse order in which they were pushed. Consequently, a stack is sometimes known as a last-in, first-out (LIFO) container.

Stacks are very straightforward to code. There are two main ways of doing so, the first by using a singly linked list and the second by using an array. As with the linked list, we'll assume that pointers represent the data items we'll be pushing on and popping off the stack. We'll discuss the linked list version first.

Stacks Using Linked Lists

With a linked list implementation of a stack, the push operation is coded as inserting a new node at the front of the list. The pop operation is coded as deleting the node at the front of the list and returning the data. Neither operation depends on the number of items in the list so we can categorize both as O(1) operations. That's it, we're done with the design.

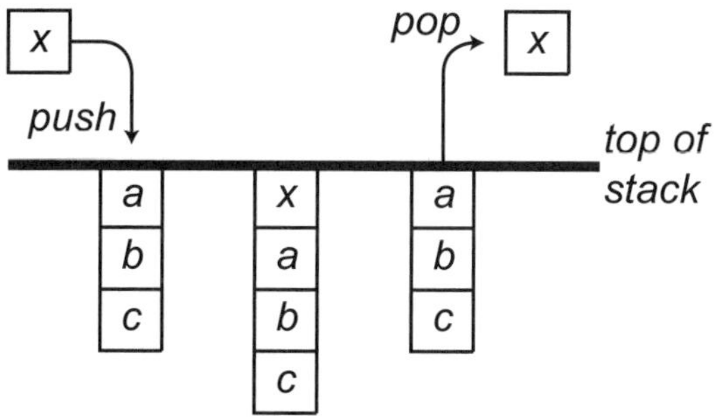

Figure 3.7: Stack push and pop

Of course, implementing this design involves a little more decision-making. We could code a stack class either to descend from the singly linked list class or to delegate the push and pop operations to an internal singly linked list instance. Personally, I don't approve of the first: we would end up with a class with Push and Pop methods, but we'd also have all of the other linked list methods hanging around as well (Insert, Delete, and so on). Not a good solution, in my view.

The other possibility, delegation, is in the spirit of Delphi, and the stack class could certainly be written that way. The Create constructor would create a new TtdSingleLinkList instance, and position the cursor after the head node; the Destroy destructor would free it; the Push method would use the instance to insert the item at the cursor; and the Pop method would delete the node at the cursor, having first saved the item so that it can be returned. A viable possibility.

Instead, we shall code the TtdStack from first principles. It's a simple class, and we'll gain a little speed and efficiency by doing so.

Listing 3.18: The TtdStack class

```
TtdStack = class
   private
     FCount   : longint;
     FDispose : TtdDisposeProc;
     FHead    : PslNode;
     FName    : TtdNameString;
   protected
     procedure sError(aErrorCode  : integer;
                const aMethodName : TtdNameString);
     class procedure sGetNodeManager;
   public
     constructor Create(aDispose : TtdDisposeProc);
     destructor Destroy; override;
     procedure Clear;
     function Examine : pointer;
     function IsEmpty : boolean;
     function Pop : pointer;
     procedure Push(aItem : pointer);
     property Count : longint read FCount;
     property Name : TtdNameString read FName write FName;
 end;
```

Examine returns the item at the top of the stack without popping it; this is a handy method to have in practice, and it saves popping the item, looking at it, and pushing it back onto the stack again. IsEmpty returns true if the stack has no items, and is equivalent to checking that Count is zero.

Listing 3.19: Examine and IsEmpty for the TtdStack class

```
function TtdStack.Examine : pointer;
begin
  if (Count = 0) then
    sError(tdeStackIsEmpty, 'Examine');
  Result := FHead^.slnNext^.slnData;
end;
function TtdStack.IsEmpty : boolean;
begin
  Result := (Count = 0);
end;
```

The Create constructor functions in the same way as the singly linked list. It checks that the node manager is present and then allocates a dummy head node using it. This node, of course, is initialized to point to nothing. Destroy clears the stack and frees the dummy head node, FHead, by returning it back to the node manager.

Listing 3.20: The constructor and destructor for the TtdStack class

```
constructor TtdStack.Create(aDispose : TtdDisposeProc);
begin
  inherited Create;
  {save the dispose procedure}
  FDispose := aDispose;
  {get the node manager}
  sGetNodeManager;
  {allocate a head node}
  FHead := PslNode(SLNodeManager.AllocNode);
  FHead^.slnNext := nil;
  FHead^.slnData := nil;
end;
destructor TtdStack.Destroy;
begin
  {remove all the remaining nodes; free the head node}
  if (Count <> 0) then
    Clear;
  SLNodeManager.FreeNode(FHead);
  inherited Destroy;
end;
```

As it happens, pushing and popping turn out to be minor routines indeed. Push allocates a new node from the node manager, and inserts it after the dummy head node. Pop checks to see if there is at least one node present, before unlinking it from the dummy head node using the "delete after" algorithm, returning the item and freeing the node by returning it to the node manager.

Listing 3.21: Push and Pop for the TtdStack class

```
procedure TtdStack.Push(aItem : pointer);
var
  Temp : PslNode;
begin
  {allocate a new node and put it at the top of the list}
  Temp := PslNode(SLNodeManager.AllocNode);
  Temp^.slnData := aItem;
  Temp^.slnNext := FHead^.slnNext;
  FHead^.slnNext:= Temp;
  inc(FCount);
end;
function TtdStack.Pop : pointer;
var
  Temp : PslNode;
begin
  if (Count = 0) then
    sError(tdeStackIsEmpty, 'Pop');
  {note that, even if we could, we don't dispose of the
   top node's data; this routine needs to return it}
  Temp := FHead^.slnNext;
  Result := Temp^.slnData;
  FHead^.slnNext := Temp^.slnNext;
  SLNodeManager.FreeNode(Temp);
  dec(FCount);
end;
```

The code for the linked list version of the stack, TtdStack, is found in the TDStkQue.pas file on the CD.

Stacks Using Arrays

Having seen the linked list version, let's consider how to implement the stack with an array. One reason we do this is that, many times, implementing a stack of some simple type (for example, characters or floating-point double values) is most efficiently implemented with an array.

For simplicity's sake, we'll use a TList as our array; in other words, we'll be implementing a stack of pointers. In the linked list version, we inserted the new node during a push operation to the front of the list, and the pop operation got the node from the same place. This is not the most efficient way to work with an array. Inserting at the front is a O(n) operation and we would prefer a O(1) operation, to mimic the linked list version. So, instead, we append the item to the end of the array during a push and delete the item from the end of the array during a pop.

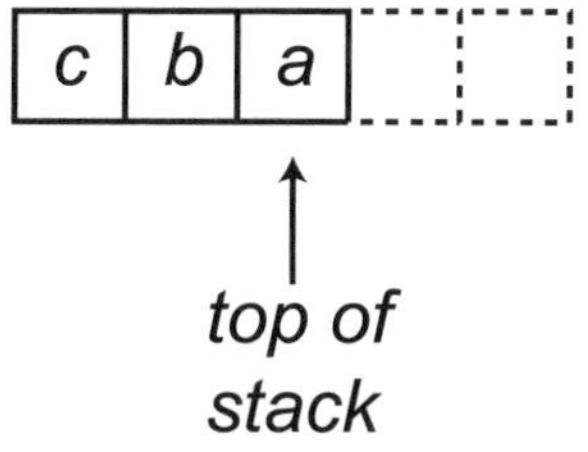

Figure 3.8: Using an array for a stack

Here's the interface for the TtdArrayStack class. As you can see, the public section is equivalent to that of the TtdStack class:

Listing 3.22: The TtdArrayStack class

```
TtdArrayStack = class
  private
    FCount   : longint;
    FDispose : TtdDisposeProc;
    FList    : TList;
    FName    : TtdNameString;
  protected
    procedure asError(aErrorCode  : integer;
                const aMethodName : TtdNameString);
    procedure asGrow;
  public
    constructor Create(aDispose  : TtdDisposeProc;
                       aCapacity : integer);
    destructor Destroy; override;
    procedure Clear;
    function Examine : pointer;
    function IsEmpty : boolean;
    function Pop : pointer;
    procedure Push(aItem : pointer);
    property Count : longint read FCount;
    property Name : TtdNameString read FName write FName;
end;
```

The constructor and destructor create and free an internal TList instance. Create accepts a capacity value for the stack. This is only an initial number of elements for the underlying TList instance, meant to make the class more efficient, rather than to serve as a concrete upper limit.

Listing 3.23: The constructor and destructor for TtdArrayStack

```
constructor TtdArrayStack.Create(aDispose  : TtdDisposeProc;
                                 aCapacity : integer);
begin
  inherited Create;
  {save the dispose procedure}
```

```
  FDispose := aDispose;
  {create the internal TList and make it have aCapacity elements}
  FList := TList.Create;
  if (aCapacity <= 1) then
    aCapacity := 16;
  FList.Count := aCapacity;
end;
destructor TtdArrayStack.Destroy;
begin
  FList.Free;
  inherited Destroy;
end;
```

The interesting code appears in the Push and Pop methods. We use the internal field FCount to serve a double purpose: first, to hold the number of items in the stack, and second, as the stack pointer. To push an item onto the stack, we write it to the element at FCount and then increase FCount. To pop an item, we do the opposite—decrement FCount and then return the element at FCount.

Listing 3.24: Pushing and popping in the TtdArrayStack

```
procedure TtdArrayStack.asGrow;
begin
  FList.Count := (FList.Count * 3) div 2;
end;
function TtdArrayStack.Pop : pointer;
begin
  {make sure we have an item to pop}
  if (Count = 0) then
    asError(tdeStackIsEmpty, 'Pop');
  {decrement the count}
  dec(FCount);
  {the item to pop is at the end of the list}
  Result := FList[FCount];
end;
procedure TtdArrayStack.Push(aItem : pointer);
begin
  {check to see whether the stack is currently full;
    if so, grow the list}
  if (FCount = FList.Count) then
    asGrow;
  {add the item to the end of the stack}
  FList[FCount] := aItem;
  {increment the count}
  inc(FCount);
end;
```

The code for the array version of the stack, TtdArrayStack, is found in the TDStkQue.pas file on the CD.

Example of Using a Stack

Stacks are used wherever you have to calculate things in reverse order but then return them in the correct one. A simple exercise that I sometimes use when conducting an interview is to ask the candidate to devise some code to reverse a string. With a character stack, the exercise is trivial: push the characters from the string onto the stack and then pop them off in reverse order. (There are other ways of completing the exercise, of course.)

An interesting variation on this theme is the problem of converting an integer value into a string. Obviously, in Object Pascal we have the Str and IntToStr routines so we wouldn't tend to write this from scratch, but it is an interesting problem nevertheless.

Let's define the problem. We want a function that takes a longint value as a parameter and returns the value expressed as a string.

Inside the function we need to calculate the digits corresponding to the integer value. The simplest way to do this is to calculate the modulus of the value with respect to 10 (this will be a number from 0 to 9 inclusive), store that somewhere, divide the value by 10 (this gets rid of the digit we just calculated), and repeat the process. We continue doing this until the value is zero.

Let's apply this algorithm (yes, it is an algorithm!) to the number 123. 123 mod 10 is 3, so store that somewhere. Divide by 10 to give 12. Repeat. 12 mod 10 is 2, store that, divide by 10 to give 1. 1 mod 10 is 1, store that, divide by 10 to give 0. We can now stop. We calculated the digits in this order: 3, 2, 1. However, we would like to return them in a string in the order 1, 2, 3. We can't just store them in a string as we calculate them (how long should we make the string?).

The answer is to push them onto a stack as we calculate them. Once we've stopped the loop, we can count the number of digits on the stack (this'll be the length of the string) and then we can pop them off and populate the string. Listing 3.25 shows the code.

Listing 3.25: Converting an integer to a string

```
function tdIntToStr(aValue : longint) : string;
var
  ChStack : array [0..10] of char;
  ChSP    : integer;
  IsNeg   : boolean;
  i       : integer;
```

```
begin
  {make the character stack empty}
  ChSP := 0;
  {force the value to be positive}
  if (aValue < 0) then begin
    IsNeg := true;
    aValue := -aValue;
  end
  else
    IsNeg := false;
  {if the value is zero, push a single 0 onto the stack}
  if (aValue = 0) then begin
    ChStack[ChSP] := '0';
    inc(ChSP);
  end
  {otherwise calculate the digits of the value in reverse order
   using the mod/div algorithm and push them onto the stack}
  else begin
    while (aValue <> 0) do begin
      ChStack[ChSP] := char((aValue mod 10) + ord('0'));
      inc(ChSP);
      aValue := aValue div 10;
    end;
  end;
  {if the original value was negative, push a minus sign}
  if IsNeg then begin
    ChStack[ChSP] := '-';
    inc(ChSP);
  end;
  {now pop the digits off the stack (there are ChSP of
   them) into the return string}
  SetLength(Result, ChSP);
  for i := 1 to ChSP do begin
    dec(ChSP);
    Result[i] := ChStack[ChSP];
  end;
end;
```

There are a couple of small tricks in this routine to note. The first is that we force the input value to be positive, if required, before we start the mod-and-div loop. If we did force the value to be positive, we make a note of the fact so that we can supply a minus sign later on. The second is to avoid the awkward case where the value is zero: as coded, the mod-and-div loop would cause the result string to be empty.

The next, and more importantly perhaps, is that I coded the character stack from scratch. Why? After all, I've just shown two variations of a stack class. Couldn't I have used that?

The answer goes back to something I noted earlier in this book: sometimes it will be more efficient to code a simple container like a stack from scratch. In this case I noted that the maximum number of digits that I would produce from a longint value would be 10 (the maximum longint value is 2,147,483,648, a 10-digit number), so the largest stack I would need should store 10 digits. I bumped this up by one so that I could store the possible minus sign as well. This is simple and small enough to declare as a short string on the stack.

Queues

Finally, in this chapter we shall look at queues, the final data structure in our basic lexicon. Whereas with a stack you get the items from it in the reverse order in which you put them, with a queue, you get them out in the same order you added them. The queue is, therefore, known as a first in, first out (FIFO) structure. The queue has two basic operations: enqueue for adding an item to a queue and dequeue for retrieving the oldest item.

Sometimes these operations are also confusingly called push and pop—I don't know about you, but in a supermarket line, I never push into it, nor do I pop out of it! Better terms in that situation might be *join* and *leave*.

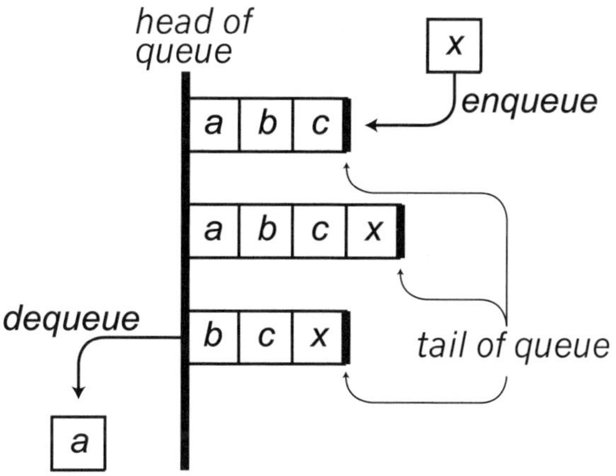

Figure 3.9: Queue enqueue and dequeue

Like stacks, we can implement queues with either singly linked lists or arrays. Unlike the stack, the latter implementation is difficult to make efficient, but the former is just as simple. So, let's look at the linked list version first.

Queues Using Linked Lists

Essentially we have to mimic the standard supermarket line with a linked list: pretty easy, since the linked list is a "line" anyway. We just have to add items to one end of the linked list and remove them from the other. If we want to use a singly linked list, we have the decision made for us: we dequeue from the front of the list and enqueue at the end of the list. With a doubly linked list we can use either end for either purpose, but we'd use more memory in the process. And, again, as it happens, neither operation depends on the number of items in the list, so they're both O(1) operations.

Like the TtdStack class, we shall design and code the TtdQueue class from first principles, making the same arguments for our choice as we did before.

Listing 3.26: The TtdQueue class

```
TtdQueue = class
  private
    FCount      : longint;
    FDispose    : TtdDisposeProc;
    FHead       : PslNode;
    FName       : TtdNameString;
    FTail       : PslNode;
  protected
    procedure qError(aErrorCode   : integer;
               const aMethodName : TtdNameString);
    class procedure qGetNodeManager;
  public
    constructor Create(aDispose : TtdDisposeProc);
    destructor Destroy; override;
    procedure Clear;
    function Dequeue : pointer;
    procedure Enqueue(aItem : pointer);
    function Examine : pointer;
    function IsEmpty : boolean;
    property Count : longint read FCount;
    property Name : TtdNameString read FName write FName;
end;
```

As with the singly linked list and the stack, the queue's Create constructor makes sure that there is a node manager instance and then allocates a dummy head node. The constructor then initializes a special FTail pointer to point to the head node. This pointer will be altered to make sure that it always points to the final node in the linked list—we can then easily insert a new item after the last node.

Listing 3.27: The constructor and destructor for TtdQueue

```
constructor TtdQueue.Create(aDispose : TtdDisposeProc);
begin
  inherited Create;
  {save the dispose procedure}
  FDispose := aDispose;
  {get the node manager}
  qGetNodeManager;
  {allocate a head node}
  FHead := PslNode(SLNodeManager.AllocNode);
  FHead^.slnNext := nil;
  FHead^.slnData := nil;
  {make the tail pointer point to the head node}
  FTail := FHead;
end;
destructor TtdQueue.Destroy;
begin
  {remove all the remaining nodes; free the head node}
  if (Count <> 0) then
    Clear;
  SLNodeManager.FreeNode(FHead);
  inherited Destroy;
end;
```

So, let us look at the Enqueue method. It allocates a new node from the node manager and sets its data pointer to the item we're inserting. Next, the FTail pointer comes into play. Assuming that it points to the last node, we add the new node right after it, and then we move the FTail pointer along to point to our new node, which is now the last node.

Listing 3.28: The Enqueue method for TtdQueue

```
procedure TtdQueue.Enqueue(aItem : pointer);
var
  Temp : PslNode;
begin
  Temp := PslNode(SLNodeManager.AllocNode);
  Temp^.slnData := aItem;
  Temp^.slnNext := nil;
  {add the new node to the tail of the list and make sure
   the tail pointer points to the newly added node}
  FTail^.slnNext := Temp;
  FTail := Temp;
  inc(FCount);
end;
```

The Dequeue method is equally simple. We first make sure that there is an item in the queue, and then we unlink the first node using the "delete after" algorithm on the dummy head node, FHead. We make sure we return the item itself and then we free the node using the node manager. Of course, we then have one less item. Now comes the interesting bit. Consider the case when we dequeue the one and only item in the queue. Prior to the dequeue operation, but the FTail pointer was pointing to the last node in the list, which, because there was only one node in the list, is also the first. After the dequeue operation, there are no more items in the queue. The first node no longer exists, but the FTail pointer is still pointing to it. We need to make sure that the FTail pointer points to the dummy head node, FHead, again. Of course, if there were more than one item in the queue the FTail pointer would still be valid, pointing to the final node.

Listing 3.29: The Dequeue method for TtdQueue

```
function TtdQueue.Dequeue : pointer;
var
  Temp : PslNode;
begin
  if (Count = 0) then
    qError(tdeQueueIsEmpty, 'Dequeue');
  Temp := FHead^.slnNext;
  Result := Temp^.slnData;
  FHead^.slnNext := Temp^.slnNext;
  SLNodeManager.FreeNode(Temp);
  dec(FCount);
  {if we've managed to empty the queue, the tail pointer
   is now invalid, so reset it to point to the head node}
  if (Count = 0) then
    FTail := FHead;
end;
```

The remaining methods, Clear, Examine, and IsEmpty, are fairly simple.

Listing 3.30: Clear, Examine, and IsEmpty

```
procedure TtdQueue.Clear;
var
  Temp : PslNode;
begin
  {delete all the nodes, except the head node;
   if we can dispose of the nodes' data, do so}
  Temp := FHead^.slnNext;
  while (Temp <> nil) do begin
    FHead^.slnNext := Temp^.slnNext;
    if Assigned(FDispose) then
      FDispose(Temp^.slnData);
    SLNodeManager.FreeNode(Temp);
    Temp := FHead^.slnNext;
  end;
```

```
  FCount := 0;
  {the queue is now empty so make the tail pointer
   point to the head node}
  FTail := FHead;
end;
function TtdQueue.Examine : pointer;
begin
  if (Count = 0) then
    qError(tdeQueueIsEmpty, 'Examine');
  Result := FHead^.slnNext^.slnData;
end;
function TtdQueue.IsEmpty : boolean;
begin
  Result := (Count = 0);
end;
```

The code for the linked list version of the queue, TtdQueue, is found in the TDStkQue.pas file on the CD.

Queues Using Arrays

Now, let's consider how to implement a queue with an array. Again, to simplify things, we'll use a TList; at least we won't have to worry about memory allocation or array growing issues.

Having seen the linked list version, your first impulse might be to call Add to append items to the end of a TList instance for the enqueue operation, and to call Delete to remove the first item in the TList for the dequeue operation (or vice versa: insert at the front of the list, delete from the end). However, consider what happens behind the scenes. For Add, nothing much, apart from the rare occasion when the TList has to be grown. It's a O(1) operation—just what we want. For Delete, all is not so hunky-dory. To implement the dequeue operation we have to delete the first item in the Tlist, and *that* requires all the subsequent items to be moved by one position toward the front. This action's speed depends on the number of items in the TList—a O(n) operation. Bad news. And we can't switch the enqueue and dequeue around so that we add to the front of the list and remove from the end; we'd *still* have a O(n) operation at the front.

> I must warn you that I have seen this method discussed as the way to implement a queue with an array in some published sources. Even worse, perhaps, the TQueue class in the Contnrs unit uses this method.

So how do we implement the queue with an array so that both queue operations are O(1), as in the linked list case?

The answer is to use the array as a *circular queue*. Imagine the waiting room at your dentist. If it's anything like my dentist's waiting room, it's a room with chairs arranged around the wall. Unlike a supermarket line where you reach the head of the queue by shuffling along pushing your shopping cart, in the waiting room you sit down. When the next person gets called in, you don't all stand up and move on to the next chair and sit down again. No, instead the head of the queue is some nebulous attribute that gets attached to a particular person for a given time. When someone gets called in, the attribute gets passed onto the next person in line, and he becomes the head of the queue. That way, no one has to get up and play musical chairs; the head of the queue is pointed to by something, the receptionist, maybe. This is a circular queue.

To implement a circular queue with an array, we define a variable that is the index of the item at the head of the queue. We also define another variable to be the index of the tail of the queue. We start off with a preallocated array of items (we size the array's capacity based on the maximum number of items we expect to be in the queue at any one time) and we set the head index equal to the tail index. In fact, if this equality holds, we define the queue to be empty.

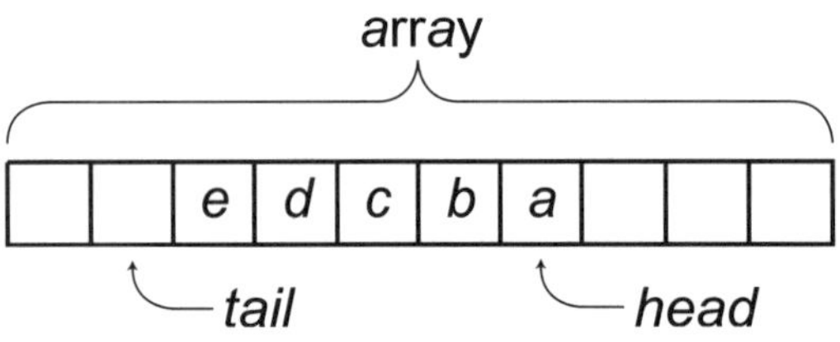

Figure 3.10: Using an array for a queue

Enqueuing an item is equivalent to setting the element at the tail index equal to the item being enqueued. Add 1 to the tail index; if it now exceeds the number of elements in the array, set it equal to 0, the index of the first element.

Dequeuing an item means returning the item at the head index. After that, we increment the head index, and again, if its value now exceeds the capacity of the array, we set it to zero. Obviously, before all this occurs, we have to make sure that there is an item to be had by checking that the head index does not equal the tail index (for if it did, the queue would be empty).

There is one slight design problem left: when we enqueue an item we have to check that the new value for the tail index does not equal that for the head. This would mean that we have managed to fill the array with items. Unfortunately, this condition also means (to the dequeue routine anyway) that the queue is empty. So, if this rather nonsensical situation occurs—empty equals full—we have to increase the size of the array, copy over all the current items, and reset the head and tail index values.

The public interface for the TtdArrayQueue class is the same as that for TtdQueue:

Listing 3.31: The TtdArrayQueue class

```
TtdArrayQueue = class
    private
      FCount      : integer;
      FDispose    : TtdDisposeProc;
      FHead       : integer;
      FList       : TList;
      FName       : TtdNameString;
      FTail       : integer;
    protected
      procedure aqError(aErrorCode  : integer;
                  const aMethodName : TtdNameString);
      procedure aqGrow;
    public
      constructor Create(aDispose  : TtdDisposeProc;
                                    aCapacity : integer);
      destructor Destroy; override;
      procedure Clear;
      function Dequeue : pointer;
      procedure Enqueue(aItem : pointer);
      function Examine : pointer;
      function IsEmpty : boolean;
      property Count : integer read FCount;
      property Name : TtdNameString read FName write FName;
  end;
```

The constructor and destructor are pretty similar to those of TtdArrayStack:

Listing 3.32: The TtdArrayQueue constructor and destructor

```
constructor TtdArrayQueue.Create(aDispose  : TtdDisposeProc;
                                  aCapacity : integer);
begin
  inherited Create;
  {save the dispose procedure}
  FDispose := aDispose;
  {create the internal TList and make it have aCapacity elements}
  FList := TList.Create;
  if (aCapacity <= 1) then
    aCapacity := 16;
  FList.Count := aCapacity;
end;
destructor TtdArrayQueue.Destroy;
```

```
begin
  FList.Free;
  inherited Destroy;
end;
```

The really interesting stuff happens in the Enqueue and Dequeue methods:

Listing 3.33: Enqueuing and dequeuing items with TtdArrayQueue

```
function TtdArrayQueue.Dequeue : pointer;
begin
  {make sure we have an item to dequeue}
  if (Count = 0) then
    aqError(tdeQueueIsEmpty, 'Dequeue');
  {the item to dequeue is at the head of the queue}
  Result := FList[FHead];
  {move the head index, making sure it's still a valid index;
    decrement the count}
  FHead := (FHead + 1) mod FList.Count;
  dec(FCount);
end;
procedure TtdArrayQueue.Enqueue(aItem : pointer);
begin
  {add the item to the tail of the queue}
  FList[FTail] := aItem;
  {move the tail index, making sure it's still a valid index;
    increment the count}
  FTail := (FTail + 1) mod FList.Count;
  inc(FCount);
  {if, having added another item we find that the tail and head
    indexes are equal, we need to grow the array in size}
  if (FTail = FHead) then
    aqGrow;
end;
```

As you can see, dequeuing involves returning the item at the head index, and then advancing that by 1; enqueuing involves setting the item at the tail index and then advancing *that*. If the tail reaches the head, we have to expand the queue by means of the protected aqGrow method:

Listing 3.34: Expanding a TtdArrayQueue instance

```
procedure TtdArrayQueue.aqGrow;
var
  i     : integer;
  ToInx : integer;
begin
  {grow the list}
  FList.Count := (FList.Count * 3) div 2;
  {the items are now down at the bottom of the list, we need to make
```

```
    them into a proper circular queue again}
  if (FHead = 0) then
    FTail := FCount
  else begin
    ToInx := FList.Count;
    for i := pred(Count) downto FHead do begin
      dec(ToInx);
      FList[ToInx] := FList[i];
    end;
    FHead := ToInx;
  end;
end;
```

This method is the most complex in the whole class. When it is called, the queue is full, the tail index temporarily equals the head index (which, if we forget, means that the queue is empty), and we need to expand the underlying TList instance in size. The first thing that happens is that we grow the list array by 50 percent. The problem now is that we have to patch up the circular queue so that it fits properly in the expanded space. If the head index is 0, the circular queue wasn't really circular, and so all we need to do is reposition the tail index. If the head index is not 0, the queue has "wrapped" within the array. To follow the items in order, we start at the head, go toward the old array limit, wrap to the start of the array, and go from there to the tail index (which is equal to the head index). The only thing is, now we have a bunch of extra elements in the array between the old limit and the new limit. So, what we need to do is move the items between the head and the old array end so that they butt up against the new array end. The queue will then be fixed again.

The entire code for the TtdArrayQueue class is found in the TDStkQue.pas file on the CD.

Summary

In this chapter we investigated linked lists, both singly linked and doubly linked. We discussed some efficiency problems with the standard linked list, and demonstrated that using a node manager improved the speed of both versions. At the end of the chapter, we looked at both stacks and queues, and implemented them with linked lists and arrays.

Having shown you both the linked list and the array versions of both the stack and the queue, I'm sure you are asking which one should be used. My timing tests with the various versions of Delphi (16- and 32-bit) show that the array version is faster in almost all cases and is the one to go for. The exception is that in Delphi 1 the array version is limited to about 16,000 items, so if you intend to have a stack with more items you'll have to use the linked list version.

Chapter 4

Searching

Searching is the act of looking through a set of items to find an item that interests us. One search routine I'm sure we've all used is the Pos function in the SysUtils unit for finding a substring within another string.

This chapter and the next one on sorting are, in many ways, linked. Often we have to search through an already sorted container to find an item. And, once a container is sorted, we can use an efficient search to enable us to find the correct spot to insert a new item so that it's in the correct order. Searching is not limited to looking through sorted items by any means; we shall also look at the simplest types of searching—algorithms that seem so simple as to be obvious and not deserving of the algorithm moniker.

This chapter also serves as a halfway point between the simpler fundamental containers, the arrays and linked lists, and the more complex ones, such as binary trees, skip lists, and hash tables. Efficient searching depends on the intricacies of the container holding the items we're using, and we'll be looking at algorithms for both arrays and linked lists in this chapter. When we introduce more complex containers in subsequent chapters, we shall always take time out to look at searching strategies for that structure.

Compare Routines

The very act of searching for an item in a set of items requires us to be able to differentiate one item from another. If we cannot tell the difference between any two items in general, there's no point in trying to look for one in particular. So the first hurdle we must overcome is how to tell the difference, how to *compare* two items that we may come across. There are two types of comparison we could make: the first is for unsorted lists of items, where we only need to know whether one item is equal to another (or, equivalently, whether the two items are different); the second is for sorted lists of items, where we can make the search more efficient if we can determine whether an item is less than, equal to, or greater than another. (In fact, if you think about it, the comparison test we make will define the order in which the items will appear in the list of items. If we are searching through a sorted list, we must use the same comparison test the list was built with in the first place.)

Obviously, if the items were integers, we'd have no problem with comparisons: we can all take two integers and determine whether they're different, and indeed if one is smaller than the other. With strings, the situation becomes more complex. We could make a case-sensitive comparison (uppercase characters being counted as different from their lowercase siblings); a case-insensitive comparison (uppercase characters equal to their lowercase equivalents), a locale comparison (comparing two strings with a country- or language-specific algorithm), and so on. With a Delphi set type, although we can tell if a set is equal to or different from another, there's no well-defined way to state whether one set is greater than another (indeed, it doesn't really make sense to say one set is greater than another, unless we're talking about the number of elements in each set). With objects, there's no well-defined way to test whether object A is equal to or different from object B (apart from testing for equality on the pointer to the object on the heap).

The best bet in this kind of situation is to make the comparison routine a black box, a function with a well-defined interface or syntax that takes two items as parameters and returns whether the first is less than the second, equal to it, or greater than it. For those item types that don't have a well-defined order (i.e., should two items be unequal, we cannot tell whether item A is less than or greater than item B), we just ensure that the comparison routine returns any value that is not "equal."

For this book, the comparison routines are all declared to be of type TtdCompareFunc (declared in the TDBasics.pas file on the CD, as are the example comparison routines):

Listing 4.1: The TtdCompareFunc prototype

```
type
  TtdCompareFunc = function (aData1, aData2 : pointer) : integer;
```

In other words, a comparison routine takes two pointers as parameters and returns an integer. The integer returned is 0 if the two data items are equal, a value less than zero if the first data item is *less* than the second, or a value greater than zero if the first is *greater* than the second. It is up to the routine to determine what aData1 and aData2 may refer to, and whether it has to cast to a non-pointer type, or a particular class, or whatever.

Here's an example comparison routine that assumes that the parameters are long integers—not pointers at all. (We assume that sizeof(longint) equals sizeof(pointer) for this routine—this applies with all current versions of Delphi.)

Listing 4.2: The TDCompareLongint function

```
function TDCompareLongint(aData1, aData2 : pointer) : integer;
var
  L1 : longint absolute aData1;
  L2 : longint absolute aData2;
begin
  if (L1 < L2) then
    Result := -1
  else if (L1 = L2) then
    Result := 0
  else
    Result := 1
end;
```

Before you throw up your hands in horror, saying that you'd never call a function like this to compare two longints, notice that you are not really supposed to. The comparison routine is going to be used by data structures that accept items as generic pointers (for example, Chapter 3's TtdSingleLinkList or Delphi's TList) and by routines that use such structures. If you are coding a search from first principles, it makes sense to code the comparison likewise, and I'm sure we can all compare two integers!

Here's a comparison routine, TDCompareNullStr, that compares two null-terminated strings in a non-country-specific manner:

Listing 4.3: The TDCompareNullStr function

```
function TDCompareNullStr(aData1, aData2 : pointer) : integer;
begin
  Result := StrComp(PAnsiChar(aData1), PAnsiChar(aData2));
end;
```

(For Delphi 1 programmers, PAnsiChar is defined in the TDBasics unit to be the same as PChar.) Luckily for us in this example, Delphi's StrComp returns the same type of value as our comparison routine requires.

As a final example, here's a locale-specific null-terminated string comparison routine, TDCompareNullStrANSI.

Listing 4.4: The TDCompareNullStrANSI function

```
function TDCompareNullStrANSI(aData1, aData2 : pointer) : integer;
begin
   {$IFDEF Delphi1}
   Result := lstrcmp(PAnsiChar(aData1), PAnsiChar(aData2));
   {$ENDIF}
```

```
  {$IFDEF Delphi2Plus}
  Result := CompareString(LOCALE_USER_DEFAULT, 0,
                          PAnsiChar(aData1), -1,
                          PAnsiChar(aData2), -1) - 2;
  {$ENDIF}
  {$IFDEF Kylix1Plus}
  Result := strcoll(PAnsiChar(aData1), PAnsiChar(aData2));
  {$ENDIF}
end;
```

Here we need to use different Windows routines in Delphi 1 and in 32-bit Windows Delphi; also notice that lstrcmp returns values in the fashion we want them, but CompareString does not. It returns 1 if the first string is less than the second, 2 if they're equal, and 3 if the first is greater than the second, so we just subtract 2 from its return value for our function result. For Kylix, we can use the strcoll routine from the Libc unit.

Sequential Search

Having nailed down the definition of a comparison routine, we can now look at searching for an item in arrays and linked lists.

Arrays

Arrays are the easiest implementation of a set of items we can search sequentially. There are two cases: one, the array's items are not in any particular order, and two, the items are sorted. Let's take the unsorted case first.

If the array is unsorted, there is only one algorithm to use to find a particular item: visit every item in the array, and compare it with the one we want. Usually this is coded as a For loop. As an example, let's search for the value 42 in an array of 100 integers:

```
var
  MyArray : array [0..99] of integer;
  Inx     : integer;
begin
  for Inx := 0 to 99 do
    if MyArray[Inx] = 42 then
      Break;
  if (Inx = 100) then
    ..42 wasn't found..
  else
    ..42 was found at element Inx..
```

Seems pretty easy, right? The code cycles through all of the items in the array, starting at the first and going to the end, and cleverly uses the Break statement to break out of the loop when it finds the first item that is equal to 42. (Break is a handy statement to use—a goto statement in all but name.) After the loop code, we check to see whether the item was found by looking at the loop counter Inx.

So, having presented the back-of-the-envelope code, I wonder how many of my readers would have spotted the bug. The problem is that Delphi's Object Pascal language specifically states that the value of the loop counter is undefined if the loop completes normally. On the other hand, the loop counter's value is defined should the loop be exited prematurely, say by use of the Break statement.

The code above assumes that the loop counter Inx is one more than the final value in the For loop if the loop goes all the way through to the end. As it happens, in the current set of 32-bit Delphi compilers (versions 2 through 6) this is what actually transpires: the final value of the loop counter is one more than the final value if the loop completes. In Delphi 1, the code is incorrect: after the loop completes, the loop counter has the final value in the For loop statement (in our example, Inx will be 99 at the end of the loop). In future versions of Delphi, who knows? Maybe the Delphi R&D team will change the compiler's optimizer so that the loop counter has another value; after all, they've left themselves the possibility by documenting the behavior of the loop counter.

So how should we code this sequential search then? We can still use a For loop (which is the fastest way of doing it), but we will have to have a flag stating whether we've found the item, instead of relying on the loop counter. The above code then becomes slightly more complex, but more strictly correct:

```
var
  MyArray : array [0..99] of integer;
  Inx     : integer;
  FoundIt : boolean;
begin
  FoundIt := false;
  for Inx := 0 to 99 do
    if MyArray[Inx] = 42 then begin
      FoundIt := true;
      Break;
    end;
  if not FoundIt then
    ..42 wasn't found..
  else
    ..42 was found at element Inx..
```

Here's a routine for finding an item in a TList, using a comparison routine (it can be found in TDTList.pas on the CD). It returns –1 if the item wasn't found; otherwise it returns the index of the item.

Listing 4.5: Sequential search through an unsorted TList

```
function TDTListIndexOf(aList : TList; aItem : pointer;
                        aCompare : TtdCompareFunc) : integer;
var
  Inx     : integer;
begin
  for Inx := 0 to pred(aList.Count) do
    if (aCompare(aList.List^[Inx], aItem) = 0) then begin
      Result := Inx;
      Exit;
    end;
  {if we get here, the item was not found}
  Result := -1;
end;
```

This works differently than the TList.IndexOf method, which finds the item in the TList by comparing pointer values for equality. It actually searches for the item as a pointer in its internal list of pointers. This routine, on the other hand, searches for an item by calling a comparison routine to compare the item we want against one in the list. This comparison routine may just compare the pointer values, or it may typecast the two pointers to something more meaningful, for example, a class or a record, and compare fields.

Notice as well that I introduced a small efficiency into the routine. Instead of comparing aItem against aList[Inx], I'm comparing against aList.List^[Inx]. Why? Well, the compiler compiles the former reference into a function call. The function that gets called, TList.Get, will check the passed index to see whether it's between 0 and the count of items (raising an exception if not) before returning the correct pointer from the internal pointer array. But we *know* that the index is valid: we're in a For loop from 0 to the count of items minus 1. We needn't access the Items property and so make a call to this method; we can instead access the pointer array directly (the List property of the TList instance).

This trick (using the List property of a TList instance) is a legitimate one to use. If you are certain your index values are bound to be in range, you can avoid the range checking implemented in the Items array by accessing the List pointer array.

I would, however, limit using this trick to code that iterates through the TList, or to code that automatically forces the indexes in range. Don't use it otherwise: Better safe than sorry.

For a TtdRecordList (introduced in Chapter 2), the class has an IndexOf method that performs a sequential search:

Listing 4.6: Sequential search with TtdRecordList.IndexOf

```
function TtdRecordList.IndexOf(aItem    : pointer;
               aCompare : TtdCompareFunc) : integer;
var
  ElementPtr : PAnsiChar;
  i  : integer;
begin
  ElementPtr := FArray;
  for i := 0 to pred(Count) do begin
    if (aCompare(aItem, ElementPtr) = 0) then begin
      Result := i;
      Exit;
    end;
    inc(ElementPtr, FElementSize);
  end;
  Result := -1;
end;
```

As you can see, the sequential search algorithm's run time depends directly on the number of items in the array. We may be lucky and find the item straight away (at the first element), or we may find it at the end of the array after wading through all of the other items. On average, for an array of n elements, we'll examine $n/2$ elements to find the one we want. In all cases, if the item is *not* present in the array, we'll examine all n elements in the array. Thus, the sequential search is a $O(n)$ operation.

What about a sorted array then? The first observation to make is that the simplistic sequential search we've shown will work equally well (or badly, depending on your viewpoint!) on a sorted array as on an unsorted array. The operation is still $O(n)$.

However, there is one improvement we can make. If the item is not in the array we can bail out of the search much earlier. Essentially, we iterate through the array as before, but this time we search for the first item that is greater than or equal to the one we want. If equal, we proceed as before; if greater than, we know that the item we're looking for is not in the array—after all, the array is sorted and we've encountered an item in the array that is larger than the one we have. All subsequent items must also be larger; hence, we can abandon the search.

Listing 4.7: Sequential search through a sorted TList

```
function TDTListSortedIndexOf(aList : TList; aItem : pointer;
                              aCompare : TtdCompareFunc) : integer;
var
  Inx, CompareResult : integer;
begin
{search for the first item >= aItem}
  for Inx := 0 to pred(aList.Count) do begin
    CompareResult := aCompare(aList.List^[Inx], aItem);
    if (CompareResult >= 0) then begin
      if (CompareResult = 0) then
        Result := Inx
      else
        Result := -1;
      Exit;
    end;
  end;
 {if we get here, the item wasn't found}
  Result := -1;
end;
```

Notice how we call the comparison routine just once for every time through the loop. We have no idea what aCompare is going to do—it is a black box—so it makes sense to call it as few times as possible. Therefore, for each time through the loop, we call it once and save the result, an integer. We can then test the integer return value as many times as we like.

As I said, this routine doesn't make the sequential search any faster if the item is in the list (it'll still take, on average, $n/2$ comparisons to find the item); it just makes the search return "not found" faster if the item is not present. As we'll see in a moment, however, the binary search will be faster still in both cases.

Linked Lists

With linked lists, the sequential search proceeds in a similar fashion. However, this time we do not visit the items by index; rather we just follow the Next links one by one until we reach the end. Using the TtdSingleLinkList class described in Chapter 3, we would end up with the following two routines, the first for searching through an unsorted linked list, and the second for searching through a sorted linked list. The routines just return whether the item was found or not. If found, the linked list will be positioned at the item in question. For the sorted version, the linked list's cursor is positioned at the point where the item would have to be inserted to maintain the list in sorted order.

Listing 4.8: Sequential search through a singly linked list

```
function TDSLLSearch(aList : TtdSingleLinkList;
                     aItem : pointer;
                  aCompare : TtdCompareFunc) : boolean;
begin
  with aList do begin
    MoveBeforeFirst;
    MoveNext;
    while not IsAfterLast do begin
      if (aCompare(Examine, aItem) = 0) then begin
        Result := true;
        Exit;
      end;
      MoveNext;
    end;
  end;
  Result := false;
end;

function TDSLLSortedSearch(aList : TtdSingleLinkList;
                           aItem : pointer;
                        aCompare : TtdCompareFunc) : boolean;
var
  CompareResult : integer;
begin
  with aList do begin
    MoveBeforeFirst;
    MoveNext;
    while not IsAfterLast do begin
      CompareResult := aCompare(Examine, aItem);
      if (CompareResult >= 0) then begin
        Result := (CompareResult = 0);
        Exit;
      end;
      MoveNext;
    end;
  end;
  Result := false;
end;
```

The corresponding routines for the TtdDoubleLinkList class are the same.

Binary Search

A better search algorithm for lists of items that are sorted is the binary search. We'll describe the standard algorithm using an array first, and then we'll discuss how to modify it for a linked list.

The binary search algorithm is for sorted containers only.

Arrays

Assume that we have an array that is in sorted order. As we have seen, the sequential search, even with the early cut-off trick, is a O(n) algorithm. What can we do to improve this?

The binary search is the answer. It is an example of a divide-and-conquer strategy: we start off with a large problem, divide it up into smaller problems, each of which is simpler and easier to solve, and thereby conquer the main problem.

This is how it works. Look at the middle item in the array. Is the item for which we're searching equal to it? If this is so then obviously we've completed the search successfully. If not, and our item is less than the middle element, then we can categorically state that the item, if it is present in the array, must be found in the first half of the array. If, on the other hand, our item is greater than the middle element, it must be found in the second half of the array, if anywhere. At a stroke, with a single comparison, we have halved the problem. We can now apply the same algorithm to the relevant half of the array: find the middle element, determine whether the item we seek is in the first half (i.e., quarter) or second half of the half-array. Again we divide the problem in two. We can continue like this, zeroing in on the sub-sub-sub-array that must contain the item we seek, or not at all.

This is the binary search algorithm. Since the size of the problem reduces by half every time we loop round trying to find the element, the run-time characteristic of the algorithm is O(log(n)); the speed of the algorithm is roughly proportional to $\log_2$ of the number of elements (essentially, squaring the number of elements only means doubling the time taken to perform the algorithm).

Here is an example of a binary search using a sorted TList (it can be found in TDTList.pas on the CD).

Listing 4.9: Binary search through a sorted TList

```
function TDTListSortedIndexOf(aList : TList; aItem : pointer;
                              aCompare : TtdCompareFunc) : integer;
var
  L, R, M : integer;
  CompareResult : integer;
begin
  {set the values of the left and right indexes}
  L := 0;
  R := pred(aList.Count);
  while (L <= R) do begin
    {calculate the middle index}
    M := (L + R) div 2;
    {compare the middle element against the given item}
    CompareResult := aCompare(aList.List^[M], aItem);
    {if middle element is less than the given item, move the left
     index to just after the middle index}
    if (CompareResult < 0) then
      L := succ(M)
    {if middle element is greater than the given item, move the right
     index to just before the middle index}
    else if (CompareResult > 0) then
      R := pred(M)
    {otherwise we found the item}
    else begin
      Result := M;
      Exit;
    end;
  end;
  Result := -1;
end;
```

We use two variables, L and R (standing for left and right), to define the sub-array we are currently considering. Initially, these two variables are set to 0 (the first item in the array) and Count–1 (the last item in the array), respectively. We then enter a While loop that we'll exit when we find the item in the array or until L crosses over past R, which we'll take to mean that the item is not present. For every cycle through the loop, we shall calculate the index of the middle element (in fact, the average of L and R). We compare the middle element against the item we need. If the middle element is less than the item, move the left index just past the middle index, making sure that the next time through the loop we'll only look at the latter half of the current sub-array. If the middle element is greater than the given item, move the right index just before the middle index. Define the new sub-array next time around, this time to be the first half of the current array. If the middle item equals the given item we're done, of course.

For illustration, Figure 4.1 shows the steps taken to find by binary search the letter *d* in the sorted array consisting of the letters from *a* to *k*. In step (a) we set the variable *L* to the first element (index 0) and *R* to the last element (index 10). That means that *M* is calculated as 5. We make the comparison: the letter at index 5 if *f* and this is larger than *d*, the letter we're trying to find.

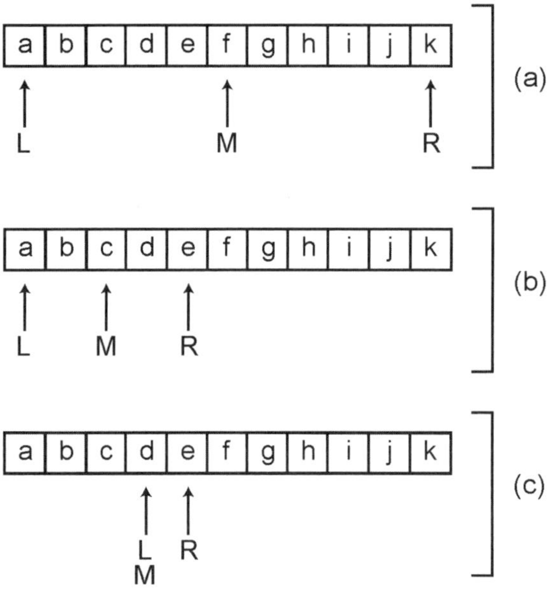

Figure 4.1: Binary search through an array

The algorithm states that we should set *R* to be $M-1$ (so that it is just before the old middle element). This means *R* is now 4. We calculate the new value of *M* to be 2, as shown in step (b). We now make the comparison: the letter *c* at index 2 is less than *d*.

Using the algorithm, we must now set *L* to be just past *M* (that is, $M+1$, or 3). We calculate the new value of *M* to be 3 in step (c). We make the comparison: the letter *d* at index 3 is equal to the letter we're looking for, so we stop: we've found the letter in the array.

Linked Lists

Looking at the code in Listing 4.9, it seems doubtful that binary search would ever work for a linked list, unless we do a bunch of indexed accesses into the linked list, which we saw was a bad idea in Chapter 3.

As it happens, it's not too difficult. Firstly, we should recognize that in general, following a link in the list is going to be much faster than calling a comparison routine. Hence, we can characterize following a link as "good," but calling the comparison routine as "bad." This means that we want to minimize the number of times we do the latter; we only want to compare as little as possible. (What I'm trying to say here is that the comparison routine is a "black box" to us—it could take a short amount of time, or it could take a very long time, at least as compared to following a link.) Secondly, we shall have to have some access to the internals of the linked list.

What we shall do is to look at a binary search for a generic linked list, and then we'll look at the code specific to TtdSingleLinkList and TtdDoubleLinkList. The generic linked list we use must know the number of items in the list, since we shall make use of this fact as we implement the binary search. We must also assume that the linked list has a dummy head node.

This is how it works:

1. Store the dummy head node in a variable called BeforeList.
2. Store the number of items in the list in a variable called ListCount.
3. If ListCount is zero, the item we seek is not in the list, and the algorithm is over. Otherwise, calculate half of ListCount, rounding up if need be, and store in MidPoint.
4. Move from BeforeList through the list, following the Next links, counting MidPoint nodes.
5. Compare the data in the node at which we stop against the item we're trying to find. If equal, we've found the item in the list and the algorithm is over.
6. If the data in the node is less than our item, store this node in BeforeList, subtract MidPoint from ListCount, and go back to step 3.
7. If the node is greater than our item, store MidPoint–1 in ListCount, and go back to step 3.

Let's step through an example to show that this algorithm works. Imagine that we have the following linked list of five nodes, and we wish to find B:

Head → A → B → C → D → E → nil

To begin with, BeforeList is set equal to Head (step 1) and ListCount equals 5 (step 2). Divide ListCount by two, rounding up, to make MidPoint equal to 3 (step 3). Follow the links from BeforeList, counting three nodes: A, B, C (step 4). Compare this node against the value we want (step 5). It's greater than the value B, so we set ListCount to 2 (step 7). Go through the loop again. Divide ListCount by two to make MidPoint equal to 1 (step 3). Follow the links from BeforeList, counting one node: A (step 4). Compare this node against the value we want (step 5). It's less than the value B, so we set

BeforeList to A, set ListCount to 1 (step 6) and go round the loop again. This time we set MidPoint to 1 (being ListCount divided by two, rounded up), and follow one link, to find the node we want.

If you were thinking that we passed over the node we wanted several times in this process, you are quite right. But, the thing to realize is, calling the comparison routine could be much slower than following several links (imagine, for example, that the items were 1,000-character strings and the comparison had to compare at least 500 characters to determine the order of two strings). If the linked list was a sorted list of integers, and we weren't using a comparison routine, then possibly the fastest way to search would be sequentially.

Here's the binary search routine for the TtdSingleLinkList class.

Listing 4.10: Binary search through a sorted singly linked list

```
function TtdSingleLinkList.SortedFind(aItem : pointer;
                  aCompare : TtdCompareFunc) : boolean;
var
  BLCursor      : PslNode;
  BLCursorIx    : longint;
  WorkCursor    : PslNode;
  WorkParent    : PslNode;
  WorkCursorIx  : longint;
  ListCount     : longint;
  MidPoint      : longint;
  i             : integer;
  CompareResult :integer;
begin
  {prepare}
  BLCursor := FHead;
  BLCursorIx := -1;
  ListCount := Count;
  {while there are still nodes to check...}
  while (ListCount <> 0) do begin
    {calculate the midpoint; it will be at least 1}
    MidPoint := (ListCount + 1) div 2;
    {move that many nodes along}
    WorkCursor := BLCursor;
    WorkCursorIx := BLCursorIx;
    for i := 1 to MidPoint do begin
      WorkParent := WorkCursor;
      WorkCursor := WorkCursor^.slnNext;
      inc(WorkCursorIx);
    end;
    {compare this node's data with the given item}
    CompareResult := aCompare(WorkCursor^.slnData, aItem);
```

```
    {if the node's data is less than the item, shrink the list, and
     try again from where we're at}
    if (CompareResult < 0) then begin
      dec(ListCount, MidPoint);
      BLCursor := WorkCursor;
      BLCursorIx := WorkCursorIx;
    end
    {if the node's data is greater than the item, shrink the list, and
     try again}
    else if (CompareResult > 0) then begin
      ListCount := MidPoint - 1;
    end
    {otherwise we found it; set the real cursor}
    else begin
      FCursor   := WorkCursor;
      FParent   := WorkParent;
      FCursorIx := WorkCursorIx;
      Result    := true;
      Exit;
    end;
  end;
  Result := false;
end;
```

The binary search for TtdDoubleLinkList is very similar.

Inserting into Sorted Containers

If we wish to have a sorted array or linked list, we have a choice as to how to maintain the order. We can either add all the items we want to the container and sort them, and resort the container every time we add a new item, or we can perform some extra work when we insert an item to ensure that it is added in the correct place to maintain the order. If we are going to use the container in a sorted fashion more often than not, it makes sense to try and maintain the order during insertion of a new item.

Of course, the problem then boils down to calculating where to insert a new item in the sorted list. Once we know that, we can just insert it. Earlier on, I indicated that the sequential search can tell us the point at which to insert an item, but we also know that the sequential search can be slow. Can the binary search help us?

As it happens, it can. Look back at the implementation of binary search for the array in Listing 4.9. When we drop out of the bottom of the loop, having determined that the item could not be found, what can we deduce about the values of L, R, and M? Firstly, and most obviously, $L > R$. Consider now the final cycle through the loop. At the start of this cycle, we must have had $L =$

R, or L = R+1, and M would have been calculated as equal to L. If there was any greater gap between L and R, say L = R+2, then M would have fallen in between them and we would have been able to go round the loop at least once more.

If, in this final cycle, the item we were looking for had been less than that at M, then R would have been set to M–1 and the loop terminated. We already know that the item was not found before that at M, and so we can deduce that the new item should be inserted between the elements at M–1 and M. In the usual parlance, we would insert it at M.

If, on the other hand, the item we were looking for had been greater than M, then L would have been set to M+1. We can assume in this case that at the start of the cycle L = R; otherwise, we would go round the loop again. We already know that the item was not found after that at M, and we can deduce that the new item should be inserted between the element at M and that at M+1. In other words, we would insert it at M+1.

So, we should either insert at M or M+1, depending on what happened in the last cycle. But look again: there is something in common between these two cases. It turns out that the value of L is the one we want both times, so we should insert the new item at L.

The following listing shows how to insert a new item into a TList. The code assumes that if the item is already in the list, the attempt to add it again will be ignored (in other words, the code does not allow any duplicates). The return value of the routine is the index of the inserted item. You can easily verify that the code still works if the list was originally empty.

Listing 4.11: Insertion into a sorted TList with binary search

```
function TDTListSortedInsert(aList : TList; aItem : pointer;
                             aCompare : TtdCompareFunc) : integer;
var
  L, R, M : integer;
  CompareResult : integer;
begin
  {set the values of the left and right indexes}
  L := 0;
  R := pred(aList.Count);
  while (L <= R) do begin
    {calculate the middle index}
    M := (L + R) div 2;
    {compare the middle element against the given item}
    CompareResult := aCompare(aList.List^[M], aItem);
    {if middle element is less than the given item,
   move the left index to just after the middle index}
    if (CompareResult < 0) then
```

```
      L := succ(M)
    {if middle element is greater than the given item,
      move the right index to just before the middle index}
    else if (CompareResult > 0) then
      R := pred(M)
    {otherwise we found the item, so just exit}
    else begin
      Result := M;
      Exit;
    end;
  end;
  Result := L;
  aList.Insert(L, aItem);
end;
```

For a linked list, the design is even simpler since we don't have to go through the discussion of how to calculate the index at which to insert the item. The search leads us directly to the point in the list where the new item should be inserted.

Summary

In this chapter we looked at searching. We showed how to perform a sequential search, and also how to cut it short if the underlying array or linked list were sorted. However, in the latter case, we showed how the binary search would dramatically reduce the time taken to search for an item. Finally, we saw how the binary search could help us insert a new item into the correct place in a sorted array.

Chapter 5

Sorting

Sorting is commonplace in regular day-to-day programming. When we display a list box on a form, it looks better and is easier to use if the items in the list are in alphabetical order. We as human beings prefer order when presented with data—patterns help us visualize the distribution of the data. Imagine how difficult a phone book would be to use if it weren't in alphabetical order but some other sequence. The chapters in this and every book are sorted by chapter number. In our development life, our programs work better if the data is in sorted order; for example, using a binary search is faster than a sequential search when you have a lot of items, so it's worth keeping data in sorted order to take advantage of this.

Tens of different sorts are known, with different characteristics and different advantages and disadvantages, each of which are optimized to work on different data sets.

Sorting Algorithms

Sorting algorithms are one of the most studied topics in computer science. In general, we can calculate the execution characteristics of sorts relatively easily. Indeed, any sorting algorithm that uses comparisons to order the items being sorted can be shown to take at least $O(n\log(n))$ time. We will discuss a couple of algorithms that can achieve this time.

Also the study and coding of sorting algorithms is ripe with clever techniques. We'll see sorts that don't require extra memory, that require a lot of extra memory, that put a binary tree into an array, that are recursive, that merge several lists of items, and so on.

The code for the generic sorts in this chapter can be found in TDSorts.pas on the CD.

Before we start, let's lay some ground rules. The sorts we'll be looking at all use comparisons to perform the ordering. Items will need to be compared to other items so that the sort algorithm "knows" how to arrange them. Rather than discuss the sorts by assuming that we are sorting integers, or strings, or TMyRecord variables, let's be a little more generic and assume that we are sorting items that are referenced by pointers. This goes along with the principle we're following with our data structures as well: our data is known via pointers. By separating the data from the manipulation of the data, we can focus on the characteristics of the algorithm or data structure without leading ourselves down a cul-de-sac of designing or optimizing methods just for integers, or strings, or whatever.

In this chapter on sorts, we shall compare items by using a comparison routine defined by the usual TtdCompareFunc function prototype. Our sort routines, therefore, must accept a comparison function as one of the parameters.

Since we are going to be comparing pointers, it makes sense to use a data structure that stores items as pointers. For our initial exposition we shall use a standard TList as an array of items that need to be sorted. The sort routines we write can therefore be completely generic: they will rearrange the pointers in the TList and will compare pointers by using a user-defined comparison routine. This initial discussion of the sorts will then easily extend to other types of arrays. We shall discuss how to sort linked lists after we are familiar with the basics of the standard sorting algorithms. Hence the majority of our sort routines will also accept a TList instance.

Finally, to be really generic, rather than just sort the entire TList, we shall also pass to the routine the range of items to sort. We'll have two parameters: the index of the first item in the range and the index item of the last item in the range. This would imply that each sort routine we write would perform the same validation test before processing: verify that the first and last indexes are valid for the TList (i.e., greater or equal to zero, and less than Count, and that the first index is less than or equal to the second).

Listing 5.1: Range validation with a TList

```
procedure TDValidateListRange(aList : TList;
                              aStart, aEnd : integer;
                              aMessage : string);
begin
  if (aList = nil) then
    raise EtdTListException.Create(
       Format(LoadStr(tdeTListIsNil), [aMessage]));
  if (aStart < 0) or (aStart >= aList.Count) or
     (aEnd   < 0) or (aEnd   >= aList.Count) or
```

```
    (aStart > aEnd) then
    raise EtdTListException.Create(
      Format(LoadStr(tdeTListInvalidRange),
             [aStart, aEnd, aMessage]));
end;
```

Doing this validation before we start sorting a TList gives us an extra advantage. The standard way of accessing an item in a TList is to use the Items property, and because this array property is the default one, we can drop the reference to Items completely: MyList[*i*]. Although this looks innocuous enough, it hides a big problem—at least as far as the efficiency of our sorts goes. The point to realize is that reading MyList[*i*], for example, causes the compiler to insert code to call MyList.Get(*i*) instead, the Get method being the read accessor method for the Items property. And the first thing that Get does is to validate the index, *i*, to be between 0 and Count–1. Yet, if we do our job properly in designing and coding the sort in question, we can *guarantee* that the index passed to the method will be valid. The same argument applies to writing a value to MyList[*i*]: the Put method is called and this validates its index parameter. So, by using the Items property we are served a double whammy: we have to call a method, and the first thing that method does is validate a perfectly valid index—not good.

Is there any way we can get around this? Luckily, the answer is yes. The TList class interfaces another property called List. This read-only property returns the pointer to the internal array of pointers used by TList to hold its items, a variable of type PPointerList. No method gets called, no validation takes place. Of course, by using this property we have taken on the responsibility of making sure that we don't try to read or write beyond the ends of the array.

Taking into account each of these points, we can see that our sort routines are all going to be of the following type:

```
type
  TtdSortRoutine = procedure (aList : TList;
                              aFirst, aLast : integer;
                              aCompare : TtdCompareFunc);
```

Since all of the comparison sorts we'll be looking at will use this prototype, it makes it easier to perform some experiments with each algorithm, such as comparing their execution times with each other.

There are three basic types of data sequences we could use to test each sort. We can sort a set of data that is in some random order (shuffled, if you like), an already sorted set of data, or a reverse sorted set of data. The second sequence would give us an indication of how the sort behaves when presented with an already sorted list—some sorts behave badly in this situation.

A list in reversed sequence also tests some sorts pretty strenuously—a lot of items have a *long* way to travel to get back into their correct sorted positions.

There is actually one more sequence of data we could use—a set of data that just consists of a small number of items repeated over and over; in other words, we use a set of items for which the comparison routine will be returning 0 for many pairs of items. This is a little bizarre, but there is at least one sort we will discuss that traditionally does not do well with this kind of data set.

Although it seems to be a little of a chicken and egg situation (to test a sort and its efficiency we need some sorted data, but what do we use to get it?), the two sorted sets of data are easy to generate. The first set of data we need for our tests, the random sequence, deserves some discussion. So, paradoxically it seems, we shall start our investigation into sorting by talking about shuffling data into a random order. In physics terms, we shall show how to increase entropy before showing how to decrease it.

Shuffling a TList

How can we shuffle the items in a TList? The algorithm most people come up with at first is a fairly easy one: visit each item in the list from the first to the last, and swap it with another, randomly chosen, item from the same list. A Delphi implementation of this algorithm would look like this:

Listing 5.2: Simple shuffling

```
procedure TDSimpleListShuffle(aList : TList;
                              aStart, aEnd : integer);
var
  Range     : integer;
  Inx       : integer;
  RandomInx : integer;
  TempPtr   : pointer;
begin
  TDValidateListRange(aList, aStart, aEnd, 'TDSimpleListShuffle');
  Range := succ(aEnd - aStart);
  for Inx := aStart to aEnd do begin
    RandomInx := aStart + Random(Range);
    TempPtr := aList.List^[Inx];
    aList.List^[Inx] := aList.List^[RandomInx];
    aList.List^[RandomInx] := TempPtr;
  end;
end;
```

Let's investigate how many sequences we could generate with this algorithm. After the first time through the loop we'll have one out of n different possibilities (the first item could be swapped with any of the others, including itself). After the second time through the loop, we'll again have one out of n different possibilities, which coupled with the n different possibilities from the first cycle, means that we have n^2 possibilities. I'm sure you can see that after exhausting the loop we will have generated 1 out of n^n possibilities.

There's just one problem with this algorithm. If we look at the shuffling from another angle, from first principles as it were, we can see that we can select a single item out of the n items for the first position. Once that has been set, we have a choice of one out of $n-1$ for the second position. Once *that* has been set, we have a possibility of one out of $n-2$ for the third, and so on and so forth. This produces a total of $n!$ different possible sequences. ($n!$ should be read n factorial and stands for $n*(n-1)*(n-2)*\ldots*1$.)

And therein lies the problem: apart from $n=1$, $n^n > n!$, and often very much larger than $n!$ Hence, by this algorithm we are generating sequences that repeat themselves, and some sequences will occur more often than others, since $n!$ does not divide n^n exactly.

A better algorithm for shuffling is to follow the method by which we calculated the correct total number of possible shuffled sequences: select the first item out of all of the n items, then select the second out of the remaining items ($n-1$), and so on. This leads to the following implementation, where, for convenience in the index calculations, we start from the end of the list instead of the beginning.

Listing 5.3: Correct shuffling of a TList

```
procedure TDListShuffle(aList : TList;
                        aStart, aEnd : integer);
var
  Range     : integer;
  Inx       : integer;
  RandomInx : integer;
  TempPtr   : pointer;
begin
  TDValidateListRange(aList, aStart, aEnd, 'TDListShuffle');
  {for each element, counting from the right...}
  for Inx := (aEnd - aStart) downto aStart + 1 do begin
    {generate a random number from aStart to the index of the
      element we're currently at}
    RandomInx := aStart + Random(Inx-aStart+1);
    {if the random index does not equal our index, swap the items}
    if (RandomInx<>Inx) then begin
      TempPtr := aList.List^[Inx];
      aList.List^[Inx] := aList.List^[RandomInx];
      aList.List^[RandomInx] := TempPtr;
```

```
      end;
    end;
  end;
```

Sort Basics

Sort algorithms separate themselves into two types: *stable* sorts and *unstable* sorts. A stable sort is one where, if there are one or more sets of items that compare equally, the order of those items will be the same in the sorted sequence as they were in the original sequence. For example, suppose that there are three items A, B, and C, all with sort value 42 (so that they compare equal), and they originally appeared in the list with A in position 12, B in position 234, and C in position 3456. In the sorted list they will appear in the sequence A, B, C; their order will not have changed. With an unstable sort, on the other hand, it is not guaranteed that items that compare equally will appear in any sequence in particular. In our example, the three items could appear as A, B, C or C, B, A, or anything in between.

In general usage, the stability of a sort doesn't matter. There are a few algorithms that require stable sorts, but in general we don't have to worry about this.

I shall illustrate each of these sorts, if possible, by means of a deck of cards. Deal yourself all of the hearts from a deck and shuffle them (only having 13 cards makes it easy to hold and manipulate them).

Slowest Sorts

We shall investigate the sorts in three separate lots. The first set is characteristically slow, $O(n^2)$ sorts, although a couple do have characteristics that make them fast in certain situations with certain data distributions.

Bubble Sort

The first sort that programmers come across when they're learning the tricks of the trade is the bubble sort. This is a shame, since, of all the sorts, it tends to be the slowest. It is perhaps the easiest to code (though not by much).

Bubble sort goes a bit like this. Fan your cards out. Look at the twelfth and thirteenth cards on the right side. If the twelfth is larger than the thirteenth, swap them. Now look at the eleventh and the twelfth cards. If the eleventh is bigger than the twelfth, swap them over. Do the same for the pairs (10, 11), (9, 10) and so on all the way down to the first and second cards. At this point, after this first sweep, you will have managed to get the ace into the first position. In fact, once you "snagged" the ace in your sweep through the hand, it "bubbles" along to the start. Now return to the twelfth and thirteenth cards. Perform the same process, stopping at the second and third card pair this time. You'll find that you managed to get the two into the second position. Continue this process, reducing the number of cards you look through every time, until you finally get the hand sorted.

```
5 King 4 2 Jack Ace 9 8 3 10 Queen 6 7
5 King 4 2 Jack Ace 9 8 3 10 Queen 6 7
5 King 4 2 Jack Ace 9 8 3 10 6 Queen 7
5 King 4 2 Jack Ace 9 8 3 6 10 Queen 7
5 King 4 2 Jack Ace 9 8 3 6 10 Queen 7
5 King 4 2 Jack Ace 9 3 8 6 10 Queen 7
5 King 4 2 Jack Ace 3 9 8 6 10 Queen 7
5 King 4 2 Jack Ace 3 9 8 6 10 Queen 7
5 King 4 2 Ace Jack 3 9 8 6 10 Queen 7
5 King 4 Ace 2 Jack 3 9 8 6 10 Queen 7
5 King Ace 4 2 Jack 3 9 8 6 10 Queen 7
5 Ace King 4 2 Jack 3 9 8 6 10 Queen 7
Ace 5 King 4 2 Jack 3 9 8 6 10 Queen 7
```

Figure 5.1: A single pass with bubble sort

I'm sure you'll agree that this was pretty tedious. When coded into Pascal, tediousness translates to a slow speed. There is, however, a small optimization we could make: if we don't swap any cards during a sweep, it means that the cards are sorted.

Listing 5.4: Bubble sort

```
procedure TDBubbleSort(aList     : TList;
                       aFirst    : integer;
                       aLast     : integer;
                       aCompare  : TtdCompareFunc);
var
  i, j : integer;
  Temp : pointer;
  Done : boolean;
begin
  TDValidateListRange(aList, aFirst, aLast, 'TDBubbleSort');
  for i := aFirst to pred(aLast) do begin
    Done := true;
    for j := aLast downto succ(i) do
      if (aCompare(aList.List^[j], aList.List^[j-1]) < 0) then begin
        {swap jth and (j-1)th elements}
        Temp := aList.List^[j];
        aList.List^[j] := aList.List^[j-1];
        aList.List^[j-1] := Temp;
        Done := false;
```

```
      end;
    if Done then
      Exit;
  end;
end;
```

Bubble sort is a $O(n^2)$ algorithm. There are two loops in the algorithm, one inside the other, and the length of each depends on the number of items. The first cycle through the first loop will do $n-1$ comparisons, the second $n-2$, the third $n-3$, and so on. There are $n-1$ cycles in all, so the total number of comparisons is

$$(n-1) + (n-2) + \ldots + 1$$

which simplifies to $n(n-1)/2$, or $(n^2-n)/2$. In other words, $O(n^2)$. The number of swaps is a little more difficult to calculate, but in the worst case (the items were originally in reverse order), there will be the same number of swaps as comparisons, so again $O(n^2)$.

The small optimization mentioned above does mean that if the original list was sorted, bubble sort is very fast: it just makes one pass through the list, finds out that no swaps are needed, and stops. $(n-1)$ comparisons and no swaps indicate a $O(n)$ algorithm in this case.

One big problem with bubble sort, and, admittedly, with a lot of others, is that items are only swapped with their immediate neighbors. If the smallest item happens to find itself at the end of the list, it will have to be swapped with every item in the list before it gets to its final resting place.

Bubble sort is not stable, since the sweeping will snag the final one of a set of equal items and hence equal items will appear in reverse order in the sorted list than they appeared in the original list. If the comparison was changed to a less than or equal test instead of a pure less than test, the sort would become stable, but the number of swaps would increase, and the little optimization we did would no longer work.

Shaker Sort

There is a minor variant of bubble sort, not known to many people, which improves the speed slightly in practice: the shaker sort.

Back to the cards. Perform the first sweep of bubble sort and get the ace into position. Instead of starting over on the right-hand side, sweep back through the cards from the left: compare the second and third cards and move the higher card into the right-hand position if necessary. Compare the third and fourth, swap if needed. Continue until you get to the twelfth and thirteenth. You will have snagged the King en route and it will be in the last position.

Now sweep back down to the second card, snagging the 2 as you go. Alternate this sweeping up and down until you've sorted the cards.

5 King 4 2 Jack Ace 9 8 3 10 Queen 6 **7**
5 King 4 2 Jack Ace 9 8 3 10 Queen **6** 7
5 King 4 2 Jack Ace 9 8 3 10 **6** Queen 7
5 King 4 2 Jack Ace 9 8 3 **6** 10 Queen 7
5 King 4 2 Jack Ace 9 8 **3** 6 10 Queen 7
5 King 4 2 Jack Ace 9 **3** 8 6 10 Queen 7
5 King 4 2 Jack Ace **3** 9 8 6 10 Queen 7
5 King 4 2 Jack **Ace** 3 9 8 6 10 Queen 7
5 King 4 2 **Ace** Jack 3 9 8 6 10 Queen 7
5 King 4 **Ace** 2 Jack 3 9 8 6 10 Queen 7
5 King **Ace** 4 2 Jack 3 9 8 6 10 Queen 7
5 **Ace** King 4 2 Jack 3 9 8 6 10 Queen 7
Ace 5 King 4 2 Jack 3 9 8 6 10 Queen 7
Ace **5** King 4 2 Jack 3 9 8 6 10 Queen 7
Ace 5 **King** 4 2 Jack 3 9 8 6 10 Queen 7
Ace 5 4 **King** 2 Jack 3 9 8 6 10 Queen 7
Ace 5 4 2 **King** Jack 3 9 8 6 10 Queen 7
Ace 5 4 2 Jack **King** 3 9 8 6 10 Queen 7
Ace 5 4 2 Jack 3 **King** 9 8 6 10 Queen 7
Ace 5 4 2 Jack 3 9 **King** 8 6 10 Queen 7
Ace 5 4 2 Jack 3 9 8 **King** 6 10 Queen 7
Ace 5 4 2 Jack 3 9 8 6 **King** 10 Queen 7
Ace 5 4 2 Jack 3 9 8 6 10 **King** Queen 7
Ace 5 4 2 Jack 3 9 8 6 10 Queen **King** 7
Ace 5 4 2 Jack 3 9 8 6 10 Queen 7 **King**

Figure 5.2: Two passes with shaker sort

Listing 5.5: Shaker sort

```
procedure TDShakerSort(aList    :TList;
                       aFirst   : integer;
                       aLast    : integer;
                       aCompare : TtdCompareFunc);
var
  i    : integer;
  Temp : pointer;
begin
  TDValidateListRange(aList, aFirst, aLast, 'TDShakerSort');
  while (aFirst < aLast) do begin
    for i := aLast downto succ(aFirst) do
      if (aCompare(aList.List^[i], aList.List^[i-1]) < 0) then begin
        Temp := aList.List^[i];
        aList.List^[i] := aList.List^[i-1];
        aList.List^[i-1] := Temp;
      end;
```

```
    inc(aFirst);
    for i := succ(aFirst) to aLast do
      if (aCompare(aList.List^[i], aList.List^[i-1]) < 0) then begin
        Temp := aList.List^[i];
        aList.List^[i] := aList.List^[i-1];
        aList.List^[i-1] := Temp;
      end;
    dec(aLast);
  end;
end;
```

This is still a O(n^2) algorithm, but in practice it manages to shave a small percentage off the execution time of the bubble sort. The reason it's called shaker sort is that items tend to oscillate around their correct position until the entire list is sorted.

Like bubble sort, shaker sort is not stable.

Selection Sort

The next sort we shall consider is selection sort. This is the first sort we'll look at that manages to have a small place in your sort algorithm arsenal (we can quite easily forget about bubble and shaker sort).

Starting at the right-hand side of your shuffled hand of hearts, scan the cards looking for the smallest (it'll be the ace, of course). Swap it with the first card. Ignoring this first, now correctly positioned, card, scan the cards from the right again until you identify the smallest. Swap it with the second card. Ignoring the first two cards, scan from the right looking for the smallest card, and swap with the card in the third position. Continue in this fashion until all the cards are sorted. Obviously the thirteenth cycle is not required since it only involves one card and that must obviously be in the correct position.

5 King 4 2 Jack Ace 9 8 3 10 Queen 6 7
Ace King 4 2 Jack **5** 9 8 3 10 Queen 6 7
Ace **2** 4 **King** Jack 5 9 8 3 10 Queen 6 7
Ace 2 **3** King Jack 5 9 8 **4** 10 Queen 6 7
Ace 2 3 **4** Jack 5 9 8 **King** 10 Queen 6 7
Ace 2 3 4 **5** **Jack** 9 8 King 10 Queen 6 7
Ace 2 3 4 5 **6** 9 8 King 10 Queen **Jack** 7
Ace 2 3 4 5 6 **7** 8 King 10 Queen Jack **9**
Ace 2 3 4 5 6 7 8 **9** 10 Queen Jack **King**
Ace 2 3 4 5 6 7 8 9 10 **Jack** **Queen** King

Figure 5.3: Selection sort

Listing 5.6: Selection sort

```
procedure TDSelectionSort(aList     : TList;
                          aFirst    : integer;
                          aLast     : integer;
                          aCompare  : TtdCompareFunc);
var
  i, j       : integer;
  IndexOfMin : integer;
  Temp       : pointer;
begin
  TDValidateListRange(aList, aFirst, aLast, 'TDSelectionSort');
  for i := aFirst to pred(aLast) do begin
    IndexOfMin := i;
    for j := succ(i) to aLast do
      if (aCompare(aList.List^[j], aList.List^[IndexOfMin]) < 0) then
        IndexOfMin := j;
    if (aIndexOfMin<>i) then begin
      Temp := aList.List^[i];
      aList.List^[i] := aList.List^[IndexOfMin];
      aList.List^[IndexOfMin] := Temp;
    end;
  end;
end;
```

As you see, there are two loops again, one inside the other, so it's a $O(n^2)$ algorithm. The first loop counts though the item positions from aFirst to aLast–1, and for each cycle through this loop, the second loop identifies the smallest item in the remaining part of the list. Unlike our card example where we knew the pip value of the smallest card at any point, the second loop doesn't know beforehand which is the smallest item: it has to examine them all. Once the smallest item has been identified, it is swapped into the correct position.

This sort is interesting for one peculiarity. The number of comparisons the sort has to do is n for the first cycle, $n-1$ for the second, and so on, for a grand total of $n(n+1)/2-1$ comparisons, or $O(n^2)$. The number of swaps, however, is much smaller; there is just one swap per cycle of the outer loop, so there are $(n-1)$ swaps, which is $O(n)$. What this means in practice is that if the cost of swapping two items is much larger than the cost of comparing two items (by *cost*, I mean the time taken or the resources required), selection sort is the way to go.

Selection sort is stable. The search for the smallest item is designed to return the first of a set of equal smallest items, and hence equal items will end up in the sorted list in the same relative order as in the original list.

Insertion Sort

The final sort in this initial set of algorithms is the insertion sort. This sort should be familiar to anyone who plays card games like whist or bridge, since this is the way that most card players sort their hands.

Start from the left of your hand of cards. Compare the first two cards and put them in order, if required. Look at the third card. Insert it into the right place amongst the first two—of course, with the understanding that it might be in the correct place to begin with. Look at the fourth card and insert it into the correct place among the three cards already sorted. Continue with the fifth, sixth, seventh cards, and so on. As you progress through the hand you'll notice that at every stage, the cards to the left of the card being considered are sorted.

```
5 King 4 2 Jack Ace 9 8 3 10 Queen 6 7
4 5 King 2 Jack Ace 9 8 3 10 Queen 6 7
2 4 5 King Jack Ace 9 8 3 10 Queen 6 7
2 4 5 Jack King Ace 9 8 3 10 Queen 6 7
Ace 2 4 5 Jack King 9 8 3 10 Queen 6 7
Ace 2 4 5 9 Jack King 8 3 10 Queen 6 7
Ace 2 4 5 8 9 Jack King 3 10 Queen 6 7
Ace 2 3 4 5 8 9 Jack King 10 Queen 6 7
Ace 2 3 4 5 8 9 10 Jack King Queen 6 7
Ace 2 3 4 5 8 9 10 Jack Queen King 6 7
Ace 2 3 4 5 6 8 9 10 Jack Queen King 7
Ace 2 3 4 5 6 7 8 9 10 Jack Queen King
```

Figure 5.4: Standard insertion sort

Listing 5.7: Standard insertion sort

```
procedure TDInsertionSortStd(aList    : TList;
                             aFirst   : integer;
                             aLast    : integer;
                             aCompare : TtdCompareFunc);
var
  i, j : integer;
  Temp : pointer;
begin
  TDValidateListRange(aList, aFirst, aLast, 'TDInsertionSortStd');
  for i := succ(aFirst) to aLast do begin
    Temp := aList.List^[i];
    j := i;
    while (j > aFirst) and
          (aCompare(Temp, aList.List^[j-1]) < 0) do begin
      aList.List^[j] := aList.List^[j-1];
      dec(j);
    end;
```

```
    aList.List^[j] := Temp;
  end;
end;
```

This implementation has a nice little wrinkle: we save the current item in a temporary variable and then, as we go back through the sorted items looking for the place to insert it (the inner loop), we slide the items that are larger along by one. In other words, the implementation creates a hole and then slides the items over by one position to the right, moving the hole leftward. Eventually we find the right place and just place the saved item into the hole.

Look at that inner loop. It stops with one of two conditions being hit: either we get the beginning of the list—in other words the current item is smaller than all of the items currently sorted—or we find an item that is less than the current one. Note however that this first test is checked every time through the inner loop, even though it's actually only needed for the fairly rare case that the current item is smaller than all of the sorted ones and we need to be able to stop running beyond the start of the loop. Traditionally, the way to get rid of this extra check is to have a sentinel item at the beginning of the list, one that is smaller than every item in the list. But, generally, we don't know what this value might be and often we don't have any room in the list to put this item anyway. (In theory, you'd have to copy the list over to another list that was one item larger, set the first item in this new list to the smallest value we'd need, sort, and then copy the sorted items back over. Just to remove a single Boolean test in a loop? No thanks.)

5 King 4 2 Jack Ace 9 8 3 10 Queen 6 7

Ace King 4 2 Jack **5** 9 8 3 10 Queen 6 7 → 1st pass of selection sort

Ace King 4 2 Jack 5 9 8 3 10 Queen 6 7 → Standard insertion sort

Ace **4 King** 2 Jack 5 9 8 3 10 Queen 6 7 →

Ace **2 4 King** Jack 5 9 8 3 10 Queen 6 7 →

Ace 2 4 **Jack King** 5 9 8 3 10 Queen 6 7 →

Ace 2 4 **5 Jack King** 9 8 3 10 Queen 6 7 →

Ace 2 4 5 **9 Jack King** 8 3 10 Queen 6 7 →

Ace 2 4 5 **8 9 Jack King** 3 10 Queen 6 7 →

Ace 2 **3 4 5 8 9 Jack King** 10 Queen 6 7 →

Ace 2 3 4 5 8 9 **10 Jack King** Queen 6 7 →

Ace 2 3 4 5 8 9 10 Jack **Queen King** 6 7 →

Ace 2 3 4 5 **6 8 9 10 Jack Queen King** 7 →

Ace 2 3 4 5 6 **7 8 9 10 Jack Queen King** →

Figure 5.5: Optimized insertion sort

A much better optimization is to scan the entire list for the smallest item and swap it into the first position (in essence, performing the first cycle of selection sort). Once that's in place we can perform the standard insertion sort and ignore the possibility of running off the beginning of the list.

Listing 5.8: Optimized insertion sort

```
procedure TDInsertionSort(aList       : TList;
                          aFirst      : integer;
                          aLast       : integer;
                          aCompare    : TtdCompareFunc);
var
  i, j        : integer;
  IndexOfMin  : integer;
  Temp        : pointer;
begin
  TDValidateListRange(aList, aFirst, aLast, 'TDInsertionSort');
  {find the smallest element and put it in the first position}
  IndexOfMin := aFirst;
  for i := succ(aFirst) to aLast do
    if (aCompare(aList.List^[i], aList.List^[IndexOfMin]) < 0) then
      IndexOfMin := i;
  if (aFirst<>IndexOfMin) then begin
    Temp := aList.List^[aFirst];
    aList.List^[aFirst] := aList.List^[IndexOfMin];
    aList.List^[IndexOfMin] := Temp;
  end;
  {now sort via insertion method}
  for i := aFirst+2 to aLast do begin
    Temp := aList.List^[i];
    j := i;
    while (aCompare(Temp, aList.List^[j-1]) < 0) do begin
      aList.List^[j] := aList.List^[j-1];
      dec(j);
    end;
    aList.List^[j] := Temp;
  end;
end;
```

Believe it or not, this initial scan for the smallest item, followed by the removal of the test for avoiding dropping off the list, improves the overall running speed of the sort by about 7 percent in my tests.

Like the three sorts we've considered so far, insertion sort is a $O(n^2)$ algorithm. Like bubble sort, if the list is already sorted, insertion sort does virtually no work apart from comparing each item to its previous neighbor. The worst-case list for insertion sort (as well as for bubble sort) is the reverse ordered list—every item has to move the maximum distance in order to get into the proper position.

However, if the list is partially sorted, with each item within a short distance of where it should be, insertion sort is very fast; in fact, it reduces to a $O(n)$ algorithm. (In other words, the outer loop performs n–1 cycles, and the inner loop only runs a small number of times to correspond to the small distance each item has to move. So we have an upper bound of a constant number of cycles, (i.e., comparisons and moves) in the inner loop, let's say d, and $n-1$ cycles in the outer loop, to make an upper bound of $d(n-1)$ comparisons and moves (a $O(n)$ algorithm). Although this type of data distribution does not appear too often in practice, there is one time when it comes up fairly often and this property of insertion sort is worth bearing in mind. We'll see where in a moment.

Insertion sort—either variety—is stable, the algorithm being designed to maintain the order of equal items since the search for the correct sorted position of an item stops when it sees an item less than *or equal to* the current item. Hence the relative order of equal items in the original list is preserved.

Like bubble sort, insertion sort has to move out-of-place items into their correct position by single moves or exchanges with their neighbors. If an item is far from its correct space, it takes a long time to get it into its spot. If only we could jump out-of-place items into the general area where they're supposed to be in one fell swoop. Enter the second set of sort algorithms.

Fast Sorts

The second set of sorts are faster than the set we've just seen. However, unlike the set of fastest sorts we'll be getting to in a moment, they are difficult to analyze mathematically. Although they can be shown to be fairly fast in practice, these fast sorts tend not to be used very much.

Shell Sort

Donald L. Shell invented Shell sort in 1959. It is based on insertion sort, and it can seem a little bizarre when you first meet it. My first encounter with it didn't explain the name and so I was continually trying to see the "shells"—there are none, which explains my initial confusion somewhat.

Shell sort tries to alleviate the problem of items that are far out of place moving to their correct sorted position by a glacial one-by-one progression. Shell sort moves out-of-place items toward their correct place by large jumps over several other items, decreasing the size of the jumps until items are being moved around in the classical insertion sort algorithm.

Doing this with cards will take some doing, but let's forge ahead. Deal out the shuffled cards into a long line. Push up the first card and every fourth card from that point (i.e., the fifth, ninth, and thirteenth cards). Insertion sort these four cards. Push them back down again. Push up the second card and every fourth card from it (i.e., the second, sixth, and tenth cards). Insertion sort them and push them down again. Continue this process with the third card and every fourth card from then on, and then the fourth card and every fourth card from that point.

After this first cycle the cards are said to be in *4-sorted order*. Whichever card you select, the cards you obtain by going forward and backward from that point by four cards at a time will be sorted. Note that the cards are not sorted as a whole, but, no matter how hard you shuffled, the cards are in the approximate vicinity of where they should be. Large jumps will have been made to get the outlying cards into roughly the right place.

Now perform a standard insertion sort and you are done. From the argument I presented with insertion sort, insertion sort is linear when items are within a small constant distance of where they should be, and our first pass will have done that.

```
5 King 4 2 Jack Ace 9 8 3 10 Queen 6 7
3 King 4 2 5 Ace 9 8 7 10 Queen 6 Jack
3 Ace 4 2 5 10 9 8 7 King Queen 6 Jack
3 Ace 4 2 5 10 9 8 7 King Queen 6 Jack
3 Ace 4 2 5 10 9 6 7 King Queen 8 Jack
Ace 3 4 2 5 10 9 6 7 King Queen 8 Jack
Ace 2 3 4 5 10 9 6 7 King Queen 8 Jack
Ace 2 3 4 5 9 10 6 7 King Queen 8 Jack
Ace 2 3 4 5 6 9 10 7 King Queen 8 Jack
Ace 2 3 4 5 6 7 9 10 King Queen 8 Jack
Ace 2 3 4 5 6 7 9 10 King Queen 8 Jack
Ace 2 3 4 5 6 7 9 10 Queen King 8 Jack
Ace 2 3 4 5 6 7 8 9 10 Queen King Jack
Ace 2 3 4 5 6 7 8 9 10 Jack Queen King
```

Figure 5.6: Shell sort

To be a little more rigorous, Shell sort works by insertion sorting subsets of the main list. Each subset is formed by taking every hth element starting at any position in the main set. There will be h subsets formed, which will be sorted by insertion sort. Once this process is done, the list is said to be h-sorted. We then reduce the value of h to a new value and then h-sort the list with this new value. We continue decreasing the value of h, and h-sorting the list, until h is 1, and the final pass is an insertion sort (which, if we were pedantic, could be called 1–sorting).

The essence of Shell sort, then, is that h-sorting rapidly jumps out-of-place items into the vicinity of where they should be, and by reducing h, we refine the jumping until the items are actually in the proper place. The migration of items to their sorted positions proceeds in leaps and bounds, with smaller and smaller jumps, until the final insertion sort doesn't do much moving at all.

So what values of h do we use? Shell, in his original paper, suggested 1, 2, 4, 8, 16, 32, etc. (in reverse order, obviously), but this suffers from a bad problem: even-numbered items are never compared with odd-numbered items until the final pass, and so there might still be some major item movement still to do (consider the artificial case where the smaller items were in the even positions and the larger items in the odd positions).

Donald Knuth proposed the sequence 1, 4, 13, 40, 121, etc. (with each value being one more than three times the previous value) in 1969. It has good performance characteristics for moderately large sets (Knuth estimated $O(n^{5/4})$ in the average case from empirical observations, and it has been proved that the worst time case is $O(n^{3/2})$), and the sequence is easy to calculate to boot. This is the one we'll use. Other sequences have better performance (though not by much), but would require the sequence values to be pre-calculated in an array since the formulae are fairly complex. An example is the fastest currently known sequence, which is by Robert Sedgewick: 1, 5, 19, 41, 109, etc. (formed by merging the two sequences $9*4i-9*2i + 1$, for $i > 0$, and $4i-3*2i + 1$, for $i > 1$) which has a worst case $O(n^{4/3})$ running time, but with an average running time of $O(n^{7/6})$. Both derivations are beyond the level of this book. It is unknown whether there might be even faster sequences.

Listing 5.9: Shell sort with Knuth's sequence

```
procedure TDShellSort(aList       : TList;
                      aFirst      : integer;
                      aLast       : integer;
                      aCompare    : TtdCompareFunc);
var
  i, j   : integer;
  h      : integer;
  Temp   : pointer;
  Ninth  : integer;
begin
  TDValidateListRange(aList, aFirst, aLast, 'TDShellSort');
  {firstly calculate the first h value we shall use: it'll
  be about one ninth of the number of the elements}
  h := 1;
  Ninth := (aLast - aFirst) div 9;
  while (h <= Ninth) do
    h := (h * 3) + 1;
  {start a loop that'll decrement h by one third each time through}
  while (h > 0) do begin
    {now insertion sort each h-subfile}
    for i := (aFirst + h) to aLast do begin
      Temp := aList.List^[i];
      j := i;
      while (j >= (aFirst+h)) and
```

```
          (aCompare(Temp, aList.List^[j-h]) < 0) do begin
        aList.List^[j] := aList.List^[j-h];
        dec(j, h);
      end;
      aList.List^[j] := Temp;
    end;
    {decrease h by a third}
    h := h div 3;
  end;
end;
```

The mathematics of analyzing Shell sort are difficult. In general, we are forced to rely on statistical methods to estimate the running time of Shell sort for various sequences. However, it does not seem worth it at this stage because there are yet faster sorts that we haven't yet met.

As for stability, any time there is an exchange of items far apart without knowing anything about the items in between, we are possibly destroying the order of equal items. So, Shell sort is not stable.

Comb Sort

A truly bizarre sort algorithm is up for discussion next, the comb sort. It's not one of the standard sorts. Indeed I only heard of it in passing on a newsgroup one day, and the research I've managed to do on it didn't turn up very much. But it does have a fairly rapid execution time and is easy to code. It was devised by Stephen Lacey and Richard Box and published in *Byte* magazine in April 1991. Essentially, it is to bubble sort what Shell sort is to insertion sort.

Comb sort requires you to deal the cards on the table again. Push up the first and ninth cards. If they are out of order, swap them. Push up the second and tenth cards and do the same; and continue for the third and eleventh, fourth and twelfth, fifth and thirteenth. Repeat for cards (1, 7), (2, 8), (3, 9), (4, 10), (5, 11), (6, 12), and (7, 13)—in other words, compare every card with the card six cards away and swap if it is greater. Now do the same for every card and its sibling four cards away. Repeat with a gap of three cards, and then two cards. Now perform a normal bubble sort (which could be viewed as having a gap of one card).

```
5 King 4 2 Jack Ace 9 8 3 10 Queen 6 7
3 King 4 2 Jack Ace 9 8 5 10 Queen 6 7 → Gap of 8
3 10 4 2 Jack Ace 9 8 5 King Queen 6 7
3 10 4 2 7 Ace 9 8 5 King Queen 6 Jack
3 8 4 2 7 Ace 9 10 5 King Queen 6 Jack → Gap of 6
3 Ace 4 2 7 8 9 10 5 King Queen 6 Jack
3 Ace 4 2 5 8 9 6 7 King Queen 10 Jack → Gap of 4
2 Ace 4 3 5 8 9 6 7 King Queen 10 Jack → Gap of 3
2 Ace 4 3 5 7 9 6 8 King Queen 10 Jack
2 Ace 4 3 5 7 9 6 8 Jack Queen 10 King
2 Ace 4 3 5 6 9 7 8 Jack Queen 10 King → Gap of 2
2 Ace 4 3 5 6 8 7 9 Jack Queen 10 King
2 Ace 4 3 5 6 8 7 9 10 Queen Jack King
Ace 2 4 3 5 6 8 7 9 10 Queen Jack King → Gap of 1
Ace 2 3 4 5 6 8 7 9 10 Queen Jack King
Ace 2 3 4 5 6 7 8 9 10 Queen Jack King
Ace 2 3 4 5 6 7 8 9 10 Jack Queen King
```

Figure 5.7: Comb sort (only showing swaps)

What we are doing here is moving cards that are way out of place into roughly the correct position by jumping over several others in one go. With cards, it's kind of awkward, just like Shell sort, but in a routine it's a couple of loops, one to reduce the gap and the other to perform a kind of bubble sort.

So where did I get the gap values of 8, 6, 4, 3, 2, 1? The inventors of this sort performed lots of experiments, and came up with the empirical answer that each gap value should be the previous one divided by 1.3. This "shrink factor" was the best one they observed and it balances the increased time due to too many gap values versus the increased time of the final bubble sort if there are too many.

Furthermore, they came up with the entirely baffling conclusion that gap values of 9 and 10 are sub-optimal. It seems that if you hit a 9 or a 10 in the gap sequence you should use 11 instead, and the sort performs much faster than if you allowed the 9 or 10 gap to stand. Again, experimentation shows this to be so. I know of no theoretical research into comb sort, nor why this particular gap sequence is the best.

Listing 5.10: Comb sort

```
procedure TDCombSort(aList    : TList;
                     aFirst   : integer;
                     aLast    : integer;
                     aCompare : TtdCompareFunc);
var
  i, j : integer;
  Temp : pointer;
  Done : boolean;
```

```
  Gap  : integer;
begin
  TDValidateListRange(aList, aFirst, aLast, 'TDCombSort');
  {start off with a gap equal to the number of elements}
  Gap := succ(aLast - aFirst);
  repeat
    {assume we'll finish this time around}
    Done := true;
    {calculate the new gap}
    Gap := (longint(Gap) * 10) div 13; {Gap := Trunc(Gap / 1.3);}
    if (Gap < 1) then
      Gap := 1
    else if (Gap = 9) or (Gap = 10) then
      Gap := 11;
    {order every item with its sibling Gap items along}
    for i := aFirst to (aLast - Gap) do begin
      j := i + Gap;
      if (aCompare(aList.List^[j], aList.List^[i]) < 0) then begin
        {swap jth and (j-Gap)th elements}
        Temp := aList.List^[j];
        aList.List^[j] := aList.List^[i];
        aList.List^[i] := Temp;
        {we swapped, so we didn't finish}
        Done := false;
      end;
    end;
  until Done and (Gap = 1);
end;
```

In my experiments, comb sort beats Shell sort (using Knuth's sequence), but only just. It's also a little easier to code, apart from the quirk of the gaps of 9 or 10. Comb sort, like Shell sort, is not stable, of course.

With comb sort we come to the end of the intermediary set of sorts and move into the stratosphere.

Fastest Sorts

Finally, we shall discuss the fastest sorts of all. These are all widely used in practice and their peculiarities should be understood so that they can be applied in your programs in the most appropriate way.

Merge Sort

Merge sort is a funny one. It's very beguiling since it is easy to describe and has some important qualities (for example, it is a $O(n\log(n))$ algorithm and doesn't have any nasty worst cases), but when you get down to actually coding it, you suddenly realize the big problem. It is, however, very important when you are sorting files that are too big to fit into memory.

We'll approach merge sort tangentially by describing the "merging" part first. We'll then see how this algorithm can be used to sort. We won't bother with the cards this time; this algorithm is pretty easy to understand.

Suppose that you have two already sorted lists and you wish to generate a destination list containing the items of both lists and which was also sorted. Plan A could be to copy the two source lists together over to the target list and then sort it, but it seems a little of a waste not to take account of the fact that the two lists are already ordered. Enter Plan B, the merge routine. Look at the two top items from both lists. Move the smaller over to the target list, removing it from the list in which it was originally found. Now look at the two top items from both lists again. Move the smaller over to the target list, removing it from the list it was originally in. Continue in this way until one of the two original lists is exhausted and has no more items, at which point you can move over the remaining items from the other source list to the target list. This algorithm is formally known as the two-way merge algorithm.

Of course, in practice we do not remove the items from the original lists. Instead we use a counter for each source list to point to the current top of the list and advance the counter for a source list when we copy an item from that list to the target list.

Listing 5.11: Merging two sorted TLists into a third

```
procedure TDListMerge(aList1, aList2, aTargetList : TList;
                      aCompare : TtdCompareFunc);
var
  Inx1, Inx2, Inx3 : integer;
begin
  {set up the target list}
  aTargetList.Clear;
  aTargetList.Capacity := aList1.Count + aList2.Count;
  {initialize the counters}
  Inx1 := 0;
  Inx2 := 0;
  Inx3 := 0;
  {do until one of the source lists is exhausted...}
  while (Inx1 < aList1.Count) and (Inx2 < aList2.Count) do begin
    {find the smaller item from both lists and copy it over to the
    target list; increment the indexes}
    if aCompare(aList1.List^[Inx1], aList2.List^[Inx2]) <= 0 then begin
      aTargetList.List^[Inx3] := aList1.List^[Inx1];
      inc(Inx1);
    end
```

```
    else begin
      aTargetList.List^[Inx3] := aList2.List^[Inx2];
      inc(Inx2);
    end;
    inc(Inx3);
  end;
  {the loop ends if one of the source lists is exhausted; if there are
  any remaining items in the first source list, copy them over}
  if (Inx1 < aList1.Count) then
    Move(aList1.List^[Inx1], aTargetList.List^[Inx3],
             (aList1.Count - Inx1) * sizeof(pointer))
  {otherwise copy over the remaining items in the second list}
  else
    Move(aList2.List^[Inx2], aTargetList.List^[Inx3],
             (aList2.Count - Inx2) * sizeof(pointer));
end;
```

Notice that the implementation copies the final items from one or the other of the source lists by means of the Move procedure. We could have written a little loop to copy the remaining items one at a time, but calling Move is much faster.

The running time of the two-way merge algorithm depends on the number of items in both of the source lists. If the first list has n items and the second m, then it's not hard to see that there will be at most $(n + m)$ comparisons, and so the algorithm has a $O(n)$ running time.

So how does the merge algorithm help us in sorting? Well, it needs two smaller sorted lists, from which it creates a larger sorted list. This leads to a recursive definition of merge sort: divide the list to be sorted into two halves, call merge sort on each half, and then use the merge algorithm to merge the two sorted sub-lists into the final sorted list. The recursive step ends when the sub-sub-sub-list passed to merge sort consists of one item, because it is obviously sorted.

There is just one problem with this scheme. The merge algorithm requires a *third* list to hold the results of the merge.

Unlike all of the sorts we've encountered so far, which sort the items in a list in place, merge sort requires a lot of extra memory to perform the sort. As a first approximation, in a naïve implementation, it would seem to require an auxiliary list equal in size to the list being sorted. We would merge the items from both sorted half-lists into the auxiliary list, and then copy the items back to the main list as the final step of the merge process. Although we could devise an algorithm that performs the merge operation without requiring the auxiliary list, in practice it robs merge sort of much of its speed. If we are to use merge sort, we have to get used to the extra memory requirement.

But how much memory do we really need? I said just now that at most we would need a list equal in size to the original, but in fact, we can refine that by using a little trick and that only requires a list half the size of the original.

Suppose we're at the very top recursion. We've just sorted the two halves of the original list (we assume that the first sorted sub-list is currently in the first half of the list, and the second sorted sub-list is in the second half—to all intents and purposes the two recursive calls to merge sort having sorted the two sub-lists in place) and now we have to merge them. Instead of proceeding with the naïve algorithm of merging into another list equal in size to the original, let's copy the first half of the list into another list (we would only need a half-sized auxiliary list in this case). We then have an auxiliary list filled with the first half of the items, and the original list, whose first half can be viewed as empty and whose second half is filled with the second set of items. We now merge the items into the original list. As we merge we won't manage to overwrite any of the second set of items—we know that the auxiliary list can fit into the empty space.

Listing 5.12: Standard merge sort

```
procedure MSS(aList     : TList;
              aFirst    : integer;
              aLast     : integer;
              aCompare  : TtdCompareFunc;
              aTempList : PPointerList);
var
  Mid        : integer;
  i, j       : integer;
  ToInx      : integer;
  FirstCount : integer;
begin
  {calculate the midpoint}
  Mid := (aFirst + aLast) div 2;
  {recursively merge sort the 1st half and the 2nd half of the list}
  if (aFirst < Mid) then
    MSS(aList, aFirst, Mid, aCompare, aTempList);
  if (succ(Mid) < aLast) then
    MSS(aList, succ(Mid), aLast, aCompare, aTempList);
  {copy the first half of the list to our temporary list}
  FirstCount := succ(Mid - aFirst);
  Move(aList.List^[aFirst], aTempList^[0], FirstCount * sizeof(pointer));
  {set up the indexes: i is the index for the temporary list (ie the
  first half of the list), j is the index for the second half of the
  list, ToInx is the index in the merged where items will be copied}
  i := 0;
  j := succ(Mid);
  ToInx := aFirst;
```

```
  {now merge the two lists}
  {repeat until one of the lists empties...}
  while (i < FirstCount) and (j <= aLast) do begin
    {calculate the smaller item from the next items in both lists and
    copy it over; increment the relevant index}
    if (aCompare(aTempList^[i], aList.List^[j]) <= 0) then begin
      aList.List^[ToInx] := aTempList^[i];
      inc(i);
    end
    else begin
      aList.List^[ToInx] := aList.List^[j];
      inc(j);
    end;
    {there's one more item in the merged list}
    inc(ToInx);
  end;
  {if there are any more items in the first list, copy them back over}
  if (i < FirstCount) then
    Move(aTempList^[i], aList.List^[ToInx], (FirstCount - i) * sizeof(pointer));
  {if there are any more items in the second list then they're already
  in place and we're done; if there aren't, we're still done}
end;

procedure TDMergeSortStd(aList    : TList;
                         aFirst   : integer;
                         aLast    : integer;
                         aCompare : TtdCompareFunc);
var
  TempList : PPointerList;
  ItemCount: integer;
begin
  TDValidateListRange(aList, aFirst, aLast, 'TDMergeSortStd');
  {if there is at least two items to sort}
  if (aFirst < aLast) then begin
    {create a temporary pointer list}
    ItemCount := succ(aLast - aFirst);
    GetMem(TempList, (succ(ItemCount) div 2) * sizeof(pointer));
    try
      MSS(aList, aFirst, aLast, aCompare, TempList);
    finally
      FreeMem(TempList, (succ(ItemCount) div 2) * sizeof(pointer));
    end;
  end;
end;
```

If you look at Listing 5.12, you'll see that it consists of a driver procedure, TDMergeSortStd, which is the one you would call to sort a list, and a separate helper procedure, MSS, that does the recursive sorting. TDMergeSortStd validates the list and range first, and then, if there are at least two items to sort, it creates an auxiliary pointer array big enough to hold half the original items. At that point, it calls the recursive MSS routine.

MSS recursively calls itself to sort the first half and the second half of the range it's passed. It then copies the first half to the auxiliary array. At this point we have a fairly standard merge implementation, copying the two half lists to the original list from the start. If, after the compare-and-copy loop is over, there are items left over in the auxiliary array, MSS copies them over. If, on the other hand, there are items left over in the second half list, we don't have to copy them over as in the traditional merge implementation: they are already in place.

Deducing the running characteristics of merge sort is a little convoluted and is best calculated assuming the list contains a power-of-2 number of items. Let's assume 32. At the first recursive level in MSS, there is just one call, and there will be at most 32 comparisons in the merge phase. At the second recursive level, there will be two calls, each with at most 16 comparisons. And so on, until the fifth level of recursion (we'll be sorting lists with two items), where we'll have 16 calls each with two comparisons. All in all, 5*32 comparisons. But the reason there are five levels is because we continually divide the list into two equal halves at each level and 2^5 is 32. Which, of course, means that $\log_2 32$ is 5. Hence, without being too rigorous in extending the proof from the particular case to the general, merge sort is a $O(n\log(n))$ algorithm.

As to stability, since items are only moved during the merge process, the stability of the overall merge sort depends on the stability of the merge operation on the two halves. Notice that if there is an item duplicated in both lists, the comparison statement ensures that the one from the first list is copied first. This means that the relative order of equal items will be maintained by the merge operation, so, overall, we can say that merge sort is stable.

If you followed the calls to MSS in a debugger, you'd notice that it is called an awful lot for very small ranges. For example, if there were 32 items to sort, MSS would be called once for a 32-item range, twice for 16 items, four times for 8 items, eight times for 4 items, and sixteen times for 2 items (the smallest range actually sorted), a grand total of 31 times. This is an awful lot, especially when you consider that the vast majority of the calls (29) are made for lists that are eight items or less. If we had 1,024 items to sort, MSS would be called 1,023 times, of which 896 would be to sort ranges with eight items or less. Horrendous. In fact, it would be better to use a simpler non-recursive sorting algorithm to sort small ranges—by doing so we would speed up the overall sort. If we did use a simpler routine, we'd also avoid all the copying of items between the main list and the auxiliary array for small ranges. The best bet in this case is the optimized insertion sort.

Listing 5.13: Optimized merge sort

```
const
  MSCutOff = 16;
procedure MSInsertionSort(aList    : TList;
                          aFirst   : integer;
                          aLast    : integer;
                          aCompare : TtdCompareFunc);
var
  i, j       : integer;
  IndexOfMin : integer;
  Temp       : pointer;
begin
  {find the smallest element in the list}
  IndexOfMin := aFirst;
  for i := succ(aFirst) to aLast do
    if (aCompare(aList.List^[i], aList.List^[IndexOfMin]) < 0) then
      IndexOfMin := i;
  if (aFirst<>IndexOfMin) then begin
    Temp := aList.List^[aFirst];
    aList.List^[aFirst] := aList.List^[IndexOfMin];
    aList.List^[IndexOfMin] := Temp;
  end;
  {now sort via fast insertion method}
  for i := aFirst+2 to aLast do begin
    Temp := aList.List^[i];
    j := i;
    while (aCompare(Temp, aList.List^[j-1]) < 0) do begin
      aList.List^[j] := aList.List^[j-1];
      dec(j);
    end;
    aList.List^[j] := Temp;
  end;
end;
procedure MS(aList     : TList;
             aFirst    : integer;
             aLast     : integer;
             aCompare  : TtdCompareFunc;
             aTempList : PPointerList);
var
  Mid        : integer;
  i, j       : integer;
  ToInx      : integer;
  FirstCount : integer;
begin
  {calculate the midpoint}
```

```
  Mid := (aFirst + aLast) div 2;
  {sort the 1st half of the list, either with merge sort, or, if there
  are few enough items, with insertion sort}
  if (aFirst < Mid) then
    if (Mid-aFirst) <= MSCutOff then
      MSInsertionSort(aList, aFirst, Mid, aCompare)
    else
      MS(aList, aFirst, Mid, aCompare, aTempList);
  {sort the 2nd half of the list likewise}
  if (succ(Mid) < aLast) then
    if (aLast-succ(Mid)) <= MSCutOff then
      MSInsertionSort(aList, succ(Mid), aLast, aCompare)
    else
      MS(aList, succ(Mid), aLast, aCompare, aTempList);
  {copy the first half of the list to our temporary list}
  FirstCount := succ(Mid - aFirst);
  Move(aList.List^[aFirst], aTempList^[0], FirstCount*sizeof(pointer));
  {set up the indexes: i is the index for the temporary list (i.e., the
  first half of the list), j is the index for the second half of the
  list, ToInx is the index in the merged where items will be copied}
  i := 0;
  j := succ(Mid);
  ToInx := aFirst;
  {now merge the two lists}
  {repeat until one of the lists empties...}
  while (i < FirstCount) and (j <= aLast) do begin
    {calculate the smaller item from the next items in both lists and
    copy it over; increment the relevant index}
    if (aCompare(aTempList^[i], aList.List^[j]) <= 0) then begin
      aList.List^[ToInx] := aTempList^[i];
      inc(i);
    end
    else begin
      aList.List^[ToInx] := aList.List^[j];
      inc(j);
    end;
    {there's one more item in the merged list}
    inc(ToInx);
  end;
  {if there are any more items in the first list, copy them back over}
  if (i < FirstCount) then
    Move(aTempList^[i], aList.List^[ToInx],
         (FirstCount - i) * sizeof(pointer));
  {if there are any more items in the second list then they're already
  in place and we're done; if there aren't, we're still done}
end;
procedure TDMergeSort(aList   : TList;
                      aFirst  : integer;
```

```
                      aLast    : integer;
                      aCompare : TtdCompareFunc);
var
  TempList : PPointerList;
  ItemCount: integer;
begin
  TDValidateListRange(aList, aFirst, aLast, 'TDMergeSort');
  {if there is at least two items to sort}
  if (aFirst < aLast) then begin
    {create a temporary pointer list}
    ItemCount := succ(aLast - aFirst);
    GetMem(TempList, (succ(ItemCount) div 2) * sizeof(pointer));
    try
      MS(aList, aFirst, aLast, aCompare, TempList);
    finally
      FreeMem(TempList, (succ(ItemCount) div 2) * sizeof(pointer));
    end;
  end;
end;
```

Although there seems to be a lot of code here, there are just three routines. The first is the driver, TDMergeSort—the routine we call. Like last time, it allocates an auxiliary pointer array on the heap and calls a recursive routine, this time called MS. In broad brushstrokes, MS works like its predecessor MSS (the recursive routine for the standard merge sort), the difference occurring when it has to sort the sub-lists. For small sub-lists, those with a number of items less than MSCutOff, MS decides to call a third routine, MSInsertionSort, to sort the items rather than calling itself recursively. For larger sub-lists, it calls itself recursively, of course. The MSInsertionSort routine is exactly the same as TDInsertionSort, except that is does not validate its input parameters (there's no need, since we've already validated them way back when in TDMergeSort).

Because we have used insertion sort, a stable sort, to order small sub-lists within merge sort, we can say that the optimized merge sort is also stable.

Although, as you have seen, merge sort requires a lot of extra memory (it's proportional to the number of items to sort), it does have some interesting properties. The first is that it is a O($n$log(n)) algorithm. Second, it is stable. The other two in-memory O($n$log(n)) sorts we'll be considering in this book are both unstable. Third, it does not care if the input list to be sorted is presorted, reverse sorted, or consists of the same item repeated n times. In other words, it has no worst-case behavior.

Toward the end of this chapter, we'll see a case where merge sort shines: sorting a linked list. Here *no* extra memory is required, and indeed is the sort of choice for linked lists.

Finally, merge sort is the sort to use when sorting files that are too big to fit into memory. The essential game plan in this case is to sort chunks of the file into temporary files, and then merge the chunks together.

Quicksort

The final algorithm we shall consider in this chapter is *quicksort*. (There is one other in-memory sort we shall consider in this book, heapsort, but this requires some extra knowledge about a data structure called a heap before we can successfully discuss it. We'll defer heapsort to Chapter 9.)

Quicksort was invented by C.A.R. Hoare in 1960, and is probably even more famous than bubble sort. It is the most widely used sorting algorithm in programming these days, mainly because of some desirable properties: it is a $O(n\log(n))$ sort in the general case, it requires only a small amount of extra memory to do its job, it works well for a wide variety of different input lists, and it is not too difficult to code. Having said that, it has some *undesirable* properties as well: it can be a bear to code properly (simple errors in implementing it can go unnoticed, causing some lists to take an excessive amount of time to sort), it has a bad worst-case running time of $O(n^2)$, and it is not stable.

Quicksort is one of the most studied sorts, as well. Since Hoare's original paper, many people have looked at quicksort and have produced voluminous mathematical studies of running times backed up with empirical evidence. Others have proposed refinements to the basic algorithm in order to speed it up, some of which we shall use here. Indeed, with the wealth of literature available on the subject, it's hard to produce a bad implementation of quicksort if you do your research properly. (Indeed, in producing the final optimized implementation of quicksort in this book, I was using no less than six different algorithms books for reference. One of them had an "optimized" quicksort that was so badly written it was slower than the version found in Borland's standard TList.Sort once converted to work with the same input.)

Quicksort turns up all over the place. In all versions of Delphi except 1, the TList.Sort method is implemented with a quicksort. The TStringList.Sort method in all versions of Delphi is implemented by means of quicksort. In C++, the standard run-time library qsort routine is a quicksort.

The basic algorithm for quicksort is a divide-and-conquer technique, much like merge sort is. It *partitions* the input list into two parts and then recursively calls itself on each part to sort the list. The focus of the quicksort algorithm is therefore the partitioning process. What happens in partitioning a list is that we select an item in the list, known as the *pivot*, and we rearrange the items in the list so that those items less than the pivot are to the left and those greater than the pivot are to the right. At that point we can deduce that the pivot item is in the correct place in the sorted list. We then recursively call the quicksort routine on the part of the list less than the pivot and on the part of the list greater than the pivot. The recursive step ends when the list passed to the quicksort routine is only one item, and hence is already sorted.

So, we need to know two sub-algorithms: how to select the pivot item and how to efficiently rearrange the list so that we have a set of items all less than the pivot, the pivot, and a set of items all greater than the pivot.

First things, first: the pivot. Ideally we would like to choose the median of all the items in the list, for then, after partitioning, the "less than" set would have the same number of items as the "greater than" set. In other words, the partition will have divided the list exactly into two halves. Calculating the median item of a list is a complex process—in fact, the standard algorithm uses the partition method of quicksort, what we are discussing—and so we abandon that suggestion before we even start.

The worst-case nightmare is to pick a pivot that turns out to be the smallest item in the list, or the largest. In that case, the partition process will produce a sub-list with no items at all, and one with all of them apart from the pivot, since all items will be on one side or another of the pivot. Of course, we can't know (not without looking through the list, anyway) whether we have selected the smallest or largest, but if we managed to with every recursive step, we'd have *n* levels of recursion for *n* items. Bad news if we were sorting a million items, even in 32-bit. (In fact, runaway recursion is something we shall be paying close attention to in our implementation of quicksort.)

So, having seen the two extremes, we would love to pick an item that approximated the first, while avoiding the second.

A lot of books choose either the first item in the list or the last as the pivot. If the list was originally in a random sequence, choosing one of these two items is as good a strategy as any other. If the list was originally sorted, however, or indeed reverse sorted, this choice of pivot would be disastrous since you'd slip into the worst-case nightmare. I'd have to say that choosing the first or last item as pivot is perfectly horrible. Don't do it.

A much better choice is to choose the middle item of the unsorted list and hope it ends up near the middle of the partitioned list. In a randomly ordered list, this value is as good as any other. In an already sorted or reverse sorted list, it's in fact the best item to choose.

Having chosen a pivot, how do we use it to partition a list? Enter the fabulously fast inner loops of the quicksort algorithm. We have two indexes into the list, one of which will be used to walk through items from the left, and the other used to walk through items from the right. We start at the right, working leftward through the list. For every item we compare it against the pivot item, and we stop when we find an item less than or equal to the pivot. That was fast inner loop 1: comparing two items and decrementing an index. Next, we do the same type of operation from the left. Work rightward from the left end of the list. We compare every item against the pivot item, and we stop when we find an item greater than or equal to the pivot. That was fast inner loop 2: comparing two items and incrementing an index.

At this point, two things might have occurred. The first one is that the left index is still less than the right index. This indicates that the two items being pointed to are out of sequence (the one on the left is greater than the pivot, whereas the one on the right is less than the pivot), so we swap them over and continue with the fast inner loops. The other situation is that the two indexes have met (the left index equals the right index) or have crossed (the left index is greater than the right index). At this point we can stop the process: we have successfully partitioned the list.

Listing 5.14: Standard quicksort

```
procedure QSS(aList    : TList;
              aFirst   : integer;
              aLast    : integer;
              aCompare : TtdCompareFunc);
var
  L, R  : integer;
  Pivot : pointer;
  Temp  : pointer;
begin
  {while there are at least two items to sort}
  while (aFirst < aLast) do begin
    {the pivot is the middle item}
    Pivot := aList.List^[(aFirst+aLast) div 2];
    {set indexes and partition}
    L := pred(aFirst);
    R := succ(aLast);
    while true do begin
      repeat dec(R); until (aCompare(aList.List^[R], Pivot) <= 0);
      repeat inc(L); until (aCompare(aList.List^[L], Pivot) >= 0);
      if (L >= R) then Break;
      Temp := aList.List^[L];
      aList.List^[L] := aList.List^[R];
      aList.List^[R] := Temp;
    end;
    {quicksort the first subfile}
    if (aFirst < R) then
```

```
      QSS(aList, aFirst, R, aCompare);
    {quicksort the second subfile - recursion removal}
    aFirst := succ(R);
  end;
end;
procedure TDQuickSortStd(aList    : TList;
                         aFirst   : integer;
                         aLast    : integer;
                         aCompare : TtdCompareFunc);
begin
  TDValidateListRange(aList, aFirst, aLast, 'TDQuickSortStd');
  QSS(aList, aFirst, aLast, aCompare);
end;
```

Because the algorithm is recursive, I've written quicksort in two routines, like I did for merge sort. The first procedure, TDQuickSortStd, is a driver routine. It validates the parameters and then calls the second routine, QSS. This is the real recursive routine, and the meat of the implementation. The first thing to note is that QSS only does something if there are two or more items in the range. It picks the pivot item as the middle item in the range. It then sets up the indexes L and R to just before the list range and just after, respectively. We then go into a loop that will go on forever—it's all right though: we'll be breaking out of it when required. The first things in this do-forever loop are the two fast inner loops, coded as Repeat..until loops. The first one decrements R until it points to an item that is less than or equal to the pivot; the second increments L until it points to an item greater than or equal to the pivot. We then check L against R. If it is greater then or equal to R, we've met or crossed and so we break out of the do-forever loop. Otherwise, we just swap over the two items being pointed to and continue round the do-forever loop.

Once we've broken out of the do-forever loop, many implementations of quicksort would have code like this:

```
QSS(aList, aFirst, R, aCompare);
QSS(aList, R+1, aLast, aCompare);
```

In other words, recursively quicksort the first half of the partition and then recursively quicksort the second half. One of the easiest tricks of the programming trade is removing a recursive call at the end of a recursive routine—it's generally a case of modifying the parameter variables for the routine and jumping back to the start of the routine. I've coded this as a while loop in QSS, with the recursion being removed by setting a new value of aFirst. A fairly simple removal of a recursive call, I'm sure you'll agree.

Presented with a routine like this, especially with some rapid loops, you naturally start trying to think of ways to improve it. This is a great danger that must be resisted with quicksort. You can make a seemingly innocuous change and suddenly performance drops or the do-forever loop lives up to its name. Let's show a couple of the pitfalls. One temptation might be to set the L and R indexes to the actual first and last items, instead of just before and after, and then replace the Repeat..until loops with While loops, switching the loop conditions, of course. After all, you'd be saving one increment and decrement, right? The first loop would become a "do while greater than" loop and the second would be a "do while less than" loop. On a randomly sequenced input list this would work. Most of the time, that is. But on a list that just consisted of one item repeated many times, the do-forever loop would live up to its name: the indexes would never change value. Changing the conditions on the loops to include equality in order to get round this problem would cause another: the indexes would run off the end of the list instead.

That last comment deserves some extra discussion. By choosing the middle item as the pivot we've not only avoided a nasty worst-case problem, but also we've ensured that the two fast inner loops actually stop within the given range. The pivot element is acting as a sentinel value for both inner loops. If worse came to worst, each loop would surely stop at the pivot. If we hadn't chosen the middle item as pivot—for example, we'd chosen the first or last item—then we would have had to alter one of the loops in order to have a check for the index running off the end (the other loop would have had the pivot as the ultimate stopping point).

I hope by arguing some of the problems that arise in writing the partitioning code, you get an appreciation for the intricacies of the quicksort algorithm, even though it's implemented with very few lines of code. By all means experiment, or check out the Delphi TStringList.Sort implementation to see how Borland performs their quicksort, but be warned and test your coding experiments with different input list sequences.

Having warned you off tinkering with the quicksort implementation, let's do exactly that in a few well-controlled ways.

The first bit of tinkering we can do is to investigate choosing different pivot items. Recall that in our first quicksort routine we chose the middle item as the pivot, and briefly investigated and rejected choosing the first or last item as pivot. Ideally we would like to choose the median item every time, or, if that's too much to ask, at least avoid choosing the smallest or largest item as the pivot (for then, quicksort would degenerate into a long series of empty sublists and sublists with just one less item). One popular way is to choose a randomly selected item as the pivot. We would then swap this random item with the middle item and proceed as before.

What does random selection of the pivot buy us? Well, providing that we have a reasonably good pseudorandom number generator, it guarantees that the probability of selecting the worst item every time grows vanishingly small. It doesn't entirely disappear, but you'd be pretty unlucky if you managed to select the worst item as pivot every time.

Listing 5.15: Quicksort with random selection of pivot

```
procedure QSR(aList       : TList;
              aFirst      : integer;
              aLast       : integer;
              aCompare    : TtdCompareFunc);
var
  L, R  : integer;
  Pivot : pointer;
  Temp  : pointer;
begin
  while (aFirst < aLast) do begin
    {choose a random item, swap with middle to become pivot}
    R := aFirst + Random(aLast - aFirst + 1);
    L := (aFirst + aLast) div 2;
    Pivot := aList.List^[R];
    aList.List^[R] := aList.List^[L];
    aList.List^[L] := Pivot;
    {set indexes and partition about the pivot}
    L := pred(aFirst);
    R := succ(aLast);
    while true do begin
      repeat dec(R); until (aCompare(aList.List^[R], Pivot) <= 0);
      repeat inc(L); until (aCompare(aList.List^[L], Pivot) >= 0);
      if (L >= R) then Break;
      Temp := aList.List^[L];
      aList.List^[L] := aList.List^[R];
      aList.List^[R] := Temp;
    end;
    {quicksort the first subfile}
    if (aFirst < R) then
      QSR(aList, aFirst, R, aCompare);
    {quicksort the second subfile - recursion removal}
    aFirst := succ(R);
  end;
end;
procedure TDQuickSortRandom(aList       : TList;
                            aFirst      : integer;
                            aLast       : integer;
                            aCompare    : TtdCompareFunc);
begin
  TDValidateListRange(aList, aFirst, aLast, 'TDQuickSortRandom');
```

```
  QSR(aList, aFirst, aLast, aCompare);
end;
```

As you can see, there's not much difference between the standard quicksort and the one with random selection. The main change is the inserted code with the light gray background; first an index is randomly chosen between aFirst and aLast inclusive, and then the item at that index is swapped with the middle item. We use the Delphi Random function for convenience; it provides good sequences of pseudorandom numbers. Swapping with the middle item provides the usual benefits that we have already discussed.

Although this change provides some probabilistic breathing room from always choosing the worst item, my tests have shown that it does not speed up quicksort. In fact, it slows it down (as you might have surmised). Generating a random number as an index for the pivot works well, in the sense that selecting a bad pivot becomes statistically remote, but this benefit just doesn't translate into an overall faster routine. The complexity of the linear congruential generator used by Delphi's Random routine kills the running time. We could investigate using a different pseudorandom number generator (and we will introduce some in Chapter 6), but it turns out that there is a much better pivot selection algorithm we could use.

The best pivot selection method I have come across is the median-of-three algorithm. Recall that ideally we would want to select the median of the items in our sublist. However, finding the median is a non-trivial exercise. A better idea would be to approximate the median. What we do is select three items in the sublist and choose the median of them to serve as our pivot. This median of three items acts as an approximation to the real median. Of course, this algorithm presupposes that the sublist has at least three items. If it has two or less, we can sort the items pretty easily anyway.

The choice of the three items we choose is arbitrary, but it makes sense to choose the first, the last, and the middle item. Why? Well, by doing so we can make a shortcut in the overall sorting process. You see, not only do we find the *median* of the three items, but also we also fully sort them so that they are *in sequence*. We place the smallest item in the first position in the sublist, the median item in the middle of the sublist, and the largest item in the final position of the sublist. At a stroke we have reduced the size of the partition by two items since we've ensured that the first item and the last item are already on the correct sides of the pivot. And this algorithm automatically places the pivot in the optimum place: the middle of the sublist.

Listing 5.16: Quicksort using the median-of-three method

```
procedure QSM(aList      : TList;
              aFirst     : integer;
              aLast      : integer;
              aCompare   : TtdCompareFunc);
var
  L, R  : integer;
  Pivot : pointer;
  Temp  : pointer;
begin
  while (aFirst < aLast) do begin
    {if there are three or more items, select the pivot as being the
    median of the first, last and middle items and store it in the
    middle}
    if (aLast - aFirst) >= 2 then begin
      R := (aFirst + aLast) div 2;
      if (aCompare(aList.List^[aFirst],
                   aList.List^[R]) > 0) then begin
        Temp := aList.List^[aFirst];
        aList.List^[aFirst] := aList.List^[R];
        aList.List^[R] := Temp;
      end;
      if (aCompare(aList.List^[aFirst],
                   aList.List^[aLast]) > 0) then begin
        Temp := aList.List^[aFirst];
        aList.List^[aFirst] := aList.List^[aLast];
        aList.List^[aLast] := Temp;
      end;
      if (aCompare(aList.List^[R],
                   aList.List^[aLast]) > 0) then begin
        Temp := aList.List^[R];
        aList.List^[R] := aList.List^[aLast];
        aList.List^[aLast] := Temp;
      end;
      Pivot := aList.List^[R];
    end
    {otherwise, there are only 2 items, so choose the first item as
    the pivot}
    else
      Pivot := aList.List^[aFirst];
    {set indexes and partition about the pivot}
    L := pred(aFirst);
    R := succ(aLast);
    while true do begin
      repeat dec(R); until (aCompare(aList.List^[R], Pivot) <= 0);
      repeat inc(L); until (aCompare(aList.List^[L], Pivot) >= 0);
      if (L >= R) then Break;
      Temp := aList.List^[L];
```

```
      aList.List^[L] := aList.List^[R];
      aList.List^[R] := Temp;
    end;
    {quicksort the first subfile}
    if (aFirst < R) then
      QSM(aList, aFirst, R, aCompare);
    {quicksort the second subfile - recursion removal}
    aFirst := succ(R);
  end;
end;
procedure TDQuickSortMedian(aList    : TList;
                            aFirst   : integer;
                            aLast    : integer;
                            aCompare : TtdCompareFunc);
begin
  TDValidateListRange(aList, aFirst, aLast, 'TDQuickSortMedian');
  QSM(aList, aFirst, aLast, aCompare);
end;
```

This time the changed code (that which has the light gray background) is much larger. The main bulk of it is the selection and sort of the three items for the median-of-three algorithm. Of course, this code only gets executed if there are more than two items.

We sort these three items using a little-known and little-used technique. Suppose the items are *a*, *b*, and *c*. Compare *a* and *b*. If *b* is less than *a*, swap them over so that $a <= b$. Compare *a* and *c*. If *c* is less than *a*, swap them over so that $a <= c$. At this point we now know that *a* is the smallest since it is less than or equal to both *b* and *c*. Compare *b* and *c*. If *c* is less than *b*, swap them over so that $b <= c$. We have arranged the items so that $a <= b <= c$; in other words, they are sorted. If the number of items in the sublist is two or less, just select the first item as pivot.

This improvement, although it looks slower theoretically, is faster in practice than the unadorned quicksort code. Not by much, it must be admitted, but certainly measurable.

We'll leave the pivot selection algorithm for now and turn to other improvements we can profitably investigate. Quicksort is a recursive algorithm, and I showed how to remove one of the recursive calls fairly easily. The other recursive call takes a little more work to remove, but it might be worth it, because we could remove some extraneous calls and setting up of stack frames and the like.

Consider the recursive call. We have to set up four parameters, of which two are fixed, as it were, and two vary with the demands of the algorithm. The two fixed parameters are aList and aCompare, and the two variable ones are aFirst and aLast. We can remove the recursion by means of an explicit stack that pushes and pops these two variable parameters, and we cycle round a loop until the stack is empty.

Listing 5.17: Quicksort without recursion

```
procedure QSNR(aList     : TList;
               aFirst    : integer;
               aLast     : integer;
               aCompare  : TtdCompareFunc);
var
  L, R    : integer;
  Pivot   : pointer;
  Temp    : pointer;
  Stack   : array [0..63] of integer; {allows for 2 billion items}
  SP      : integer;
begin
  {initialize stack}
  Stack[0] := aFirst;
  Stack[1] := aLast;
  SP := 2;
  while (SP<>0) do begin
    {pop off the top subfile}
    dec(SP, 2);
    aFirst := Stack[SP];
    aLast := Stack[SP+1];
    {while there are at least two items to sort}
    while (aFirst < aLast) do begin
      {the pivot is the middle item}
      Pivot := aList.List^[(aFirst+aLast) div 2];
      {set indexes and partition}
      L := pred(aFirst);
      R := succ(aLast);
      while true do begin
        repeat dec(R); until (aCompare(aList.List^[R], Pivot) <= 0);
        repeat inc(L); until (aCompare(aList.List^[L], Pivot) >= 0);
        if (L >= R) then Break;
        Temp := aList.List^[L];
        aList.List^[L] := aList.List^[R];
        aList.List^[R] := Temp;
      end;
      {push the larger subfile onto the stack, go round loop again
      with the smaller subfile}
      if (R - aFirst) < (aLast - R) then begin
        Stack[SP] := succ(R);
        Stack[SP+1] := aLast;
        inc(SP, 2);
        aLast := R;
      end
```

```
      else begin
        Stack[SP] := aFirst;
        Stack[SP+1] := R;
        inc(SP, 2);
        aFirst := succ(R);
      end;
    end;
  end;
end;
procedure TDQuickSortNoRecurse(aList     : TList;
                               aFirst    : integer;
                               aLast     : integer;
                               aCompare  : TtdCompareFunc);
begin
  TDValidateListRange(aList, aFirst, aLast, 'TDQuickSortNoRecurse');
  QSNR(aList, aFirst, aLast, aCompare);
end;
```

I've left the code as a driver routine and an internal routine, so that the overall picture looks the same as the standard quicksort. Of course, this time the internal routine, QSNR, is called only once.

The internal routine declares a stack of 64 longints, Stack, and a stack pointer, SP, to reference the top of the stack. The comment blithely states that the stack is good enough for 2 billion items, and we shall show that this is true in a moment. When we enter the routine, we set up the stack to contain the first and last indexes that we were passed. We make the convention that the first index is the item at the stack pointer and the last index is the item at the pointer + 1. The stack pointer is then advanced by 2. (This can also be coded as two stacks, one for the aFirst indexes and one for the aLast indexes, both controlled by the same stack pointer variable.)

We now enter a While loop that will terminate when the stack is empty, which is equivalent to SP being zero.

The first thing we do is to pop off the aFirst and aLast variables from the stack and decrement the stack pointer. We now enter the loop we had in the standard quicksort, repeating until the aFirst value overtakes the aLast value. The ending statements for this loop, where we would have recursively called the internal routine before, are where the clever stuff happens. At this point, the pivot is in the correct place and we have successfully partitioned the sublist. We now have two sub-sublists, the one to the left of the pivot and the one to the right. We find out which is the larger sublist, push it onto the stack (i.e., we push the index of its first and last items), and continue with the smaller sublist.

Think about what this means for a moment. If we were amazingly fortunate and managed to select the actual median as pivot for each sublist we came across, then each sublist would be exactly half the size of its "owning" sublist. If the overall list had 32 items, for example, we would partition it into two 16-item sublists, each of which would be partitioned into two 8-item sublists and so on. We would reach a maximum depth of five items on the stack, since 2^5 is 32. Think about it. We'd push a 16-item sublist, partition the other 16-item sublist into two 8-item sublists, push one of the 8-item sublists onto the stack, and partition the other into two 4-items sublists, and so on and so forth. By the time we reach the first 1-item sublist, the stack will contain a 16-item sublist, an 8-item sublist, a 4-item sublist, a 2-item sublist, and a 1-item sublist. Five levels. So, to sort a maximum of 2 billion items, with pure luck in choosing a pivot every time, would require the stack to hold 32 levels, the size of the declared stack in QSNR.

But that argument only holds if we're lucky, surely? Not really. If we always push the larger sublist onto the stack and continue to partition the smaller sublist, then it is the smaller sublist that determines how deep the stack goes. Since the smaller sublist is less than or equal to half the partitioned list, the depth of the stack resulting from that sublist will be less than or equal to that of our fortunate case. Hence, our pre-declared stack will always suffice.

Notice that, if we wanted to, we could do the same trick with the recursive quicksort. In this case, we would recursively call the internal quicksort routine with the smaller sublist. This minor change would ensure that we don't have a runaway stack if the quicksort was presented with the worst-case list.

That clears up the non-recursive quicksort. Funnily enough, the time savings from removing recursion aren't that great. Indeed, sometimes the quicksort runs slower (I would guess that it's the checking for the smaller sublist that's slowing us down). There are some improvements, but no great breakthrough, yet.

Some of my readers might have looked at the median-of-three code in Listing 5.16 and balked a little at the idea of the code that gets executed if the sublist has less than three items. In fact, this is the next area we can target for improvement.

By using the same argument we made for merge sort, we can see that quicksort will attempt to partition smaller and smaller sublists, sublists that could be far better sorted by another means.

Suppose we only partitioned sublists that had more than a given number of items. What would be the result at the end of the quicksort in that case? We'd have a list that was roughly sorted, in the sense that all items were roughly in the right spot. The sublists we eventually obtained before abandoning the partition process would be sorted in the sense that if sublist X were before sublist Y, then all items in X would be before all items in Y, for any sublist X and Y. This is *exactly* the situation where insertion sort excels. If we partially sorted the list with quicksort in this manner, we could finish off the job with insertion sort very quickly.

This is the final optimization of quicksort we shall consider. We'll show a super-optimized quicksort with recursion removed, the median-of-three method for selecting the pivot, and insertion sort to finally polish off the sort.

Listing 5.18: Optimized quicksort

```
const
  QSCutOff = 15;
procedure QSInsertionSort(aList     : TList;
                          aFirst    : integer;
                          aLast     : integer;
                          aCompare  : TtdCompareFunc);
var
  i, j       : integer;
  IndexOfMin : integer;
  Temp       : pointer;
begin
  {find the smallest element in the first QSCutOff items and put it in
  the first position}
  IndexOfMin := aFirst;
  j := QSCutOff;
  if (j > aLast) then
    j := aLast;
  for i := succ(aFirst) to j do
    if (aCompare(aList.List^[i], aList.List^[IndexOfMin]) < 0) then
      IndexOfMin := i;
  if (aFirst<>IndexOfMin) then begin
    Temp := aList.List^[aFirst];
    aList.List^[aFirst] := aList.List^[IndexOfMin];
    aList.List^[IndexOfMin] := Temp;
  end;
  {now sort via fast insertion method}
  for i := aFirst+2 to aLast do begin
    Temp := aList.List^[i];
    j := i;
    while (aCompare(Temp, aList.List^[j-1]) < 0) do begin
      aList.List^[j] := aList.List^[j-1];
      dec(j);
    end;
    aList.List^[j] := Temp;
  end;
```

```
end;
procedure QS(aList       : TList;
             aFirst      : integer;
             aLast       : integer;
             aCompare    : TtdCompareFunc);
var
  L, R  : integer;
  Pivot : pointer;
  Temp  : pointer;
  Stack : array [0..63] of integer; {allows for 2 billion items}
  SP    : integer;
begin
  {initialize stack}
  Stack[0] := aFirst;
  Stack[1] := aLast;
  SP := 2;

  {while there are subfiles on the stack...}
  while (SP<>0) do begin

    {pop off the top subfile}
    dec(SP, 2);
    aFirst := Stack[SP];
    aLast := Stack[SP+1];

    {repeat while there are sufficient items in the subfile...}
    while ((aLast - aFirst) > QSCutOff) do begin

      {sort the first, middle and last items, then set the pivot to
      the middle one - the median-of-3 method}
      R := (aFirst + aLast) div 2;
      if aCompare(aList.List^[aFirst], aList.List^[R]) > 0 then begin
        Temp := aList.List^[aFirst];
        aList.List^[aFirst] := aList.List^[R];
        aList.List^[R] := Temp;
      end;
      if aCompare(aList.List^[aFirst], aList.List^[aLast]) > 0 then begin
        Temp := aList.List^[aFirst];
        aList.List^[aFirst] := aList.List^[aLast];
        aList.List^[aLast] := Temp;
      end;
      if aCompare(aList.List^[R], aList.List^[aLast]) > 0 then begin
        Temp := aList.List^[R];
        aList.List^[R] := aList.List^[aLast];
        aList.List^[aLast] := Temp;
      end;
      Pivot := aList.List^[R];
```

```
      {set indexes and partition}
      L := aFirst;
      R := aLast;
      while true do begin
        repeat dec(R); until (aCompare(aList.List^[R], Pivot) <= 0);
        repeat inc(L); until (aCompare(aList.List^[L], Pivot) >= 0);
        if (L >= R) then Break;
        Temp := aList.List^[L];
        aList.List^[L] := aList.List^[R];
        aList.List^[R] := Temp;
      end;

      {push the larger subfile onto the stack, go round loop again
      with the smaller subfile}
      if (R - aFirst) < (aLast - R) then begin
        Stack[SP] := succ(R);
        Stack[SP+1] := aLast;
        inc(SP, 2);
        aLast := R;
      end
      else begin
        Stack[SP] := aFirst;
        Stack[SP+1] := R;
        inc(SP, 2);
        aFirst := succ(R);
      end;
    end;
  end;
end;
procedure TDQuickSort(aList    : TList;
                      aFirst   : integer;
                      aLast    : integer;
                      aCompare : TtdCompareFunc);
begin
  TDValidateListRange(aList, aFirst, aLast, 'TDQuickSort');
  QS(aList, aFirst, aLast, aCompare);
  QSInsertionSort(aList, aFirst, aLast, aCompare);
end;
```

We have three routines in this optimized quicksort. The first is the routine we call, TDQuickSort. This routine validates the parameters, calls the QS routine to partially sort the list, and then calls QSInsertionSort to finish off the sort. QS performs a non-recursive partitioning process with a cutoff for small sublists. QSInsertionSort performs an optimized insertion sort on the partially sorted list. Note in particular that the smallest item is in the first QSCutOff items in the list; this is as a result of the partitioning process and the fact that we cutoff partitioning small sublists.

And was it worth it? My tests showed an unequivocal yes. In sorting 100,000 longint items, the optimized quicksort took 18 percent less time than the standard quicksort.

Merge Sort with Linked Lists

The final sort we shall consider in this chapter is merge sort again, but this time with linked lists. Recall that, although it's a speedy sort—O($n$log(n))—using merge sort with arrays suffered from a requirement for a auxiliary array, at least half the size of the array being sorted. The reason for this is that the merge phase of the sort needed somewhere to put the items without having to perform some kind of insert operation.

With linked lists, mergesort does *not* require this auxiliary array at all; we can move items around with impunity, since the links can be broken and remade at will in O(1), or constant time.

The code for the linked list sorts can be found in TDLnkLst.pas on the CD.

Let's see how it's done with the singly linked list and then we'll extend the concept to the doubly linked list.

We shall assume that we have a linked list with a dummy head node; the algorithm is much easier with such an assumption. Every node that we are trying to arrange in sorted order therefore has a parent. Consider the merge phase of the sort. Suppose we have two linked lists, both defined by a node that is the parent of the first node. These two lists are in order. We can easily devise an algorithm for doing the merge such that the merged sorted list is attached to the first parent node: it merely turns into a bunch of deletes and inserts.

Compare the two items pointed to by the two parent nodes. If the smallest item is in the first list, it's in the right place, so advance, making this node the new parent node. If the smallest item is in the second list, delete it from that list and insert it after the parent node of the first list, and advance to make it the new parent node. Continue in the same manner until one of the lists is exhausted. If it is the first list that is exhausted, add the remainder of the second list onto the first.

Pretty easy stuff. However, it seems that we'd have to divide the original list into a whole bunch of small one-node lists, all pointed to by their own dummy head nodes and then stitch them together. This is not so, as we can use other nodes in the list to act as temporary dummy head nodes and not even break the list up. Here's how.

Firstly, we write a driver method to do the merge sort. All it does is call a recursive method, and that's the one that does the hard work. We pass two parameters: the node from which the to-be-sorted list hangs and a count of items in that list. We *won't* be using the nil node at the end of a list to signal that there are no more items to sort; we shall use a count instead. Listing 5.19 shows this very simple driver method, Sort.

Listing 5.19: The driver method for merge sorting single linked lists

```
procedure TtdSingleLinkList.Sort(aCompare : TtdCompareFunc);
begin
 {perform a mergesort if there is more than one item in the list}
 if (Count > 1) then
  sllMergesort(aCompare, FHead, Count);
  MoveBeforeFirst;
  FIsSorted := true;
end;
```

As you can see, the driver method calls sllMergesort to do the work. sllMergesort first calls itself with the first half of the list, then calls itself with the second half of the list, and finally merges the two half lists. To aid in this endeavor, sllMergesort will return the last node that it sorted.

Listing 5.20: The recursive merge sort for single linked lists

```
function TtdSingleLinkList.sllMergesort(aCompare   : TtdCompareFunc;
                                        aPriorNode : PslNode;
                                        aCount     : longint)
                                                   : PslNode;
var
  Count2     : longint;
  PriorNode2 : PslNode;
begin
  {easy case first: if there is only one item in the sublist, it must
  be sorted, so return}
  if (aCount = 1) then begin
    Result := aPriorNode^.slnNext;
    Exit;
  end;
  {split the list into two parts}
  Count2 := aCount div 2;
  aCount := aCount - Count2;
  {mergesort the first half: this'll return the head node for the
  second half}
  PriorNode2 := sllMergeSort(aCompare, aPriorNode, aCount);
  {mergesort the second half}
  sllMergeSort(aCompare, PriorNode2, Count2);
  {now merge the two halves, return the final node}
```

```
  Result := sllMerge(aCompare, aPriorNode, aCount, PriorNode2, Count2);
end;
```

The merge sort method is called knowing the prior node for the list and the number of items in the list. It could then work out where the second half of the list starts by walking the list and counting the nodes, but instead we get the last node of the first half as a return value of merge sorting the first half of the list. We have to walk the list during the merge sort anyway, so why waste time walking the list again to find the halfway point?

The final piece of the puzzle is the actual merge routine itself. This is shown in Listing 5.21 and is fairly easy to understand. The parent of the first sublist is the one to which we attach the merged list, and we return the final item in the merged list (this will become the parent of the unsorted sublist that remains).

Listing 5.21: The merge phase of single linked list merge sort

```
function TtdSingleLinkList.sllMerge(
                                   aCompare    : TtdCompareFunc;
                                   aPriorNode1 : PslNode; aCount1 : longint;
                                   aPriorNode2 : PslNode; aCount2 : longint) : PslNode;
var
  i : integer;
  Node1     : PslNode;
  Node2     : PslNode;
  LastNode  : PslNode;
  Temp      : PslNode;
begin
  LastNode := aPriorNode1;
  {get the two top nodes}
  Node1 := aPriorNode1^.slnNext;
  Node2 := aPriorNode2^.slnNext;
  {repeat until one of the lists empties}
  while (aCount1<>0) and (aCount2<>0) do begin
    if (aCompare(Node1^.slnData, Node2^.slnData) <= 0) then begin
      LastNode := Node1;
      Node1 := Node1^.slnNext;
      dec(aCount1);
    end
    else begin
      Temp := Node2^.slnNext;
      Node2^.slnNext := Node1;
      LastNode^.slnNext := Node2;
      LastNode := Node2;
      Node2 := Temp;
      dec(aCount2);
    end;
```

```
  end;
  {if it was the first list that emptied, link the last node up to the
  remaining part of the second list, and walk it to get the very last
  node}
  if (aCount1 = 0) then begin
    LastNode^.slnNext := Node2;
    for i := 0 to pred(aCount2) do
      LastNode := LastNode^.slnNext;
  end
  {if it was the second list that emptied, Node2 is the first node of
  the remaining list; walk the remaining part of the first list and
  link it up to Node2}
  else begin
    for i := 0 to pred(aCount1) do
      LastNode := LastNode^.slnNext;
    LastNode^.slnNext := Node2;
  end;
  {return the last node}
  Result := LastNode;
end;
```

Notice that throughout the singly linked list merge sort we did not need to backtrack at any time. We were never left in a position of requiring the parent node of a given node, but in fact not knowing it. This means that merge sorting a doubly linked list can be performed in exactly the same way as merge sorting a singly linked list, followed by a pass that patches up all of the backward links.

Listing 5.22: Merge sort for a doubly linked list

```
function TtdDoubleLinkList.dllMerge(
                                     aCompare    : TtdCompareFunc;
                                     aPriorNode1: PdlNode; aCount1 : longint;
                                     aPriorNode2: PdlNode; aCount2 : longint) : PdlNode;
var
  i : integer;
  Node1     : PdlNode;
  Node2     : PdlNode;
  LastNode  : PdlNode;
  Temp      : PdlNode;
begin
  LastNode := aPriorNode1;
  {get the two top nodes}
  Node1 := aPriorNode1^.dlnNext;
  Node2 := aPriorNode2^.dlnNext;
  {repeat until one of the lists empties}
  while (aCount1<>0) and (aCount2<>0) do begin
    if (aCompare(Node1^.dlnData, Node2^.dlnData) <= 0) then begin
      LastNode := Node1;
      Node1 := Node1^.dlnNext;
```

```
      dec(aCount1);
    end
    else begin
      Temp := Node2^.dlnNext;
      Node2^.dlnNext := Node1;
      LastNode^.dlnNext := Node2;
      LastNode := Node2;
      Node2 := Temp;
      dec(aCount2);
    end;
  end;
  {if it was the first list that emptied, link the last node up to the
  remaining part of the second list, and walk it to get the very last
  node}
  if (aCount1 = 0) then begin
    LastNode^.dlnNext := Node2;
    for i := 0 to pred(aCount2) do
      LastNode := LastNode^.dlnNext;
  end
  {if it was the second list that emptied, Node2 is the first node of
  the remaining list; walk the remaining part of the first list and
  link it up to Node2}
  else begin
    for i := 0 to pred(aCount1) do
      LastNode := LastNode^.dlnNext;
    LastNode^.dlnNext := Node2;
  end;
  {return the last node}
  Result := LastNode;
end;
function TtdDoubleLinkList.dllMergesort(aCompare       : TtdCompareFunc;
                                        aPriorNode     : PdlNode;
                                        aCount         : longint)
                                                       : PdlNode;
var
  Count2     : longint;
  PriorNode2 : PdlNode;
begin
  {easy case first: if there is only one item in the sublist, it must
  be sorted, so return}
  if (aCount = 1) then begin
    Result := aPriorNode^.dlnNext;
    Exit;
  end;
  {split the list into two parts}
  Count2 := aCount div 2;
  aCount := aCount - Count2;
  {mergesort the first half: this'll return the head node for the
```

```
  second half}
  PriorNode2 := dllMergeSort(aCompare, aPriorNode, aCount);
  {mergesort the second half}
  dllMergeSort(aCompare, PriorNode2, Count2);
  {now merge the two halves, return the final node}
  Result := dllMerge(aCompare, aPriorNode, aCount, PriorNode2, Count2);
end;
procedure TtdDoubleLinkList.Sort(aCompare : TtdCompareFunc);
var
  Dad, Walker : PdlNode;
begin
  {perform a singly linked mergesort if there are more than one item
  in the list; then patch up the prior links}
  if (Count > 1) then begin
    dllMergesort(aCompare, FHead, Count);
    Dad := FHead;
    Walker := FHead^.dlnNext;
    while (Walker<>nil) do begin
      Walker^.dlnPrior := Dad;
      Dad := Walker;
      Walker := Dad^.dlnNext;
    end;
  end;
  MoveBeforeFirst;
  FIsSorted := true;
end;
```

Summary

In this chapter we have looked at various sorting algorithms and have obtained a feel for the complexities and efficiencies of each. We saw the basic algorithms: bubble, shaker, selection, and insertion sort and saw that they were all $O(n^2)$ in nature. Then we looked at two medium speed algorithms: Shell sort and comb sort, both of which are complex to analyze but are faster than the basic ones. Finally, we looked at two advanced sorts: merge sort and quicksort, both $O(n\log(n))$ algorithms. We observed that, unlike all the other sorts mentioned, merge sort required an auxiliary array to aid in the algorithm.

With quicksort in particular, we stepped through a series of possible enhancements for the algorithm, discussing each in turn and seeing how the optimization worked in practice. Each optimization didn't alter the overall big-Oh nature of quicksort, but instead reduced the algorithm's big-Oh proportionality constant, speeding up the routine.

Finally, we saw how to apply merge sort to linked lists, where we didn't need the auxiliary array, and allowed merge sort to achieve its true potential.

Chapter 6

Randomized Algorithms

Those of you who flipped through this book in a bookstore might have stopped at this chapter and wondered what *randomized algorithms* might possibly be. Algorithms that work in a random fashion, perhaps? Nothing so existential. In this book, a randomized algorithm is one that generates or uses random numbers.

If you think about the phrase "generating random numbers" for a moment, you'll realize what nonsense it is. Computers are deterministic machines: once you've written a program or a routine to do a particular job, you expect it to produce exactly the same answer for the same input. (If it didn't, you'd be sending it straight back to the manufacturers.) Without using specialized hardware for generating random numbers, the random number generators we all use are simply routines, too. How can the numbers they produce be random? If you start the generator in a particular state, by reading the source code you can predict the next number it'll produce, and the one after that, and so on. Hardly random, right? We'll look at this dilemma in more detail shortly.

Linux comes with a module in the kernel that analyzes the way a user types and the intervals between each keystroke, and uses the results as a randomizing factor. Thus, if you use the kernel's routines for random numbers, you'll find them to be more random, in a sense.

As far as using random numbers in an algorithm goes, we've already come across one in Chapter 5: quicksort with the selection of a partitioning pivot by random means. The reason for using random numbers in this kind of algorithm is that the algorithm concerned has some good overall qualities, but that it also has a very bad worst-case scenario. By using random numbers, we ensure that there is a very small probability of encountering the worst-case scenario. In this chapter, we will discuss the skip list data structure, a way of maintaining a sorted linked list by using random numbers to improve the speed of its insert operations.

There are other algorithms that use random numbers, either because their solution space is very large and searching through it all for a particular solution would be horrendously slow, or because we wish to emulate a physical system in order to gain some optimization or provide some other benefit.

All of the code to generate random numbers can be found in the TDRandom.pas file on the CD.

Random Number Generation

One of the first things we need to consider is the definition of *random number.* Without a good definition of such a beast, we'd be shooting blindfolded in trying to design or write a random number generator.

Is the number 2 a random number? Well, on its own, devoid of context, you can't really say one way or another. If you throw a die once, it may come up 2. But that singular event doesn't really tell us anything. It could be just pure luck that it came up 2, or it could be that all six sides of the die were 2s, or the die could be subtly biased or weighted toward the 2. To determine whether the 2 were a random number, we'd have to look at a *sequence* of numbers produced by the generator in which the 2 appeared and make our conclusions from that.

So, what could we determine if it were in a sequence and it came after a 1 and was followed by a 3, and then a 4? It doesn't look very random, does it? Well, if we had a random digit generator that used a quantum source (i.e., something that produces true random events), we'd expect that sequence, or indeed any other predetermined four-digit sequence, to occur once every 10,000 tries. Our intuition just doesn't help us at all here. We would have to perform some kind of test and use probability or statistics to help us determine whether a given sequence, and hence the generator that created it, was, to all intents and purposes, random.

This leads us to a definition of a random number generator. A random number generator is a routine that produces a sequence of numbers that would pass statistical or probabilistic tests for randomness. To be really strict, routines that generate random numbers are said to be *pseudorandom number generators* (often abbreviated to PRNG) to differentiate them from true random number generators that rely on some kind of random events happening at a quantum level. (Current theories state that quantum events are truly random. The time of the decay of a radioactive atom into its byproducts cannot be predicted; all we can say is that there is a certain probability that it will decay within a certain period of time, and we can estimate that probability by observing the decay of many, many atoms.)

So, what kind of tests could we perform on a sequence of numbers to determine whether they were random or not? The tests we do would all be statistical in nature; by observing many events we can make conclusions about the statistical patterns in the data. One simple test we could do is to "bucket" the numbers in the sequence. Suppose that we have a sequence of single digits that we wanted to test for randomness. We put the digits into "buckets," essentially counting the number of zeros, ones, twos, and so on, in the sequence. For a random sequence, we would expect the number of occurrences of each digit to be roughly one-tenth of the total number of digits in the sequence. For a sequence of 1,000 random digits, we'd expect there to be about 100 zeros, 100 ones, 100 twos, and so on. Not exactly, of course, but pretty close.

"Expect." "About." "Roughly." These words don't give us much confidence that our tests are really objective, rather than subjective. After all, having 110 zeros in our test, for example, might look fine to one person, but very fishy to another.

Chi-Squared Tests

Imagine that we have a pair of coins that we think someone has tampered with. How could we prove that they were biased? Of course, one putative crook might be completely dumb and have weighted them to always show heads, but he'd have been caught long ago, leaving a master crook full rein. Let's throw the coins 100 times, say, and plot the number of times we toss individual scores in a table. Our table might look like Table 6.1.

Table 6.1: The results of tossing a pair of "biased" coins 100 times

	Two Heads (1)	One of Each (2)	Two Tails (3)
Our tests (100 tosses)	28	51	21
Probability of event	¼	½	¼
Expected number for 100 tosses	25	50	25

I've added the probability of each event to Table 6.1, and also the expected number of tosses for each event, if we do 100 tosses overall. (The expected number of a given event is merely its probability multiplied by the total number of events.)

Well, just looking at the table we could argue that the coins are biased to heads, but is the difference that great? Let's look at the spread (i.e., the difference) of our results from the expected values. We'll square these differences to accentuate them and to get rid of any negative values. The sum of these squared differences would be a measure of how biased these coins are. Calculating this sum, I get 26 (= $3^2 + 1^2 + (-4)^2$). But, wait a moment—we should incorporate the probability of each event somehow. We should get a bigger squared difference for "one of each" than for "two heads" just because the former is more likely to happen. To put it another way, the difference of 3 for "two heads" is more significant than the difference of 1 for "one of each." So let us divide each squared difference by the expected result of that event. The new sum we calculate is

$$X = \sum_{1}^{3} \frac{(C_i - 100p_i)^2}{100p_i}$$

where C_i is our observed counts and p_i is the probability of each event i. I get a value of 1.02 for X. What we've just calculated is known as the *chi-squared value* for our tests. We can look up this value in a standard table of the chi-squared distribution (Table 6.2).

Table 6.2: Percentage points of the chi-squared distribution

	1%	5%	95%	99%
$\nu = 1$	0.000157	0.00393	3.84	6.63
$\nu = 2$	0.0201	0.103	5.99	9.21
$\nu = 3$	0.115	0.352	7.81	11.3
$\nu = 4$	0.297	0.711	9.49	13.3
$\nu = 5$	0.554	1.15	11.1	15.1
$\nu = 6$	0.872	1.64	12.6	16.8

The table looks slightly daunting, but is quite easy to understand, once explained. The values shown are selected values from the chi-square distribution with ν degrees of freedom (the Greek character ν is the traditional symbol used to denote the number of degrees of freedom). Without being rigorous, the number of degrees of freedom is one less than the number of buckets we are counting things or events into. In our case, we have three buckets: one for "two heads," one for "one of each," and one for "two tails," so the number of degrees of freedom for our experiment is 2. If we look along the $\nu = 2$ line we see that there are four values, one in each of four columns. Looking at the value in the 1% column (0.0201), it should be read as: "The value we calculated for X should be less than 0.0201 only 1 percent of the time." In other words, if we repeated our experiment 100 times, only about one of them would have an X value of less than 0.0201. If we found that a lot of these experiments had a value less than 0.0201, then it would give a very strong indication that flipping the coins is not a random event, and that they are biased. A similar interpretation can be made for the 5% column. Moving to the 95 percent column, the value there should be read as: "The value X should be less than 5.99 about 95% of the time," or "X should be greater than 5.99 only 5 percent of the time." Similarly we can make an equivalent statement for the 99% column.

We see that our X value falls in between the 5% value and the 95% value, so we can't make a strong conclusion either way. We have to assume that the coins are true. If, on the other hand, our calculated X value was as high as 10, we see that this result should occur in less than 1 percent of our trials (10 is greater than 9.21, which is the 99% value). And this is therefore a strong indication that the coins are biased. Of course, we should perform more experiments and see how our spread of X values fits into the chi-squared distribution; from an extended set of experiments we'd get a better feel for the bias, if any, of the coins. We don't want to be caught out with a rogue result, one which probability theory tells us should happen, albeit infrequently.

Generally, we take the same boundaries at either end of the range of the chi-squared distribution, say 5% and 95%, and then say that our experiment is *significant* at the 5% level if it falls outside these boundaries, or is *not significant* at the 5% level if it falls in between.

One thing I haven't mentioned so far is this: How many individual events should we generate? In our coin test we did 100 flips. Is this enough? Can we get away with less, or should it be more? Unfortunately, the answer is unclear. Knuth states that a common rule of thumb is to make sure that the expected number of events for each bucket should be at least five (our expected numbers are 25, 50, and 25 so we're all right there), but the more events to bucket, the merrier [11].

Let's leave our coins and go back to our hypothetical random number sequence, and apply what we've just learned. We calculate the count of each digit in our sequence and then calculate the X value and then check it against the chi-square distribution with nine degrees of freedom (here we have 10 buckets, one for each digit, and so the number of degrees of freedom would be one less than this, or nine). We would have to have at least 50 digits to make the expected number for each bucket at least 5, although many more would be better.

We can go even further. If we take our sequence and view it as a series of pairs of digits from 00 to 99, then we can bucket the sequence again (counting each pair this time). There will be 100 buckets—and hence 99 degrees of freedom—each having a probability of 1/100. We would have to have at least 500 pairs of digits (1,000 digits) to make the test worthwhile.

We could go on, using triplets of digits for example, but the space requirements grow tremendously quickly, and there are other tests we could do. Before we look at these other tests, let's have a look at how to generate random number sequences. Once we have a few random number sequence generators under our belt, we can test their output against the tests I've shown so far and against the tests to come.

Again, at the risk of being repetitive, I repeat that the first thing to realize is that a deterministic algorithm can never generate random number sequences in the same way that throwing an unbiased die does, or that counting beta particles from a radioactive source can. The whole point about a deterministic algorithm is that it generates the same result from the same starting point. If I told you that Generator X, using a particular well-defined algorithm, generates the new random number 65584256 from a starting value (or *seed*) of 12345678, then you'd know five months from now that X would calculate exactly the same next value from this same seed. There is absolutely no randomness present in the *calculation* of the random number sequence at all. Instead, it is the *sequence of* numbers so generated that can be shown (by statistical tests) to be random.

Indeed, sometimes we would like this repetition of our random number generator. It enables us to use the generator to produce a sequence of random numbers, over and over again. There are some instances where this could be of value, for example, in a test to reproduce a bug.

Middle-Square Method

The history of random number generators starts off with one of the most illustrious names in computing: John von Neumann. He put forward the following scheme for calculating random number sequences in about 1946: take an N-digit number, square it and from the result (expressed as a 2N-digit number, padded on the left with zeros if required) take the middle N-digits as the next number in the sequence. If we take N as 4, for example, and have 1234 as our starting point, the next few numbers in the random number sequence are 5227, 3215, 3362, 3030, 1809, and so on. This method is known as the middle-square method.

Listing 6.1: The middle-square method in action

```
var
  MidSqSeed : integer;
function GetMidSquareNumber : integer;
var
```

```
  Seed : longint;
begin
  Seed := longint(MidSqSeed) * MidSqSeed;
  MidSqSeed := (Seed div 100) mod 10000;
  Result := MidSqSeed;
end;
```

There are a couple of *big* problems with this algorithm, which is why it's never used any more. Using our four-digit example again, suppose we hit upon a value in the sequence that is less than 10. In calculating the square, we get a number less than 100. This, in turn, means that the next value in the sequence is 0 (we would be taking the middle four digits from 000000xx). This again is less than 10, so the next and all subsequent random numbers in the sequence would also be 0. Hardly random! (Starting off with 1234 as the seed, the middle-square method generates 55 numbers before hitting zero.) Also, if you start off with a number like 4100, you'll end up with the sequence 8100, 6100, 2100, 4100, ad infinitum. There are other pathological sequences like this and it's quite easy to hit them but difficult to do anything about it.

Using a 16-bit integer, it is easy to calculate random numbers using the middle-square method. Squaring a 16-bit word results in a 32-bit integer and calculating the middle 16-bit part is merely shifting the answer right by eight, and then ANDing with $FFFF. However, if you do so, you'll still find the algorithm producing hopeless results. Within about 50 or 60 random numbers, the algorithm settles down into generating a series of zeros, or generating a cycle. The same happens with 32-bit integers with their 64-bit intermediary values. All in all, although simple to describe, the middle-square method is quite dreadful in practice.

Linear Congruential Method

The next big step forward in random number generators came from D.H. Lehmer in 1949, in the process hammering several nails into the coffin of the middle-square method, if not all of them. What he proposed is known as the linear congruential method for generating random number sequences. Choose three numbers, m, a, and c, and a starting seed X_0 and use the following formula to generate a sequence of numbers X_i:

$$X_{n+1} = (aX_n + c) \bmod m$$

The operation mod m is calculated as the remainder after dividing by m, for example, 24 mod 10 is 4.

If we choose our numbers well, the sequence generated will be random. For example, the standard system random number generator in Delphi uses a =

134775813 ($8088405), $c = 1$, and $m = 2^{32}$; and it is up to us, the programmers, to set the starting seed X_0. (It's the RandSeed global variable. We can set it directly or use the Randomize procedure to set it from the system clock.)

It must be noted that if we get a particular value x in the generated sequence at two different points, then the sequence in fact must repeat at those two points—the algorithm is deterministic, remember. Because of the modulus operation, no value in the sequence can be greater or equal to m, so all values must be between 0 and m-1. Hence, the sequence will repeat itself after, at most, m values. It may, if we are pretty inept at choosing a, c, and m, repeat much sooner. A simple example is $a = 0$: the sequence boils down to {c, c, c...}, repeating itself after only one term.

So what are good values for these magic numbers a, c, and m? Much has been conjectured, posited, and proved in the literature. Generally, we choose m to be as large as possible so that our repeat cycle is as large as possible as well. We try and make it at least as large as the word size of the operating system (in other words, for a 32-bit operating system we make m 31 or 32 bits in size). a is chosen to be relatively prime to m (two numbers are *relatively prime* if their greatest common divisor is 1). c is usually chosen to be either 0 or 1, although the general rule is that if you choose a non-zero value, you have to make sure that c and m are relatively prime.

If we choose c to be 0, the generator is said to be a *multiplicative linear congruential generator.* To be sure we obtain a maximal cycle with such a generator, we *have* to ensure that m is prime. The most famous such random number generator is the so-called *minimal standard random number generator,* proposed by Stephen Park and Keith Miller in 1988. This generator has a=16807 and m=2147483647 (or 2^{31}–1). In the intervening years since Park and Miller's proposal, the generator has had numerous statistical tests done on it and it has passed most of them (although it does have some undesirable properties as we'll see in a moment).

There is one anomaly with multiplicative linear congruential generators though: they will never generate the number 0. (The proof relies in the fact that, first, m is prime; second, that a mod m is non-zero; and, third, if the seed is also non-zero, the seed mod m is also non-zero. Hence the next seed value must also be non-zero.) Indeed, if they did ever produce a zero, the output of the generator would no longer be random. In practice, the fact that the generator cannot produce zero is usually ignored—after all, on a 32-bit machine, we're missing out on one number in about 2 billion.

In coding the minimal standard random number generator (or indeed, any generator) we have to be aware of overflow and cater for it. After all, the current seed multiplied by *a* could easily overflow a 32-bit integer. If we do not recognize this case we are likely to cause errors that would destroy the good qualities of the generator. What we do is apply Schrage's method (the derivation of which is beyond this book, but can be found in Park and Miller's paper [16]).

In order to compare and test different random number generators, we shall create a hierarchy of classes, the base class of which will define a virtual method that encapsulates the basic functionality of a random number generator, namely, creating a floating-point random number (we'll use the double type) between 0 and 1. This method will be overridden in descendant classes to generate a random number according to the algorithm for that class. The base class will use this virtual method to create other types of random numbers, such as a random integer up to a particular value or a uniform random number in a certain range.

Having a hierarchy of random number generator classes gives us a benefit in another way, too. Since the data for the random number generator is contained solely within the object itself, we could have different generators for different purposes within our applications and they'd be totally independent. Contrast this with the standard Random function where there is one and only one seed, and this gets to be shared amongst all calls to Random wherever they may occur. In this kind of situation, where many separate routines are calling Random, it is hard to get a replicable test case since all the disparate calls would be interfering with each other, maybe at separate times.

Listing 6.2: Base random number generator class

```
type
  TtdBasePRNG = class
    private
      FName : TtdNameString;
    protected
      procedure bError(aErrorCode  : integer;
                 const aMethodName : TtdNameString);
    public
      function AsDouble : double; virtual; abstract;
      {-returns a random number between 0 inclusive and 1 exclusive}
      function AsLimitedDouble(aLower, aUpper : double) : double;
      {-returns a random number between aLower inclusive and aUpper
      exclusive}
      function AsInteger(aUpper : integer) : integer;
      {-returns a random integer between 0 inclusive and aUpper
      exclusive}
      property Name : TtdNameString read FName write FName;
  end;
function TtdBasePRNG.AsLimitedDouble(aLower, aUpper : double) : double;
```

```
begin
  if (aLower < 0.0) or (aUpper < 0.0) or (aLower >= aUpper) then
    bError(tdeRandRangeError, 'AsLimitedDouble');
  Result := (AsDouble * (aUpper - aLower)) + aLower;
end;
function TtdBasePRNG.AsInteger(aUpper : integer) : integer;
begin
  if (aUpper <= 0) then
    bError(tdeRandRangeError, 'AsInteger');
  Result := Trunc(AsDouble * aUpper);
end;
procedure TtdBasePRNG.bError(aErrorCode  : integer;
                       const aMethodName : TtdNameString);
begin
  raise EtdRandGenException.Create(
     FmtLoadStr(aErrorCode,
               [UnitName, ClassName, aMethodName, Name]));
end;
```

Listing 6.2 shows our base class. It defines a virtual method called AsDouble that returns a random number x, such that $0 <= x < 1$. It also defines two simple methods, one that returns a floating-point random number in a certain range, and another that returns a random integer between 0 and some upper limit (in the same way that Random(Limit) works with Limit as an integer value). Now that we have defined a base class, we can easily define a descendant to perform Park and Miller's algorithm.

Listing 6.3: Minimal standard PRNG

```
type
  TtdMinStandardPRNG = class(TtdBasePRNG)
    private
      FSeed : longint;
    protected
      procedure msSetSeed(aValue : longint);
    public
      constructor Create(aSeed : longint);

      function AsDouble  : double; override;
      property Seed : longint read FSeed write msSetSeed;
  end;
constructor TtdMinStandardPRNG.Create(aSeed : longint);
begin
  inherited Create;
  Seed := aSeed;
end;

function TtdMinStandardPRNG.AsDouble  : double;
```

```
const
  a = 16807;
  m = 2147483647;
  q = 127773; {equals m div a}
  r = 2836;   {equals m mod a}
  OneOverM : double = 1.0 / 2147483647.0;
var
  k : longint;
begin
  k := FSeed div q;
  FSeed := (a * (FSeed - (k * q))) - (k * r);
  if (FSeed <= 0) then
    inc(FSeed, m);
  Result := FSeed * OneOverM;
end;

function GetTimeAsLong : longint;
{$IFDEF Delphi1}
assembler;
asm
  mov ah, $2C
  call DOS3Call
  mov ax, cx
end;
{$ENDIF}
{$IFDEF Delphi2Plus}
begin
  Result := longint(GetTickCount);
end;
{$ENDIF}
{$IFDEF Kylix1Plus}
var
  T : TTime_t;
begin
  __time(@T);
  Result := longint(T);
end;
{$ENDIF}

procedure TtdMinStandardPRNG.msSetSeed(aValue : longint);
const
  m = 2147483647;
begin
  if (aValue > 0) then
    FSeed := aValue
  else
    FSeed := GetTimeAsLong;
  {make sure that the seed is between 1 and m-1 inclusive}
```

```
  if (FSeed >= m-1) then
    FSeed := FSeed - (m - 1) + 1;
end;
```

As you can see by looking at the AsDouble method, Schrage's method does not look anything like the formula $X_{n+1} = aX_n \bmod m$ with a = 16807 and $m = 2^{32}-1$, yet some fairly involved algebra can show it to be so.

Also, as we've already said, with this type of random number generator, using the value of zero for the seed is bad news indeed: if it were used, all random numbers emitted by the generator would be zero. So, the msSetSeed method uses zero as a flag to cause the random number seed to be set from the system clock. This, out of necessity, requires separate code for 16-bit Windows and 32-bit Windows.

We can easily create a random number class that uses the system random number generator, Random. Listing 6.4 shows the AsDouble method for this class.

Listing 6.4: Using the System Random function in a class

```
function TtdSystemPRNG.AsDouble  : double;
var
  OldSeed : longint;
begin
  OldSeed := System.RandSeed;
  System.RandSeed := Seed;
  Result := System.Random;
  Seed := System.RandSeed;
  System.RandSeed := OldSeed;
end;
```

Now that we have a couple of random number generators in our arsenal, we can start discussing how to test them.

Testing

The tests all follow the same logic. We'll generate a lot of random numbers between 0.0 (inclusive) and 1.0 (exclusive). We categorize various events derived from these random numbers into separate buckets, count them, calculate the probability associated with each bucket, from which we can work out the chi-square value, and apply the chi-square test with the number of degrees of freedom being one less than the number of buckets. A little abstract, but you'll see the idea in a moment.

The Uniformity Test

The first test is the simplest: the uniformity test. This is the one we were discussing earlier. Basically, the random numbers we generate are going to be checked to see that they uniformly cover the range 0.0 to 1.0. We create 100 buckets, generate 1,000,000 random numbers, and slot them into each bucket. Bucket 0 gets all the random numbers from 0.0 to 0.01, bucket 1 gets them from 0.01 to 0.02, and so on. The probability of a random number falling into a particular bucket is obviously 0.01. We calculate the chi-square value for our test and check that against the standard table, using the 99 degrees of freedom line.

Listing 6.5: The uniformity test

```
procedure UniformityTest(RandGen        : TtdBasePRNG;
                         var ChiSquare  : double;
                         var DegsFreedo : integer);
var
  BucketNumber,
  i : integer;
  Expected, ChiSqVal : double;
  Bucket : array [0..pred(UniformityIntervals)] of integer;
begin
  {Fill buckets}
  FillChar(Bucket, sizeof(Bucket), 0);
  for i := 0 to pred(UniformityCount) do begin
    BucketNumber := trunc(RandGen.AsDouble * UniformityIntervals);
    inc(Bucket[BucketNumber]);
  end;
  {calc chi squared}
  Expected := UniformityCount / UniformityIntervals;
  ChiSqVal := 0.0;
  for i := 0 to pred(UniformityIntervals) do
    ChiSqVal := ChiSqVal + (Sqr(Expected - Bucket[i]) / Expected);
  {return values}
  ChiSquare := ChiSqVal;
  DegsFreedom := pred(UniformityIntervals);
end;
```

The Gap Test

The second test is a little more interesting: the gap test. The gap test ensures that you don't get runs of values in one particular range followed by runs in another, flip-flopping between the two, even though, as a whole, the random numbers are evenly spread out. Define a sub-range of the range 0.0 to 1.0, let's say the first half, 0.0 to 0.5. Generate the random numbers. For each random number, we test to see whether it lands in our sub-range (a *hit*), or whether it lands outside (a *miss*). You'll get a sequence of hits and misses. Look at the runs of one or more misses (these are called the gaps between the hits, hence the gap test). You'll get some runs with just one miss, some with two misses, and so on. Bucket these lengths. If we say the probability of a hit is p (it'll be the width of the sub-range expressed as a decimal), the probability of a miss is $(1-p)$. We can now calculate the probability of a run of one miss: $(1-p)p$; of two misses: $(1-p)^2p$; of n misses: $(1-p)^np$, and hence calculate the expected numbers for each run length. From then it's a short step to the chi-squared test. We shall use 10 buckets (since the probability of 11 misses or more is so small, we'll toss runs of 10 misses or more into the last bucket, remembering to alter the probability for that last bucket, of course); hence, there are nine degrees of freedom. Generally, we repeat the gap test five times: for the first and second halves of the range, and for the first, second, and third thirds.

Listing 6.6: The gap test

```
procedure GapTest(RandGen        : TtdBasePRNG;
                  Lower, Upper   : double;
                  var ChiSquare  : double;
                  var DegsFreedom : integer);
var
  NumGaps   : integer;
  GapLen    : integer;
  i         : integer;
  p         : double;
  Expected  : double;
  ChiSqVal  : double;
  R         : double;
  Bucket    : array [0..pred(GapBucketCount)] of integer;
begin
  {calc gaps and fill buckets}
  FillChar(Bucket, sizeof(Bucket), 0);
  GapLen := 0;
  NumGaps := 0;
  while (NumGaps < GapsCount) do begin
    R := RandGen.AsDouble;
    if (Lower <= R) and (R < Upper) then begin
      if (GapLen >= GapBucketCount) then
        GapLen := pred(GapBucketCount);
      inc(Bucket[GapLen]);
      inc(NumGaps);
      GapLen := 0;
    end
    else
      if (GapLen < GapBucketCount) then
        inc(GapLen);
```

```
  end;
  p := Upper - Lower;
  ChiSqVal := 0.0;
  {do all but the last bucket}
  for i := 0 to GapBucketCount-2 do begin
    Expected := p * IntPower(1-p, i) * NumGaps;
    ChiSqVal := ChiSqVal + (Sqr(Expected - Bucket[i]) / Expected);
  end;
  {do the last bucket}
  i := pred(GapBucketCount);
  Expected := IntPower(1-p, i) * NumGaps;
  ChiSqVal := ChiSqVal + (Sqr(Expected - Bucket[i]) / Expected);
  {return values}
  ChiSquare := ChiSqVal;
  DegsFreedom := pred(GapBucketCount);
end;
```

The Poker Test

The third test is known as the poker test. The random numbers are grouped into sets or "hands" of five, and the numbers are converted into "cards," each card actually being a digit from 0 to 9. The number of different cards in each hand is then counted (it'll be from one to five), and this result is bucketed. Because the probability of only one digit repeated five times is so low, it is generally grouped into the "two different digits" category. Apply the chi-squared test to the four buckets; there will be three degrees of freedom. The probability for each bucket is somewhat difficult to calculate (and involves some combinatorial values called Stirling numbers) so we won't present it here. If you are interested, the details can be found in *The Art of Computer Programming: Fundamental Algorithms* [11].

Listing 6.7: The poker test

```
procedure PokerTest(RandGen         : TtdBasePRNG;
                    var ChiSquare   : double;
                    var DegsFreedom : integer);
var
  i, j,
  BucketNumber,
  NumFives : integer;
  Accum, Divisor,
  Expected, ChiSqVal : double;
  Bucket : array [0..4] of integer;
  Flag : array [0..9] of boolean;
  p : array [0..4] of double;
begin
  {prepare}
  FillChar(Bucket, sizeof(Bucket), 0);
```

```
  NumFives := PokerCount div 5;
  {calc probabilities for each bucket, algorithm from Knuth}
  Accum := 1.0;
  Divisor := IntPower(10.0, 5);
  for i := 0 to 4 do begin
    Accum := Accum * (10.0 - i);
    p[i] := Accum * Stirling(5, succ(i)) / Divisor;
  end;
  {for each group of five random numbers, convert all five to a
  number between 1 and 10, count the number of different digits}
  for i := 1 to NumFives do begin
    FillChar(Flag, sizeof(Flag), 0);
    for j := 1 to 5 do begin
      Flag[trunc(RandGen.AsDouble * 10.0)] := true;
    end;
    BucketNumber := -1;
    for j := 0 to 9 do
      if Flag[j] then inc(BucketNumber);
    inc(Bucket[BucketNumber]);
  end;
  {Accumulate the first bucket into the second, do calc separately -
  it'll be the sum of the 'all the same' and 'two different digits'
  buckets}
  inc(Bucket[1], Bucket[0]);
  Expected := (p[0]+p[1]) * NumFives;
  ChiSqVal := Sqr(Expected - Bucket[1]) / Expected;
  {write the other buckets}
  for i := 2 to 4 do begin
    Expected := p[i] * NumFives;
    ChiSqVal := ChiSqVal + (Sqr(Expected - Bucket[i]) / Expected);
  end;
  {return values}
  ChiSquare := ChiSqVal;
  DegsFreedom := 3;
end;
```

The Coupon Collector's Test

The fourth test we'll use here is the coupon collector's test. The random numbers are read one by one and converted into a "coupon" or a number from 0 to 4. The length of the sequence required to get a complete set of the coupons (i.e., the digits 0 to 4) is counted; this will obviously vary from five onward. Once a full set is obtained, we start over. We bucket the lengths of these sequences and then apply the chi-squared test to the buckets. We'll use buckets for the sequence lengths from 5 to 19, and then have a composite bucket for every length after that. So, there are 16 buckets and hence 15 degrees of freedom. Again, like the poker test, the calculation of the probability for each bucket is somewhat mathematically intensive, so we won't present it here. Again, *The Art of Computer Programming: Fundamental Algorithms* [11] has the details.

Listing 6.8: The coupon collector's test

```
procedure CouponCollectorsTest(RandGen       : TtdBasePRNG;
                               var ChiSquare   : double;
                               var DegsFreedom : integer);
var
  NumSeqs, LenSeq, NumVals, NewVal,
  i : integer;
  Expected, ChiSqVal : double;
  Bucket : array [5..20] of integer;
  Occurs : array [0..4] of boolean;
  p : array [5..20] of double;
begin
  {calc probabilities for each bucket, algorithm from Knuth}
  p[20] := 1.0;
  for i := 5 to 19 do begin
    p[i] := (120.0 * Stirling(i-1, 4)) / IntPower(5.0, i);
    p[20] := p[20] - p[i];
  end;
  NumSeqs := 0;
  FillChar(Bucket, sizeof(Bucket), 0);
  while (NumSeqs < CouponCount) do begin
    {keep getting coupons (ie random numbers) until we have collected
    all five}
    LenSeq := 0;
    NumVals := 0;
    FillChar(Occurs, sizeof(Occurs), 0);
    repeat
      inc(LenSeq);
      NewVal := trunc(RandGen.AsDouble * 5);
      if not Occurs[NewVal] then begin
        Occurs[NewVal] := true;
        inc(NumVals);
      end;
    until (NumVals = 5);
    {update the relevant bucket depending on the number of coupons we
    had to collect}
    if (LenSeq > 20) then
      LenSeq := 20;
    inc(Bucket[LenSeq]);
    inc(NumSeqs);
  end;
  {calculate chi-square value}
  ChiSqVal := 0.0;
  for i := 5 to 20 do begin
```

```
    Expected := p[i] * NumSeqs;
    ChiSqVal := ChiSqVal + (Sqr(Expected - Bucket[i]) / Expected);
  end;
  {return values}
  ChiSquare := ChiSqVal;
  DegsFreedom := 15;
end;
```

Results of Applying Tests

On the book's CD is a test program that applies each of these tests to the standard Delphi random number generator and to the minimal standard random number generator. Figure 6.1 shows the result of one of these tests on the Delphi generator.

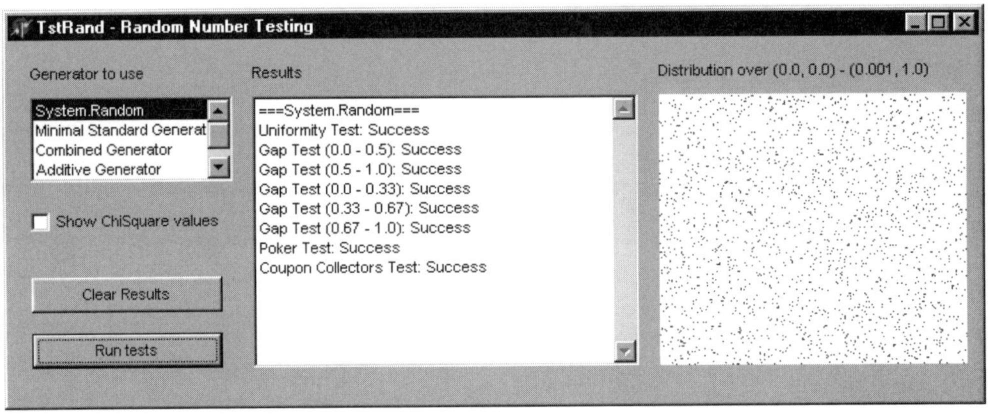

Figure 6.1: Testing the Delphi generator

As you can see, this particular test shows that the Delphi generator passes all of the tests. (By passing a test, the program means that the random number sequences applied to the test are not producing results that are significant at the 5% level.)

The display on the right-hand side of the window is a snapshot of the random numbers produced by the generator in a very thin slice of the unit square. The points are generated by calculating two random numbers: one for the *x* coordinate and one for the *y* coordinate. The points are then plotted if they fall in the rectangle (0.0, 0.0, 0.001, 1.0); in other words, the rectangle whose lower-left corner is at (0.0, 0.0) and whose upper-right corner is at (0.001, 1.0). To make it easier to see the points, this thin slice is stretched along the *x* axis. As you can see, the points are randomly scattered around this area; there is no pattern that we can discern.

You may be wondering why I'm making such a big deal about this display. Well, Figure 6.2 shows the same program displaying the results for the minimal standard random number generator. As you can see, the generator passes all the tests, but this time look at the distribution of the random points on the thin slice. You can see that the generator is producing a sequence of random numbers that, when plotted in this manner, is showing some regularity.

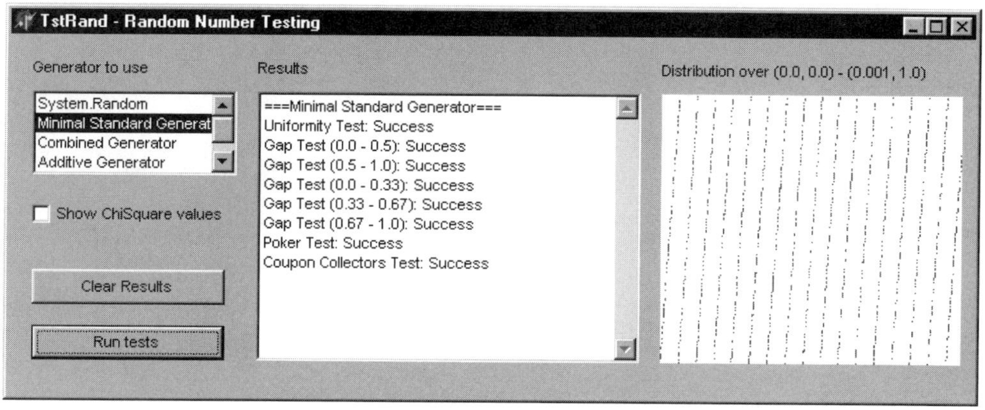

Figure 6.2: Testing the minimal standard generator

This regularity is certainly enough to reject the minimal standard generator in certain applications, especially those that require random numbers in pairs. This subtle regularity would be enough to skew the results of the application. Also, just because the Delphi generator does not show these kinds of regularities in a two-dimensional plane, maybe it shows them in hyper-planes of greater dimensions. There are tests we can run that show these regularities in *k*-dimensional space, but instead of getting bogged down in fairly esoteric random number sequence tests, let's look at how to use these simple random number generators in some way to further randomize their output. We'll look at three distinct methods, the first being known as a *combinatorial* method, the second as an *additive* method, and the final one as a *shuffling* method.

Combining Generators

What we do here is use two (or maybe more) multiplicative linear congruential generators with different cycle lengths in parallel. We generate the next number in sequence from both the first and second generators, and then subtract one from the other. If the answer is negative we add the cycle length from the first generator to force it positive.

Listing 6.9: Combining generators

```
type
  TtdCombinedPRNG = class(TtdBasePRNG)
    private
```

```
      FSeed1 : longint;
      FSeed2 : longint;
    protected
      procedure cpSetSeed1(aValue : longint);
      procedure cpSetSeed2(aValue : longint);
    public
      constructor Create(aSeed1, aSeed2 : longint);

      function AsDouble  : double; override;
      property Seed1 : longint read FSeed1 write cpSetSeed1;
      property Seed2 : longint read FSeed2 write cpSetSeed2;
  end;
constructor TtdCombinedPRNG.Create(aSeed1, aSeed2 : longint);
begin
  inherited Create;
  Seed1 := aSeed1;
  Seed2 := aSeed2;
end;
function TtdCombinedPRNG.AsDouble  : double;
const
  a1 = 40014;
  m1 = 2147483563;
  q1 = 53668;  {equals m1 div a1}
  r1 = 12211;  {equals m1 mod a1}
  a2 = 40692;
  m2 = 2147483399;
  q2 = 52774;  {equals m2 div a2}
  r2 = 3791;   {equals m2 mod a2}
  OneOverM1 : double = 1.0 / 2147483563.0;
var
  k : longint;
  Z : longint;
begin
  {advance first PRNG}
  k := FSeed1 div q1;
  FSeed1 := (a1 * (FSeed1 - (k * q1))) - (k * r1);
  if (FSeed1 <= 0) then
    inc(FSeed1, m1);
  {advance second PRNG}
  k := FSeed2 div q2;
  FSeed2 := (a2 * (FSeed2 - (k * q2))) - (k * r2);
  if (FSeed2 <= 0) then
    inc(FSeed2, m2);
  {combine the two seeds}
  Z := FSeed1 - FSeed2;
  if (Z <= 0) then
    Z := Z + m1 - 1;
  Result := Z * OneOverM1;
```

```
end;
procedure TtdCombinedPRNG.cpSetSeed1(aValue : longint);
const
  m1 = 2147483563;
begin
  if (aValue > 0) then
    FSeed1 := aValue
  else
    FSeed1 := GetTimeAsLong;
  {make sure that the seed is between 1 and m-1 inclusive}
  if (FSeed1 >= m1-1) then
    FSeed1 := FSeed1 - (m1 - 1) + 1;
end;
procedure TtdCombinedPRNG.cpSetSeed2(aValue : longint);
const
  m2 = 2147483399;
begin
  if (aValue > 0) then
    FSeed2 := aValue
  else
    FSeed2 := GetTimeAsLong;
  {make sure that the seed is between 1 and m-1 inclusive}
  if (FSeed2 >= m2-1) then
    FSeed2 := FSeed2 - (m2 - 1) + 1;
end;
```

As you can see from the AsDouble method in Listing 6.9 the combined generator has two multiplicative linear congruential generators, the first defined by $\{a, m\}=\{40014, 2147483563\}$ and the second by $\{a, m\}=\{40692, 2147483399\}$. The cycles of these are different but both are still of the order 2^{31}. The generator with the longest cycle is used to convert the longint intermediary value to a double value.

This generator removes the two-dimensional regularity of the simple multiplicative linear congruential generator, as can be seen by running the test program. The cycle of the combined generator can be shown to be approximately $2*10^{18}$. (For comparison, the Delphi generator has a cycle of about $4*10^{9}$.) The output of this combined generator is completely defined by two seeds, one for each internal generator, compared with just the one seed for the simple multiplicative generator.

Additive Generators

The second standard method of producing output that is "more random" from a simple generator is the *additive* method.

Here we initialize an array of floating-point numbers from a simple generator, such as the minimal standard random number generator. We have two indexes into this array, which we'll use to generate the sequence of random numbers in the following fashion. Add the two values pointed at by the two indexes and store the result in the element pointed at by the first index (if the sum is greater than 1.0, subtract 1.0 before storing the result). Return this value as the next random number. Now advance the two indexes by one, wrapping at the end of the array, if necessary. That's all there is to it.

Listing 6.10: Additive generator

```
type
  TtdAdditiveGenerator = class(TtdBasePRNG)
    private
      FInx1  : integer;
      FInx2  : integer;
      FPRNG  : TtdMinStandardPRNG;
      FTable : array [0..54] of double;
    protected
      procedure agSetSeed(aValue : longint);
      procedure agInitTable;
    public
      constructor Create(aSeed : longint);
      destructor Destroy; override;
      function AsDouble  : double; override;
      property Seed : longint write agSetSeed;
  end;
constructor TtdAdditiveGenerator.Create(aSeed : longint);
begin
  inherited Create;
  FPRNG := TtdMinStandardPRNG.Create(aSeed);
  agInitTable;
  FInx1 := 54;
  FInx2 := 23;
end;
destructor TtdAdditiveGenerator.Destroy;
begin
  FPRNG.Free;
  inherited Destroy;
end;
procedure TtdAdditiveGenerator.agSetSeed(aValue : longint);
begin
  FPRNG.Seed := aValue;
  agInitTable;
end;
procedure TtdAdditiveGenerator.agInitTable;
var
  i : integer;
```

```
begin
  for i := 54 downto 0 do
    FTable[i] := FPRNG.AsDouble;
end;
function TtdAdditiveGenerator.AsDouble  : double;
begin
  Result := FTable[FInx1] + FTable[FInx2];
  if (Result >= 1.0) then
    Result := Result - 1.0;
  FTable[FInx1] := Result;
  inc(FInx1);
  if (FInx1 >= 55) then
    FInx1 := 0;
  inc(FInx2);
  if (FInx2 >= 55) then
    FInx2 := 0;
end;
```

If you look closely at Listing 6.10, you'll see that we create and use a minimal standard random number generator to seed the table used by the additive generator. Although we can't read the "seed" for this generator (once it has been running for a while, the seed is equivalent to the whole table; the delegated internal PRNG is only used 55 times), we can set it. The write method will cause the internal PRNG to be seeded and then it will be used to initialize the internal table again.

The values for the size of the table, 55, and the initial values for the indexes, 54 and 23, are not guessed at; instead they have been shown to have good properties when the generator is used with integer values rather than the floating-point values that we are using. (*The Art of Computer Programming: Fundamental Algorithms* provides a table of other tables' sizes and initial index values [11].)

The great thing about this particular generator is its cycle length. To put it mildly, it is huge (with an implementation that uses longints, it can be shown that the cycle length is $2^{30}(2^{55}-1)$, or approximately $3*10^{25}$). Even if you could generate a trillion random numbers from this generator every second on your computer, it would still take over a million years to start the cycle afresh.

Shuffling Generators

The final generator we'll discuss that produces a "more random" sequence of random numbers is the shuffling algorithm. In this book, we'll discuss the variant that uses just one internal PRNG, although there is another that uses two in a similar manner.

Like the additive generator, we make use of a separate table of floating-point random numbers. The number of elements in this table is not overly important; Knuth suggests a number in the neighborhood of 100, and we'll use 97, a close prime [11]. (There is no reason for us to use a prime, by the way; to my eyes it just seems more fitting.) Fill the table with random numbers from a minimal standard random number generator. Set a further auxiliary variable to the next random number in the sequence.

When we need to generate the next random number from our shuffle generator, we calculate a random number between 0 and 96 using our auxiliary variable. Set the auxiliary variable to the number at that index in the table and replace that element with the next random number from our internal PRNG. The result is equal to the value of the auxiliary variable.

Listing 6.11: Shuffle generator

```
type
  TtdShuffleGenerator = class(TtdBasePRNG)
    private
      FAux        : double;
      FPRNG       : TtdMinStandardPRNG;
      FTable      : array [0..96] of double;
    protected
      procedure sgSetSeed(aValue : longint);
      procedure sgInitTable;
    public
      constructor Create(aSeed : longint);
      destructor Destroy; override;
      function AsDouble : double; override;
      property Seed : longint write sgSetSeed;
  end;
constructor TtdShuffleGenerator.Create(aSeed : longint);
begin
  inherited Create;
  FPRNG := TtdMinStandardPRNG.Create(aSeed);
  sgInitTable;
end;
destructor TtdShuffleGenerator.Destroy;
begin
  FPRNG.Free;
  inherited Destroy;
end;
function TtdShuffleGenerator.AsDouble : double;
var
  Inx : integer;
begin
  Inx := Trunc(FAux * 97.0);
  Result := FTable[Inx];
```

```
  FAux := Result;
  FTable[Inx] := FPRNG.AsDouble;
end;
procedure TtdShuffleGenerator.sgSetSeed(aValue : longint);
begin
  FPRNG.Seed := aValue;
  sgInitTable;
end;
procedure TtdShuffleGenerator.sgInitTable;
var
  i : integer;
begin
  for i := 96 downto 0 do
    FTable[i] := FPRNG.AsDouble;
  FAux := FPRNG.AsDouble;
end;
```

Considering that this generator produces the exact same random numbers as the minimal standard random number generator, it is impressive to use it in the test program on the CD and to notice that the regularity exhibited by the original generator has completely gone.

Against this we note that the cycle length for the shuffle generator is the same as for its internal generator. All that is happening here is that the numbers are coming out in a different order. We could change things by using another random number generator to supply the sequence of index values, and in this case the cycle would grow correspondingly. (If we use the two PRNGs provided in the combined generator, we would get the same cycle length.)

Summary of Generator Algorithms

In the preceding section we've seen various random number generators, all fairly simple. The final two generators provide the best sequences, but unfortunately have some hefty memory requirements (the final one needing nearly 800 bytes for its internal table). The minimal standard random number generator is probably the "worst," at least in the sense that it can have some bad regularities, but this can easily be hidden by using the shuffling algorithm. Personally speaking, I prefer the additive generator: it's simple, only requires the addition operator, has a huge cycle, and produces a good sequence of statistically independent random numbers. Its drawback is that, in order to save its state, you would have to save the entire table and the two indexes, which is enormous compared to the single longint seed of the minimal standard random number generator.

Other Random Number Distributions

If we are using random numbers to simulate a process, we'll find that the generators we've discussed so far are probably not up to the task. This is because they all produce a *uniform distribution* of random numbers—each random number is equally likely to appear as any other. If we were performing some kind of simulation, we'd probably require another probability distribution altogether. It turns out that we can use the random number generators we've been discussing up to now to calculate sequences with other distributions.

The next most important distribution after the uniform one is the *normal distribution* or *Gaussian distribution*. This distribution is also known as the *bell-shaped curve*, where all the data points are grouped equally about their mean, and data points far away from the mean are much more unlikely than data points closer to the mean. This distribution is important in statistics where we see it cropping up everywhere. For example, the heights of men of age 42 in a population follow a normal distribution. If we got a large number of people to measure a table with a ruler that is much smaller than the length of the table (in other words, there's an element of error involved), we'd get answers that follow a normal distribution. And so on and so forth.

For a normally distributed set of random numbers, we need to know the mean and the standard deviation of the numbers. Once this is known, we can easily produce a sequence of random numbers that would be normally distributed with this mean and standard deviation. We shall use the Box-Muller transformation, the derivation of which is beyond this book. This transformation requires two uniformly distributed random numbers and generates two normally distributed random numbers. This is awkward since we only generally want one random number at a time, but we can easily store the other ready for the next time the function is called. Note that, for multithreaded applications, this would make the function non-thread-safe since we must store the unused random number in a global variable. This can be avoided by encapsulating the calculation as a class.

Listing 6.12: Normally distributed random numbers

```
var
  NRGNextNumber : double;
  NRGNextIsSet  : boolean;
function NormalRandomNumber(aPRNG   : TtdBasePRNG;
                            aMean   : double;
                            aStdDev : double) : double;
var
  R1, R2     : double;
  RadiusSqrd : double;
```

```
  Factor      : double;
begin
  if NRGNextIsSet then begin
    Result := NRGNextNumber;
    NRGNextIsSet := false;
  end
  else begin
    {get two random numbers that define a point in the unit circle}
    repeat
      R1 := (2.0 * aPRNG.AsDouble) - 1.0;
      R2 := (2.0 * aPRNG.AsDouble) - 1.0;
      RadiusSqrd := sqr(R1) + sqr(R2);
    until (RadiusSqrd < 1.0) and (RadiusSqrd > 0.0);
    {apply Box-Muller transformation}
    Factor := sqrt(-2.0 * ln(RadiusSqrd) / RadiusSqrd);
    Result := R1 * Factor;
    NRGNextNumber := R2 * Factor;
    NRGNextIsSet := true;
end;
end;
```

Notice that we specifically avoid the extremely rare case that both uniform random numbers are 0, causing the radius-squared value to also be 0. Since we need to take the natural logarithm of this value (which is infinity), this situation should be avoided.

The other important distribution is the *exponential distribution*. These random numbers are used in simulation of "arrival time" situations, such as people arriving at a supermarket checkout. If people are arriving at a checkout one every x seconds on average, then the time in between two people arriving is exponentially distributed with mean x.

Generating random numbers with this distribution is fairly easy. Without going into the mathematics, if u is a uniformly distributed random number between 0.0 and 1.0, then the value e, where

$$e = -x \ln(u)$$

is exponentially distributed with mean x.

Listing 6.13: Exponentially distributed random numbers

```
function ExponentialRandomNumber(aPRNG  : TtdBasePRNG;
                                 aMean : double) : double;
var
  R : double;
begin
  repeat
    R := aPRNG.AsDouble;
```

```
  until (R<>0.0);
  Result := -aMean * ln(R);
end;
```

Notice again that we are avoiding the rare case where the uniform random number is 0, since we need to take the natural logarithm of this value.

Skip Lists

Having described in detail several random number generators, let's now look at a data structure that uses random numbers in order to provide probabilistic good run-time characteristics.

The code for the skip list class we shall be discussing can be found in TDSkpLst.pas on the CD.

Recall from Chapter 4 that if we wanted to find a particular item in a linked list, we had to start at the beginning and walk the list, following the Next pointers one by one, until we found the item we were seeking. If the list was sorted, we could employ a binary search technique to minimize the amount of comparisons we were doing, but still we had to follow the Next pointers in order to move along the list.

William Pugh, in his 1990 paper "Skip Lists: A Probabilistic Alternative to Balanced Trees" [18], showed that there was a better alternative to this with sorted linked lists if we were prepared to use bigger nodes with more forward links.

What Pugh invented was a variant of a linked list, but one that was a little out of the ordinary to say the least. At its lowest level it is a doubly linked list, with a forward link to the next node in the list and a backward link to the previous. However, he made some of the nodes in the skip list have another forward link that pointed to a node that was several nodes in front. This link skipped over a whole sequence of other, standard nodes. He then had some of these bigger nodes have yet another forward link that jumped even further ahead. And then again, some of these nodes had another link that skipped over even more nodes. The structure looks a little like Figure 6.3. Notice that eventually all links end at the tail node, and that the head node is the start for all forward links at every level.

Looking at Figure 6.3, you can see that, providing you use some of the new links, you'd be able to jump over huge swaths of smaller nodes, gradually taking smaller and smaller jumps, zeroing in on the item for which you're searching. We'll describe this search process a little more rigorously in a moment.

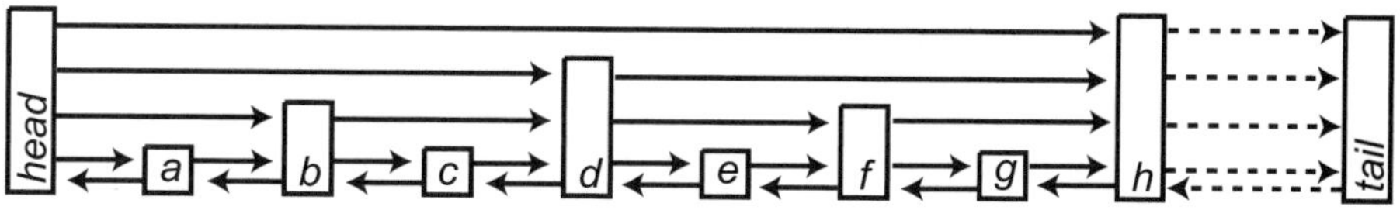

Figure 6.3: Diagrammatic representation of a skip list

Searching through a Skip List

If you look again at Figure 6.3, you'll notice that you can characterize the list as being several singly and doubly linked lists merged together. There is a doubly linked list at level 0, a singly linked list at level 1 that skips over single nodes (i.e., it links every second node), another singly linked list at level 2 that skips over three nodes (i.e., it links every fourth node), and another singly linked list at level 3 that skips over seven nodes (i.e., it links every eighth node). So, to find the node named *g*, for example, we could follow the link at level 2 from the head node to node *d*, then the link at level 1 to node *f*, and then the link at level 0 to get to node *g*. Hence, in theory, we only need to follow three links to get to that seventh node.

Having seen the search algorithm in general terms, let's be a little more rigorous. We shall assume that we have a skip list already built for our purposes. (We'll be looking at how to build it in a moment, but part of that process is going to be the search algorithm we're about to describe.) The search algorithm works like this:

1. Set a variable called LevelNumber to the highest level of links in our skip list (we assume that we have made a note of this through all our inserts and deletes as we built up the skip list).
2. Set a variable called BeforeNode to the dummy head node.
3. Follow the forward link at level LevelNumber from BeforeNode. Call the node we reach NextNode.
4. Compare the item at NextNode with the item we're seeking. If NextNode has the item we want, we're finished.
5. If the item at NextNode is less than the one we want, then the latter must be beyond NextNode, so set BeforeNode equal to NextNode, and continue at step 3.
6. If the item at NextNode is greater than the one we want, our item—if it exists at all in the skip list—must lie in between BeforeNode and NextNode. We decrease LevelNumber by one (in other words, we want to reduce the number of nodes we skip over).

7. If LevelNumber is 0 or greater, we continue at step 3. Otherwise, the item we seek is not to be found in the skip list and, if we were to insert it, it would appear in between BeforeNode and NextNode.

Following this algorithm to find *g* in Figure 6.3 we would start at level 3 and the head node. Follow the link at level 3 from the head node and we get to node *h*. We compare and find that *h* is greater than *g*. We, therefore, drop a level and start over. Follow the link at level 2 from the head node and we get to node *d*. Compare—*d* is less than *g* so we advance to node *d*. Follow the link at level 2 again and we get to *h*. Compare—it's larger, therefore, we drop a level. Follow the link from *d* at level 1 and we reach *f*. This is smaller so we advance. Follow the link at level 1 and we reach *h* again, which is greater. So we drop a level again and follow the link to finally reach *g*.

In doing so, we have followed six links and made six comparisons. This doesn't sound too hot; after all, if we were using a simple doubly linked list without a binary search we have followed seven links and made seven comparisons. However, Figure 6.3 makes an assumption that I've glossed over. The assumption is that a link at level $n+1$ jumps a distance twice that of level n. But why should it? Why not three times as far, or four, or five? In the skip list we'll build in this chapter, we shall jump four nodes at a time for level 1, 16 (i.e., 4*4 nodes) for level 2, 64 (i.e., 4^3 nodes) for level 3, and 4^n nodes for level n.

The reason for choosing four as our multiplier is that we have to balance the need for jumping major distances at high levels versus the length of the slower level 0 search at the end as we home in on the node we want. Four is a good compromise.

How big should the nodes grow then? If we assume that an item we are storing in the skip list is a pointer (much as we did for the linked lists in Chapter 3) then nodes at level 0 are at least three pointers in size (one data pointer, one forward pointer, one backward pointer), nodes at level 1 are four pointers in size (because now there are two forward pointers), at level 2 they're five pointers in size, and so on. Hence, at level n, nodes are at least $n+3$ pointers in size. (If we assume that the size of a pointer is 4 bytes, then these values are 12, 16, 20, and $4n+12$ bytes respectively.) In reality, to make a workable skip list, the nodes have to be at least 1 byte larger than this, because we will have to store the number of the level to which a node belongs.

Remember that a node at level n is able to point to another node 4^n nodes in front. If n were 16, we'd be able to jump over approximately 4 billion nodes, which is unachievable to say the least. In 32-bit operating systems, for example, each process only has access to 4 billion bytes, let alone 4 billion nodes of varying sizes. In reality, we would probably only use less than a million nodes, and so a maximum level of 11 (giving a total of 12 levels) will be ample. At the maximum level, we'd be jumping ahead 4 million nodes at a time.

From this discussion, we can easily work out a structure for a node in a skip list. It's a variable length structure, so that makes it a little more complicated to allocate and free nodes, but not especially so. Listing 6.14 shows the layout of a skip list node.

Listing 6.14: The layout of a skip list node

```
const
  tdcMaxSkipLevels = 12;
type
  PskNode = ^TskNode;
  TskNodeArray = array [0..pred(tdcMaxSkipLevels)] of PskNode;
  TskNode = packed record
    sknData      : pointer;
    sknLevel     : longint;
    sknPrev      : PskNode;
    sknNext      : TskNodeArray;
  end;
```

We won't actually ever declare a variable of type TskNode; instead, we will be dealing exclusively with variables of type PskNode, allocated on the heap. The size of the variable will be calculated as (3+sknLevel)*sizeof(pointer) + sizeof(longint).

Given the layout of a skip list node, we can now see Listing 6.15, which shows an implementation of the search routine for a skip list. This is an internal method to the TtdSkipList class that we'll be introducing. I designed the method to be used from both the Add and Remove methods of this class, and, as we'll see in a moment, one of its jobs is to build up a list of "before nodes" at every level.

Listing 6.15: Searching through a skip list

```
function TtdSkipList.slSearchPrim(aItem : pointer;
                              var aBeforeNodes : TskNodeArray) : boolean;
var
  Level  : integer;
  Walker : PskNode;
  Temp   : PskNode;
  CompareResult : integer;
begin
  {set the entire BeforeNodes array to refer to the head node}
  for Level := 0 to pred(tdcMaxSkipLevels) do
    aBeforeNodes[Level] := FHead;
```

```
  {initialize}
  Walker := FHead;
  Level := MaxLevel;
  {start zeroing in on the item we want}
  while (Level >= 0) do begin
    {get the next node at this level}
    Temp := Walker^.sknNext[Level];
    {if the next node is the tail, pretend that it is greater than the
     item we're looking for}
    if (Temp = FTail) then
      CompareResult := 1
    {otherwise, compare the next node's data with our item}
    else
      CompareResult := FCompare(Temp^.sknData, aItem);
    {if the node's data and item are equal, we found it; exit now,
    there's no need to go any further }
    if (CompareResult = 0) then begin
      aBeforeNodes[Level] := Walker;
      FCursor := Temp;
      Result := true;
      Exit;
    end;
    {if less than, then advance the walker node}
    if (CompareResult < 0) then begin
      Walker := Temp;
    end
    {if greater than, save the before node, drop down a level}
    else begin
      aBeforeNodes[Level] := Walker;
      dec(Level);
    end;
  end;
  {reaching this point means that the item was not found}
  Result := false;
end;
```

The method starts off by initializing every level of the aBeforeNodes array to the head node. Then we start off at the highest level of the skip list so far (MaxLevel) and follow the links at that level until we reach a node whose data is greater than the item we seek. Notice that we have a special case for the tail node, where we assume that the tail node compares greater than any node in the skip list. Unfortunately, with a class designed for any type of data, this check is necessary since we cannot preset the data for the tail node to be the largest value. If, on the other hand, we were designing the skip list class for strings, say, we could preset the tail node's data with a string that was guaranteed to be the largest string we'd encounter.

We then check the result of the comparison. If equal, we've found the node, so we can escape out of the method after setting various variables. If less than, we follow the link. If greater than, we set this level in the aBeforeNodes array and then drop a level.

Insertion into a Skip List

Having seen how to search for an item in a pre-existing skip list, we should consider how to build one by inserting items. Looking back at Figure 6.3, it looks like an impossible task to build this extremely regular structure through a series of unknown item insertions and deletions.

The cleverness of Pugh's insertion algorithm is that he realized that it was impossible—or rather, much too long-winded and time-consuming—to build the completely regular structure, so he proposed building a skip list that *on the average* approximated the regular structure. In a regular skip list with a jump factor of four, one node in four is a larger node with at least one extra forward pointer. One node out of four of these larger nodes is, in turn, itself a larger node with at least one extra forward pointer. We can continue in this vein, leading to the result that, for a large completely regular skip list, three-quarters of the nodes are level 0 nodes, three-sixteenths of them are level 1 nodes, three-sixty-fourths of them are level 2 nodes and so on. In other words, if we selected a node at random, we could state that the probability that it is a level 0 node is 0.75, that it is a level 1 node as 0.1875, a level 2 node as 0.046875, and so on.

Pugh's algorithm for insertion in a skip list replicates these probabilities, so that overall, there are approximately the right numbers of nodes at each level. This means that, *on the average*, the probabilistic skip list will work with the same efficiency as the fully "regular" skip list: some nodes will take longer to find, some a shorter time, but, averaged out, the probabilistic skip list performs the same as its regular yet unachievable cousin.

Armed with this information, we can now describe the insertion algorithm. We start off with an empty skip list. An empty skip list consists of a head node of level 11 and a tail node of level 0. All of the forward pointers in the head node point to the tail node. The tail node's backward pointer is set to point to the head node. The insertion algorithm works as follows.

1. Perform the search algorithm to find the item we are about to insert, with one extra detail. Every time we need to descend a level, store the value of BeforeNode before doing so. We'll end up with a set of values of BeforeNode, one for each level (since we've limited the number of levels to 12, we can use a simple array for this, one node per level).

2. If the item was found, we raise an error (we'll discuss why in a minute) and stop.
3. The node was not found. As I stated before, we know between which two nodes we have to insert the item. In addition, we know that we reached level zero during the search.
4. Set a variable called NewLevel to 0.
5. Using a random number generator, calculate a random number between 0 and 1.
6. If the number is less than 0.25, increment NewLevel.
7. If NewLevel is less than or equal to the current maximum level for the skip list (or 11), return to step 5.
8. If NewLevel is greater than the current maximum level for the skip list, set this latter value to NewLevel.
9. Create a node of level NewLevel and set its data pointer to the item we are inserting.
10. We now have to insert this node into the links at all levels up to NewLevel (that's why we stored all those values of BeforeNode during the search in step 1). This is done by merely applying the insert after method for the doubly linked list at level 0, and for each of the singly linked lists at levels 1 to NewLevel.

There are a couple of weird steps in this algorithm that need a little further explanation. Steps 5, 6, 7 and 8, for example, where we seem to be calculating a value for NewLevel: what is happening here? Well, firstly, we're calculating the size of the new node. Remember that we are trying to make the skip list have the required numbers of each size of node. So, we would like to create a node for level 0 three-fourths of the time, for level 1 three-sixteenths of the time, and so on. The loop described in steps 5, 6, and 7 is performing this calculation. Secondly, step 8 is making sure that we don't go off the deep end. There's no point in creating a node that is much larger than the current maximum, so we should limit it to only one more than the largest level.

Step 2 also bears some discussion. Essentially, what it is saying is that a skip list cannot have duplicate items—or, to be more strict, items that compare equal. Why? Imagine a skip list containing 42 nodes, all of value *a*. What does it mean then to search for item *a*? Because of the nature of the skip list, we'll jump over a whole set of items in the first step of the search algorithm to, say, the thirty-fifth, and find item *a*. We certainly didn't find the first one, or the last, but we did find one. Should we add a few steps to the algorithm to walk backward until we don't find any more items equal to *a* (and hence find the first one)? Some might say that we ought to add duplicate items in the order they were inserted. This would mean that when we insert an item, we should add it at the end of the set of possible duplicate items, and when we search for an item we should find the first in the set of possible duplicates. Of course, for the insertion algorithm we are supposed to maintain a list of "before nodes" as we descend the levels, and this would also get messier. In my view, the extra complexity is not worth it and is unnecessary. Presumably, if there was a possibility of duplicate items, we would know how to differentiate them; otherwise, they would truly be the same item. If we can differentiate them then presumably the comparison function should be able to do so as well. Hence, they are no longer duplicates.

Listing 6.16 shows the Add method for the skip list class. For the random number part of the algorithm, it uses a minimal standard random number generator from the first part of this chapter. Other than that, it follows the insertion algorithm pretty well.

Listing 6.16: Insertion into a skip list

```
procedure TtdSkipList.Add(aItem : pointer);
var
  i, Level    : integer;
  NewNode     : PskNode;
  BeforeNodes : TskNodeArray;
begin
  {search for the item and initialize the BeforeNodes array}
  if slSearchPrim(aItem, BeforeNodes) then
    slError(tdeSkpLstDupItem, 'Add');
  {calculate the level for the new node}
  Level := 0;
  while (Level <= MaxLevel) and (FPRNG.AsDouble < 0.25) do
    inc(Level);
  {if we've gone beyond the maximum level, save it}
  if (Level > MaxLevel) then
    inc(FMaxLevel);
  {allocate the new node}
  NewNode := slAllocNode(Level);
  NewNode^.sknData := aItem;
  {patch up the links on level 0 - a doubly linked list}
  NewNode^.sknPrev := BeforeNodes[0];
  NewNode^.sknNext[0] := BeforeNodes[0].sknNext[0];
  BeforeNodes[0].sknNext[0] := NewNode;
  NewNode^.sknNext[0]^.sknPrev := NewNode;
  {patch up the links on the other levels - all singly linked lists}
  for i := 1 to Level do begin
    NewNode^.sknNext[i] := BeforeNodes[i].sknNext[i];
    BeforeNodes[i].sknNext[i] := NewNode;
```

```
  end;
  {we now have one more node in the skip list}
  inc(FCount);
end;
```

Notice the check right at the start to make sure we don't add duplicate items. Another reason for this limitation is that the deletion process would become completely unwieldy, so let's discuss that algorithm now.

Deletion from a Skip List

Deleting a node from a skip list is fairly easy, albeit long-winded. The algorithm goes like this.

1. Find the item we wish to delete by the usual method.
2. Assume we find it at level *i*. Store the node just prior to ours that's on the same level as the *i*th item in an array. Set LevelNumber to *i*, and the node before in BeforeNode.
3. Decrease LevelNumber by one.
4. If LevelNumber is negative, continue at step 7.
5. Starting at BeforeNode, follow the links on level LevelNumber until we reach the item again. As we walk the forward links on level LevelNumber, keep a note of the parent of each node so that we can identify the node prior to ours on level LevelNumber.
6. Store this prior node in the array, in element LevelNumber. Set BeforeNode to this node. Continue at step 3.
7. When we reach this point, we have an array of prior nodes from level *i* down to 0. Perform the usual linked list "delete after" operations on each level.

Step 5 is guaranteed to work (i.e., we are guaranteed to always find the item we are trying to delete at every level) because a node at level *n* has a link at each level up to *n* pointing to it.

Listing 6.17 shows the Remove method from the skip list class. It is this method that performs the deletion code as described above.

Listing 6.17: Deletion from a skip list

```
procedure TtdSkipList.Remove(aItem : pointer);
var
  i, Level    : integer;
  Temp        : PskNode;
  BeforeNodes : TskNodeArray;
begin
```

```
  {search for the item and initialize the BeforeNodes array}
  if not slSearchPrim(aItem, BeforeNodes) then
    slError(tdeSkpLstItemMissing, 'Remove');
  {the only valid before nodes are from the skip list's maximum level
  down to this node's level; we need to get the before nodes for the
  others}
  Level := FCursor^.sknLevel;
  if (Level > 0) then begin
    for i := pred(Level) downto 0 do begin
      BeforeNodes[i] := BeforeNodes[i+1];
      while (BeforeNodes[i]^.sknNext[i]<>FCursor) do
        BeforeNodes[i] := BeforeNodes[i]^.sknNext[i];
    end;
  end;
  {patch up the links on level 0 - doubly linked list}
  BeforeNodes[0]^.sknNext[0] := FCursor^.sknNext[0];
  FCursor^.sknNext[0]^.sknPrev := BeforeNodes[0];
  {patch up the links on the other levels - all singly linked lists}
  for i := 1 to Level do
    BeforeNodes[i].sknNext[i] := FCursor^.sknNext[i];
  {reset cursor, dispose of the node}
  Temp := FCursor;
  FCursor := FCursor^.sknNext[0];
  slFreeNode(Temp);
  {we now have one less node in the skip list}
  dec(FCount);
end;
```

Full Skip List Class Implementation

Having shown the three complex operations for the skip list, we can now reveal the interface to the class itself. Unlike its simpler linked list brethren, the skip list class does not provide any array-like functionality. It's not that we couldn't add an access by index; it's just that the skip list is the first of the data structures in this book where it no longer makes sense to do so (others being the hash table and the binary tree). The reason for this is that providing the correct index for an item in the skip list necessitates walking the lowest level counting nodes. If we do that then there's no point any more for the complex structure of nodes and links to support longer jumps. Hence, we shall only provide the database-style MoveNext and MovePrior type functionality in our skip list class. To support this, of course, we provide an implicit, internal cursor for the class. Methods like MoveNext and MovePrior move the cursor along, Examine will return the item at the cursor, Delete will delete the item at the cursor, and so on.

Listing 6.18: Skip list class interface

```
type
  TtdSkipList = class
    private
      FCompare    : TtdCompareFunc;
      FCount      : integer;
      FCursor     : PskNode;
      FDispose    : TtdDisposeProc;
      FHead       : PskNode;
      FMaxLevel   : integer;
      FName       : TtdNameString;
      FPRNG       : TtdMinStandardPRNG;
      FTail       : PskNode;
    protected
      class function slAllocNode(aLevel : integer) : PskNode;
      procedure slError(aErrorCode  : integer;
                  const aMethodName : TtdNameString);
      procedure slFreeNode(aNode : PskNode);
      class procedure slGetNodeManagers;
      function slSearchPrim(aItem : pointer;
                        var aBeforeNodes : TskNodeArray) : boolean;
    public
      constructor Create(aCompare : TtdCompareFunc;
                         aDispose : TtdDisposeProc);
      destructor Destroy; override;
      procedure Add(aItem : pointer);
      procedure Clear;
      procedure Delete;
      function Examine : pointer;
      function IsAfterLast : boolean;
      function IsBeforeFirst : boolean;
      function IsEmpty : boolean;
      procedure MoveAfterLast;
      procedure MoveBeforeFirst;
      procedure MoveNext;
      procedure MovePrior;
      procedure Remove(aItem : pointer);
      function Search(aItem : pointer) : boolean;
      property Count : integer read FCount;
      property MaxLevel : integer read FMaxLevel;
      property Name : TtdNameString read FName write FName;
  end;
```

If you refer back to Chapter 3 on linked lists, you'll be able to determine the purpose of most of these methods and properties.

Like the linked list classes, we shall use a node manager to efficiently allocate and free nodes. However, with the skip list there is a small but important distinction: the nodes in a skip list are different sizes. In fact, there can be up to 12 different sized nodes in a skip list, and hence we should have 12 different node managers to manage them all. The slGetNodeManagers class procedure will make sure that all 12 node managers are properly initialized; this method is called from the Create constructor for the class. All skip list objects will use the same node managers. The finalization section of the unit will eventually destroy these node managers.

Listing 6.19: Constructor and destructor for the skip list class

```
constructor TtdSkipList.Create(aCompare : TtdCompareFunc;
                               aDispose : TtdDisposeProc);
var
  i : integer;
begin
  inherited Create;
  {the compare function cannot be nil}
  if not Assigned(aCompare) then
    slError(tdeSkpLstNoCompare, 'Create');
  {get the node managers}
  slGetNodeManagers;
  {allocate a head node}
  FHead := slAllocNode(pred(tdcMaxSkipLevels));
  FHead^.sknData := nil;
  {allocate a tail node}
  FTail := slAllocNode(0);
  FTail^.sknData := nil;
  {set the forward and back links in both the head and tail nodes}
  for i := 0 to pred(tdcMaxSkipLevels) do
    FHead^.sknNext[i] := FTail;
  FHead^.sknPrev := nil;
  FTail^.sknNext[0] := nil;
  FTail^.sknPrev := FHead;
  {set the cursor to the head node}
  FCursor := FHead;
  {save the compare function and the dispose procedure}
  FCompare := aCompare;
  FDispose := aDispose;
  {create a random number generator}
  FPRNG := TtdMinStandardPRNG.Create(0);
end;
destructor TtdSkipList.Destroy;
begin
  Clear;
  slFreeNode(FHead);
  slFreeNode(FTail);
  FPRNG.Free;
```

```
  inherited Destroy;
end;
```

The constructor takes a compare routine so that the skip list can properly order the items that will be added (this routine cannot be nil, obviously). It also takes a dispose procedure. If this routine is nil, the skip list is not a data owner and will not dispose of any of its items; if it is non-nil, the skip list is a data owner and will dispose of any items it needs to. The Create constructor creates the head and tail nodes and sets all their links to point to each other. Finally, a random number generator is created; this will be used in the Add method, as we've already seen.

The Destroy destructor clears the skip list by calling Clear, deallocates the head and tail nodes, and frees the random number generator.

The Clear method frees all the nodes between the head and tail nodes by walking the lowest level of the skip list and disposing of nodes as it goes.

Listing 6.20: Clearing a skip list

```
procedure TtdSkipList.Clear;
var
  i : integer;
  Walker, Temp : PskNode;
begin
  {walk level 0, freeing all the nodes}
  Walker := FHead^.sknNext[0];
  while (Walker<>FTail) do begin
    Temp := Walker;
    Walker := Walker^.sknNext[0];
    slFreeNode(Temp);
  end;
  {patch up the head and tail nodes}
  for i := 0 to pred(tdcMaxSkipLevels) do
    FHead^.sknNext[i] := FTail;
  FTail^.sknPrev := FHead;
  FCount := 0;
end;
```

The node allocation and disposal methods are fairly trivial. They use the node managers for the class and identify the particular node manager to use by means of a level value. For the allocation method, this value is passed in as a parameter; for the dispose method, this value is obtained from the node being freed.

Listing 6.21: Allocating and freeing nodes for the skip list

```
class function TtdSkipList.slAllocNode(aLevel : integer) : PskNode;
begin
  Result := SLNodeManager[aLevel].AllocNode;
  Result^.sknLevel := aLevel;
end;
procedure TtdSkipList.slFreeNode(aNode : PskNode);
begin
  if (aNode<>nil) then begin
    if Assigned(FDispose) then
      FDispose(aNode^.sknData);
    SLNodeManager[aNode^.sknLevel].FreeNode(aNode);
  end;
end;
class procedure TtdSkipList.slGetNodeManagers;
var
  i : integer;
begin
  {if the node managers haven't been allocated yet, do so}
  if (SLNodeManager[0] = nil) then
    for i := 0 to pred(tdcMaxSkipLevels) do
      SLNodeManager[i] := TtdNodeManager.Create(NodeSize[i]);
end;
```

Notice that the dispose method will free the item if the skip list was created as a data owner.

The remaining skip list methods are simple—none is more than a few lines of code.

Listing 6.22: Remaining skip list methods

```
procedure TtdSkipList.Delete;
begin
  {we can't delete at the head or tail}
  if (FCursor = FHead) or (FCursor = FTail) then
    slError(tdeListCannotDelete, 'Delete');
  {remove the cursor's item}
  Remove(FCursor^.sknData);
end;
function TtdSkipList.Examine : pointer;
begin
  Result := FCursor^.sknData;
end;
```

```
function TtdSkipList.IsAfterLast : boolean;
begin
  Result := FCursor = FTail;
end;
function TtdSkipList.IsBeforeFirst : boolean;
begin
  Result := FCursor = FHead;
end;
function TtdSkipList.IsEmpty : boolean;
begin
  Result := Count = 0;
end;
procedure TtdSkipList.MoveAfterLast;
begin
  FCursor := FTail;
end;
procedure TtdSkipList.MoveBeforeFirst;
begin
  FCursor := FHead;
end;
procedure TtdSkipList.MoveNext;
begin
  if (FCursor<>FTail) then
    FCursor := FCursor^.sknNext[0];
end;
procedure TtdSkipList.MovePrior;
begin
  if (FCursor<>FHead) then
    FCursor := FCursor^.sknPrev;
end;
```

There's one small problem, though, with using a set of node managers for the skip list that's not so readily apparent with the linked lists. The problem is one of thrashing. This becomes more and more obvious when you have millions of nodes. The thing about using node managers for the skip list is that neighboring nodes in the skip list will most likely be from different memory pages. If you sequentially walk the skip list from start to finish, you will come across nodes of different sizes and hence from different memory pages as you go, causing page swaps to occur. There's not a great deal we can do about this (and indeed, if we are using millions of nodes, the items for those nodes will probably be on different memory pages anyway) apart from using the standard Delphi heap manager. However, under these conditions, it is also likely that nodes directly allocated from the Delphi heap manager will also cause similar thrashing.

Summary

In this chapter we've looked at random numbers from two different viewpoints: the problem of generating a sequence of random numbers and an application of random numbers to create a data structure that has probabilistic run-time characteristics, rather than predictive ones.

We saw how to generate uniformly distributed random numbers using various methods, including a multiplicative congruential method, a combined method, an additive method, and a shuffle method. Not content with just presenting these methods as a fait accompli, we also discussed how to statistically show that the sequences produced were, to all intents and purposes, random. We also showed two important algorithms for generating random numbers with other distributions: the normal and the exponential distributions.

Finally, we discussed the skip list, a data structure used for storing items in sorted order. We saw how random numbers helped the structure attain good run-time characteristics.

Chapter 7

Hashing and Hash Tables

In Chapter 4, we looked at searching algorithms for finding an item in an array (for example, a TList) or in a linked list. The fastest general method we discussed was binary search, which required a sorted container. Binary search is a O(log(n)) algorithm. Thus, for 1,000 items, we'd need approximately 10 comparisons to either find a given item in a list, or to discover that it wasn't actually there (since $2^{10} = 1024$). Can we do better?

If we had to rely on a comparison function to help us identify an item, the answer would be no. Binary search is the best we could do.

However, if we could uniquely associate an index with an item, we can find the item at a stroke with just one access: simply retrieve the item at MyList[ItemIndex]. This is an example of a key-indexed search where the key for an item is transformed into an index and the item is retrieved from an array using this index. This is a completely different approach to binary search where, in essence, the key for an item is used to navigate through a data structure using a comparison-based method.

The transformation of the key for an item into an index value is called *hashing* and is performed by means of a *hash function*. The array used to store the items, with which the index value is used, is known as the *hash table*.

Enabling a search by use of hashing requires two separate algorithms. The first is a hashing process by which a key for an item is converted into an array index value. In a perfect world, different keys would hash to different index values, but we cannot guarantee this and often we'll find that two distinct keys will map to the same index value. Hence, the second algorithm we would need to consider is what we do when this happens. Two or more keys mapping to the same index is called, with obvious reasons, a *collision*, and the second algorithm required to correct this is known as *collision resolution*.

Hash tables are an excellent example of a tradeoff between speed and space. If the keys for the items we're considering were unique values of type word, all we would need to do would be to create an array of 65,536 elements, and we could guarantee to find an item with a particular word key in one operation. However, if we only wanted to store a maximum of 100 items, say, this is clearly excessive. Fast it may be, but 99.85% of the array would be empty. Going to the other extreme, we could get away with exactly the right amount of memory by allocating an array of the correct size, keeping the items in sorted order and using binary search. Slower, agreed, but no longer so wasteful of space. Hashing and hash tables allow us to strike a happy medium between these two opposing points of view. Hash tables will take up more room with some elements empty, but the hash function will enable us to find an item will very few accesses—usually one, if we're careful.

Eventually, what we want to do with our hash tables is this: we would like to insert items into the hash table; we would like to see if a particular item is in the hash table (the very fast search that prompted all this discussion); we would like to delete items from the hash table. We would also like to make the hash table extensible if required; in other words to be able to grow the hash table to accommodate more items than we expected.

Notice that the proposed functionality for a hash table says nothing about retrieving the entries in key order. All we're trying to do is design a data structure with very fast access to a particular record given a key, or to quickly return the fact that the key doesn't exist in the structure. Obviously, we also need to insert new records and their keys, and possibly delete existing ones. That's it.

If we also need that data structure to return the records in key sequence, we should look at binary search trees or skip lists or TStringLists. Hash tables don't do retrieval in key sequence.

First, however, we need to investigate the hash functions that would make these operations possible.

Hash Functions

The first algorithm we need to discuss is the hash function. This is the routine that will take the key for an item and magically transform it into an index value. If the hash table has room for *n* items, then the hash function obviously has to produce index values that lie in the range 0 to $n-1$ (we shall assume zero-based index values, as usual).

Since I've not really stated what type an item key may be, it's fairly clear that we'll have different hash functions for different key types. The hash function for an integer key will be different than a hash function for a string key. Ideally, the hash function should produce index values that seem to bear no relation to the keys; in other words, it should resemble a randomizing function in some sense. Thus, keys that are very similar would produce different hash values.

This is all a little theoretical. Let's investigate some hash functions to get an idea of what's good or bad.

The simplest case is that of integer keys where an item is uniquely known by an integer value. The easiest hash function we could use is the mod operator. If there are n elements in the hash table, we calculate the hash of key k by computing k mod n (if the answer comes out negative, just add n). For example, if n were 16, then key 6 would be hashed to index 6, key 44 to index 12, and so on. If the set of key values were randomly distributed this would be perfectly fine, but generally we'll find that the universe of key values is not so nicely distributed and we need to use a prime number as the hash table size.

> In fact, this can be codified as a rule for hash tables: always make the number of hash table entries prime. For full mathematical details, see *The Art of Computer Programming: Sorting and Searching* [13].

For string keys, the method of attack is to convert the string into an integer value and then apply the mod operator as above to get the index as a value in the range 0 to n–1.

So how do we convert a string into an integer? One way might be to use the length of the string key. This has the advantage of being very simple and fast, but has the disadvantage of generating numerous collisions. In fact, way too many collisions. For example, suppose we wanted to create a hash table to contain the names of the albums in your CD collection. Looking at my collection of several hundred CDs, the vast majority of the album titles are between 2 and 20 characters long. Using the length of the album title would result in collisions galore: *Bilingual* by Pet Shop Boys would clash with *Technique* by New Order and with *Mind Bomb* by The The. Altogether, a bad hash function.

Another, better hash function would be to typecast the first two characters of the key as a word value. We could then mod this with the hash table size to produce an index. This isn't a bad hash function with a pop or rock CD collection, but it's pretty dire with a classical CD collection: all of Beethoven's symphonies would hash to the same value, which would be the same value for all of Rachmaninov's symphonies and for the majority of Vaughan-Williams' symphonies.

We can take this idea a little further and make the hash function be the sum of all the ASCII values of the characters in the key, and mod the hash table size. For a CD collection this isn't too bad. Unfortunately, with many applications, the keys can be anagrams of each other and, of course, anagrams would collide with this scheme.

Simple Hash Function for Strings

The argument with the previous idea would seem to indicate that we should weight each character according to its position in the string to avoid collisions when using anagrams as keys. This results in the following implementation (the source code can be found in TDHshBse.pas on the CD).

Listing 7.1: Simple hash function for string keys

```
function TDSimpleHash(const aKey   : string;
                            aTableSize : integer) : integer;
var
  i : integer;
  Hash : longint;
begin
  Hash := 0;
  for i := 1 to length(aKey) do
    Hash := ((Hash * 17) + ord(aKey[i])) mod aTableSize;
  Result := Hash;
  if (Result < 0) then
    inc(Result, aTableSize);
end;
```

The routine accepts two parameters, the first being the string whose hash value is required, and the second being the hash table size (which we assume to be a prime number). The algorithm maintains a running hash value, initially set to zero. This hash value is modified for each character in the string by multiplying with a small prime number, 17, adding in the next character, and taking the modulus of the hash table size.

This routine is pretty good. It consists of just a couple of arithmetic operations per character—including a divide operation, unfortunately—and so is reasonably efficient. It so happens, in real life, string keys are pretty similar (think of the titles of pieces of classical music, for example), and this routine creates random-looking hashes from similar input. The final If statement is there because the intermediary value of the Hash variable could be negative (it's an annoying "feature" of Delphi's mod operator) and the caller of this routine will be expecting an answer between 0 and aTableSize–1.

The PJW Hash Functions

During the discussion on hash tables, the Dragon Book (*Compilers: Principles, Techniques, and Tools* by Aho, et al [2]) shows a hash function by P.J.

Weinberger (this routine is also known as the Executable and Linking Format (ELF) hash). This follows a similar algorithm to the routine in Listing 7.1, except it throws in a randomizing effect where the topmost nibble of the longint hash work variable (the nibble that is going to disappear due to the overflow from the next multiplication), if it is non-zero, is fed back into the low end of the variable by an XOR operation. The algorithm then ensures that the top nibble is set to zero, meaning that the final hash value will always be non-negative. (The source code can be found in TDHshBse.pas on the CD.)

Listing 7.2: PJW hash function for string keys

```
function TDPJWHash(const aKey   : string;
                         aTableSize  : integer) : integer;
var
  G    : longint;
  i    : integer;
  Hash : longint;
begin
  Hash := 0;
  for i := 1 to length(aKey) do begin
    Hash := (Hash shl 4) + ord(aKey[i]);
    G := Hash and $F0000000;
    if (G<>0) then
      Hash := Hash xor (G shr 24) xor G;
  end;
  Result := Hash mod aTableSize;
end;
```

This hash function is better than the simple hash function in a couple of ways. First is the randomization effect I discussed. Second, all operations performed for each character are bit shifts and fast logical AND, OR, NOT, and XOR operations (although it is finished off with a mod operation—inevitable, I'm afraid). This is probably the best hash function to use in a general case.

I won't say too much about other key data types, since they generally map quite nicely into either the integer case or the string case. As an example, let us consider hashing dates held in TDateTime variables. In the vast majority of applications, the values will be limited to a date later than a given date, say January 1, 1975. A pretty good hash function would be to take the date value you wish to hash and subtract the date for January 1, 1975, from it to give you the number of days from that start date. Now calculate the modulus using the hash table size.

We've been happily discussing generic hash functions with the understanding that they will sometimes generate equal hashes for different keys. But suppose we have a known list of 100 string keys. Is there any hash function that would generate a different hash value for each of these known keys so that we could use a hash table of exactly 100 elements? A hash function of this type is known as a perfect hash function. The theoretical answer is yes, of course; there are very many such functions (it's essentially a case of finding a permutation of the original keys). But how to find one? Unfortunately, the answer lies beyond the scope of this book. Indeed, even Knuth skips the topic [13]. In reality, perfect hashes tend to be of theoretical interest only. As soon as another key is required, the perfect hash function is broken and we need to develop another. Far better is to assume that there are no perfect hash functions and instead deal with the inevitable collisions that will occur.

Collision Resolution with Linear Probing

If we know the number of items the hash table is likely to contain, we could allocate a hash table to contain that number of items, plus a small extra reserve "just in case." There are several algorithms that have been devised that enable you to store the items in a table, using empty slots in the table to store items that collide with ones that are already present. This class of algorithms is called *open-addressing schemes*. The simplest open-addressing scheme is one called *linear probing*.

Let's explain by using a simple example. Suppose we are inserting surnames into a hash table. I know that I haven't really described what a hash table looks like yet, but for now imagine that it is a simple array of item pointers. Assume that we have a hash function of some pedigree or other.

To start off, we shall insert the name "Smith" into the empty hash table (i.e., insert the item whose key is "Smith"). We hash the key Smith with our hash function, and get the index value 42. We set element 42 of our hash table to Smith. The hash table now looks like this around this element:

```
Element 41: <empty>
Element 42: Smith
Element 43: <empty>
```

That was pretty easy. Let's now insert the name "Jones." We shall proceed as before: hash the key Jones and then insert Jones at the resulting index. Unfortunately, our hash function is of dubious provenance and hashes Jones to the value 42 again. We go to the hash table and notice that we have a collision: slot 42 is already taken up with Smith. What do we do? With linear probing, we try the next slot to see if it is empty. It is, so we set element 43 of our hash table to Jones. (If 43 were taken, we would have a look at the next slot, and so on, wrapping back to the beginning if we reach the end of the hash table. Eventually we'd find an empty slot, or we'd get back to where we started only to find that the table was full.) The act of checking a slot in the hash table is called a *probe*, whence the name of the algorithm, linear probing.

The hash table now looks like this around the area of interest:

```
Element 41: <empty>
Element 42: Smith
Element 43: Jones
Element 44: <empty>
```

Having inserted two items in our hypothetical hash table, let's see if we can find them again. We hash "Smith" to give an index of 42. We look at element 42 and find the Smith item right there. We hash Jones to give an index of 42. We look at element 42. It's the Smith item, which isn't the one we want. What we do then is the same as when we were inserting: we visit the next element in the hash table to see if it ours. As it happens, it is.

How about searching for an item that's not in the table? Let's search for "Brown." We hash with our hash function and get the index value 43. We visit element 43 and see that it's the item for Jones. We advance one step to element 44 and notice that it is empty. We can conclude that Brown is not in the hash table.

Advantages and Disadvantages of Linear Probing

In general, if there are few occupied slots in the hash table, we'd expect most searches, whether successful or unsuccessful, to take just one or two probes. Once the table gets pretty loaded with items, the number of empty slots would be very few, so we'd expect unsuccessful searches to take very many probes, even as much as n–1 probes if there was only one empty slot. In fact, if we are using an open addressing scheme like linear probing, it makes sense to ensure that the hash table *doesn't* get overloaded. Our probing sequences would get incredibly long otherwise.

All this is not too difficult. However, there are a couple of points worth mentioning about linear probing. The first thing to realize is that if there are n elements in a hash table, you can only insert n items (in fact, this is true for *any* open-addressing scheme). We'll investigate ways of expanding a hash table that uses open addressing in a moment. These dynamic hash tables would also enable us to avoid the long linear probe sequences that drastically cut efficiency.

The second point is the problem of clustering. If you use linear probing, you'll find that items tend to form clumps or clusters of occupied slots. Adding more items causes the clumps to grow in size, since it gets more and more likely that the inserted items collide with an item in a cluster. And, of course, as collisions get more likely, so the clusters grow in size.

We can illustrate this mathematically by using an ideal hash function that randomizes its input. Insert an item into an empty hash table. Let's say it ends up at index x. Insert another item. Since the hash function is essentially random there is a $1/n$ chance the new item ends up at any given slot. In particular, there is a $1/n$ chance it will collide with x and be inserted at $x+1$. It could end up directly at $x-1$ or $x+1$ as well, both with probability $1/n$, and therefore the probability that the second item starts a two-slot cluster is $3/n$.

After inserting the second item, we have three possible situations: the two items form a cluster, the two items are separated by one empty slot, or the two items are separated by more than one empty slot. These three cases have probabilities $3/n$, $2/n$, and $(n-5)/n$, respectively.

Insert a third item. In the first situation, it can grow the cluster with probability $4/n$. In the second situation, it can form a cluster with probability $5/n$. In the third situation, it can form a cluster with probability $6/n$. Add this lot up and you'll get a cluster after three items are inserted with probability $6/n-8/n^2$, roughly double the previous probability. We could continue calculating probabilities for more and more items, but it's not really profitable to do so. Instead we'll note that, when you insert an item, if there is a cluster with two items already present, you have a $4/n$ probability of growing that cluster. If there is a cluster with three items, the probability rises to $5/n$, and so on.

I'm sure you see that clusters, once they form, have a greater and greater probability of growing.

Clusters affect both the average number of probes required to find an existing item (known as a *hit*) and also the average number of probes required to show that an item does not exist in the hash table (known as a *miss*). In fact, Knuth showed that the average number of probes for a hit is approximately $\frac{1}{2}(1+1/(1-x))$ where x is the number of items in the hash table divided by the hash table size (this is known as the *load factor*), and the average number of probes for a miss is approximately $\frac{1}{2}(1+1/(1-x)^2)$ [13]. Despite the simple nature of these expressions, the mathematics required to prove them is hard indeed.

Using these formulae, we can work out that if the hash table is about half full, a hit requires about 1.5 probes, whereas a miss requires 2.5 probes, on average. If the table is two-thirds full, a hit requires about 2 probes and a miss 5 probes. If the table is 90 percent full, a hit requires on average 5.5 probes, but a miss requires an amazing 55.5 probes on average. As you can see, using a hash table with linear probing as its collision resolution scheme requires us to keep the table at most two-thirds full to enjoy acceptable efficiency. If we do manage to do this we'll reduce the effect clustering has on the efficiency of the hash table.

> This is an important point for hash tables that use linear probing as a collision method. You *cannot* let the hash table get too full; if you do, probe sequence lengths go through the roof. I've used "two-thirds full" as a limit for many years now and hash tables perform very well with it. Don't go above this, but, by all means, experiment with smaller values, for example, half full.

Deleting Items from a Linear Probe Hash Table

Before we look at some code, let us discuss deleting items from our hash table. It seems easy enough: hash the key for the item to delete, find it (using as many linear probes as required), and then mark the slot as empty. Unfortunately, this simplistic method causes some problems.

Suppose that our hash function hashes the keys Smith, Jones, and Brown to 42, 42, and 43 respectively. We add them in that order to an empty hash table, to result in the following situation:

```
Element 41: <empty>
Element 42: Smith
Element 43: Jones
Element 44: Brown
Element 45: <empty>
```

In other words, Smith inserts directly into slot 42, Jones collides with Smith and instead goes into slot 43, and Brown collides with Jones and goes into slot 44.

Delete Jones using our proposed deletion algorithm. The following situation results:

```
Element 41: <empty>
Element 42: Smith
Element 43: <empty>
Element 44: Brown
Element 45: <empty>
```

Now, the problem: try and find Brown. It hashes to the index 43. When we look at 43, though, it's empty, and according to our search algorithm that means that Brown is not present in the hash table. Wrong, of course.

Deleting an item from a hash table using linear probing therefore means that we cannot mark the slot as empty: the slot may form part of a linear probe sequence. We will have to mark the slot as “deleted” instead, and modify the search algorithm slightly to continue searching if a deleted slot is found.

We’d also have to modify the insertion algorithm slightly as well. Currently, to insert an item, we search for the item concerned (i.e., hash the item’s key and probe the resulting index and possible subsequent slots) until we either find it or we come across the first empty space. If we end up at an empty slot, we insert the new item there. (If we do find the item, we can either raise an error or we can just replace the existing item.)

Now, for efficiency’s sake, we will have to make a note of the first deleted slot we come across in our probe sequence. If we hit an empty slot, the item is not present. However, we don’t insert the item there at the empty slot; instead we back up and insert it at the first deleted slot we came across.

There is, of course, an important corollary to allowing the ability to delete items: if we do it too often we’ll populate the hash table with slots marked as deleted. This, in turn, will raise the average number of probes required for a hit or a miss, reducing the efficiency of the hash table. If the number of deleted slots rises too high, it will be highly advantageous to allocate a new hash table and copy all the items over.

So, given that deleting items will cause the efficiency of the hash table to decay, is there any other algorithm we could use? The answer, surprisingly perhaps, is yes. The algorithm goes like this. Delete the item according to our simplistic deletion scheme; in other words, mark the slot as empty. Once we’ve done this, we know that subsequent items may become unreachable by this operation—not *all* subsequent items, to be sure, only those *in the same cluster* as the item we just deleted. So, all we do is temporarily delete all items in the cluster that lie after the item we permanently deleted and reinsert them. We do it one at a time, obviously. In code, we would start at the slot after the one we just marked as empty and loop until we hit an empty slot (note that we don’t have to worry about an infinite loop here; we know there is at least one empty slot in the hash table since we created it). We mark each item’s slot as empty and then reinsert it.

Finally, let us consider the possibility of making the hash table dynamic. Making a hash table dynamic is really pretty easy, albeit time-consuming. If the load factor rises too much, we allocate a new hash table that is larger than the old one (say, roughly twice as large), transfer the items in the original hash table to the new one (note that the hash values for the items will change because the new hash table is larger), and finally free the old hash table. That’s all there is to it. The only small “gotcha” is that we ideally would want the new size of the hash table to be prime, like the original.

The Linear Probe Hash Table Class

Listing 7.3 shows the interface for our linear probe hash table (the entire source code for this class can be found in TDHshLnP.pas on the CD). There are a couple of things to note about this implementation. First, we make the convention that the key for an item is a string, separate from the item itself. This makes the underlying code a lot easier to understand, and also makes designing and using the hash table easier. In the vast majority of cases, keys will be strings anyway, and converting other data types to strings is usually pretty easy.

Another convention is that although the class will accept any hash function, the function must be of type TtdHashFunc.

```
type
  TtdHashFunc = function (const aKey   : string;
                          aTableSize   : integer) : integer;
```

If you look back to listings 7.1 and 7.2, you'll see that they're both of this type.

Listing 7.3: A linear probe hash table, TtdHashTableLinear

```
type
  TtdHashTableLinear = class
    {-a hash table that uses linear probing to resolve collisions}
    private
      FCount   : integer;
      FDispose: TtdDisposeProc;
      FHashFunc   : TtdHashFunc;
      FName    : TtdNameString;
      FTable   : TtdRecordList;
    protected
      procedure htlAlterTableSize(aNewTableSize : integer);
      procedure htlError(aErrorCode  : integer;
                   const aMethodName : TtdNameString);
      procedure htlGrowTable;
      function htlIndexOf(const aKey  : string;
                            var aSlot : pointer) : integer;
    public
      constructor Create(aTableSize : integer;
                         aHashFunc  : TtdHashFunc;
                         aDispose   : TtdDisposeProc);
      destructor Destroy; override;
      procedure Delete(const aKey : string);
      procedure Empty;
      function Find(const aKey  : string;
                      var aItem : pointer) : boolean;
      procedure Insert(const aKey : string; aItem : pointer);
```

```
    property Count : integer
      read FCount;
    property Name : TtdNameString
      read FName write FName;
end;
```

The public interface holds no surprises. There's a method to insert an item with its key, delete an item through its key, and search for an item given its key. We can empty the hash table of all items through the Clear method.

As you can see, we will be using a TtdRecordList instance to hold the hash table itself. The class interface doesn't give us any idea about the structure of the hash table elements, i.e., the slots; the unit hides it in the implementation section.

```
type
  PHashSlot = ^THashSlot;
  THashSlot = packed record
    {$IFDEF Delphi1}
    hsKey  : PString;
    {$ELSE}
    hsKey  : string;
    {$ENDIF}
    hsItem : pointer;
    hsInUse: boolean;
  end;
```

The slot is a record with three fields: the key, the item itself, and the state of the slot (whether it is in use or not). In Delphi 1, the key is a pointer to a string, whereas in later versions, it's a long string (which, of course, is a pointer in disguise).

The Create constructor allocates the record list instance, and the Destroy destructor frees it.

Listing 7.4: TtdHashTableLinear's constructor and destructor

```
constructor TtdHashTableLinear.Create(aTableSize : integer;
                                      aHashFunc  : TtdHashFunc;
                                      aDispose   : TtdDisposeProc);
begin
  inherited Create;
  FDispose := aDispose;
  if not Assigned(aHashFunc) then
    htlError(tdeHashTblNoHashFunc, 'Create');
  FHashFunc := aHashFunc;
  FTable := TtdRecordList.Create(sizeof(THashSlot));
  FTable.Name := ClassName + ': hash table';
  FTable.Count := TDGetClosestPrime(aTableSize);
```

```
end;
destructor TtdHashTableLinear.Destroy;
begin
  if (FTable<>nil) then begin
    Clear;
    FTable.Destroy;
  end;
  inherited Destroy;
end;
```

The constructor does make sure that the hash function is assigned. It's kind of pointless using a hash table without a hash function. The FTable instance is set up to contain a prime number of elements—the nearest prime number to the passed aTableSize value. The destructor makes sure to empty the hash table (contained items may need to be disposed of first) before freeing the FTable instance.

Let's take a look at the insertion of a new item. The Insert method takes a key for the item and the item and adds it to the hash table.

Listing 7.5: Inserting an item into a linear probe hash table

```
procedure TtdHashTableLinear.Insert(const aKey   : string;
                                          aItem  : pointer);
var
  Slot : pointer;
begin
  if (htlIndexOf(aKey, Slot)<>-1) then
    htlError(tdeHashTblKeyExists, 'Insert');
  if (Slot = nil) then
    htlError(tdeHashTblIsFull, 'Insert');
  with PHashSlot(Slot)^ do begin
    {$IFDEF Delphi1}
    hsKey := NewStr(aKey);
    {$ELSE}
    hsKey := aKey;
    {$ENDIF}
    hsItem := aItem;
    hsInUse := true;
  end;
  inc(FCount);
  {grow the table if we're over 2/3 full}
  if ((FCount * 3) > (FTable.Count * 2)) then
    htlGrowTable;
end;
```

There are several things going on here that are taken care of with protected helper methods. The first of these is htlIndexOf. This method tries to find a key in the hash table and returns its index if it was found together with a pointer to the slot containing the item (the Insert method takes this to be an error). If the key was *not* found, it returns –1, and this time it will return with a pointer to a slot where the item can be placed, which is exactly what happens next. (There is a third possibility: htlIndexOf returns –1 for the index and nil for the slot; this is taken to mean that the table is full.) At the end of the routine there is a check to see if the hash table is now over two-thirds full, which, as we discussed earlier, is a good trigger point to expand the hash table in size so that the load factor is reduced (the new expanded hash table would then be about one-third full). htlGrowTable does this for us.

The Delete method removes an item and its key from the hash table. As we already saw, the method must patch up any linear probe chains.

Listing 7.6: Deleting an item from a linear probe hash table

```
procedure TtdHashTableLinear.Delete(const aKey : string);
var
  Inx      : integer;
  ItemSlot : pointer;
  Slot     : PHashSlot;
  Key      : string;
  Item     : pointer;
begin
  {find the key}
  Inx := htlIndexOf(aKey, ItemSlot);
  if (Inx = -1) then
    htlError(tdeHashTblKeyNotFound, 'Delete');
  {delete the item and the key in this slot}
  with PHashSlot(ItemSlot)^ do begin
    if Assigned(FDispose) then
      FDispose(hsItem);
    {$IFDEF Delphi1}
    DisposeStr(hsKey);
    {$ELSE}
    hsKey := '';
    {$ENDIF}
    hsInUse := false;
  end;
  dec(FCount);
  {now reinsert all subsequent items until we reach an empty slot}
  inc(Inx);
  if (Inx = FTable.Count) then
    Inx := 0;
  Slot := PHashSlot(FTable[Inx]);
  while Slot^.hsInUse do begin
    {save the item and key; remove key from slot}
    Item := Slot^.hsItem;
    {$IFDEF Delphi1}
```

```
    Key := Slot^.hsKey^;
    DisposeStr(Slot^.hsKey);
    {$ELSE}
    Key := Slot^.hsKey;
    Slot^.hsKey := '';
    {$ENDIF}
    {mark the slot as empty}
    Slot^.hsInUse := false;
    dec(FCount);
    {reinsert the item and its key}
    Insert(Key, Item);
    {move to the next slot}
    inc(Inx);
    if (Inx = FTable.Count) then
      Inx := 0;
    Slot := PHashSlot(FTable[Inx]);
  end;
end;
```

Again, we call htlIndexOf, though this time it's an error if the key was not found. Once found, a pointer to the slot is returned, so we dispose of the item (if required) and the key. We set the state of the slot to "unused."

Now we reinsert all items that follow the one just deleted and are in the same cluster. This looks a little messy because of all the palaver with the key strings in the slots we visit. In order to avoid memory leaks, we have to make sure we free the key strings; the Insert method will reallocate them no matter what we do here.

A method that is closely allied to Delete is Clear, which is used for removing all items in the hash table.

Listing 7.7: Emptying a linear probe hash table

```
procedure TtdHashTableLinear.Clear;
var
  Inx : integer;
begin
  for Inx := 0 to pred(FTable.Count) do begin
    with PHashSlot(FTable[Inx])^ do begin
      if hsInUse then begin
        if Assigned(FDispose) then
          FDispose(hsItem);
        {$IFDEF Delphi1}
        DisposeStr(hsKey);
        {$ELSE}
        hsKey := '';
        {$ENDIF}
      end;
```

```
      hsInUse := false;
    end;
  end;
  FCount := 0;
end;
```

Because we are getting rid of all the items in the hash table, we can set the state of all the slots (once we've disposed of the keys and items in those slots that are in use) to "unused."

Searching for an item using its key is performed by the Find method. I'm sure that, having seen Insert and Delete, you can guess that it's merely a call to the ubiquitous htlIndexOf method.

Listing 7.8: Finding an item in a hash table given its key

```
function TtdHashTableLinear.Find(const aKey  : string;
                                   var aItem  : pointer) : boolean;
var
  Slot : pointer;
begin
  if (htlIndexOf(aKey, Slot)<>-1) then begin
    Result := true;
    aItem  := PHashSlot(Slot)^.hsItem;
  end
  else begin
    Result := false;
    aItem  := nil;
  end;
end;
```

As you see, nothing very challenging.

The methods that grow the hash table make use of a second method, htlAlterTableSize. Here are the two methods.

Listing 7.9: Changing the size of a linear probe hash table

```
procedure TtdHashTableLinear.htlAlterTableSize(aNewTableSize : integer);
var
  Inx      : integer;
  OldTable : TtdRecordList;
begin
  {save the old table}
  OldTable := FTable;
  {allocate a new table}
  FTable := TtdRecordList.Create(sizeof(THashSlot));
  try
    FTable.Count := aNewTableSize;
    {read through the old table and transfer over the keys & items}
```

```
    FCount  := 0;
    for Inx := 0 to pred(OldTable.Count) do
      with PHashSlot(OldTable[Inx])^ do
        if (hsState = hssInUse) then begin
          {$IFDEF Delphi1}
          Insert(hsKey^, hsItem);
          DisposeStr(hsKey);
          {$ELSE}
          Insert(hsKey, hsItem);
          hsKey := ''
          {$ENDIF}
        end;
  except
    {if we get an exception, try to clean up and leave the hash
     table in a consistent state}
     FTable.Free;
     FTable := OldTable;
     raise;
  end;
  {finally free the old table}
  OldTable.Free;
end;
procedure TtdHashTableLinear.htlGrowTable;
begin
  {make the table roughly twice as large as before}
  htlAlterTableSize(GetClosestPrime(succ(FTable.Count * 2)));
end;
```

The htlAlterTableSize method contains the meat of these operations. The method works by saving off the current hash table (i.e., the record list instance), allocating a new one, and then going through all the items in the old table (they'll be in the slots marked "in use") and inserting them into the new table. Finally, the old table is freed. Notice the Try..except block to attempt to make sure that the hash table is in a consistent state if an exception occurs. It does assume that the hash table is in a consistent state when the method is called, of course.

It should go without saying that to expand a hash table is time-consuming (and requires a lot of extra memory—double the amount we already have allocated). It is always far better to estimate the total number of strings we wish to insert into the hash table, and add, say, half that number again. Use the resulting value as an estimate to the hash table size when we create it. This estimate would give us some leeway in using our hash table.

After all that, let's take a look at the final piece of the puzzle: the shadowy htlIndexOf method, the primitive used by Insert, Delete, and Find.

Listing 7.10: Primitive to find a key in the hash table

```
function TtdHashTableLinear.htlIndexOf(const aKey  : string;
                                        var aSlot  : pointer)
                                                    : integer;
var
  Inx      : integer;
  CurSlot  : PHashSlot;
  FirstInx : integer;
begin
  {calculate the hash for the string, make a note of it so we can
   find out when (if) we wrap around the table completely}
  Inx := FHashFunc(aKey, FTable.Count);
  FirstInx := Inx;
  {do forever - we'll be exiting out of the loop when needed}
  while true do begin
    {with the current slot...}
    CurSlot := PHashSlot(FTable[Inx]);
    with CurSlot^ do begin
      if not hsInUse then begin
        {the slot is 'empty', we must stop the linear
         probe and return this slot}
        aSlot := CurSlot;
        Result := -1;
        Exit;
      end
      else begin
        {the slot is 'in use', we check to see if it's our
         key, if it is, exit returning the index and slot}
        {$IFDEF Delphi1}
        if (hsKey^ = aKey) then begin
        {$ELSE}
        if (hsKey = aKey) then begin
        {$ENDIF}
          aSlot := CurSlot;
          Result := Inx;
          Exit;
        end;
      end;
    end;
    {we didn't find the key or an empty slot this time around, so
    increment the index (taking care of the wraparound) and exit if
    we've got back to the start again}
    inc(Inx);
    if (Inx = FTable.Count) then
      Inx := 0;
    if (Inx = FirstInx) then begin
      aSlot := nil; {this signifies the table is full}
      Result:= -1;
```

```
      Exit;
    end;
  end;{forever loop}
end;
```

After some simple initialization, the htlIndexOf method calculates the hash value (i.e., the index value) for the passed key. It saves this value so that we can detect the case should we manage to wrap completely around the hash table.

A pointer to the reference slot is obtained. We look at the slot and perform different operations depending on the state of the slot. The first case is one where the slot is empty. If this point is reached, it means that the key was not found, and so we return the pointer to this very slot. Of course, the function result is –1 in this case to signify "not found."

The second case is that the slot is in use. We compare the key stored in the slot with the passed key to see if they are the same (notice we look for exact equality, i.e., a case-sensitive comparison; if you want case insensitivity, you'll have to use uppercased keys). If they are the same, the routine has found the correct item, so we return the slot pointer and set the function result to the index of the slot.

If we didn't exit from the method via these comparisons, we need to look at the next slot along. Hence we advance the index, Inx, making sure we check for wraparound and go around the loop again.

Note that the check to see whether we managed to visit every single slot is slightly superfluous. The hash table is dynamic and will keep the load factor between one-sixth and two-thirds, meaning that there should always be slots that aren't in use. However, it's good programming practice to perform the check, just in case the hash table gets enhanced in the future and some code causes the situation to occur.

The complete code for the TtdHashTableLinear class can be found in the TDHshLnP.pas file on the book's CD.

Other Open-Addressing Schemes

Although the hash table class we have just described has been designed to get around the main problem with the linear probe open-addressing scheme (the tendency for occupied slots to cluster), we'll take a brief look at some other open-addressing schemes.

Quadratic Probing

The first one is the quadratic probe. With this algorithm we try and avoid creating clusters by not always checking the next slot in sequence. Instead, we check slots that are farther and farther away. If the first probe is unsuccessful, we check the next slot. If that probe is unsuccessful, we check the slot four slots along. If *that* probe is unsuccessful, we check the slot nine slots along—and so on, with subsequent probes jumping 16, 25, 36, etc., slots along. This would help break up the clusters that we can see with linear probing, but it can lead to a couple of undesirable problems. The first one is that if many keys hash to the same index, their probe sequences would all follow the same path. They'd form a cluster, but one that seems to be spread throughout the hash table. The bigger problem, however, is the second one: quadratic probing does not guarantee to visit all the slots. In fact, the most that can be proven is that quadratic probing will visit at least half of the slots in a hash table if the table size is prime. That's all we have, an at least, not an at most.

You can show this for yourself. Start at slot 0 for an 11-slot hash table and see which slots you visit with quadratic probing. The sequence runs 0, 1, 5, 3, 8 before starting over at 0 again. We never visit slots 2, 4, 6, 7, and so on. This problem is enough to avoid quadratic probing altogether in my view, although it could be avoided by never letting the hash table get more than half full.

Pseudorandom Probing

The next alternative is pseudorandom probing. This algorithm needs a random number generator that we can reset at a particular point. Of the ones we introduced in Chapter 6, the best one for this algorithm would be the minimal standard random number generator since its state is completely defined by one longint value, the seed. The algorithm uses the following steps. Hash the key to give a hash value, but do *not* take the modulus with the table size. Set the generator's seed value to this hash value. Generate the first random floating-point number (it'll be between 0 and 1) and multiply it by the table size to give a integer value between 0 and the table size minus 1. This is the first probe point. If the slot is taken, generate the next random number, multiply by the table size, and then probe. Continue until you find an empty slot. Because the random number generator will produce the same random numbers in the same sequence given a particular starting value of the seed, we are guaranteed to have the same probe sequence for the same hash value.

Sounds pretty good. At the cost of some complex and lengthy calculations to get a random number, this algorithm will avoid all the clustering that's a consequence of linear probing. It has a small problem, though: there is no guarantee that the randomized sequence will visit every slot in the table.

Agreed, the probability of it continually missing an empty slot is pretty remote, but it could happen if the table is very full. What's worse is that the probe sequence could get very large before hitting an empty slot. Hence, it makes sense to ensure the table doesn't get very full, and to resize it if it does. At that point we might as well continue to use linear probing with a self-expanding hash table. It's simpler and faster.

Double Hashing

The final open-addressing scheme we will consider is that of double hashing. This is actually the most successful of the alternative open-addressing schemes. Here, we hash the item's key to an index value; call it h_1. Probe that slot. If it is occupied, we hash the key with another, totally separate and independent hashing algorithm to give another index value; call this one h_2. We probe slot h_1+h_2. If this is occupied, we probe slot h_1+2h_2, then h_1+3h_2, and so on (obviously, all calculations are done modulus the table size). The reasoning behind this algorithm goes like this: if two keys hash to the same index with the first hash function, it is extremely unlikely that they will hash to the same value with the second hash function. Thus, two keys that hash to the same slot initially will not follow the same probe sequence after that. We can avoid the "unavoidable" clustering with linear probing. If the table size is prime, the probe sequence will visit all slots before starting over, avoiding the problems with quadratic and pseudorandom probing. The only real problem with double hashing—apart from that of having to calculate an extra hash value—is that the second hash function must never return the value 0 for obvious reasons. This is simple to get around in practice by taking the modulus table size minus one (this will give a value between 0 and TableSize–2), and then adding one.

When using string keys, for example, you could call the Weinberger hash function, TDPJWHash, to calculate the primary hash, and then call the simple hash function, TDSimpleHash, to calculate the hash value used for skipping. I leave it as an easy exercise for the reader to implement this double hashing hash table.

Collision Resolution through Chaining

If we are willing to use extra space beyond the requirements of the hash table itself, there is another effective scheme for resolving collisions, a closed-addressing scheme. This method is called *chaining*. The principle behind it is very simple: hash the item's key to give an index value. Instead of storing the item at the slot given by the index value, we store the item in a singly linked list rooted at that slot.

Searching for an item is pretty easy. We hash the key to give an index, and we then search through the linked list rooted at that slot for the item we want.

We have several choices as to where to insert the item in the linked list. We could store it at the beginning of the linked list or at the end, or we could ensure that the linked lists are in sorted order and store the item into its correct sorted position. All three places have their advantages. The first option means that newly inserted items will be the ones found first when we search for them (a kind of stack-like effect), so it's for those applications where we will probably be searching for newer items more often than older ones. The second option means the opposite: the items found first will be the "oldest" (a queue-like effect), so it's for those cases where we are more likely to search for older items than newer ones. The third option is for those cases where we don't have a preference for finding the newest or oldest items, but we just want to find any item equally as quickly, in which case we can use a binary search to aid the search through the linked list. In fact, in my tests, the third option only has a noticeable effect if there are many items in each linked list. In practice, it's better to limit the average length of the linked lists by expanding the hash table if required. Some people have experimented by using binary search trees (see Chapter 8) at each slot instead of linked lists, but the benefits are not all that worthwhile.

The first option we mentioned above for inserting an item into a linked list has a nice corollary. When we successfully search for an item, we can move it to the beginning of its linked list on the premise that if we search for an item we will probably be searching for it again pretty soon. The items we search for most often will migrate to the tops of their respective linked lists.

Deleting an item is laughably easy, compared with the gyrations we went through in deleting an item from a linear probe hash table. Just search for the item in its correct linked list and unlink it. Chapter 3 showed us how to do that for a singly linked list.

Advantages and Disadvantages of Chaining

The advantages of chaining are fairly obvious. Firstly, we never run out of space in a hash table that uses chaining; we can continue adding items ad nauseam to the hash table and all that happens is that the linked lists just keep on growing. Insertion and deletion are extremely simple to implement—indeed, we've done most of the work in Chapter 3.

Despite its simple nature, chaining has one main disadvantage. This is that we never run out of space! The problem here is that the linked lists grow longer and longer and longer. The time taken to search through the linked lists grows as well, and since *every* meaningful operation we can do on a hash table involves searching for an item (recall the ubiquitous htlIndexOf method for the linear probe hash table class), we end up spending most of our time searching through the linked lists.

Notice something else though. For the linear probe collision resolution algorithm, we were deliberately trying to minimize the amount of probing we were doing by expanding the hash table when its load factor rose to a value above two-thirds. At that point, the analysis told us that, on average, a successful search would take two probes, and an unsuccessful one, five. Think about what a probe means; it is essentially a comparison of keys. The whole point of the hash table was to reduce the number of key comparisons to one or two; otherwise we might as well do binary search on a sorted array of strings. Well, in the case of using chaining to resolve collisions, each time we wander down a linked list trying to find a particular key, we are using comparisons to do it. Each comparison should equate to a "probe," using the terminology of the open-addressing case. So how many probes does chaining take, on average, for a successful search? For the chaining algorithm, the load factor is still calculated as the number of items divided by the number of slots (although this time it can rise above 1.0), and can be thought of as the average length of the linked lists attached to the hash table slots. If the load factor is F, then the average number of probes for a successful search is $F/2$. For an unsuccessful search, the average number of probes is F. (These results are for unsorted linked lists; if the linked lists were sorted, the values would be smaller, both equal to $\log_2(F)$ in theory). Suddenly, although chaining seems a better idea than open addressing on the surface, it doesn't look so good once you look at it under the hood.

The thrust of the previous argument is that, ideally, we should also grow a hash table that uses the chaining method of collision resolution. Using the methodology of migrating most-recently used items to the tops of their linked lists is also a valuable efficiency benefit

The Chained Hash Table Class

Time to look at some code. The public interface to the TtdHashTableChained class is roughly the same as that for the TtdHashTableLinear class, the differences between the classes manifesting themselves in the private and protected sections.

Listing 7.11: The TtdHashTableChained class

```
type
  TtdHashChainUsage = (        {Usage of hash table chains...}
                hcuFirst,      {..insert at the beginning}
                hcuLast);      {..insert at the end}
type
  TtdHashTableChained = class
    {-a hash table that uses chaining to resolve collisions}
    private
      FChainUsage   : TtdHashChainUsage;
      FCount        : integer;
      FDispose      : TtdDisposeProc;
      FHashFunc     : TtdHashFunc;
      FName         : TtdNameString;
      FTable        : TList;
      FNodeMgr      : TtdNodeManager;
      FMaxLoadFactor : integer;
    protected
      procedure htcSetMaxLoadFactor(aMLF : integer);

      procedure htcAllocHeads(aTable : TList);
      procedure htcAlterTableSize(aNewTableSize : integer);
      procedure htcError(aErrorCode : integer;
                    const aMethodName : TtdNameString);
      function htcFindPrim(const aKey    : string;
                           var aInx    : integer;
                           var aParent : pointer) : boolean;
      procedure htcFreeHeads(aTable : TList);
      procedure htcGrowTable;
    public
      constructor Create(aTableSize : integer;
                         aHashFunc  : TtdHashFunc;
                         aDispose   : TtdDisposeProc);
      destructor Destroy; override;

      procedure Delete(const aKey : string);
      procedure Clear;
      function Find(const aKey  : string;
                    var aItem : pointer) : boolean;
      procedure Insert(const aKey : string; aItem : pointer);

      property Count : integer
                 read FCount;
      property MaxLoadFactor : integer
                 read FMaxLoadFactor write htcSetMaxLoadFactor;
      property Name : TtdNameString
                 read FName write FName;
      property ChainUsage : TtdHashChainUsage
```

```
                   read FChainUsage write FChainUsage;
  end;
```

We declare a small enumerated type, TtdHashChainUsage, to denote whether we insert items at the front or end of a linked list. The class has a property, ChainUsage, that shows the class which method you wish to use.

The MaxLoadFactor property serves another tuning function. It details how long, on average, you wish to grow the linked lists at each slot. If the average length of the linked lists gets too large, the class will grow the internal hash table used to store the items and reinsert them all.

The MaxLoadFactor property can be difficult to use. What value should it have? Remember that one way to look at it is that it is equal to the average linked list length at each slot. If we were to follow the rule for linear probing where we select the load factor such that a search that misses takes five probes on average, then the value we should use for MaxLoadFactor should be a maximum of five.

There are other considerations though. Every probe makes a comparison between the key we search and the key in the hash table item. If the comparison takes a long time, such as a lengthy string, MaxLoadFactor must be smaller. If the comparison is much faster (for example, a shorter string, or an integer), the value for MaxLoadFactor can be larger. As with all tuning devices, you have to experiment to get the best results.

If you look carefully, you'll see our old friend the TtdNodeManager class being used (we'll see how in a moment). The Create constructor will allocate one, as well as a TList instance to hold the hash table. The Destroy destructor will free both of these instances.

Listing 7.12: The constructor and destructor for TtdHashTableChained

```
constructor TtdHashTableChained.Create(aTableSize : integer;
                                       aHashFunc  : TtdHashFunc;
                                       aDispose   : TtdDisposeProc);
begin
  inherited Create;
  FDispose := aDispose;
  if not Assigned(aHashFunc) then
    htcError(tdeHashTblNoHashFunc, 'Create');
  FHashFunc := aHashFunc;
  FTable := TList.Create;
  FTable.Count := TDGetClosestPrime(aTableSize);
  FNodeMgr := TtdNodeManager.Create(sizeof(THashedItem));
  htcAllocHeads(FTable);
  FMaxLoadFactor := 5;
```

```
end;
destructor TtdHashTableChained.Destroy;
begin
  if (FTable<>nil) then begin
    Clear;
    htcFreeHeads(FTable);
    FTable.Destroy;
  end;
  FNodeMgr.Free;
  inherited Destroy;
end;
```

The node manager that we create is for THashedItem nodes. This is the layout of this record type; it's much the same as that for TtdHashTableLinear except that we need a link field and we don't need an "in use" field (all items in the linked list are by definition "in use"; items that have been deleted from the hash table are not present in a linked list).

```
type
  PHashedItem = ^THashedItem;
  THashedItem = packed record
    hiNext : PHashedItem;
    hiItem : pointer;
    {$IFDEF Delphi1}
    hiKey  : PString;
    {$ELSE}
    hiKey  : string;
    {$ENDIF}
  end;
```

The constructor calls a method called htcAllocHeads to set up the initial empty hash table. This is what is going to happen. Each slot in the hash table will hold a pointer to a singly linked list (that's why we can use a TList for the hash table, since each slot holds just a pointer). To make the insertion and deletion of items easier, we allocate head nodes for each possible linked list, as discussed in Chapter 3. The destructor, of course, has to free these head nodes—this operation being done by the htcFreeHeads method.

Listing 7.13: Allocating and freeing the head nodes for the linked lists

```
procedure TtdHashTableChained.htcAllocHeads(aTable : TList);
var
  Inx  : integer;
begin
  for Inx := 0 to pred(aTable.Count) do
    aTable.List^[Inx] := FNodeMgr.AllocNodeClear;
end;
procedure TtdHashTableChained.htcFreeHeads(aTable : TList);
var
```

```
  Inx   : integer;
begin
  for Inx := 0 to pred(aTable.Count) do
    FNodeMgr.FreeNode(aTable.List^[Inx]);
end;
```

Let's now look at how we insert a new item and its string key into a hash table that uses chaining.

Listing 7.14: Inserting a new item into a chained hash table

```
procedure TtdHashTableChained.Insert(const aKey  : string;
                                           aItem : pointer);
var
  Inx     : integer;
  Parent  : pointer;
  NewNode : PHashedItem;
begin
  if htcFindPrim(aKey, Inx, Parent) then
    htcError(tdeHashTblKeyExists, 'Insert');
  NewNode := FNodeMgr.AllocNodeClear;
  {$IFDEF Delphi1}
  NewNode^.hiKey := NewStr(aKey);
  {$ELSE}
  NewNode^.hiKey := aKey;
  {$ENDIF}
  NewNode^.hiItem := aItem;
  NewNode^.hiNext := PHashedItem(Parent)^.hiNext;
  PHashedItem(Parent)^.hiNext := NewNode;
  inc(FCount);
  {grow the table if we're over the maximum load factor}
  if (FCount  > (FMaxLoadFactor * FTable.Count)) then
    htcGrowTable;
end;
```

The first thing that happens is we call a routine called htcFindPrim. This routine performs the same kind of operation that htlIndexOf did in the linear probe case: it attempts to find the key and return the item to where it was found. The method, however, is written with linked lists in mind. If it is successful in finding the key, it returns true, and also gives us the index of the slot in the hash table and a pointer to the parent of the item in the linked list. Why the parent? Well, if you recall from Chapter 3, the basic operations for a singly linked list involve inserting after a node and deleting the node after a given node. So, it makes more sense for htcFindPrim to return the parent of the node in which we are interested.

If the key isn't found, htcFindPrim returns false obviously, and also the index of the slot where the item should be inserted and the parent node after which it can successfully be inserted.

So, back to Insert. If the key was found, it's an error, of course. Otherwise, we allocate a new node from the node manager, set the item and the key, and then insert it immediately after the parent node we're given.

If the load factor of the hash table now reaches the maximum, we expand the hash table.

As you might have guessed, Delete works in a similar way.

Listing 7.15: Deleting an item from a chained hash table

```
procedure TtdHashTableChained.Delete(const aKey : string);
var
  Inx    : integer;
  Parent : pointer;
  Temp   : PHashedItem;
begin
  {find the key}
  if not htcFindPrim(aKey, Inx, Parent) then
    htcError(tdeHashTblKeyNotFound, 'Delete');
  {delete the item and the key in this node}
  Temp := PHashedItem(Parent)^.hiNext;
  if Assigned(FDispose) then
    FDispose(Temp^.hiItem);
  {$IFDEF Delphi1}
  DisposeStr(Temp^.hiKey);
  {$ELSE}
  Temp^.hiKey := '';
  {$ENDIF}
  {unlink the node and free it}
  PHashedItem(Parent)^.hiNext := Temp^.hiNext;
  FNodeMgr.FreeNode(Temp);
  dec(FCount);
end;
```

We try to find the key (if not found, it's an error) and then dispose of the returned item's contents and free it from the linked list. Notice, by the way, in both the Insert and the Delete methods, the ease of coding that the presence of the head node in each linked list gives us. There are no worries about the parent node being nil or not; htcFindPrim will always give us a valid parent node.

The Clear method is closely allied to Delete except that we just delete all the nodes from each linked list (apart from the head nodes, of course) in the standard manner.

Listing 7.16: Emptying a TtdHashTableChained hash table

```
procedure TtdHashTableChained.Clear;
var
  Inx : integer;
  Temp, Walker : PHashedItem;
begin
  for Inx := 0 to pred(FTable.Count) do begin
    Walker := PHashedItem(FTable.List^[Inx])^.hiNext;
    while (Walker<>nil) do begin
      if Assigned(FDispose) then
        FDispose(Walker^.hiItem);
      {$IFDEF Delphi1}
      DisposeStr(Walker^.hiKey);
      {$ELSE}
      Walker^.hiKey := '';
      {$ENDIF}
      Temp := Walker;
      Walker := Walker^.hiNext;
      FNodeMgr.FreeNode(Temp);
    end;
    PHashedItem(FTable.List^[Inx])^.hiNext := nil;
  end;
  FCount := 0;
end;
```

The Find method is simple since the main work is done by the ever-present htcFindPrim method.

Listing 7.17: Finding an item in a chained hash table

```
function TtdHashTableChained.Find(const aKey  : string;
                                    var aItem  : pointer) : boolean;
var
  Inx    : integer;
  Parent : pointer;
begin
  if htcFindPrim(aKey, Inx, Parent) then begin
    Result := true;
    aItem  := PHashedItem(Parent)^.hiNext^.hiItem;
  end
  else begin
    Result := false;
    aItem  := nil;
  end;
end;
```

The only slight weirdness is the fact that we must remember the htcFindPrim method returns the parent of the node we're really interested in.

Growing the hash table is not something we would really want to do, since it involves a lot of data movement. However, the class has an automatic operation to grow the table; the MaxLoadFactor property governs when this happens by calling htcGrowTable when we insert one too many items.

Listing 7.18: Growing a chained hash table

```
procedure TtdHashTableChained.htcGrowTable;
begin
  {make the table roughly twice as large as before}
  htcAlterTableSize(TDGetClosestPrime(succ(FTable.Count * 2)));
end;
procedure TtdHashTableChained.htcAlterTableSize(aNewTableSize : integer);
var
  Inx      : integer;
  OldTable : TList;
  Walker, Temp : PHashedItem;
begin
  {save the old table}
  OldTable := FTable;
  {allocate a new table}
  FTable := TList.Create;
  try
    FTable.Count := aNewTableSize;
    htcAllocHeads(FTable);
    {read through the old table and transfer over the keys and items to
    the new table by inserting them}
    FCount := 0;
    for Inx := 0 to pred(OldTable.Count) do begin
      Walker := PHashedItem(OldTable.List^[Inx])^.hiNext;
      while (Walker<>nil) do begin
        {$IFDEF Delphi1}
        Insert(Walker^.hiKey^, Walker^.hiItem);
        {$ELSE}
        Insert(Walker^.hiKey, Walker^.hiItem);
        {$ENDIF}
        Walker := Walker^.hiNext;
      end;
    end;
  except
    {if we get an exception, try to clean up and leave the hash
    table in a consistent state}
    Clear;
    htcFreeHeads(FTable);
    FTable.Free;
    FTable := OldTable;
    raise;
  end;
```

```
  {the new table is now fully populated with all the items and their
  keys, so destroy the old table and its linked lists}
  for Inx := 0 to pred(OldTable.Count) do begin
    Walker := PHashedItem(OldTable.List^[Inx])^.hiNext;
    while (Walker<>nil) do begin
      {$IFDEF Delphi1}
      DisposeStr(Walker^.hiKey);
      {$ELSE}
      Walker^.hiKey := '';
      {$ENDIF}
      Temp := Walker;
      Walker := Walker^.hiNext;
      FNodeMgr.FreeNode(Temp);
    end;
    PHashedItem(OldTable.List^[Inx])^.hiNext := nil;
  end;
  htcFreeHeads(OldTable);
  OldTable.Free;
end;
```

The htcAlterTableSize method is much more complex in this class than in the linear probe one. To enable us to recover gracefully from exceptions while we're growing the table, we do it in two stages. First, copy the items and their keys to the new larger table; second, dispose of the nodes in the old smaller table once the first stage is complete.

Finally we take a look at the powerhouse method used by many methods in the hash table, the htcFindPrim method (Listing 7.19).

Listing 7.19: Primitive to find an item in a chained hash table

```
function TtdHashTableChained.htcFindPrim(const aKey    : string;
                                           var aInx    : integer;
                                           var aParent : pointer) : boolean;
var
  Inx  : integer;
  Head, Walker, Parent : PHashedItem;
begin
  {calculate the hash for the string}
  Inx := FHashFunc(aKey, FTable.Count);
  {assume there's a linked list at the Inx'th slot}
  Head := PHashedItem(FTable.List^[Inx]);
  {start walking the linked list looking for the key}
  Parent := Head;
  Walker := Head^.hiNext;
  while (Walker<>nil) do begin
    {$IFDEF Delphi1}
    if (Walker^.hiKey^ = aKey) then begin
    {$ELSE}
```

```
    if (Walker^.hiKey = aKey) then begin
    {$ENDIF}
      if (ChainUsage = hcuFirst) and (Parent  Head) then begin
        Parent^.hiNext := Walker^.hiNext;
        Walker^.hiNext := Head^.hiNext;
        Head^.hiNext := Walker;
        Parent := Head;
      end;
      aInx := Inx;
      aParent := Parent;
      Result  := true;
      Exit;
    end;
    Parent := Walker;
    Walker := Walker^.hiNext;
  end;
  {if we reach here, the key was not found}
  aInx := Inx;
  if ChainUsage = hcuLast then
    aParent := Parent
  else
    aParent := Head;
  Result := false;
end;
```

We start out by hashing the passed key. This gives us the index of the slot, where we find the head of the linked list. We walk down the linked list until we find the item we are searching for or we hit the nil pointer signifying the end of the list. As we walk down the list we maintain a parent variable, since it is this node we have to return to the caller, not the pointer to the node for the item.

If the key was not found, we return either the node at the end of the list or the head node, the value being determined by the ChainUsage property. If this is set to hcuLast, we return the final node, if it is set to hcuFirst, the default for the class, we return the head node. That way, if the caller was the Insert method, we know that the new item will be inserted at the correct place. We return the index of the slot as well.

If the key was found and the ChainUsage property is set to hcuFirst, we must use the "move to front" methodology and move the found item to the first position in the linked list. With a singly linked list, this operation is of course simple and efficient. Finally, we return the parent node and the index of the slot.

The full source to the TtdHashTableChained class can be found in the TDHshChn.pas file on the CD.

Collision Resolution through Bucketing

There is a variant of the chaining method for collision resolution called *bucketing*. Instead of having a linked list at each slot, there is a *bucket*, essentially a fixed size array of items. When the hash table is created, we have to allocate the bucket for each slot and mark all the elements in each bucket as "empty."

To insert an item, we hash the key for the item to find the slot number. We then look at each element in the bucket until we find one that is marked as empty and set it to the item we're trying to insert (obviously, if we find the item already in the bucket, we signal an error).

But what happens when there are no more empty elements in the bucket? What do we do then? There are two possibilities, one that follows the linear probe approach and one that uses overflow buckets.

When we run out of space in the required bucket, plan A is to have a look at the bucket in the next slot and see if there's room there. We continue like this, visiting slots and their buckets until we find an element that is empty and we put our item there. This method is the direct analogue of the linear probe algorithm (indeed, if the buckets are all one element long, this *is* the linear probe method). As a consequence, it suffers from the same kind of problems. For example, deleting items from the hash table requires us not to break probe chains. If the bucket is not full, we can just remove the item from the bucket and move the subsequent items in the bucket up by one. If the bucket is full, items for this bucket may have overflowed into another bucket, so we either mark the item as deleted, or we reinsert subsequent items, including those in following buckets until we reach an empty bucket element.

Plan B is to have overflow buckets. What happens here is that the hash table has an extra bucket that doesn't take part in the normal usage of the hash table; this bucket is known as the *overflow bucket*. If, when inserting an item, there is no room for it in the bucket, we have a look in the overflow bucket for an empty element and place it there. The overflow bucket thus has overflow items from every normal bucket. If the overflow bucket itself fills, we just allocate another and continue. Finding an item with this data structure involves our looking at every item in the bucket we hashed the key to, and if it is full, looking at every item in every overflow bucket until we reach an empty element. Deleting an item from such a hash table is inefficient indeed, even to the point of not allowing it. The only method that makes sense is to mark elements as deleted; otherwise, if we wanted to delete an item from the correct full bucket, we'd have to reinsert every item that's present in the overflow buckets.

So why consider bucketing at all? Well, it's probably the best data structure for hash tables on disk.

Hash Tables on Disk

The controllers for permanent storage devices such as disks, floppies, Zip drives, and tapes are designed to read and write data a block at a time. These blocks are usually some power-of-two bytes in size, like 512 bytes, 1,024 bytes, or 4,096 bytes. Since the controller must read a complete block even when it only needs a few bytes, it makes sense to capitalize on this behavior.

Suppose you wish to write an application that uses a large number of records stored on disk. The records are to be randomly accessed by key, each record having a separate, unique string key. This is an ideal use of a hash table, but the records are so numerous and large that you can't read them all into memory at once. Indeed, it doesn't make sense to do so, since we can assume that the majority of them wouldn't even be required in any one run of the program.

An example of such an application is a point-of-sale system at a large grocery supermarket. There may be hundreds of thousands of different items for sale in the store, of which the average shopper only buys a hundred, let's say. This is an ideal application for a hash table: each item in the store is known by its UPC code, a 12-digit string value, which is a unique key for each item. Thus the application at the checkout uses the scanned UPC code to hash into a hash table and then to the item's record.

Notice, however, that a disk-based hash table is only good for retrieval-type processing: given a key, it returns the record. Like its in-memory cousin, a disk-based hash table is no good for returning records in sequence.

The first file we shall create is the data file, consisting of many equal-sized records, each one describing a single item. We will, of course, use the TtdRecordFile class from Chapter 2 for this purpose.

The index file is the second file in our hash database duo. Again, we don't want to read the entire index into memory; for example, if each key was 10 digits long, and the record number associated with each key was 4 bytes long, the minimum amount of storage per key would be 15 bytes (we assume the key either has a zero terminator or a preceding length byte). If we have 100,000 items, that makes a minimum of 1,500,000 bytes for the hash table index in memory. Of course, we are allocating the key strings in our hash table on the heap, and so there will be yet more overhead (for example, in

32-bit, each string on the heap has an extra three longints of overhead). Far better would be to read chunks of the index when we need them.

Enter bucketing. We shall make use of fixed size buckets in our hash table index, so that when we have a key, we can hash it to obtain the bucket number required, read it from the index file, and then search through the bucket for the key we want. Sounds simple enough, but of course, we must consider what happens when a bucket overflows.

Extendible Hashing

The algorithm we need to use is called *extendible hashing*, and to use it we need to go back to square one with our hash function.

Originally, we knew the size of our hash table and so, when we hashed a key, we would then immediately mod it with the table size and use the result as an index into our hash table. With extendible hashing, on the other hand, we do not know how big our hash table is, since it will grow whenever required to avoid a bucket overflow. In previous versions of our hash tables, we've grown them when we needed to, in a rehash-everything-in-sight fashion. With hash tables on disk, this method is overkill; the majority of our time would be spent in disk I/O. With extendible hashing, we only reorganize a very small part of the hash table—basically just the bucket that is overflowing.

Our hash function is now going to return a longint value instead. If you look back at the original PJW hash function, you'll see that it was calculating a 32-bit hash value (actually a 28-bit value since the top four bits were always forced to zero), and then the result was this value mod the table size. Well, with extensible hashing, we don't do the final mod, we just use the entire hash value.

Does that mean we have a hash table with 268 million slots? No, and this is where the clever stuff comes in. What we use is just a couple of bits of the hash value, and as the table fills up, we start to use more and more bits of the hash value.

Let's see how this works by filling up a hypothetical hash table. Initially, there is one bucket. We shall assume that each bucket will hold 10 hash values, plus a record number for each hash value so that we can retrieve the record. Notice that we do not place the keys themselves in the buckets; with a 28-bit hash value, we will be unlucky to have two keys hash to the same value. (It will happen so rarely, in fact, that we can retrieve the record itself in order to check its key, without slowing down the entire process. Of course, this argument assumes that our hash function is a good randomizer.)

Let's start inserting hash values and their record numbers into the table. With only one bucket, there's only one place for them to go, so after 10 insertions we've filled the bucket. We split the full bucket into two buckets the same size, and reinsert all the items we had in the original bucket into the two buckets. We insert all items that have a hash that ends in a zero bit into one bucket and those that end in a one bit into the other. These two buckets are said to have a *bit-depth* of one bit. Each time we now insert a hash/record number pair, we shall look at the last bit of the hash and this tells us which bucket to put it in.

Eventually, we'll fill up another of the buckets. Let's assume that it's the bucket where we're inserting all hashes that end in 0. Again, we split the bucket into two separate buckets. This time we say that all items with hashes that end in two zero bits, 00, go into the first bucket and all those with hashes that end in 10 go into the second bucket. Both buckets have a bit-depth of 2, since we need to look at the bottom two bits of a hash to decide where to insert it. We now have three buckets, one accepting hashes ending in 00, one for those ending in 10, and one for those just ending in 1.

Let's suppose we continue and manage to fill up the 10 bucket. Again we split the full bucket into two and reinsert all the items in the bucket into the two new buckets. This time the two new buckets will accept hashes ending in 010 and 110. So now we have four buckets: one of bit-depth 1 accepting hashes ending in 1, one of bit-depth 2 holding hashes ending in 00, and two of bit-depth 3 for hashes ending in 010 and 110.

I'm sure you now have a flavor of how extendible hashing works—the rest is merely housekeeping.

To maintain the mapping of which hashes go into which buckets, we use a structure called a *directory*. Essentially, the directory has a list of possible hash endings and the associated bucket number for each. Rather than try and maintain some bizarre set of bit-depths and values, the directory maintains its own bit-depth value equal to the maximum bucket bit-depth value, and has a slot for every value that can be expressed with that bit-depth.

At the point where we stopped with our example, the maximum bucket bit-depth was 3, and so the directory bit-depth has this value, too. There are eight possible bit patterns that can be formed of three bits: 000, 001, 010, 011, 100, 101, 110, and 111. All those patterns that end in 1 (i.e., the second, fourth, sixth, and eighth values) all point to the same bucket, the one that accepts items with hashes ending in 1. Similarly, the directory entries for 000 and 100 both point to the same bucket, the one that accepts items with hashes ending in 00.

However, this scheme leaves something to be desired. The two directory entries that point to the bucket for items whose hashes end in 00 are separated by three other directory entries. Similarly, the single bucket that accepts all items whose hashes end in 1 has four directory entries spread equally through the directory. When we split a bucket, it and its buddy bucket (the one that will take half of its items) will not be neighbors in the directory. In the discussion that follows, it will be simpler to assume that directory entries for the same bucket are neighbors so that when a bucket is split, it will be next to its buddy bucket.

The answer is to *reverse* the last bits in the hash to calculate the directory index entry. So, for example, if the hash ends in 001, we don't go to directory entry 001 to look for the bucket. Instead we use entry 100 (4, which is 001 reversed). This makes the directory much simpler to use. In our example, hashes ending in 00 go to either directory entry 000 (0) or 001 (1); hashes ending in 010 go to directory entry 010 (2); hashes ending in 110 go to entry 011 (3); and hashes ending in a 1 go to 100, 101, 110, or 111 (4, 5, 6, 7).

Let's go back and insert items into an empty extendible hash table in the same manner as before. Figure 7.1 shows the steps. We start off with a directory with only one entry at index 0 (a). This is counted as having bit-depth 0. We fill the single bucket up (call it *A*) and need to split it. First, we increase the directory to bit-depth 1, in other words, to have two entries (b). This will create two buckets, one pointed to by entry 0 (the original *A*) and one pointed to by entry 1, *B* (c). We put all items with hashes ending in 0 in *A* and the rest in *B*. We fill up bucket *A* again. We now need to increase the directory bit- depth from 1 to 2, in order to have a possible four buckets. Before we split the bucket that's full, directory entries 00 and 01 will point to the original bucket *A*, and entries 10 and 11 will point to bucket *B* (d). The *A* bucket gets split into a bucket that accepts 00 hashes (*A* again) and one that accepts 10 hashes, *C*. *A* will be pointed at by the 00 directory entry and *C* by the 01 entry (e). Finally, bucket *C* (which is pointed to by the 01 directory entry) fills up. We have to increase the directory bit-depth again, this time to 3 bits. Entries 000 and 001 now point to the *A* bucket, entries 010 and 011 point to the *C* bucket, and entries 100, 101, 110, and 111 all point to the *B* bucket (f). We create a new bucket, *D*, and reinsert all the items in *C* to be in *C* and *D*, with the former at directory entry 010 (2) accepting hashes ending in 010 and the latter at directory entry 011 (3) accepting hashes ending in 110(g).

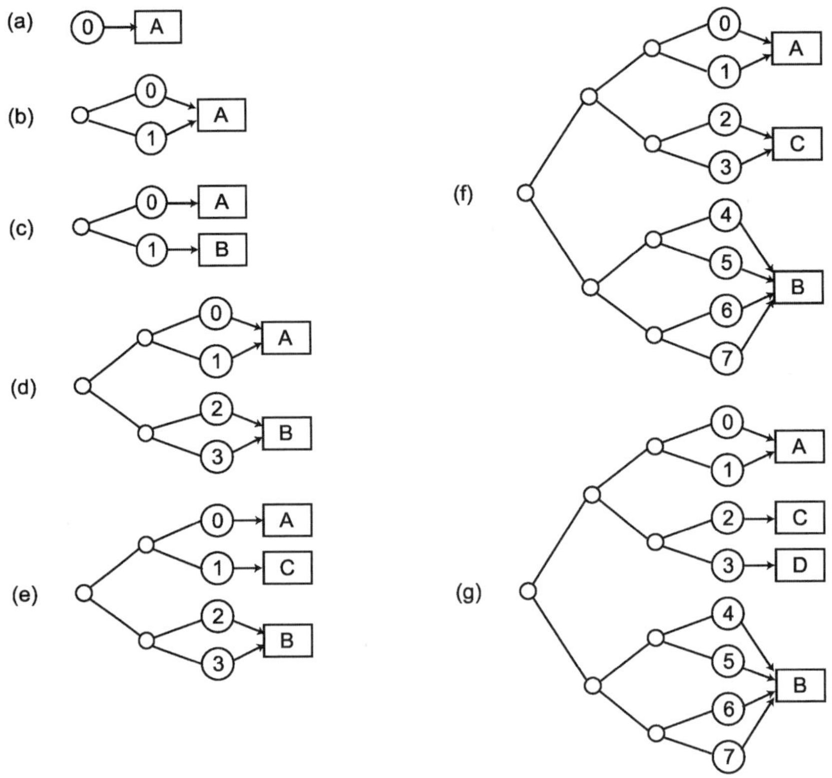

Figure 7.1: Inserting into an extendible hash table

Now that we've seen the basic algorithm, it's time to flesh it out in practical terms. Firstly, we store all of the pieces of an extendible hash table in separate files: the directory, the buckets, and the records. For the buckets and the records we use the TtdRecordStream to store them (actually we'll use the file-based descendant TtdRecordFile, but internally to the extendible hash table we'll assume it's just a stream). The directory can be stored in and retrieved from any TStream descendant, though it obviously makes sense to use a TFileStream for permanency.

The directory is the next easiest part to extract and implement. The interface to it is shown in Listing 7.20.

Listing 7.20: The interface to the TtdHashDirectory class

```
type
  TtdHashDirectory = class
    private
      FCount  : integer;
      FDepth  : integer;
      FList   : TList;
      FName   : TtdNameString;
```

```
    FStream : TStream;
  protected
    function hdGetItem(aInx : integer) : longint;
    procedure hdSetItem(aInx : integer; aValue : longint);
    function hdErrorMsg(aErrorCode  : integer;
                  const aMethodName : TtdNameString;
                        aIndex      : integer) : string;
    procedure hdLoadFromStream;
    procedure hdStoreToStream;
  public
    constructor Create(aStream : TStream);
    destructor Destroy; override;
    procedure DoubleCount;
    property Count : integer read FCount;
    property Depth : integer read FDepth;
    property Items[aInx : integer] : longint
                read hdGetItem write hdSetItem; default;
    property Name : TtdNameString
                read FName write FName;
end;
```

This public interface is enough to get us going. We can double the number of items in the directory using the DoubleCount method, and we can get the current number of items (the Count property) and the directory bit-depth (the Depth property). In theory we could get away with just the one property since Count equals 2^{Depth}. Maintaining both is minor work though, compared with calculating the power on demand. Finally, we can access the individual items as longints in the directory. These are, of course, going to be the bucket numbers.

Hidden in the private and protected sections we can see some other methods and fields. First are the set and get methods for the Items property, and then two methods to read and write the directory to and from a stream. We can also see that the real container for the directory entries is an instance of a TList.

In Listing 7.21, the constructor creates an instance of a hash directory, creates the internal TList, and reads itself from the stream, if required.

Listing 7.21: Creating an instance of the TtdHashDirectory class

```
constructor TtdHashDirectory.Create(aStream : TStream);
begin
  Assert(sizeof(pointer) = sizeof(longint),
         hdErrorMsg(tdePointerLongSize, 'Create', 0));
  {create the ancestor}
  inherited Create;
  {create the directory as a TList}
```

```
  FList := TList.Create;
  FStream := aStream;
  {if there's nothing in the stream, initialize the directory to
  have one entry and be of depth 0}
  if (FStream.Size = 0) then begin
    FList.Count := 1;
    FCount := 1;
    FDepth := 0;
  end
  {otherwise load from the stream}
  else
  hdLoadFromStream;
  end;
procedure TtdHashDirectory.hdLoadFromStream;
begin
  FStream.Seek(0, soFromBeginning);
  FStream.ReadBuffer(FDepth, sizeof(FDepth));
  FStream.ReadBuffer(FCount, sizeof(FCount));
  FList.Count := FCount;
  FStream.ReadBuffer(FList.List^, FCount * sizeof(longint));
end;
```

I've left in an Assert statement in the Create constructor. It checks to see that the size of a pointer is equal to the size of a longint. The reason is that I'm "cheating" a little, by storing the values for the directory directly as typecast pointers in a TList. If the size of either one changes, pointer or longint, this would no longer work. So, I've put an assertion in there, just in case. If the compiler complains in the future, I can fix it; if not, then I'll see the assertion failure at run time.

At the moment, LoadFromStream does minimal checking to see whether the stream contains a valid directory. Since I'm reading directly from the stream into a fixed size buffer, it might make sense to beef this up a little in the future by including a signature in the stream, or by adding CRC checking, etc.

Destroying an instance of the hash directory (Listing 7.22), involves writing its current contents out to the stream again, and freeing the internal TList.

Listing 7.22: Destroying an instance of the TtdHashDirectory class

```
destructor TtdHashDirectory.Destroy;
begin
  hdStoreToStream;
  FList.Free;
  inherited Destroy;
end;
procedure TtdHashDirectory.hdStoreToStream;
begin
```

```
  FStream.Seek(0, soFromBeginning);
  FStream.WriteBuffer(FDepth, sizeof(FDepth));
  FStream.WriteBuffer(FCount, sizeof(FCount));
  FStream.WriteBuffer(FList.List^, FCount * sizeof(longint));
end;
```

The accessor methods (Listing 7.23) for the Items property merely get the data from the internal TList, typecast to a longint.

Listing 7.23: Setting and getting the directory values

```
function TtdHashDirectory.hdGetItem(aInx : integer) : longint;
begin
  Assert((0 <= aInx) and (aInx < FList.Count),
         hdErrorMsg(tdeIndexOutOfBounds, 'hdGetItem', aInx));
  Result := longint(FList.List^[aInx]);
end;
procedure TtdHashDirectory.hdSetItem(aInx : integer; aValue : longint);
begin
  Assert((0 <= aInx) and (aInx < FList.Count),
         hdErrorMsg(tdeIndexOutOfBounds, 'hdGetItem', aInx));
  FList.List^[aInx] := pointer(aValue);
end;
```

Finally, in Listing 7.24, we can see the interesting method in the class that doubles the size of the directory.

Listing 7.24: Doubling the number of entries in a directory

```
procedure TtdHashDirectory.DoubleCount;
var
  Inx : integer;
begin
  {double the count, increment the depth}
  FList.Count := FList.Count * 2;
  FCount := FCount * 2;
  inc(FDepth);
  {each entry in the original directory is now doubled up in the new
  one; for example, the value in the old dir entry 0 is now the value
  for the new dir entries 0 and 1}
  for Inx := pred(FList.Count) downto 1 do
    FList.List^[Inx] := FList.List^[Inx div 2];
end;
```

The first thing that happens is that it doubles the count of items in the internal TList. The TList implementation guarantees that the new items will be set to nil, not that it makes any difference to us as we'll see. We double the internal count and increment bit-depth. Now we copy and double up all the old items in the TList (to see that the loop works as expected, read it in conjunction with the transition between Figure 7.1 (e) and (f)).

That class has got some important things out of the way ready for our main TtdHashTableExtendible class, whose interface is shown in Listing 7.25.

Listing 7.25: The interface to the TtdHashTableExtendible class

```
type
  TtdHashTableExtendible = class
    private
      FCompare  : TtdCompareRecordKey;
      FCount    : longint;
      FDirectory: TtdHashDirectory;
      FHashFunc : TtdHashFuncEx;
      FName     : TtdNameString;
      FBuckets  : TtdRecordStream;
      FRecords  : TtdRecordStream;
      FRecord   : pointer;
    protected
      procedure hteCreateNewHashTable;
      procedure hteError(aErrorCode : integer;
                   const aMethodName : TtdNameString);
      function hteErrorMsg(aErrorCode : integer;
                     const aMethodName : TtdNameString) : string;
      function hteFindBucket(const aKey : string;
                               var aFindInfo) : boolean;
      procedure hteSplitBucket(var aFindInfo);
    public
      constructor Create(aHashFunc     : TtdHashFuncEx;
                         aCompare      : TtdCompareRecordKey;
                         aDirStream    : TStream;
                         aBucketStream : TtdRecordStream;
                         aRecordStream : TtdRecordStream);
      destructor Destroy; override;
      function Find(const aKey   : string;
                     var aRecord) : boolean;
      procedure Insert(const aKey : string; var aRecord);
      property Count : longint read FCount;
      property Name : TtdNameString read FName write FName;
  end;
```

The class supports the usual constructor and destructor as well as the abilities to insert a record with its key and find a record given its key later on.

The Create constructor, as shown in Listing 7.26, is passed three streams as well as two function pointers. The three streams are for the directory, the buckets, and the records. The first function pointer is the usual hash function (although hash functions for this hash table have to produce 32-bit answers; no mod with the table size here). The second function pointer is a function to compare a Key value against a record read from the record stream.

Listing 7.26: Constructing an instance of the TtdHashTableExtendible class

```
constructor TtdHashTableExtendible.Create(
                                  aHashFunc     : TtdHashFuncEx;
                                  aCompare      : TtdCompareRecordKey;
                                  aDirStream    : TStream;
                                  aBucketStream : TtdRecordStream;
                                  aRecordStream : TtdRecordStream);
begin
  {create the ancestor}
  inherited Create;
  {create the directory}
  FDirectory := TtdHashDirectory.Create(aDirStream);
  {save parameters}
  FHashFunc := aHashFunc;
  FCompare := aCompare;
  FBuckets := aBucketStream;
  FRecords := aRecordStream;
  {get a buffer for any records we have to read}
  GetMem(FRecord, FRecords.RecordLength);
  {if the bucket stream is empty, create the first bucket}
  if (FBuckets.Count = 0) then
    hteCreateNewHashTable;
end;
procedure TtdHashTableExtendible.hteCreateNewHashTable;
var
  NewBucket : TBucket;
begin
  FillChar(NewBucket, sizeof(NewBucket), 0);
  FDirectory[0] := FBuckets.Add(NewBucket);
end;
```

The constructor creates the directory, passing it the directory stream and saving the parameters in internal fields. If the bucket stream contains no buckets yet, the constructor calls the protected method hteCreateNew-HashTable to set up the new table. This method adds the first empty bucket to the bucket stream, and stores the bucket number as the first directory entry.

The destructor merely cleans up as shown in Listing 7.27.

Listing 7.27: Destroying an instance of the TtdHashTableExtendible class

```
destructor TtdHashTableExtendible.Destroy;
begin
  FDirectory.Free;
  if (FRecord<>nil) then
    FreeMem(FRecord, FRecords.RecordLength);
```

```
  inherited Destroy;
end;
```

Now let's look at the Find method and its protected helper method, hteFindBucket, which, in the tradition of helper routines, does most of the work. Listing 7.28 shows us that, indeed, Find merely makes a call to hteFindBucket, and if it returns true, copies the record from the internal buffer to the user's buffer and itself returns true. If hteFindBucket returned false, then the record was not found, and so Find returns false in its turn.

Listing 7.28: Finding a record using its key

```
type
  THashElement = packed record
    heHash : longint;
    heItem : longint;
  end;
  PBucket = ^TBucket;
  TBucket = packed record
    bkDepth  : longint;
    bkCount  : longint;
    bkHashes : array [0..pred(tdcBucketItemCount)] of THashElement;
  end;
  PFindItemInfo = ^TFindItemInfo;
  TFindItemInfo = packed record
    fiiHash      : longint;      {hash of key parameter}
    fiiDirEntry  : integer;      {directory entry}
    fiiSlot      : integer;      {slot in bucket}
    fiiBucketNum : longint;      {bucket number in stream}
    fiiBucket    : TBucket;      {bucket}
  end;
function TtdHashTableExtendible.Find(const aKey   : string;
                                     var aRecord) : boolean;
var
  FindInfo  : TFindItemInfo;
begin
  if hteFindBucket(aKey, FindInfo) then begin
    Result := true;
    Move(FRecord^, aRecord, FRecords.RecordLength);
  end
  else
    Result := false;
end;
function TtdHashTableExtendible.hteFindBucket(
                                          const aKey : string;
                                          var aFindInfo) : boolean;
var
  FindInfo  : PFindItemInfo;
  Inx       : integer;
```

```
  IsDeleted : boolean;
begin
  FindInfo := PFindItemInfo(@aFindInfo);
  with FindInfo^ do begin
    {calculate the hash for the string}
    fiiHash := FHashFunc(aKey);
    {calculate the entry in the directory for this hash, which gives
     us the bucket number}
    fiiDirEntry := ReverseBits(fiiHash, FDirectory.Depth);
    fiiBucketNum := FDirectory[fiiDirEntry];
    {retrieve the bucket}
    FBuckets.Read(fiiBucketNum, fiiBucket, IsDeleted);
    if IsDeleted then
      hteError(tdeHashTblDeletedBkt, 'hteFindBucket');
    {search for the hash value in the bucket, assume we won't succeed}
    Result := false;
    with fiiBucket do begin
      for Inx := 0 to pred(bkCount) do begin
        {if the hash matches...}
        if (bkHashes[Inx].heHash = fiiHash) then begin
          {read the record}
          FRecords.Read(bkHashes[Inx].heItem, FRecord^, IsDeleted);
          if IsDeleted then
            hteError(tdeHashTblDeletedRec, 'hteFindBucket');
          {compare the record to the key}
          if FCompare(FRecord^, aKey) then begin
            Result := true;
            fiiSlot := Inx;
            Exit;
          end;
        end;
      end;
    end;
  end;
end;
```

The hteFindBucket method is the most interesting. First, like a "normal" hash table, it calculates the hash for the key. Now it calculates the directory entry to which this hash refers. As discussed above, this involves taking the required number of least significant bits and reversing them. The number of bits required is equal to the directory bit-depth, and the work is done by a small routine called ReverseBits.

Listing 7.29: Calculating the directory entry

```
function ReverseBits(aValue : longint; aBitCount : integer) : longint;
var
  i : integer;
begin
```

```
  Result := 0;
  for i := 0 to pred(aBitCount) do begin
    Result := (Result shl 1) or (aValue and 1);
    aValue := aValue shr 1;
  end;
end;
```

Once we have the directory entry we can read it to get the bucket number. Once we have that, we can read the bucket out of the bucket stream. And, once we have that, we search through the hashes in the bucket to find the one for the key we were given. If this was found, we will have the record number for the record required and we can read it from the records stream.

As written, the Insert and Find methods don't assume anything about the ordering of the hash numbers in the bucket, and hence the search we use is a sequential one. With a little extra work, we could make sure that the items in the bucket are sorted in hash order and therefore be able to use a binary search.

There is one caveat though: there is nothing to stop the hash function from generating the same hash for two or more keys. If that happened, they would be added to the same bucket, and so we would have to make sure that we visited each record with the same key hash to find the record we wanted.

If the record was found, the hteFindBucket method returns, in a private record structure, the hash, the directory entry, the bucket number, the bucket itself, and the slot in the bucket where the hash was found. At the moment, all this information is discarded. A later version of the TtdHashTable-Extendible class will support deletion, and this extra information will be required.

If the record was not found, everything except the slot number is still returned. We'll see how this is used right now, looking at the Insert method in Listing 7.30.

Listing 7.30: Inserting a key/record pair into the hash table

```
procedure TtdHashTableExtendible.Insert(const aKey : string;
                                        var aRecord);
var
  FindInfo  : TFindItemInfo;
  RRN       : longint;
begin
  if hteFindBucket(aKey, FindInfo) then
    hteError(tdeHashTblKeyExists, 'Insert');
  {check to see if there's enough room in this bucket, if not we'll
  split the bucket, and re-find where to insert the item; continue
  until the bucket found has enough room}
```

```
  while (FindInfo.fiiBucket.bkCount >= tdcBucketItemCount) do begin
    hteSplitBucket(FindInfo);
    if hteFindBucket(aKey, FindInfo) then
      hteError(tdeHashTblKeyExists, 'Insert');
  end;
  {add the record to the record stream to get the record number}
  RRN := FRecords.Add(aRecord);
  {add the hash to the end of the hash list, update the bucket}
  with FindInfo, FindInfo.fiiBucket do begin
    bkHashes[bkCount].heHash := fiiHash;
    bkHashes[bkCount].heItem := RRN;
    inc(bkCount);
    FBuckets.Write(fiiBucketNum, fiiBucket);
  end;
  {we have one more record}
  inc(FCount);
end;
```

The first thing to do when inserting is to try and find the key/record. If we do, it's an error. If we don't, the hteFindBucket will return various pieces of information: the hash for the key (so we don't have to recalculate it), the directory entry and the bucket number and the bucket itself, where the key's hash should have been found.

We check to see whether the bucket is full. Let's assume for now that it isn't. We add the record to the records stream—giving us the record number—and then we add the hash/record number pair onto the end of the bucket, incrementing the usual counts.

If the bucket is full, we have to split it. This is done by another hidden protected method, hteSplitBucket. Once this returns, we have to try and find the item again, to set up the required information so that we can easily add the key/record pair. Although I added the code to check for finding the key/record and raising an error, if we ever did at this point, the hash table is well and truly trashed—we've already ascertained that it is not present.

So, the last method: hteSplitBucket. This is, by far, the most complex method of the class. Listing 7.31 has the details, but we should refer back to Figure 7.1 for clarification.

Listing 7.31: Splitting a bucket

```
procedure TtdHashTableExtendible.hteSplitBucket(var aFindInfo);
var
  FindInfo  : PFindItemInfo;
  Inx       : integer;
  NewBucket : TBucket;
  Mask      : longint;
```

```
  OldValue  : longint;
  OldInx    : integer;
  NewInx    : integer;
  NewBucketNum     : longint;
  StartDirEntry    : longint;
  NewStartDirEntry : longint;
  EndDirEntry      : longint;
begin
  FindInfo := PFindItemInfo(@aFindInfo);
  {if the bucket we are splitting has the same bit depth as the
  directory, then we need to double the capacity of the directory}
  if (FindInfo^.fiiBucket.bkDepth = FDirectory.Depth) then begin
    FDirectory.DoubleCount;
    {update the directory entry for the bucket we're splitting}
    FindInfo^.fiiDirEntry := FindInfo^.fiiDirEntry * 2;
 end;
 {calculate the range of directory entries pointing to the original
  bucket, and the range for the new}
 StartDirEntry := FindInfo^.fiiDirEntry;
 while (StartDirEntry >= 0) and
       (FDirectory[StartDirEntry] = FindInfo^.fiiBucketNum) do
  dec(StartDirEntry);
 inc(StartDirEntry);
 EndDirEntry := FindInfo^.fiiDirEntry;
 while (EndDirEntry < FDirectory.Count) and
       (FDirectory[EndDirEntry] = FindInfo^.fiiBucketNum) do
  inc(EndDirEntry);
 dec(EndDirEntry);
 NewStartDirEntry := (StartDirEntry + EndDirEntry + 1) div 2;
 {increase the bit depth of the bucket being split}
 inc(FindInfo^.fiiBucket.bkDepth);
 {initialize the new bucket; it will have the same bucket depth as
 the bucket we're splitting}
 FillChar(NewBucket, sizeof(NewBucket), 0);
 NewBucket.bkDepth := FindInfo^.fiiBucket.bkDepth;
 {calculate the AND mask we'll use to identify where hash entries go}
 Mask := (1 shl NewBucket.bkDepth) - 1;
 {calculate the ANDed value for hash entries for the old bucket}
 OldValue := ReverseBits(StartDirEntry, FDirectory.Depth) and Mask;
 {read through the old bucket and transfer hashes that belong to the
 new bucket over to it}
 OldInx := 0;
 NewInx := 0;
 with FindInfo^.fiiBucket do
   for Inx := 0 to pred(bkCount) do begin
     if (bkHashes[Inx].heHash and Mask) = OldValue then begin
       bkHashes[OldInx] := bkHashes[Inx];
       inc(OldInx);
```

```
      end
      else begin
    NewBucket.bkHashes[NewInx] := bkHashes[Inx];
    inc(NewInx);
  end;
end;
{set the counts for both buckets}
FindInfo^.fiiBucket.bkCount := OldInx;
NewBucket.bkCount := NewInx;
{add the new bucket to the bucket stream, update the old bucket}
NewBucketNum := FBuckets.Add(NewBucket);
FBuckets.Write(FindInfo^.fiiBucketNum, FindInfo^.fiiBucket);
{set all the entries in the new directory range to the new bucket}
for Inx := NewStartDirEntry to EndDirEntry do
  FDirectory[Inx] := NewBucketNum;
end;
```

The first check is to see whether the bucket we're splitting has the same bit-depth as the directory. If it does, we need to double the directory in size, and make sure that the directory entry value we're tracking is also updated. For example, if FindInfo^.fiiDirEntry had a value of 3, and we doubled the directory in size, then it now should be 6 (or 7, admittedly, since both new directory entries point to the same bucket).

What happens now is that we have to work out the range of directory entries that point to the bucket being split. In Figure 7.1 (g), if we had to split *B* the range would be 4 to 7. What's going to happen is that the bucket being split is going to remain in the first half of this range, whereas the new bucket we're about to fill will occupy the second half of the directory range.

Since we're splitting the bucket, we need to increase its bit-depth (we've already made sure that this can be done without exceeding the directory bit-depth). Since the new bucket is a buddy to this one, it will have the same depth.

We now have to split the items in the full bucket between it and the new one. If we were to do it the long-winded way, we would copy the items into a temporary array, clear the full bucket, update the directory entries, and then add the items back. For each item, this would entail taking the hash and calculating the reversed bits to define the directory entry, from which we know which bucket to add the item to. Perfectly doable, but long-winded, as I said.

Better would be to work out a method whereby we can identify which bucket the hash would go into directly. Suppose we had the following case: the directory bit-depth is 3, but the bucket bit-depth is 2. Directory entries 4 and 5 point to bucket *A*, the full one, and directory entries 6 and 7 point to bucket *B*, the empty one. Given a hash, where would it go? First thing is to realize that bucket *A* only contains hashes ending in 001, 101, 011, or 111 (to see this, reverse the bits in each to get the directory entries 4, 5, 6, 7). If the hash ends in 001 or 101, it would go into bucket *A*; if it ends in 011 or 111, it would go into bucket *B*. Still looks hard, doesn't it? Well, the first two possibilities end in 01, whereas the second two end in 11. Why two bits? Well, the bucket bit-depth is 2. The plan is to calculate the directory entry for the start of the range (which we know), reverse the bits up to the directory bit-depth, and AND the result with a mask generated from the bucket bit-depth. We can then use this as a mask to categorize the hashes. That's what the middle section of the routine is doing.

After all that, it's just housekeeping—making sure the buckets have the correct counts, adding the new bucket, updating the original bucket, and ensuring that the directory entries that need changing point to the new bucket.

The complete code for the TtdHashTableExtendible class is found in the TDHshExt.pas source file on the CD.

Summary

In this chapter we have been discussing hash tables, a data structure that tries to give you access to its items in O(1) time.

We've seen various in-memory tables, including the two most important: the hash table with linear probing and the hash table with chaining. We discussed the benefits and drawbacks of each, and how to keep them tuned.

Finally, we saw how to maintain a hash table on disk, where we want to minimize the number of disk accesses. We saw the bucketing algorithm and how to implement it to provide a hash-based database.

Chapter 8

Binary Trees

Much like arrays and linked lists, trees of one variety or another are ubiquitous data structures in the programmer's world. In Chapter 3, we looked at singly linked lists, where there was a single link that joined one node to another (doubly linked lists had a link the other way as well). Normally, we view linked lists as horizontal structures (it saves on paper!), with the initial node being the leftmost node, and the linked list extending to the right. Consider now this linked list turned 90 degrees clockwise, so that the initial node is at the top and the final node is at the bottom. This is a specialized example of a multiway tree, where each node has just one *child*, the node underneath it. Each node, similarly, has one *parent*, which is the node immediately above it. The nomenclature, of course, reflects family trees. We make the convention that the lowest node has a nil link, i.e., it has no child. Since each node has at most one child, we could call a singly linked list a unary tree.

A *multiway tree* is a generalization of this concept. It is a collection of nodes organized so that all nodes apart from the root (we define the node at the top of the tree as the *root* and a node with no child as a *leaf*) have exactly *one* parent and can have zero or more children. A linked list is, therefore, a specialized multiway tree where each node (apart from the bottommost one) has exactly one child. If each node can have at most *n* children, the tree is known as an *n*-ary tree.

Consider now the case where each node has up to two children nodes; in other words, for every node there are at most two links to nodes on the next level down. This structure is known as a binary tree. By convention, a node's two children are known as the left child and the right child since when we draw a tree with the root at the top, a node's children are arrayed horizontally underneath it, one to the left of the other. Figure 8.1 shows a classical representation of a binary tree.

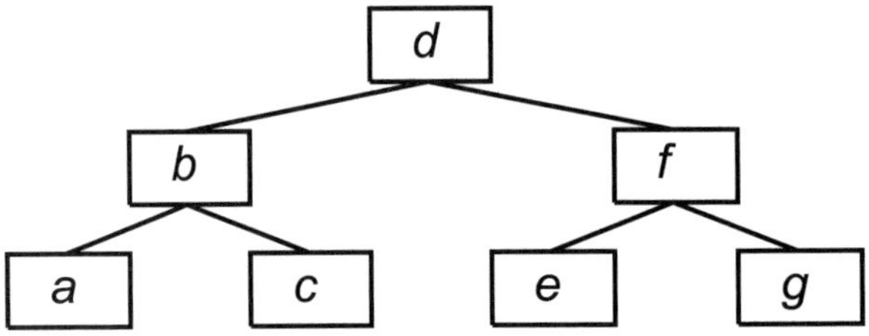

Figure 8.1: A binary tree

From this discussion, you can see that when we define a node for use in a binary tree in Delphi, we must have two links (i.e., pointers) to its children, a link to its parent (this link is optional, but we'll find that some tree algorithms are easier with it), and the actual data that we want to store in the node. To make everything easier all around, we'll assume that the data in a node can be represented by a pointer, just like the TList and the data structures we've seen so far in this book. Because the node has a fixed size, you can be sure that we will be using the node manager from Chapter 3 again when it's time to write a binary tree class. Listing 8.1 has the node record layout.

Listing 8.1: The layout for a node in a binary tree

```
type
  TtdChildType = (        {types of children}
         ctLeft,          {..left child}
         ctRight);        {..right child}
  TtdRBColor = (          {colors for the red-black tree}
         rbBlack,         {..black}
         rbRed);          {..red}
  PtdBinTreeNode = ^TtdBinTreeNode;
  TtdBinTreeNode = packed record
    btParent : PtdBinTreeNode;
    btChild  : array [TtdChildType] of PtdBinTreeNode;
    btData   : pointer;
    case boolean of
      false : (btExtra  : longint);
      true  : (btColor  : TtdRBColor);
  end;
```

Notice that we define the two child links as a two-element array. At first this might seem like overkill, but when it comes to implementing binary tree operations, this definition will make things much simpler. Also, the binary tree node declares an extra field that is not required for normal binary trees, but will make things easier for the red-black variant of the binary search tree.

Creating a Binary Tree

Creating a binary tree is trivial. At its most simple, the root node in a binary tree defines the binary tree.

```
var
  MyBinaryTree : PtdBinTreeNode;
```

If MyBinaryTree is nil, there is no binary tree, so this value serves as the initial value of the binary tree.

```
{initialize the binary tree}
MyBinaryTree := nil;
```

However, in practice, we tend to use a dummy node analogous to the dummy head node in a singly linked list, so that every real node in the tree has a parent, including the root. The root node can be either the left or right child from the dummy head node, but we'll hereby make the rule that it is the left child.

Insertion and Deletion with a Binary Tree

If we are to use a binary tree in earnest we shall have to consider how to add items (i.e., nodes) to the tree, how to delete items from the tree, and how to visit all the items in the tree. The latter operation will enable us to search for a particular item. Since we can't do the latter two operations without considering the first, let's start by discussing how to insert a node into a binary tree.

To be able to insert a node in a binary tree, we must select a parent node to which we can attach the new node as a child, and furthermore, that node cannot already have two children. We must also know which child, left or right, the new node must become.

Given a parent node and a left/right child indication, the code to insert a node is very simple. We create the node, set its data field to the item we're adding to the tree, and set both its child links to nil. Then, in pretty much the same manner as inserting a node in a doubly linked list, we set the relevant child pointer of the parent to the new child node, and the parent pointer of the child to the parent node.

Listing 8.2: Insertion into a binary tree

```
function TtdBinaryTree.InsertAt(aParentNode : PtdBinTreeNode;
                                aChildType  : TtdChildType;
                                aItem       : pointer)
                                            : PtdBinTreeNode;
begin
```

```
  {if the parent node is nil, assume this is inserting the root}
  if (aParentNode = nil) then begin
    aParentNode := FHead;
    aChildType := ctLeft;
  end;
  {check to see the child link isn't already set}
  if (aParentNode^.btChild[aChildType]<>nil) then
    btError(tdeBinTreeHasChild, 'InsertAt');
  {allocate a new node and insert as the required child of the parent}
  Result := BTNodeManager.AllocNode;
  Result^.btParent := aParentNode;
  Result^.btChild[ctLeft] := nil;
  Result^.btChild[ctRight] := nil;
  Result^.btData := aItem;
  Result^.btExtra := 0;
  aParentNode^.btChild[aChildType] := Result;
  inc(FCount);
end;
```

Notice that the code in Listing 8.2 first checks to see if we are adding the root node; if so, the parent node passed in is nil. In this case, the method initializes the parent node to an internal head node.

Apart from that check, the InsertAt method ensures that the child link we wish to use for the new node is actually unused; otherwise it would be an egregious error.

Notice that the binary tree class (of which this method is part) uses a node manager for allocation and disposal of nodes. Since all the nodes are the same size, this makes eminent sense, as discussed in Chapter 3.

What about deleting a node? This is a little more complicated because the node may have a child or two children. The first rule is that a leaf node (that is, a node with no children) can be deleted with impunity. We work out which child the leaf is of the parent and set that child link to nil. The node can then be freed.

The second rule for deletion from a binary tree is for the case where the node we are deleting has one child. Again this is pretty easy: we merely move the child up the tree to become the same child of the parent as is the node we are deleting.

The third rule is for the case where the node we are deleting has *two* children. This is a simple rule, perhaps: the node cannot be deleted. It is an error to try to do so. Later on we'll discuss a variant of the binary tree, the binary search tree, where there is sufficient extra information embedded in the tree to allow us to get around this restriction.

Listing 8.3: Deletion from a binary tree

```
procedure TtdBinaryTree.Delete(aNode : PtdBinTreeNode);
var
  OurChildsType : TtdChildType;
  OurType       : TtdChildType;
begin
  if (aNode = nil) then
    Exit;
  {find out whether we have a single child and which one it is; if we
  find that there are two children raise an exception}
  if (aNode^.btChild[ctLeft]<>nil) then begin
    if (aNode^.btChild[ctRight]<>nil) then
      btError(tdeBinTree2Children, 'Delete');
    OurChildsType := ctLeft;
  end
  else
    OurChildsType := ctRight;
  {find out whether we're a left or right child of our parent}
  OurType := GetChildType(aNode);
  {set the child link of our parent to our child link}
  aNode^.btParent^.btChild[OurType] :=
  Node^.btChild[OurChildsType];
  if (aNode^.btChild[OurChildsType]<>nil) then
    aNode^.btChild[OurChildsType]^.btParent := aNode^.btParent;
  {free the node}
  if Assigned(FDispose) then
    FDispose(aNode^.btData);
  BTNodeManager.FreeNode(aNode);
  dec(FCount);
end;
```

In Listing 8.3, we ignore the case where the node to be deleted is nil. There's not a lot we can do there, anyway, and it seems overkill to raise an exception. The method then makes sure that the node being deleted does not have two children. However, it does not separate out the other two deletion cases (that is, no children and only one child), instead merging them into one where one child replaces the node, even if it may be nil. The GetChildType routine is a small function that returns whether its node parameter is a left child or a right child of its parent.

Navigating through a Binary Tree

Now we've seen how to build a binary tree we can discuss how to visit all the nodes in such a structure. By *visit*, I mean process the item in the node in some fashion. This could be something as simple as writing out the data in the node, or it could be more complex.

Unlike a linked list where the navigation of the structure is pretty well defined (follow all the Next pointers until we reach the end), in a binary tree there are two ways we could take at each node and so the process becomes a little more complex. For a tree, the navigation procedure is known as a *traversal*. There are four main traversal algorithms, known as *pre-order, in-order, post-order,* and *level-order* traversals. The latter, level-order traversal, is the easiest to visualize but the most complicated to code. With level-order traversal we visit each of the nodes starting at the root and working our way down level by level. At each level we visit the nodes on that level from left to right. So, we visit the root, the root's left child, the root's right child, the root's left child's left child, the root's left child's right child, and so on. Looking at Figure 8.1 again, if we were to perform a level-order traversal, we would visit the nodes in the order *d, b, f, a, c, e, g*.

Pre-order, In-order, and Post-order Traversals

Before describing the other three traversal algorithms, which are all inter-related, let's define a binary tree in a different fashion. A binary tree consists of a root node with pointers to the root nodes of two other binary trees, known as the children. The pointers to either or both children could be nil. This definition describes a binary tree very succinctly, albeit recursively, yet it provides an ideal way to define the other three traversals.

A pre-order traversal visits the root node, then traverses the left child tree using the pre-order algorithm, and then traverses the right child tree in the same fashion. (In Figure 8.1, we'd visit the nodes in the order *d, b, a, c, f, e, g*.) An in-order traversal traverses the root's left child tree using the in-order algorithm, then visits the root node, and then traverses the right child tree in-order. (In Figure 8.1, we'd visit the nodes in the order *a, b, c, d, e, f, g*.) A post-order traversal traverses the root's left child tree using the post-order algorithm, traverses the right child tree in the same manner, and then visits the root node. (In Figure 8.1, we'd visit the nodes in the order *a, c, b, e, g, f, d*.)

Post-order traversals are used most often for destroying all of the nodes in a binary tree, where the destroy process could be couched as "to destroy all the nodes in a binary tree, destroy the left child tree of the root, destroy the right child tree of the root, and then destroy the root."

Coding these three traversals is simple: we just write a recursive routine that calls itself for each node. Listing 8.4 shows some simple code for performing recursive traversals.

Listing 8.4: Pre-, in-, and post-order traversals

```
type
  TtdProcessNode = procedure (aNode : PtdBinaryNode);
procedure PreOrderTraverse(aRoot : PtdBinaryNode;
                     aProcessNode : TtdProcessNode);
begin
  if (aNode<>nil) then begin
    aProcessNode(aRoot);
    PreOrderTraverse(aRoot^.bnChild[ciLeft], aProcessNode);
    PreOrderTraverse(aRoot^.bnChild[ciRight], aProcessNode);
  end;
end;
procedure InOrderTraverse(aRoot : PtdBinaryNode;
                    aProcessNode : TtdProcessNode);
begin
  if (aNode<>nil) then begin
    InOrderTraverse(aRoot^.bnChild[ciLeft], aProcessNode);
    aProcessNode(aRoot);
    InOrderTraverse(aRoot^.bnChild[ciRight], aProcessNode);
  end;
end;
procedure PostOrderTraverse(aRoot : PtdBinaryNode;
                      aProcessNode : TtdProcessNode);
begin
  if (aNode<>nil) then begin
    PostOrderTraverse(aRoot^.bnChild[ciLeft], aProcessNode);
    PostOrderTraverse(aRoot^.bnChild[ciRight], aProcessNode);
    aProcessNode(aRoot);
  end;
end;
```

Notice the way that each recursive routine checks to see whether the node passed in is nil. In this case it does nothing, exiting immediately, and therefore the recursion will end eventually (since presumably the tree is not infinite in extent).

However, any time we have a recursive routine we should consider how many times it would be executed through a recursive chain of calls. The reason for this is that recursive routines store their state on the program stack, and this stack is generally limited in size. If we determine that the recursive routine could run to too many levels, we should consider how to remove the recursion by means of an external stack. Using an external stack rather than the program stack, we know that we can grow the stack on the heap whenever needed (until we run out of heap space, but in general the amount of heap space is much larger than the size of the program stack).

We use a stack based on a linked list, the TtdStack class from Chapter 3. For a pre-order traversal, push the root node onto the stack and enter a loop that continues until the stack is empty. Pop the top node off the stack and visit it. If the node's right child link is not nil, push it onto the stack. Then, if the node's left child link is not nil, push it onto the stack. (Pushing the children in this order means that we'll pop off the left child first.) If the stack is not empty, go around the loop again. Once the stack is exhausted, the traversal is over.

Listing 8.5: Non-recursive pre-order traversal

```
type
  TtdVisitProc = procedure (aData       : pointer;
                            aExtraData  : pointer;
                        var aStopVisits : boolean);
function TtdBinaryTree.btNoRecPreOrder(aAction    : TtdVisitProc;
                                       aExtraData : pointer)
                                                  : PtdBinTreeNode;
var
  Stack   : TtdStack;
  Node    : PtdBinTreeNode;
  StopNow : boolean;
begin
  {assume we won't get a node selected}
  Result := nil;
  StopNow := false;
  {create the stack}
  Stack := TtdStack.Create(nil);
  try
    {push the root}
    Stack.Push(FHead^.btChild[ctLeft]);
    {continue until the stack is empty}
    while not Stack.IsEmpty do begin
      {get the node at the head of the queue}
      Node := Stack.Pop;
      {perform the action on it, if this returns StopNow as
      true, return this node}
      aAction(Node^.btData, aExtraData, StopNow);
      if StopNow then begin
        Result := Node;
        Stack.Clear;
      end
      {otherwise, continue}
      else begin
        {push the right child, if it's not nil}
        if (Node^.btChild[ctRight]<>nil) then
          Stack.Push(Node^.btChild[ctRight]);
        {push the left child, if it's not nil}
```

```
        if (Node^.btChild[ctLeft]<>nil) then
          Stack.Push(Node^.btChild[ctLeft]);
      end;
    end;
  finally
    {destroy the stack}
    Stack.Free;
  end;
end;
```

There are a couple of points to be made about the code in Listing 8.5. Firstly, we're using an action routine that is a little more complicated than before. The TtdVisitProc procedure type allows the user of the traversal method more control over the process, namely the ability to stop the traversal. This means that the user of the binary tree class could perform for each type processing (visiting all the nodes), or a first that type search (looking for the first node that satisfies a condition). The third parameter of the action procedure, aStopVisits, is set to false by the calling routine, and if the action procedure wishes to stop the traversal it can be set to true (the traversal method will return the item that caused the action procedure to return true).

The big point, however, about the code in Listing 8.5 is that the routine assumes the tree is not empty. In fact, this routine is an internal routine to the eventual binary tree class, and it will only get called for a tree containing at least one node.

Having seen how easy removing recursion for pre-order traversal was, we might expect that the other two traversals would be equally as easy. However, we run into a snag doing the same for in-order and post-order traversals. To see what I mean, let's consider removing the recursion for the in-order traversal in the same manner as we did for the pre-order method. Inside the loop we would, in theory, push the right child, push the node itself and then push the left child. Then, eventually, we would pop off a node and want to process it. But when we pop off a node, how do we know whether we've seen it before? If we have seen it before we would want to visit it; if not, we would want to push its children and itself in the correct order.

We should really do the following: pop off the node; if we haven't seen it before, push the right child, mark the node as "seen," push it, and then push the left child; if we *have* seen the node before (it's marked, remember), then just process it. But how do we mark a node? After all, a node is a pointer, and we don't really want to mess with that. My solution for this is to push a nil node onto the stack after pushing the "seen" node. Then, when we pop off a nil node, we know that the next node on the stack is one to be processed.

The non-recursive algorithm for in-order traversal works as follows. Push the root node onto the stack and enter a loop that runs until the stack is empty. Pop the top node off the stack. If this node is nil, pop the next node off the stack and visit it. If the popped node isn't nil, push the right child node onto the stack (if it is non-nil), push the node itself onto the stack, push a nil pointer, then finally push the left child node onto the stack (if it is non-nil). Go around the loop again.

Listing 8.6: Non-recursive in-order traversal

```
function TtdBinaryTree.btNoRecInOrder(aAction    : TtdVisitProc;
                                      aExtraData : pointer)
                                                 : PtdBinTreeNode;
var
  Stack   : TtdStack;
  Node    : PtdBinTreeNode;
  StopNow : boolean;
begin
  {assume we won't get a node selected}
  Result := nil;
  StopNow := false;
  {create the stack}
  Stack := TtdStack.Create(nil);
  try
    {push the root}
    Stack.Push(FHead^.btChild[ctLeft]);
    {continue until the stack is empty}
    while not Stack.IsEmpty do begin
      {get the node at the head of the queue}
      Node := Stack.Pop;
      {if it's nil, pop the next node, perform the action on it. If
      this returns with a request to stop then return this node}
      if (Node = nil) then begin
        Node := Stack.Pop;
        aAction(Node^.btData, aExtraData, StopNow);
        if StopNow then begin
          Result := Node;
          Stack.Clear;
        end;
      end
      {otherwise, the children of the node have not been pushed yet}
      else begin
        {push the right child, if it's not nil}
        if (Node^.btChild[ctRight]<>nil) then
          Stack.Push(Node^.btChild[ctRight]);
        {push the node, followed by a nil pointer}
        Stack.Push(Node);
        Stack.Push(nil);
```

```
        {push the left child, if it's not nil}
        if (Node^.btChild[ctLeft]<>nil) then
          Stack.Push(Node^.btChild[ctLeft]);
      end;
    end;
  finally
    {destroy the stack}
    Stack.Free;
  end;
end;
```

As in the pre-order traversal case, the method assumes that the tree is not empty, that there is at least one node present. This is even more important this time, since the method can go terribly wrong if a nil node is pushed onto the stack that is not part of the algorithm.

The non-recursive algorithm for post-order traversal works in a similar fashion. Push the root node onto the stack and enter a loop that runs until the stack is empty. Pop the top node off the stack. If it is nil, pop the next node off the stack and process it. If it isn't nil, push the node itself onto the stack, push a nil pointer, push the right child node onto the stack (if it is non-nil), then push the left child node onto the stack (if it is non-nil). Go around the loop again.

Listing 8.7: Non-recursive post-order traversal

```
function TtdBinaryTree.btNoRecPostOrder(aAction    : TtdVisitProc;
                                        aExtraData : pointer)
                                                   : PtdBinTreeNode;
var
  Stack   : TtdStack;
  Node    : PtdBinTreeNode;
  StopNow : boolean;
begin
  {assume we won't get a node selected}
  Result := nil;
  StopNow := false;
  {create the stack}
  Stack := TtdStack.Create(nil);
  try
    {push the root}
    Stack.Push(FHead^.btChild[ctLeft]);
    {continue until the stack is empty}
    while not Stack.IsEmpty do begin
      {get the node at the head of the queue}
      Node := Stack.Pop;
      {if it's nil, pop the next node, perform the action on it, if
      this returns false (ie, don't continue), return this node}
```

```
      if (Node = nil) then begin
        Node := Stack.Pop;
        aAction(Node^.btData, aExtraData, StopNow);
        if StopNow then begin
          Result := Node;
          Stack.Clear;
        end;
      end
      {otherwise, the children of the node have not been pushed yet}
      else begin
        {push the node, followed by a nil pointer}
        Stack.Push(Node);
        Stack.Push(nil);
        {push the right child, if it's not nil}
        if (Node^.btChild[ctRight]<>nil) then
          Stack.Push(Node^.btChild[ctRight]);
        {push the left child, if it's not nil}
        if (Node^.btChild[ctLeft]<>nil) then
          Stack.Push(Node^.btChild[ctLeft]);
      end;
    end;
  finally
    {destroy the stack}
    Stack.Free;
  end;
end;
```

Again, the method assumes that the tree is not empty for the same reasons as before.

Level-order Traversals

The one traversal method we have not yet looked at is level-order, where we visit the root, visit the two possible nodes at level 1 from left to right, visit the four possible nodes at level 2 from left to right, and so on. This traversal method looks to be difficult to code, but in fact is very simple once you know the trick. The trick is to use a queue in the following manner. Enqueue the root node and enter a loop until the queue is empty. Dequeue the top node. Visit it. If its left child link is not nil, enqueue it. If its right child link is not nil, enqueue it too. If the queue is not empty, go around the loop again. That's all there is to it.

Listing 8.8: Level-order traversal

```
function TtdBinaryTree.btLevelOrder(aAction    : TtdVisitProc;
                                    aExtraData : pointer)
                                               : PtdBinTreeNode;
var
```

```
  Queue   : TtdQueue;
  Node    : PtdBinTreeNode;
  StopNow : boolean;
begin
  {assume we won't get a node selected}
  Result := nil;
  StopNow := false;
  {create the queue}
  Queue := TtdQueue.Create(nil);
  try
    {enqueue the root}
    Queue.Enqueue(FHead^.btChild[ctLeft]);
    {continue until the queue is empty}
    while not Queue.IsEmpty do begin
      {get the node at the head of the queue}
      Node := Queue.Dequeue;
      {perform the action on it, if this returns with a request to
      stop then return this node}
      aAction(Node^.btData, aExtraData, StopNow);
      if StopNow then begin
        Result := Node;
        Queue.Clear;
      end
      {otherwise, continue}
      else begin
        {enqueue the left child, if it's not nil}
        if (Node^.btChild[ctLeft]<>nil) then
          Queue.Enqueue(Node^.btChild[ctLeft]);
        {enqueue the right child, if it's not nil}
        if (Node^.btChild[ctRight]<>nil) then
          Queue.Enqueue(Node^.btChild[ctRight]);
      end;
    end;
  finally
    {destroy the queue}
    Queue.Free;
  end;
end;
```

Like the non-recursive traversal methods, the btLevelOrder method must only be called for a tree that is not empty.

Class Implementation of a Binary Tree

As with the other data structures we've been discussing up to now, we will encapsulate a standard binary tree as a class. Indeed, we've already made a start by showing various methods of the finished class.

Ideally, as we did with linked lists, for example, we don't want to bore the user of the class with the structure of nodes (it allows us to alter their structure without inconveniencing the user of the class), but with these ordinary binary trees we have to assume some knowledge of the node structure so that the user can insert a new node (he has to tell the tree class which node is the parent and which child the new node becomes). So our implementation won't quite be as black a box as we'd like.

The binary tree class will support the standard operations such as insert and delete. It will also support the various traversals in a Traverse method. One method that would prove beneficial to a task like expression parsing would be the operation of joining two trees at a new root node.

Listing 8.9: Interface to the binary tree class

```
type
  TtdBinaryTree = class
    {the binary tree class}
    private
      FCount   : integer;
      FDispose : TtdDisposeProc;
      FHead    : PtdBinTreeNode;
      FName    : TtdNameString;
    protected
      procedure btError(aErrorCode  : integer;
                  const aMethodName : TtdNameString);
      function btLevelOrder(aAction    : TtdVisitProc;
                            aExtraData : pointer) : PtdBinTreeNode;
      function btNoRecInOrder(aAction    : TtdVisitProc;
                              aExtraData : pointer) : PtdBinTreeNode;
      function btNoRecPostOrder(aAction    : TtdVisitProc;
                                aExtraData : pointer) : PtdBinTreeNode;
      function btNoRecPreOrder(aAction    : TtdVisitProc;
                               aExtraData : pointer) : PtdBinTreeNode;
      function btRecInOrder(aNode      : PtdBinTreeNode;
                            aAction    : TtdVisitProc;
                            aExtraData : pointer) : PtdBinTreeNode;
      function btRecPostOrder(aNode      : PtdBinTreeNode;
                              aAction    : TtdVisitProc;
                              aExtraData : pointer) : PtdBinTreeNode;
      function btRecPreOrder(aNode      : PtdBinTreeNode;
                             aAction    : TtdVisitProc;
                             aExtraData : pointer) : PtdBinTreeNode;
    public
      constructor Create(aDisposeItem : TtdDisposeProc);
      destructor Destroy; override;
      procedure Clear;
      procedure Delete(aNode : PtdBinTreeNode);
```

```
    function InsertAt(aParentNode : PtdBinTreeNode;
                      aChildType  : TtdChildType;
                      aItem       : pointer) : PtdBinTreeNode;
    function Root : PtdBinTreeNode;
    function Traverse(aMode         : TtdTraversalMode;
                      aAction       : TtdVisitProc;
                      aExtraData    : pointer;
                      aUseRecursion : boolean) : PtdBinTreeNode;
    property Count : integer read FCount;
    property Name : TtdNameString read FName write FName;
  end;
```

As usual with the data structures in this book, we make sure that the class can own the data it holds, and therefore be able to dispose of it when needed, or assume that the data is taken care of elsewhere, in which case the tree will not dispose of any data. The Create constructor therefore takes a parameter for the dispose routine for an item of data. If this is nil, the tree does not own the data and hence will not dispose of it. If the aDisposeItem parameter is the address of a routine, then it will get called whenever an item needs to be freed.

Listing 8.10: Create and Destroy for the binary tree class

```
constructor TtdBinaryTree.Create(aDisposeItem : TtdDisposeProc);
begin
  inherited Create;
  FDispose := aDisposeItem;
  {make sure the node manager is available}
  if (BTNodeManager = nil) then
    BTNodeManager := TtdNodeManager.Create(sizeof(TtdBinTreeNode));
  {allocate a head node, eventually the root node of the tree will be
  its left child}
  FHead := BTNodeManager.AllocNodeClear;
end;
destructor TtdBinaryTree.Destroy;
begin
  Clear;
  BTNodeManager.FreeNode(FHead);
  inherited Destroy;
end;
```

Create will make sure that the binary tree node manager is active and then allocate itself a dummy head node. It is from the left child of this node that the tree's root node is found. Destroy makes sure that the tree is cleared (that is, all the nodes in the tree freed) and then free the dummy head node.

The next method is Clear. Here we have to dispose of all the nodes in the tree. As mentioned before, this is done by means of a post-order traversal of the whole tree. We code this traversal as a non-recursive one; it is safer.

Listing 8.11: Clearing a binary tree

```
procedure TtdBinaryTree.Clear;
var
  Stack : TtdStack;
  Node  : PtdBinTreeNode;
begin
  if (FCount = 0) then
    Exit;
  {create the stack}
  Stack := TtdStack.Create(nil);
  try
    {push the root}
    Stack.Push(FHead^.btChild[ctLeft]);
    {continue until the stack is empty}
    while not Stack.IsEmpty do begin
      {get the node at the head of the queue}
      Node := Stack.Pop;
      {if it's nil, pop the next node and free it}
      if (Node = nil) then begin
        Node := Stack.Pop;
        if Assigned(FDispose) then
          FDispose(Node^.btData);
        BTNodeManager.FreeNode(Node);
      end
      {otherwise, the children of the node have not been pushed yet}
      else begin
        {push the node, followed by a nil pointer}
        Stack.Push(Node);
        Stack.Push(nil);
        {push the right child, if it's not nil}
        if (Node^.btChild[ctRight]<>nil) then
          Stack.Push(Node^.btChild[ctRight]);
        {push the left child if it's not nil}
        if (Node^.btChild[ctLeft]<>nil) then
          Stack.Push(Node^.btChild[ctLeft]);
      end;
    end;
  finally
    {destroy the stack}
    Stack.Free;
  end;
  {patch up the tree to be empty}
  FCount := 0;
```

```
  FHead^.btChild[ctLeft] := nil;
end;
```

If you compare this against the generic non-recursive code in Listing 8.7, you'll see that it is much the same, the only real difference being that there is no action procedure; we already know what we will do to each node.

The Traverse method just acts as a wrapper around the various internal traversal methods, most of which we've already discussed. The others that we haven't seen yet are the proper recursive methods for traversing a tree.

Listing 8.12: Traversing the binary tree class

```
function TtdBinaryTree.btRecInOrder(aNode      : PtdBinTreeNode;
                                    aAction    : TtdVisitProc;
                                    aExtraData : pointer)
                                               : PtdBinTreeNode;
var
  StopNow : boolean;
begin
  Result := nil;
  if (aNode^.btChild[ctLeft]<>nil) then begin
    Result := btRecInOrder(aNode^.btChild[ctLeft],
                           aAction, aExtraData);
    if (Result<>nil) then
      Exit;
  end;
  StopNow := false;
  aAction(aNode^.btData, aExtraData, StopNow);
  if StopNow then begin
    Result := aNode;
    Exit;
  end;
  if (aNode^.btChild[ctRight]<>nil) then begin
    Result := btRecInOrder(aNode^.btChild[ctRight],
                           aAction, aExtraData);
  end;
end;
function TtdBinaryTree.btRecPostOrder(aNode      : PtdBinTreeNode;
                                      aAction    : TtdVisitProc;
                                      aExtraData : pointer)
                                                 : PtdBinTreeNode;
var
  StopNow : boolean;
begin
  Result := nil;
  if (aNode^.btChild[ctLeft]<>nil) then begin
    Result := btRecPostOrder(aNode^.btChild[ctLeft],
                             aAction, aExtraData);
```

```
    if (Result<>nil) then
      Exit;
  end;
  if (aNode^.btChild[ctRight]<>nil) then begin
    Result := btRecPostOrder(aNode^.btChild[ctRight],
                             aAction, aExtraData);
    if (Result<>nil) then
      Exit;
  end;
  StopNow := false;
  aAction(aNode^.btData, aExtraData, StopNow);
  if StopNow then
    Result := aNode;
end;
function TtdBinaryTree.btRecPreOrder(aNode      : PtdBinTreeNode;
                                     aAction    : TtdVisitProc;
                                     aExtraData : pointer)
                                                : PtdBinTreeNode;
var
  StopNow : boolean;
begin
  Result := nil;
  StopNow := false;
  aAction(aNode^.btData, aExtraData, StopNow);
  if StopNow then begin
    Result := aNode;
    Exit;
  end;
  if (aNode^.btChild[ctLeft]<>nil) then begin
    Result := btRecPreOrder(aNode^.btChild[ctLeft],
                            aAction, aExtraData);
    if (Result<>nil) then
      Exit;
  end;
  if (aNode^.btChild[ctRight]<>nil) then begin
    Result := btRecPreOrder(aNode^.btChild[ctRight],
                            aAction, aExtraData);
  end;
end;
function TtdBinaryTree.Traverse(aMode         : TtdTraversalMode;
                                aAction       : TtdVisitProc;
                                aExtraData    : pointer;
                                aUseRecursion : boolean)
                                              : PtdBinTreeNode;
var
  RootNode : PtdBinTreeNode;
begin
  Result := nil;
```

```
    RootNode := FHead^.btChild[ctLeft];
    if (RootNode <> nil) then begin
      case aMode of
        tmPreOrder :
          if aUseRecursion then
            Result := btRecPreOrder(RootNode, aAction, aExtraData)
          else
            Result := btNoRecPreOrder(aAction, aExtraData);
        tmInOrder :
          if aUseRecursion then
            Result := btRecInOrder(RootNode, aAction, aExtraData)
          else
            Result := btNoRecInOrder(aAction, aExtraData);
        tmPostOrder :
          if aUseRecursion then
            Result := btRecPostOrder(RootNode, aAction, aExtraData)
          else
            Result := btNoRecPostOrder(aAction, aExtraData);
        tmLevelOrder :
          Result := btLevelOrder(aAction, aExtraData);
      end;
    end;
  end;
```

As you can see from the internal recursive routines, the ability to stop the traversal at any time makes the code a little more illegible and complicated.

The source code for the TtdBinaryTree class can be found in the TDBinTre.pas file on the CD.

Binary Search Trees

Although binary trees are interesting data structures in their own right, people generally use binary trees containing items in a sorted form. Such binary trees are known as *binary search trees*.

In a binary search tree, each node has a *key*. (In the binary search trees we build in this chapter, the key is assumed to be part of the item we'll be inserting into the tree. We will use a TtdCompareFunc routine to compare two items, and therefore their keys.) An ordering is applied to all of the nodes in the tree: for each node, the key of the left child node is less than or equal to the node's key, and this key in turn is less than or equal to the key of the right child node. If this ordering is consistently applied during insertion (we'll see how in a moment) this ordering also means that, for any node, all of the keys in the left child tree are less than or equal to the node's key, and all of the keys in the right child tree are greater than or equal to the node's key.

If we use a binary search tree instead of an ordinary binary tree, what basic operations have changed? Well, the traversals all work in the same way as before (in fact, an in-order traversal visits the nodes in a binary search tree in key order—hence the name "in-order"). Insert and delete, though, must change, since they may upset the binary search tree's ordering. Searching for an item can be made much faster.

The search algorithm for a binary search tree makes use of the ordering in the tree. To look for an item, we proceed as follows. Start at the root, and make this the current node. Compare the key of the item we are looking for with the key at the current node. If they are equal, we're done since we've found the correct item in the tree. Otherwise, if the item's key is less than that at the current node, make the left child the current node; if greater than, make the right child the current node, and return to the comparison step. Eventually, we will either find the node we want or we will get to a child that is nil, in which case, the item we are searching for is not in the tree.

There is one thing to notice about this algorithm should we have several items in the tree with equal keys: we are not guaranteed to get any particular item with an equal key; it could be the first, the last, or any in between. In fact, for much of the same reasons as with the skip list, I prefer making sure that the items in a binary search tree all have unique, different keys. Duplicate keys are not allowed. This rule does not pose too much difficulty in practice: if we can differentiate between two items, it should not be too difficult to enable the binary search tree to differentiate between them as well, usually by the use of minor keys (for example, using the last name as the main key and using the first name as a "tie-breaker" when two last names are equal). Henceforth, the binary search trees in this chapter will enforce the "no duplicates" rule. The definition of our binary search tree is now one where the left child key is strictly less than the node's key and this key is strictly less than the right child's key.

The search algorithm in a binary search tree mimics the standard binary search in an array or linked list. At every node we make a decision about which child link we are going to follow and we can ignore all of the nodes that appear in the other child's tree. If the tree is *balanced*, the search algorithm is a $O(\log(n))$ operation, the time taken to find any item being proportional to the $\log_2$ of the number of items in the tree. By balanced I mean that the path from every leaf to the root is approximately the same, with the tree having the minimum number of levels for the number of nodes present.

Listing 8.13: Searching in a binary search tree

```
function TtdBinarySearchTree.bstFindItem(aItem : pointer;
                                     var aNode  : PtdBinTreeNode;
                                     var aChild : TtdChildType)
                                                : boolean;
var
  Walker    : PtdBinTreeNode;
  CmpResult : integer;
begin
  Result := false;
  {if the tree is empty, return nil and left to signify that a new
  node, if inserted, would be the root}
  if (FCount = 0) then begin
    aNode := nil;
    aChild := ctLeft;
    Exit;
  end;
  {otherwise, walk the tree}
  Walker := FBinTree.Root;
  CmpResult := FCompare(aItem, Walker^.btData);
  while (CmpResult<>0) do begin
    if (CmpResult < 0) then begin
      if (Walker^.btChild[ctLeft] = nil) then begin
        aNode := Walker;
        aChild := ctLeft;
        Exit;
      end;
      Walker := Walker^.btChild[ctLeft];
    end
    else begin
      if (Walker^.btChild[ctRight] = nil) then begin
        aNode := Walker;
        aChild := ctRight;
        Exit;
      end;
      Walker := Walker^.btChild[ctRight];
    end;
    CmpResult := FCompare(aItem, Walker^.btData);
  end;
  Result := true;
  aNode := Walker;
end;
function TtdBinarySearchTree.Find(aKeyItem : pointer) : pointer;
var
  Node      : PtdBinTreeNode;
  ChildType : TtdChildType;
begin
  if bstFindItem(aKeyItem, Node, ChildType) then
```

```
    Result := Node^.btData
else
    Result := nil;
end;
```

The code in Listing 8.13 does not make use of a separate key for each item. Instead, it assumes that the binary search tree's ordering property is defined by a compare function, much as we did with the sorted linked lists and skip lists and so on. The compare function is declared to the binary search tree with the Create constructor.

The Find method makes use of an internal method called bstFindItem. This method is designed to be called for two different purposes. The first is the Find method itself, and the other is the method that inserts new nodes into the tree (which we'll be looking at in a moment). Consequently, the method will, if the item was not found, return the place where it should be inserted. This functionality, of course, is not required for a simple search: all that we would like to know is whether the item exists or not, and if so to get the complete item back.

Another thing to note about the code is that the class uses an internal TtdBinaryTree instance called FBinTree to hold the actual binary tree. The binary search tree class, as we shall see, delegates all binary tree operations to this internal binary tree. As you can see, all we need from this internal object is the root; from that point, we just walk the nodes.

Insertion with a Binary Search Tree

For a user of a binary search tree, we can make the insert operation a lot easier to use: all that has to be provided is the item itself. No longer does the user have to worry about which node becomes the parent and as which child the new node is added. Instead, the binary search tree can do it all, hiding all the details, by using the ordering of the items within the tree as a guide.

In fact, it is relatively easy to insert a new item into a binary search tree, and we've seen the majority of the process already. We search for the item, until we get to the point where we can't move down any more because the child link we would like to follow is nil. At this point we know where the item should be: it's the point where we had to stop. We know which child we want, and we, of course, stopped at the parent of the new node. So, we allocate a new node and add it to the parent node as the required child. Notice, as well, that our search for the place to insert the new item ensures that the order of the binary search tree is not violated.

There is, however, a problem with this insertion algorithm. Although the method is guaranteed to produce a valid binary search tree after the operation, the tree produced may not be optimal or efficient. To see what I mean, let's insert the items *a*, *b*, *c*, *d*, *e*, and *f* into an empty binary search tree. *a* is easy: it becomes the root node. *b* gets added as the right child of *a*. *c* gets added as the right child of *b*, and so on. The first image in Figure 8.2 is the result: a long spindly tree that can be viewed as a linked list. Ideally, we would want the tree to be more balanced. The degenerate binary search tree we just produced has search times that are proportional to the number of items in the tree (O(*n*)), not to $\log_2$ of the number (O(log(*n*))). There are other degenerate cases as well; try this series of inserts for another example: *a*, *f*, *b*, *e*, *c*, and *d*, which produces the kinky degenerate tree as shown in the second image of Figure 8.2.

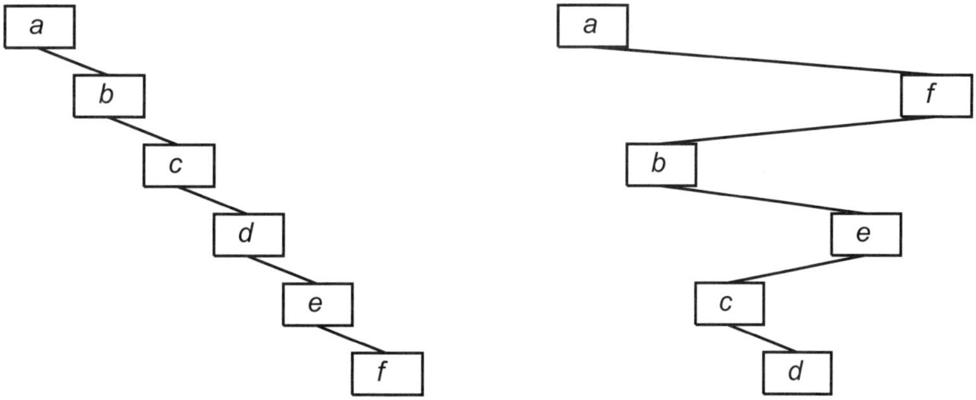

Figure 8.2: Degenerate binary search trees

In fact, this simple insertion algorithm is hardly ever used, just because of these problems. If the keys and items being inserted were guaranteed to be in a random sequence, or the total number of items is going to be fairly small, this insertion algorithm is acceptable. In general, however, we just can't provide this type of guarantee, and we need to use a more complex insertion algorithm that attempts to balance the binary search tree as part of the algorithm. We'll take a look at this balancing methodology in a moment, when we discuss red-black trees.

> This is an important point to bear in mind. The insertion and deletion algorithms we're discussing here are guaranteed to produce a valid binary search tree; however, it is very likely that the tree will be cockeyed and unbalanced. For small binary search trees, it doesn't much matter (after all for small *n*, log(*n*) and *n* are of the same magnitude more or less, so the big-Oh number doesn't help us much), but for large ones it's dreadful.

Going back to the simple insertion algorithm, we can see that inserting *n* items into a binary search tree is, on average, a O(nlog(*n*)) process (in layman's terms: each insertion uses a O(log(*n*)) search algorithm to find where the new item should be put, and there are *n* items to be inserted). In the degenerate case, inserting *n* items becomes a O(n^2) operation instead.

Listing 8.14: Insertion in a binary search tree

```
function TtdBinarySearchTree.bstInsertPrim(aItem      : pointer;
                                       var aChildType : TtdChildType)
                                                      : PtdBinTreeNode;
begin
  {first, attempt to find the item; if found, it's an error}
  if bstFindItem(aItem, Result, aChildType) then
    bstError(tdeBinTreeDupItem, 'bstInsertPrim');
  {this returns a node, so insert there}
  Result := FBinTree.InsertAt(Result, aChildType, aItem);
  inc(FCount);
end;
procedure TtdBinarySearchTree.Insert(aItem : pointer);
var
  ChildType : TtdChildType;
begin
  bstInsertPrim(aItem, ChildType);
end;
```

We make use of an internal routine, bstInsertPrim, to do most of the work. The reason for this is to separate the actual insertion code from the Insert method so that when we eventually write descendants of the binary search tree to perform balancing operations, we'll have an easier time. bstInsertPrim returns the node that was inserted, and as you can see, it makes use of the bstFindItem method we encountered in Listing 8.13.

As you can see, we delegate the actual insertion to the binary tree object, using its InsertAt method.

Deletion from a Binary Search Tree

Again, for the user of a binary search tree, we can hide most of the difficulties. The tree, however, has some more complex work to do.

The first step is, of course, to search for the item in the tree using the standard algorithm. If we don't manage to find the item, we would have to report a failure in some way. If we do find the item, there are three types of node we could end up at, just as with the standard binary tree.

The first type of node is the one with no children, both child links being nil; a leaf, in other words. To delete this type of node, we merely unlink it from its parent and dispose of it. This deletion does not disturb the ordering of the tree—after all, the node was a leaf and had no child nodes.

The second type of node is the one with just one child. With the standard binary tree, we merely promoted the child up a level to replace the node being deleted. Can we do the same here? Consider the parent of the node to be deleted. Either the deleted node is the left child (in which case the key of the node is less than that of the parent), or the deleted node is the right child (in which case the key of the node is greater than that of the parent). Not only that, but all children, grandchildren, etc., of the deleted node have the same property; they will either all be less than the parent node or all be greater than the parent node. So as far as the parent is concerned, if we replace the node with its one child, the ordering property will be preserved. If the child node has children nodes of its own, this promotion has no effect on them or their ordering. So, we can still do this simple operation in the binary search tree case.

The third type of node is the one with two children. In the standard binary tree, we deemed that deleting this type of node was an error; it couldn't be done since there was no generic way to perform a delete operation that made sense. With the binary search tree this is no longer the case: we can use the ordering property of the binary search tree to help us out.

The situation we have is this: we want to delete a given node (i.e., the item in that node), but it has two children (both of which may have children of their own). The algorithm is a little peculiar, so I'll first describe it and then show that it works. What we do is find the node containing the largest item that is just smaller than the one we are trying to delete. We then swap the items in these two nodes. Finally, we delete the second node; it will always be one of the first two deletion cases.

The first step is to find the largest item that is smaller than the item we are trying to delete. This is obviously found in the left child tree (it is smaller than the item we're deleting). It is also the largest item there; in other words, all the other items that can be found in the left child tree are less than this item. It so happens that all the items in the *right* child tree are greater than this selected item (since it's less than the item to be deleted and this latter item is less than all the items in the right child tree). Hence it can easily replace the item we're deleting, and in doing so still maintain the proper ordering of the tree.

But what about the node it came from, the one we now have to delete? The important thing to realize about this particular node is that it has *no right child*. If it did have a right child, the item in this child would have been larger than the item we swapped, and hence the item we originally selected could not have been the largest. It might have a left child, to be sure, but whether it does or not, we know how to delete a node with at most one child.

This still leaves the problem of how to find the largest item that is smaller than our original item, the one we want to delete. Essentially, we walk the tree. Starting at the item we want to delete, we take the left child link. From this point we continue taking right child links until we get to a node without any right child. This node is guaranteed to have the largest item in it that is just smaller than the one we are trying to delete.

Notice also that deletion, just like insertion, has the capability to create a degenerate tree. The balancing algorithms that we'll discuss as part of the red-black variant will address this problem.

Listing 8.15: Deletion from a binary search tree

```
function TtdBinarySearchTree.bstFindNodeToDelete(aItem : pointer)
                                                       : PtdBinTreeNode;
var
  Walker : PtdBinTreeNode;
  Node   : PtdBinTreeNode;
  Temp   : pointer;
  ChildType : TtdChildType;
begin
  {attempt to find the item; signal error if not found}
  if not bstFindItem(aItem, Node, ChildType) then
    bstError(tdeBinTreeItemMissing, 'bstFindNodeToDelete');
  {if the node has two children, find the largest node that is smaller
  than the one we want to delete, and swap over the items}
  if (Node^.btChild[ctLeft]<>nil) and
     (Node^.btChild[ctRight]<>nil) then begin
    Walker := Node^.btChild[ctLeft];
    while (Walker^.btChild[ctRight]<>nil) do
      Walker := Walker^.btChild[ctRight];
    Temp := Walker^.btData;
    Walker^.btData := Node^.btData;
    Node^.btData := Temp;
    Node := Walker;
  end;
  {return the node to delete}
  Result := Node;
end;
procedure TtdBinarySearchTree.Delete(aItem : pointer);
begin
  FBinTree.Delete(bstFindNodeToDelete(aItem));
```

```
  dec(FCount);
end;
```

It is the bstFindNodeToDelete method that does most of the work. It calls bstFindItem to find the item to delete (of course, if it wasn't found we signal an error), and then checks to see whether the node found has two children or not. If it does, we find the node with the largest item that is smaller than the item we want to delete. We swap over the items between the nodes and return the second one.

Class Implementation of a Binary Search Tree

As usual, we shall encapsulate a binary search tree as a class, although I would warn you again that you should only use it if you can be sure that the items being inserted are sufficiently random or small in number that the tree doesn't degenerate into a spindly affair. What we are trying to achieve with a binary search tree class is hiding the mechanics of the tree from the user. This means that the user should be able to use the class to keep a set of items in sorted order, and traverse through them, without having to know how the internal nodes are structured.

In implementing the binary search tree, we will not descend from the binary tree class we described in the first part of this chapter. The main reason for this is that the binary tree class exposed too much of the internal node structure for our goal. Instead, we will delegate the mechanics of inserting, deleting, and traversing to an internal binary tree object. Just in case the user needs the underlying tree object we'll expose it through a property.

Listing 8.16: Binary search tree interface

```
type
  TtdBinarySearchTree = class
    {binary search tree class}
    private
      FBinTree : TtdBinaryTree;
      FCompare : TtdCompareFunc;
      FCount   : integer;
      FName    : TtdNameString;
    protected
      procedure bstError(aErrorCode  : integer;
                   const aMethodName : TtdNameString);
      function bstFindItem(aItem  : pointer;
                       var aNode  : PtdBinTreeNode;
                       var aChild : TtdChildType) : boolean;
      function bstFindNodeToDelete(aItem : pointer) : PtdBinTreeNode;
      function bstInsertPrim(aItem      : pointer;
                         var aChildType : TtdChildType)
```

```
                                          : PtdBinTreeNode;
  public
    constructor Create(aCompare : TtdCompareFunc;
                       aDispose : TtdDisposeProc);
    destructor Destroy; override;
    procedure Clear;
    procedure Delete(aItem : pointer); virtual;
    function Find(aKeyItem : pointer) : pointer; virtual;
    procedure Insert(aItem : pointer); virtual;
    function Traverse(aMode         : TtdTraversalMode;
                      aAction       : TtdVisitProc;
                      aExtraData    : pointer;
                      aUseRecursion : boolean) : pointer;
    property BinaryTree : TtdBinaryTree read FBinTree;
    property Count : integer read FCount;
    property Name : TtdNameString read FName write FName;
end;
```

Looking at this class definition, you can see that we've already met most of the methods.

The source code for the TtdBinarySearchTree class can be found in the TDBinTre.pas file on the CD.

Binary Search Tree Rearrangements

When discussing the binary search tree, I stated that adding items to a binary tree could make it woefully unbalanced, sometimes even degenerating into a long spindly tree like a linked list.

The problem with this degeneration is not that the binary search tree stops functioning properly (items are still being stored in sorted order), it's that the tree's good efficiency takes a fatal knock if it happens. For a perfectly balanced tree (on average, all parent nodes have two children, and all leaves appear at the same level, plus or minus one), search time, insertion time, and deletion time are all O(log(n)). In other words, if a basic operation takes time t for a tree with 1,000 nodes, it will only take time $2t$ for a tree with 1,000,000 nodes. On the other hand, for a degenerate tree, the basic operations all become O(n) operations, and the time taken for 1,000,000 nodes would instead be $1{,}000t$.

So, how do we avoid this descent into degenerate trees? The answer is to devise an algorithm that balances the binary search tree during insertion and deletion of items. Before we actually look at balancing algorithms, let's investigate various methods of rearranging binary search trees and then we can use these methods to balance our trees.

Recall that in a binary search tree, for every node, all of the nodes in the left child tree are all less than it, and all those in the right child tree are greater than it. (By a node being less than another, I mean, of course, that the key for the item in the one node is less than the key for the item in the other. However, it is certainly easier to write "one node is less than another" than continually having to refer to the keys for the nodes.) Let's explore this axiom a little more.

Look at the left child of a node in a binary search tree. What do we know about it? Well, it has a left child tree and a right child tree of its own, of course. It is greater than all of the nodes in its left child tree; it is less than all of the nodes in its right child tree. Furthermore, since it is a left child, its parent is greater than all of the nodes in its right child tree. So if we rotate the left child into its parent's position, such that its right child tree becomes the parent's new left child tree, the resulting binary search tree is still valid. Figure 8.3 shows this rotation. In this figure, the little triangles represent child trees that contain zero or more nodes—the exact number is not germane to the rotation algorithm.

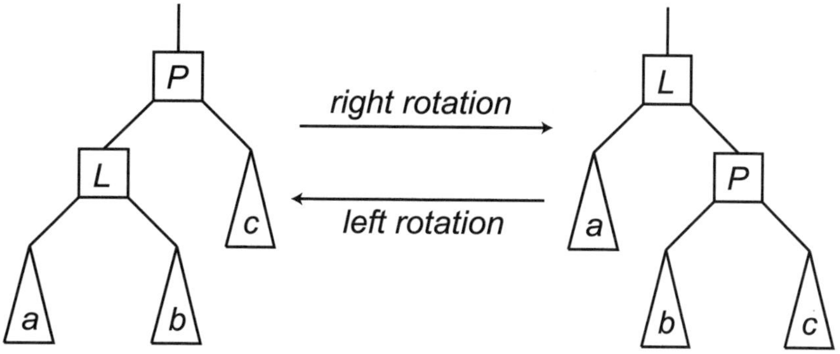

Figure 8.3: Promoting the left child (and vice versa)

Using the original tree, we could write the following inequality: $(a<L<b)<P<c$. In the new tree, we have $a<L<(b<P<c)$, which, of course, is the same thing when the brackets are removed, because < is commutative. (Read the first inequality as: all the nodes in a are less than L, which is less than all of the nodes in b, and that tree taken as a whole is less than P, which in turn is less than all the nodes in c. We can interpret the second inequality in a similar manner.)

The operation we have just seen is known as a *right rotation*. It is said to *promote* the left child L and *demote* the parent P; in other words L is moved up a level and P is moved down a level. The rotation is said to be about P.

Of course, having seen the right rotation operation, we can easily conceive of another rotation, a *left rotation*: the rotation that would produce the first tree from the second. A left rotation promotes the right child P and demotes the parent L. Listing 8.17 shows both rotations, but coded from the viewpoint of the node being promoted.

Listing 8.17: Promotion of a node

```
function TtdSplayTree.stPromote(aNode  : PtdBinTreeNode)
                                       : PtdBinTreeNode;
var
  Parent : PtdBinTreeNode;
begin
  {make a note of the parent of the node we're promoting}
  Parent := aNode^.btParent;
  {in both cases there are 6 links to be broken and remade: the node's
  link to its child and vice versa, the node's link with its parent
  and vice versa and the parent's link with its parent and vice
  versa; note that the node's child could be nil}
  {promote a left child = right rotation of parent}
  if (Parent^.btChild[ctLeft] = aNode) then begin
    Parent^.btChild[ctLeft] := aNode^.btChild[ctRight];
    if (Parent^.btChild[ctLeft]<>nil) then
      Parent^.btChild[ctLeft]^.btParent := Parent;
    aNode^.btParent := Parent^.btParent;
    if (aNode^.btParent^.btChild[ctLeft] = Parent) then
      aNode^.btParent^.btChild[ctLeft] := anode
    else
      aNode^.btParent^.btChild[ctRight] := aNode;
    aNode^.btChild[ctRight] := Parent;
    Parent^.btParent := aNode;
  end
  {promote a right child = left rotation of parent}
  else begin
    Parent^.btChild[ctRight] := aNode^.btChild[ctLeft];
    if (Parent^.btChild[ctRight]<>nil) then
      Parent^.btChild[ctRight]^.btParent := Parent;
    aNode^.btParent := Parent^.btParent;
    if (aNode^.btParent^.btChild[ctLeft] = Parent) then
      aNode^.btParent^.btChild[ctLeft] := anode
    else
      aNode^.btParent^.btChild[ctRight] := aNode;
    aNode^.btChild[ctLeft] := Parent;
    Parent^.btParent := aNode;
  end;
  {return the node we promoted}
  Result := aNode;
end;
```

This method is from the splay tree class, which we'll be discussing in a moment, but the essential point to see is the way the links are broken and reformed for both types of promotion. Since the node passed in could be a left child or a right child, with different links to break and reform, this method is essentially an If statement for the two possibilities.

These two rotations rearrange the tree at a local level, but the main node ordering property of a binary search tree remains invariant. For a right rotation, all of the nodes in *a* move one level closer to the root, those in *b* stay at the same level and those in c move down by one level. For a left rotation, all of the nodes in *a* move one level farther from the root, those in *b* stay at the same level and those in c move up by one level. As you may imagine, assuming the control of some overall balancing algorithm, a series of these two rotations could help rebalance a binary search tree.

Frequently, these two rotations are combined in pairs and used in what are known as *zig-zag* and *zig-zig forms*. There are two zig-zag operations and two zig-zig operations. A zig-zag operation consists either of a right rotation followed by a left rotation or a left rotation followed by a right rotation, and the net result of both is to promote a node two levels up. Zig-zig operations, on the other hand, consist of two right rotations or two left rotations performed in sequence. The intent of all these paired operations is to promote a node up two levels.

Figure 8.4 shows a zig-zag operation starting with a left rotation about P. This promotes R and demotes P. In the next step we have a right rotation about G, and this promotes R yet again and demotes G. The overall effect of the zig-zag operation is to balance the tree locally.

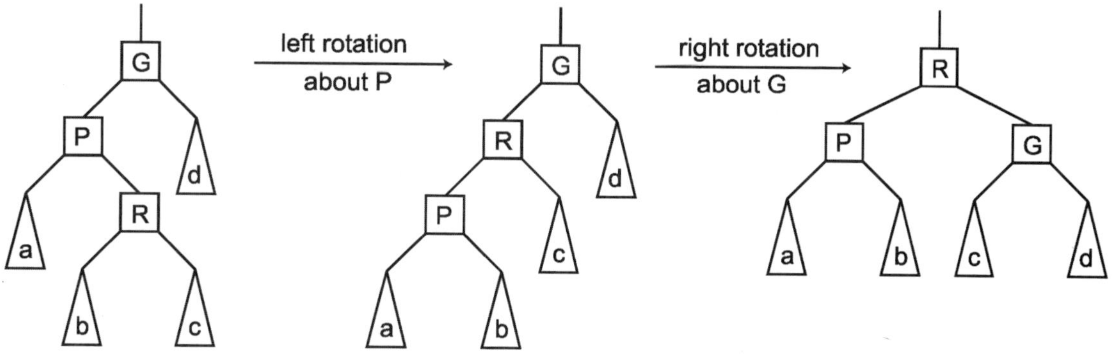

Figure 8.4: The zig-zag operation

Figure 8.5 shows both zig-zig operations since it turns out they are complementary. Notice that in a zig-zig operation you always start out with the upper rotation first.

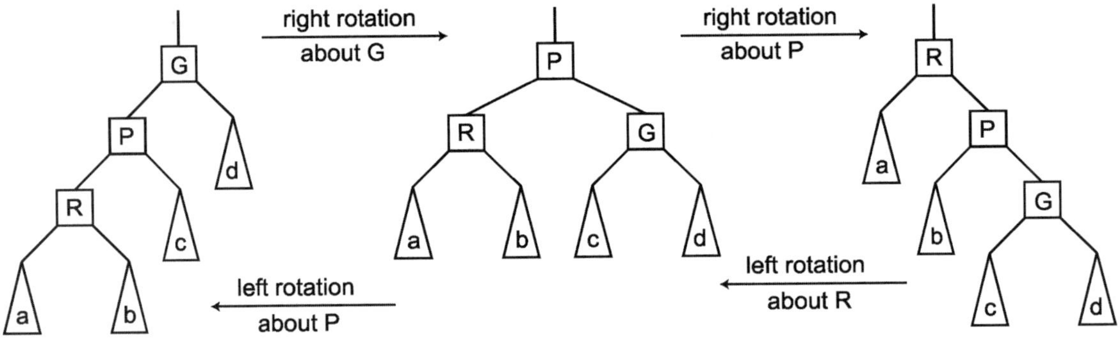

Figure 8.5: Both zig-zag operations

Splay Trees

Anyway, having seen these rotations and zig-zag and zig-zig operations, we can use them in a data structure known as a splay tree. A *splay tree* is a binary search tree constructed such that any access to a node results in the node being *splayed* to the root. Splaying is the application of zig-zag or zig-zig operations until the node being splayed is at the root of the tree, or is one level down from the root, in which case a single rotation can promote it to the root. Splay trees were invented by D.D. Sleator and R.E. Tarjan in 1985 [22].

The first operation we look at is the search operation, i.e., finding a particular node. We start off with the standard search algorithm for a binary search tree. Once we've found the node for which we were searching, we splay it to the root of the tree. In other words, we apply either zig-zag operations or zig-zig operations, moving the node up the tree, until it reaches the root. If the node ends up on the second level, we can't apply a zig-zag or a zig-zig operation any more, so instead we perform either a left or a right rotation to move the node into the root spot.

If the search was unsuccessful, we shall hit a nil node during the search. In this case, we splay the node that would have been the parent, if the node we were looking for existed. Of course, we would report the failure to find the item in some manner.

Insertion is easily described as well: perform the normal algorithm for binary search tree insertion and then splay the newly added node.

For deletion, we perform the normal binary search tree deletion and then splay the parent of the node that was deleted.

Overall, what the splay tree gives us is a self-modifying data structure; one that tends to keep frequently accessed nodes near the top of the tree, with infrequently accessed nodes out toward the leaves. The frequently accessed nodes would tend to have faster access times than the average, whereas the rarely accessed nodes would have longer access times than the average. It is important to note that the splay tree doesn't have any explicit balancing features, but we do find in practice that the splaying action does help keep the tree balanced reasonably well. On average, the splay tree has O(log(*n*)) search times.

Class Implementation of a Splay Tree

The TtdSplayTree class is a simple decendant of the TtdBinarySearchTree class, overriding the Delete, Find and Insert methods and declaring new internal methods to splay and promote a node. Listing 8.18 shows the interface to this class.

Listing 8.18: The interface to TtdSplayTree

```
type
  TtdSplayTree = class(TtdBinarySearchTree)
    private
    protected
      function stPromote(aNode  : PtdBinTreeNode) : PtdBinTreeNode;
      procedure stSplay(aNode : PtdBinTreeNode);
    public
      procedure Delete(aItem : pointer); override;
      function Find(aKeyItem : pointer) : pointer; override;
      procedure Insert(aItem : pointer); override;
  end;
```

The overridden Find method (Listing 8.19) performs the usual binary search tree find operation and, if the node was found, splays it to the root.

Listing 8.19: The TtdSplayTree.Find method

```
function TtdSplayTree.Find(aKeyItem : pointer) : pointer;
var
  Node      : PtdBinTreeNode;
  ChildType : TtdChildType;
begin
  if bstFindItem(aKeyItem, Node, ChildType) then begin
    Result := Node^.btData;
    stSplay(Node);
  end
```

```
  else
    Result := nil;
end;
```

The overridden Insert method (Listing 8.20) performs the usual binary search tree insert operation and splays the new node to the root.

Listing 8.20: The TtdSplayTree.Insert method

```
procedure TtdSplayTree.Insert(aItem : pointer);
var
  ChildType : TtdChildType;
begin
  stSplay(bstInsertPrim(aItem, ChildType));
end;
```

The overridden Delete method (Listing 8.21) performs the usual binary search tree delete operation and splays the deleted node's parent to the root.

Listing 8.21: The TtdSplayTree.Delete method

```
procedure TtdSplayTree.Delete(aItem : pointer);
var
  Node : PtdBinTreeNode;
  Dad  : PtdBinTreeNode;
begin
  Node := bstFindNodeToDelete(aItem);
  Dad  := Node^.btParent;
  FBinTree.Delete(Node);
  dec(FCount);
  if (Count<>0) then
    stSplay(Dad);
end;
```

These three overridden methods are all pretty easy to understand because they defer the real processing to the stSplay method. Listing 8.22 shows this method.

Listing 8.22: The TtdSplayTree.stSplay method

```
procedure TtdSplayTree.stSplay(aNode : PtdBinTreeNode);
var
  Dad      : PtdBinTreeNode;
  Grandad  : PtdBinTreeNode;
  RootNode : PtdBinTreeNode;
begin
  {as we've got to splay until we reach the root, get the root as a
  local variable: it'll make things a little faster}
  RootNode := FBinTree.Root;
  {if we're at the root, there's no splaying to do}
  if (aNode = RootNode) then
```

```
    Exit;
  {get the parent and the grandparent}
  Dad := aNode^.btParent;
  if (Dad = RootNode) then
    Grandad := nil
  else
    Grandad := Dad^.btParent;
  {while we can, perform zig-zag and zig-zig promotions}
  while (Grandad<>nil) do begin
    {determine the kind of double-promotion we need to do}
    if ((Grandad^.btChild[ctLeft] = Dad) and
        (Dad^.btChild[ctLeft] = aNode)) or
       ((Grandad^.btChild[ctRight] = Dad) and
        (Dad^.btChild[ctRight] = aNode)) then begin
      {zig-zig promotion}
      stPromote(Dad);
      stPromote(aNode);
    end
    else begin
      {zig-zag promotion}
      stPromote(stPromote(aNode));
    end;
    {now we've promoted the node, get the new parent and grandparent}
    RootNode := FBinTree.Root;
    if (aNode = RootNode) then begin
      Dad := nil;
      Grandad := nil;
    end
    else begin
      Dad := aNode^.btParent;
      if (Dad = RootNode) then
        Grandad := nil
      else
        Grandad := Dad^.btParent;
    end;
  end;
  {once this point is reached, the node is either at the root, or one
  level down; make one last promotion if necessary}
  if (Dad<>nil) then
    stPromote(aNode);
end;
```

Although this routine looks complex, all it is doing is promoting the node passed in all the way to the root. This is done through a series of zig-zig or zig-zag promotions: if the node, parent, and grandparent are all in a line, it's a zig-zig promotion; otherwise it's a zig-zag promotion. This process is continued in a loop until either the node is promoted to the root, or the parent of the node is the root. In the latter case, there is one more promotion to do.

The rearrangement code for the promotions is supplied by the stPromote method, shown in Listing 8.17.

Red-Black Trees

Having looked at rotations, zig-zags, and zig-zigs, and familiarized ourselves with the reorganization of binary search trees with splay trees, we shall now investigate a proper balancing algorithm.

What should a balancing algorithm do? Ideally, it should ensure that the path from every leaf to the root is exactly the same length, plus or minus one. In practice, this rigorous requirement is somewhat difficult to enforce (AVL trees use this definition and their balancing algorithm enforces the rule), so we'd settle for some algorithm that provided a "looser" requirement, just so long as it wasn't so loose that we're back where we started.

In 1978, Guibas and Sedgewick invented the red-black tree, which provides this loose-but-not-too-loose requirement. Red-black trees are the data structure of choice for implementing maps in C++'s Standard Template Library (STL). The red-black algorithm provides a fast, efficient method of balancing a binary search tree—one that doesn't require too much extra space per node to hold the information required for balancing (indeed, a single extra bit will do).

So, what is a red-black tree? Well, to begin with, it is a binary search tree, having the usual simple search algorithm. In a red-black tree, though, we impose some extra information onto every node: each one is marked to be in one of two states. These two states are called red and black.

Obviously there must be more to this than just coloring nodes, and, in fact, there are three other rules that we must follow:

1. The nil child links in nodes on the periphery of the tree are assumed to point to other nodes (non-existent, of course). These invisible nil nodes are known as *external nodes* and are always colored black.
2. The black condition: Each path from root to every external node contains exactly the same number of black nodes.
3. The red condition: Each red node that is not the root has a black parent.

Rule 1 seems a little bizarre considering the construction of our trees so far where we've pretty well ignored these nil links, but the clause is required in order to help satisfy rule 2. Hence, a tree with a single node has two external nodes as well, being the two nil links from the single actual node (which is itself known as an internal node). The second rule is the balancing rule; it tries to make every path from root to external node roughly the same length, the only difference between different paths being the number of red nodes along them.

Figure 8.6 shows some simple red-black trees, with red nodes shown in gray (the limitations of a black and white book!) and external nodes shown as little black squares. The first tree (a) is supposed to represent an empty tree—it consists of just one external node, which is black—and hence by definition is a red-black tree. From the second and third trees (b and c), those containing just one internal node, you can see that whether we color the root node red or black, we have a red-black tree. The three rules are definitely being satisfied.

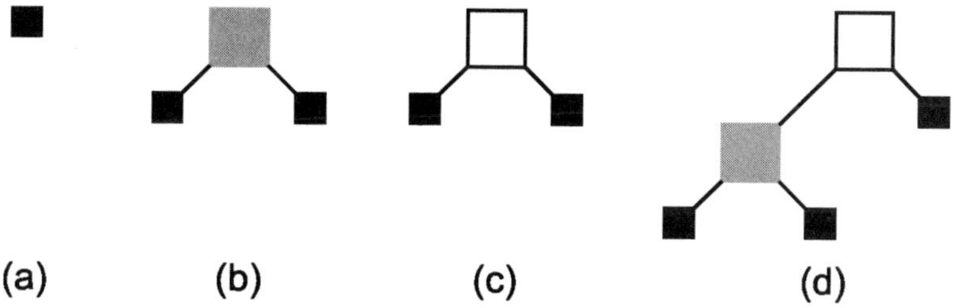

Figure 8.6: Some simple red-black trees

Before you look at the answer, try and construct a red-black tree that has two nodes, the root and its left child, and three external nodes (d). No matter how hard you try, you will find that the root has to be colored black and its left child red. That is the only way to color the nodes such that the tree satisfies our rules.

Let's approach this from a different angle. Take a look at Figure 8.7. The internal nodes have not yet been colored. Can you color them so that the tree satisfies rules 2 and 3? There is no possible solution. It is impossible to color the internal nodes such that both the black and red conditions are satisfied. Figure 8.7 can never be a red-black tree—which is good, because it is the start of a degenerate tree. So this is an important principle to grasp: not all trees can be colored red-black.

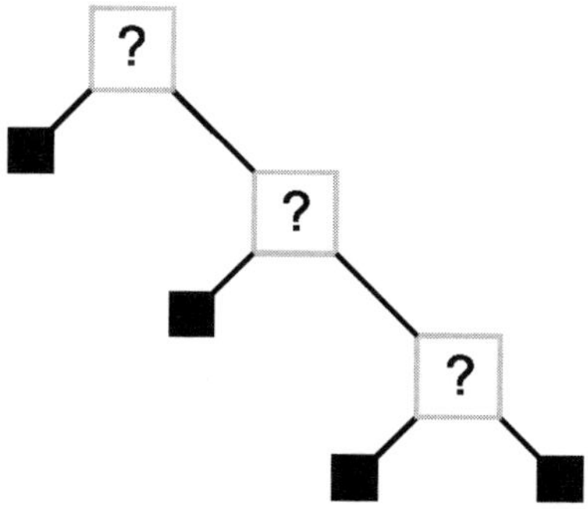

Figure 8.7: A tree that cannot be colored red-black

In fact, it can be shown that a red-black tree with n internal nodes has a height that is proportional to log n. In other words, a red-black tree has a proven worst-case search time of O(log(n)). This is exactly the result we want from a binary search tree; it is the degenerate trees which have search times of O(n).

Insertion into a Red-Black Tree

Having seen the rules for a red-black tree, how do we use them to insert a new node into a red-black tree? Well, we start off in the familiar way and search for the node. If we find it, we signal an error (we don't allow duplicates in a red-black tree, in the same manner that we didn't allow them in the standard binary search tree). Otherwise, we'll reach a node that we can use as the parent of our new node and an indication of which child the new node is to be. We replace the external node (remember, this is a grand name for the non-existent node at the end of the nil link) with our new node. Our new node will automatically come with two external nodes, which are colored black by rule 1, but what color do we make the new node?

Well, we start off by coloring it red. What impact does this have on the red-black rules? The first thing to notice is that the black condition is still satisfied: we are replacing a black external node with a red node and two black external nodes. The path to the root from each of the two new external nodes will still have the same number of black nodes as the path to the root from the replaced external node. But what about the red condition? Is that still satisfied? It may be, or it may not be. If the new node is the root, and therefore has no parent, we still have a proper red-black tree (actually, we could, if we wanted to, recolor the new node black and still have a red-black tree). If the new node is not the root, it will have a parent. If this parent node is black, the red condition, rule 3, still applies, and we still have a red-black tree. If the new node's parent is the root, then all we have to do is recolor the parent black, if necessary, to ensure that the tree remains red-black. (In fact, in a red-black tree, if both the root's children are black the root can be either red or black: it makes no difference to the rules.)

If the parent of the new node is not the root and is red, we would have two red nodes in sequence. The red condition would be violated and we would need to address the problem to make the tree red-black once more.

There are several sub-cases to consider. Let us first name some of the nodes so that we can see what is going on more easily. Then we can describe some of the transformations we need to do in order to return the tree to its red-black state.

Call the new node *s* (for Son), its parent *d* (for Dad), its parent's parent *g* (for Granddad), and its parent's sibling *u* (for Uncle). Just after adding the new node *s*, we have the following situation: *s* and *d* are red nodes (this is the violation of rule 2), *g* must be a black node (from rule 2), and *u* could be either red or black.

Let's assume that *u* is black for our first case. What we shall do is either a single rotation or a zig-zag rotation, and then recolor some nodes. In the first case, shown as the first transformation in Figure 8.8, we right rotate *d* into *g*'s place so that *g* becomes a child of *d*. We then recolor *d* to be black and *g* to be red. In the second case (the lower part of Figure 8.8) we zig-zag *s* into *g*'s place, and then recolor *s* to be black and *g* to be red. Note that we do not care whether *u* is an external node or an internal node; it just has to be black.

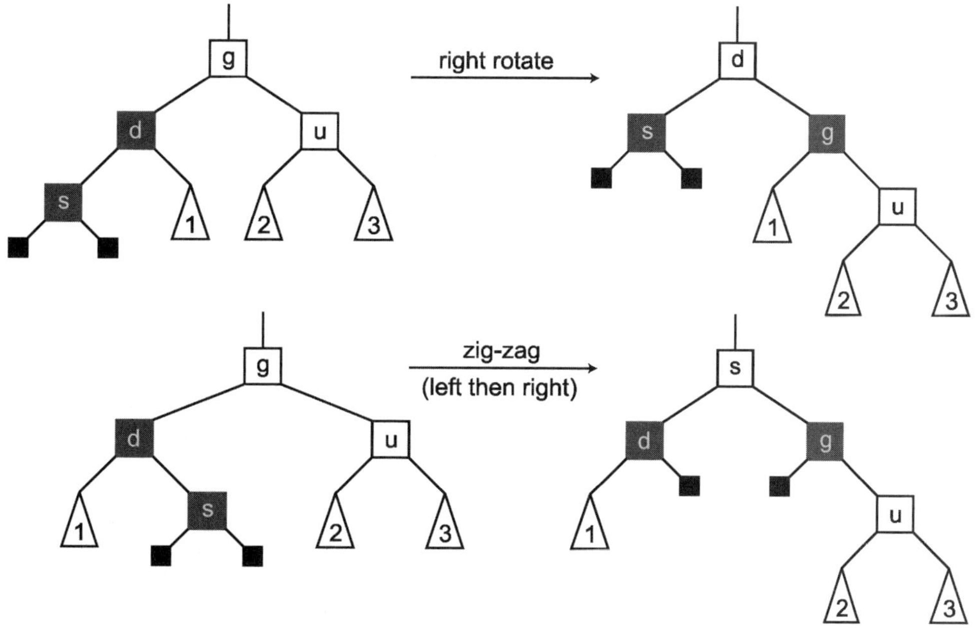

Figure 8.8: Balancing after insertion: the two simple cases

There are, of course, two other mirror-image possibilities as well, but we won't show them here. By looking at Figure 8.8, I'm sure that you can see that the red condition is now satisfied and that the rotations and recolor operations have not violated the black condition.

That was the easy case. Now for the more difficult. We assume *u*, the uncle, is red as well. The first step is simple: we recolor *d* and *u* to be black and *g* to be red. The black condition is still satisfied, but we seem to have made this worse as far as the red condition goes. Instead of node *s* being the violator of the red condition, we now have to assume that *g* could be; after all, *g*'s parent could be red. In other words, this recolor operation hasn't really solved anything; all we've done is shift the problem elsewhere. But is it really worse? Consider what we've done: we've moved the problem node farther up the tree. There's only so far we can go upward because eventually we will hit the root.

So we shift our attention two levels up the tree, consider *g* to be a new *s* and see whether we've violated any of the rules. In other words, we reapply the algorithm we've discussed so far, but starting at *g* this time. Figure 8.9 shows these two cases (and of course there are two mirror cases as well that are not shown). I've marked the *g* node in both resulting trees with a triple exclamation mark to indicate that it might violate one of our two rules and that we need to continue the process by repeating the algorithm again.

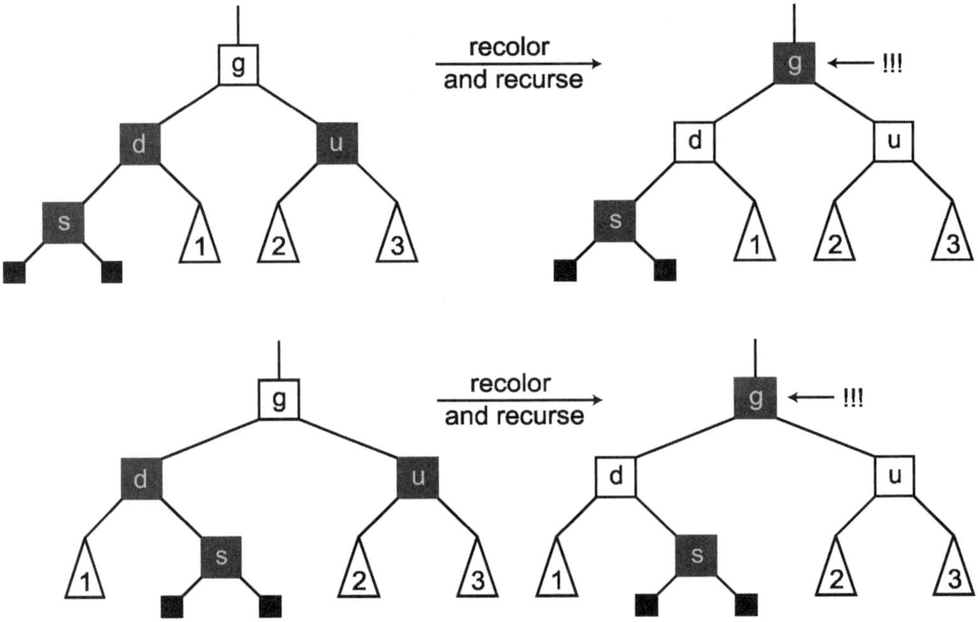

Figure 8.9: Balancing after insertion: the two recursive cases

Without delving too deeply into the mathematics, the red-black insertion algorithm is O(log(n)), just like the simple binary tree case, although there is a larger constant factor associated with the red-black tree to account for the possible rotations and promotions.

The implementation of this insertion and rebalancing algorithm is shown in Listing 8.23. The method has an internal loop that exits when the tree has been rebalanced. We assume at the beginning of the loop that we shall rebalance the tree in this cycle, and it is only if we have to shift our attention up the tree that we make sure that we go around the loop once more. Apart from that, the code is a pretty faithful representation of the red-black insertion algorithm. The only part that tends to be long-winded is the fact we have to maintain knowledge about whether certain nodes are left children or right children of their parents.

Listing 8.23: Red-black tree insertion

```
procedure TtdRedBlackTree.Insert(aItem : pointer);
var
  Node        : PtdBinTreeNode;
  Dad        : PtdBinTreeNode;
  Grandad    : PtdBinTreeNode;
  Uncle      : PtdBinTreeNode;
  OurType    : TtdChildType;
  DadsType   : TtdChildType;
  IsBalanced : boolean;
begin
  {insert the new item, get back the node that was inserted and its
  relationship to its parent}
  Node := bstInsertPrim(aItem, OurType);
  {color it red}
  Node^.btColor := rbRed;
  {in a loop, continue applying the red-black insertion balancing
  algorithms until the tree is balanced}
  repeat
    {assume we'll balance it this time}
    IsBalanced := true;
    {if the node is the root, we're done and the tree is balanced, so
    assume we're not at the root}
    if (Node<>FBinTree.Root) then begin
      {as we're not at the root, get the parent of this node}
      Dad := Node^.btParent;
      {if the parent is black, we're done and the tree is balanced, so
      assume that the parent is red}
      if (Dad^.btColor = rbRed) then begin
        {if the parent is the root, just recolor it black and we're
        done}
        if (Dad = FBinTree.Root) then
          Dad^.btColor := rbBlack
        {otherwise the parent has a parent of its own}
        else begin
          {get the grandparent (it must be black) and color it red}
          Grandad := Dad^.btParent;
          Grandad^.btColor := rbRed;
          {get the uncle node}
          if (Grandad^.btChild[ctLeft] = Dad) then begin
            DadsType := ctLeft;
            Uncle := Grandad^.btChild[ctRight];
          end
          else begin
            DadsType := ctRight;
```

```
            Uncle := Grandad^.btChild[ctLeft];
          end;
          {if the uncle is also red (note that the uncle can be nil!),
          color the parent black, the uncle black and start over with
          the grandparent}
          if IsRed(Uncle) then begin
            Dad^.btColor := rbBlack;
            Uncle^.btColor := rbBlack;
            Node := Grandad;
            IsBalanced := false;
          end
          {otherwise the uncle is black}
          else begin
            {if the current node has the same relationship with its
            parent as the parent has with the grandparent (ie, both
            are left children or both are right children), color the
            parent black and promote it; we're then done}
            OurType := GetChildType(Node);
            if (OurType = DadsType) then begin
              Dad^.btColor := rbBlack;
              rbtPromote(Dad);
            end
            {otherwise color the node black and zig-zag promote it;
            we're then done}
            else begin
              Node^.btColor := rbBlack;
              rbtPromote(rbtPromote(Node));
            end;
          end;
        end;
      end;
    end;
  until IsBalanced;
end;
```

There is a small catch that you should be aware of: we have to test nodes for their color. Some of the nodes we will be testing will be external nodes, in other words, nil. To make the code more legible, I wrote a small routine called IsRed that tests for a nil node (returning false) before testing the color field of the node.

Listing 8.24: Intelligent IsRed routine

```
function IsRed(aNode : PtdBinTreeNode) : boolean;
begin
  if (aNode = nil) then
    Result := false
  else
```

```
    Result := aNode^.btColor = rbRed;
end;
```

Deletion from a Red-Black Tree

Compared with insertion, deletion from a red-black tree is filled with special cases, and can be difficult to follow.

As usual with binary search trees, we start off by searching for the node to be deleted. Like before, we'll have three initial cases: the node has no children (or, in red-black tree terms, both of its children are external nodes); the node has one actual child and one external child; and, finally, the node has two real children. We delete the node in exactly the same way as we did with the standard uncolored binary search tree.

Let's look at these three cases in terms of red-black trees now. The first case has the node with two external children (i.e., the links are nil). By rule 1, these two children are assumed to be black. The node we want to delete, however, can be red or black. Suppose it is red. By deleting it, we replace the parent's child link with a nil pointer—in other words, an external black node. However, we will not have altered the number of black nodes from the new external node to the root, compared with the two paths we had before. Hence, rule 2 is still satisfied. Rule 3 is obviously not violated (we're removing a red node, so we won't run into any problems with this rule). Therefore, the binary tree is still red-black after the deletion. The first transformation in Figure 8.10 shows this possibility.

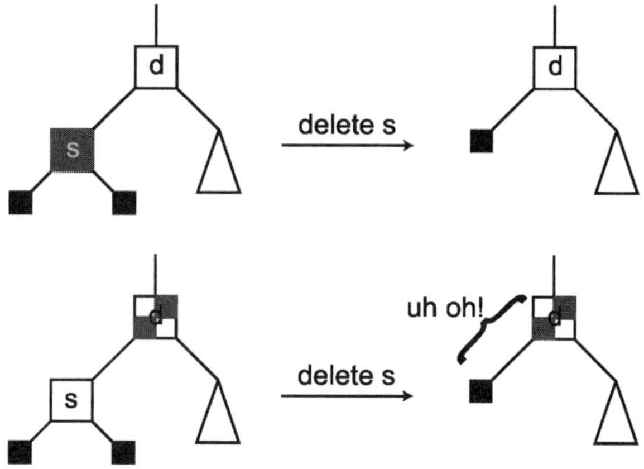

Figure 8.10: Deletion of a node with two external children

How about the other alternative (the node we remove is black)? Well, here rule 2, the black condition, is well and truly violated. We are reducing the number of black nodes in a path through the tree, by one. The second transformation in Figure 8.10 shows the problem. Let's metaphorically place a bookmark at this point, and consider some more cases.

The second deletion case is the one where we have a single actual child and an external child node. Suppose the node we're deleting is red; its one real child will be black. We can remove the node and replace it with its one child. Rule 2 will not be violated—we're removing a red node after all—and rule 3 does not come into play, so the tree remains red-black. This is the first transformation of Figure 8.11.

Assume now that the node we're removing is black. The one child could be either red or black. Suppose it is red. Rule 2 is going to be violated straight

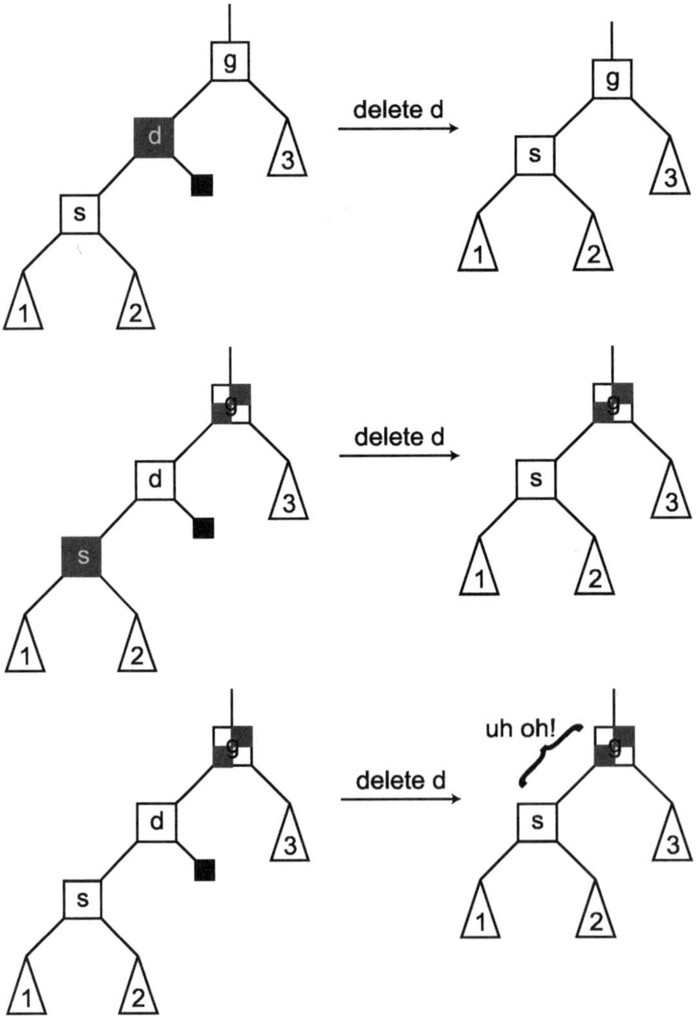

Figure 8.11: Deletion of a node with one internal and one external child

away since we're removing a black node, and rule 3 may be violated, since the red child's new parent may also be red. However, this case is fairly easy: we merely recolor the red child to be black as we move it up to replace the node being removed. At a stroke we satisfy rule 2 again, and rule 3 does not come into play. The tree is red-black once more. The second transformation in Figure 8.11 shows this possibility.

However, the alternative where the one child is black is not so easy (the third transformation in Figure 8.11). We'll bookmark this problem and consider the third and final deletion case.

The final binary search tree deletion case is not really different from the two we've already considered, because, if you recall, we swap over the node we would like to delete with the largest node from the left child tree and then delete this latter node instead. This latter node is either going to be the first deletion case or the second one, and so we will have to discuss the two bookmarked problems sooner than we thought.

Let's briefly recap. The node we are deleting has at least one external node. If the node we are deleting is red, then its other child must also be black (it can be an external node, of course, since external nodes are automatically black). We can delete the node, replace it with this second child, and the resulting tree is still red-black. If the node we are deleting is black and has one internal child that is red, then we can delete the node and replace it with its one child, recoloring the child black in the process.

If, however, the node we are deleting is black and has at least one external node as a child and the other child is either black or is external, then we have the two problems we identified earlier. The child node being promoted by the deletion is the start of a rule 2 violation (call this the *violating node*). The last two transformations in Figures 8.10 and 8.11 show these cases.

Let's start whittling away at the individual possibilities. It so happens that we have to take into account the parent and the brother of the violating node and the two children of the brother (the nephews). Notice that we can assume that the brother *does* have two children (in other words, that the brother is not an external node). Why? Well, consider the original tree. It was red-black; therefore all of the paths that went through the deleted node and the parent had the same number of black nodes as those that went through the brother and the parent. Since we're assuming that the parent is black, and the node we deleted and the child that replaced it were black as well, then all of the paths through the brother must have at least two black nodes in them as well. This translates, at a minimum, to the brother being black and having black nephews.

Anyway, look at the brother node. The following discussion will be easier if the brother is black. If it isn't, recolor the parent red and the brother black, and rotate the parent and promote the brother. This still leaves the tree as red-black except for the original violating node, but it does ensure that the brother node is black. So, from now on, we shall assume that the brother node is black. (Note that if the brother were red, then its children must be black, and furthermore they would have to have children of their own so that rule 2 is originally satisfied. Hence, this transformation still leaves us with a brother with children, as well as a red-black tree.)

The first possibility we shall look at is the one where the violating node has a black parent, and the two nephews are also black. If we recolor the brother red, we shift the problem area up to the parent node, and we can just repeat the full algorithm with that node as the violating node. This possibility is shown in Figure 8.12.

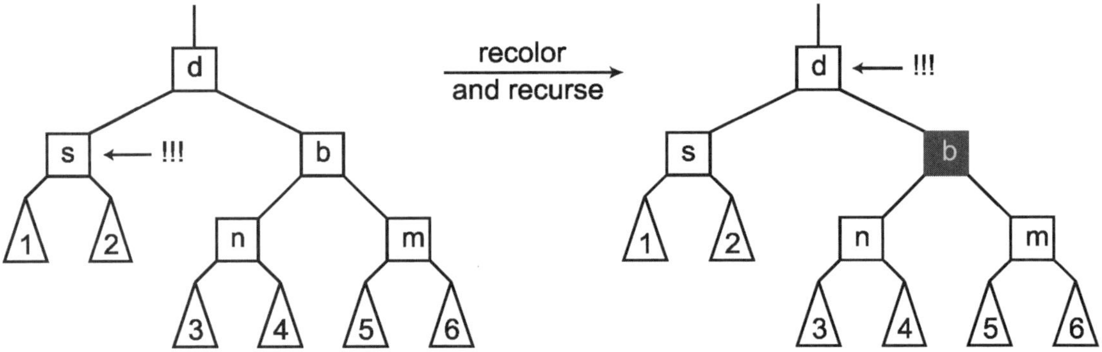

Figure 8.12: Balancing after deletion: the first case

The second possibility has a red parent and two black nephews. This is even easier: recolor the parent black and the brother red. The path through the violating node now has the correct number of black nodes again (satisfying rule 2), and the path through the brother node has the correct number of black nodes as well (again, satisfying rule 2). The newly colored red node has a black parent, so we're not violating rule 3. Hence, we have a red-black tree again. Figure 8.13 shows this case.

For the next possibility, suppose that the opposite nephew from the violating node is red. (In other words, if the violating node is a left child of its parent, I'm talking about the right nephew, and if the violating node is a right child, the left nephew.) Recolor this nephew to black. Color the brother the same color as the parent (we don't care what color the parent was originally), and color the parent black. Then rotate the parent to promote the brother. Let's

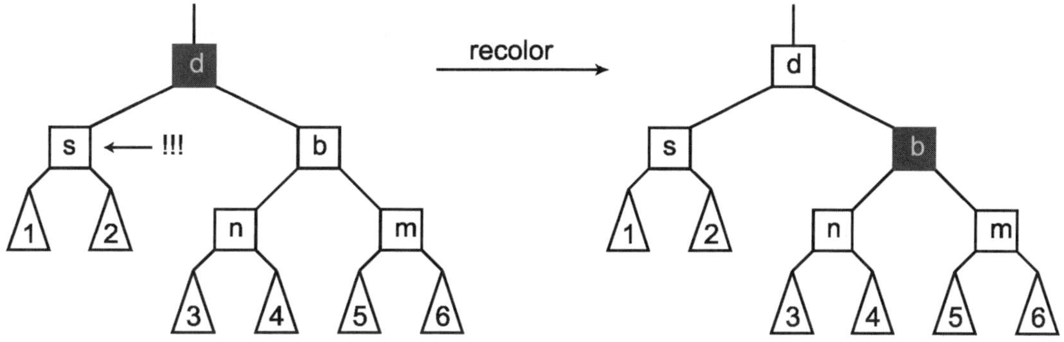

Figure 8.13: Balancing after deletion: the second case

take this one carefully, looking at Figure 8.14. Rule 3 first: obviously we haven't introduced any new red nodes so we know that it is satisfied. Now consider rule 2. All paths through the violating node now have an extra black node in them to rectify the problem we had by deleting the original node. All paths through child trees 3 and 4 have the same number of black nodes as before. All paths through the child trees 5 and 6 also have the same number of black nodes as before. Hence, in all cases, we've satisfied rule 2 and therefore the tree is red-black again.

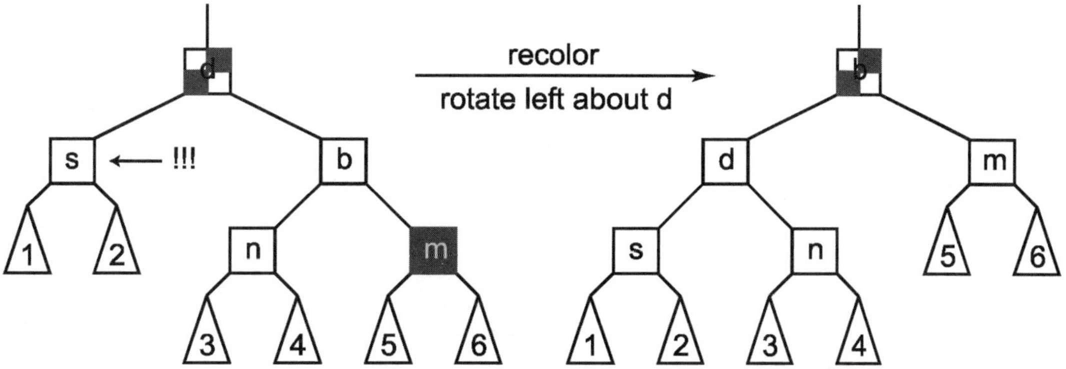

Figure 8.14: Balancing after deletion: the third case

We now consider the last case. Suppose that the opposite nephew is black, but that the one with the same relationship is red. This time we shall do a zig-zag rotation. First, recolor the nephew to be the same color as the parent (again, we don't care what color it was originally), and then recolor the parent black. Second, rotate the brother to promote the nephew, and then rotate the parent to promote the nephew again. Figure 8.15 shows the transformation. Rule 3 hasn't inadvertently been violated anywhere: we haven't introduced any new red nodes. Rule 2: all paths through the violating node have one extra black node so we've removed that problem. All paths through child tree 3 still have the same number of black nodes. Similarly, we can see that all the paths through child trees 4, 5, and 6 have not had an extra black node introduced or removed, so rule 3 still applies. The tree is red-black once again.

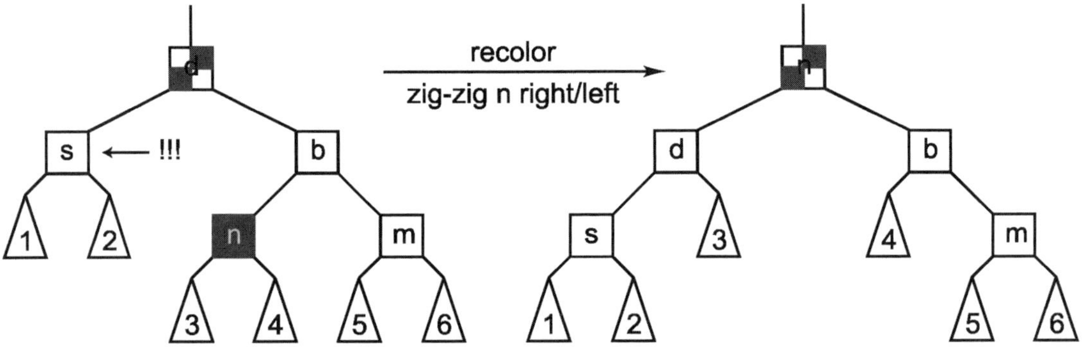

Figure 8.15: Balancing after deletion: the final case

There is one ultimate case if we manage to push the violating node all the way up to the root. In this case, the violating node has no parent, and hence has no brother. In this case, it turns out that the violating node is no longer a problem.

Of course, all these cases have mirror-image variants as well, but the analysis of each deletion case will not change. When we code the deletion routine, we shall have to make sure that we cover both the left and right variants properly.

We've at last exhausted all possibilities. There were two recursive steps, or, to be stricter, two steps that required further rebalancing efforts. The first one was that the brother was red, and we wanted it to be black. The second one was that the parent, brother, and nephews were all black. There were three other cases: the parent was red and the brother and nephews were black; the brother was black and the furthest nephew was red (the parent and the nearest nephew were "don't cares"); and finally the brother was black, the furthest nephew was black, and the nearest nephew was red. If you look at Figures 8.12, 8.13, 8.14, and 8.15 you'll see that we've covered all variants.

Without going into the mathematics, it turns out that the red-black deletion algorithm is O(log(n)), although the extra constant time is larger than that of a simple binary tree.

The node deletion operation in a red-black tree is implemented by the code in Listing 8.25.

Listing 8.25: Red-black tree deletion

```
procedure TtdRedBlackTree.Delete(aItem : pointer);
var
  Node       : PtdBinTreeNode;
  Dad        : PtdBinTreeNode;
  Child      : PtdBinTreeNode;
  Brother    : PtdBinTreeNode;
  FarNephew  : PtdBinTreeNode;
  NearNephew : PtdBinTreeNode;
  IsBalanced : boolean;
  ChildType  : TtdChildType;
begin
  {find the node to delete; this node will have but one child}
  Node := bstFindNodeToDelete(aItem);
  {if the node is red, or is the root, delete it with impunity}
  if (Node^.btColor = rbRed) or (Node = FBinTree.Root) then begin
    FBinTree.Delete(Node);
    dec(FCount);
    Exit;
  end;
  {if the node's only child is red, recolor the child black, and
  delete the node}
  if (Node^.btChild[ctLeft] = nil) then
    Child := Node^.btChild[ctRight]
  else
    Child := Node^.btChild[ctLeft];
  if IsRed(Child) then begin
    Child^.btColor := rbBlack;
    FBinTree.Delete(Node);
    dec(FCount);
    Exit;
  end;
  {at this point, the node we have to delete is Node, it is black, and
  we know that its one Child that will replace it is black (and also
  maybe nil!), and there is a parent of Node (which will soon be the
  parent of Child); Node's brother also exists because of the black
  node rule}
  {if the Child is nil, we'll have to help the loop a little bit and
  set the parent and brother and whether Node is a left child or not}
  if (Child = nil) then begin
    Dad := Node^.btParent;
```

```
    if (Node = Dad^.btChild[ctLeft]) then begin
      ChildType := ctLeft;
      Brother := Dad^.btChild[ctRight];
    end
    else begin
      ChildType := ctRight;
      Brother := Dad^.btChild[ctLeft];
    end;
  end
  else begin
    {the following three lines are merely to fool the compiler and
    remove some spurious warnings}
    Dad := nil;
    Brother := nil;
    ChildType := ctLeft;
  end;
  {delete the node we want to remove, we have no more need of it}
  FBinTree.Delete(Node);
  dec(FCount);
  Node := Child;
  {in a loop, continue applying the red-black deletion balancing
  algorithms until the tree is balanced}
  repeat
    {assume we'll balance it this time}
    IsBalanced := true;
    {we are balanced if the node is the root, so assume it isn't}
    if (Node<>FBinTree.Root) then begin
      {get the parent and the brother}
      if (Node<>nil) then begin
        Dad := Node^.btParent;
        if (Node = Dad^.btChild[ctLeft]) then begin
          ChildType := ctLeft;
          Brother := Dad^.btChild[ctRight];
        end
        else begin
          ChildType := ctRight;
          Brother := Dad^.btChild[ctLeft];
        end;
      end;
      {we need a black brother, so if the brother is currently red,
      color the parent red, the brother black, and promote the
      brother; then go round loop again}
      if (Brother^.btColor = rbRed) then begin
        Dad^.btColor := rbRed;
        Brother^.btColor := rbBlack;
        rbtPromote(Brother);
        IsBalanced := false;
      end
```

```
{otherwise the brother is black}
else begin
  {get the nephews, denoted as far and near}
  if (ChildType = ctLeft) then begin
    FarNephew := Brother^.btChild[ctRight];
    NearNephew := Brother^.btChild[ctLeft];
  end
  else begin
    FarNephew := Brother^.btChild[ctLeft];
    NearNephew := Brother^.btChild[ctRight];
  end;
  {if the far nephew is red (note that it could be nil!), color
  it black, color the brother the same as the parent, color the
  parent black, and then promote the brother; we're then done}
  if IsRed(FarNephew) then begin
    FarNephew^.btColor := rbBlack;
    Brother^.btColor := Dad^.btColor;
    Dad^.btColor := rbBlack;
    rbtPromote(Brother);
  end
  {otherwise the far nephew is black}
  else begin
    {if the near nephew is red (note that it could be nil!),
    color it the same color as the parent, color the parent
    black, and zig-zag promote the nephew; we're then done}
    if IsRed(NearNephew) then begin
      NearNephew^.btColor := Dad^.btColor;
      Dad^.btColor := rbBlack;
      rbtPromote(rbtPromote(NearNephew));
    end
    {otherwise the near nephew is also black}
    else begin
      {if the parent is red, color it black and the brother red,
      and we're done}
      if (Dad^.btColor = rbRed) then begin
        Dad^.btColor := rbBlack;
        Brother^.btColor := rbRed;
      end
      {otherwise the parent is black: color the brother red and
      start over with the parent}
      else begin
        Brother^.btColor := rbRed;
        Node := Dad;
        IsBalanced := false;
      end;
    end;
  end;
end;
```

```
    end;
  until IsBalanced;
end;
```

Apart from the overridden Insert and Delete methods, there's not much else to the TtdRedBlackTree class. Listing 18.26 shows the interface and the remaining internal method, the one that promotes a node.

Listing 8.26: The TtdRedBlackTree class and node promotion method

```
type
  TtdRedBlackTree = class(TtdBinarySearchTree)
    private
    protected
      function rbtPromote(aNode  : PtdBinTreeNode) : PtdBinTreeNode;
    public
      procedure Delete(aItem : pointer); override;
      procedure Insert(aItem : pointer); override;
  end;
function TtdRedBlackTree.rbtPromote(aNode : PtdBinTreeNode)
                                          : PtdBinTreeNode;
var
  Parent : PtdBinTreeNode;
begin
  {make a note of the parent of the node we're promoting}
  Parent := aNode^.btParent;
  {in both cases there are 6 links to be broken and remade: the node's
  link to its child and vice versa, the node's link with its parent
  and vice versa and the parent's link with its parent and vice
  versa; note that the node's child could be nil}
  {promote a left child = right rotation of parent}
  if (Parent^.btChild[ctLeft] = aNode) then begin
    Parent^.btChild[ctLeft] := aNode^.btChild[ctRight];
    if (Parent^.btChild[ctLeft]<>nil) then
      Parent^.btChild[ctLeft]^.btParent := Parent;
    aNode^.btParent := Parent^.btParent;
    if (aNode^.btParent^.btChild[ctLeft] = Parent) then
      aNode^.btParent^.btChild[ctLeft] := anode
    else
      aNode^.btParent^.btChild[ctRight] := aNode;
    aNode^.btChild[ctRight] := Parent;
    Parent^.btParent := aNode;
  end
  {promote a right child = left rotation of parent}
  else begin
    Parent^.btChild[ctRight] := aNode^.btChild[ctLeft];
    if (Parent^.btChild[ctRight]<>nil) then
      Parent^.btChild[ctRight]^.btParent := Parent;
    aNode^.btParent := Parent^.btParent;
```

```
    if (aNode^.btParent^.btChild[ctLeft] = Parent) then
      aNode^.btParent^.btChild[ctLeft] := anode
    else
      aNode^.btParent^.btChild[ctRight] := aNode;
    aNode^.btChild[ctLeft] := Parent;
    Parent^.btParent := aNode;
  end;
  {return the node we promoted}
  Result := aNode;
end;
```

The source code for the TtdRedBlackTree class can be found in the TDBinTre.pas file on the CD.

Summary

In this chapter, we looked at binary trees, an important data structure that can be used in many applications. We saw the standard binary tree, then moved on quickly to its sorted cousin, the binary search tree.

With the binary search tree, we saw the problems that could occur during insertion and deletion—the degeneracy problem—so we investigated ways of removing it. The first solution, the splay tree, is a good possibility, even though its insertion and deletion efficiency turns out to be an average, rather than a firm, O(log(n)). It is, however, a good compromise between a standard binary search tree and a true balanced tree, such as the red-black tree.

With the red-black tree, we finally had a complete binary search tree that contained balancing algorithms on both insertion and deletion.

Chapter 9

Priority Queues and Heapsort

In Chapter 3, we looked at a couple of very simple data structures. One of them was the queue. With this structure, we could add items and then retrieve the oldest first. We didn't actually calculate how long an item had been in the queue by storing its date and time of entry; rather, we just arranged the items in order of arrival in a linked list or an array and then removed them in order. We had two main operations: the "add an item to the queue" (known as enqueue) and the "remove the oldest item in the queue" (or dequeue).

All fine and dandy, and the queue is an important data structure in its own right. However, it has a limitation in that items are processed in the order of their arrival. Suppose we want to process items in some other order entirely. In other words, a queue that still has the "add an item" operation, but whose second operation is not "remove the oldest," but "remove the largest" or "remove the smallest." We would like to replace the simplistic "age" ordering with another ordering criterion completely. For example, the items in the queue are jobs to be processed and we want to retrieve the job that has the highest priority.

The Priority Queue

In fact, this example gives this new data structure its name: it is known as a priority queue. A *priority queue* has two main operations: add an item (as before) and retrieve the item with the largest priority. (We, of course, assume that each item has an associated priority value that we can inspect.) What do I mean by "priority" in this context? Well, it can be anything. Classically, it's a numeric value that denotes the item's priority in some process. Examples include print queues in operating systems, job queues, or threads in a multithreaded environment. Taking the print queue as an example, each print job is assigned a priority, a value that indicates how important that particular print job is. High priority print jobs would need to be processed before low priority print jobs. The operating system would finish off a particular print job, go to the print queue, and retrieve the print job with the highest priority. As work is done in the operating system, other print jobs get added to the print queue with various priorities, and the print queue will organize them in some fashion so that it can determine the highest priority print job when required.

Do note however that the value we are using as "priority" doesn't need to be a classic priority number. It can be any type or meaning, just so long as it has an ordering relation so that the queue is able to determine the item with the largest value. (An *ordering relation* on a set of objects is a rule that enables us to order the objects in such a way that we can say that object x is "smaller" than object y. If x is less than y, then y cannot be less than x. Also, if x is less than y and y is less than z, then x is less than z. The common ordering rule for integers, 2 is less than 3, etc., is an ordering relation.)

For example, the priority value could be a name (in other words, a string), and the ordering could be the standard alphabetic order. So the retrieval operation of getting the item with the largest priority would instead become getting the item earliest in alphabetic sequence (that is, the As before the Bs, etc.).

To recap then, the priority queue must be able to (1) store an arbitrary number of items, (2) add an item with associated priority to the queue, and (3) identify and remove the item with the largest priority.

First Simple Implementation

In designing a priority queue, the first attribute (storing an arbitrary number of items) would indicate the use of some extensible data structure like a linked list or an extensible array, such as a TList. Let's use, for now at least, a TList.

The next attribute (adding an item to the queue) is easy with a TList: we just call the TList's Add method. We'll make the assumption that the items we add to the priority queue will be objects of some description, with their priority as a property of the object. This gives us a simple enough item that we don't get distracted away from the properties of the priority queue.

The third attribute (finding the highest priority and returning the associated object, removing it from the priority queue in the process) is a little more involved but still relatively simple. Essentially we iterate through the items in the TList and for each item we see whether its priority is larger than the largest priority we've found so far. If it is, we take note of the index of the item in the TList with this newer largest priority, and move on to the next item. This is a simple sequential search. After we've checked all of the items in the TList, we know which is the largest (we took note of its index) and so we just remove it from the TList and pass it back.

The code in Listing 9.1 shows this simple priority queue. It uses a comparison function that you pass to the priority queue when you create it in order to determine whether one item's priority is greater than another's. The priority queue therefore doesn't need to know how to compare priorities (and hence whether they're numbers or strings or something else): it merely calls the comparison function, passing the two items whose priorities it needs to compare. Note also that the queue doesn't need to know *what* the items are, it just stores them, so we can just declare the queue to use pointer variables and typecast as necessary.

Listing 9.1: Simple TList-based priority queue

```
type
  TtdSimplePriQueue1 = class
    private
      FCompare : TtdCompareFunc;
      FList    : TList;
    protected
      function pqGetCount : integer;
    public
      constructor Create(aCompare : TtdCompareFunc);
      destructor Destroy; override;
      function Dequeue : pointer;
      procedure Enqueue(aItem : pointer);
      property Count : integer read pqGetCount;
  end;
constructor TtdSimplePriQueue1.Create(aCompare : TdCompareFunc);
begin
  inherited Create;
  FCompare := aCompare;
  FList := TList.Create;
end;
destructor TtdSimplePriQueue1.Destroy;
begin
  FList.Free;
  inherited Destroy;
end;
function TtdSimplePriQueue1.Dequeue : pointer;
var
  Inx     : integer;
  PQCount : integer;
  MaxInx  : integer;
  MaxItem : pointer;
begin
```

```
  PQCount := Count;
  if (PQCount = 0) then
    Result := nil
  else if (PQCount = 1) then begin
    Result := FList.List^[0];
    FList.Clear;
  end
  else begin
    MaxItem := FList.List^[0];
    MaxInx := 0;
    for Inx := 1 to pred(PQCount) do
      if (FCompare(FList.List^[Inx], MaxItem) > 0) then begin
        MaxItem := FList.List^[Inx];
        MaxInx := Inx;
      end;
    Result := MaxItem;
    FList.List^[MaxInx] := FList.Last;
    FList.Count := FList.Count - 1;
  end;
end;
procedure TtdSimplePriQueue1.Enqueue(aItem : pointer);
begin
  FList.Add(aItem);
end;
function TtdSimplePriQueue1.pqGetCount : integer;
begin
  Result := FList.Count;
end;
```

Looking at Listing 9.1, you can see that the class is really quite trivial and even adding the missing error checking wouldn't bulk it up. The only interesting piece of code is in the removal of an item: we don't call TList's Delete method (a O(n) operation); instead we just replace the item to be removed with the last item and decrement the count of items (a O(1) operation).

The source code for the TtdSimplePriQueue1 class can be found in the TDPriQue.pas file on the CD.

Having seen how simple this priority queue was to design and write, let's consider its efficiency. Firstly, adding an item to the priority queue will get done in constant time; in other words, it is a O(1) operation. Whether the queue has no items or thousands of them, adding a new item will take roughly the same amount of time: all we're doing is appending it to the end of the list.

Secondly, let's look at the opposite operation: removing an item. Here, we need to read through all of the items in the TList in order to find the one with the largest priority. It is a sequential search and, as we saw in Chapter 4, this is a O(n) operation. The time taken is proportional to the number of items in the queue.

So we have designed and written a data structure that implements a priority queue in which adding an item is a O(1) operation and removing it is a O(n) operation. For small numbers of items this structure is perfectly acceptable and efficient.

Second Simple Implementation

However, for large numbers of items, or when we add and remove large numbers of items from the queue, it is not as efficient as we'd like. I'm sure you can think of one possible efficiency improvement straight away: maintain the TList in priority order; in other words, keep it sorted through all the additions. Thinking about it, this improvement means that we shift the real work of the queue from item removal to item insertion. When we add an item we have to find its correct place inside the TList, which is after all items with lower priority and before all those with higher priority. If we do this extra work during the add phase, the TList will have all the items in priority order and hence, when we remove an item, all we need to do is to delete the last item. In fact, removal becomes a O(1) operation (we know exactly where the item with the largest priority is—it's at the end, so removing it doesn't depend on how many items there are).

Calculating the time required for insertion in this sorted TList is a little more involved. The simplest way to think of how this is done is to think of it as an insertion sort (introduced in Chapter 5). We grow the TList by one item, and then move items along by one into the spare element, like beads on a thread, starting from the end of the TList. You stop when you reach an item that has a priority less than the one you are trying to insert. You then have a "hole" in the TList where you can put the new item. Think about this for a moment: on average, you'd move $n/2$ items for n items in the TList. Hence, insertion is a O(n) operation (the time taken is again proportional to the number of items in the queue), although with this improvement, the time taken would be somewhat less than the previous implementation. Listing 9.2 shows how these two operations are coded with this kind of internal structure.

Listing 9.2: A priority queue using a sorted TList

```
type
  TtdSimplePriQueue2 = class
    private
      FCompare : TtdCompareFunc;
      FList    : TList;
    protected
```

```
      function pqGetCount : integer;
    public
      constructor Create(aCompare : TtdCompareFunc);
      destructor Destroy; override;
      function Dequeue : pointer;
      procedure Enqueue(aItem : pointer);
      property Count : integer read pqGetCount;
  end;

constructor TtdSimplePriQueue2.Create(aCompare : TtdCompareFunc);
begin
  inherited Create;
  FCompare := aCompare;
  FList := TList.Create;
end;
destructor TtdSimplePriQueue2.Destroy;
begin
  FList.Free;
  inherited Destroy;
end;
function TtdSimplePriQueue2.Dequeue : pointer;
begin
  Result := FList.Last;
  FList.Count := FList.Count - 1;
end;
procedure TtdSimplePriQueue2.Enqueue(aItem : pointer);
var
  Inx : integer;
begin
  {increment the number of items in the list}
  FList.Count := FList.Count + 1;
  {find where to put our new item}
  Inx := FList.Count - 2;
  while (Inx >= 0) and
        (FCompare(FList.List^[Inx], aItem) > 0) do begin
    FList.List^[Inx+1] := FList.List^[Inx];
    dec(Inx);
  end;
  {put it there}
  FList.List^[Inx+1] := aItem;
end;
function TtdSimplePriQueue2.pqGetCount : integer;
begin
  Result := FList.Count;
end;
```

The source code for the TtdSimplePriQueue2 class can be found in the TDPriQue.pas file on the CD.

In designing and implementing this improved priority queue, we've moved from fast insertion/slow deletion to slow insertion/fast deletion. Can we do better than this?

Another possibility is to abandon the TList entirely and move to another data structure: the binary search tree from Chapter 8 or the skip list from Chapter 6. With these two structures, insertions and deletions are both O(log(n)) operations—in other words, the time taken for both item insertion and item deletion are proportional to the logarithm of the number of items in the structure. But both of these structures are somewhat complicated to use; the skip list because it is a probabilistic structure and the binary search tree because we have to worry about balancing the resulting tree on insertion and deletion. Is there something simpler?

The Heap

The classical data structure for a priority queue is known as the heap. A *heap* is a binary tree with some special properties and a couple of special operations. (Don't confuse this heap with the Delphi heap, the pool of memory from which all allocations are made.)

In a binary search tree, the nodes are arranged so that every node is greater than its left child and less than its right child. This is known as strict ordering. The heap uses a less strict ordering called the heap property. The *heap property* merely states that any node in the tree must be greater than both its children. Note that the heap property doesn't say anything about the ordering of the children for a given node, it does not state, for example, that the left child must be less than the right child.

There's another attribute that the heap possesses: the binary tree must be *complete*. A binary tree is called complete when all its levels are full, except for possibly the last. In the last level all nodes appear as far to the left as possible. A complete tree is as balanced as it can be. Figure 9.1 shows a complete binary tree.

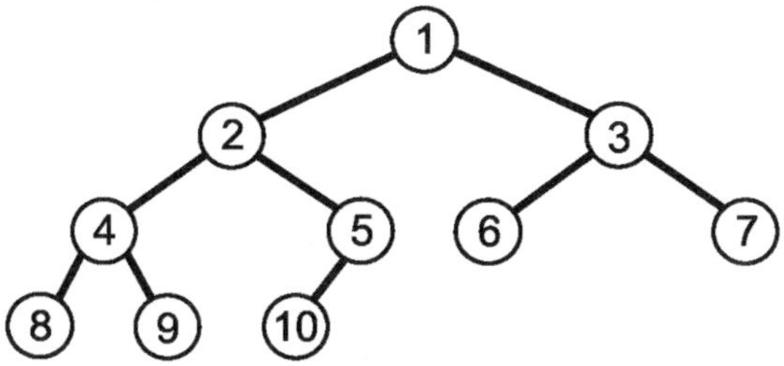

Figure 9.1: A heap

So how does this help us in our quest for the perfect priority queue structure? Well, it turns out that the insertion and deletion operations with a heap are O(log(n)), but they are significantly faster than the same operations with a binary search tree, balanced or not. This is one instance where the big-Oh notation seems to fall short—it doesn't give any quantitative feel for which of two operations with the same big-Oh value is actually *faster*.

Insertion into a Heap

Let's now discuss the insertion and deletion algorithms, insertion first. To insert an item into a heap, we add it to the end of the heap in the only place that continues to maintain the completeness attribute—in Figure 9.1 that would be the right child of node 5. That's one of the attributes of the heap that is satisfied. The other, the heap property, may be violated—the new node may be larger than its parent—so we need to patch up the tree and reestablish the heap property.

If this new child node is greater than its parent, we swap it with the parent. In its new position, it may still be greater than its new parent, and so we need to swap it again. In this manner we continue working our way up the heap until we reach a point where our new node is no longer greater than its parent or we've reached the root of the tree. By performing this algorithm, we've again ensured that all nodes are greater than both their children and so the heap property has been restored. This algorithm is known as the *bubble up* algorithm because we bubble up the new node until it reaches its correct place (either the root or just under a node that is larger than it).

If you think about it, the heap property ensures that the largest item is at the root. This is simple enough to prove: if the largest node weren't at the root, it would have a parent. Since it is the largest node we would have to conclude that it is larger than its parent—a violation of the heap property. Hence, our original supposition that the largest node was not at the root is false.

Deletion from a Heap

We can now move on to the removal of the largest node since we've just shown that the item we want is at the root. Deleting the root node and passing that item back to the caller is not a good idea. We would be left with two separate child trees—a complete violation of the completeness attribute of the heap. Instead, we replace the root node with the last node of the heap and shrink the heap, thereby ensuring that the heap remains complete. But, again, we've probably violated the heap property. The new root will, in all probability, be smaller than one or both of its children, so we have to patch up the heap again to restore the heap property. We find the larger of the node's two children and exchange it with the node. Again, this new position may violate the heap property, so we verify whether it's smaller than one (or both) of its two children, and repeat the process. Eventually, we'll find that the node has sunk, or trickled down, to a level where it is greater than both its children, or it's now a leaf with no children. Either way we've again restored the heap property. This algorithm is called the *trickle down* algorithm.

If we implement a heap with an actual binary tree in the manner of Chapter 8 we'll find that it's pretty wasteful of space. For every node we have to maintain three pointers: one for each child, so that we can trickle down the tree, and one for the parent, so that we can bubble up. Every time we swap nodes we will have to update umpteen different pointers for numerous nodes. The usual trick is to leave the nodes where they are and just swap the items around inside the nodes instead.

However, there is a simpler way. A complete binary tree can be easily represented by an array. Look at Figure 9.1 again. Scan the tree using a level-order traversal. Notice that in a complete tree, a level-order traversal does not come across any gaps where there's a position for a node but no node is present (until, of course, we've visited every node and reached the end of the tree). We can map the nodes easily onto elements of an array so that walking the elements sequentially in the array is equivalent to visiting the nodes with a level-order traversal. Element 1 of the array would be the root of the heap, element 2 the root's left child, element 3 the root's right child, and so on—in fact, exactly how the nodes are numbered in Figure 9.1.

Now have a look at the numbers of the children for each node. The children for node 1, the root, are 2 and 3 respectively. The children for node 4 are 8 and 9, and for node 6 they are 12 and 13. Notice any pattern? The children for node n are nodes $2n$ and $2n+1$, and the parent for node n is n div 2. We no longer require a node to contain pointers to its children and its parent; we have a simple arithmetic relationship that we can use instead. We have discovered a method of implementing a heap with an array, and in fact we could use a TList again once we've solved a minor problem.

The problem is this: the heap-as-an-array implementation we've seen so far seems to require that the array start counting its elements from one, not zero like a TList. This is easy enough to change; we just alter the arithmetic formulae for calculating the index of the parent and the children. The children for node n would be at $2n+1$ and $2n+2$, and the parent for node n is at $(n-1)$ div 2.

Implementation of a Priority Queue with a Heap

Listing 9.3 shows the interface for our final priority queue which uses a heap implemented by a TList.

Listing 9.3: TtdPriorityQueue class interface

```
type
  TtdPriorityQueue = class
    private
      FCompare : TtdCompareFunc;
      FDispose : TtdDisposeProc;
      FList    : TList;
      FName    : TtdNameString;
    protected
      function pqGetCount : integer;
      procedure pqError(aErrorCode   : integer;
                  const aMethodName : TtdNameString);
      procedure pqBubbleUp(aFromInx : integer);
      procedure pqTrickleDown;
      procedure pqTrickleDownStd;
    public
      constructor Create(aCompare : TtdCompareFunc;
                         aDispose : TtdDisposeProc);
      destructor Destroy; override;
      procedure Clear;
      function Dequeue : pointer;
      procedure Enqueue(aItem : pointer);
      function Examine : pointer;
      function IsEmpty : boolean;

      property Count : integer read pqGetCount;
      property Name  : TtdNameString read FName write FName;
  end;
```

The Create constructor and Destroy destructor are both fairly simple to implement: the former has to create the internal TList instance, and the latter just needs to free the internal TList. Like a standard queue, Create requires an item disposal routine so that it can free items if need be, but unlike the standard queue, we now need a comparison routine so that we can compare two items to find the larger.

Listing 9.4: The constructor and destructor for the priority queue

```
constructor TtdPriorityQueue.Create(aCompare : TtdCompareFunc;
                                    aDispose : TtdDisposeProc);
begin
  inherited Create;
  if not Assigned(aCompare) then
```

```
    pqError(tdePriQueueNoCompare, 'Create');
  FCompare := aCompare;
  FDispose := aDispose;
  FList    := TList.Create;
end;
destructor TtdPriorityQueue.Destroy;
begin
  Clear;
  FList.Free;
  inherited Destroy;
end;
```

Listing 9.5 shows the insertion algorithm, together with the routine that performs the actual bubble up operation. The insertion operation has been written to ensure that the largest item is found at the root. This type of priority queue is usually known as a *max-heap*. If we change the sense of the comparison routine so that a negative number is returned if the first item is larger than the second, the priority queue will have the smallest item at the root, and it is known as a *min-heap* instead.

Listing 9.5: Insertion into a TtdPriorityQueue: Enqueue

```
procedure TtdPriorityQueue.pqBubbleUp(aFromInx : integer);
var
  ParentInx : integer;
  Item      : pointer;
begin
  Item := FList.List^[aFromInx];
  {while the item under consideration is larger than its parent, swap
  it with its parent and continue from its new position}
  {Note: the parent for the child at index n is at n-1 div 2}
  ParentInx := (aFromInx - 1) div 2;
  {while our item has a parent, and it's greater than the parent...}
  while (aFromInx > 0) and
        (FCompare(Item, FList.List^[ParentInx]) > 0) do begin
    {move our parent down the tree}
    FList.List^[aFromInx] := FList.List^[ParentInx];
    aFromInx := ParentInx;
    ParentInx := (aFromInx - 1) div 2;
  end;
  {store our item in the correct place}
  FList.List^[aFromInx] := Item;
end;
procedure TtdPriorityQueue.Enqueue(aItem : pointer);
begin
  {add the item to the end of the list and bubble it up as far as it
  will go}
  FList.Add(aItem);
```

```
  pqBubbleUp(pred(FList.Count));
end;
```

Listing 9.6 shows the final jigsaw piece for the priority queue: the deletion algorithm together with the routine that performs the trickle down operation.

Listing 9.6: Deletion from a TtdPriorityQueue: Dequeue

```
procedure TtdPriorityQueue.pqTrickleDownStd;
var
  FromInx  : integer;
  ChildInx : integer;
  MaxInx   : integer;
  Item     : pointer;
begin
  FromInx := 0;
  Item := FList.List^[0];
  MaxInx := FList.Count - 1;
  {while the item under consideration is smaller than one of its
  children, swap it with the larger child and continue from its new
  position}
  {Note: the children for the parent at index n are at 2n+1 and 2n+2}
  ChildInx := (FromInx * 2) + 1;
  {while there is at least a left child...}
  while (ChildInx <= MaxInx) do begin
    {if there is a right child as well, calculate the index of the
    larger child}
    if (succ(ChildInx) <= MaxInx) and
       (FCompare(FList.List^[ChildInx],
                 FList.List^[succ(ChildInx)]) < 0) then
      inc(ChildInx);
    {if our item is greater or equal to the larger child, we're done}
    if (FCompare(Item, FList.List^[ChildInx]) >= 0) then
      Break;
    {otherwise move the larger child up the tree, and move our item
    down the tree and repeat}
    FList.List^[FromInx] := FList.List^[ChildInx];
    FromInx := ChildInx;
    ChildInx := (FromInx * 2) + 1;
  end;
  {store our item in the correct place}
  FList.List^[FromInx] := Item;
end;
function TtdPriorityQueue.Dequeue : pointer;
begin
  {make sure we have an item to dequeue}
  if (FList.Count = 0) then
    pqError(tdeQueueIsEmpty, 'Dequeue');
  {return the item at the root}
```

```
  Result := FList.List^[0];
  {if there was only one item in the queue, it's now empty}
  if (FList.Count = 1) then
    FList.Count := 0
  {if there were two, just replace the root with the one remaining
  child; the heap property is obviously satisfied}
  else if (FList.Count = 2) then begin
    FList.List^[0] := FList.List^[1];
    FList.Count := 1;
  end
  {otherwise we have to restore the heap property}
  else begin
    {replace the root with the child at the lowest, rightmost
    position, shrink the list, and finally trickle down the root item
    as far as it will go}
    FList.List^[0] := FList.Last;
    FList.Count := FList.Count - 1;
    pqTrickleDownStd;
  end;
end;
```

Notice that at each stage through the loop in the trickle down algorithm, as we move down the heap, we make at most two comparisons: comparing the two children to find the larger and comparing the larger child with the parent to see if we need to exchange them. Compared with the bubble up operation with its single comparison at each level as we move up the heap, it seems a little excessive. Is there anything we can do to alleviate the situation?

Robert Floyd pointed out that the first step of the dequeue operation involves removing the item with the largest priority and replacing it with one of the smallest items in the heap. Not necessarily *the* smallest, mind you, but it's certainly going to move down to near the bottom level of the tree when we apply the trickle down algorithm. In other words, the majority of the comparisons we make between the parent and its larger child during the trickle down process are probably not worth doing, as the result of the comparison is going to be a foregone conclusion: the parent will be less than its larger child. What Floyd proposed was this: completely ignore the parent-larger child comparisons in the trickle down process and always exchange the parent with its larger child. Eventually, of course, we shall reach the bottom of the heap, and the item may be in the wrong place (in other words, it may be larger than its parent). No matter; we then just apply the bubble up operation. Since the item we were trickling down was one of the smallest items in the heap, it is likely that we won't have to bubble it up very far, if at all.

This optimization cuts the number of comparisons made during a dequeue operation by roughly half. If the comparisons are time-intensive (for example, comparing strings), this optimization is worthwhile. In our implementation of a priority queue, where we use a comparison function rather than a simple comparison between integers, etc., it is also worthwhile to apply this optimization.

Listing 9.7: Optimized trickle down operation

```
procedure TtdPriorityQueue.pqTrickleDown;
var
  FromInx  : integer;
  ChildInx : integer;
  MaxInx   : integer;
  Item     : pointer;
begin
  FromInx := 0;
  Item := FList.List^[0];
  MaxInx := pred(FList.Count);
  {swap the item under consideration with its larger child until it
  has no children}
  {Note: the children for the parent at index n are at 2n+1 and 2n+2}
  ChildInx := (FromInx * 2) + 1;
  {while there is at least a left child...}
  while (ChildInx <= MaxInx) do begin
    {if there is a right child as well, calculate the index of the
    larger child}
    if (succ(ChildInx) <= MaxInx) and
       (FCompare(FList.List^[ChildInx],
                 FList.List^[succ(ChildInx)]) < 0) then
      inc(ChildInx);
    {move the larger child up the tree, and move our item
    down the tree and repeat}
    FList.List^[FromInx] := FList.List^[ChildInx];
    FromInx := ChildInx;
    ChildInx := (FromInx * 2) + 1;
  end;
  {store our item where we end up}
  FList.List^[FromInx] := Item;
  {now bubble this item up the tree}
  pqBubbleUp(FromInx);
end;
```

The source code for the TtdPriorityQueue class can be found in the TDPriQue.pas file on the CD.

Heapsort

Now that we've implemented the heap version of a priority queue, we can observe that it can be used as a sorting algorithm: add a bunch of items all at once to the heap and then pick them off one by one in the correct order. (Note that, as written, the items are picked off in reverse order, that is, largest first, but using a reversed comparison method, we can get them in the correct ascending order instead.)

The algorithm to sort with a heap, unsurprisingly, is known as *heapsort*. If you recollect from Chapter 5, this was the other sort that we left until later, until we had the required background.

The heapsort algorithm I've just posited is this: assume we have a min-heap priority queue, add all the items to it, and then remove them one by one. If the unsorted items were being held in a TList in the first place, this algorithm would mean that all the items would be copied from one TList to another, and then copied back. Far better would be an in-place sort where we don't have to copy the items from one array to another. In other words, can we organize an existing array into a heap by applying the heap properties to it?

Floyd's Algorithm

Robert Floyd devised such an algorithm, and interestingly enough, the heap created is generated in $O(n)$ time, which is much better than the $O(n\log(n))$ time required by adding the items one by one to a separate heap.

Floyd's Algorithm proceeds like this. We start out with the parent of the rightmost child node (i.e., the node furthest to the right on the last level of the heap). Apply the trickle down algorithm to this parent. Select the node to the left of the parent on the same level (it'll be a parent as well, of course). Apply the trickle down algorithm again. Keep on moving left, applying the trickle down algorithm, until you run out of nodes. Move up a level, to the rightmost node. Continue the same process from right to left, going up level by level, until you reach the root node. At this point the array has been ordered into a heap.

To prove the $O(n)$ time, suppose we have a heap with 31 items in it (it'll be a heap with five full layers). The first stage would make heaps of all the nodes in the fourth level; there are eight of these, and each would take at most one demotion to do so—eight in all. The next stage would make mini heaps on level 3: there are four of these, each taking at most two demotions, making eight demotions in all. The next stage would be to make heaps on level 2: there are two possible ones, each taking at most three demotions, and so we'd have six demotions maximum. The last stage requires at most four demotions to make a heap. The grand total would be a maximum of 26 demotions, less than the original number of nodes. If we follow the same argument for a heap with 2^n-1 nodes, we find that it takes at most 2^n-n-1 demotions to create a heap—hence the original assertion that Floyd's Algorithm is a $O(n)$ operation.

Completing Heapsort

Having ordered an array into a heap, what then? Removing the items one by one still means we need somewhere to put them in sorted order, presumably some auxiliary array. Or does it? Think about it for a moment. If we peel off the largest item, the heap size reduces by one, leaving space at the end of the array for the item we just removed. In fact, the algorithm to remove an item from a heap requires the lowest, rightmost node to be copied to the root before being trickled down, so all we need to do is to swap the root with the lowest, rightmost node, reduce the count of items in the heap, and then apply the trickle down algorithm. Continue doing this until we run out of items in the heap. What we're left with are the items in the original array, but sorted.

Listing 9.8 shows the full heapsort routine, implemented in the same manner as we saw all the sorts in Chapter 5.

Listing 9.8: The heapsort algorithm

```
procedure HSTrickleDown(aList    : PPointerList;
                        aFromInx : integer;
                        aCount   : integer;
                        aCompare : TtdCompareFunc);
var
  Item     : pointer;
  ChildInx : integer;
  ParentInx: integer;
begin
  {first do a simple trickle down continually replacing parent with
  larger child until we reach the bottom level of the heap}
  Item := aList^[aFromInx];
  ChildInx := (aFromInx * 2) + 1;
  while (ChildInx < aCount) do begin
    if (succ(ChildInx) < aCount) and
       (aCompare(aList^[ChildInx], aList^[succ(ChildInx)]) < 0) then
      inc(ChildInx);
    aList^[aFromInx] := aList^[ChildInx];
    aFromInx := ChildInx;
    ChildInx := (aFromInx * 2) + 1;
  end;
  {now bubble up from where we ended up}
  ParentInx := (aFromInx - 1) div 2;
```

```
  while (aFromInx > 0) and
        (aCompare(Item, aList^[ParentInx]) > 0) do begin
    aList^[aFromInx] := aList^[ParentInx];
    aFromInx := ParentInx;
    ParentInx := (aFromInx - 1) div 2;
  end;
  {save the item where we ended up after the bubble up}
  aList^[aFromInx] := Item;
end;
procedure HSTrickleDownStd(aList    : PPointerList;
                           aFromInx : integer;
                           aCount   : integer;
                           aCompare : TtdCompareFunc);
var
  Item     : pointer;
  ChildInx : integer;
begin
  Item := aList^[aFromInx];
  ChildInx := (aFromInx * 2) + 1;
  while (ChildInx < aCount) do begin
    if (succ(ChildInx) < aCount) and
       (aCompare(aList^[ChildInx], aList^[succ(ChildInx)]) < 0) then
      inc(ChildInx);
    if aCompare(Item, aList^[ChildInx]) >= 0 then
      Break;
    aList^[aFromInx] := aList^[ChildInx];
    aFromInx := ChildInx;
    ChildInx := (aFromInx * 2) + 1;
  end;
  aList^[aFromInx] := Item;
end;
procedure TDHeapSort(aList    : TList;
                     aFirst   : integer;
                     aLast    : integer;
                     aCompare : TtdCompareFunc);
var
  ItemCount : integer;
  Inx       : integer;
  Temp      : pointer;
begin
  TDValidateListRange(aList, aFirst, aLast, 'TDHeapSort');
  {convert the list into a heap-Floyd's Algorithm}
  ItemCount := aLast - aFirst + 1;
  for Inx := pred(ItemCount div 2) downto 0 do
    HSTrickleDownStd(@aList.List^[aFirst], Inx, ItemCount, aCompare);
  {now remove the items one at a time from the heap, placing them at
  the end of the array}
```

```
  for Inx := pred(ItemCount) downto 0 do begin
    Temp := aList.List^[aFirst];
    aList.List^[aFirst] := aList.List^[aFirst+Inx];
    aList.List^[aFirst+Inx] := Temp;
    HSTrickleDown(@aList.List^[aFirst], 0, Inx, aCompare);
  end;
end;
```

Notice that we use the standard trickle down algorithm for the first stage when we create a heap from the array (Floyd's Algorithm), but make use of Floyd's optimized trickle down for the second stage when we are removing the largest item from the steadily reducing heap. In the first stage, we have no knowledge about the distribution of the items in the array, so it makes sense to just apply the standard trickle down algorithm; after all, Floyd's Algorithm is a O(n) operation overall. In the second stage, however, we know that we are exchanging the largest item with one of the smallest items, and so it makes sense to apply the optimization.

There's one point that I haven't yet clarified. If you are using a max-heap as a priority queue, you will retrieve the items in reverse order, from largest to smallest. However, if you are using a max-heap to perform a heapsort, you will get the items sorted in ascending order, not in reverse order. With a min-heap you'd remove items in ascending order, but you'd heapsort in descending order.

Heapsort is an important sorting algorithm for a couple of reasons. Firstly, it runs in O($n$log(n)) time, so it's fast. Secondly, heapsort has no worst-case scenario. Compare this behavior with quicksort. Generally, quicksort tends to be faster than heapsort (heapsort will use more item comparisons than quicksort, and the internal loop in heapsort has more going on than the one in quicksort), but quicksort does have cases that can easily trip it up, causing it to slow to a crawl. (It can become a O(n^2) algorithm in the worst case, unless we apply some algorithm improvements.) When we compare heapsort with merge sort instead, we note that it is an in-place sort and does not require large amounts of extra space like merge sort does. Finally, we should state that heapsort is not a stable sort algorithm.

The source code for the TDHeapSort procedure and its helper routines can be found in the TDSorts.pas file

Extending the Priority Queue

Having made a brief diversion to look at heapsort, we should return to priority queues and consider extending the data structure we've implemented so far.

We have designed a data structure with two main operations: enqueue, which adds a new item to the structure, and dequeue, which returns the item in the structure with the highest priority (and we got to define how we determined this priority through the use of an external comparison function). We called the resulting structure a priority queue.

However, operating system structures like thread priority queues or print queues enable us to perform two more operations: remove to delete an item from the queue wherever it may appear in the queue and return it (it doesn't necessarily have to be the largest item), and change priority to change the priority for an arbitrary item in the queue.

With a print queue, the remove operation enables us to cancel a print job that we no longer want to print, or to remove a print job from one queue and add it to another (for example, if the printer associated with the first queue is tied up printing a large report). With a thread priority queue, we can temporarily increase the priority of a thread to give it a better chance of resuming execution the next time the operating system decides to swap threads.

At first glance, these operations would be difficult to implement using a heap. Consider the problem for a moment. The priority queue class would be given a reference to an item that's already in the queue somewhere, so that it could be deleted or its priority changed. How do we find the item in the queue? This is one place where the "loose" sorting in the heap works against us. The only possible method at this stage seems to be a sequential search, but that's pretty slow. Once we find the item, we either have to remove it or change its priority and then re-establish the completeness of the heap, or the heap property, or both.

Re-establishing the Heap Property

It turns out that the second problem (making the heap a valid heap again) is easier than the first (finding the item we wish to delete or whose priority we wish to change), so we'll deal with that first.

To delete an arbitrary item from the heap, we would exchange it with the last item in the heap, and reduce the size of the heap. At that point, we have an item that may be invalidating the heap property.

To change the priority of an arbitrary item, we would simply make the change and be left with an item that may be invalidating the heap property.

In both cases, we have an item that could be in the wrong place in the heap, i.e., the heap property is violated at this particular item. But we know how to deal with this situation; we've done it before in the standard priority queue. If the item's priority is greater than its parent's, we bubble the item up the heap. If not, we check it against its children. If it's smaller than one or both of its children, we trickle it down the heap. Eventually, it'll settle into a position where it is less than its parent and greater than both its children.

Finding an Arbitrary Item in the Heap

We are now left with the initial problem: efficiently finding the item in the heap. This problem seems intractable—the heap does not store any information to help since it was designed merely to enable the largest item to be easily identified. It almost seems as if we need to revert to a balanced binary search tree (then we can use the standard search algorithm to find the item in $O(\log(n))$ time).

What we will do instead is create what's called an *indirect heap*. When you add an item to the priority queue, you're passing control of that item to the queue. In return, you'll be given a *handle*. The handle is a value by which the queue "knows" the item that was added; if you like, the handle is an indirect reference to the actual item in the heap.

So, to remove an item from the priority queue, you pass the item's handle to the queue. The queue uses this handle to identify the position of the item in the heap, and then deletes it in the manner we've just described.

To change the priority of an item, we merely change the priority value in the item and tell the queue what has happened by passing the handle of the item to the queue. The queue can then re-establish the heap priority. The dequeue operation works as before (we don't need to pass the handle of the item because it is the queue that will determine the largest item); however, the queue will destroy the handle of the item that was returned since it no longer appears in the queue. If the items are records or objects, we can store the handle for a given item within the item itself alongside its priority and other fields.

When using the operating system, the type of a handle is usually a long integer, which is usually some kind of disguised pointer. For this implementation, we'll just use a typeless pointer.

Implementation of the Extended Priority Queue

As far as the user of the priority queue is concerned, this new interface is only slightly more complicated than before. Listing 9.9 shows the class interface to TtdPriorityQueueEx, the extended priority queue.

Listing 9.9: The TtdPriorityQueueEx class interface

```
type
  TtdPQHandle = pointer;

  TtdPriorityQueueEx = class
    private
      FCompare : TtdCompareFunc;
      FHandles : pointer;
      FList    : TList;
      FName    : TtdNameString;
    protected
      function pqGetCount : integer;
      procedure pqError(aErrorCode   : integer;
                  const aMethodName : TtdNameString);
      procedure pqBubbleUp(aHandle : TtdPQHandle);
      procedure pqTrickleDown(aHandle : TtdPQHandle);
    public
      constructor Create(aCompare : TtdCompareFunc);
      destructor Destroy; override;
      procedure ChangePriority(aHandle : TtdPQHandle);
      procedure Clear;
      function Dequeue : pointer;
      function Enqueue(aItem : pointer) : TtdPQHandle;
      function Examine : pointer;
      function IsEmpty : boolean;
      function Remove(aHandle : TtdPQHandle) : pointer;

      property Count : integer read pqGetCount;
      property Name : TtdNameString read FName write FName;
  end;
```

As you can see, the only real differences from the TtdPriorityQueue class are the Remove and ChangePriority methods and the fact that Enqueue returns a handle.

Now, how do we implement this interface? Internally, the queue has a heap as usual, but this time it must maintain some extra information so that it can track where each item may appear in the heap. It must also identify each item with a handle in such a way that finding an item given a handle is fast and efficient—in theory, faster than a binary search tree's O(log(n)) search time.

What we will do is this: when the user enqueues an item, we will add the item to a linked list. This will involve defining and using a node with at least two pointers, a next pointer and the item itself, although for reasons that will become apparent we'll be making the list a doubly linked list so we'll need a prior pointer as well. The handle to the item that we pass back will be the address of the node. Now comes the clever bit. The node also stores an integer value—the position of the item in the array that implements the heap. The heap does not store the items themselves; it stores the handles instead (that is, the linked list nodes). Whenever it needs to access the item itself, for comparison purposes, it will dereference the handle.

Unfortunately, we cannot use the doubly linked list class introduced in Chapter 3 since we need access to the nodes, and that class was designed to hide the node structure from us. This is one of those cases where we cannot use prepackaged classes, but instead must code from first principles. This isn't too bad in the case of the doubly linked list, since it is such a simple structure. We create a linked list with an explicit head and tail node, and this will make deleting a normal node especially easy. These node deletions will occur with both the Dequeue and Remove methods of the extended priority queue class.

The enqueue and bubble up operations are made only slightly more complicated. We first create a handle by allocating a node for the item and add it to our linked list of nodes. Since we are adding the handles to the heap, we shall need to dereference the handles to access the items, and when we move an item around in the heap we need to store the index of its new resting place inside the node. Listing 9.10 shows the enqueue and bubble up methods.

Listing 9.10: Enqueue and bubble up in the extended priority queue

```
procedure TtdPriorityQueueEx.pqBubbleUp(aHandle : pointer);
var
  FromInx      : integer;
  ParentInx    : integer;
  ParentHandle : PpqexNode;
  Handle       : PpqexNode absolute aHandle;
begin
  {while the handle under consideration is larger than its parent,
  swap it with its parent and continue from its new position}
  {Note: the parent for the child at index n is at (n-1) div 2}
  FromInx := Handle^.peInx;
  if (FromInx > 0) then begin
    ParentInx := (FromInx - 1) div 2;
    ParentHandle := PpqexNode(FList.List^[ParentInx]);
    {while our item has a parent, and it's greater than the parent...}
    while (FromInx > 0) and
          (FCompare(Handle^.peItem, ParentHandle^.peItem) > 0) do begin
      {move our parent down the tree}
      FList.List^[FromInx] := ParentHandle;
      ParentHandle^.peInx := FromInx;
      FromInx := ParentInx;
      ParentInx := (FromInx - 1) div 2;
      ParentHandle := PpqexNode(FList.List^[ParentInx]);
    end;
```

```
  end;
  {store our item in the correct place}
  FList.List^[FromInx] := Handle;
  Handle^.peInx := FromInx;
end;
function TtdPriorityQueueEx.Enqueue(aItem : pointer) : TtdPQHandle;
var
  Handle : PpqexNode;
begin
  {create a new node for the linked list}
  Handle := AddLinkedListNode(FHandles, aItem);
  {add the handle to the end of the queue}
  FList.Add(Handle);
  Handle^.peInx := pred(FList.Count);
  {now bubble it up as far as it will go}
  if (FList.Count > 1) then
    pqBubbleUp(Handle);
  {return the handle}
  Result := Handle;
end;
```

Like Enqueue, Dequeue is made a little more complicated by all the indirection going on, but the code is still recognizable as the standard dequeue and trickle down operations.

Listing 9.11: Dequeue and trickle down in the extended priority queue.

```
procedure TtdPriorityQueueEx.pqTrickleDown(aHandle : TtdPQHandle);
var
  FromInx     : integer;
  MaxInx      : integer;
  ChildInx    : integer;
  ChildHandle : PpqexNode;
  Handle      : PpqexNode absolute aHandle;
begin
  {while the item under consideration is smaller than one of its
  children, swap it with the larger child and continue from its new
  position}
  FromInx := Handle^.peInx;
  MaxInx := pred(FList.Count);
  {calculate the left child index}
  ChildInx := succ(FromInx * 2);
  {while there is at least a left child...}
  while (ChildInx <= MaxInx) do begin
    {if there is a right child, calculate the index of the larger
    child}
    if ((ChildInx+1) <= MaxInx) and
       (FCompare(PpqexNode(FList.List^[ChildInx])^.peItem,
                 PpqexNode(FList.List^[ChildInx+1])^.peItem) < 0) then
```

```
    inc(ChildInx);
    {if our item is greater or equal to the larger child, we're done}
    ChildHandle := PpqexNode(FList.List^[ChildInx]);
    if (FCompare(Handle^.peItem, ChildHandle^.peItem) >= 0) then
      Break;
    {otherwise move the larger child up the tree, and move our item
    down the tree and repeat}
    FList.List^[FromInx] := ChildHandle;
    ChildHandle^.peInx := FromInx;
    FromInx := ChildInx;
    ChildInx := succ(FromInx * 2);
  end;
  {store our item in the correct place}
  FList.List^[FromInx] := Handle;
  Handle^.peInx := FromInx;
end;
function TtdPriorityQueueEx.Dequeue : pointer;
var
  Handle : PpqexNode;
begin
  {make sure we have an item to dequeue}
  if (FList.Count = 0) then
    pqError(tdeQueueIsEmpty, 'Dequeue');
  {return the item at the root, remove it from the handles list}
  Handle := FList.List^[0];
  Result := Handle^.peItem;
  DeleteLinkedListNode(FHandles, Handle);
  {if there was only one item in the queue, it's now empty}
  if (FList.Count = 1) then
    FList.Count := 0
  {if there were two, just replace the root with the one remaining
  child; the heap property is obviously satisfied}
  else if (FList.Count = 2) then begin
    Handle := FList.List^[1];
    FList.List^[0] := Handle;
    FList.Count := 1;
    Handle^.peInx := 0;
  end
  {otherwise we have to restore the heap property}
  else begin
    {replace the root with the child at the lowest, rightmost
    position, and shrink the list; then trickle down the root item as
    far as it will go}
    Handle := FList.Last;
    FList.List^[0] := Handle;
    Handle^.peInx := 0;
    FList.Count := FList.Count - 1;
    pqTrickleDown(Handle);
```

```
  end;
end;
```

Having seen the enqueue and dequeue operations, we can now look at the new operations: remove and change priority. The ChangePriority method is the simplest. The class assumes that the item's priority has been altered before the method is called. The method first checks to see if the item has a parent, and if so, whether the item with the new priority is greater than its parent. If so, the item is bubbled up the heap. If a bubble up wasn't possible or wasn't required, the method then checks to see if a trickle down operation could be done.

Listing 9.12: Re-establishing the heap property after changing the priority

```
procedure TtdPriorityQueueEx.ChangePriority(aHandle : TtdPQHandle);
var
  Handle : PpqexNode absolute aHandle;
  ParentInx    : integer;
  ParentHandle : PpqexNode;
begin
  {check to see whether we can bubble up}
  if (Handle^.peInx > 0) then begin
    ParentInx := (Handle^.peInx - 1) div 2;
    ParentHandle := PpqexNode(FList[ParentInx]);
    if (FCompare(Handle^.peItem, ParentHandle^.peItem) > 0) then begin
      pqBubbleUp(Handle);
      Exit;
    end;
  end;
  {otherwise trickle down}
  pqTrickleDown(Handle);
end;
```

The final operation is implemented by the Remove method. Here, we return the item denoted by the handle and then replace it with the last item in the heap. The handle is removed from the linked list, this operation being simplified by using a doubly linked list. The count of items in the heap is then reduced by one. At this point, the process works in exactly the same manner as changing the priority and so we merely call that particular method.

Listing 9.13: Removing an item given by its handle

```
function TtdPriorityQueueEx.Remove(aHandle : TtdPQHandle) : pointer;
var
  Handle    : PpqexNode absolute aHandle;
  NewHandle : PpqexNode;
  HeapInx   : integer;
begin
  {return the item, then delete the handle}
```

```
  Result := Handle^.peItem;
  HeapInx := Handle^.peInx;
  DeleteLinkedListNode(FHandles, Handle);
  {check to see whether we deleted the last item, if so just shrink
  the heap - the heap property will still apply}
  if (HeapInx = pred(FList.Count)) then
    FList.Count := FList.Count - 1
  else begin
    {replace the heap element with the child at the lowest, rightmost
     position, and shrink the list}
    NewHandle := FList.Last;
    FList.List^[HeapInx] := NewHandle;
    NewHandle^.peInx := HeapInx;
    FList.Count := FList.Count - 1;
    {now treat it as a change priority operation}
    ChangePriority(NewHandle);
  end;
end;
```

The full code can be found in the TDPriQue.pas file on the CD.

Summary

In this chapter we have looked primarily at priority queues, queues that do not return the oldest item but instead the item with the largest priority. Having investigated a couple of simple implementations, we saw an implementation using a heap. We discussed the basic heap properties and operations and saw how to apply these as a heapsort algorithm, as well as our original requirement for a priority queue.

Finally, we extended the definition of a priority queue to allow a couple of further operations: removing an arbitrary item and changing the priority of a given item. We discussed how the implementation would have to change to support these operations.

Chapter 10

State Machines and Regular Expressions

There is a whole class of problems that can be solved by recourse to pen and paper. For me, it's a fun part of programming: being able to map something out by drawing and then coding. I'm referring to algorithms involving state machines.

State Machines

Unlike most of the algorithms in this book, state machines are a technique to help solve other algorithms. They are a means to an end, the end being the implementation of an algorithm. Nevertheless they have some interesting qualities, as we shall see. We shall mainly be looking at state machines that implement *parsing* algorithms. To parse is to read through a string (or a text file) and break up the characters into individual tokens. A state machine that parses is usually known as a *parser.*

Using State Machines: Parsing

An example will help us understand the process. Let us suppose we wish to devise an algorithm that would extract the individual words in a string of text. We'll put the words we extract into a string list. Moreover, there's a wrinkle: we would like quoted text inside the string to be considered as a single word. So, if we had the string:

```
He said, "State machines?"
```

the routine would ignore the punctuation and white space and return:

```
He
said
"State machines?"
```

Notice that the white space and punctuation inside the quoted text are left alone.

The simplest way to solve this particular parsing algorithm is to use a *state machine*. A state machine is a system (usually digital) that moves from one state to another according to input it receives. The moves are called *transitions*. You can think of a state machine as a specialized flowchart, and, indeed, Figure 10.1 shows the flowchart for our algorithm.

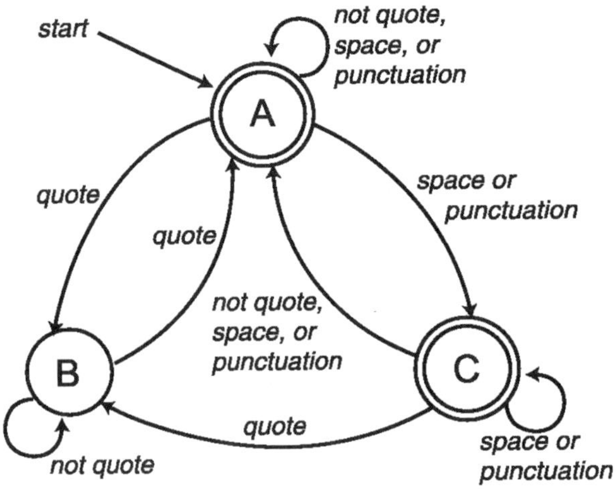

Figure 10.1: State machine to extract words from a string

The state machine shown has three states: A, B, and C. We enter the flowchart in state A. At this point, we read a character from the input string. If it is a double quote, we move to state B. If it is a space character or a punctuation character we move to state C. If it is any other character we keep it in A (this is shown by the loop).

If we reach state B, we stay there reading characters until we read the closing double quote. At that point we move back to state A.

If we reach state C, on the other hand, we stay there reading characters until one of two things happens: we read a double quote character and therefore move to state B, or we read a character that is not a double quote, space, or puctuation character and therefore move back to state A.

When we make a move, we may also have an action to do. Assume that we use a string to collect the characters for the current word. The initial move to state A will clear this string. The loop from A to itself will append the character to the current word. The move from A to B will first add the current word (if there is one) to the string list and then set the current word to the opening double quote. The loop from B to itself appends the character to the current word. The transition from B back to A will append the closing double quote to the current word; add this to the string list and then clear it. From A to C, the current word is added to the string list and it is then cleared. The move from C to itself does nothing (this is where we are, in effect, discarding the white space and punctuation). From C to A, we set the current word equal to the character read. From C to B, we set the current word equal to the opening double quote.

By tracing Figure 10.1 with the above paragraph, you can see that the state machine implements the algorithm perfectly.

```
Move to A; clear word
Read 'H', stay in A; word = 'H'
Read 'e', stay in A; word = 'He'
Read ' ', move to C; output 'He', clear word
Read 's', move to A; word = 's'
Read 'a', stay in A; word = 'sa'
Read 'i', stay in A; word = 'sai'
Read 'd', stay in A; word = 'said'
Read ',', move to C; output 'said', clear word
Read ' ', stay in C
Read '"', move to B; word = '"'
Read 'S', stay in B; word = '"S'
..and so on..
```

There is, however, one more property of the state machine in Figure 10.1 that I have glossed over up to now. States A and C are circled with a double line, whereas B is not. By convention, state machine diagrams use the double circle for a state to mean that it is a *terminating state* (also known as a *halt state* or an *accepting state*). When the input string is completely read, the state machine will be in a particular state (for the example string above, the final state of the state machine is A). If that final state is a terminating state, the state machine is said to *accept* the input string. No matter which characters (or, more strictly, *tokens*) were found in the input string, and no matter what moves were made, the state machine "understood" the string. If, on the other hand, the state machine ended up in a non-terminating state, the string was not accepted and the state machine did not understand the string.

In our case, state B is not an accepting state. What does that mean in practical terms? Well, if we're in state B when the input string is exhausted, then we've read one double quote but not a second. The state machine has been reading a string containing text with an unbalanced double quote. Depending on how strict we were being, this could be viewed as an error or we could just ignore it. Figure 10.1 views it as an error.

Speaking of errors, although our particular example doesn't show this possibility, we could get into a state that doesn't have a move for a particular character or token. This would cause an immediate error. We'll see later how to incorporate this into the state machine itself.

Having drawn the picture, we should now implement it. For ease of understanding, we tend to invert it slightly so that reading the input string drives the state machine rather than having each state read the next character from the input string. Doing it this way makes it easier to see how to exit the state machine.

Listing 10.1 shows the code that implements the state machine from Figure 10.1 (the source code can be found in the TDStates.pas file on the CD). Notice that I've decided not to name the states unimaginatively as A, B, and C to mimic the figure, but instead gave them descriptive names like ScanNormal, ScanQuoted, and ScanPunctuation.

Listing 10.1: Extracting words from a string

```
procedure TDExtractWords(const S : string; aList : TStrings);
type
  TStates = (ScanNormal, ScanQuoted, ScanPunctuation);
const
  WordDelim = ' !<>[]{}(),./?;:-+=*&';
var
  State   : TStates;
  Inx     : integer;
  Ch      : char;
  CurWord : string;
begin
  {initialize by clearing the string list, and
  starting in ScanNormal state with empty word}
  Assert(aList <> nil, 'TDExtractWords: list is nil');
  aList.Clear;
  State := ScanNormal;
  CurWord := '';
  {read through all the characters in the string}
  for Inx := 1 to length(S) do begin
    {get the next character}
    Ch := S[Inx];
    {switch processing on the state}
    case State of
      ScanNormal :
        begin
          if (Ch = '"') then begin
            if (CurWord <> '') then
              aList.Add(CurWord);
```

```
          CurWord := '"';
          State := ScanQuoted;
        end
        else if (TDPosCh(Ch, WordDelim) <> 0) then begin
          if (CurWord <> '') then begin
            aList.Add(CurWord);
            CurWord := '';
          end;
          State := ScanPunctuation;
        end
        else
          CurWord := CurWord + Ch;
      end;
    ScanQuoted :
      begin
        CurWord := CurWord + Ch;
        if (Ch = '"') then begin
          aList.Add(CurWord);
          CurWord := '';
          State := ScanNormal;
        end;
      end;
    ScanPunctuation :
      begin
        if (Ch = '"') then begin
          CurWord := '"';
          State := ScanQuoted;
        end
        else if (TDPosCh(Ch, WordDelim) = 0) then begin
          CurWord := Ch;
          State := ScanNormal;
        end
      end;
    end;
  end;
  {if we are in the ScanQuoted state at the end of the
  string, there was a mismatched double quote}
  if (State = ScanQuoted) then
    raise EtdStateException.Create(
       FmtLoadStr(tdeStateMisMatchQuote,
                  [UnitName, 'TDExtractWords']));
  {if the current word is not empty, add it to the list}
  if (CurWord <> '') then
    aList.Add(CurWord);
end;
```

The code gets a character from the input string and then enters a Case statement that switches on the current state. For each state, we have If statements to implement the actions and the moves depending on the value of the current character. At the end, we signal an exception if we're left in the ScanQuoted state.

There is an inefficiency in this code for 32-bit Delphi. The code builds up the current word character by character by use of the string + operator. For long strings, this is very inefficient because the operator has to periodically reallocate the string's memory block to accommodate extra characters.
The string is initially empty. The first character is then added. Since an empty string is a nil pointer, some memory gets allocated (8 bytes worth) and the string is changed to point to it. The character is added. After seven more are appended, the string must be reallocated to accept another character.
The other inefficiency concerns the operation of adding a character. The compiler emits code to convert the character into a one-character temporary string and then concatenates that. This conversion of a character into a long string requires memory to be allocated, obviously.

Both of these inefficiencies degrade the speed of the TDExtract- Words routine. To counteract this we can implement the following changes to the code, although it does muddy what we are trying to do, at least from a maintenance programmer's viewpoint.

- Instead of setting the CurWord variable to '', call SetLength to preallocate the string memory. Use a reasonable value for the number of bytes depending on your requirements. (For example, a good value might be the length of S. We know that a word we extract can never be longer than that.)
- Maintain a CurInx variable that details where the next character is to go. It starts off as zero.
- For each character we wish to add, increment CurInx and set CurWord[CurInx] equal to the character.
- When we wish to add the current word to the string list, call SetLength again, this time passing the value of CurInx. This will reset the string length to be exactly the number of characters in the string. Reset CurInx to zero.

With this algorithm, we are deliberately trying to minimize the number of times CurWord is reallocated (we've got it down to two, pretty much the minimum) and we're removing the compiler's automatic conversion of a character into a long string.

As you can see, the code implements the state machine perfectly. The code is even fairly simple to extend. Suppose, for example, we wanted to cover the use of single quotes as well. Simple enough: we create a new state, D, that functions in the same manner as state B except that the transitions to and from it use single instead of double quotes. In the code, this means a copy-and-paste action so that we duplicate the state B functionality as state D.

Parsing Comma-Delimited Files

A common problem is the requirement to parse comma-delimited files. A comma-delimited file is a text file describing a table of records. Each line in the file is a separate record, and the lines are further subdivided into fields of the record, with each field being separated from its neighbor by commas. (Sometimes this arrangement is known as comma-separated values (CSV) format.) There are several wrinkles (as always!). A field can be surrounded by quotes (this enables a field's value to contain commas). A field could be missing, in which case the two commas defining the field are next to each other.

Here's an example of a CSV line of text.

```
Julian,Bucknall,,43,"Author, and Columnist"
```

There are five fields here. The first two have values [Julian] and [Bucknall], the third has no value, the fourth is [43], and the fifth is [Author, and Columnist]. (I'm using brackets here to delimit the string values to show that the double quotes in the original string are discarded.)

We'll assume that our ultimate aim is to write a routine that takes a string and a string list, breaks up the string into separate fields, and inserts the fields into the string list. Before we start drawing the state machine diagram, let's lay down a couple of specific rules about the format the CSV string can take. The first rule is that all characters are significant and the only ones we will throw away are the commas (after we've used them for splitting the CSV text, of course) and the double quotes that enclose a field's value. Furthermore, a double quote only has significance as an opening double quote if it appears after a comma (or as the first character in the string). That rule means, for example, that if there were a single space between the comma and the opening double quote in the example string, our routine would parse it as six fields, with the last two being ["Author] and [and Columnist"]. Furthermore, if a double quote was identified as an opening double quote, then the next double quote closes the field value, and the very next character must be a comma (or it must be the end of the string). If not, it is an error and the string is rejected.

Now we can draw the state machine. I came up with Figure 10.2 comprising five states. The initial state I named FieldStart. If the next character is a double quote, we move to ScanQuoted where we gather characters until the next double quote when we move to the EndQuoted state. If we get a comma, we can move back to FieldStart; if not, we move to the error state and stop. From FieldStart we can also get a comma (the field is counted as being empty), or if we get something that's not a comma or a double quote we move to the ScanField state. Here we gather characters until we get a comma.

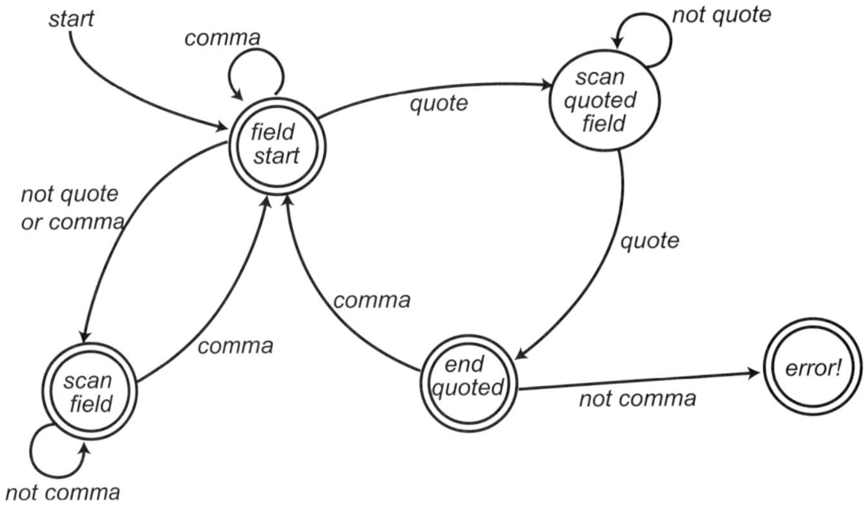

Figure 10.2: State machine to parse a CSV formatted string

As you can see, we can show error conditions in a state machine by creating a special state. (On the other hand, we could take it as written. Without the move to the error state, there is only one character that can get us out of the EndQuoted state, the comma, and any other character causes an "exception" in the state machine.)

Converting the state machine diagram to code is as easy as the previous example. Listing 10.2 shows the implementation.

Listing 10.2: Parsing a CSV string

```
procedure TDExtractFields(const S : string; aList : TStrings);
type
  TStates = (FieldStart, ScanField, ScanQuoted, EndQuoted, GotError);
var
  State    : TStates;
  Inx      : integer;
  Ch       : char;
  CurField: string;
begin
  {initialize by clearing the string list, and
```

```
 starting in FieldStart state}
Assert(aList <> nil, 'TDExtractFields: list is nil');
aList.Clear;
State := FieldStart;
CurField := '';
{read through all the characters in the string}
for Inx := 1 to length(S) do begin
  {get the next character}
  Ch := S[Inx];
  {switch processing on the state}
  case State of
    FieldStart :
      begin
        case Ch of
          '"' :
            begin
              State := ScanQuoted;
            end;
          ',' :
            begin
              aList.Add('');
            end;
        else
          CurField := Ch;
          State := ScanField;
        end;
      end;
    ScanField :
      begin
        if (Ch = ',') then begin
          aList.Add(CurField);
          CurField := '';
          State := FieldStart;
        end
        else
          CurField := CurField + Ch;
      end;
    ScanQuoted :
      begin
        if (Ch = '"') then
          State := EndQuoted
        else
          CurField := CurField + Ch;
      end;
    EndQuoted :
      begin
        if (Ch = ',') then begin
          aList.Add(CurField);
```

```
          CurField := '';
          State := FieldStart;
        end
        else
          State := GotError;
      end;
    GotError :
      begin
        raise EtdStateException.Create(
           FmtLoadStr(tdeStateBadCSV,
                      [UnitName, 'TDExtractFields']));
      end;
  end;
 end;
 {if we are in the ScanQUoted or GotError state at the end
 of the string, there was a problem with a closing quote}
 if (State = ScanQuoted) or (State = GotError) then
   raise EtdStateException.Create(
      FmtLoadStr(tdeStateBadCSV,
                 [UnitName, 'TDExtractFields']));
 {if the current field is not empty, add it to the list}
 if (CurField <> '') then
   aList.Add(CurField);
end;
```

The source code for TDExtractFields can be found in the TDStates.pas file on the CD.

Deterministic and Non-deterministic State Machines

Now that we have seen a couple of fairly complex state machines and are more familiar with them, I will introduce a couple of new terms. The first is *automaton* (plural: *automata*). This is nothing more than another name for a state machine, but it is used extensively in computer science classes and textbooks. A *finite state machine* or *finite automaton* is merely a state machine whose number of states is not infinite. Both of our examples are finite automata; the first has three states and the second five.

The last new term is *deterministic*. Look at the state machine in Figure 10.2. No matter what state we're in, no matter what the next character is, we know without fail where to move to next. The moves are all well defined. This state machine is deterministic; there is no guesswork involved or choice to be made. If we get a double quote while in state FieldStart, for example, we have to move to the ScanQuoted state.

Figures 10.1 and 10.2 are examples of *deterministic finite state machines* (DFSM) or *deterministic finite automata* (DFA). The opposite of these is a state machine that involves some kind of choice with some of its states. In using this latter type of state machine we will have to make a choice as to whether to move to state X or state Y for a particular character. As you might imagine, the processing of this kind of state machine involves some more intricate code. These state machines are known, not surprisingly, as *non-deterministic finite state machines* (NDFSM) or *non-deterministic finite automata* (NFA).

Let us now consider an NFA. Figure 10.3 shows an NFA that can convert a string containing a number in decimal format to a double value. Looking at it, you may be wondering what the moves are that have the peculiar lowercase e (ε). These are *no-cost* or *free moves*, where you can make the move without using up the current character or token. So, for example, you can move from the start token A to the next token B by using up a "+" sign, using up a "–" sign, or by just moving there (the no-cost move). These free moves are a feature of non-deterministic state machines.

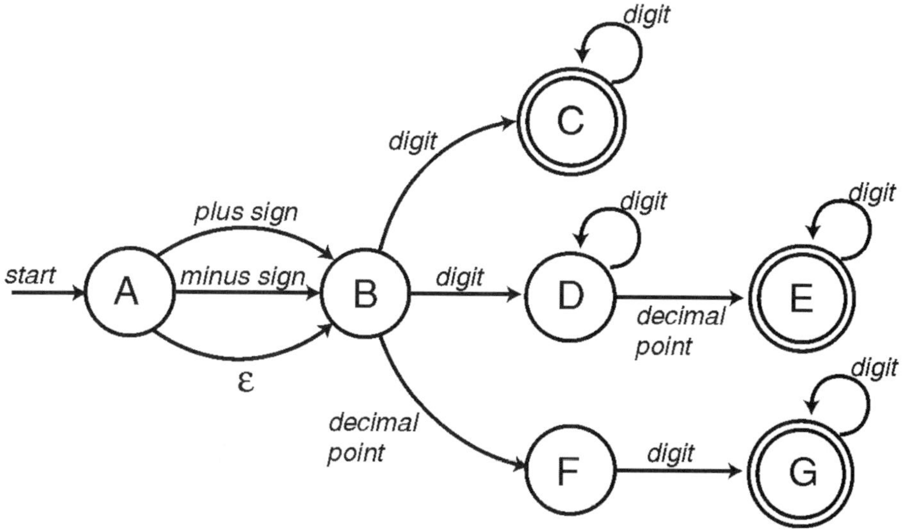

Figure 10.3: NFA to validate a string to be a number

Take a moment to browse the figure and use it to validate strings such as "1", "1.23", "+.7", "–12". You'll see that the upper branch is for integer values (those without a decimal radix point); the middle one is for strings that consist of at least one digit before the decimal point but maybe none afterward; and the lower one for strings that may not have any digits before the decimal point but must have at least one afterward. If you think about it for a while, you'll see that the state machine won't be able to accept the decimal point on its own.

The problem still remains though: although the state machine will accept "1.2", how does it "know" to take the middle path? An even more basic question might be: why bother with NFAs at all? It all looks too complicated; let's stick to DFAs.

The second question is actually easier to answer than the first. NFAs are the natural state machines for evaluating regular expressions. Once we understand how to use an NFA, we are more than half way toward being able to apply regular expression matching to a string, the eventual goal of this chapter.

Back to the first question: how does the NFA know to take the middle path for the string "1.2"? The answer is, of course, it doesn't. There are a couple of ways of processing a string with such a state machine, the easiest to describe being a trial-and-error algorithm. To help in this trial-and-error algorithm we make use of another algorithm: the backtracking algorithm.

> Note that we are only interested in finding *one* path through the state machine that accepts the string. There may well be others, but we're not interested in enumerating them all.

Let's see how it works by tracing through what happens when we try to see whether the state machine accepts "12.34".

We start off in state A. The first token is "1". We can't make the "+" move to B, nor the "–" move. So we take the free move (the ε link). We're now at state B with the same token, the "1". We now have two choices: move either to C or to D, consuming the token in the process. Let's take the first choice. Before we move though, we make a note of what we are about to do, so that if it was wrong we know not to do it again. So we arrive at C, consuming the digit as we do so. We get the next token, the "2". Simple enough; we stay in the same state, using the token.

We get the next token, the ".". There are no possible moves at all. We're now stuck. There are no moves and yet we have a token to process. This is where the backtracking algorithm comes in. We look back at our notes and see that in state B we made a choice when we were trying to use the "1" . Maybe it was the wrong choice, so we backtrack to find out. We reset the state machine back to state B, and we reset the input string so that we are at the "1". Since the first choice resulted in a problem, we try the second choice: the move to D. We make the transition to state D, consuming the "1". The next token is "2"; we use it up and stay in state D. The next token is ".": a move to state E, which, in fact, consumes the next two digits. We're finished with the input string, and we're in a terminating state, E, and so we can say the NFA accepts the string "12.34".

When converting this state machine into code, we have a couple of problems to solve.

The first thing to note is that we can no longer have a simple For loop to cycle through the characters in the string. With a deterministic automaton, every character read from the input string resulted in a move (even if it was to the same state), and there was no possibility of backtracking, or going back to a character we'd already visited. For the non-deterministic case then, we'll have to replace the For loop with a While loop and make sure we increment the string index variable when we need to.

The next thing to notice is that we cannot have a simple Case or If statement on the input character for some states. We have a plurality of "move choices" to worry about. Some of these choices will be rejected immediately because the current character doesn't match the condition for the move. Some will be followed, with some of these being rejected at a later stage and another choice being followed. For now, we'll simply enumerate the possible moves and make sure we follow them in order. We'll use an integer variable for that purpose.

We now must consider the final piece: the backtracking implementation. Whenever we choose a move that is valid (compare this with rejecting a move because the current character doesn't match the conditions for the move), we want to save the fact that we made that particular move. Then, if we need to backtrack to the same state, with the same input character, we can easily select the next move and try that. Of course, with any state we may be making choices about our moves, so we must save them all and revisit them in reverse order; the backtrack goes to the most recent choice we made. In other words, we must use a last-in first-out type structure—a stack. We'll use one of those we implemented in Chapter 3.

What shall we save on the stack? Well, we need to save the state where we made the choice, the move number we were making (so we know which is the next one we have to try), and finally, the character index where we made the choice. Using these three items of information we can easily rewind the state machine to a previous point so that we can make the next, and possibly better, choice for a move.

Listing 10.3 shows the implementation of the decimal number NFA. This state machine will accept a string when the string is exhausted and the automaton is in a terminating state. It will fail a string if the string is exhausted and we're not in a terminating state, or if we reach a state and the current character cannot be matched against a move. This second condition has a further caveat: the backtracking stack must be empty.

Listing 10.3: Validating a string to be a number using an NFA

```
type
  TnfaState = (StartScanning,              {state A in figure}
               ScannedSign,                {state B in figure}
               ScanInteger,                {state C in figure}
               ScanLeadDigits,             {state D in figure}
               ScannedDecPoint,            {state E in figure}
               ScanLeadDecPoint,           {state F in figure}
               ScanDecimalDigits);         {state G in figure}
  PnfaChoice = ^TnfaChoice;
  TnfaChoice = packed record
    chInx   : integer;
    chMove  : integer;
    chState : TnfaState;
  end;
procedure DisposeChoice(aData : pointer); far;
begin
  if (aData <> nil) then
    Dispose(PnfaChoice(aData));
end;
procedure PushChoice(aStack : TtdStack;
                     aInx   : integer;
                     aMove  : integer;
                     aState : TnfaState);
var
  Choice : PnfaChoice;
begin
  New(Choice);
  Choice^.chInx := aInx;
  Choice^.chMove := aMove;
  Choice^.chState := aState;
  aStack.Push(Choice);
end;
procedure PopChoice(aStack : TtdStack;
                var aInx   : integer;
                var aMove  : integer;
                var aState : TnfaState);
var
  Choice : PnfaChoice;
begin
  Choice := PnfaChoice(aStack.Pop);
  aInx := Choice^.chInx;
  aMove := Choice^.chMove;
  aState := Choice^.chState;
  Dispose(Choice);
end;
function IsValidNumberNFA(const S : string) : boolean;
var
```

```
  StrInx: integer;
  State : TnfaState;
  Ch    : AnsiChar;
  Move  : integer;
  ChoiceStack : TtdStack;
begin
  {assume the number is invalid}
  Result := false;
  {initialize the choice stack}
  ChoiceStack := TtdStack.Create(DisposeChoice);
  try
    {prepare for scanning}
    Move := 0;
    StrInx := 1;
    State := StartScanning;
    {read through all the characters in the string}
    while StrInx <= length(S) do begin
      {get the current character}
      Ch := S[StrInx];
      {switch processing based on state}
      case State of
        StartScanning :
          begin
            case Move of
              0 : {move to ScannedSign with +}
                begin
                  if (Ch = '+') then begin
                    PushChoice(ChoiceStack, StrInx, Move, State);
                    State := ScannedSign;
                    Move := 0;
                    inc(StrInx);
                  end
                  else
                    inc(Move);
                end;
              1 : {move to ScannedSign with -}
                begin
                  if (Ch = '-') then begin
                    PushChoice(ChoiceStack, StrInx, Move, State);
                    State := ScannedSign;
                    Move := 0;
                    inc(StrInx);
                  end
                  else
                    inc(Move);
                end;
              2 : {no-cost move to ScannedSign}
                begin
```

```
          PushChoice(ChoiceStack, StrInx, Move, State);
          State := ScannedSign;
          Move := 0;
        end;
      else
        {we've run out of moves for this state}
        Move := -1;
      end;
    end;
  ScannedSign :
    begin
      case Move of
        0 : {move to ScanInteger with digit}
          begin
            if TDIsDigit(Ch) then begin
              PushChoice(ChoiceStack, StrInx, Move, State);
              State := ScanInteger;
              Move := 0;
              inc(StrInx);
            end
            else
              inc(Move);
          end;
        1 : {move to ScanLeadDigits with digit}
          begin
            if TDIsDigit(Ch) then begin
              PushChoice(ChoiceStack, StrInx, Move, State);
              State := ScanLeadDigits;
              Move := 0;
              inc(StrInx);
            end
            else
              inc(Move);
          end;
        2 : {move to ScanLeadDigits with decimal separator}
          begin
            if (Ch = DecimalSeparator) then begin
              PushChoice(ChoiceStack, StrInx, Move, State);
              State := ScanLeadDecPoint;
              Move := 0;
              inc(StrInx);
            end
            else
              inc(Move);
          end;
      else
        {we've run out of moves for this state}
        Move := -1;
```

```
      end;
    end;
  ScanInteger :
    begin
      case Move of
        0 : {stay in same state with digit}
          begin
            if TDIsDigit(Ch) then
              inc(StrInx)
            else
              inc(Move);
          end;
      else
        {we've run out of moves for this state}
        Move := -1;
      end;
    end;
  ScanLeadDigits :
    begin
      case Move of
        0 : {stay in same state with digit}
          begin
            if TDIsDigit(Ch) then
              inc(StrInx)
            else
              inc(Move);
          end;
        1 : {move to ScannedDecPoint with decimal separator}
          begin
            if (Ch = DecimalSeparator) then begin
              PushChoice(ChoiceStack, StrInx, Move, State);
              State := ScannedDecPoint;
              Move := 0;
              inc(StrInx);
            end
            else
              inc(Move);
          end;
      else
        {we've run out of moves for this state}
        Move := -1;
      end;
    end;
  ScannedDecPoint :
    begin
      case Move of
        0 : {stay in same state with digit}
          begin
```

```
            if TDIsDigit(Ch) then
              inc(StrInx)
            else
              inc(Move);
          end;
      else
        {we've run out of moves for this state}
        Move := -1;
      end;
    end;
  ScanLeadDecPoint :
    begin
      case Move of
        0 : {move to ScannedDecPoint with digit}
          begin
            if TDIsDigit(Ch) then begin
              PushChoice(ChoiceStack, StrInx, Move, State);
              State := ScanDecimalDigits;
              Move := 0;
              inc(StrInx);
            end
            else
              inc(Move);
          end;
      else
        {we've run out of moves for this state}
        Move := -1;
      end;
    end;
  ScanDecimalDigits :
    begin
      case Move of
        0 : {stay in same state with digit}
          begin
            if TDIsDigit(Ch) then
              inc(StrInx)
            else
              inc(Move);
          end;
      else
        {we've run out of moves for this state}
        Move := -1;
      end;
    end;
end;
{if we've run out of moves for a particular state, backtrack by
popping off the topmost choice, and incrementing the move}
if (Move = -1) then begin
```

```
        {if the stack is empty, there is no more backtracking}
        if ChoiceStack.IsEmpty then
          Exit;
        {pop the top choice, advance on by one move}
        PopChoice(ChoiceStack, StrInx, Move, State);
        inc(Move);
      end;
    end;
    {if we reach this point, the number is valid if we're in a
    terminating state}
    if (State = ScanInteger) or
       (State = ScannedDecPoint) or
       (State = ScanDecimalDigits) then
      Result := true;
  finally
    ChoiceStack.Free;
  end;
end;
```

The source code for the IsValidNumberNFA routine can be found in the TDStates.pas file on the CD.

Looking at Listing 10.3 you can see that the code for all states has the same basic structure. We assume that we have a series of moves for each state, starting at 0 (referring back to Figure 10.3, the moves are counted clockwise). For each state, we test to see whether we can follow each possible move in turn. If we can make a move, we push the choice we made onto the stack, and then make the move. If we can't make a move, we try the next.

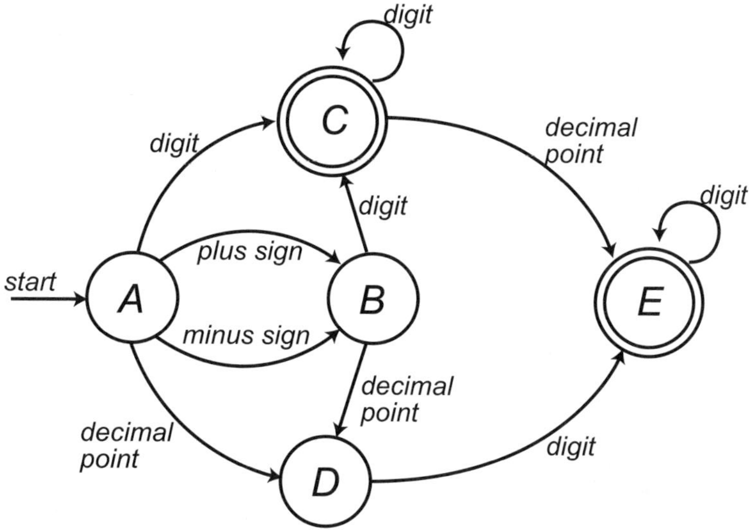

Figure 10.4: DFA to validate a string to be a number

If we need to backtrack, we pop off the topmost choice on the stack, and try the move after it. The information held on the stack is enough to reset the state of the routine to the point at which the choice was made.

For comparison, Figure 10.4 shows a deterministic automaton that performs the same validation, and its implementation is shown in Listing 10.4.

Listing 10.4: Validating a string to be a number using a DFA

```
function IsValidNumber(const S : string) : boolean;
type
  TStates = (StartState, GotSign,
             GotInitDigit, GotInitDecPt, ScanDigits);
var
  State   : TStates;
  Inx     : integer;
  Ch      : AnsiChar;
begin
  {assume the string is not a valid number}
  Result := false;
  {prepare for the scan loop}
  State := StartState;
  {read all the characters in the string}
  for Inx := 1 to length(S) do begin
    {get the current character}
    Ch := S[Inx];
    {switch processing on state}
    case State of
      StartState :
        begin
          if (Ch = '+') or (Ch = '-') then
            State := GotSign
          else if (Ch = DecimalSeparator) then
            State := GotInitDecPt
          else if TDIsdigit(Ch) then
            State := GotInitDigit
          else
            Exit;
        end;
      GotSign :
        begin
          if (Ch = DecimalSeparator) then
            State := GotInitDecPt
          else if TDIsDigit(Ch) then
            State := GotInitDigit
          else
            Exit;
        end;
      GotInitDigit :
```

```
          begin
            if (Ch = DecimalSeparator) then
              State := ScanDigits
            else if not TDIsDigit(Ch) then
              Exit;
          end;
        GotInitDecPt :
          begin
            if TDIsDigit(Ch) then
              State := ScanDigits
            else
              Exit;
          end;
        ScanDigits :
          begin
            if not TDIsDigit(Ch) then
              Exit;
          end;
      end;
    end;
    {if we reach this point, the number is valid if
    we're in a terminating state}
    if (State = GotInitDigit) or
       (State = ScanDigits) then
      Result := true;
end;
```

The source code for the IsValidNumber routine can be found in the TDStates.pas file on the CD.

If you compare the code in Listings 10.3 and 10.4, you can't help but see that the NFA code is much more complicated. There's a whole set of supporting routines we need to code and maintain. It's prone to error as well (we have to worry about the stack, about rewinding the state machine, about selecting another move, and so on).

In general, if we need a fixed, predefined automaton, we should try to devise and use a deterministic one. We try to leave the implementation of non-deterministic automatons to automatic algorithms; doing it by hand is too time-consuming.

Of course, with this NFA example (and its DFA cousin), all we're doing is validating a string to be the textual representation of an integer or floating-point number. Usually we would also like to calculate the number concerned and this would be piecemeal as we make the moves. For the DFA, that's pretty easy. We set an accumulator variable to 0. As we decode each digit before the decimal point, we multiply the accumulator by 10.0 and add the new digit value. For digits after the decimal point, maintain a counter for the decimal place, incrementing it by one for each digit after the point. For each such digit, we add that digit value multiplied by the power of one-tenth that we've reached for that decimal place.

What about the NFA? Well, that's pretty difficult. The problem all lies in the backtracking algorithm. At any time, we could suddenly find the state machine rewinding to a previous position. For the string to floating-point number example, this is not too bad: when we push a choice, we just save the current accumulator value on the stack as well (together with any minor variables we need to store). When we backtrack, we'll pop off the accumulator value as well as the data for the point where we made the bad choice.

Regular Expressions

To go back to our original reason for considering NFAs, let's now talk about regular expressions. First, let's recap what they are. Essentially they're a mini-language for describing, in a simple way, a pattern for searching text (or, more rigorously, matching text). At its most basic, a regular expression merely consists of a word or set of characters. However, using the standard metacharacters (or regular expression operators), you can search for more complex patterns. The standard metacharacters are "." (matches any character except newline), "?" (matches zero or one occurrence of the previous subexpression), "*" (matches zero or more occurrences of the previous subexpression), "+" (matches one or more occurrences of the previous subexpression), and "|" (the OR operator, which matches either the left subexpression or the right one). You can also define a character class to match one of a set of characters. If the first character of a character class is "^", the class is negated, meaning that class should not match the rest of the set.

Figure 10.5 shows the grammar for the regular expressions with which we'll be dealing. It's written in standard BNF (*Backus-Naur Form*). The "::=" means "is defined as" and the "|" means "OR." Hence the first line says that an <expr> is either a <term>, or is a <term> followed by the pipe character, followed by another <expr>. The second line says that a <term> is either a <factor>, or is a <factor> followed by a <term>, and so on. This grammar definition (it's called a "grammar" definition because it defines a language. If you search in the Delphi help you will find the grammar for Object Pascal: it's defined in the same way) can be used to generate a routine to evaluate a regular expression; we'll see how in a moment. But for now, be aware that we could use the grammar definition to desk-check that a given regular expression is valid.

```
<expr>    ::= <term> |
              <term> '|' <expr>                    - alternation
<term>    ::= <factor> |
              <factor><term>                       - concatenation
<factor> ::= <atom> |
              <atom> '?' |                         - zero or one
              <atom> '*' |                         - zero or more
              <atom> '+'                           - one or more
<atom> ::= <char> |
            '.' |                                  - any char
            '(' <expr> ') |                        - parentheses
            '[' <charclass> ']' |                  - normal class
            '[^' <charclass> ']'                   - negated class
<charclass> ::= <charrange> |
                <charrange><charclass>
<charrange> ::= <ccchar> |
                <ccchar> '-' <ccchar>
<char> ::= <any character except metacharacters> |
            '\' <any character at all>
```

Figure 10.5: Regular expression grammar in BNF

It's probably best to see some examples of regular expressions. This will help you understand how they're used.

```
[a-zA-Z_][a-zA-Z0-9_]*
```

This matches an identifier name in Pascal. The first bracketed subexpression is a character class and says that the first character in the string to be matched must be a letter, upper or lowercase, or an underscore. The second bracketed subexpression is another character class, the same as the first but with the addition of the digits. This pattern occurs zero or more times (the * operator at the end). So, a letter or underscore, followed by zero or more letters, underscores, or digits.

```
(+|-)?[0-9]+(.[0-9]+)?
```

This regular expression matches an integer or a floating-point number in Pascal. The expression reads as an optional sign, one or more digits, and an optional tail. The tail consists of a decimal point, followed by one or more digits. If the tail is not present, the number is an integer; if it is present, the number is a floating-point number.

```
{[^}]*}
```

This final example matches a comment in Pascal, one that is surrounded by braces. The expression is read as an opening brace, followed by zero or more characters, none of which are a closing brace, followed by a closing brace.

Using Regular Expressions

There are three stages to using a regular expression. The first is to parse the expression into its constituent tokens, the next is to convert those tokens into a form that we can use for matching (compiling the regular expression), and the final one is to use the compiled form of the regular expression to match strings. The reason why this all appears in this chapter is that the compiled form of the regular expression is an NFA.

Parsing Regular Expressions

Let us take these three steps in order. The first problem we'll attack then is the one of parsing a given regular expression string. In this process, our objective is merely to validate a regular expression string to show that the regular expression follows the syntax defined by the grammar.

Given this grammar definition and a regular expression, how can we read through the characters in the string and verify that the regular expression as a whole satisfies the grammar? The easiest way is to write a *top-down parser* (sometimes called a *recursive descent parser*). Providing the grammar is well defined, this is a fairly easy task.

For top-down parsing, each of the *productions* in the grammar becomes a separate routine. (A production is one of the definitions in the grammar, that is, one of the lines that has a "::=" operator.) Take the first production in the grammar, the one for <expr>. Make it into a method called ParseExpr.

So what does ParseExpr do? Well, the production states that an <expr> is either a <term> on its own or a <term> followed by the pipe character followed by another <expr>. So let's assume that we have a method that parses a <term> called ParseTerm. The first thing we do either way is to call this routine to parse a <term>. If, on return from this routine, the current character is the pipe character, then we go ahead and call ParseExpr recursively to parse the next <expr>. That's all there is to ParseExpr.

We'll leave the implementation of ParseTerm for last (you'll see why in a moment) and proceed with ParseFactor to parse a <factor>. Again, the code is simple enough. The first thing is to parse an <atom> by calling ParseAtom, and then check for one of three metacharacters: "*", "+", or "?". (A *metacharacter* is a character that has special meaning within the grammar, for example, the asterisk, the plus sign, the parentheses, and so on. Other characters have no special meaning.) ParseAtom is fairly trivial to code. It can be a <char> or a period; an opening parenthesis followed by an <expr> followed by the closing parenthesis; an opening bracket followed by a <charclass> followed by a closing bracket; or an opening bracket followed by a caret followed by a <charclass> followed by a closing bracket. We code it in exactly that form. The other methods that implement the other productions are equally as trivial. Notice that it's the very lowest methods that have the actual validation in them. For example, ParseAtom will check that a closing parenthesis is present after parsing the opening parenthesis and the <expr>. ParseChar checks that the current character is not a metacharacter. And so on. Listing 10.5 shows the code we have so far.

Listing 10.5: Regular expression parser

```
type
  TtdRegexParser = class
    private
      FRegexStr : string;
      {$IFDEF Delphi1}
      FRegexStrZ: PAnsiChar;
      {$ENDIF}
      FPosn     : PAnsiChar;
    protected
      procedure rpParseAtom;
      procedure rpParseCCChar;
      procedure rpParseChar;
      procedure rpParseCharClass;
      procedure rpParseCharRange;
      procedure rpParseExpr;
      procedure rpParseFactor;
      procedure rpParseTerm;
    public
      constructor Create(const aRegexStr : string);
      destructor Destroy; override;
      function Parse(var aErrorPos : integer) : boolean;
  end;
constructor TtdRegexParser.Create(const aRegexStr : string);
begin
  inherited Create;
  FRegexStr := aRegexStr;
  {$IFDEF Delphi1}
  FRegexStrZ := StrAlloc(succ(length(aRegexStr)));
  StrPCopy(FRegexStrZ, aRegexStr);
  {$ENDIF}
end;
destructor TtdRegexParser.Destroy;
begin
  {$IFDEF Delphi1}
  StrDispose(FRegexStrZ);
  {$ENDIF}
  inherited Destroy;
end;
```

```
function TtdRegexParser.Parse(var aErrorPos : integer) : boolean;
begin
  Result := true;
  aErrorPos := 0;
  {$IFDEF Delphi1}
  FPosn := FRegexStrZ;
  {$ELSE}
  FPosn := PAnsiChar(FRegexStr);
  {$ENDIF}
  try
    rpParseExpr;
    if (FPosn^ <> #0) then begin
      Result := false;
      {$IFDEF Delphi1}
      aErrorPos := FPosn - FRegexStrZ + 1;
      {$ELSE}
      aErrorPos := FPosn - PAnsiChar(FRegexStr) + 1;
      {$ENDIF}
    end;
  except
    on E:Exception do begin
      Result := false;
      {$IFDEF Delphi1}
      aErrorPos := FPosn - FRegexStrZ + 1;
      {$ELSE}
      aErrorPos := FPosn - PAnsiChar(FRegexStr) + 1;
      {$ENDIF}
    end;
  end;
end;
procedure TtdRegexParser.rpParseAtom;
begin
  case FPosn^ of
    '(' : begin
            inc(FPosn);
            writeln('open paren');
            rpParseExpr;
            if (FPosn^ <> ')') then
              raise Exception.Create(
              'Regex error: expecting a closing parenthesis');
            inc(FPosn);
            writeln('close paren');
          end;
    '[' : begin
            inc(FPosn);
            if (FPosn^ = '^') then begin
              inc(FPosn);
              writeln('negated char class');
```

```
          rpParseCharClass;
        end
        else begin
          writeln('normal char class');
          rpParseCharClass;
        end;
        inc(FPosn);
      end;
    '.' : begin
        inc(FPosn);
        writeln('any character');
      end;
  else
    rpParseChar;
  end;{case}
end;
procedure TtdRegexParser.rpParseCCChar;
begin
  if (FPosn^ = #0) then
    raise Exception.Create(
    'Regex error: expecting a normal character, found null terminator');
  if FPosn^ in [']', '-'] then
    raise Exception.Create(
    'Regex error: expecting a normal character, found a metacharacter');
  if (FPosn^ = '\') then begin
    inc(FPosn);
    writeln('escaped ccchar ', FPosn^);
    inc(FPosn);
  end
  else begin
    writeln('ccchar ', FPosn^);
    inc(FPosn);
  end;
end;
procedure TtdRegexParser.rpParseChar;
begin
  if (FPosn^ = #0) then
    raise Exception.Create(
    'Regex error: expecting a normal character, found null terminator');
  if FPosn^ in MetaCharacters then
    raise Exception.Create(
    'Regex error: expecting a normal character, found a metacharacter');
  if (FPosn^ = '\') then begin
    inc(FPosn);
    writeln('escaped char ', FPosn^);
    inc(FPosn);
  end
  else begin
```

```
    writeln('char ', FPosn^);
    inc(FPosn);
  end;
end;
procedure TtdRegexParser.rpParseCharClass;
begin
  rpParseCharRange;
  if (FPosn^ <> ']') then
    rpParseCharClass;
end;
procedure TtdRegexParser.rpParseCharRange;
begin
  rpParseCCChar;
  if (FPosn^ = '-') then begin
    inc(FPosn);
    writeln('--range to--');
    rpParseCCChar;
  end;
end;
procedure TtdRegexParser.rpParseExpr;
begin
  rpParseTerm;
  if (FPosn^ = '|') then begin
    inc(FPosn);
    writeln('alternation');
    rpParseExpr;
  end;
end;
procedure TtdRegexParser.rpParseFactor;
begin
  rpParseAtom;
  case FPosn^ of
    '?' : begin
            inc(FPosn);
            writeln('zero or one');
          end;
    '*' : begin
            inc(FPosn);
            writeln('zero or more');
          end;
    '+' : begin
            inc(FPosn);
            writeln('one or more');
          end;
  end;{case}
end;
```

The full source code for the TtdRegexParser class can be found in the TDRegex.pas file on the CD.

If you look at Listing 10.5, you'll see that all I'm doing with this parser is writing the current grammar item to the console and raising an exception if we reach a point where we can determine whether the regular expression is invalid. Neither of these things would be done in a production environment, of course; the first because our goal is to compile the regular expression into an NFA, and the second because we shouldn't use exceptions for validation as it's too inefficient. The code does, however, show the structure and design of a simplistic top-down parser: you design the grammar and then convert it into code in this fairly trivial fashion.

The remaining method is the ParseTerm method. Compared with what we've just done, it's a little more complicated. The problem is that the production says that a <term> is either a <factor>, or a <factor> followed by another <term> (that is, concatenation). There is no operator that links the two, such as the plus sign or something similar. If there were, we could easily write ParseTerm in the same manner as all the other ParseXxx methods. However, since there is no metacharacter for concatenation, we have to rely on another trick.

Consider the problem here. Suppose we were parsing the regular expression "ab". We would parse it as an <expr>, which means parsing it as a <term>, then a <factor>, then an <atom>, then a <char>. That takes care of the "a" part. We then continue up the grammar until we reach <term> again, which says that after the first <factor> we can have another <term>. Proceeding down the productions again, we parse the "b" as a <char> again, and we're done.

Sounds simple enough, so where's the problem? Do the same for "(a)". This time we go down the productions until we reach the point where it says that an <atom> could consist of a "(", followed by an <expr>, followed by a ")". So the "(" is taken care of and we start over at the top of the grammar parsing an <expr>. Wander down again: <expr>, then <term>, then <factor>, then <atom>, then <char>—that takes care of the "a". On the way up again, we encounter the alternative for the <term> production. So, why don't we take the alternative this time and try to parse a concatenation? Obviously we can't because this time the current character is a ")". In the first example we decided to parse a concatenation because the current character was a "b" but this time we don't because the current character is a ")". We need to take a quick peek at the current character before deciding whether to parse another concatenated <term> or not. If it could be counted as the start of another <atom>, then we go ahead and parse it as such. If not, we assume that someone else (that is, a caller method) will do something with it and that there is no concatenation.

This is known as *breaking the grammar.* We are going to have to assume that, if there is concatenation, the current character will serve as the starting character for an <atom>. In other words, if the current character is a ".", a "(", a "[", or an ordinary character, we shall parse another <term>. If not, we assume there is no concatenation and exit the ParseTerm method. We are using the information for the <atom> production, a "lower" production, to determine what to do about the <term> production, a "higher" production. It bears repeating that this is only necessary because we don't have a concatenation metacharacter.

Listing 10.6 shows the two final methods for the regular expression parser class: ParseTerm and the interfaced Parse.

Listing 10.6: The ParseTerm and Parse methods

```
procedure TtdRegexParser.rpParseTerm;
begin
  rpParseFactor;
  if (FPosn^ = '(') or
     (FPosn^ = '[') or
     (FPosn^ = '.') or
     ((FPosn^ <> #0) and not (FPosn^ in MetaCharacters)) then
    rpParseTerm;
end;
function TtdRegexParser.Parse(var aErrorPos : integer) : boolean;
begin
  Result := true;
  aErrorPos := 0;
  {$IFDEF Delphi1}
  FPosn := FRegexStrZ;
  {$ELSE}
  FPosn := PAnsiChar(FRegexStr);
  {$ENDIF}
  try
    rpParseExpr;
    if (FPosn^ <> #0) then begin
      Result := false;
      {$IFDEF Delphi1}
      aErrorPos := FPosn - FRegexStrZ + 1;
      {$ELSE}
      aErrorPos := FPosn - PAnsiChar(FRegexStr) + 1;
      {$ENDIF}
    end;
  except
    on E:Exception do begin
```

```
      Result := false;
      {$IFDEF Delphi1}
      aErrorPos := FPosn - FRegexStrZ + 1;
      {$ELSE}
      aErrorPos := FPosn - PAnsiChar(FRegexStr) + 1;
      {$ENDIF}
    end;
  end;
end;
```

We now know how to parse a regular expression. We can take a string and return whether it forms a valid regular expression or not.

Compiling Regular Expressions

The next step is to create the NFA for the regular expression. To attack this problem, we'll start off by drawing the state machine for a regular expression. Creating a state machine diagram for a particular regular expression is pretty easy. The language basically states that a regular expression consists of various subexpressions (which are themselves regular expressions) arranged or joined together in various ways. Each subexpression has a single start state and a single terminating state, and like Legos, we fit these simple building blocks together to show the entire regular expression. Figure 10.6 has the most important constructions.

The first one is a state machine for recognizing a single character in the alphabet. The second is equally as simple: a state machine for recognizing any character in the alphabet (the "." operator, in other words). The fourth construction shows you how to draw concatenation (one expression followed by another). We simply merge the start state of the second subexpression to the terminating state of the first subexpression. Following that construction is the one for alternation. We create a new start state and have two no-cost moves, one to each of the subexpressions. The end state of the first subexpression is joined to the end state of the second subexpression, and that latter state becomes the end state of the overall expression. The next one is a state machine for the "?" operator: here we create a new start state with two ε paths; the first connects to the start state of the subexpression, and the second to its end state. This terminating state is the end state for the whole expression. The most complicated constructions are probably for the "+" and "*" operators.

If you look at Figure 10.6, you'll notice some interesting properties. Some constructions define and use extra states in order to create their state machine, but they do it in a well-defined way: every state has either one or two moves coming from it, and, if there are two moves, both are no-cost moves. There's a reason for this: it just makes it simpler to code.

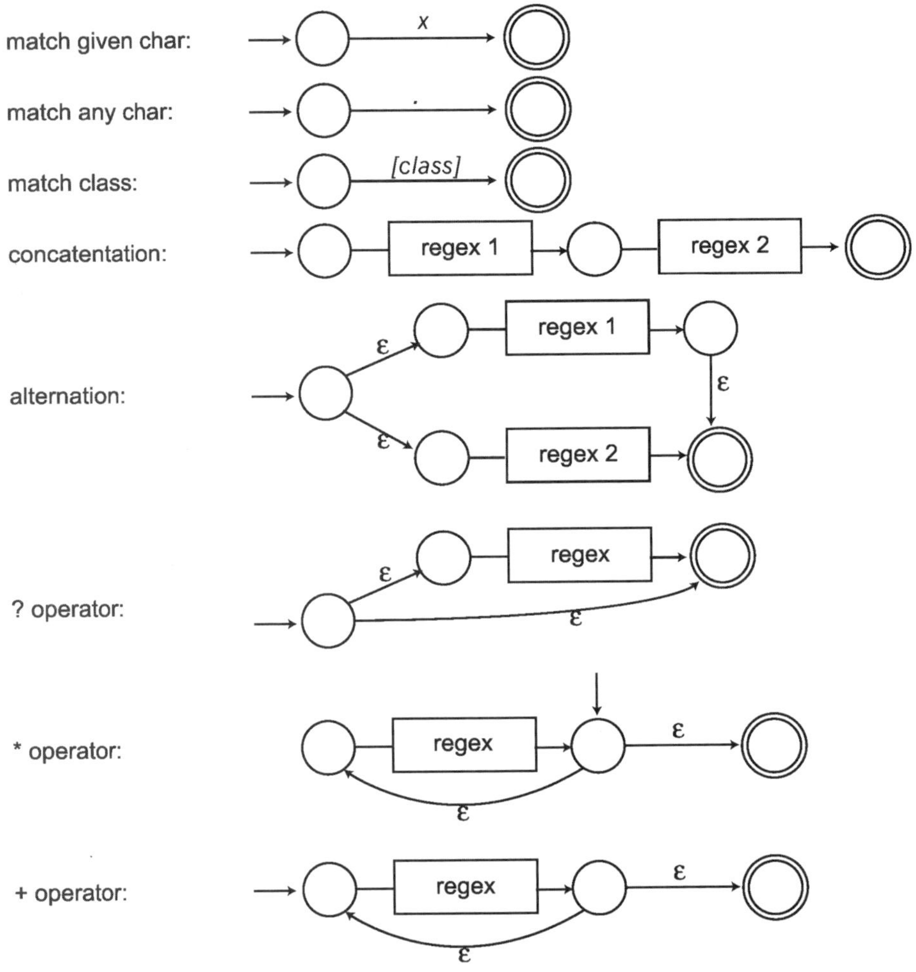

Figure 10.6: NFAs for regular expression operators

Let's take a simple example: the regular expression "(a|b)*bc" (an *a* or a *b*, repeated zero or more times, followed by a *b* and *c*). Using these construction pieces, we can build up its NFA step by step. Figure 10.7 shows how. Notice that at every step, we have an NFA with one start state and one terminating state, and we make sure that there are at most two moves from every new state we create.

Because of the construction method we used, we can create a very simple tabular representation for each state. Each state will be represented by a record in an array of such records (the state number being the index of the record in the array). Each state record will consist of something to match and two state numbers for the next state (NextState1, NextState2). The "something to match" is a character pattern to match; it can be ε, an actual character, the "." operator for any character, a character class (i.e., a set of characters, one of which must match the input character), or a negated character class (the input character cannot be part of the set to match). Once built, this array is known as the *transition table*; it shows all the transitions or moves from one state to another.

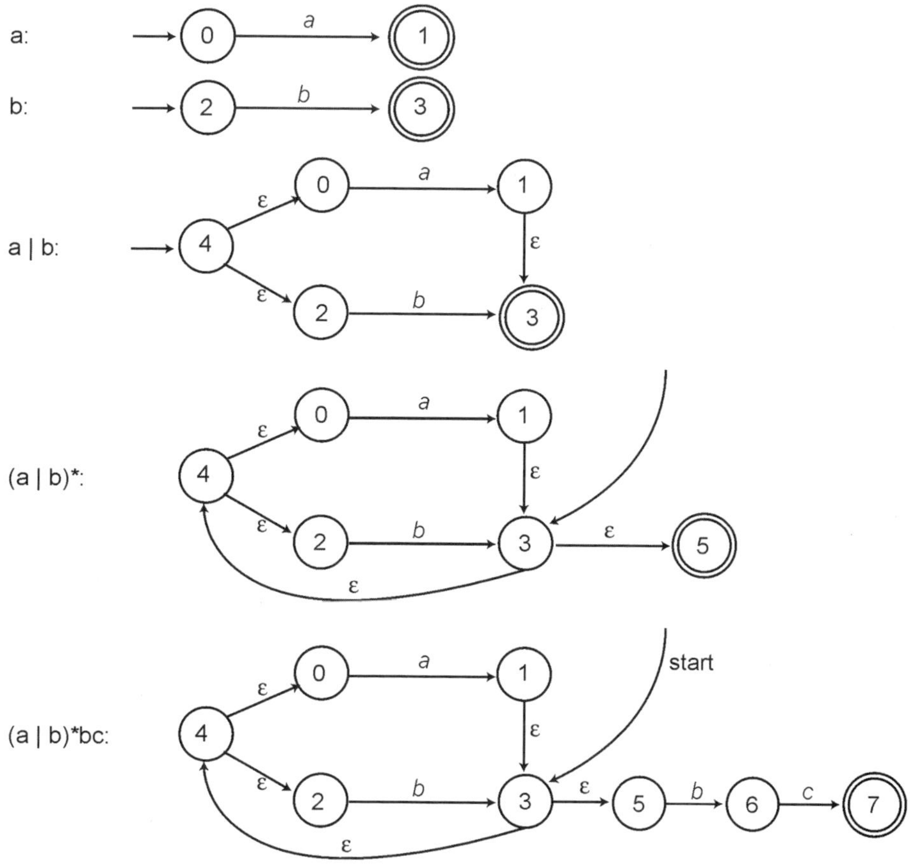

Figure 10.7: Building an NFA step by step

Using the final NFA in Figure 10.7, we can build the transition table by hand for "(a|b)*bc." Table 10.1 shows the results. We start off in state 0, and move through, matching each character in the input string, until we reach state 7. Implementing a matching algorithm to use a transition table like this should be very easy.

Table 10.1: The transition table for (a|b)*bc

State:	0	1	2	3	4	5	6	7
Match char:		a		b		b	c	
Next state 1:	1	3	3	5	0	6	7	–1
Next state 2:	–1	–1	–1	4	2	–1	–1	–1

Now that we have seen how to visually create the NFA for a particular regular expression and that a simple transition table can represent that NFA, we have to marry both algorithms inside the regular expression parser so that the parser can compile the transition table directly. Once we have that, we can discuss the final part of the jigsaw: matching strings using the transition table.

The first thing we need to decide is how to represent the transition table. The most obvious choice is the TtdRecordList from Chapter 2. This class will grow the internal array if needed; we don't have to work out beforehand how many states there might be for a given regular expression.

We use the individual construction pieces in Figure 10.6 as our guide. The simplest one is the expression that recognizes a single character. As you see from the first image in Figure 10.6, we need a start state, which will recognize the character and will have a single link to the end state (we'll need one of those too). We'll write a simple routine that will create a new state (as a record) and append it to our transition table. Listing 10.7 shows this simple method. As you can see, it takes in a match type, a character, a pointer to a character class, and two links to other states. Not all of these parameters will be required for every state we want to create, of course, but it makes it a little easier to have one method that can create any type of state record rather than a whole bunch of them, one for each type of state we may need.

Listing 10.7: Adding a new state to the transition table

```
function TtdRegexEngine.rcAddState(aMatchType  : TtdNFAMatchType;
                                   aChar       : AnsiChar;
                                   aCharClass  : PtdCharSet;
                                   aNextState1: integer;
                                   aNextState2: integer) : integer;
var
  StateData : TNFAState;
begin
  {set up the fields in the state record}
  if (aNextState1 = NewFinalState) then
```

```
    StateData.sdNextState1 := succ(FTable.Count)
  else
    StateData.sdNextState1 := aNextState1;
  StateData.sdNextState2 := aNextState2;
  StateData.sdMatchType := aMatchType;
  if (aMatchType = mtChar) then
    StateData.sdChar := aChar
  else if (aMatchType = mtClass) or (aMatchType = mtNegClass) then
    StateData.sdClass := aCharClass;
  {add the new state}
  Result := FTable.Count;
  FTable.Add(@StateData);
end;
```

From the first image in Figure 10.6 it seems that we need to create two new states for this simple character recognizer. Actually, we can get away with only creating one, the start state, and assume that the end state will be the next state to be added to the list. We leave it as a "virtual" end state. If we do this with every parsing routine, we may be able to get away with making the end state equal to the start state of another subexpression. Let's say that from now on, all parsing routines will return their start state, and we'll assume that the end state, if it really existed, would be the index number of the next state to be added to the transition table.

Looking at Listing 10.7, if we pass the special state number NewFinalState as a next state number, you can see that we actually set the link to the index of the next item to be added to the transition table. This item doesn't exist yet, of course, but we're assuming that it will or that something else will come along and patch a new link in.

Listing 10.8 shows the parsing method to recognize a single character. By referring back to Listing 10.5, notice how we've reengineered the original character parsing method. The first thing we've changed is that we don't raise any exceptions on errors any more; instead, we return a special state number: ErrorState. We also track the error code for any error that occurred. If there is no error, we add a new state to the transition table and return it as the function result. This is, of course, the start state for this expression. This routine is actually a method of a regular expression engine class.

Listing 10.8: Parsing a single character and adding its state

```
function TtdRegexEngine.rcParseChar : integer;
var
  Ch : AnsiChar;
begin
  {if we hit the end of the string, it's an error}
  if (FPosn^ = #0) then begin
```

```
    Result := ErrorState;
    FErrorCode := recSuddenEnd;
    Exit;
  end;
  {if the current char is one of the metacharacters, it's an error}
  if FPosn^ in MetaCharacters then begin
    Result := ErrorState;
    FErrorCode := recMetaChar;
    Exit;
  end;
  {otherwise add a state for the character}
  {..if it's an escaped character: get the next character instead}
  if (FPosn^ = '\') then
    inc(FPosn);
  Ch := FPosn^;
  Result := rcAddState(mtChar, Ch, nil, NewFinalState, UnusedState);
  inc(FPosn);
end;
```

That was easy enough, so let's look at another, more complex, parsing method—the one that parses an atom. The first case, the parenthesized expression, is pretty much the same as before: we don't need to add any states for this. The second case, the character class or the negated one, is definitely one that needs a new state machine. We parse the character class as before (by treating it as a set of ranges, each of which can be a single character or two characters separated by a dash). This time, however, we must record the characters in the class. We use a set of characters allocated on the heap for this purpose. The final step is to add a new state to the transition table that recognizes this character class, much as we did for the character recognizer. The final case, apart from the single character we've already discussed, is the state machine for the "any character" operator, the period. This is pretty simple: create a new state that matches any character. The complete listing for the atom parser is shown in Listing 10.9. Again, the start state for these expressions is returned as the function result and the end state is the virtual end state.

Listing 10.9: Parsing an <atom> and subsidiary parts

```
function TtdRegexEngine.rcParseAtom : integer;
var
  MatchType : TtdNFAMatchType;
  CharClass : PtdCharSet;
begin
  case FPosn^ of
    '(' :
      begin
        {move past the open parenthesis}
```

```
      inc(FPosn);
      {parse a complete regex between the parentheses}
      Result := rcParseExpr;
      if (Result = ErrorState) then
        Exit;
     {if the current character is not a close parenthesis,
     there's an error}
     if (FPosn^ <> ')') then begin
       FErrorCode := recNoCloseParen;
       Result := ErrorState;
       Exit;
     end;
     {move past the close parenthesis}
     inc(FPosn);
   end;
 '[' :
   begin
     {move past the open square bracket}
     inc(FPosn);
     {if the first character in the class is a '^' then the
     class if negated, otherwise it's a normal one}
     if (FPosn^ = '^') then begin
       inc(FPosn);
       MatchType := mtNegClass;
     end
     else begin
       MatchType := mtClass;
     end;
     {allocate the class character set and parse the character
     class; this will return either with an error, or when the
     closing square bracket is encountered}
     New(CharClass);
     CharClass^ := [];
     if not rcParseCharClass(CharClass) then begin
       Dispose(CharClass);
       Result := ErrorState;
       Exit;
     end;
     {move past the closing square bracket}
     inc(FPosn);
     {add a new state for the character class}
     Result := rcAddState(MatchType, #0, CharClass,
                          NewFinalState, UnusedState);
   end;
 '.' :
   begin
     {move past the period metacharacter}
     inc(FPosn);
```

```
        {add a new state for the 'any character' token}
        Result := rcAddState(mtAnyChar, #0, nil,
                             NewFinalState, UnusedState);
      end;
  else
    {otherwise parse a single character}
    Result := rcParseChar;
  end;{case}
end;
```

So far we've been creating states without any reference to each other, but if you look at the NFA construction diagram for the "|" operator, you'll see that we need to finally join some states together. We need to save the start states for each subexpression, and we need to create a new start state that will have no-cost links to each of these two start states. The final state of the first subexpression must be linked to the final state of the second, which then becomes the final state of the alternation expression.

There is a small problem, though. The final state for the first expression *does not exist*. So we'll have to create one, but we'll have to do it carefully so as not to get other states pointing to it in error.

The first thing we must do, of course, is to parse the initial <term>. We'll get back the start state (so we save it in a variable) and we know that the final state is the virtual end state just beyond the end of the list. If the next character is a "|" we know that we're parsing an alternation clause and that we should be parsing another <expr>. It's at this point that we have to take things carefully. The first thing we do is create a state for the end state of that initial <term>. We don't care at present where its links point; we'll patch that up in a moment. Creating this end state now also means that whichever states in the <term> point to the virtual end state will, in fact, point to the state we just made real. Now we will create the alternation start state. We know one of the links (the initial <term>) but we don't know the other yet; after all, we haven't parsed the second <expr> yet. Now we can parse the second <expr>. We'll get back a start state that we use to patch up the second link in the alternation start state. The new virtual end state can be used to link up from the initial <term>'s end state.

After all these shenanigans, we had to create two new states (the first being the start state for the alternation, the second being the end state for the initial <term>), and we were careful enough so that the virtual end state of the second <expr> was the virtual end state of the overall alternation. Listing 10.10 shows this bit of intricacy (notice that I wrote another method that sets the links for a state after it was created).

Listing 10.10: Parsing the "|" operator

```
function TtdRegexEngine.rcSetState(aState     : integer;
                                   aNextState1: integer;
                                   aNextState2: integer) : integer;
var
  StateData : PNFAState;
begin
  {get the state record and change the transition information}
  StateData := PNFAState(FTable[aState]);
  StateData^.sdNextState1 := aNextState1;
  StateData^.sdNextState2 := aNextState2;
  Result := aState;
end;
function TtdRegexEngine.rcParseExpr : integer;
var
  StartState1 : integer;
  StartState2 : integer;
  EndState1   : integer;
  OverallStartState : integer;
begin
  {assume the worst}
  Result := ErrorState;
  {parse an initial term}
  StartState1 := rcParseTerm;
  if (StartState1 = ErrorState) then
    Exit;
  {if the current character is *not* a pipe character, no alternation
  is present so return the start state of the initial term as our
  start state}
  if (FPosn^ <> '|') then
    Result := StartState1
  {otherwise, we need to parse another expr and join the two together
  in the transition table}
  else begin
    {advance past the pipe}
    inc(FPosn);
    {the initial term's end state does not exist yet (although there
    is a state in the term that points to it), so create it}
    EndState1 := rcAddState(mtNone, #0, nil, UnusedState, UnusedState);
    {for the OR construction we need a new initial state: it will
    point to the initial term and the second just-about-to-be-parsed
    expr}
    OverallStartState := rcAddState(mtNone, #0, nil,
                                    UnusedState, UnusedState);
    {parse another expr}
    StartState2 := rcParseExpr;
    if (StartState2 = ErrorState) then
      Exit;
```

```
    {alter the state state for the overall expr so that the second
    link points to the start of the second expr}
    Result := rcSetState(OverallStartState, StartState1, StartState2);
    {now set the end state for the initial term to point to the final
    end state for the second expr and the overall expr}
    rcSetState(EndState1, FTable.Count, UnusedState);
  end;
end;
```

Having seen this particular construction, creating the state machines for the three closures (the *, +, and ? operators) is equally simple, providing that we are careful about the order in which we create the states. Follow along with Listing 10.11.

Listing 10.11: Parsing the closure operators

```
function TtdRegexEngine.rcParseFactor : integer;
var
  StartStateAtom : integer;
  EndStateAtom   : integer;
begin
  {assume the worst}
  Result := ErrorState;
  {first parse an atom}
  StartStateAtom := rcParseAtom;
  if (StartStateAtom = ErrorState) then
    Exit;
  {check for a closure operator}
  case FPosn^ of
    '?' : begin
            {move past the ? operator}
            inc(FPosn);
            {the atom's end state doesn't exist yet, so create one}
            EndStateAtom := rcAddState(mtNone, #0, nil,
                                       UnusedState, UnusedState);
            {create a new start state for the overall regex}
            Result := rcAddState(mtNone, #0, nil,
                                 StartStateAtom, EndStateAtom);
            {make sure the new end state points to the next unused
            state}
            rcSetState(EndStateAtom, FTable.Count, UnusedState);
          end;
    '*' : begin
            {move past the * operator}
            inc(FPosn);
            {the atom's end state doesn't exist yet, so create one;
            it'll be the start of the overall regex subexpression}
            Result := rcAddState(mtNone, #0, nil,
                                 NewFinalState, StartStateAtom);
```

```
        end;
    '+' : begin
          {move past the + operator}
          inc(FPosn);
          {the atom's end state doesn't exist yet, so create one}
          rcAddState(mtNone, #0, nil, NewFinalState, StartStateAtom);
          {the start of the overall regex subexpression will be the
          atom's start state}
          Result := StartStateAtom;
        end;
  else
    Result := StartStateAtom;
  end;{case}
end;
```

For the zero or one closure (the "?" operator), we need to create the end state for the atom's expression to which we're applying the operator, and we need to create a start state for the overall state machine. These new states are linked up as shown in Figure 10.5.

For the zero or more closure (the "*" operator), it's even easier: we just need to create the end state for the atom. This becomes the start state for the overall expression. The virtual end state is the end state for the expression.

For the one or more closure (the "+" operator), it's just as easy again. Create the end state for the atom and link it to the start state for the atom (which is also the start state for the expression). The virtual end state is again the end state for the expression.

The final operator to code is the concatenation operator. It looks easy in Figure 10.6: the end state for the first subexpression becomes the start state for the second, and they're linked. In practice, it's not quite so easy. The end state for the first expression is the virtual end state, and there's no guarantee that this will be equal to the start state of the next expression (in which case, they would be automatically linked). No, instead we have to create the end state for the first expression and link it to the second's start state. Listing 10.12 shows the final piece of the jigsaw, including the creation of the terminating state.

Listing 10.12: Parsing concatenation

```
function TtdRegexEngine.rcParseTerm : integer;
var
  StartState2 : integer;
  EndState1   : integer;
begin
  {parse an initial factor, the state number returned will also be our
  return state number}
```

```
  Result := rcParseFactor;
  if (Result = ErrorState) then
    Exit;
  if (FPosn^ = '(') or
      (FPosn^ = '[') or
      (FPosn^ = '.') or
      ((FPosn^ <> #0) and not (FPosn^ in MetaCharacters)) then begin
    {the initial factor's end state does not exist yet (although there
    is a state in the term that points to it), so create it}
    EndState1 := rcAddState(mtNone, #0, nil, UnusedState, UnusedState);
    {parse another term}
    StartState2 := rcParseTerm;
    if (StartState2 = ErrorState) then begin
      Result := ErrorState;
      Exit;
    end;
    {join the first factor to the second term}
    rcSetState(EndState1, StartState2, UnusedState);
  end;
end;
```

At this point we've successfully married the parsing and the compiling aspects, so that we can take a regular expression and parse it to generate the compiled transition table. The compilation phase will work out and store the initial state of the complete NFA for the regular expression.

There are, however, a couple of small inefficiencies we should take care of before proceeding. In a couple of cases we had to add some states that had just one no-cost move leaving them, the most egregious case being the extra state needed for concatenation. A state with a single no-cost move leaving it is, of course, a waste of time, and so we need to optimize them out of the transition table. These states are called *do-nothing states*.

Instead of removing them though, we'll just skip over them. The algorithm to do this is fairly easy: read through all the states. For each state, follow its NextState1 field. If it links to one of these do-nothing states, replace the link with the do-nothing state's NextState1 link. Do the same with each state's NextState2's link if it exists. Listing 10.13 shows this iterative procedure.

Listing 10.13: Optimizing do-nothing states

```
procedure TtdRegexEngine.rcLevel1Optimize;
var
  i : integer;
  Walker : PNFAState;
begin
  {level 1 optimization removes all states that have only a single
  no-cost move to another state}
```

```
    {cycle through all the state records, except for the last one}
    for i := 0 to (FTable.Count - 2) do begin
      {get this state}
      with PNFAState(FTable[i])^ do begin
        {walk the chain pointed to by the first next state, unlinking
        the states that are simple single no-cost moves}
        Walker := PNFAState(FTable[sdNextState1]);
        while (Walker^.sdMatchType = mtNone) and
              (Walker^.sdNextState2 = UnusedState) do begin
          sdNextState1 := Walker^.sdNextState1;
          Walker := PNFAState(FTable[sdNextState1]);
        end;
        {walk the chain pointed to by the second next state, unlinking
        the states that are simple single no-cost moves}
        if (sdNextState2 <> UnusedState) then begin
          Walker := PNFAState(FTable[sdNextState2]);
          while (Walker^.sdMatchType = mtNone) and
                (Walker^.sdNextState2 = UnusedState) do begin
            sdNextState2 := Walker^.sdNextState1;
            Walker := PNFAState(FTable[sdNextState2]);
          end;
        end;
      end;
    end;
  end;
end;
```

Matching Strings to Regular Expressions

It is time now to complete the final part of the regular expression jigsaw, that of matching strings to the regular expression. Instead of using the backtracking algorithm we've already seen, we shall instead use a different algorithm. We shall traverse the NFA (that is, the transition table) with the input string, tracing every possible path through the state machine *simultaneously*. We shall make no choices since we're following every possible path with every single character in the string. Eventually we shall exhaust the characters in the string and have one or more paths that got us to that point, or we shall run out of possible paths part way through the string.

To perform this algorithm, though, we shall need an implementation of a *deque*. A deque (pronounced *deck*) is a double-ended queue, one where you can enqueue or dequeue at either end of the queue. The features we shall need are the ability to enqueue items at the tail of the deque and to push and pop items at the front of the queue (in other words, we shall only dequeue items from the head of the deque, never from the tail). The items we shall be enqueuing are integers, in fact, state numbers. Listing 10.14 has the code for this simple integer deque (it can be found in the TDIntDeq.pas file on the CD).

Listing 10.14: An integer deque class

```
type
  TtdIntDeque = class
    private
      FList : TList;
      FHead : integer;
      FTail : integer;
    protected
      procedure idGrow;
      procedure idError(aErrorCode   : integer;
                  const aMethodName : TtdNameString);
    public
      constructor Create(aCapacity : integer);
      destructor Destroy; override;
      function IsEmpty : boolean;
      procedure Enqueue(aValue : integer);
      procedure Push(aValue : integer);
      function Pop : integer;
  end;
constructor TtdIntDeque.Create(aCapacity : integer);
begin
  inherited Create;
  FList := TList.Create;
  FList.Count := aCapacity;
  {let's help out the user of the deque by putting the head and
  tail pointers in the middle-it's probably more efficient}
  FHead := aCapacity div 2;
  FTail := FHead;
end;
destructor TtdIntDeque.Destroy;
begin
  FList.Free;
  inherited Destroy;
end
procedure TtdIntDeque.Enqueue(aValue : integer);
begin
  FList.List^[FTail] := pointer(aValue);
  inc(FTail);
  if (FTail = FList.Count) then
    FTail := 0;
  if (FTail = FHead) then
    idGrow;
end;
procedure TtdIntDeque.idGrow;
var
```

```
  OldCount : integer;
  i, j     : integer;
begin
  {grow the list by 50%}
  OldCount := FList.Count;
  FList.Count := (OldCount * 3) div 2;
  {expand the data into the increased space, maintaining the deque}
  if (FHead = 0) then
    FTail := OldCount
  else begin
    j := FList.Count;
    for i := pred(OldCount) downto FHead do begin
      dec(j);
      FList.List^[j] := FList.List^[i]
    end;
    FHead := j;
  end;
end;
function TtdIntDeque.IsEmpty : boolean;
begin
  Result := FHead = FTail;
end;
procedure TtdIntDeque.Push(aValue : integer);
begin
  if (FHead = 0) then
    FHead := FList.Count;
  dec(FHead);
  FList.List^[FHead] := pointer(aValue);
  if (FTail = FHead) then
    idGrow;
end;
function TtdIntDeque.Pop : integer;
begin
  if FHead = FTail then
    idError(tdeDequeIsEmpty, 'Pop');
  Result := integer(FList.List^[FHead]);
  inc(FHead);
  if (FHead = FList.Count) then
    FHead := 0;
end;
```

The algorithm works like this. Enqueue the value –1 onto the deque. This is a special value that is a signal to advance by one through the input string. Now, enqueue the number of the initial state onto the deque. Set an integer value to 0; this will be the index of the current character in the string being matched.

With the preparation complete, we enter into a loop. For each cycle through the loop, we do the same thing: pop off the top value from the deque. If it is –1 (as it will be initially, of course), increment the current character index and get this character from the string being matched. Enqueue the value –1 onto the deque again, so that we'll know when to read another character. If it is not –1, it must be an actual state number. Look at the state record in the transition table. Check to see if the current input character matches that state's character pattern. If it does, enqueue the state's NextState1 value. If the state's character pattern was ε, the character didn't match, obviously. We push the state's NextState1 value on to the deque, followed by the state's NextState2 value.

The loop terminates once the deque is empty (no paths match the input string) or it has read all the characters from the string being matched (the deque then contains the set of states reached by the end of the string, which can be popped off until we find the one-and-only terminating state or not, as the case may be).

The overall effect of this algorithm is this: we have a "get next character" value (–1) on the deque. To the "left" of it is a set of states that we still need to test the current character against (we're continually popping these off and pushing states we can reach via the no-cost move). To its "right" is a set of states derived from states that have already matched the current character. We'll be getting to them once we have popped the –1 and retrieved the next character. As you can see, the algorithm is trying every path through the NFA simultaneously.

Listing 10.15 shows the matching routine. It has been written to be a method of the regular expression engine. It is passed a string to be matched and an index value. The index value states where in the string the matching is supposed to start. This gives us the ability to apply the regular expression to any part of the string rather than the entire string as we have been doing with our simple state machine examples. The method will return true if the regular expression, through its transition table, matches the string at that point.

Listing 10.15: Matching a substring against a transition table

```
function TtdRegexEngine.rcMatchSubString(const S   : string;
                                         StartPosn : integer) : boolean;
var
  Ch     : AnsiChar;
  State  : integer;
  Deque  : TtdIntDeque;
  StrInx : integer;
begin
  {assume we fail to match}
```

```
Result := false;
{create the deque}
Deque := TtdIntDeque.Create(64);
try
  {enqueue the special value to start scanning}
  Deque.Enqueue(MustScan);
  {enqueue the first state}
  Deque.Enqueue(FStartState);
  {prepare the string index}
  StrInx := StartPosn - 1;
  {loop until the deque is empty or we run out of string}
  while (StrInx <= length(S)) and not Deque.IsEmpty do begin
    {pop the top state from the deque}
    State := Deque.Pop;
    {process the "must scan" state first}
    if (State = MustScan) then begin
      {if the deque is empty at this point, we might as well give up
      since there are no states left to process new characters}
      if not Deque.IsEmpty then begin
        {if we haven't run out of string, get the character, and
        enqueue the "must scan" state again}
        inc(StrInx);
        if (StrInx <= length(S)) then begin
          Ch := S[StrInx];
          Deque.Enqueue(MustScan);
        end;
      end;
    end
    {otherwise, process the state}
    else with PNFAState(FTable[State])^ do begin
      case sdMatchType of
        mtNone :
          begin
            {for free moves, push the next states onto the deque}
            Deque.Push(sdNextState2);
            Deque.Push(sdNextState1);
          end;
        mtAnyChar :
          begin
            {for a match of any character, enqueue the next state}
            Deque.Enqueue(sdNextState1);
          end;
        mtChar :
          begin
            {for a match of a character, enqueue the next state}
            if (Ch = sdChar) then
              Deque.Enqueue(sdNextState1);
          end;
```

```
      mtClass :
        begin
          {for a match within a class, enqueue the next state}
          if (Ch in sdClass^) then
            Deque.Enqueue(sdNextState1);
        end;
      mtNegClass :
        begin
          {for a match not within a class, enqueue the next state}
          if not (Ch in sdClass^) then
            Deque.Enqueue(sdNextState1);
        end;
      mtTerminal :
        begin
          {for a terminal state, the string successfully matched
          if the regex had no end anchor, or we're at the end
          of the string}
          if (not FAnchorEnd) or (StrInx > length(S)) then begin
            Result := true;
            Exit;
          end;
        end;
    end;
  end;
end;
{if we reach this point we've either exhausted the deque or we've
run out of string; if the former, the substring did not match
since there are no more states. If the latter, we need to check
the states left on the deque to see if one is the terminating
state; if so, the string matched the regular expression defined by
the transition table}
while not Deque.IsEmpty do begin
  State := Deque.Pop;
  with PNFAState(FTable[State])^ do begin
    case sdMatchType of
      mtNone :
        begin
          {for free moves, push the next states onto the deque}
          Deque.Push(sdNextState2);
          Deque.Push(sdNextState1);
        end;
      mtTerminal :
        begin
          {for a terminal state, the string successfully matched
          if the regex had no end anchor, or we're at the end
          of the string}
          if (not FAnchorEnd) or (StrInx > length(S)) then begin
            Result := true;
```

```
                Exit;
              end;
            end;
        end;{case}
      end;
    end;
  finally
    Deque.Free;
  end;
end;
```

Having shown that it would be nice for the matching routine to be designed so that it can be applied to any starting point in the string, we would also like the opportunity to just match the entire string only, if need be.

We therefore introduce two new regular expression operators to enable us to do just that: the anchor operators "^" and "$". The caret means that any matching must only occur from the beginning of the string. The dollar sign means that the matching must proceed all the way to the end of the string. Thus, for example, the regular expression "^function" means "match the word 'function' at the beginning of the string," whereas "^end.$" means "the entire string should just consist of the characters e, n, d, and the period; no other characters at all." The ^ and $ can only appear at the start and at the end of the regular expression respectively; they cannot occur anywhere else.

This entails a small change to our grammar, not too drastic, but, as we've seen, designing the grammar properly makes writing the code much easier. The new rule is shown in Listing 10.16, together with the relevant parsing method. The interfaced Parse method is changed to call this method instead of the original, of course.

Listing 10.16: Using the anchor operators

```
<anchorexpr> ::= <expr> |
                 '^' <expr> |
                 <expr> '$' |
                 '^' <expr> '$'
function TtdRegexEngine.rcParseAnchorExpr : integer;
begin
  {check for an initial '^'}
  if (FPosn^ = '^') then begin
    FAnchorStart := true;
    inc(FPosn);
  end;
  {parse an expression}
  Result := rcParseExpr;
  {if we were successful, check for the final '$'}
  if (Result <> ErrorState) then begin
```

```
    if (FPosn^ = '$') then begin
      FAnchorEnd := true;
      inc(FPosn);
    end;
  end;
end;
```

We can now change the string matching code to match complete strings as well as substrings. If the regular expression starts with a ^, we just try to match the string starting from the first character. If not, then we try to match each of the substrings formed from the original string. Listing 10.17 shows the interfaced MatchString method where this decision is made.

Listing 10.17: The MatchString method

```
function TtdRegexEngine.MatchString(const S : string) : integer;
var
  i : integer;
  ErrorPos  : integer;
  ErrorCode : TtdRegexError;
begin
  {if the regex string hasn't been parsed yet, do so}
  if (FTable.Count = 0) then begin
    if not Parse(ErrorPos, ErrorCode) then
      rcError(tdeRegexParseError, 'MatchString', ErrorPos);
  end;
  {now see if the string matches (empty strings don't)}
  Result := 0;
  if (S <> '') then
    {if the regex specified a start anchor, then we only need to check
    the string starting at the first position}
    if FAnchorStart then begin
      if rcMatchSubString(S, 1) then
        Result := 1;
    end
    {otherwise we try to match the string at every position and
    return at the first success}
    else begin
      for i := 1 to length(S) do
        if rcMatchSubString(S, i) then begin
          Result := i;
          Break;
        end;
    end;
end;
```

If you look carefully back at Listing 10.15, you'll see that the matching code already allows for the end anchor. The code only accepts the terminating state as indicating a match if the regular expression had no ending anchor, or if we managed to reach the end of the string. If either of these conditions were not met, the terminating state would be ignored.

The full source code for the TtdRegexEngine class can be found in the TDRegex.pas file on the CD.

Summary

In this chapter we've seen both finite deterministic state machines and finite non-deterministic ones. We experimented with a couple of simple DFA examples.

We also observed that, when coding by hand, DFAs are easier to devise, understand, and write, whereas NFAs are better suited to automatic processes. To close the chapter, we implemented a complete regular expression engine that parses and compiles a regular expression to an NFA (represented by a transition table). This NFA could then be used for matching strings.

Chapter 11

Data Compression

When we think of data, we usually just think of the information conveyed by data: a customer list, an audio CD, a letter, and so on. We don't usually think too much about the physical representation of that data; the program that manipulates that data—displaying the customer list, playing the CD, printing the letter—takes care of that.

Representations of Data

Let's consider this split in the nature of data: its information content versus its physical representation. In the 1950s Claude Shannon laid the foundations of information theory, including the notion that data can be represented by some minimal number of bits, called its entropy (a term taken from thermodynamics). He also realized that data is usually represented physically by more bits than its entropy would suggest.

For a simple example, consider a probability experiment with a coin. We would like to toss the coin many times, build up a large table of results, and then do some statistical analysis on this large dataset to posit or prove some theorem. To build the dataset, we could record the results of each coin toss in several different ways: we could write down the word "heads" or "tails"; we could write down the letter "H" or "T"; or we could record a single bit (on or off, with on meaning tails for example). Information theory would say that the result of each coin toss could be encoded in a single bit, so the final possibility I gave would be the most efficient in terms of space needed to encode the results. The first possibility is the most wasteful of space, taking five characters to record a single coin toss.

Think of it another way, though: from the first example of recording the data to the last, we are storing the same results—the same information—in less and less space. We are compressing the data, in other words.

Data Compression

Data compression is an algorithm for encoding information in a different way so that it occupies less space than before. We are removing *redundancy*, that is, getting rid of the bits from the physical representation of the data that aren't really required, to get at just the right number of bits that entropy would predict we should need for the information. There is a metric by which we measure how successfully we are compressing the data: the *compression ratio*. This is calculated as the size of the compressed data divided by the size of the original data, subtracted from 1 and usually expressed as a percentage. For example, if the compressed data were 1,000 bits and the uncompressed 4,000 bits, the compression ratio is 75 percent—we've squeezed out three-fourths of the original bits.

Of course, the compressed data may then be in a form that we, as imperfect calculating machines, couldn't actually read and understand. Humans require some level of redundancy in the representation of data to aid our recognition and understanding of that data. In the coin toss experiment, we would find a series of H's and T's easier to comprehend rather than the values of the bytes formed 8 bits at a time. (And we'd probably need the H's and T's to be separated into blocks of 10 or so to help our comprehension even further.) In other words, the ability to compress data would be useless without the ability to decompress the data at a later time. This reverse operation is known as *decoding*.

Types of Compression

There are two main types of data compression: *lossy* and *lossless*. Lossless compression is the easiest to understand; it is a method of compressing data so that when the encoded data is decompressed, an exact copy of the original data is returned. This is the type of compression used by the PKZIP™ program: unzipping an archived file results in a file that has exactly the same content as the original had when it was compressed. Lossy compression, on the other hand, does not produce the same uncompressed data as the original. This seems like a step backward, but for certain types of data like images and audio, the fact that the uncompressed data is different than the original doesn't matter: our eyes and ears cannot tell the difference. Lossy algorithms generally allow us better compression than lossless algorithms (otherwise it wouldn't be worth using them). An example of a lossy algorithm is the JPEG format for storing images, compared to the lossless GIF format. The numerous streaming audio and video formats used on the Internet for downloading multimedia material are lossy algorithms.

For the coin toss experiment, it was fairly easy to determine the best way of storing the dataset, but for other data, it gets more difficult. There are several algorithmic approaches we can take. The two classes of compression we will look at in this chapter are both lossless and are known as *minimum redundancy coding* and *dictionary compression*.

Minimum redundancy coding is a method of encoding bytes (or, more formally, *symbols*) that occur more often with fewer bits than those that occur less often. For example, for text in the English language the letters E, T, and A occur more often than the letters Q, X, and Z. So, if we were able to code E, T, and A with less than 8 bits (as ASCII insists they should have), and Q, X, and Z with more, we should be able to store English text in less bits than ASCII can.

Dictionary compression divides the data into larger pieces (known as *tokens*) than symbols. The algorithms then encode the tokens with some minimal number of bits. For instance, the words "the," "and," and "to" would occur with more frequency than other words like "eclectic," "ambiguous," and "irresistible," and so we should encode them with fewer bits than ASCII would have us do.

Bit Streams

Before we discuss the actual compression algorithms we shall cover in this book, we should take a moment to discuss bit manipulation. Most of the compression algorithms we will look at compress data using a varying number of bits, whether we consider the data as a sequence of symbols or tokens. We cannot assume that we will always be using a group of 8 bits as bytes.

We shall need to perform two basic operations: read a single bit and write a single bit. Building on these, there could be operations that read and write several bits at a time. What we shall do is design and write a *bit stream*, a data structure that encapsulates a set of bits. Obviously, the bit stream will be using some other data structure that stores the bit data as a sequence of bytes; it will extract the bits as required from the bytes in the underlying data. Because we're using Delphi, we will make the bit stream use a TStream object (or a descendant) as the underlying data structure. That way, for example, we would be able to view a memory stream or a file stream as a stream of bits. In fact, since we will only use bit streams as a sequential series of bits, we will create two distinct types: the input bit stream and the output bit stream. We can also dispense with the usual Seek method since we will not be seeking into a bit stream.

The interface for the TtdInputBitStream and TtdOutputBitStream classes are shown in Listing 11.1.

Listing 11.1: The interface to the bit stream classes

```
type
  TtdInputBitStream = class
    private
      FAccum     : byte;
      FBufEnd    : integer;
      FBuffer    : PAnsiChar;
      FBufPos    : integer;
      FMask      : byte;
      FName      : TtdNameString;
      FStream    : TStream;
    protected
      procedure ibsError(aErrorCode  : integer;
                   const aMethodName : TtdNameString);
      procedure ibsReadBuffer;
    public
      constructor Create(aStream : TStream);
      destructor Destroy; override;

      function ReadBit : boolean;
      procedure ReadBits(var aBitString : TtdBitString;
                             aBitCount  : integer);
      function ReadByte : byte;

      property Name : TtdNameString read FName write FName;
  end;
  TtdOutputBitStream = class
    private
      FAccum     : byte;
      FBuffer    : PAnsiChar;
      FBufPos    : integer;
      FMask      : byte;
      FName      : TtdNameString;
      FStream    : TStream;
      FStrmBroken : boolean;
    protected
      procedure obsError(aErrorCode  : integer;
                   const aMethodName : TtdNameString);
      procedure obsWriteBuffer;
    public
      constructor Create(aStream : TStream);
      destructor Destroy; override;

      procedure WriteBit(aBit : boolean);
      procedure WriteBits(const aBitString : TtdBitString);
```

```
    procedure WriteByte(aByte : byte);

    property Name : TtdNameString read FName write FName;
  end;
```

The Create constructors both require an already created TStream descendant as a parameter. It is this stream of bytes from which the bit stream class will retrieve or store individual bytes. Listing 11.2 shows the Create constructors and Destroy destructors for these classes.

Listing 11.2: Creating and destroying bit stream objects

```
constructor TtdInputBitStream.Create(aStream : TStream);
begin
  inherited Create;
  FStream := aStream;
  GetMem(FBuffer, StreamBufferSize);
end;
destructor TtdInputBitStream.Destroy;
begin
  if (FBuffer <> nil) then
    FreeMem(FBuffer, StreamBufferSize);
  inherited Destroy;
end;
constructor TtdOutputBitStream.Create(aStream : TStream);
begin
  inherited Create;
  FStream := aStream;
  GetMem(FBuffer, StreamBufferSize);
  FMask := 1; {ready for the first bit to be written}
end;
destructor TtdOutputBitStream.Destroy;
begin
  if (FBuffer <> nil) then begin
    {if Mask is not equal to 1, it means that there are some bits in
     the accumulator that need to be written to the buffer; make sure
     the buffer is written to the underlying stream}
    if not FStrmBroken then begin
      if (FMask <> 1) then begin
        byte(FBuffer[FBufPos]) := FAccum;
        inc(FBufPos);
      end;
      if (FBufPos > 0) then
        obsWriteBuffer;
    end;
    FreeMem(FBuffer, StreamBufferSize);
  end;
  inherited Destroy;
end;
```

Notice that both Create constructors allocate a large buffer of bytes (4 KB worth) so that the underlying stream is only accessed for blocks of data. In other words, we will be buffering the underlying stream. Hence, Destroy must free this buffer, after making sure that, for the output bit stream, any data that is still buffered is written to the underlying stream.

Notice the reference to the peculiar FStrmBroken class field. This is a workaround for a possible error condition. Suppose that the underlying stream was a TFileStream instance, and that, during the use of the output bit stream we had filled the disk. The output bit stream has been written to signal this kind of problem as an exception. Once this exception is raised, it no longer makes sense to try and write to the underlying stream, so the code at that point sets the FStrmBroken field to true, signifying that the stream is broken.

Now that we know how to create and destroy our bit streams, we should look at how to read or write a single bit. Listing 11.3 has the details for reading a single bit. The ReadBit method returns a Boolean value: true if the next bit read from the stream was set, and false otherwise.

Listing 11.3: Reading a single bit from a TtdInputBitStream object

```
function TtdInputBitStream.ReadBit : boolean;
begin
  {if we have no bits left in the current accumulator, read another
   accumulator byte and reset the mask}
  if (FMask = 0) then begin
    if (FBufPos >= FBufEnd) then
      ibsReadBuffer;
    FAccum := byte(FBuffer[FBufPos]);
    inc(FBufPos);
    FMask := 1;
  end;
  {take the next bit}
  Result := (FAccum and FMask) <> 0;
  FMask := FMask shl 1;
end;
```

We make use of a mask byte (FMask) that has a single set bit and an AND that mask against the current byte (FAccum) from the underlying stream. If the result is non-zero, the bit in the byte was set, and we have to return true; if zero, the bit in the byte was clear, and we return false. We then shift the mask left by one to move the single mask bit onward by one position. When we start, if the mask was zero, it means that we need to read a new byte from the buffer and reset the mask. If the buffer was empty or had been fully read, we have to read another buffer-full from the underlying stream.

Having seen how to read a single bit, we shall now see that writing a single bit is the same process, but reversed. Listing 11.4 shows the WriteBit method, where we pass in a single bit as a Boolean value—true for set, false for clear.

Listing 11.4: Writing a single bit to a TtdOutputBitStream object

```
procedure TtdOutputBitStream.WriteBit(aBit : boolean);
begin
  {set the next spare bit}
  if aBit then
    FAccum := (FAccum or FMask);
  FMask := FMask shl 1;
  {if we have no spare bits left in the current accumulator, write it
  to the buffer, and reset the accumulator and the mask}
  if (FMask = 0) then begin
    byte(FBuffer[FBufPos]) := FAccum;
    inc(FBufPos);
    if (FBufPos >= StreamBufferSize) then
      obsWriteBuffer;
    FAccum := 0;
    FMask := 1;
  end;
end;
```

Since we always start off with our accumulator byte (FAccum) as zero, we only have to record set bits, not clear bits. Again, we make use of a mask (FMask) with a single set bit, but this time we OR it into the accumulator to set the relevant bit. We then shift the mask left by one to move the single mask bit onward by one position, ready for the next bit. If, however, the mask is now zero, we have to save the accumulator byte into the buffer (writing the buffer to the underlying stream if full), and then reset the accumulator byte and the mask.

The full code for both the TtdInputBitStream and TtdOutputBitStream classes are found in the TDStrms.pas unit on the CD. The full code also has routines to read or write several bits at a time, either eight of them in a single byte (ReadByte and WriteByte), or a variable number from an array of bytes (ReadBits and WriteBits). All these extra routines use the same bit-twiddling methodology to access individual bits; they just do it in a loop.

Minimum Redundancy Compression

Now that we have a bit stream class, we can use it in discussing compression and decompression algorithms. We will start off by discussing minimum redundancy coding algorithms and then move on to the more complex dictionary compression.

We will look at three minimum redundancy coding algorithms: Shannon-Fano encoding, Huffman encoding, and splay tree compression, although we will provide implementations for only the last two (Huffman encoding provides as good as or better encoding than Shannon-Fano). Each of them analyzes the input data as a stream of bytes and somehow assigns different bit sequences to different byte values.

Shannon-Fano Encoding

The first compression algorithm is Shannon-Fano encoding, named after two researchers who invented it separately and simultaneously, Claude Shannon and R.M. Fano. This algorithm analyzes the input data and builds a minimum encoding binary tree from them. Using this tree, we can then reread the input data and encode it.

To illustrate the algorithm, we will compress the phrase "How much wood could a woodchuck chuck?" The first step of the algorithm is the analysis phase. We make a pass through the data and calculate how many times each character occurs and draw up a table of the counts. Table 11.1 shows the result.

Table 11.1: Counts of characters for the sample phrase

Character	Count
space	6
c	6
o	6
u	4
d	3
h	3
w	3
k	2
H	1
a	1
l	1
m	1
?	1

We now divide this table up into two portions by placing a line between two letters such that the count of characters above the line is approximately the same as below. There are 38 characters in all, so the line should divide the table after about 19 characters. This is easy; just place the line in between the o line and the u line, and there are 18 characters above, and 20 below. This gives us Table 11.2.

Now we do the same to each of the portions: insert a line in between two characters so that we divide each portion into two further portions. We continue to do this until each letter is divided from each other. I get Table 11.3 as my final Shannon-Fano tree.

Table 11.2: Starting to build the Shannon-Fano tree

Character	Count	
space	6	
c	6	
o	6	
		division 1
u	4	
d	3	
h	3	
w	3	
k	2	
H	1	
a	1	
l	1	
m	1	
?	1	

Table 11.3: The Shannon-Fano tree is complete

Character	Count	
space	6	
		division 2
c	6	
		division 3
o	6	
		division 1
u	4	
		division 3
d	3	
		division 4
h	3	
		division 2
w	3	
		division 4
k	2	
		division 3
H	1	
		division 5
a	1	
		division 4
l	1	
		division 5
m	1	
		division 6
?	1	

I've deliberately shown each division as a shorter and shorter line, with division 1 as the longest line, the two division 2 lines being shorter, and so on, until we reach division 6, which is the shortest of all. The reason for these shenanigans is that the division lines form a binary tree on its side. (To see this, rotate the book counter-clockwise by 90 degrees.) The division 1 line is the root of the tree, the division 2 lines its two children, and so on. The characters form the leaves of the tree. Figure 11.1 has the resulting tree in the normal orientation.

All very well, but how does this help with encoding each character and compressing the phrase? Well, to get to the space character we start at the root, go left, and then go left again. To get to the c, we go left from the root, go right, and then left. The o is found after going left, then right twice. If we say that going left is equal to a zero bit and going right a one bit, we can draw up the encoding table shown in Table 11.4.

We can now calculate the encoding for the entire phrase. It starts with

```
1110001111000011111010001010110 0...
```

and there are 131 bits in all. If we assume that the original phrase was encoded in ASCII, one character per byte, the original phrase was 286 bits in length, and so our compression ratio is about 54 percent.

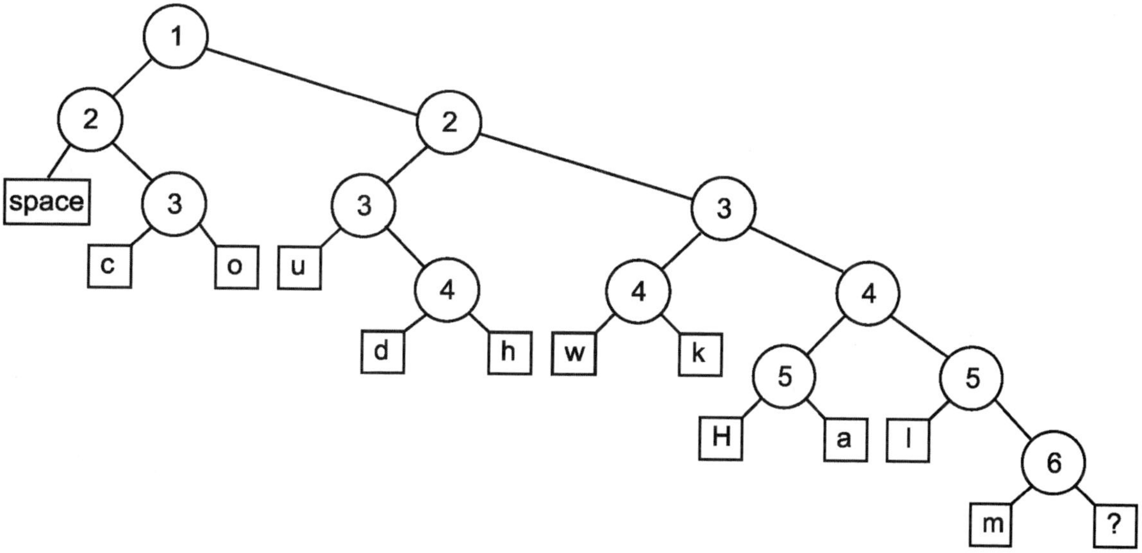

ure 11.1:
hannon-
no tree

Table 11.4: The Shannon-Fano encodings for the sample phrase

Character	Encoding
space	00
c	010
o	011
u	100
d	1010
h	1011
w	1100
k	1101
H	11100
a	11101
l	11110
m	111110
?	111111

To decode a compressed bit stream, we use the same tree we built up in the compression phase. We start at the root and pick off one bit at a time from the compressed bit stream. If the bit is clear, we go left; if set, we go right. We continue like this until we reach a leaf, that is, a character, and we output the character to the stream for the uncompressed data. At this point we start off from the root of the tree again with the next bit. Notice that, since characters are only found on the leaves, the encoding for one character does not form the first part of the encoding for another. Because of this, we cannot decode the compressed data incorrectly. (The name for a binary tree where the data only appears at the leaves is a *prefix tree*.)

We have a slight problem though: how do we recognize the end of the bit stream? After all, underneath the covers of the bit stream class, we will be packing the bits eight to a byte and writing the bytes out. It is unlikely that we will have an exact multiple of 8 bits in our bit stream. There are two solutions to this dilemma, the first being to encode a special character not found in the original data and call it an end-of-file character, and the second to record the length of the uncompressed data to the compressed stream prior to compressing the data itself. The former requires us to find a symbol that is not present in the original data and use that (presumably we would have to pass this on to the decompressor as part of the compressed data so that it would know what to look for). An alternative would be to assume that, although the data symbols were all byte-sized, the end-of-file symbol was word-sized (and given the value 256, say). We will use the latter solution, however. We will store the length of the uncompressed data prior to the compressed data, and so, on decompression, we know exactly how many symbols we need to decode.

The other problem with Shannon-Fano encoding that we have managed to gloss over so far is the tree. Usually we wish to compress data to save space or to save on transmission times. The time and place we decompress the data is usually far removed from the time and place we compressed it. However, the decompression algorithm requires the tree; otherwise, we have no hope of decoding the encoded bit stream. We have two alternatives. The first one is to make the tree static; in other words, the same tree will be used to compress *all* data. For some data, the resulting compression will be fairly optimal; for others it will be pretty hopeless. The second alternative is to attach the tree itself to the compressed bit stream, in some form or other. Of course, attaching the tree to the compressed data is bound to make the compression ratio worse, but there's nothing we can do about it. We'll see how to add the tree to the compressed data in a moment, with the next compression algorithm.

Huffman Encoding

A very similar compression algorithm to Shannon-Fano is Huffman encoding. This algorithm was invented in 1952 by David Huffman ("A Method for the Construction of Minimum-Redundancy Codes") and was even more successful than Shannon-Fano. The reason for this is that Huffman's algorithm is mathematically guaranteed to produce the smallest encoding for each character in the original data.

Like the Shannon-Fano algorithm, we have to build a binary tree, and again, it will be a prefix tree with all the data at the leaves. Unlike Shannon-Fano, which is a top-down algorithm, we build it from the bottom up. First, we make a pass through the input data counting the number of times each byte value appears, just like we did with Shannon-Fano. Once we have this table of character counts, we can start to build the tree.

Consider these character-and-count pairs as a "pool" of nodes for the eventual Huffman tree. Remove the two nodes that have the smallest count from this pool. Join the two nodes to a new parent node, and set the parent's count to the sum of its two children. Add the parent node back to the pool. We continue this process of removing two nodes, and adding back a single parent node, until the pool has only one node in it. At this point we can remove the one node; it is the root of the Huffman tree.

This is a little hard to see, so let's create the Huffman tree for the sample phrase "How much wood could a woodchuck chuck?" We've already calculated the character counts in Table 11.1, so now we have to apply the algorithm to build the full Huffman tree. Select two nodes that have the smallest count. We have ample nodes to choose from, but we'll select the m and ? nodes, both of count 1. We create a parent node of count 2, and attach these two nodes as children. The parent goes back into the pool. Round the loop again. This time we select the a and l nodes, combine them as a mini-tree and put the parent node (of count 2 again) back into the pool. Round the loop again. This time we have a single node of count 1 (the H node), and a choice of three nodes of count 2 (the k node and the two parent nodes we've added previously). We choose the k node, join it to the H node, and add the new parent of count 3 to the pool again. We now select the two parent nodes of count 2, join them to a new parent of count 4, and add that back into the pool. Figure 11.2 shows the first few steps of building the Huffman tree and also the final tree.

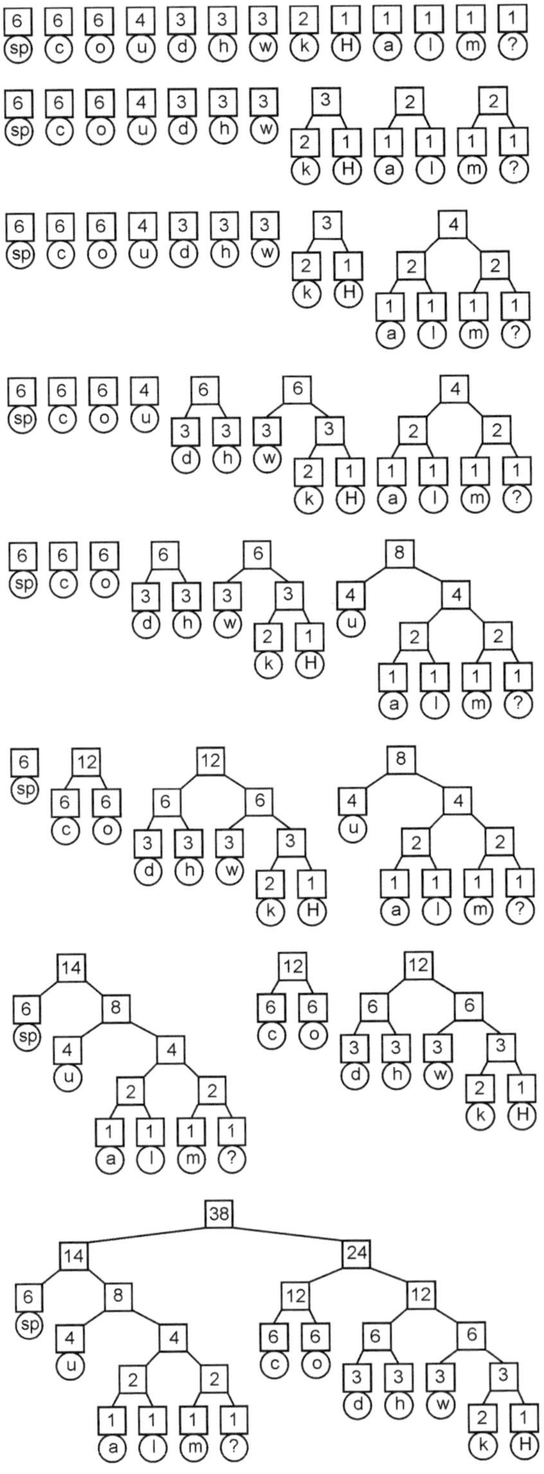

Figure 11.2: Building a Huffman tree

Using this tree in exactly the same manner as the tree we obtained for Shannon-Fano encoding, we can calculate the encoding for each character in the original phrase and obtain Table 11.5.

Table 11.5: The Huffman encodings for the sample phrase

Character	Encoding
space	00
c	100
o	101
u	010
d	1100
h	1101
w	1110
k	11110
H	11111
a	01100
l	01101
m	01110
?	01111

Notice that this table of encodings is not the only one we could have calculated. Every time we had three or more nodes from which to choose two, we would have altered the shape of the final tree and hence the final encodings. But, in reality, each of these possible trees and encodings would produce the best compression; they are all equivalent.

We can now calculate the encoding for the entire phrase. It starts with

```
1111110111100001110010100...
```

and there are 131 bits in all. If we assume that the original phrase was encoded in ASCII, one character per byte, the original phrase was 286 bits in length, and so our compression ratio is about 54 percent.

Again, just as in the Shannon-Fano case, we will have to compress the tree in some fashion and include it with the compressed data.

Decompressing is exactly the same as with the Shannon-Fano case: rebuild the tree from the data in the compressed stream and then use this tree to read the compressed bit stream.

Let's take a look at the Huffman encoding from a high-level viewpoint. With every implementation of the compression methods we shall describe in this chapter, we will write a simple routine that takes both an input stream and an output stream and that compresses all the data in the input stream to the output stream. Listing 11.5 shows this high-level routine TDHuffmanCompress for Huffman encoding.

Listing 11.5: High-level Huffman encoding

```
procedure TDHuffmanCompress(aInStream, aOutStream : TStream);
var
  HTree     : THuffmanTree;
  HCodes    : PHuffmanCodes;
  BitStrm   : TtdOutputBitStream;
  Signature : longint;
  Size      : longint;
begin
  {output the header information (the signature and the size of the
  uncompressed data)}
  Signature := TDHuffHeader;
  aOutStream.WriteBuffer(Signature, sizeof(longint));
  Size := aInStream.Size;
  aOutStream.WriteBuffer(Size, sizeof(longint));
  {if there's nothing to compress, exit now}
  if (Size = 0) then
    Exit;
  {prepare}
  HTree := nil;
  HCodes := nil;
  BitStrm := nil;
  try
    {create the compressed bit stream}
    BitStrm := TtdOutputBitStream.Create(aOutStream);
    BitStrm.Name := 'Huffman compressed stream';
    {allocate the Huffman tree}
    HTree := THuffmanTree.Create;
    {get the distribution of characters in the input stream, and build
    the Huffman tree from the bottom up}
    HTree.CalcCharDistribution(aInStream);
    {output the tree to the bit stream to aid the decompressor}
    HTree.SaveToBitStream(BitStrm);
    {if the root of the Huffman tree is a leaf, the input stream just
    consisted of repetitions of one character, so we're done; other-
    wise we compress the input stream}
    if not HTree.RootIsLeaf then begin
      {allocate the codes array}
      New(HCodes);
      {calculate all the codes}
```

```
      HTree.CalcCodes(HCodes^);
      {compress the characters in the input stream to the bit stream}
      DoHuffmanCompression(aInStream, BitStrm, HCodes^);
    end;
  finally
    BitStrm.Free;
    HTree.Free;
    if (HCodes <> nil) then
      Dispose(HCodes);
  end;
end;
```

There's a lot going on here that we haven't talked about yet; however, we can certainly discuss what's going on in layman's terms first and then start dissecting each individual step. The first thing that happens is that we write a small header to the output stream, followed by the input stream length. This will help us later during decompression to ensure that the compressed stream is one we created. We then create a bit stream object wrapping the output stream. The next step is to create an instance of a THuffmanTree class. This class, as we shall see in a moment, will be used to set up a Huffman tree and has various methods to aid in that endeavor. One of the first methods of this new object that we call, CalcCharDistribution, sets up the distribution statistics for the characters in the input stream, and then builds the Huffman prefix tree.

Now that we have the Huffman tree built, we call the SaveToBitStream method to write the structure of the tree to the output bit stream.

Then comes a special case and a little optimization. If the input stream just consists of multiple occurrences of the same character, the root of the Huffman tree will be a leaf node; the entire prefix tree just consists of one node. In this case, it turns out that we will have written enough information to the output bit stream to enable the decompressor to reconstruct the original file (we have written the input stream size and the single node to the bit stream).

Otherwise, there must have been at least two separate characters in the input stream, and the Huffman tree looks like a proper tree, rather than just one node. In this case, we perform an optimization: we calculate the encoding table for every character that occurs in the input stream. This will save us time in the next stage, the actual compression, because we won't have to continually walk the tree to encode each character. The HCodes array is a simple 256-element array that holds the encoding for each and every character and is built by calling the CalcCodes method of the Huffman tree object.

Finally, having set up all these data structures, we call the DoHuffman-Compression routine to perform the actual compression. Listing 11.6 shows this routine.

Listing 11.6: The Huffman compression loop

```
procedure DoHuffmanCompression(aInStream : TStream;
                               aBitStream: TtdOutputBitStream;
                           var aCodes    : THuffmanCodes);
var
  i         : integer;
  Buffer    : PByteArray;
  BytesRead : longint;
begin
  GetMem(Buffer, HuffmanBufferSize);
  try
    {reset the input stream to the start}
    aInStream.Position := 0;
    {read the first block from the input stream}
    BytesRead := aInStream.Read(Buffer^, HuffmanBufferSize);
    while (BytesRead <> 0) do begin
      {for each character in the block, write out its bit string}
      for i := 0 to pred(BytesRead) do
        aBitStream.WriteBits(aCodes[Buffer^[i]]);
      {read the nextblock from the input stream}
      BytesRead := aInStream.Read(Buffer^, HuffmanBufferSize);
    end;
  finally
    FreeMem(Buffer, HuffmanBufferSize);
  end;
end;
```

The DoHuffmanCompression procedure allocates a large buffer to hold blocks of data from the input stream, and will continually read blocks from the input stream, compressing them, until the stream is exhausted. Buffering the data in this way is a simple optimization to increase the efficiency of the whole process. For every character in the block, the routine writes the corresponding encoding from the aCodes array to the output bit stream.

Having seen the high-level Huffman compression, we should now look at the workhorse class that does most of the clever stuff. This is the internal class THuffmanTree. Its associated types are shown in Listing 11.7.

Listing 11.7: The Huffman tree class

```
type
  PHuffmanNode = ^THuffmanNode;
  THuffmanNode = packed record
    hnCount    : longint;
```

```
    hnLeftInx  : longint;
    hnRightInx : longint;
    hnIndex    : longint;
  end;
  PHuffmanNodeArray = ^THuffmanNodeArray;
  THuffmanNodeArray = array [0..510] of THuffmanNode;
type
  THuffmanCodeStr = string[255];
type
  PHuffmanCodes = ^THuffmanCodes;
  THuffmanCodes = array [0..255] of TtdBitString;
type
  THuffmanTree = class
    private
      FTree : THuffmanNodeArray;
      FRoot : integer;
    protected
      procedure htBuild;
      procedure htCalcCodesPrim(aNodeInx : integer;
                            var aCodeStr : THuffmanCodeStr;
                            var aCodes   : THuffmanCodes);
      function htLoadNode(aBitStream : TtdInputBitStream) : integer;
      procedure htSaveNode(aBitStream : TtdOutputBitStream;
                           aNode : integer);
    public
      constructor Create;

      procedure CalcCharDistribution(aStream : TStream);
      procedure CalcCodes(var aCodes : THuffmanCodes);
      function DecodeNextByte(aBitStream : TtdInputBitStream) : byte;
      procedure LoadFromBitStream(aBitStream : TtdInputBitStream);
      function RootIsLeaf : boolean;
      procedure SaveToBitStream(aBitStream : TtdOutputBitStream);

      property Root : integer read FRoot;
  end;
```

First, we declare a node of the Huffman tree, THuffmanNode, and a fixed-size array of them, THuffmanNodeArray. This array will be used for the actual tree structure and has exactly 511 elements. Why that particular number?

Well, there is a small theorem (or *lemma*) with binary trees that I haven't introduced yet. Assume that a tree has only two types of nodes: internal nodes with exactly two children and leaf nodes with no children (in other words, there are no nodes with just one child—this is what a prefix tree looks like). If there are n leaf nodes in this tree, how many internal nodes are there? Well, the lemma states that there are exactly $n-1$ internal nodes. This is proven by induction. When $n=1$, the lemma is obviously satisfied since this describes a tree with just a root node. Now assume that the lemma is true for all $i<n$, where $n>1$, and let's look at the case where $i=n$. Well, we must have a tree with at least one internal node: the root. This root has two child trees, the left child tree and the right child tree. If the left child tree has x leaves, then it must have $x-1$ internal nodes by our assumption, since $x<n$. Similarly, if the right child tree has y leaves, it must have $y-1$ internal nodes, using our assumption. The tree, as a whole, has n leaves, which must be equal to $x+y$ (remember the root is an internal node). The number of internal nodes is therefore $(x-1) + (y-1) + 1$ which is equal to $n-1$.

How does this lemma help us? Well, in a prefix tree we must have all the characters in leaf nodes; otherwise we wouldn't get unambiguous encodings. Hence, a prefix tree like the Huffman tree will have at most 511 nodes in it, a maximum of 256 nodes for the leaves and at most 255 nodes for the internal nodes, no matter what the tree ends up looking like. Hence, we should be able to implement a Huffman tree (at least one that encodes byte values) as a 511-element array.

The node structure has a count field (to hold the total character count for itself and all its children nodes), an index for the left child and one for the right child, and finally a field to hold its own index (this is helpful when we start building the Huffman tree).

The reason for the Huffman code types (THuffmanCodeStr and THuffmanCodes) will become obvious when we discuss generating the encoding for each character.

The Create constructor for the Huffman tree class merely initializes the internal tree array.

Listing 11.8: Constructing a Huffman tree object

```
constructor THuffmanTree.Create;
var
  i : integer;
begin
  inherited Create;
  FillChar(FTree, sizeof(FTree), 0);
  for i := 0 to 510 do
    FTree[i].hnIndex := i;
end;
```

Since the constructor does not allocate any memory, nor is any allocated elsewhere in the class, there is nothing for an explicit destructor to do, so the class defaults to TObject.Destroy.

The first method we called for the Huffman tree in the compression routine was CalcCharDistribution. This reads the input stream, calculates the number of occurrences for each character and then builds the tree.

Listing 11.9: Calculating the character counts

```
procedure THuffmanTree.CalcCharDistribution(aStream : TStream);
var
  i         : integer;
  Buffer    : PByteArray;
  BytesRead : integer;
begin
  {starting at the beginning of the stream, read all the bytes,
  maintain counts for each byte value}
  aStream.Position := 0;
  GetMem(Buffer, HuffmanBufferSize);
  try
    BytesRead := aStream.Read(Buffer^, HuffmanBufferSize);
    while (BytesRead <> 0) do begin
      for i := pred(BytesRead) downto 0 do
        inc(FTree[Buffer^[i]].hnCount);
      BytesRead := aStream.Read(Buffer^, HuffmanBufferSize);
    end;
  finally
    FreeMem(Buffer, HuffmanBufferSize);
  end;
  {now build the tree}
  htBuild;
end;
```

As you can see by looking at Listing 11.9, the majority of the method's code calculates the character counts and stores them in the first 256 nodes of the array. The method does make sure that it reads the input stream in blocks for efficiency (it allocates a large memory block on the heap prior to performing the calculation loop and releases it afterward). Finally, at the end of the routine, it calls the internal htBuild method to build the tree.

Before we look at the implementation of this important internal method, consider how we might implement the tree-building algorithm. Recall that we start off with a "pool" of nodes, one per character. We select the two smallest (that is, the two nodes with the smallest counts) and join them to a new parent (setting its count to the sum of its two children), and then put the parent back into the pool. We continue like this until we only have one node left in the pool. If you think back to Chapter 9, it should be obvious which data structure we can use to implement this nebulous "pool": the priority queue. To be really strict we should use a min-heap (normally a priority queue is implemented to return the largest item).

Listing 11.10: Building the Huffman tree

```
function CompareHuffmanNodes(aData1, aData2 : pointer) : integer; far;
var
  Node1 : PHuffmanNode absolute aData1;
  Node2 : PHuffmanNode absolute aData2;
begin
  {NOTE: this comparison routine is for the Huffman priority queue,
         which is a *min heap*, therefore this comparison routine
         should return the reverse of what we expect}
  if (Node1^.hnCount) > (Node2^.hnCount) then
    Result := -1
  else if (Node1^.hnCount) = (Node2^.hnCount) then
    Result := 0
  else
    Result := 1;
end;
procedure THuffmanTree.htBuild;
var
  i        : integer;
  PQ       : TtdPriorityQueue;
  Node1    : PHuffmanNode;
  Node2    : PHuffmanNode;
  RootNode : PHuffmanNode;
begin
  {create a priority queue}
  PQ := TtdPriorityQueue.Create(CompareHuffmanNodes, nil);
  try
    PQ.Name := 'Huffman tree minheap';
    {add all the non-zero nodes to the queue}
    for i := 0 to 255 do
      if (FTree[i].hnCount <> 0) then
        PQ.Enqueue(@FTree[i]);
    {SPECIAL CASE: there is only one non-zero node, ie the input
    stream consisted of just one character, repeated one or more
    times; set the root to the index of the single character node}
    if (PQ.Count = 1) then begin
      RootNode := PQ.Dequeue;
      FRoot := RootNode^.hnIndex;
    end
    {otherwise we have the normal, many different chars, case}
    else begin
      {while there is more than one item in the queue, remove the two
      smallest, join them to a new parent, and add the parent to the
       queue}
      FRoot := 255;
      while (PQ.Count > 1) do begin
        Node1 := PQ.Dequeue;
        Node2 := PQ.Dequeue;
```

```
        inc(FRoot);
        RootNode := @FTree[FRoot];
        with RootNode^ do begin
          hnLeftInx := Node1^.hnIndex;
          hnRightInx := Node2^.hnIndex;
          hnCount := Node1^.hnCount + Node2^.hnCount;
        end;
        PQ.Enqueue(RootNode);
      end;
    end;
  finally
    PQ.Free;
  end;
end;
```

We start off by creating an instance of the TtdPriorityQueue class. We pass to it the CompareHuffmanNodes routine. Recall that the priority queue we created in Chapter 9 used the comparison routine to return the largest items first. To create the min-heap we need for the Huffman tree, we alter the sense of the comparison routine so that it returns a positive value if the first item is less than the second, and a negative value if it is greater.

Once the priority queue has been created, we enqueue all of the nodes with non-zero counts. If there was only one such node, we set the Huffman tree's root field, FRoot, to the index of this one node. Otherwise, we go through the Huffman algorithm, with the first parent node being available at index 256. As we dequeue two nodes and enqueue a new parent node, we maintain the FRoot variable to point to the latest parent node, ensuring that, at the end, we know the index of the element that represents the root of the tree.

Finally, we free the priority queue object, and the Huffman tree has been completely built.

The next method we called in the high-level compression routine is the one that writes the Huffman tree to the output bit stream. Essentially, we have to devise some algorithm that writes enough information to rebuild the tree. One possibility is to write out the characters and their counts. Once we have this information, the decompressor can easily rebuild the Huffman tree by merely calling the htBuild method. This seems like a good idea until you consider the amount of space occupied by the character-and-count table in the compressed output stream. Each character would occupy a complete byte in the output stream, and its count would occupy some fixed number of bytes (say two bytes per character to allow a count up to 65,535). If there were 100 separate characters in the input stream, this makes a grand total of 300 bytes for the table. If all characters were represented, it would make a total of 768 bytes.

An alternative is to store the counts for each character. We'd have a fixed two bytes for all characters, including those not present in the input stream, making a total of 512 bytes for the table in every situation. Not much better, admittedly.

Of course, if the input stream were large enough, some of these counts might overflow a 2-byte word, and so we'd have to use three or even four bytes per character.

A better idea is to ignore the character counts and store the actual *structure* of the tree. There are two different kinds of nodes in a prefix tree: internal nodes with two children and external nodes with no children. The external nodes are the ones that have the characters. What we will do is traverse the tree using one of the normal traversal methods (in fact, we'll use the preorder method). For every node we reach we'll write a clear bit if the node is internal, or a set bit if the node is external, followed by the character the node represents. Listing 11.11 shows the SaveToBitStream method and the recursive method it calls, htSaveNode, that does the actual work of traversing the tree and writing the information to the bit stream.

Listing 11.11: Writing Huffman tree to a bit stream

```
procedure THuffmanTree.htSaveNode(aBitStream : TtdOutputBitStream;
                                  aNode : integer);
begin
  {if this is an internal node, write a clear bit, and then the left
   child tree followed by the right child tree}
  if (aNode >= 256) then begin
    aBitStream.WriteBit(false);
    htSaveNode(aBitStream, FTree[aNode].hnLeftInx);
    htSaveNode(aBitStream, FTree[aNode].hnRightInx);
  end
  {otherwise it is a leaf, write a set bit, and the character}
  else begin
    aBitStream.WriteBit(true);
    aBitStream.WriteByte(aNode); {aNode equals the char value}
  end;
end;
procedure THuffmanTree.SaveToBitStream(aBitStream : TtdOutputBitStream);
begin
  htSaveNode(aBitStream, FRoot);
end;
```

If there were 100 separate characters in the input stream then there would be 99 internal nodes, making a grand total of 199 bits to store the node information, plus 100 bytes for the characters themselves, about 125 bytes. If all characters were represented in the input stream, there would be a maximum of 511 bits for the nodes, plus 256 characters, making 320 bytes to store the tree.

The full code for the Huffman tree compression can be found in the TDHuffmn.pas file on the CD.

Having seen Huffman compression, let us now look at the decompression side. Listing 11.12 shows the controlling routine, TDHuffmanDecompress.

Listing 11.12: The TDHuffmanDecompress routine

```
procedure TDHuffmanDecompress(aInStream, aOutStream : TStream);
var
  Signature : longint;
  Size      : longint;
  HTree     : THuffmanTree;
  BitStrm   : TtdInputBitStream;
begin
  {make sure that the input stream is a valid Huffman encoded stream}
  aInStream.Seek(0, soFromBeginning);
  aInStream.ReadBuffer(Signature, sizeof(Signature));
  if (Signature <> TDHuffHeader) then
    raise EtdHuffmanException.Create(
       FmtLoadStr(tdeHuffBadEncodedStrm,
                  [UnitName, 'TDHuffmanDecompress']));
  aInStream.ReadBuffer(Size, sizeof(longint));
  {if there's nothing to decompress, exit now}
  if (Size = 0) then
    Exit;
  {prepare for the decompression}
  HTree := nil;
  BitStrm := nil;
  try
    {create the bit stream}
    BitStrm := TtdInputBitStream.Create(aInStream);
    BitStrm.Name := 'Huffman compressed stream';
    {create the Huffman tree}
    HTree := THuffmanTree.Create;
    {read the tree data from the input stream}
    HTree.LoadFromBitStream(BitStrm);
    {if the root of the Huffman tree is a leaf, the original stream
    just consisted of repetitions of one character}
    if HTree.RootIsLeaf then
      WriteMultipleChars(aOutStream, AnsiChar(HTree.Root), Size)
    {otherwise, using the Huffman tree, decompress the characters in
    the input stream}
    else
      DoHuffmanDecompression(BitStrm, aOutStream, HTree, Size);
  finally
```

```
    BitStrm.Free;
    HTree.Free;
  end;
end;
```

First, we check to see if the stream starts with the correct signature. If not, there's no point in continuing: the stream is obviously faulty.

We then read the length of the uncompressed data, and if this is zero, we have finished. Otherwise, there's some work to do. We create the input bit stream to wrap the input stream. We create the Huffman tree object that'll be doing most of the work for us, and get it to read itself from the input bit stream (the LoadFromBitStream method). If the Huffman tree happened to represent a single character, we re-create the original stream as multiples of that character. If not, we call DoHuffmanDecompression to do the decoding work. Listing 11.13 shows this routine.

Listing 11.13: The DoHuffmanDecompression routine

```
procedure DoHuffmanDecompression(aBitStream : TtdInputBitStream;
                                 aOutStream : TStream;
                                 aHTree     : THuffmanTree;
                                 aSize      : longint);
var
  CharCount : longint;
  Ch        : byte;
  Buffer    : PByteArray;
  BufEnd    : integer;
begin
  GetMem(Buffer, HuffmanBufferSize);
  try
    {preset the loop variables}
    BufEnd := 0;
    CharCount := 0;
    {repeat until all the characters have been decompressed}
    while (CharCount < aSize) do begin
      {read the next byte}
      Ch := aHTree.DecodeNextByte(aBitStream);
      Buffer^[BufEnd] := Ch;
      inc(BufEnd);
      inc(CharCount);
      {if we've filled the buffer, write it out}
      if (BufEnd = HuffmanBufferSize) then begin
        aOutStream.WriteBuffer(Buffer^, HuffmanBufferSize);
        BufEnd := 0;
      end;
    end;
    {if there's anything left in the buffer, write it out}
    if (BufEnd <> 0) then
```

```
      aOutStream.WriteBuffer(Buffer^, BufEnd);
  finally
    FreeMem(Buffer, HuffmanBufferSize);
  end;
end;
```

The routine is essentially a loop within which we decode bytes and fill a buffer repeatedly. When the buffer is full, we write it out to the output stream and start filling it again. The decoding is done by the DecodeNextByte method of the THuffmanTree class.

Listing 11.14: The DecodeNextByte method

```
function THuffmanTree.DecodeNextByte(
                       aBitStream : TtdInputBitStream) : byte;
var
  NodeInx : integer;
begin
  NodeInx := FRoot;
  while (NodeInx >= 256) do begin
    if not aBitStream.ReadBit then
      NodeInx := FTree[NodeInx].hnLeftInx
    else
      NodeInx := FTree[NodeInx].hnRightInx;
  end;
  Result := NodeInx;
end;
```

This method is simple to the extreme. It merely starts at the root of the Huffman tree, and then for each bit read from the input bit stream, it follows the links either left or right, depending on whether the bit read was clear or set. Once the routine reaches a leaf (the node index will be less than or equal to 255), it returns the node index reached; this is the decoded byte.

The full code for the Huffman tree decompression can be found in the TDHuffmn.pas file on the CD.

Splay Tree Encoding

As we've seen, one big problem with both Shannon-Fano and Huffman encoding is the requirement to ship the tree with the compressed data. This is a drawback, since we can't compress the tree very well and the compression ratio is reduced. Another drawback is that we must read the input data twice: first, to calculate the character frequencies in the data and, second, once the tree has been built, to actually encode the data.

Is there any way we can remove the requirement to ship the tree, or avoid reading the input data twice, or, preferably, both? There is a variant of

Huffman compression called adaptive Huffman encoding that enables us to do this. However, in this chapter we will look at a little-known adaptive technique that uses splaying, which we first met in Chapter 8.

Douglas W. Jones devised splay tree compression in 1988 [8]. If you recollect from Chapter 8, splay trees were a method of balancing a binary search tree by splaying a node to the root after accessing the node. So, after searching for and finding a node, we would move it up to the root by a series of rotations, called zig-zag and zig-zig operations. The result of splaying meant that the most frequently accessed nodes tended to find themselves at the top of the tree, the least frequently accessed nodes out toward the leaves. If we employ this strategy in a prefix tree and encode characters as we did for Huffman and Shannon-Fano (left link = a zero bit, right link = a one bit), we will find that the encoding for a given character will change over time: the tree will adapt to the frequency of the characters encoded. Not only that, but the most often used characters will be nearer the top of the tree and hence will tend to have smaller encodings than those that aren't used that often.

Now, it must be admitted that splay trees were designed for binary search trees, that is, binary trees with an ordering. Part of their usefulness was that the splaying operations maintained the ordering during the various rotations and transformations. With a prefix tree, there is no ordering, so we can avoid most of the intricate pointer fiddling that accompanies rotations. Also we must ensure that leaf nodes remain leaf nodes; otherwise, the tree would no longer remain a prefix tree. The splaying we use moves a leaf's parent closer to the root.

The basic compression works as shown in Listing 11.15.

Listing 11.15: Basic splay tree compression algorithm

```
procedure TDSplayCompress(aInStream, aOutStream : TStream);
var
  STree     : TSplayTree;
  BitStrm   : TtdOutputBitStream;
  Signature : longint;
  Size      : longint;
begin
  {output the header information (the signature and the size of the
  uncompressed data)}
  Signature := TDSplayHeader;
  aOutStream.WriteBuffer(Signature, sizeof(longint));
  Size := aInStream.Size;
  aOutStream.WriteBuffer(Size, sizeof(longint));
  {if there's nothing to compress, exit now}
  if (Size = 0) then
    Exit;
```

```
  {prepare}
  STree := nil;
  BitStrm := nil;
  try
    {create the compressed bit stream}
    BitStrm := TtdOutputBitStream.Create(aOutStream);
    BitStrm.Name := 'Splay compressed stream';
    {create the Splay tree}
    STree := TSplayTree.Create;
    {compress the characters in the input stream to the bit stream}
    DoSplayCompression(aInStream, BitStrm, STree);
  finally
    BitStrm.Free;
    STree.Free;
  end;
end;
```

We write out a longint signature to the output stream to mark it as being a splay-compressed stream, and then we write out the size of the uncompressed stream. If the input stream were empty, we exit at this point: we're done. Otherwise, we create an output bit stream to wrap the output stream and a splay tree. We then call DoSplayCompression to do the actual compression. This latter routine is shown in Listing 11.16.

Listing 11.16: The splay tree compression loop

```
procedure DoSplayCompression(aInStream  : TStream;
                             aBitStream : TtdOutputBitStream;
                             aTree      : TSplayTree);
var
  i         : integer;
  Buffer    : PByteArray;
  BytesRead : longint;
  BitString : TtdBitString;
begin
  GetMem(Buffer, SplayBufferSize);
  try
    {reset the input stream to the start}
    aInStream.Position := 0;
    {read the first block from the input stream}
    BytesRead := aInStream.Read(Buffer^, SplayBufferSize);
    while (BytesRead <> 0) do begin
      {for each character in the block, write out its bit string}
      for i := 0 to pred(BytesRead) do
       aTree.EncodeByte(aBitStream, Buffer^[i]);
      {read the next block from the input stream}
      BytesRead := aInStream.Read(Buffer^, SplayBufferSize);
    end;
  finally
```

```
    FreeMem(Buffer, SplayBufferSize);
  end;
end;
```

This routine is actually a loop within a loop. The outer loop reads the input stream in blocks, and the inner loop encodes each byte in the current block and writes out the encoding to the output bit stream by calling the splay tree's EncodeByte method.

It's time to talk about the internal TSplayTree class, the workhorse of the splay compression algorithm. Listing 11.17 shows the interface to the class.

Listing 11.17: The splay tree compression class

```
type
  PSplayNode = ^TSplayNode;
  TSplayNode = packed record
    hnParentInx: longint;
    hnLeftInx  : longint;
    hnRightInx : longint;
    hnIndex    : longint;
  end;
  PSplayNodeArray = ^TSplayNodeArray;
  TSplayNodeArray = array [0..510] of TSplayNode;
type
  TSplayTree = class
    private
      FTree : TSplayNodeArray;
      FRoot : integer;
    protected
      procedure stConvertCodeStr(const aRevCodeStr : ShortString;
                                 var aBitString   : TtdBitString);
      procedure stInitialize;
      procedure stSplay(aNodeInx : integer);
    public
      constructor Create;
      procedure EncodeByte(aBitStream : TtdOutputBitStream;
                           aValue     : byte);
      function DecodeByte(aBitStream : TtdInputBitStream) : byte;
  end;
```

Although we could use a node-based tree as we did in Chapter 8, because we know how many characters are in our alphabet (basically, there are 256 characters), it is easier to use an array-based system, much as we did with the heap data structure and the Huffman tree. Another consideration to switch structures is that with the non-adaptive compression methods we were able to build a table of encodings because they were static. With splay tree compression, the bit encoding for a character depends on the state of the splay tree at the time the character is encoded. We can no longer have a static table. Hence, one of the requirements is going to be that we can find a character in the tree easily and efficiently (preferably through a O(1) algorithm—we *don't* want to search for it). Once we have the character and its leaf node, we can easily walk the tree up to the root to calculate the encoding for the character (admittedly we'll get the bit encoding in reverse order, but with a stack we can easily reverse the bits).

We start off with the tree in a known state. We could set up the tree to mimic the frequency of letters in the English language, or some other distribution, but in practice it is much easier to create a perfectly balanced tree. Each node has three "pointers," actually just indexes of other nodes in the array, and we set it up in the same manner as we did with a heap: the children for a node at index n are at $2n+1$ and $2n+2$, and its parent is at $(n-1)$ div 2. Since the nodes won't actually move in the array (we're just going to be manipulating the indexes), we will always know where to find the leaves; they will always occupy the same positions in the array: #0 will be found at index 255, #1 at index 256, etc. Listing 11.18 shows the method that initializes the tree; it is called from the Create constructor.

Listing 11.18: The stInitialize method

```
procedure TSplayTree.stInitialize;
var
  i : integer;
begin
  {create a perfectly balanced tree, the root will be at element 0;
  for node n, its parent is at (n-1) div 2 and its children are at
  2n+1 and 2n+2}
  FillChar(FTree, sizeof(FTree), 0);
  for i := 0 to 254 do begin
    FTree[i].hnLeftInx := (2 * i) + 1;
    FTree[i].hnRightInx := (2 * i) + 2;
  end;
  for i := 1 to 510 do
    FTree[i].hnParentInx := (i - 1) div 2;
end;
constructor TSplayTree.Create;
begin
  inherited Create;
  stInitialize;
end;
```

When we compress a character, we find its node in the tree. We then walk up the tree saving the bits so described in a stack (if we came up a left link, that's a zero bit, if a right link, a one bit). Once at the root, we can then pop the bits off the stack to give the encoding for the character. (The code in Listing 11.19 uses a short string to act as the stack.)

At that point we then splay that node's parent to the root. The reason we don't splay the character's node itself to the root is that we must maintain the characters in leaf nodes; otherwise, it is entirely possible that one character's encoding becomes the start of another's. Splaying the parent will "drag" the child along with it. Frequently used characters will, therefore, find themselves nearer the top of the tree.

Listing 11.19: The EncodeByte and stSplay methods

```
procedure TSplayTree.EncodeByte(aBitStream : TtdOutputBitStream;
                                aValue     : byte);
var
  NodeInx    : integer;
  ParentInx  : integer;
  RevCodeStr : ShortString;
  BitString  : TtdBitString;
begin
  {starting at the node for aValue, work our way up the tree, saving
  whether we moved up a left link (0) or a right link (1) at every
  step}
  RevCodeStr := '';
  NodeInx := aValue + 255;
  while (NodeInx <> 0) do begin
    ParentInx := FTree[NodeInx].hnParentInx;
    inc(RevCodeStr[0]);
    if (FTree[ParentInx].hnLeftInx = NodeInx) then
      RevCodeStr[length(RevCodeStr)] := '0'
    else
      RevCodeStr[length(RevCodeStr)] := '1';
    NodeInx := ParentInx;
  end;
  {convert the string code into a bit string}
  stConvertCodeStr(RevCodeStr, BitString);
  {write the bit string to the bit stream}
  aBitStream.WriteBits(BitString);
  {now splay the node}
  stSplay(aValue + 255);
end;
procedure TSplayTree.stConvertCodeStr(const aRevCodeStr : ShortString;
                                      var aBitString  : TtdBitString);
var
  ByteNum : integer;
  i       : integer;
  Mask    : byte;
  Accum   : byte;
```

```
begin
  {prepare for the conversion loop}
  ByteNum := 0;
  Mask := 1;
  Accum := 0;
  {convert the bits in reverse}
  for i := length(aRevCodeStr) downto 1 do begin
    if (aRevCodeStr[i] = '1') then
      Accum := Accum or Mask;
    Mask := Mask shl 1;
    if (Mask = 0) then begin
      aBitString.bsBits[ByteNum] := Accum;
      inc(ByteNum);
      Mask := 1;
      Accum := 0;
    end;
  end;
  {if there are some bits left over, store them}
  if (Mask <> 1) then
    aBitString.bsBits[ByteNum] := Accum;
  {store binary code in the codes array}
  aBitString.bsCount := length(aRevCodeStr);
end;
procedure TSplayTree.stSplay(aNodeInx : integer);
var
  Dad      : integer;
  GrandDad : integer;
  Uncle    : integer;
begin
  {splay the node}
  repeat
    {get the parent of the node}
    Dad := FTree[aNodeInx].hnParentInx;
    {if the parent is the root, we're done}
    if (Dad = 0) then
      aNodeInx := 0
    {otherwise, semi-rotate the node up the tree}
    else begin
      {get the parent of the parent}
      GrandDad := FTree[Dad].hnParentInx;
      {semi-rotate (ie, swap the node with its uncle)}
      if (FTree[GrandDad].hnLeftInx = Dad) then begin
        Uncle := FTree[GrandDad].hnRightInx;
        FTree[GrandDad].hnRightInx := aNodeInx;
      end
      else begin
        Uncle := FTree[GrandDad].hnLeftInx;
        FTree[GrandDad].hnLeftInx := aNodeInx;
```

```
      end;
      if (FTree[Dad].hnLeftInx = aNodeInx) then
        FTree[Dad].hnLeftInx := Uncle
      else
      FTree[Dad].hnRightInx := Uncle;
      FTree[Uncle].hnParentInx := Dad;
      FTree[aNodeInx].hnParentInx := GrandDad;
      {start again at the grandparent}
      aNodeInx := GrandDad;
    end;
  until (aNodeInx = 0);
end;
```

On decompression, we set up the tree to the initial configuration as we did in the compression phase. We then pick off bits from the bit stream one by one and walk down the tree in the usual manner, and, once we'd reached the leaf with the character (which we output as uncompressed data), we would splay the node's parent to the root. Providing we update the tree in exactly the same manner for both compression and decompression, the decoding algorithm can keep the tree in exactly the same state at the same time as the encoding algorithm.

Listing 11.20: Basic splay tree decompression algorithm

```
procedure TDSplayDecompress(aInStream, aOutStream : TStream);
var
  Signature : longint;
  Size      : longint;
  STree     : TSplayTree;
  BitStrm   : TtdInputBitStream;
begin
  {make sure that the input stream is a valid Splay encoded stream}
  aInStream.Seek(0, soFromBeginning);
  aInStream.ReadBuffer(Signature, sizeof(Signature));
  if (Signature <> TDSplayHeader) then
    raise EtdSplayException.Create(
       FmtLoadStr(tdeSplyBadEncodedStrm,
                  [UnitName, 'TDSplayDecompress']));
  aInStream.ReadBuffer(Size, sizeof(longint));
  {if there's nothing to decompress, exit now}
  if (Size = 0) then
    Exit;
  {prepare for the decompression}
  STree := nil;
  BitStrm := nil;
  try
    {create the bit stream}
    BitStrm := TtdInputBitStream.Create(aInStream);
```

```
    BitStrm.Name := 'Splay compressed stream';
    {create the Splay tree}
    STree := TSplayTree.Create;
    {using the Splay tree, decompress the characters in the input
    stream}
    DoSplayDecompression(BitStrm, aOutStream, STree, Size);
  finally
    BitStrm.Free;
    STree.Free;
  end;
end;
```

On decompressing a stream, we first check that the stream is a splay-compressed stream by validating the signature. We then read the size of the uncompressed data and exit if this is zero.

If there is data to decompress, we create an input bit stream to wrap the input stream and the splay tree. We then call DoSplayDecompression to do the actual decoding (Listing 11.21).

Listing 11.21: The splay tree decompression loop

```
procedure DoSplayDecompression(aBitStream : TtdInputBitStream;
                               aOutStream : TStream;
                               aTree      : TSplayTree;
                               aSize      : longint);
var
  CharCount : longint;
  Ch        : byte;
  Buffer    : PByteArray;
  BufEnd    : integer;
begin
  GetMem(Buffer, SplayBufferSize);
  try
    {preset the loop variables}
    BufEnd := 0;
    CharCount := 0;
    {repeat until all the characters have been decompressed}
    while (CharCount < aSize) do begin
      {read the next byte}
      Buffer^[BufEnd] := aTree.DecodeByte(aBitStream);
      inc(BufEnd);
      inc(CharCount);
      {if we've filled the buffer, write it out}
      if (BufEnd = SplayBufferSize) then begin
        aOutStream.WriteBuffer(Buffer^, SplayBufferSize);
        BufEnd := 0;
      end;
    end;
```

```
    {if there's anything left in the buffer, write it out}
    if (BufEnd <> 0) then
      aOutStream.WriteBuffer(Buffer^, BufEnd);
  finally
    FreeMem(Buffer, SplayBufferSize);
  end;
end;
```

As in the Huffman tree decoding loop, we fill a buffer with decoded bytes and write them out to the output stream. The real work is done by the DecodeByte method of the splay tree.

Listing 11.22: The TSplayTree.DecodeByte method

```
function TSplayTree.DecodeByte(aBitStream : TtdInputBitStream) : byte;
var
  NodeInx : integer;
begin
  {starting at the root, walk down the tree as dictated by the bits
  from the bit stream}
  NodeInx := 0;
  while NodeInx < 255 do begin
    if not aBitStream.ReadBit then
      NodeInx := FTree[NodeInx].hnLeftInx
    else
      NodeInx := FTree[NodeInx].hnRightInx;
  end;
  {calculate the byte from the final node index}
  Result := NodeInx - 255;
  {now splay the node}
  stSplay(NodeInx);
end;
```

This method simply walks down the tree, reading bits from the input bit stream and following the left or right link depending on whether the current bit is clear or set. Finally, the leaf node reached is splayed toward the root of the tree, to mimic what happened to the tree during compression. Since the splaying at the compressor and decompressor is the same, the data can be decoded properly.

The full code for the splay tree compression algorithm can be found in the TDSplyCm.pas file on the CD.

Dictionary Compression

Up until 1977, the main thrust of compression research centered on minimum redundancy encoding, such as the Shannon-Fano or the Huffman algorithms, either in making them dynamic (so that the code table didn't have to be part of the compressed file), or in various speed, space, and efficiency improvements. Then, suddenly, two Israeli researchers, Jacob Ziv and Abraham Lempel, came up with a new radically different method of compression and opened up research into a completely different direction. Their main idea was not to try and encode single characters or symbols, but instead to encode *strings* of characters. Their idea was to use a *dictionary* of previously seen *phrases* from the file being compressed to help encode later phrases.

Suppose you had a normal English dictionary. Every word you'd encounter in a given text file would appear in the dictionary. If the compressor and decompressor programs had access to an electronic version of this dictionary, they could encode individual words in the text file by finding them in the dictionary, and outputting the page number and the number of the word on the page. We could assume a 2-byte integer would be able to hold the page number (there are not that many dictionaries with more than 65,536 pages) and a byte should be able to hold the word number on the page (again there are never usually more than 256 words defined on a page in a dictionary), hence each word in the text file, no matter how long, would be replaced by three bytes. Obviously small words like "a," "in," "up," and so on, would grow in size instead of being compressed, but the majority of words are three or more letters long and so the overall size of the compressed file would tend to decrease.

LZ77 Compression Description

Ziv and Lempel's idea followed the lines of dictionary compression. Instead of having a static pre-built dictionary though, their algorithm generated one on the fly from the data that the compressor had already seen in the input file. And, instead of using page numbers and word numbers on the page, they output distance and length values. It works a little like this: as you read through the input file, you attempt to match up the set of characters at your current position with something you've already seen in the input file. If you do find a match, you calculate the distance of the matching string from your current position and the number of bytes (the length) that match. If you manage to find several matches, you choose the longest one.

A small example that we can work through would serve us here. Suppose we were compressing the sentence:

```
a cat is a cat is a cat
```

The first character, "a," doesn't match with anything yet seen (because we haven't seen anything yet!), so we just output it to the compressed bit stream as is. We would do the same thing with the following space and "c." The next "a" matches a previous "a" but that's all; we can't match anything more. Let us impose the rule that we only want to match at least three characters before we do something different. So, we output the "a" to the output stream, as well as the "t," space, "i," "s," and space. We can visualize the current state of play as the following:

```
---------+
a cat is |a cat is a cat
---------+^
```

where the characters we've seen are in the box (this is technically known as a *sliding window*), and the current position is marked with a caret.

Now it gets really interesting. The set of characters "a cat is " at the current position matches something we've already seen before. The matching string occurs nine characters before our current position and we can match nine characters. So we can output a distance/length pair, represented here by <9,9> (or some sequence of bits), to the output file and then advance nine characters. The state of play is then:

```
------------------+
a cat is a cat is |a cat
------------------+^
```

But, again, we can match the set of characters at the current position with something that's gone before. We have a choice to either match five characters nine characters before, or five characters 18 characters before. Let's choose the first option, <9,5>. Our compressed stream ends up looking like this

```
a cat is <9,9><9,5>
```

Decompressing this bit stream is quite easy, too. As we decompress, we build up a buffer of decompressed characters so that we can decode the distance/length pairs or codes. Literal characters in the compressed stream are output to the decompressed stream as they are.

The first nine codes in the compressed stream are literal characters, so we output them to the decompressed stream as is, and also we create a buffer (called a sliding window) at the same time. The buffer looks like this at this point:

```
---------+
a cat is |
---------+
```

The next code in the compressed stream is a distance/length pair, <9,9>. We understand this as saying "output the nine characters found at a distance of nine bytes back in the buffer." Those nine characters are "a cat is " and so we output those to our uncompressed stream and add them to our buffer, or sliding window:

```
------------------+
a cat is a cat is |
------------------+
```

Again, the next code in the compressed stream is a distance/length pair, <9,5>, and I'm sure you can decode that using the buffer we have.

With this small example we haven't needed a dictionary per se; we just used our visual acumen to find the longest match in the set of previously seen characters. In practice, we would add previously seen phrases or tokens to a dictionary (actually a hash table) and then look up the token at the current position in this dictionary to try and find a previously seen match.

By the way, in case you were wondering, defining the buffer of previously seen characters as a "sliding window" means that we only consider the previous *n* bytes in trying to find a possible match; *n* is usually something like 4 KB or 8 KB (the Deflate algorithm in PKZIP can use a sliding window of up to 32 KB in size). As we advance the current position, we slide the window forward on the data we've already seen. Why do we do this? Why not use the entirety of the previously seen text? The answer to this boils down to how text is generally structured. In general, text we read and write obeys a rule called *locality of reference*. What this term means is that characters in a text file tend to match other characters close by rather than far away. In a novel, for example, the protagonists and locations the narrative is describing tend to be "clumped" together in chapters or sections of chapters. The standard words and phrases like "and," "the," and "he said" occur throughout the novel.

Other text, like reference books such as this one, also exhibit locality of reference. Hence, it makes sense to limit the amount of previously seen text we have to search through for a matching string—locality of reference tells us that it makes sense. Another strong reason for limiting the size of the sliding window is that the more text we have to search through, the slower the compression becomes.

Consider also how we are to encode the distance/length pair. I've glossed over this so far, but it makes sense to pack them in as small a space as possible. If we have a sliding window over the last 4 KB of text, we can encode a distance value in 12 bits (2^{12} is 4 KB). If we limit the maximum length we try and match to 15 characters, we can encode that in 4 bits, and we see that we can manage to encode a distance/length pair in two complete bytes. We could also use an 8 KB window and a maximum of seven matched characters and still fit in 2 bytes. Our compressed stream can be viewed as a byte stream rather than the admittedly more fiddly bit stream we used for minimum length encoding. Also, if we limit the distance/length encoding to 2 bytes, it means that strings of at least three characters that match with something we're already seen can get compressed, whereas matches of one or two characters can be safely ignored since they won't compress.

Without being too rigorous, this is the essence of Ziv and Lempel's algorithm, usually known these days as LZ77.

Encoding Literals Versus Distance/Length Pairs

The above discussion does leave out a small implementation detail: how do you tell the difference between a literal character and a distance/length code as you are reading through the compressed data? After all, there is nothing intrinsically different between a literal character and the first byte of a distance/length pair. One simple answer is to output a single flag bit before the literal character or distance/length code. If the flag bit is clear, the next code read will be a literal character; if the flag bit is set, the next code read will be a distance/length pair. However, using this method would result in having to output single bits again, losing the advantage of just using bytes.

The general way around this disadvantage is to have a byte of eight flag bits that tells you what the next eight codes are going to be. The first bit denotes what the first code after the flag byte is going to be; the second bit what the second code is going to be and so on for 8 bits and codes, after which there will be another flag byte. Using this scheme we can write (and read) the compressed stream as a sequence of bytes.

A similar scheme was used, for example, by the old Microsoft EXPAND.EXE program you used to get with MS-DOS or Windows 3.1 (nowadays, Microsoft products use cabinet files instead). You may remember that the files on the DOS diskettes used to have names like FILENAME.EX_, and the EXPAND.EXE program would decompress them and fix the final character of the extension in the decompressed file. In Microsoft's version of LZ77, the distance/length codes were always 2 bytes in size, 12 bits being the distance value (in fact, the Microsoft version used a circular queue of bytes and the distance value was an offset from the start of the queue), with the other 4 bits being the length value.

Having seen the theory, it is time to think about the implementation and nail down some rules. We shall assume that a distance/length pair will always be 2 bytes in length, a word value, with the upper 13 bits for the distance value and the lower 3 bits for the length value. Because we have 13 bits for the distance value, in theory, we can encode distances from 0 to 8,191 bytes, and so our sliding window will be 8 KB in size. Notice that, in determining the distance, we will never use the value 0 (otherwise, we'd be matching with the current position). So we'll interpret these 13 bits as being values from 1 to 8,192 rather than 0 to 8,191, by the simple expedient of adding one.

Consider now the length value. In theory, using 3 bits, we can only encode lengths from 0 to 7. Remember, though, we only try and convert matching strings of three characters or more into distance/length pairs. Any less, and there would be no compression. So, it makes sense to interpret the 3 bits as being lengths of 3 to 10 bytes by simply adding 3.

Hence, to convert a distance and a length amount into a word value, we'd write something like this:

```
Code := ((Distance-1) shl 3)
        + (Length-3);
```

And to get the distance and length values back, we'd code this:

```
Length := (Code and $7)+3;
Distance := (Code shr 3)+1;
```

LZ77 Decompression

Before discussing how we compress data, let's implement the decompression algorithm, since conceptually it is the easiest to visualize. With decompression, we read a flag byte and then use it to determine how we should read the next eight codes from the stream. If the current bit in the flag byte is clear, we read 1 byte from the stream and interpret it as a literal character to be written straight to the output stream. If, on the other hand, the current bit is set, we read 2 bytes from the input stream and split the value into distance and length values. We then use these with our current sliding window of previously decoded data to interpret what characters should be written to the output stream.

Every time we decode a single character or a set of three to 10 characters, not only do we have to write them to the output stream, as I have already indicated, but we have to add them onto the end of the sliding window buffer and advance the start of the sliding window by a commensurate amount so that the window size never exceeds 8,192 bytes. Obviously, we don't want to reconstruct the buffer every time we decode a character or a string of characters—it would take too long. In practice we use a circular queue, a queue of a fixed size whose head and tail are defined by indexes. Since the compression phase would also use a similar sliding window—we'll discuss how in a moment—it makes sense to have a shareable class implementation.

Before we go on to describe the decompression methods we'd need for this class, I want to describe a little trick that's employed by PKZIP's Deflate method. Look back to the sample sentence we were compressing above. At one stage in describing the algorithm we had the following position:

```
---------+
a cat is |a cat is a cat
---------+^
```

and we calculated the distance/length pair of <9,9>. However, there is a little trick we can use. Why stop at matching nine characters? We can, in fact, match more than that by going beyond the right boundary of the sliding window, and continuing matching with the current character and others to its right. We could, in fact, match 14 characters in all, to give a code of <9,14>, with the length being greater than the distance. All very well, and pretty clever, but what happens on decoding? At the point where we have to decode <9,14> we have this in our sliding window:

```
---------+
a cat is |
---------+
```

We go back nine characters into the window and start copying characters, one by one until we reach 14 of them. It turns out that we end up copying characters we have managed to set as part of the same operation. After copying nine characters we have

```
---------+
a cat is |a cat is
---------+^        ^
       from       to
```

with the places we are copying from and copying to shown. As you can see, we can easily copy the remaining five characters with no problem at all. Hence, it is simple to have a length value greater than a distance value (although, it must be admitted, we couldn't just use the Move procedure to copy the data).

What we will do with the sliding window class during decompression is pass it the output stream to which the data is to be written. That way, when the object determines that it needs to slide the active data in the buffer back to the start, it can first copy the data it is about to overwrite to the stream. There are two main methods we need for decompression: adding a single character and converting a distance/length pair. Note that we make the sliding window class perform these actions since we need to update the sliding window and advance in both cases, and also the class is the best agent for converting the distance and length values. The class interface, housekeeping, and output related code is shown in Listing 11.23.

Listing 11.23: The sliding window class output-related code

```
type
  TtdLZSlidingWindow = class
    private
      FBuffer       : PAnsiChar;      {the circular buffer}
      FBufferEnd    : PAnsiChar;      {the end point of the buffer}
      FCompressing  : boolean;        {true=for compressing data}
      FCurrent      : PAnsiChar;      {current character}
      FLookAheadEnd : PAnsiChar;      {end of the look-ahead}
      FMidPoint     : PAnsiChar;      {mid-point of the buffer}
      FName         : TtdNameString;  {name of the sliding window}
      FStart        : PAnsiChar;      {start of the sliding window}
      FStartOffset  : longint;        {stream offset for FStart}
      FStream       : TStream;        {underlying stream}
    protected
      procedure swAdvanceAfterAdd(aCount : integer);
      procedure swReadFromStream;
      procedure swSetCapacity(aValue : longint);
      procedure swWriteToStream(aFinalBlock : boolean);
    public
      constructor Create(aStream       : TStream;
                         aCompressing : boolean);
      destructor Destroy; override;

      {methods used for both compression and decompression}
      procedure Clear;

      {methods used during compression}
      procedure Advance(aCount : integer);
      function Compare(aOffset    : longint;
                   var aDistance : integer) : integer;
      procedure GetNextSignature(var aMS     : TtdLZSignature;
                                 var aOffset : longint);

      {methods used during decompression}
      procedure AddChar(aCh : AnsiChar);
      procedure AddCode(aDistance : integer; aLength : integer);

      property Name : TtdNameString
                 read FName write FName;
  end;
```

```
constructor TtdLZSlidingWindow.Create(aStream      : TStream;
                                      aCompressing : boolean);
begin
  inherited Create;
  {save parameters}
  FCompressing := aCompressing;
  FStream := aStream;
  {set capacity of sliding window: by definition this is 8,192 bytes of
  sliding window and 10 bytes of lookahead}
  swSetCapacity(tdcLZSlidingWindowSize + tdcLZLookAheadSize);
  {reset the buffer and, if we're compressing, read some data from the
  stream to be compressed}
  Clear;
  if aCompressing then
    swReadFromStream;
end;
destructor TtdLZSlidingWindow.Destroy;
begin
  if Assigned(FBuffer) then begin
    {finish writing to the output stream if we're decompressing}
    if not FCompressing then
      swWriteToStream(true);
    {free the buffer}
    FreeMem(FBuffer, FBufferEnd - FBuffer);
  end;
  inherited Destroy;
end;
procedure TtdLZSlidingWindow.AddChar(aCh : AnsiChar);
begin
  {add the character to the buffer}
  FCurrent^ := aCh;
  {advance the sliding window by one character}
  swAdvanceAfterAdd(1);
end;
procedure TtdLZSlidingWindow.AddCode(
                          aDistance : integer; aLength : integer);
var
  FromChar : PAnsiChar;
  ToChar   : PAnsiChar;
  i        : integer;
begin
  {set up the pointers to do the data copy; note we cannot use Move
  since part of the data we are copying may be set up by the actual
  copying of the data}
  FromChar := FCurrent - aDistance;
  ToChar := FCurrent;
  for i := 1 to aLength do begin
    ToChar^ := FromChar^;
```

```
      inc(FromChar);
      inc(ToChar);
    end;
    {advance the start of the sliding window}
    swAdvanceAfterAdd(aLength);
end;
procedure TtdLZSlidingWindow.swAdvanceAfterAdd(aCount : integer);
begin
  {advance the start of the sliding window, if required}
  if ((FCurrent - FStart) >= tdcLZSlidingWindowSize) then begin
    inc(FStart, aCount);
    inc(FStartOffset, aCount);
  end;
  {advance the current pointer}
  inc(FCurrent, aCount);
  {check to see if we have advanced into the overflow zone}
  if (FStart >= FMidPoint) then begin
    {write some more data to the stream (from FBuffer to FStart)}
    swWriteToStream(false);
    {move current data back to the start of the buffer}
    Move(FStart^, FBuffer^, FCurrent - FStart);
    {reset the various pointers}
    dec(FCurrent, FStart - FBuffer);
    FStart := FBuffer;
  end;
end;
procedure TtdLZSlidingWindow.swSetCapacity(aValue : longint);
var
  NewQueue   : PAnsiChar;
begin
  {round the requested capacity to nearest 64 bytes}
  aValue := (aValue + 63) and $7FFFFFC0;
  {get a new buffer}
  GetMem(NewQueue, aValue * 2);
  {destroy the old buffer}
  if (FBuffer <> nil) then
    FreeMem(FBuffer, FBufferEnd - FBuffer);
  {set the head/tail and other pointers}
  FBuffer := NewQueue;
  FStart := NewQueue;
  FCurrent := NewQueue;
  FLookAheadEnd := NewQueue;
  FBufferEnd := NewQueue + (aValue * 2);
  FMidPoint := NewQueue + aValue;
end;
procedure TtdLZSlidingWindow.swWriteToStream(aFinalBlock : boolean);
var
  BytesToWrite : longint;
```

```
begin
  {write the data before the current sliding window}
  if aFinalBlock then
    BytesToWrite := FCurrent - Fbuffer
  else
    BytesToWrite := FStart - FBuffer;
  FStream.WriteBuffer(FBuffer^, BytesToWrite);
end;
```

The AddChar method adds a single literal character to the sliding window and advances the window by 1 byte. The internal swAdvanceAfterAdd method does the actual advancing, and after sliding the window along, it checks to see if another block can't be written to the output stream. The AddCode method adds a distance/length pair to the sliding window, by copying the characters one by one from the already decoded part of the sliding window to the current position. The sliding window is then advanced.

That done, it is fairly easy to write the decompression code. (It seems a bit bizarre to write the decompression code before the compression code, but, in reality, we've defined the format of the compressed data to such a level of detail that we can. Also, it's easier!) We'll code the main loop as a state machine with three states: read and process a flag byte, read and process a character, and, finally, read and process a distance/length code. The code is shown in Listing 11.24. Notice that we determine when to end the decompression by utilizing the fact that the compressor writes the number of bytes in the uncompressed stream to the start of the compressed stream.

Listing 11.24: The main LZ77 decompression code

```
procedure TDLZDecompress(aInStream, aOutStream : TStream);
type
  TDecodeState = (dsGetFlagByte, dsGetChar, dsGetDistLen);
var
  SlideWin      : TtdLZSlidingWindow;
  BytesUnpacked : longint;
  TotalSize     : longint;
  LongValue     : longint;
  DecodeState   : TDecodeState;
  FlagByte      : byte;
  FlagMask      : byte;
  NextChar      : AnsiChar;
  NextDistLen   : longint;
  CodeCount     : integer;
  Len           : integer;
begin
  SlideWin := TtdLZSlidingWindow.Create(aOutStream, false);
  try
    SlideWin.Name := 'LZ77 Decompress sliding window';
```

```
{read the header from the stream: 'TDLZ' followed by uncompressed
size of input stream}
aInStream.ReadBuffer(LongValue, sizeof(LongValue));
if (LongValue <> TDLZHeader) then
  RaiseError(tdeLZBadEncodedStream, 'TDLZDecompress');
aInStream.ReadBuffer(TotalSize, sizeof(TotalSize));
{prepare for the decompression}
BytesUnpacked := 0;
NextDistLen := 0;
DecodeState := dsGetFlagByte;
CodeCount := 0;
FlagMask := 1;
{while there are still bytes to decompress...}
while (BytesUnpacked < TotalSize) do begin
  {given the current decode state, read the next item}
  case DecodeState of
    dsGetFlagByte :
      begin
        aInStream.ReadBuffer(FlagByte, 1);
        CodeCount := 0;
        FlagMask := 1;
      end;
    dsGetChar :
      begin
        aInStream.ReadBuffer(NextChar, 1);
        SlideWin.AddChar(NextChar);
        inc(BytesUnpacked);
      end;
    dsGetDistLen :
      begin
        aInStream.ReadBuffer(NextDistLen, 2);
        Len := (NextDistLen and tdcLZLengthMask) + 3;
        SlideWin.AddCode(
           (NextDistLen shr tdcLZDistanceShift) + 1, Len);
        inc(BytesUnpacked, Len);
      end;
  end;
  {calculate the next decode state}
  inc(CodeCount);
  if (CodeCount > 8) then
    DecodeState := dsGetFlagByte
  else begin
    if ((FlagByte and FlagMask) = 0) then
      DecodeState := dsGetChar
    else
      DecodeState := dsGetDistLen;
    FlagMask := FlagMask shl 1;
  end;
```

```
    end;
  finally
    SlideWin.Free;
  end;{try..finally}
end;
```

After checking that the input stream is a valid LZ77-compressed stream, we read the number of decompressed bytes. We then enter a simple state machine, with the states being determined by the flag bytes we'll be reading from the input stream. If the current state is dsGetFlagByte, we read another flag byte from the input stream. If it is dsGetChar, we read a literal from the input stream and add it to the sliding window. Otherwise, the state is dsGetDistLen and we read a distance/length pair from the input stream and add the pair to the sliding window. We continue like this until we've decompressed all the data from the input stream.

LZ77 Compression

Now we've seen how the decompression works, we need to discuss the compression implementation. This quickly boils down to one problem: searching for the longest match to the current position in the previous 8,192 bytes. There is one method we shall ignore completely as being too inefficient: searching through the entire buffer.

It turns out that Ziv and Lempel didn't suggest much of anything in their original paper. Some people use a binary search tree built over the sliding window to store the maximum length match strings previously seen (an example is Mark Nelson's implementation [15]). This does, however, cause problems in that we need to worry about balancing the tree and how to get rid of strings that are about to leave the sliding window. Instead, we'll make use of a hint presented in the Internet document Deflate Compressed Data Format Specification (RFC1951) and use a hash table.

The algorithm goes like this: we look at the three characters at the current position—we'll call it the signature. We hash the signature using some method and use the hash value to access an element in a hash table, one that uses chaining. The chains or linked lists at each element of the hash table will consist of a sequence of items, each item consisting of a three-character signature as well as the offset in the input stream where the signature occurred.

So, we have the signature at the current position and we've hashed it to a linked list, one of the chains in our hash table. We walk the linked list and compare each item's signature in it to ours. If we find one that is equal, we go to the sliding window using the item's offset value and then compare the characters in the sliding window with those at the current position. We do this with every item in the linked list that equals our signature, and keep a note of the longest match we find.

After this search, be it successful or not, we'll need to add the current signature to the hash table so that we may find it with later signatures. We add it to the front of the linked list, thereby ensuring that the linked list becomes sorted in reverse order by offset value.

However, unless we do something about it, the number of items in the hash table will just keep on growing when, in reality, we don't need the items that no longer appear in our 8 KB sliding window. The first solution might be to remove the item that's just about to disappear out of the sliding window when we slide the window along. We would find the signature of the position (or, indeed, positions) just about to disappear from the start of the sliding window, hash it, follow the linked list at that position in the hash table until we find the relevant item, and then delete it.

A more efficient way, at the expense of having more items in the hash table than there should be, is to prune the linked list as we are searching it for the current signature. Recall that the linked lists are sorted in descending order by offset value. As we are stepping along a linked list trying to find a maximum match for the current position, if we should get to an item with an offset value that no longer appears in the sliding window, we should delete it and all subsequent items in that linked list. Using this method, we defer removal of old items to our search through the linked list routine—when we're actually there in the middle of the linked list, in fact. This does mean that the hash table contains more items than it needs to, but this is minor compared with the benefit of a speedier algorithm.

We should decide on a hash function, of course. Rather than use one of the general-purpose hash routines discussed in Chapter 7, we'll take advantage of the fact that signatures are three characters long. We make the signature the least significant three bytes of a longint, with the most significant byte being zero. The result is a hash value with virtually no calculation required. As usual, we should make the hash table size a prime number: I chose 521, the smallest prime greater than 512. This means that, on average, 16 signatures from our 8 KB sliding window will map to the same element number—forming a reasonably sized linked list to step along during our search.

It makes sense to create a specialized hash table class for LZ77 decompression since there are some specialized things going on. The code for this hash table class is shown in Listing 11.25.

Listing 11.25: The LZ77 hash table

```
type
  TtdLZSigEnumProc = procedure (aExtraData : pointer;
                          const aSignature : TtdLZSignature;
                                aOffset    : longint);
  PtdLZHashNode = ^TtdLZHashNode;
  TtdLZHashNode = packed record
    hnNext   : PtdLZHashNode;
    hnSig    : TtdLZSignature;
    hnOffset : longint;
  end;
type
  TtdLZHashTable = class
    private
      FHashTable : TList;
      FName      : TtdNameString;
    protected
      procedure htError(aErrorCode  : integer;
                  const aMethodName : TtdNameString);
      procedure htFreeChain(aParentNode : PtdLZHashNode);
    public
      constructor Create;
      destructor Destroy; override;

      procedure Empty;
      function EnumMatches(const aSignature : TtdLZSignature;
                                 aCutOffset : longint;
                                 aAction    : TtdLZSigEnumProc;
                                 aExtraData : pointer) : boolean;
      procedure Insert(const aSignature : TtdLZSignature;
                             aOffset    : longint);

      property Name : TtdNameString
                 read FName write FName;
  end;
constructor TtdLZHashTable.Create;
var
  Inx : integer;
begin
  inherited Create;
  if (LZHashNodeManager = nil) then begin
    LZHashNodeManager := TtdNodeManager.Create(sizeof(TtdLZHashNode));
    LZHashNodeManager.Name := 'LZ77 node manager';
  end;
  {create the hash table, make all elements linked lists with a dummy
  head node}
  FHashTable := TList.Create;
  FHashTable.Count := LZHashTableSize;
```

```
  for Inx := 0 to pred(LZHashTableSize) do
    FHashTable.List^[Inx] := LZHashNodeManager.AllocNodeClear;
end;
destructor TtdLZHashTable.Destroy;
var
  Inx : integer;
begin
  {destroy the hash table completely, including dummy head nodes}
  if (FHashTable <> nil) then begin
    Empty;
    for Inx := 0 to pred(FHashTable.Count) do
      LZHashNodeManager.FreeNode(FHashTable.List^[Inx]);
    FHashTable.Free;
  end;
  inherited Destroy;
end;
procedure TtdLZHashTable.Empty;
var
  Inx : integer;
begin
  for Inx := 0 to pred(FHashTable.Count) do
    htFreeChain(PtdLZHashNode(FHashTable.List^[Inx]));
end;
function TtdLZHashTable.EnumMatches(const aSignature : TtdLZSignature;
                                    aCutOffset : longint;
                                    aAction    : TtdLZSigEnumProc;
                                    aExtraData : pointer) : boolean;
var
  Inx : integer;
  Temp : PtdLZHashNode;
  Dad  : PtdLZHashNode;
begin
  {assume we don't find any}
  Result := false;
  {calculate the hash table index for this signature}
  Inx := (aSignature.AsLong shr 8) mod LZHashTableSize;
  {walk the chain at this index}
  Dad := PtdLZHashNode(FHashTable.List^[Inx]);
  Temp := Dad^.hnNext;
  while (Temp <> nil) do begin
    {if this node has an offset that is less than the cutoff offset,
    then remove the rest of this chain and exit}
    if (Temp^.hnOffset < aCutOffset) then begin
      htFreeChain(Dad);
      Exit;
    end;
    {if the node's signature matches ours, call the action routine}
    if (Temp^.hnSig.AsLong = aSignature.AsLong) then begin
```

```
      Result := true;
      aAction(aExtraData, aSignature, Temp^.hnOffset);
    end;
    {advance to the next node}
    Dad := Temp;
    Temp := Dad^.hnNext;
  end;
end;
procedure TtdLZHashTable.htFreeChain(aParentNode : PtdLZHashNode);
var
  Walker, Temp : PtdLZHashNode;
begin
  Walker := aParentNode^.hnNext;
  aParentNode^.hnNext := nil;
  while (Walker <> nil) do begin
    Temp := Walker;
    Walker := Walker^.hnNext;
    LZHashNodeManager.FreeNode(Temp);
  end;
end;
procedure TtdLZHashTable.Insert(const aSignature : TtdLZSignature;
                                      aOffset    : longint);
var
  Inx      : integer;
  NewNode  : PtdLZHashNode;
  HeadNode : PtdLZHashNode;
begin
  {calculate the hash table index for this signature}
  Inx := (aSignature.AsLong shr 8) mod LZHashTableSize;
  {allocate a new node and insert at the head of the chain at this
  index in the hash table; this ensures that the nodes in the chain
  are in reverse order of offset value}
  NewNode := LZHashNodeManager.AllocNode;
  NewNode^.hnSig := aSignature;
  NewNode^.hnOffset := aOffset;
  HeadNode := PtdLZHashNode(FHashTable.List^[Inx]);
  NewNode^.hnNext := HeadNode^.hnNext;
  HeadNode^.hnNext := NewNode;
end;
```

For efficiency purposes, the hash table makes use of a node manager since we are going to be allocating and deallocating several thousand nodes; this is done inside the Create constructor. We'll be seeing the EnumMatches method again in a moment; it goes through all of the items in the hash table for a particular signature and for each one it finds, it calls the aAction procedure. This is the main matching logic for the LZ77 algorithm.

The sliding window class also has some important functionality apart from storing the previously seen bytes. First, the sliding window reads data from the input stream in large blocks during encoding, so that we don't have to worry about it in the compression routine. Second, it returns the current signature, together with its offset in the input stream. A third method performs the matching: it takes in an offset into the input stream, converts it to an offset in the sliding window buffer, and then compares the characters there with the characters at the current position. It will return the number of characters that match and the distance value so that we can construct a distance/length pair. Listing 11.26 has the remaining implementation of this sliding window class (the code for the other methods can be found in Listing 11.23).

Listing 11.26: The sliding window methods used during compression

```
procedure TtdLZSlidingWindow.Advance(aCount : integer);
var
  ByteCount : integer;
begin
  {advance the start of the sliding window, if required}
  if ((FCurrent - FStart) >= tdcLZSlidingWindowSize) then begin
    inc(FStart, aCount);
    inc(FStartOffset, aCount);
  ebnd;
  {advance the current pointer}
  inc(FCurrent, aCount);
  {check to see if we have advanced into the overflow zone}
  if (FStart >= FMidPoint) then begin
    {move current data back to the start of the buffer}
    ByteCount := FLookAheadEnd - FStart;
    Move(FStart^, FBuffer^, ByteCount);
    {reset the various pointers}
    ByteCount := FStart - FBuffer;
    FStart := FBuffer;
    dec(FCurrent, ByteCount);
    dec(FLookAheadEnd, ByteCount);
    {read some more data from the stream}
    swReadFromStream;
  end;
end;
function TtdLZSlidingWindow.Compare(aOffset   : longint;
                                var aDistance : integer) : integer;
var
  MatchStr  : PAnsiChar;
  CurrentCh : PAnsiChar;
begin
  {Note: when this routine is called it is assumed that at least three
         characters will match between the passed position and the
         current position}
```

```
  {calculate the position in the sliding window for the passed offset
  and its distance from the current position}
  MatchStr := FStart + (aOffset - FStartOffset);
  aDistance := FCurrent - MatchStr;
  inc(MatchStr, 3);
  {calculate the length of the matching characters between this and
  the current position. Don't go above the maximum length. Have a
  special case for the end of the input stream}
  Result := 3;
  CurrentCh := FCurrent + 3;
  if (CurrentCh <> FLookAheadEnd) then begin
    while (Result < tdcLZMaxMatchLength) and
          (MatchStr^ = CurrentCh^) do begin
      inc(Result);
      inc(MatchStr);
      inc(CurrentCh);
      if (CurrentCh = FLookAheadEnd) then
       Break;
    end;
  end;
end;
procedure TtdLZSlidingWindow.GetNextSignature(
                               var aMS     : TtdLZSignature;
                               var aOffset : longint);
var
  P : PAnsiChar;
  i : integer;
begin
  {calculate the length of the match string; usually it's 3, but at
  the end of the input stream it could be 2 or less.}
  if ((FLookAheadEnd - FCurrent) < 3) then
    aMS.AsString[0] := AnsiChar(FLookAheadEnd - FCurrent)
  else
    aMS.AsString[0] := #3;
  P := FCurrent;
  for i := 1 to length(aMS.AsString) do begin
    aMS.AsString[i] := P^;
    inc(P);
  end;
  aOffset := FStartOffset + (FCurrent - FStart);
end;
procedure TtdLZSlidingWindow.swReadFromStream;
var
  BytesRead   : longint;
  BytesToRead : longint;
begin
  {read some more data into the look ahead zone}
  BytesToRead := FBufferEnd - FLookAheadEnd;
```

```
  BytesRead := FStream.Read(FLookAheadEnd^, BytesToRead);
  inc(FLookAheadEnd, BytesRead);
end;
```

And now, with these classes in our armory, we can write the compressor routine shown in Listing 11.27. The routine is slightly complicated by the need to accumulate compression codes eight at a time. This is so we can calculate a flag byte for all eight, and then write the flag byte followed by the eight codes; that's what the Encodings array is all about. However, since we have a lot of supporting code all worked out, the routine itself is not too hard to understand.

Listing 11.27: The LZ77 compression routine

```
type
  PEnumExtraData = ^TEnumExtraData;     {extra data record for the    }
  TEnumExtraData = packed record        {  hash table's FindAll method}
    edSW          : TtdLZSlidingWindow;{..sliding window object}
    edMaxLen      : integer;            {..maximum match length so far}
    edDistMaxMatch: integer;            I
  end;
type
  TEncoding = packed record
    AsDistLen : cardinal;
    AsChar    : AnsiChar;
    IsChar    : boolean;
    {$IFNDEF Delphi1}
    Filler    : word;
    {$ENDIF}
  end;
  TEncodingArray = packed record
    eaData : array [0..7] of TEncoding;
    eaCount: integer;
  end;
procedure MatchLongest(aExtraData : pointer;
                 const aSignature : TtdLZSignature;
                       aOffset    : longint); far;
var
  Len  : integer;
  Dist : integer;
begin
  with PEnumExtraData(aExtraData)^ do begin
    Len := edSW.Compare(aOffset, Dist);
    if (Len > edMaxLen) then begin
      edMaxLen := Len;
      edDistMaxMatch := Dist;
    end;
  end;
```

```
end;
procedure WriteEncodings(aStream    : TSTream;
                     var aEncodings : TEncodingArray);
var
  i : integer;
  FlagByte : byte;
  Mask     : byte;
begin
  {build flag byte, write it to the stream}
  FlagByte := 0;
  Mask := 1;
  for i := 0 to pred(aEncodings.eaCount) do begin
    if not aEncodings.eaData[i].IsChar then
      FlagByte := FlagByte or Mask;
    Mask := Mask shl 1;
  end;
  aStream.WriteBuffer(FlagByte, sizeof(FlagByte));
  {write out the encodings}
  for i := 0 to pred(aEncodings.eaCount) do begin
    if aEncodings.eaData[i].IsChar then
      aStream.WriteBuffer(aEncodings.eaData[i].AsChar, 1)
    else
      aStream.WriteBuffer(aEncodings.eaData[i].AsDistLen, 2);
  end;
  aEncodings.eaCount := 0;
end;
procedure AddCharToEncodings(aStream : TStream;
                             aCh : AnsiChar;
                     var aEncodings : TEncodingArray);
begin
  with aEncodings do begin
    eaData[eaCount].AsChar := aCh;
    eaData[eaCount].IsChar := true;
    inc(eaCount);
    if (eaCount = 8) then
      WriteEncodings(aStream, aEncodings);
  end;
end;
procedure AddCodeToEncodings(aStream   : TStream;
                           aDistance : integer;
                           aLength   : integer;
                       var aEncodings : TEncodingArray);
begin
  with aEncodings do begin
    eaData[eaCount].AsDistLen :=
      (pred(aDistance) shl tdcLZDistanceShift) + (aLength - 3);
    eaData[eaCount].IsChar := false;
    inc(eaCount);
```

```
    if (eaCount = 8) then
      WriteEncodings(aStream, aEncodings);
  end;
end;
procedure TDLZCompress(aInStream, aOutStream : TStream);
var
  HashTable : TtdLZHashTable;
  SlideWin  : TtdLZSlidingWindow;
  Signature : TtdLZSignature;
  Offset    : longint;
  Encodings : TEncodingArray;
  EnumData  : TEnumExtraData;
  LongValue : longint;
  i         : integer;
begin
  HashTable := nil;
  SlideWin := nil;
  try
    HashTable := TtdLZHashTable.Create;
    HashTable.Name := 'LZ77 Compression hash table';
    SlideWin := TtdLZSlidingWindow.Create(aInStream, true);
    SlideWin.Name := 'LZ77 Compression sliding window';
    {write the header to the stream: 'TDLZ' followed by uncompressed
    size of input stream}
    LongValue := TDLZHeader;
    aOutStream.WriteBuffer(LongValue, sizeof(LongValue));
    LongValue := aInStream.Size;
    aOutStream.WriteBuffer(LongValue, sizeof(LongValue));
    {prepare for the compression}
    Encodings.eaCount := 0;
    EnumData.edSW := SlideWin;
    {get the first signature}
    SlideWin.GetNextSignature(Signature, Offset);
    {while the signature is three characters long...}
    while (length(Signature.AsString) = 3) do begin
      {find the longest match in the sliding window using the hash
      table to identify matches}
      EnumData.edMaxLen := 0;
      if HashTable.EnumMatches(Signature,
                               Offset - tdcLZSlidingWindowSize,
                               MatchLongest,
                               @EnumData) then begin
        {we have at least one match: save the distance/length pair
        of the longest match and advance the sliding window by its
        length}
        AddCodeToEncodings(aOutStream,
                           EnumData.edDistMaxMatch,
                           EnumData.edMaxLen,
```

```
                              Encodings);
          SlideWin.Advance(EnumData.edMaxLen);
        end
        else begin
          {we don't have a match: save the current character and
          advance by 1}
          AddCharToEncodings(aOutStream,
                             Signature.AsString[1],
                             Encodings);
          SlideWin.Advance(1);
        end;
        {now add this signature to the hash table}
        HashTable.Insert(Signature, Offset);
        {get the next signature}
        SlideWin.GetNextSignature(Signature, Offset);
      end;
      {if the last signature of all was at most two characters, save
      them as literal character encodings}
      if (length(Signature.AsString) > 0) then begin
        for i := 1 to length(Signature.AsString) do
          AddCharToEncodings(aOutStream,
                             Signature.AsString[i],
                             Encodings);
      end;
      {make sure we write out the final encodings}
      if (Encodings.eaCount > 0) then
        WriteEncodings(aOutStream, Encodings);
    finally
      SlideWin.Free;
      HashTable.Free;
    end;{try..finally}
end;
```

The compression routine works like this. We create the hash table and the sliding window. We write out a signature to the output stream, followed by the length of the uncompressed data. Now we enter the loop. Each time round the loop we get the current signature and try and match it with something we've already seen (the hash table's EnumMatches method). If there were no match, the literal is added to the encoding array and the sliding window advanced by one character; otherwise, the distance/length pair for the longest match is added instead and the sliding window advanced by the number of characters matched.

The code for LZ77 compression is split over several files on the CD: TDLZBase.pas for some common constants, TDLZHash.pas for the specialized hash table, TDLZSWin.pas for the sliding window class, and TDLZCmpr.pas for the compression and decompression code.

Now that we've seen the algorithm and all the code for LZ77 compression and decompression, we can work out some theoretical compression ratios. If we could compress all 10 byte strings in a file down to 2 bytes—in other words, a maximal match every time—for every 80 bytes of the file we'd write out 17 (one flag byte and eight 2-byte codes): a compression ratio of 79 percent. If, on the other hand, we could find no matches in the file at all, we'd actually write out nine bytes for every eight in the original file, a compression ratio of –13 percent. Generally, compressing files with this method would tend to fall somewhere between these two extremes.

Summary

In this chapter we have looked at data compression. We started off with two static minimum redundancy coding algorithms: Shannon-Fano encoding and Huffman encoding. We discussed the drawbacks to these methods—having to read the input data twice and somehow encoding the tree in order that it could be shipped with the compressed data. We then showed an adaptive algorithm, splay tree compression, that removed both of these problems. Finally, we discussed LZ77 compression, an algorithm that uses a dictionary to enable us to compress strings of characters, instead of just singly. Although all four algorithms were interesting in their own right, to implement them we had to make use of several simpler algorithms and data structures that we'd been introduced to in earlier chapters.

Chapter 12

Advanced Topics

In this chapter we'll break free of some of the standard, classical algorithms and move on to some more advanced subjects. Sometimes we'll be using some of the simpler algorithms and data structures in this chapter, but always as stepping stones toward a more complex algorithm. Indeed, this is how we should use the classical algorithms and data structures: as building blocks in our own code, to create new algorithms to implement our own designs (after all, a design is merely the blueprint for our own specialized algorithm).

Readers-Writers Algorithm

In 32-bit Windows multithreaded applications, we have a whole set of problems to master that simply do not occur in single-threaded programs. Certainly, the first problem is how to start and stop threads, but essentially this is an operating system problem: we read the operating system programming documentation and apply our findings.

> This section applies to 32-bit Windows programmers only. Delphi 1 does not support multithreading at all, whereas Kylix and Linux do not have the requisite primitive synchronization objects with which to solve the readers-writers problem.

The bigger problem is that of sharing data between threads, be the data a single integer value or a more complex data structure. Essentially, we have to worry about concurrency issues. If a particular thread is updating a piece of data, then it doesn't make sense for another thread to be reading it at the same time. The reading thread (usually known as a *reader*) may get a partially updated value because the updating thread (the *writer*) hasn't finished its update but the operating system has switched away from it.

If we have two or more writers, we shall get into great trouble fairly quickly if they are updating the same data. However, we won't get any concurrency issues should we have several readers reading the same data.

At the time of writing, people tend to have single processor PCs. The operating system will switch very quickly between threads by stopping a particular thread and then starting up another, in a round robin fashion. The method by which it does this is not of importance (we shouldn't program to a particular scheme since it may change from operating system to operating system), but we should realize early on that we cannot guarantee anything about thread switching, such as when it occurs, whether certain operations are atomic, and so on. Indeed, one of the best pieces of advice I have ever received is that multithreaded applications must always be tested on a multiprocessor machine. On such a machine, the operating system will indeed run two or more threads at the same time. Concurrency problems will rear their ugly head with a vengeance when run on a PC with two or more processors. If you've been lucky running your test program on a single processor PC (maybe the thread switches always seem to be in your favor), your code might crash with bizarre errors on a multiple processor machine.

What we need is a locking mechanism. A writer needs to be able to "lock" some data so that while it is updating the data, no other writer or reader can access it. Similarly, when a reader is reading the data, no writer can update it, and yet other readers can continue accessing it.

With 32-bit Windows we seem to have a lot of synchronization objects: the critical section, the mutex, the semaphore, the event, but nothing that fits the bill particularly well. The critical section and the mutex come close, but they wouldn't allow several readers to access the data at the same time.

If you are using the TList class for your multithreaded shared data, Delphi provides the TThreadedList class, available in Delphi 3 and above. Essentially, the synchronization strategy used by this class is implemented in the following manner: every access to the TList is protected with a critical section or a mutex. In Delphi's version, the TThreadedList provides a method called LockList that enters a critical section and returns the internal TList. The thread is then free to use this TList object until it has finished, at which point the thread routine is supposed to call UnlockList to leave the critical section.

Although this solution works, and works very well, it has a blindingly obvious drawback: only one thread can access the TList at any one time. There is no differentiation between read access (which doesn't alter the list) and write access (which does). As we saw, there could be many readers of the TList at any one time; the restriction is that there should be only one writer. This solution, although simple to implement, is overkill. It does not enable us to make the most efficient use of the TList in a multithreaded manner.

Let's define what we'd like our synchronization object to do. We need a single object that can be used by reader and writer threads to synchronize access to a data structure. It should allow several reader threads to be active at once. It should allow only one writer thread to be active at any one time, and, if one is, no reader threads should be allowed either (they might access something in the data structure that is in the middle of being updated).

Ideally, we should set up the following behavior as well. If a thread wishes to write to the data structure, it should be able to tell the object so. The object will then block any new reader threads from running until all the current reader threads have finished. It will then allow the writer thread to continue. If there is no writer thread waiting, a reader thread should be allowed to access the data structure without hindrance. We should allow several writer threads to become queued in some fashion. This specification means that, in essence, the synchronization object forces a cycle of many reader threads using the TList, followed by a single writer thread, followed by many reader threads, etc.

It seems clear from the definition that there must be some primitive synchronization object that a writer thread can signal, once it has completed its update, to allow reader threads to run (by *primitive* I mean something that is provided by the operating system). Conversely, there must be a synchronization object that the final reader thread of a set of reader threads can signal, once complete, in order to release a writer thread.

The compound object that we're designing requires at least four methods. A reader thread calls the first method in order to start reading (note that it may get blocked inside this routine, waiting for a writer thread to finish its work). This method is sometimes called the *reader registration routine*. Once a reader thread has completed, it needs to call another routine to terminate its use of the synchronization object and maybe release a writer thread (the reader deregistration routine). Similarly there must be two such routines for a writer thread. We'll call these four routines StartReading, StopReading, StartWriting, and StopWriting.

It's fairly easy to describe how this might now work; harder is the actual implementation. StartReading has several jobs. It must first check to see if a writer is waiting. If there is at least one, it must start waiting on a synchronization object of some sort, the most likely candidates being a semaphore or an event (these objects, when signaled, allow several threads to start at once, whereas a mutex or critical section does not). If a writer is actually running at this time, StartReading must block in the same manner. If there is no writer running or waiting, StartReading registers the thread as a reader, the routine exits, and the thread can continue its work immediately.

In the StopReading method, the reader must work out if it is the last reader to be running. If it is, and a writer is waiting, it must release the writer by signaling the object the writer is waiting on. If there is no writer waiting, there can't be any readers waiting either, so the method must leave the object in such a state that either a reader or writer thread could start immediately when the relevant start routine is called.

The StartWriting method does several things, too. If a writer thread is active, it waits on the synchronization object that will be used to release the next writer. If there are one or more reader threads active, it does the same. Otherwise, it registers itself as writing, and exits, allowing the writer to continue.

The StopWriting method deregisters the thread running it as a writer and then checks to see if one or more readers are ready to go. If so, it signals the synchronization object that the readers are waiting on and finishes. If there are no readers, it then checks for a writer waiting. If so, it releases one writer by signaling the object they're all waiting on and then terminates. If neither case applies, it leaves the compound object in a state such that either a reader or a writer could start immediately.

From this functional description, we can extract various pieces of information. One, we need a variable to hold the number of readers waiting. Two, we need a variable to hold the number of writers waiting. Three, we need a variable to hold the number of readers currently executing. Finally, we need a Boolean flag to say that a writer is executing. Finally we need some primitive synchronization objects to wrap it all up.

Since there are four variables, very much interrelated, we shall have to wrap the calls to read and update them inside a critical section or a mutex. We'll use a critical section since they're more efficient. That's synchronization object number one. Each of the four methods would acquire the critical section as a first step, and release it as the final one. However, recall that the methods that allow the reader to start may block inside the routine. It would be an automatic deadlock should this block occur in between the code to acquire or release the controlling critical section, so we must make sure that it occurs outside, after the critical section is released.

Since there can only be one writer active at once, it would seem to make sense for the synchronization object that serializes the writer threads to be a critical section as well since a critical section can only be owned by one thread. In reality, it is easier if we use a semaphore. The reason is simple: we don't actually want to acquire the synchronization object, because there is no great place to release it. Indeed, you will see that we shall wait for a semaphore in one thread and release it from another. This is not possible with a critical section: the thread that acquires the critical section owns it.

The synchronization object for the readers? Either a semaphore or a manual-reset event would be our best choices. Again, our best bet is to use a semaphore since the use of an event object would cause problems (when it is signaled it is only the threads waiting on it that will be released; in our implementation, a thread could be in a state where it hadn't called the WaitFor routine yet).

Listing 12.1 shows the interface for the synchronization class we're creating, the TtdReadWriteSync class. If you look at it, you'll see the various private fields that we'll be using in the four main methods.

Listing 12.1: The TtdReadWriteSync class interface

```
type
  TtdReadWriteSync = class
    private
      FActiveReaders  : integer;
      FActiveWriter   : boolean;
      FBlockedReaders : THandle; {a semaphore}
      FBlockedWriters : THandle; {a semaphore}
      FController     : TRTLCriticalSection;
      FWaitingReaders : integer;
      FWaitingWriters : integer;
    protected
    public
      constructor Create;
      destructor Destroy; override;

      procedure StartReading;
      procedure StartWriting;
      procedure StopReading;
      procedure StopWriting;
  end;
```

The private FBlockedReaders field is the semaphore for the waiting readers, whereas the FBlockedWriters field is the one for the waiting writers. The FController field is the critical section for accessing the object in a serialized manner (unfortunately, we have to have a serializing mechanism like this to ensure that each thread gets a complete uncorrupted picture of the class as a whole).

Listing 12.2 gives the code for the StartReading method.

Listing 12.2: The StartReading method

```
procedure TtdReadWriteSync.StartReading;
var
  HaveToWait : boolean;
begin
```

```
  {acquire the controlling critical section}
  EnterCriticalSection(FController);

  {if there is a writer executing or there is at least one writer
   waiting, add ourselves as a waiting reader, make sure we wait}
  if FActiveWriter or (FWaitingWriters <> 0) then begin
    inc(FWaitingReaders);
    HaveToWait := true;
  end

  {otherwise, add ourselves as another executing reader,
   and make sure we don't wait}
  else begin
    inc(FActiveReaders);
    HaveToWait := false;
  end;

  {release the controlling critical section}
  LeaveCriticalSection(FController);

  {if we have to wait, then do so}
  if HaveToWait then
    WaitForSingleObject(FBlockedReaders, INFINITE);
end;
```

We first acquire the controlling critical section. After this point we have control of the values of the internal fields. If there is at least one writer waiting to have a go, or there is one currently executing, we increment the number of waiting readers, release the controlling critical section and then wait for the "blocked readers" semaphore to become signaled. If there are no writers waiting or running, we increment the number of executing readers, and release the critical section. Once we exit this method, we've either been released from waiting for the semaphore, or we went straight through. Notice that in the second case we incremented the number of running readers, but that in the first we did not. This looks like a bug in the making, but we see how to get around it in a moment.

Let's now look at the StopReading method, shown in Listing 12.3.

Listing 12.3: The StopReading method

```
procedure TtdReadWriteSync.StopReading;
begin
  {acquire the controlling critical section}
  EnterCriticalSection(FController);

  {we've finished reading}
  dec(FActiveReaders);
```

```
    {if we are the last reader reading and there is at
    least one writer waiting, then release it}
   if (FActiveReaders = 0) and (FWaitingWriters <> 0) then begin
     dec(FWaitingWriters);
     FActiveWriter := true;
     ReleaseSemaphore(FBlockedWriters, 1, nil);
   end;

   {release the controlling critical section}
   LeaveCriticalSection(FController);
 end;
```

We first acquire the controlling critical section, as usual. This thread wishes to stop its reading activities and so it decrements the executing readers count. If the resulting value is non-zero, there are other reader threads still active, and so we just release the controlling critical section and exit. If, however, it was the last active reader, the count is now zero, and we need to release a waiting writer (if there is one). To do this we release the blocked writers semaphore; in other words, we increment the count by one, and the system will release one and only one blocked writer thread, immediately reducing the count back to zero again, making sure that all the other writer threads remain blocked. Just before this though, the StopReading method decrements the number of waiting writers and increments the number of running writers. The controlling critical section is then released. The overall effect of this code is that a writing thread is released and the two counts for the writers are adjusted.

On to the StartWriting method, shown in Listing 12.4.

Listing 12.4: The StartWriting method

```
procedure TtdReadWriteSync.StartWriting;
var
  HaveToWait : boolean;
begin
  {acquire the controlling critical section}
  EnterCriticalSection(FController);

  {if there is another writer running or there are active readers, add
   ourselves as a waiting writer, and make sure we wait}
  if FActiveWriter or (FActiveReaders <> 0) then begin
    inc(FWaitingWriters);
    HaveToWait := true;
  end

  {otherwise, add ourselves as another executing writer, and make sure
   we don't wait}
  else begin
    FActiveWriter := true;
```

```
    HaveToWait := false;
  end;

  {release the controlling critical section}
  LeaveCriticalSection(FController);

  {if we have to wait, then do so}
  if HaveToWait then
    WaitForSingleObject(FBlockedWriters, INFINITE);
end;
```

First thing again is to acquire the controlling critical section. If there are any running readers or writers, we increment the number of waiting writers, release the controlling critical section and then wait for the blocked writers semaphore to be released. If there are no other running threads at all, we can start writing straight away. We increment the number of executing writers, release the controlling critical section, and exit the routine. Either way, once we exit the routine, the number of active writers is set to one, either by the method itself or by the StopReading method (if you remember, this happens just before the blocked writers semaphore is signaled).

Finally, we can look at the StopWriting method in Listing 12.5.

Listing 12.5: The StopWriting method

```
procedure TtdReadWriteSync.StopWriting;
var
  i : integer;
begin
  {acquire the controlling critical section}
  EnterCriticalSection(FController);

  {we've finished writing}
  FActiveWriter := false;

  {if there is at least one reader waiting then release them all}
  if (FWaitingReaders <> 0) then begin
    FActiveReaders := FWaitingReaders;
    FWaitingReaders := 0;
    ReleaseSemaphore(FBlockedReaders, FActiveReaders, nil);
  end

  {otherwise, if there is at least one waiting writer, release one}
  else if (FWaitingWriters <> 0) then begin
    dec(FWaitingWriters);
    FActiveWriter := true;
    ReleaseSemaphore(FBlockedWriters, 1, nil);
  end;
```

```
  {release the controlling critical section}
  LeaveCriticalSection(FController);
end;
```

Again, the initial task is to acquire the controlling critical section. Then, because we've finished writing, we decrement the number of active writers. We now check the number of waiting readers. If it is greater than zero, we need to release them all. We enter a loop that decrements the number of waiting readers, increments the number of active readers, and releases the semaphore. This will in turn release one reader from waiting. Eventually at the end of the loop, all reader threads will have been released, and they can be considered to be all active (notice that they will all be exiting their respective call to the StartReading method). If, on the other hand, there are no readers waiting, the method checks for any writers waiting. If there are, it releases just one in the manner already described in StopReading. Finally, no matter what, it releases the controlling critical section.

Finally, the only two methods left are the Create constructor and the Destroy destructor, and they're shown in Listing 12.6.

Listing 12.6: Creating and destroying the synchronization object

```
constructor TtdReadWriteSync.Create;
var
  NameZ : array [0..MAX_PATH] of AnsiChar;
begin
  inherited Create;
  {create the primitive synchronization objects}
  GetRandomObjName(NameZ, 'tdRW.BlockedReaders');
  FBlockedReaders := CreateSemaphore(nil, 0, MaxReaders, NameZ);
  GetRandomObjName(NameZ, 'tdRW.BlockedWriters');
  FBlockedWriters := CreateSemaphore(nil, 0, 1, NameZ);
  InitializeCriticalSection(FController);
end;
destructor TtdReadWriteSync.Destroy;
begin
  CloseHandle(FBlockedReaders);
  CloseHandle(FBlockedWriters);
  DeleteCriticalSection(FController);
  inherited Destroy;
end;
```

As you can see, the Create constructor will create the three primitive synchronization objects, and the destructor Destroy will destroy them.

The full source code for the TtdReadWriteSync class can be found in the TDRWSync.pas file on the CD.

Producers-Consumers Algorithm

Another multithreading algorithm that's closely allied to the readers and writers problem is the one that solves the producers and consumers problem.

> This section applies to 32-bit Windows programmers only. Delphi 1 does not support multithreading at all, whereas Kylix and Linux do not have the requisite primitive synchronization objects with which to solve the producers-consumers problem.

In this situation, we have one or more threads producing data (known as the *producers*) that will be used or consumed by one or more other threads (known as the *consumers*). As you can see, this is a close relation to the readers-writers algorithm: the consumers could be considered as the readers of the data written by the producers. An example of the use of this algorithm is a video streaming program: there will be a thread that downloads the video from a site on the Internet and another thread that plays the downloaded stream. Neither thread has to worry about what the other has to do.

We'll mimic this process with a multithreaded stream copy routine. The producer will copy data from a stream into a queue of buffers. The consumer will then copy the data from the buffers to another stream. We could, for example, have the producer reading an uncompressed data stream and have two consumers of the data: the first compressing the data to another stream using one algorithm, and the other compressing it with another algorithm, presumably so that we can choose the smaller compressed data. In this way the producer can go ahead and try and fill up the buffers in the queue as fast as it can and the consumers can, in turn, try to read them as fast as they can. The producer will stall if the consumers aren't fast enough and the queue fills up with unread buffers; similarly, the consumers will stall if the producer is slow and the queue empties.

Single Producer, Single Consumer Model

Let us discuss the single producer, single consumer model first. We'll then extend this into the single producer, multiple consumer model. What we want to happen is that, once the producer has generated "enough" data, the consumer can be released to start using the data already generated. Therefore, we have three situations to consider: the producer and the consumer are both running in tandem; the consumer is stopped or blocked because the producer hasn't produced enough data; or the producer is blocked because the consumer hasn't read the data it's already produced.

With our stream copy example, the producer will stop if it manages to fill up all the buffers before the consumer has managed to read and process the first. The consumer will block if it manages to process all the buffers before the producer manages to fill another.

The synchronization class we're designing, therefore, has to have four methods: a method the producer calls to start producing; one that's called when there is some data for the consumer to use; one for the consumer to start consuming; and the final one when the consumer has finished consuming enough data that the producer can recommence generating data. As in the readers-writers case, both the start methods can block the threads that call them.

Listing 12.7 shows the complete interface and implementation to the producer-consumer class. As you can see, the implementation is pretty simple.

Listing 12.7: The single producer single consumer synchronization class

```
type
  TtdProduceConsumeSync = class
    private
      FHasData   : THandle; {a semaphore}
      FNeedsData : THandle; {a semaphore}
    protected
    public
      constructor Create(aBufferCount : integer);
      destructor Destroy; override;

      procedure StartConsuming;
      procedure StartProducing;
      procedure StopConsuming;
      procedure StopProducing;
  end;
```

The first method we look at, StartProducing (in Listing 12.8), is the one the producer calls to start producing data. The method will block if the consumer has not used enough data for the producer to replace with more. The method is simple enough: it's a simple wait for a semaphore to be signaled. This "needs data" semaphore will be signaled by the consumer, as we'll see.

Listing 12.8: The StartProducing method

```
procedure TtdProduceConsumeSync.StartProducing;
begin
  {to start producing, the "needs data" semaphore needs to be
  signaled}
  WaitForSingleObject(FNeedsData, INFINITE);
end;
```

The producer will call the second method, StopProducing (in Listing 12.9), to tell the consumer that it has generated some, maybe all, the data and therefore there is data to be consumed. Again a simple implementation: the code merely signals the semaphore the consumer is waiting on, the "has data" semaphore.

Listing 12.9: The StopProducing method

```
procedure TtdProduceConsumeSync.StopProducing;
begin
  {if we've produced some more data, we should signal the
  consumer to use it up}
  ReleaseSemaphore(FHasData, 1, nil);
end;
```

The third method, StartConsuming (in Listing 12.10), is the one the consumer calls before it wants to start consuming data produced by the producer. The method will block when waiting on the "has data" semaphore, which, if the producer has already generated some data, will immediately fall through.

Listing 12.10: The StartConsuming method

```
procedure TtdProduceConsumeSync.StartConsuming;
begin
  {to start consuming, the "has data" semaphore needs to be signaled}
  WaitForSingleObject(FHasData, INFINITE);
end;
```

The last method, StopConsuming (in Listing 12.11), is the method that the consumer calls when it has read enough of (or all) the data so that the producer can generate some more. Obviously, this merely signals the "needs data" semaphore, which will release the producer if it is waiting.

Listing 12.11: The StopConsuming method

```
procedure TtdProduceConsumeSync.StopConsuming;
begin
  {if we've consumed some data, we should signal the
  producer to generate some more}
  ReleaseSemaphore(FNeedsData, 1, nil);
end;
```

The full source code for the TtdProduceConsumeSync class can be found in the TDPCSync.pas file on the CD.

Notice that in using the Windows semaphore object we are implicitly assuming that the data can only be held in 127 buffers or less since every time the producer signals that the consumer can use some more data, the "has data" semaphore's value is incremented by one (and there is a maximum limit of 127 for this value). A similar argument holds for the consumer signaling the "needs data" semaphore. In general, though, that is not a great limitation. A lot of producer-consumer scenarios only use one buffer to transfer data, and the stream copy routine we shall be looking at now uses a queue of buffers with 20 items.

The buffer queue for our stream copy example is implemented as a circular queue. The queue is created with all of its buffers preallocated. Listing 12.12 shows this class.

Note that we do *not* want to use the heap manager during the stream copy process since a critical section protects the heap manager in a multithreaded program. If we start to call memory allocation and deallocation routines from our threads, they will block each other too easily and possibly defeat the purpose of the producer-consumer synchronization class.

The producer will fill up the buffer at the head of the queue and then advance the head pointer. The consumer, on the other hand, will read the data in the buffer at the tail of the queue and then advance the tail. The fill and read processes can occur at the same time since they use different buffers.

Listing 12.12: The TQueuedBuffers class for the stream copy

```
type
  PBuffer = ^TBuffer;
  TBuffer = packed record
    bCount : longint;
    bBlock : array [0..pred(BufferSize)] of byte;
  end;
  PBufferArray = ^TBufferArray;
  TBufferArray = array [0..1023] of PBuffer;
type
  TQueuedBuffers = class
    private
      FBufCount   : integer;
      FBuffers    : PBufferArray;
      FHead       : integer;
      FTail       : integer;
    protected
      function qbGetHead : PBuffer;
      function qbGetTail : PBuffer;
    public
      constructor Create(aBufferCount : integer);
      destructor Destroy; override;
      procedure AdvanceHead;
      procedure AdvanceTail;
      property Head : PBuffer read qbGetHead;
```

```
    property Tail : PBuffer read qbGetTail;
  end;
constructor TQueuedBuffers.Create(aBufferCount : integer);
var
  i : integer;
begin
  inherited Create;
  {allocate the buffers}
  FBuffers := AllocMem(aBufferCount * sizeof(pointer));
  for i := 0 to pred(aBufferCount) do
    GetMem(FBuffers^[i], sizeof(TBuffer));
  FBufCount := aBufferCount;
end;
destructor TQueuedBuffers.Destroy;
var
  i : integer;
begin
  {free the buffers}
  if (FBuffers <> nil) then begin
    for i := 0 to pred(FBufCount) do
      if (FBuffers^[i] <> nil) then
        FreeMem(FBuffers^[i], sizeof(TBuffer));
    FreeMem(FBuffers, FBufCount * sizeof(pointer));
  end;
  inherited Destroy;
end;
procedure TQueuedBuffers.AdvanceHead;
begin
  inc(FHead);
  if (FHead = FBufCount) then
    FHead := 0;
end;
procedure TQueuedBuffers.AdvanceTail;
begin
  inc(FTail);
  if (FTail = FBufCount) then
    FTail := 0;
end;
function TQueuedBuffers.qbGetHead : PBuffer;
begin
  Result := FBuffers^[FHead];
end;
function TQueuedBuffers.qbGetTail : PBuffer;
begin
  Result := FBuffers^[FTail];
end;
```

Less obvious is that the changing of the head and tail pointers do not have to be protected with critical sections and the like. This seems counterintuitive and against all the rules for sharing data between threads; however, the consumer thread never needs to look at the tail pointer. It will be signaled by the producer thread when there is data to be read from the head pointer (and at that point the head and tail pointers will be different), and similarly the producer thread never needs to look at the head pointer since the consumer thread will signal the producer that there is room at the tail of the queue to add more data.

Listing 12.13 shows the producer and consumer classes. These are descended from the TThread class. The code for each overridden Execute method is as previously described. The producer thread enters a loop. Each time through the loop, it calls the StartProducer method of the synchronization object, and then reads a block of data from the source stream into the buffer at the tail of the queue. It then advances the tail pointer. Finally, it calls the StopProducing method and goes around the loop again. The loop terminates once the producer thread has set a buffer to contain no data (the consumer takes this as meaning "end of stream").

The consumer thread's loop, on the other hand, proceeds as follows. First, it calls the StartConsuming method of the synchronization method. Once this method returns, it knows that there is data present in the queued buffers object for it to read. It reads the data in the buffer at the head pointer and writes it to the destination stream. It then advances the head pointer. Since it has just consumed a bufferful of data, it calls the StopConsuming method of the synchronization object, and goes around the loop again. The consumer stops once it receives a buffer that is empty.

Listing 12.13: The producer and consumer classes

```
type
  TProducer = class(TThread)
    private
      FBuffers : TQueuedBuffers;
      FStream  : TStream;
      FSyncObj : TtdProduceConsumeSync;
    protected
      procedure Execute; override;
    public
      constructor Create(aStream  : TStream;
                         aSyncObj : TtdProduceConsumeSync;
                         aBuffers : TQueuedBuffers);
  end;
constructor TProducer.Create(aStream  : TStream;
                             aSyncObj : TtdProduceConsumeSync;
```

```
                                aBuffers : TQueuedBuffers);
begin
  inherited Create(true);
  FStream := aStream;
  FSyncObj := aSyncObj;
  FBuffers := aBuffers;
end;
procedure TProducer.Execute;
var
  Tail : PBuffer;
begin
  {do until the stream is exhausted...}
  repeat
    {signal that we want to start producing}
    FSyncObj.StartProducing;
    {read a block from the stream into the tail buffer}
    Tail := FBuffers.Tail;
    Tail^.bCount := FStream.Read(Tail^.bBlock, BufferSize);
    {advance the tail pointer}
    FBuffers.AdvanceTail;
    {as we've now written a new buffer, signal that we've produced}
    FSyncObj.StopProducing;
  until (Tail^.bCount = 0);
end;
type
  TConsumer = class(TThread)
    private
      FBuffers : TQueuedBuffers;
      FStream  : TStream;
      FSyncObj : TtdProduceConsumeSync;
    protected
      procedure Execute; override;
    public
      constructor Create(aStream  : TStream;
                         aSyncObj : TtdProduceConsumeSync;
                         aBuffers : TQueuedBuffers);
  end;
constructor TConsumer.Create(aStream  : TStream;
                             aSyncObj : TtdProduceConsumeSync;
                             aBuffers : TQueuedBuffers);
begin
  inherited Create(true);
  FStream := aStream;
  FSyncObj := aSyncObj;
  FBuffers := aBuffers;
end;
procedure TConsumer.Execute;
var
```

```
  Head : PBuffer;
begin
  {signal that we want to start consuming}
  FSyncObj.StartConsuming;
  {get the head buffer}
  Head := FBuffers.Head;
  {while the head buffer is not empty...}
  while (Head^.bCount <> 0) do begin
    {write a block from the head buffer into the stream}
    FStream.Write(Head^.bBlock, Head^.bCount);
    {advance the head pointer}
    FBuffers.AdvanceHead;
    {as we've read and processed a buffer, signal that we've consumed}
    FSyncObj.StopConsuming;
    {signal that we want to start consuming again}
    FSyncObj.StartConsuming;
    {get the head buffer}
    Head := FBuffers.Head;
  end;
end;
```

Finally, we can see the stream copy routine in Listing 12.14. The routine accepts two parameters: the input stream and the output stream. It creates a special object of type TQueuedBuffers. This object contains all the resources and methods necessary to implement a queued set of buffers. It also creates an instance of the TtdProducerConsumerSync class to act as the synchronization object to keep the producer and the consumer in sync.

Listing 12.14: Multithreaded stream copy

```
procedure ThreadedCopyStream(aSrcStream, aDestStream : TStream);
var
  SyncObj  : TtdProduceConsumeSync;
  Buffers  : TQueuedBuffers;
  Producer : TProducer;
  Consumer : TConsumer;
  WaitArray : array [0..1] of THandle;
begin
  SyncObj := nil;
  Buffers := nil;
  Producer := nil;
  Consumer := nil;
  try
    {create the synchronization object, the queued
    buffer object (with 20 buffers) and the two threads}
    SyncObj := TtdProduceConsumeSync.Create(20);
    Buffers := TQueuedBuffers.Create(20);
    Producer := TProducer.Create(aSrcStream, SyncObj, Buffers);
    Consumer := TConsumer.Create(aDestStream, SyncObj, Buffers);
```

```
    {save the thread handles so we can wait on them}
    WaitArray[0] := Producer.Handle;
    WaitArray[1] := Consumer.Handle;
    {start the threads up}
    Consumer.Resume;
    Producer.Resume;
    {wait for the threads to finish}
    WaitForMultipleObjects(2, @WaitArray, true, INFINITE);
  finally
    Producer.Free;
    Consumer.Free;
    Buffers.Free;
    SyncObj.Free;
  end;
end;
```

The copy routine then creates the two threads that between them will perform the copy, and resumes them (they are created suspended). It then waits for both threads to complete and cleans up. The full code can be found in the TstCopy.dpr and TstCopyu.pas files on the CD.

Single Producer, Multiple Consumer Model

That particular application of the producer-consumer model was fairly easy to implement, so now let's consider the single producer, multiple consumer model. Here we have a thread that is providing data. We assume that we have a number of threads that want to read the data being produced. The example we mentioned earlier used two consumers that compressed the data with different algorithms. Another example could be found in an HTML browser. Let's say the producer is downloading a Web page from a remote site and one consumer is reading the HTML code to save the page to disk, another is reading the HTML in order to display it on screen, and a third is reading the data in order to display a progress bar. Writing these processes as separate consumers makes each of them easier to write; each only has one task to accomplish.

What, then, is required for a synchronization object to keep the producer and consumers in step? Firstly, the producer has to let all of the consumers know that there is data to be read. Each of these consumers will presumably work at different speeds and so they will get through the data at different rates. This implies that there must be one "has data" semaphore per consumer. We assume that there is a list of buffers for the producer to replenish with data, and furthermore, that this list is organized as a circular queue. We therefore need a single tail pointer (under the exclusive control of the producer) and a head pointer per consumer, since presumably each consumer will read the buffers at a different rate.

What about the producer? When does it know that it can refill a data buffer? Obviously, it can only do so once the last (and presumably the slowest) consumer has read enough data so that there is room to replenish with new data (if you like, once a buffer comes free again). This implies in turn that there be a count of consumers for each data buffer. Every time a consumer reads a buffer, it decrements this count (the number of consumers that have yet to read this buffer) so that the last consumer to use some data knows that it is the last consumer since the count would then be zero after decrementing. Notice that the consumers are threads and therefore we need to perform the decrementing in a thread-safe manner.

Listing 12.15 shows this expanded class, TtdProduceManyConsumeSync, which enables several consumers to consume data generated by a single producer. Each consumer thread is assumed to have a unique identifier starting at zero (in practice this isn't hard to arrange, but if necessary, this class could be expanded to allow for consumers to register and deregister themselves and be allocated identifiers on the fly). The consumer then uses this identifier, a numerical value, in its calls to the StartConsumer and StopConsumer methods.

Listing 12.15: The single producer multiple consumer synchronization class

```
type
  TtdProduceManyConsumeSync = class
    private
      FBufferCount   : integer; {count of data buffers}
      FBufferInfo    : TList;   {a circular queue of buffer info}
      FBufferTail    : integer; {tail of the buffer circular queue}
      FConsumerCount : integer; {count of consumers}
      FConsumerInfo  : TList;   {info for each consumer}
      FNeedsData     : THandle; {a semaphore}
    protected
    public
      constructor Create(aBufferCount   : integer;
                         aConsumerCount : integer);
      destructor Destroy; override;

      procedure StartConsuming(aId : integer);
      procedure StartProducing;
      procedure StopConsuming(aId : integer);
      procedure StopProducing;
  end;
```

It is assumed in this class that the producer is filling buffers that the consumers then use. The buffers have no tangible existence in the class itself; providing them is up to the user of the class.

The StartProducing method in Listing 12.16 works in much that same way as the previous case: it merely waits for the "needs data" semaphore to be signaled. (This semaphore is created such that it has a signal value equal to the number of buffers, so that the producer could fill up all the buffers.)

The StopProducing method, also in Listing 12.16, has a little more work this time. Firstly, the buffer it has just filled must have its consumer usage count set equal to the number of consumers. Note the producer thread must signal all of the "has data" semaphores, one per consumer, so say that there is one more buffer to use.

Listing 12.16: The StartProducing and StopProducing methods

```
type
  PBufferInfo = ^TBufferInfo;
  TBufferInfo = packed record
    biToUseCount : integer; {count of consumers still to use buffer}
  end;
type
  PConsumerInfo = ^TConsumerInfo;
  TConsumerInfo = packed record
    ciHasData : THandle; {a semaphore}
    ciHead    : integer; {head pointer into the buffer queue}
  end;
procedure TtdProduceManyConsumeSync.StartProducing;
begin
  {to start producing, the "needs data" semaphore needs to be
  signaled}
  WaitForSingleObject(FNeedsData, INFINITE);
end;
procedure TtdProduceManyConsumeSync.StopProducing;
var
  i : integer;
  BufInfo      : PBufferInfo;
  ConsumerInfo : PConsumerInfo;
begin
  {if we've produced some more data, set the count of consumers for
  the buffer at the tail to cover all of them}
  BufInfo := PBufferInfo(FBufferInfo[FBufferTail]);
  BufInfo^.biToUseCount := FConsumerCount;
  inc(FBufferTail);
  if (FBufferTail >= FBufferCount) then
    FBufferTail := 0;
  {now signal all the consumers that there is more data}
  for i := 0 to pred(FConsumerCount) do begin
    ConsumerInfo := PConsumerInfo(FConsumerInfo[i]);
    ReleaseSemaphore(ConsumerInfo^.ciHasData, 1, nil);
```

```
  end;
end;
```

To look at the consumer's side of things, see Listing 12.17. The StartConsuming method must wait on the "has data" semaphore for the consumer thread concerned (each thread has a consumer ID). The StopConsuming method is the most complex of the entire synchronization class. It first gets the buffer information record for its own head pointer. It then safely decrements the count of consumers that have yet to read (consume) this buffer. (The InterlockedDecrement routine is part of the Win32 API. It decrements its parameter in a thread-safe manner, and returns the new value of the parameter.) The method then increments the head pointer for this consumer thread and, if the number of consumers yet to read this buffer is now zero, it signals the "needs data" semaphore to get the producer to generate more data.

Listing 12.17: The StartConsuming and StopConsuming methods

```
procedure TtdProduceManyConsumeSync.StartConsuming(aId : integer);
var
  ConsumerInfo : PConsumerInfo;
begin
  {to start consuming, the "has data" semaphore needs to be signaled
  for that particular consumer id}
  ConsumerInfo := PConsumerInfo(FConsumerInfo[aId]);
  WaitForSingleObject(ConsumerInfo^.ciHasData, INFINITE);
end;
procedure TtdProduceManyConsumeSync.StopConsuming(aId : integer);
var
  BufInfo      : PBufferInfo;
  ConsumerInfo : PConsumerInfo;
  NumToRead    : integer;
begin
  {we've consumed the data in the buffer at our head pointer}
  ConsumerInfo := PConsumerInfo(FConsumerInfo[aId]);
  BufInfo := PBufferInfo(FBufferInfo[ConsumerInfo^.ciHead]);
  NumToRead := InterlockedDecrement(BufInfo^.biToUseCount);
  {advance our head pointer}
  inc(ConsumerInfo^.ciHead);
  if (ConsumerInfo^.ciHead >= FBufferCount) then
    ConsumerInfo^.ciHead := 0;
  {if we were the last to use this buffer, we should signal the
  producer to generate some more}
  if (NumToRead = 0) then
    ReleaseSemaphore(FNeedsData, 1, nil);
end;
```

The constructor and destructor for this class have a large number of synchronization objects to create and destroy, as well as all the buffer information and the consumer information.

Listing 12.18: Creating and destroying the synchronization object

```
constructor TtdProduceManyConsumeSync.Create(aBufferCount   : integer;
                                             aConsumerCount : integer);
var
  NameZ : array [0..MAX_PATH] of AnsiChar;
  i     : integer;
  BufInfo : PBufferInfo;
  ConsumerInfo : PConsumerInfo;
begin
  inherited Create;
  {create the "needs data" semaphore}
  GetRandomObjName(NameZ, 'tdPMC.NeedsData');
  FNeedsData := CreateSemaphore(nil, aBufferCount, aBufferCount, NameZ);
  if (FNeedsData = INVALID_HANDLE_VALUE) then
    RaiseLastWin32Error;
  {create the buffer circular queue and populate it}
  FBufferCount := aBufferCount;
  FBufferInfo := TList.Create;
  FBufferInfo.Count := aBufferCount;
  for i := 0 to pred(aBufferCount) do begin
    New(BufInfo);
    BufInfo^.biToUseCount := 0;
    FBufferInfo[i] := BufInfo;
  end;
  {create the consumer info list and populate it}
  FConsumerCount := aConsumerCount;
  FConsumerInfo := TList.Create;
  FConsumerInfo.Count := aConsumerCount;
  for i := 0 to pred(aConsumerCount) do begin
    New(ConsumerInfo);
    FConsumerInfo[i] := ConsumerInfo;
    GetRandomObjName(NameZ, 'tdPMC.HasData');
    ConsumerInfo^.ciHasData :=
       CreateSemaphore(nil, 0, aBufferCount, NameZ);
    if (ConsumerInfo^.ciHasData = INVALID_HANDLE_VALUE) then
      RaiseLastWin32Error;
    ConsumerInfo^.ciHead := 0;
  end;
end;
destructor TtdProduceManyConsumeSync.Destroy;
var
  i : integer;
  BufInfo : PBufferInfo;
  ConsumerInfo : PConsumerInfo;
```

```
begin
  {destroy the "needs data" semaphore}
  if (FNeedsData <> INVALID_HANDLE_VALUE) then
    CloseHandle(FNeedsData);
  {destroy the consumer info list}
  if (FConsumerInfo <> nil) then begin
    for i := 0 to pred(FConsumerCount) do begin
      ConsumerInfo := PConsumerInfo(FConsumerInfo[i]);
      if (ConsumerInfo <> nil) then begin
        if (ConsumerInfo^.ciHasData <> INVALID_HANDLE_VALUE) then
          CloseHandle(ConsumerInfo^.ciHasData);
        Dispose(ConsumerInfo);
      end;
    end;
    FConsumerInfo.Free;
  end;
  {destroy the buffer info list}
  if (FBufferInfo <> nil) then begin
    for i := 0 to pred(FBufferCount) do begin
      BufInfo := PBufferInfo(FBufferInfo[i]);
      if (BufInfo <> nil) then
        Dispose(BufInfo);
    end;
    FBufferInfo.Free;
  end;
  inherited Destroy;
end;
```

Although there seems to be a lot going on in Listing 12.18, in reality it's all very easy. The Create constructor must create a list of buffers, and populate the list with the required number of buffer records. It must also create a list of consumers, and populate that list with the required number of consumer records. Each consumer record requires a semaphore to be created for it. The Destroy destructor must tear all this down and free everything.

The full source code for the TtdProduceManyConsumeSync class can be found in the TDPCSync.pas file on the CD.

For an example program, we'll show a multithreaded stream copy routine, one that copies a stream to three other streams. As with the example in Listing 12.14, the producer will read the source stream into up to 20 buffers. The consumers, of which there are now three, will read the buffers and write to their own streams.

The TQueuedBuffers class (Listing 12.19) has to change a little since it has to store the head pointer for several consumers and hence must have an array of them.

Listing 12.19: The TQueuedBuffers class for the multiple consumer model

```
type
  PBuffer = ^TBuffer;
  TBuffer = packed record
    bCount : longint;
    bBlock : array [0..pred(BufferSize)] of byte;
  end;
  PBufferArray = ^TBufferArray;
  TBufferArray = array [0..pred(MaxBuffers)] of PBuffer;
  TQueuedBuffers = class
    private
      FBufCount      : integer;
      FBuffers       : PBufferArray;
      FConsumerCount : integer;
      FHead          : array [0..pred(MaxConsumers)] of integer;
      FTail          : integer;
    protected
      function qbGetHead(aInx : integer) : PBuffer;
      function qbGetTail : PBuffer;
    public
      constructor Create(aBufferCount   : integer;
                         aConsumerCount : integer);
      destructor Destroy; override;
      procedure AdvanceHead(aConsumerId : integer);
      procedure AdvanceTail;
      property Head[aInx : integer] : PBuffer read qbGetHead;
      property Tail : PBuffer read qbGetTail;
      property ConsumerCount : integer read FConsumerCount;
  end;
constructor TQueuedBuffers.Create(aBufferCount   : integer;
                                  aConsumerCount : integer);
var
  i : integer;
begin
  inherited Create;
  {allocate the buffers}
  FBuffers := AllocMem(aBufferCount * sizeof(pointer));
  for i := 0 to pred(aBufferCount) do
    GetMem(FBuffers^[i], sizeof(TBuffer));
  FBufCount := aBufferCount;
  FConsumerCount := aConsumerCount;
end;
destructor TQueuedBuffers.Destroy;
var
  i : integer;
begin
  {free the buffers}
  if (FBuffers <> nil) then begin
```

```
    for i := 0 to pred(FBufCount) do
      if (FBuffers^[i] <> nil) then
        FreeMem(FBuffers^[i], sizeof(TBuffer));
    FreeMem(FBuffers, FBufCount * sizeof(pointer));
  end;
  inherited Destroy;
end;
procedure TQueuedBuffers.AdvanceHead(aConsumerId : integer);
begin
  inc(FHead[aConsumerId]);
  if (FHead[aConsumerId] = FBufCount) then
    FHead[aConsumerId] := 0;
end;
procedure TQueuedBuffers.AdvanceTail;
begin
  inc(FTail);
  if (FTail = FBufCount) then
    FTail := 0;
end;
function TQueuedBuffers.qbGetHead(aInx : integer) : PBuffer;
begin
  Result := FBuffers^[FHead[aInx]];
end;
function TQueuedBuffers.qbGetTail : PBuffer;
begin
  Result := FBuffers^[FTail];
end;
```

The producer and consumer classes are next (Listing 12.20). The producer class hasn't changed much from its previous incarnation, whereas the consumer class now has an ID number with which it accesses the buffers object to get the correct head pointer.

Listing 12.20: The producer and consumer classes

```
type
  TProducer = class(TThread)
    private
      FBuffers : TQueuedBuffers;
      FStream  : TStream;
      FSyncObj : TtdProduceManyConsumeSync;
    protected
      procedure Execute; override;
    public
      constructor Create(aStream  : TStream;
                         aSyncObj : TtdProduceManyConsumeSync;
                         aBuffers : TQueuedBuffers);
  end;
constructor TProducer.Create(aStream  : TStream;
```

```
                              aSyncObj : TtdProduceManyConsumeSync;
                              aBuffers : TQueuedBuffers);
begin
  inherited Create(true);
  FStream := aStream;
  FSyncObj := aSyncObj;
  FBuffers := aBuffers;
end;
procedure TProducer.Execute;
var
  Tail : PBuffer;
begin
  {do until the stream is exhausted...}
  repeat
    {signal that we're about to start producing}
    FSyncObj.StartProducing;
    {read a block from the stream into the tail buffer}
    Tail := FBuffers.Tail;
    Tail^.bCount := FStream.Read(Tail^.bBlock, 1024);
    {advance the tail pointer}
    FBuffers.AdvanceTail;
    {signal that we've stopped producing}
    FSyncObj.StopProducing;
  until (Tail^.bCount = 0);
end;
type
  TConsumer = class(TThread)
    private
      FBuffers : TQueuedBuffers;
      FID      : integer;
      FStream  : TStream;
      FSyncObj : TtdProduceManyConsumeSync;
    protected
      procedure Execute; override;
    public
      constructor Create(aStream  : TStream;
                         aSyncObj : TtdProduceManyConsumeSync;
                         aBuffers : TQueuedBuffers;
                         aID      : integer);
  end;
constructor TConsumer.Create(aStream  : TStream;
                             aSyncObj : TtdProduceManyConsumeSync;
                             aBuffers : TQueuedBuffers;
                             aID      : integer);
begin
  inherited Create(true);
  FStream := aStream;
  FSyncObj := aSyncObj;
```

```
  FBuffers := aBuffers;
  FID := aID;
end;
procedure TConsumer.Execute;
var
  Head : PBuffer;
begin
  {signal that we want to start consuming}
  FSyncObj.StartConsuming(FID);
  {get our head buffer}
  Head := FBuffers.Head[FID];
  {while the head buffer is not empty...}
  while (Head^.bCount <> 0) do begin
    {write a block from the head buffer into the stream}
    FStream.Write(Head^.bBlock, Head^.bCount);
    {advance our head pointer}
    FBuffers.AdvanceHead(FID);
    {we've now finished with this buffer}
    FSyncObj.StopConsuming(FID);
    {signal that we want to start consuming again}
    FSyncObj.StartConsuming(FID);
    {get our head buffer}
    Head := FBuffers.Head[FID];
  end;
  {we've now finished with the final buffer}
  FSyncObj.StopConsuming(FID);
end;
```

The last piece of the jigsaw is the stream copy routine in Listing 12.21.

Listing 12.21: Stream copy using the producer-consumer model

```
procedure ThreadedMultiCopyStream(aSrcStream   : TStream;
                                  aDestCount   : integer;
                                  aDestStreams : PStreamArray);
var
  i : integer;
  SyncObj   : TtdProduceManyConsumeSync;
  Buffers   : TQueuedBuffers;
  Producer  : TProducer;
  Consumer  : array [0..pred(MaxConsumers)] of TConsumer;
  WaitArray : array [0..MaxConsumers] of THandle;
begin
  SyncObj := nil;
  Buffers := nil;
  Producer := nil;
  for i := 0 to pred(MaxConsumers) do
    Consumer[i] := nil;
  for i := 0 to MaxConsumers do
```

```
    WaitArray[i] := 0;
  try
    {create the synchronization object}
    SyncObj := TtdProduceManyConsumeSync.Create(20, aDestCount);
    {create the queued buffer object}
    Buffers := TQueuedBuffers.Create(20, aDestCount);
    {create the producer thread, save its handle}
    Producer := TProducer.Create(aSrcStream, SyncObj, Buffers);
    WaitArray[0] := Producer.Handle;
    {create the consumer threads, save their handles}
    for i := 0 to pred(aDestCount) do begin
      Consumer[i] := TConsumer.Create(
                       aDestStreams^[i], SyncObj, Buffers, i);
      WaitArray[i+1] := Consumer[i].Handle;
    end;
    {start the threads up}
    for i := 0 to pred(aDestCount) do
      Consumer[i].Resume;
    Producer.Resume;
    {wait for the threads to finish}
    WaitForMultipleObjects(1+aDestCount, @WaitArray, true, INFINITE);
  finally
    Producer.Free;
    for i := 0 to pred(aDestCount) do
      Consumer[i].Free;
    Buffers.Free;
    SyncObj.Free;
  end;
end;
```

Most of it is the same housekeeping as in the single consumer model in Listing 12.14, except that this time there are several consumers to take care of. The full code is in the TstNCpy.dpr and TstNCpyu.pas files on the CD.

Finding Differences between Two Files

Consider this problem. You have two versions of a source file, one of which is a later version with some changes. How can you find the differences between these two files? Which lines were added, and which deleted? Which were changed?

Programs that do this kind of functionality abound. There's diff, the grandfather of all file difference programs. With the Microsoft Windows SDK, you get one called WinDiff. Microsoft's Visual SourceSafe product also has a feature whereby you can select two versions of a file stored in the database and view their differences.

> This section applies to 32-bit programmers only. The algorithm shown is recursive and is a heavy user of the program stack. Delphi 1 does not support a stack large enough to implement the algorithm, even for moderately sized files.

Spend a couple of minutes trying to devise an algorithm to do this. I've tried before, and it's difficult. We can simplify things a little straight away: changes to a line can be viewed as a deletion of the old line and an insertion of the new one. We needn't get into semantic problems trying to decide whether a line has changed a little or a lot; we'll just view all text file changes as a set of lines being deleted and another set of new lines being inserted.

Calculating the LCS of Two Strings

The algorithm we need is known as the longest common subsequence (LCS) algorithm. We'll first take a look at how it works with strings, and then we'll extend our discoveries to text files.

I'm sure we've all played those children's word puzzles where you change one word into another by altering a single letter at a time. All the intermediary steps should be words as well. So, to take a simple example, to change CAT into DOG, we might take the following steps: CAT, COT, COG, DOG.

These word games consist merely of deleting a letter and inserting a new one at each step. If we didn't have the limitations imposed by the rules of the puzzle, we could certainly transform any word into another by deleting all the old characters and inserting all the new ones. That's the sledgehammer approach, but we'd like to be a little subtler.

Suppose our goal is to find the smallest number of edits needed to convert one word to another. Let's take as an example changing BEGIN to FINISH. Looking at this you can see that we should delete B, E, G, and then insert F before what's left, and I, S, H afterward. So how do we implement this as an algorithm?

One way is to look at the subsequences of each word and see if we can't find a common subsequence between the two words. A *subsequence* of a string is formed by removing one or more characters from the string. The remaining characters should not be rearranged. For example, the four-letter subsequences of BEGIN are EGIN, BGIN, BEIN, BEGN, and BEGI. As you can see, you form them by dropping each character in turn. The three-letter subsequences are BEG, BEI, BEN, BGI, BGN, BIN, EGI, EGN, EIN, and GIN. There are 10 two-letter subsequences and five single-letter ones. So, for a five-letter word there are a total of 30 possible subsequences, and in fact, it can be shown that for an n letter sequence the number of subsequences is about 2^n. Make a note of that conclusion for now.

The brute-force algorithm, if I may call it that, is to look at the two words BEGIN and FINISH and enumerate their five-letter subsequences to see if any match. None do, so do the same for the four-letter subsequences of each word. Again, none match, so proceed to the three-letter subsequences. Yet another no, so we move on to the two-letter subsequences. There's IN, the longest common subsequence between the two words. From that we can work out what to delete and what to insert.

Now for small words, like our example, this process isn't too bad. But now imagine that we're looking at enumerating all of the subsequences of a 100-character string. As we've already seen, the number of these is 2^{100}. The brute-force algorithm is exponential; it is $O(2^n)$. For even medium-sized strings, the algorithm's search space grows alarmingly fast. With the growth in the search space comes a dramatic decrease in the time taken to find the solution. To drive home the point: suppose we could generate one thousand billion subsequences per second (that is, 2^{40}, or one thousand subsequences per cycle on a one gigahertz PC). A year is about 2^{25} seconds, so, to generate the entire set of subsequences for a 100-character string would take 2^{35} years—a number with 11 digits. And remember here that the 100-character string is merely a simplification of what we want to do: find differences for a 600-line source file, for example.

The subsequence idea does have its merits though; we just need to approach it from a different angle. Instead of enumerating all of the subsequences in the two words and comparing, let's see if we can't do it in a stepwise progression.

To start, let's suppose we have managed to work out a longest common subsequence for two words (we'll abbreviate "longest common subsequence" to "LCS" from now on). We could then draw lines between the letters in the LCS from the first word to the corresponding ones in the second word. These lines would not cross. (Why? Because a subsequence is defined so that no rearrangement of the letters is allowed; therefore the letters in the LCS would appear in the same order in both words.) Figure 12.1 shows the LCS for the words "banana" and "abracadabra" (that is, b, a, a, a) with lines drawn to show the equivalent subsequence letters. Notice that there are several possible longest common subsequences for this word pair; the figure just shows the first (the one that appears closest to the left).

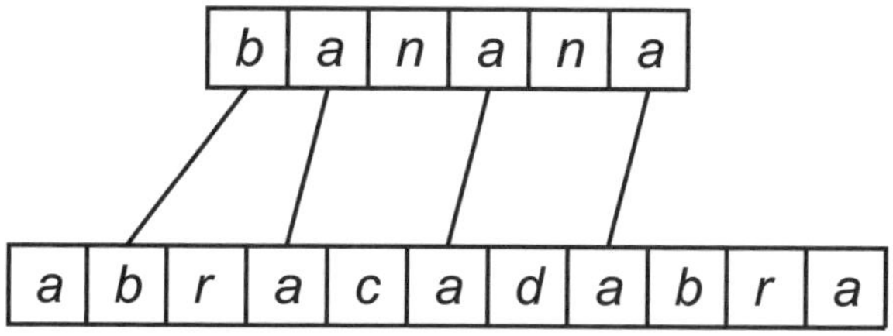

Figure 12.1: The LCS for banana and abracadabra

So, we've worked out, one way or another, an LCS between the two words. The length of this subsequence is x, let's say. Take a look at the final letters for the two words. If neither is part of a linking line, and they are the same letter, then this *must* appear as the final letter in the LCS, and there would be a linking line between them. (If it doesn't appear as the final letter of the subsequence, then we could add it, making the LCS one letter longer, contradicting our assumption about having the longest one in the first place.) Remove this final letter from both the two words and the subsequence. This shortened subsequence of length $x-1$ is an LCS of the two abbreviated words. (If it weren't, then there would be a common subsequence of x or larger for the two abbreviated words. Adding in the final letters would increase the length of this new common subsequence by one, so that there would be a common subsequence between the complete words of $x+1$ letters or longer. This contradicts our assumption that we had an LCS.)

Suppose now that the final letter in the LCS were not the same as the final letter of the first word. This would mean that the LCS between the two complete words was also the LCS between the first word less its final letter and the second word (if it weren't, we could add back the final letter of the first word and find a longer LCS for the two words). The same argument applies to the case where the final letter of the second word was not the same as the final letter in the LCS.

This is all very well, but what does this show? A longest common subsequence contains within it a longest common subsequence of truncated parts of the two words. To find an LCS of X and Y, we break the problem down into smaller problems. If the final character of X and Y were the same, we would have to find the LCS of X and Y minus their final letters, and then add in this common letter. If not, we would have to find out the LCS of X minus its final letter and Y, and that of X and Y minus its final letter, and choose the longer of the two. A simple recursive algorithm.

We should describe the algorithm is a little more detail first, though, to avoid a problem that the simple solution would raise.

We are trying to calculate the LCS of two strings, *X* and *Y*. First, we define that the *X* string has *n* characters and the *Y* string *m*. We shall write X_i to mean the string formed from the first *i* characters of *X*. *i* can also take the value zero to mean the empty string (this convention will make things easier to understand in a moment). X_n is then the whole string. Using this nomenclature, the algorithm reduces to this: if the last two characters of X_n and Y_m are the same, the longest common subsequence is equal to the LCS of X_{n-1} and Y_{m-1} plus this last character. If they are not the same, the LCS is equal to the longer of the LCS of X_{n-1} and Y_m and the LCS of X_n and Y_{m-1}. To calculate these "smaller" LCSs, we recursively call the same routine.

However, note that to calculate the LCS of X_{n-1} and Y_m, we may have to calculate the LCS of X_{n-2} and Y_{m-1}, the LCS of X_{n-1} and Y_{m-1}, and the LCS of X_{n-2} and Y_m. The second of these might have been calculated already. If we're not careful we could end up calculating the same LCSs over and over again. Ideally, we would need a cache of previously calculated results to avoid this problem of recalculation. Since we have two indexes, one for the *X* string and one for the *Y* string, it make sense to use a matrix.

What should we store at each element of this matrix cache? The obvious answer is the LCS itself, a string. However, this isn't too helpful: it helps us calculate the LCS, yes, but it doesn't help us in calculating which characters need to be deleted from *X* and which new characters need to be inserted to produce *Y*. A better answer is to store enough information at each element to enable us to generate the LCS as a O(1) algorithm, and also enough information to calculate the edit commands to go from *X* to *Y*.

One item of information we really need is the length of the LCS at every point. Using this, we can easily work out the length of the LCS for the two complete strings, using the recursive algorithm. To be able to generate the LCS string itself, we'd need to know which path we took through the matrix cache. For this we'd need to store a pointer at each element that pointed to the previous element that was used to build the LCS for this one.

However, before we can discuss walking the LCS matrix, we have to build one. For now, we'll assume that each element of the matrix will store two pieces of information: the length of the LCS at that point and the position of the previous matrix element that forms the prequel for this LCS. There are only three possible cells for this latter value: the one just above (north), the one to the left (west), and the one on the upper left diagonal (northwest), so we might as well use an enumerated type for this.

Let's calculate the LCS by hand for the BEGIN/FINISH case. We'll have a 6x7 matrix (we take into account empty substrings, so we should start indexing at 0). Rather than fill in the matrix recursively (it's hard for us to keep all those recursive calls straight), we'll calculate all the cells iteratively from the top left all the way down to the bottom right, going from left to right along each row for every row. The first row and column are easy: all zeros. Why? Because the longest common subsequence between an empty string and any other string is zero, that's why. From this we can start working out the LCS for cell (1,1), or the two strings B and F. The two final characters of these one-character strings are not equal; therefore the length of the LCS is the maximum of the previous cells to the north and west. These are both zero, so their maximum value and hence the value of this cell is zero. Cell (1,2) is for the strings B and FI. Again, zero. Cell (2,1) is for BE and F: the LCS length is zero again. Continuing like this we can fill in all the 42 cells in the matrix. Notice the cells for the matching characters: this is where the LCS length gets greater. Table 12.1 shows the answer.

Table 12.1: The LCS matrix for BEGIN and FINISH

		F	I	N	I	S	H
	0	0	0	0	0	0	0
B	0	0	0	0	0	0	0
E	0	0	0	0	0	0	0
G	0	0	0	0	0	0	0
I	0	0	1	1	1	1	1
N	0	0	1	2	2	2	2

Writing this manual process in code is not too difficult. For starters, I decided early on to make the matrix cache a class. Internally to this class, the matrix is held as a TList of TLists, with the major TList being rows in the matrix and the minor TLists being cells across the columns for a particular row. The matrix class is also specific to the problem at hand; it would be overkill to design, code, and use a generic matrix class. The code for the matrix class is shown in Listing 12.22.

Listing 12.22: The matrix class for the LCS algorithm

```
type
  TtdLCSDir = (ldNorth, ldNorthWest, ldWest);
  PtdLCSData = ^TtdLCSData;
  TtdLCSData = packed record
    ldLen  : integer;
    ldPrev : TtdLCSDir;
  end;
type
  TtdLCSMatrix = class
    private
      FCols     : integer;
      FMatrix   : TList;
```

```
      FRows     : integer;
    protected
      function mxGetItem(aRow, aCol : integer) : PtdLCSData;
      procedure mxSetItem(aRow, aCol : integer;
                          aValue : PtdLCSData);
    public
      constructor Create(aRowCount, aColCount : integer);
      destructor Destroy; override;
      procedure Clear;
      property Items[aRow, aCol : integer] : PtdLCSData
                 read mxGetItem write mxSetItem; default;
      property RowCount : integer read FRows;
      property ColCount : integer read FCols;
  end;
constructor TtdLCSMatrix.Create(aRowCount, aColCount : integer);
var
  Row     : integer;
  ColList : TList;
begin
  {create the ancestor}
  inherited Create;
  {simple validation}
  Assert((aRowCount > 0) and (aColCount > 0),
         'TtdLCSMatrix.Create: Invalid Row or column count');
  FRows := aRowCount;
  FCols := aColCount;
  {create the matrix: it'll be a TList of TLists in row order}
  FMatrix := TList.Create;
  FMatrix.Count := aRowCount;
  for Row := 0 to pred(aRowCount) do begin
    ColList := TList.Create;
    ColList.Count := aColCount;
    TList(FMatrix.List^[Row]) := ColList;
  end;
end;
destructor TtdLCSMatrix.Destroy;
var
  Row : integer;
begin
  {destroy the matrix}
  if (FMatrix <> nil) then begin
    Clear;
    for Row := 0 to pred(FRows) do
      TList(FMatrix.List^[Row]).Free;
    FMatrix.Free;
  end;
  {destroy the ancestor}
  inherited Destroy;
```

```
end;
procedure TtdLCSMatrix.Clear;
var
  Row, Col : integer;
  ColList  : TList;
begin
  for Row := 0 to pred(FRows) do begin
    ColList := TList(FMatrix.List^[Row]);
    if (ColList <> nil) then
      for Col := 0 to pred(FCols) do begin
        if (ColList.List^[Col] <> nil) then
          Dispose(PtdLCSData(ColList.List^[Col]));
        ColList.List^[Col] := nil;
      end;
  end;
end;
function TtdLCSMatrix.mxGetItem(aRow, aCol : integer) : PtdLCSData;
begin
  if not ((0 <= aRow) and (aRow < RowCount) and
          (0 <= aCol) and (aCol < ColCount)) then
    raise Exception.Create(
        'TtdLCSMatrix.mxGetItem: Row or column index out of bounds');
  Result := PtdLCSData(TList(FMatrix.List^[aRow]).List^[aCol]);
end;
procedure TtdLCSMatrix.mxSetItem(aRow, aCol : integer;
                       aValue : PtdLCSData);
begin
  if not ((0 <= aRow) and (aRow < RowCount) and
          (0 <= aCol) and (aCol < ColCount)) then
    raise Exception.Create(
        'TtdLCSMatrix.mxSetItem: Row or column index out of bounds');
  TList(FMatrix.List^[aRow]).List^[aCol] := aValue;
end;
```

The next step is to write a class that implemented the LCS algorithm for strings. Listing 12.23 shows the interface and the housekeeping parts of the TtdStringLCS class.

Listing 12.23: The TtdStringLCS class

```
type
  TtdStringLCS = class
    private
      FFromStr : string;
      FMatrix  : TtdLCSMatrix;
      FToStr   : string;
    protected
      procedure slFillMatrix;
      function slGetCell(aFromInx, aToInx : integer) : integer;
```

```
    procedure slWriteChange(var F : System.Text;
                            aFromInx, aToInx : integer);
  public
    constructor Create(const aFromStr, aToStr : string);
    destructor Destroy; override;
    procedure WriteChanges(const aFileName : string);
end;
constructor TtdStringLCS.Create(const aFromStr, aToStr : string);
begin
  {create the ancestor}
  inherited Create;
  {save the strings}
  FFromStr := aFromStr;
  FToStr := aToStr;
  {create the matrix}
  FMatrix := TtdLCSMatrix.Create(succ(length(aFromStr)),
                                 succ(length(aToStr)));
  {now fill in the matrix}
  slFillMatrix;
end;
destructor TtdStringLCS.Destroy;
begin
  {destroy the matrix}
  FMatrix.Free;
  {destroy the ancestor}
  inherited Destroy;
end;
```

I had a dilemma when I first implemented the LCS algorithm: should I follow the recursive algorithm already outlined, or should I follow the manual process I just described? I wrote both in order to answer some questions (which is easier, which uses less memory, which is faster?), and I started with the iterative method. Listing 12.24 shows this iterative solution.

Listing 12.24: Calculating the LCS iteratively

```
procedure TtdStringLCS.slFillMatrix;
var
  FromInx : integer;
  ToInx   : integer;
  NorthLen: integer;
  WestLen : integer;
  LCSData : PtdLCSData;
begin
  {Create the empty items along the top and left sides}
  for ToInx := 0 to length(FToStr) do begin
    New(LCSData);
    LCSData^.ldLen := 0;
    LCSData^.ldPrev := ldWest;
```

```
    FMatrix[0, ToInx] := LCSData;
  end;
  for FromInx := 1 to length(FFromStr) do begin
    New(LCSData);
    LCSData^.ldLen := 0;
    LCSData^.ldPrev := ldNorth;
    FMatrix[FromInx, 0] := LCSData;
  end;
  {fill in the matrix, row by row, from left to right}
  for FromInx := 1 to length(FFromStr) do begin
    for ToInx := 1 to length(FToStr) do begin
      {create the new item}
      New(LCSData);
      {if the two current chars are equal, increment the count
      from the northwest, that's our previous item}
      if (FFromStr[FromInx] = FToStr[ToInx]) then begin
        LCSData^.ldPrev := ldNorthWest;
        LCSData^.ldLen := succ(FMatrix[FromInx-1, ToInx-1]^.ldLen);
      end
      {otherwise the current characters are different: use the
      maximum of the north or west (west preferred)}
      else begin
        NorthLen := FMatrix[FromInx-1, ToInx]^.ldLen;
        WestLen := FMatrix[FromInx, ToInx-1]^.ldLen;
        if (NorthLen > WestLen) then begin
          LCSData^.ldPrev := ldNorth;
          LCSData^.ldLen := NorthLen;
        end
        else begin
          LCSData^.ldPrev := ldWest;
          LCSData^.ldLen := WestLen;
        end;
      end;
      {set the item in the matrix}
      FMatrix[FromInx, ToInx] := LCSData;
    end;
  end;
  {at this point the item in the bottom right hand corner has
  the length of the LCS and the calculation is complete}
end;
```

We start off by filling the top row and the left column of the matrix with null cells. These cells all have an LCS length of zero (remember that they describe an LCS between an empty string and another), and I just set the direction flag to point to the previous cell that's closer to (0,0). Next comes the loop within a loop (the column-by-column loop within the row-by-row loop). For every row, we calculate the LCS for each of the cells from left to right. We do this for all rows from top to bottom. First we test to see whether the two characters referenced by the cell are equal. (A cell in the matrix is at the junction of a character in the From string and one in the To string.) If they are, then we know that the LCS length at this cell is equal to the LCS length from the cell adjacent at the northwest, plus one. Notice that the way we're calculating the cells means that this cell being referenced has already been calculated (that's one reason why we precalculated the cells along the top and left sides). If the two characters are not equal, we have to look at the cells to the north and the west. We select the one that has the longest LCS length, and use that length for this cell. If the two lengths are equal, we could select either one. We will, however, make a rule that we would preferentially choose the one to the left. The reason for this is that, once we have calculated a path through the matrix to produce the LCS of both strings, the deletions from the first string will occur before the insertions into the second string.

Notice that the method shown in Listing 12.24 takes a constant time for two strings, no matter how many similarities or differences there are. If the two strings have length *n* and *m*, the time taken in the main loop will be proportional to *n*m*, since that's the number of cells that have to be calculated. (Remember: the cell for which you really want the answer is the last one to be calculated, the one at the bottom right corner).

Listing 12.25 shows the LCS algorithm implemented using a recursive method. The recursive routine is coded as a function that returns the LCS length for a particular cell, given by its row and column index (which are, after all, indexes into the From string and the To string).

Listing 12.25: Calculating the LCS recursively

```
function TtdStringLCS.slGetCell(aFromInx, aToInx : integer) : integer;
var
  LCSData : PtdLCSData;
  NorthLen: integer;
  WestLen : integer;
begin
  if (aFromInx = 0) or (aToInx = 0) then
    Result := 0
  else begin
    LCSData := FMatrix[aFromInx, aToInx];
    if (LCSData <> nil) then
      Result := LCSData^.ldLen
    else begin
      {create the new item}
      New(LCSData);
      {if the two current chars are equal, increment the count
      from the northwest, that's our previous item}
      if (FFromStr[aFromInx] = FToStr[aToInx]) then begin
```

```
          LCSData^.ldPrev := ldNorthWest;
          LCSData^.ldLen := slGetCell(aFromInx-1, aToInx-1) + 1;
        end
        {otherwise the current characters are different: use the
        maximum of the north or west (west preferred)}
        else begin
          NorthLen := slGetCell(aFromInx-1, aToInx);
          WestLen := slGetCell(aFromInx, aToInx-1);
          if (NorthLen > WestLen) then begin
            LCSData^.ldPrev := ldNorth;
            LCSData^.ldLen := NorthLen;
          end
          else begin
            LCSData^.ldPrev := ldWest;
            LCSData^.ldLen := WestLen;
          end;
        end;
        {set the item in the matrix}
        FMatrix[aFromInx, aToInx] := LCSData;
        {return the length of this LCS}
        Result := LCSData^.ldLen;
      end;
    end;
end;
```

The first big difference is that we don't have to generate the null cells along the top and down the left side; that's now taken care of with a simple If statement. (To be fair, we could get away without calculating them in the iterative case, but the inner code in the loop would become that much more complicated to understand and maintain, so in the interest of simplicity, we precalculated those cells.) If the cell has already been calculated, we simply return its LCS length. If not, then we do the same checking as before: are the two characters equal? If yes, add one to the LCS length from the cell at the northwest. If no, use the larger LCS length value from the cells at the north or at the west. These LCS values are, of course, calculated from recursive calls to this routine.

Using both the iterative and recursive versions, I generated the matrix for calculating the LCS of "illiteracy" and "innumeracy." (This pair of words has an LCS of length 6: ieracy.) Tables 12.2 and 12.3 show the results. With the recursive version, a large number of cells are not calculated at all (these are the ones denoted by a question mark). They form no part in the final LCS.

Table 12.2: The iterative LCS matrix for "illiteracy" and "innumeracy"

<table>
<tr><th></th><th></th><th>i</th><th>n</th><th>n</th><th>u</th><th>m</th><th>e</th><th>r</th><th>a</th><th>c</th><th>y</th></tr>
<tr><td></td><td>–0</td><td>–0</td><td>–0</td><td>–0</td><td>–0</td><td>–0</td><td>–0</td><td>–0</td><td>–0</td><td>–0</td><td>–0</td></tr>
<tr><td>i</td><td>| 0</td><td>\ 1</td><td>–1</td><td>–1</td><td>–1</td><td>–1</td><td>–1</td><td>–1</td><td>–1</td><td>–1</td><td>–1</td></tr>
<tr><td>l</td><td>| 0</td><td>| 1</td><td>–1</td><td>–1</td><td>–1</td><td>–1</td><td>–1</td><td>–1</td><td>–1</td><td>–1</td><td>–1</td></tr>
<tr><td>l</td><td>| 0</td><td>| 1</td><td>–1</td><td>–1</td><td>–1</td><td>–1</td><td>–1</td><td>–1</td><td>–1</td><td>–1</td><td>–1</td></tr>
<tr><td>i</td><td>| 0</td><td>\ 1</td><td>–1</td><td>–1</td><td>–1</td><td>–1</td><td>–1</td><td>–1</td><td>–1</td><td>–1</td><td>–1</td></tr>
<tr><td>t</td><td>| 0</td><td>| 1</td><td>–1</td><td>–1</td><td>–1</td><td>–1</td><td>–1</td><td>–1</td><td>–1</td><td>–1</td><td>–1</td></tr>
<tr><td>e</td><td>| 0</td><td>| 1</td><td>–1</td><td>–1</td><td>–1</td><td>–1</td><td>\ 2</td><td>–2</td><td>–2</td><td>–2</td><td>–2</td></tr>
<tr><td>r</td><td>| 0</td><td>| 1</td><td>–1</td><td>–1</td><td>–1</td><td>–1</td><td>| 2</td><td>\ 3</td><td>–3</td><td>–3</td><td>–3</td></tr>
<tr><td>a</td><td>| 0</td><td>| 1</td><td>–1</td><td>–1</td><td>–1</td><td>–1</td><td>| 2</td><td>| 3</td><td>\ 4</td><td>–4</td><td>–4</td></tr>
<tr><td>c</td><td>| 0</td><td>| 1</td><td>–1</td><td>–1</td><td>–1</td><td>–1</td><td>| 2</td><td>| 3</td><td>| 4</td><td>\ 5</td><td>–5</td></tr>
<tr><td>y</td><td>| 0</td><td>| 1</td><td>–1</td><td>–1</td><td>–1</td><td>–1</td><td>| 2</td><td>| 3</td><td>| 4</td><td>| 5</td><td>\ 6</td></tr>
</table>

Table 12.3: The recursive LCS matrix for "illiteracy" and "innumeracy"

<table>
<tr><th></th><th></th><th>i</th><th>n</th><th>n</th><th>u</th><th>m</th><th>e</th><th>r</th><th>a</th><th>c</th><th>y</th></tr>
<tr><td></td><td>? 0</td><td>? 0</td><td>? 0</td><td>? 0</td><td>? 0</td><td>? 0</td><td>? 0</td><td>? 0</td><td>? 0</td><td>? 0</td><td>? 0</td></tr>
<tr><td>i</td><td>? 0</td><td>\ 1</td><td>–1</td><td>–1</td><td>–1</td><td>–1</td><td>? 0</td><td>? 0</td><td>? 0</td><td>? 0</td><td>? 0</td></tr>
<tr><td>l</td><td>? 0</td><td>| 1</td><td>–1</td><td>–1</td><td>–1</td><td>–1</td><td>? 0</td><td>? 0</td><td>? 0</td><td>? 0</td><td>? 0</td></tr>
<tr><td>l</td><td>? 0</td><td>| 1</td><td>–1</td><td>–1</td><td>–1</td><td>–1</td><td>? 0</td><td>? 0</td><td>? 0</td><td>? 0</td><td>? 0</td></tr>
<tr><td>i</td><td>? 0</td><td>\ 1</td><td>–1</td><td>–1</td><td>–1</td><td>–1</td><td>? 0</td><td>? 0</td><td>? 0</td><td>? 0</td><td>? 0</td></tr>
<tr><td>t</td><td>? 0</td><td>| 1</td><td>–1</td><td>–1</td><td>–1</td><td>–1</td><td>? 0</td><td>? 0</td><td>? 0</td><td>? 0</td><td>? 0</td></tr>
<tr><td>e</td><td>? 0</td><td>? 0</td><td>? 0</td><td>? 0</td><td>? 0</td><td>? 0</td><td>\ 2</td><td>? 0</td><td>? 0</td><td>? 0</td><td>? 0</td></tr>
<tr><td>r</td><td>? 0</td><td>? 0</td><td>? 0</td><td>? 0</td><td>? 0</td><td>? 0</td><td>? 0</td><td>\ 3</td><td>? 0</td><td>? 0</td><td>? 0</td></tr>
<tr><td>a</td><td>? 0</td><td>? 0</td><td>? 0</td><td>? 0</td><td>? 0</td><td>? 0</td><td>? 0</td><td>? 0</td><td>\ 4</td><td>? 0</td><td>? 0</td></tr>
<tr><td>c</td><td>? 0</td><td>? 0</td><td>? 0</td><td>? 0</td><td>? 0</td><td>? 0</td><td>? 0</td><td>? 0</td><td>? 0</td><td>\ 5</td><td>? 0</td></tr>
<tr><td>y</td><td>? 0</td><td>? 0</td><td>? 0</td><td>? 0</td><td>? 0</td><td>? 0</td><td>? 0</td><td>? 0</td><td>? 0</td><td>? 0</td><td>\ 6</td></tr>
</table>

At this point we have a matrix that defines the longest common subsequence. How can we use it? One possibility is to write a routine that creates a text file describing the changes, the *edit sequence*. This would make it easier for us to write the equivalent for the text file case—the ultimate aim of this section.

Listing 12.26 shows a simple traversal technique, which we can modify to suit our needs. It comprises two methods: the first gets called by the user with a file name, and the second is a recursive routine that writes the data to the file. All the hard work occurs inside this second routine. Since the matrix encodes the LCS path backward (in other words, you have to start at the finish, and work your way back to the start to discover the path that you then follow forward) we write the method to call itself recursively first and then write out the data for the current position. We have to make sure a recursive routine terminates. This is taken to be the case where the routine is called for cell (0,0). We don't write anything to the file for this case. If the index into the To string is zero, we make the recursive call moving up the matrix (the index into the From string is decremented) and the action is taken to be the deletion of the current character in the From string. If the index into the From string is zero, we make the recursive call moving left through the matrix, and the action is inserting the current character into the To string. Finally, if both indexes are non-zero, we find the cell in the matrix, make the requisite recursive call, and write the action to the file. For a down move, it's a deletion; for a right move, it's an insertion; for a diagonal move, it's neither (the character is "carried over"). For a deletion we use a right facing arrow (->); for an insertion, a left facing arrow (<-); and for a carry over, nothing.

Listing 12.26: Printing the edit sequence

```
procedure TtdStringLCS.slWriteChange(var F : System.Text;
                                     aFromInx, aToInx : integer);
var
  Cell : PtdLCSData;
begin
  {if both indexes are zero, this is the first
  cell of the LCS matrix, so just exit}
  if (aFromInx = 0) and (aToInx = 0) then
    Exit;
  {if the from index is zero, we're flush against the left
  hand side of the matrix, so go up; this'll be a deletion}
  if (aFromInx = 0) then begin
    slWriteChange(F, aFromInx, aToInx-1);
    writeln(F, '-> ', FToStr[aToInx]);
  end
  {if the to index is zero, we're flush against the top side
  of the matrix, so go left; this'll be an insertion}
  else if (aToInx = 0) then begin
    slWriteChange(F, aFromInx-1, aToInx);
    writeln(F, '<- ', FFromStr[aFromInx]);
  end
  {otherwise see what the cell says to do}
  else begin
    Cell := FMatrix[aFromInx, aToInx];
    case Cell^.ldPrev of
      ldNorth :
        begin
          slWriteChange(F, aFromInx-1, aToInx);
          writeln(F, '<- ', FFromStr[aFromInx]);
        end;
      ldNorthWest :
```

```
        begin
          slWriteChange(F, aFromInx-1, aToInx-1);
          writeln(F, '    ', FFromStr[aFromInx]);
        end;
      ldWest :
        begin
          slWriteChange(F, aFromInx, aToInx-1);
          writeln(F, '-> ', FToStr[aToInx]);
        end;
    end;
  end;
end;
procedure TtdStringLCS.WriteChanges(const aFileName : string);
var
  F : System.Text;
begin
  System.Assign(F, aFileName);
  System.Rewrite(F);
  try
    slWriteChange(F, length(FFromStr), length(FToStr));
  finally
    System.Close(F);
  end;
end;
```

Here is the text file that was generated for converting "illiteracy" into "innumeracy."

```
<- i
<- l
<- l
   i
<- t
-> n
-> n
-> u
-> m
   e
   r
   a
   c
   y
```

This representation is easy to understand at a glance, but can be expanded as needed. You can easily see the longest common subsequence (i, e, r, a, c, y), and you can identify the deletions and insertions.

Given that the method is a recursive method, we should think about the stack depth required to run it. If the strings had nothing in common at all, the edit sequence would be to delete all of the characters in the first and insert all of the characters in the second. If the first has *n* characters and the second, *m*, then the stack depth would be proportional to *n*+*m*.

Calculating the LCS of Two Text Files

Having seen the solution for two strings, we can now modify it to calculate the LCS and generate the edit commands for two text files. To make it easier for ourselves, we shall read both files into TStringLists. Obviously we're now comparing whole text lines (strings) at a time, instead of characters, but the main implementation remains pretty much the same. Listing 12.27 shows the interface and housekeeping methods.

Listing 12.27: The TtdFileLCS class

```
type
  TtdFileLCS = class
    private
      FFromFile : TStringList;
      FMatrix   : TtdLCSMatrix;
      FToFile   : TStringList;
    protected
      function slGetCell(aFromInx, aToInx : integer) : integer;
      procedure slWriteChange(var F : System.Text;
                                  aFromInx, aToInx : integer);
    public
      constructor Create(const aFromFile, aToFile : string);
      destructor Destroy; override;
      procedure WriteChanges(const aFileName : string);
  end;
constructor TtdFileLCS.Create(const aFromFile, aToFile : string);
begin
  {create the ancestor}
  inherited Create;
  {read the files}
  FFromFile := TStringList.Create;
  FFromFile.LoadFromFile(aFromFile);
  FToFile := TStringList.Create;
  FToFile.LoadFromFile(aToFile);
  {create the matrix}
  FMatrix := TtdLCSMatrix.Create(FFromFile.Count, FToFile.Count);
  {now fill in the matrix}
  slGetCell(pred(FFromFile.Count), pred(FToFile.Count));
end;
destructor TtdFileLCS.Destroy;
begin
  {destroy the matrix}
```

```
  FMatrix.Free;
  {free the string lists}
  FFromFile.Free;
  FToFile.Free;
  {destroy the ancestor}
  inherited Destroy;
end;
```

There is one problem to address, though: with strings, we start counting the characters at 1; with a string list, we start counting the strings (the lines in the original file) at 0. Therefore, there must be some changes.

The first change is to just code the recursive method. If you recall, the iterative method required the cells along the top and left of the matrix to be preallocated and set to 0, whereas the recursive method used an If statement to do the work. That potentially saves us a lot of memory (after all, text files might have several hundred or thousand lines).

The next change is to count from 0, as already specified. The recursive routine takes care of this automatically.

Listing 12.28 shows the recursive method for generating the LCS for a pair of files.

Listing 12.28: Generating the LCS of a pair of files

```
function TtdFileLCS.slGetCell(aFromInx, aToInx : integer) : integer;
var
  LCSData : PtdLCSData;
  NorthLen: integer;
  WestLen : integer;
begin
  if (aFromInx = -1) or (aToInx = -1) then
    Result := 0
  else begin
    LCSData := FMatrix[aFromInx, aToInx];
    if (LCSData <> nil) then
      Result := LCSData^.ldLen
    else begin
      {create the new item}
      New(LCSData);
      {if the two current lines are equal, increment the count
      from the northwest, that's our previous item}
      if (FFromFile[aFromInx] = FToFile[aToInx]) then begin
        LCSData^.ldPrev := ldNorthWest;
        LCSData^.ldLen := slGetCell(aFromInx-1, aToInx-1) + 1;
      end
      {otherwise the current lines are different: use the
      maximum of the north or west (west preferred)}
```

```
      else begin
        NorthLen := slGetCell(aFromInx-1, aToInx);
        WestLen := slGetCell(aFromInx, aToInx-1);
        if (NorthLen > WestLen) then begin
          LCSData^.ldPrev := ldNorth;
          LCSData^.ldLen := NorthLen;
        end
        else begin
          LCSData^.ldPrev := ldWest;
          LCSData^.ldLen := WestLen;
        end;
      end;
      {set the item in the matrix}
      FMatrix[aFromInx, aToInx] := LCSData;
      {return the length of this LCS}
      Result := LCSData^.ldLen;
    end;
  end;
end;
```

The method to write out the edit sequence to convert the first file into the other hasn't changed much, apart from writing out the lines instead of the characters. Listing 12.29 shows the routine.

Listing 12.29: Writing out the edit sequence for a pair of files

```
procedure TtdFileLCS.slWriteChange(var F : System.Text;
                                   aFromInx, aToInx : integer);
var
  Cell : PtdLCSData;
begin
  {if both indexes are less than zero, this is the first
  cell of the LCS matrix, so just exit}
  if (aFromInx = -1) and (aToInx = -1) then
    Exit;
  {if the from index is less than zero, we're flush against the
  left hand side of the matrix, so go up; this'll be a deletion}
  if (aFromInx = -1) then begin
    slWriteChange(F, aFromInx, aToInx-1);
    writeln(F, '-> ', FToFile[aToInx]);
  end
  {if the to index is less than zero, we're flush against the
  top side of the matrix, so go left; this'll be an insertion}
  else if (aToInx = -1) then begin
    slWriteChange(F, aFromInx-1, aToInx);
    writeln(F, '<- ', FFromFile[aFromInx]);
  end
  {otherwise see what the cell says to do}
  else begin
```

```
    Cell := FMatrix[aFromInx, aToInx];
    case Cell^.ldPrev of
      ldNorth :
        begin
          slWriteChange(F, aFromInx-1, aToInx);
          writeln(F, '<- ', FFromFile[aFromInx]);
        end;
      ldNorthWest :
        begin
          slWriteChange(F, aFromInx-1, aToInx-1);
          writeln(F, '   ', FFromFile[aFromInx]);
        end;
      ldWest :
        begin
          slWriteChange(F, aFromInx, aToInx-1);
          writeln(F, '-> ', FToFile[aToInx]);
        end;
    end;
  end;
end;
procedure TtdFileLCS.WriteChanges(const aFileName : string);
var
  F : System.Text;
begin
  System.Assign(F, aFileName);
  System.Rewrite(F);
  try
    slWriteChange(F, pred(FFromFile.Count), pred(FToFile.Count));
  finally
    System.Close(F);
  end;
end;
```

Summary

In this chapter we looked at three advanced algorithms, the first two dealing with multithreaded applications, and the third with an important but little-known algorithm to find the differences in two editions of a file.

For multithreaded applications, we saw how to solve both the readers-writers problem, an important algorithm in many such programs, and the producers-consumers problem, an algorithm which can be used in many situations where large amounts of data have to be processed simultaneously in different ways.

The longest common subsequence algorithm is more specialized, but finds its way into source control systems as well as diff-type programs.

Epilogue

To put it mildly, this book has been an interesting exercise (as well as bloody hard work).

It has been my viewpoint for years that Delphi, Visual Basic, and now Kylix, have produced/are producing/will produce programmers that have no real knowledge of our craft. Yes, they can write applications with drag-and-drop and a little glue code and some event handlers. But any application that is worth writing needs some of the skills and expertise and background that traditional computer science and programming can teach us. We can muddle though, certainly, and the program will work, but it'll turn out like the difference between a hard-boiled and a Fabergé egg.

I admit the only computer science background I have is self-taught. I obtained a mathematics degree at Kings College, University of London, during which I took a single programming course—FORTRAN on decks of punched cards, results later this afternoon, thank you—but as far as I remember there was no real attempt at teaching us formal computer science (there was also none of the immediacy you get these days programming PCs). I would have loved to have seen linked lists in a language that didn't have local variables or pointers. But that didn't stop me. I started to investigate and learn all this stuff. I wrestled to try and convert it from Knuth's MIX language, or C, or worse. I tried to distill practical viewpoints from textbooks that left the Delete operation as Exercise 4.25. Doing all this was also a great way to learn the language.

I contend that if you are shown what possibilities there are, in the language with which you are most familiar, you'll know next time to use a hash table, or to push the keyboard away and draw a state machine on a pad, or to write YATLD (Yet Another TList Delegate). That's the main reason for this book: it shows you what you can achieve once you know what's available. The main reason for the book's code is to use it directly. (Do you need a regular expression evaluator? Then use the one we develop in Chapter 10. Add the unit to the Uses list, and go on.)

I warn you that this book is incomplete. In planning it, I had more to leave out than I thought possible ("So, where are the B-trees, Julian?"). Read it, then go forth and discover what else is out there.

References

This is a list of all the references that I used to write this book. Some of them are vital—without them I would not have been able to understand some algorithms and explain them to you in terms of Delphi code. Others just contain minor expositions of topics covered elsewhere, yet they've done so in a way that I found illuminating.

1. Abramowitz, Milton, and Irene A. Stegun. *Handbook of Mathematical Functions*. Dover Publications, Inc., 1964.
2. Aho, Alfred V., Ravi Sethi, and Jeffrey D. Ullman. *Compilers: Principles, Techniques, and Tools*. Addison-Wesley, 1986.
3. Beck, Kent. *Extreme Programming Explained*. Addison-Wesley, 2000.
4. Binstock, Andrew, and John Rex. *Practical Algorithms for Programmers*. Addison-Wesley, 1995.
5. Cormen, Thomas H., Charles E. Leiserson, and Ronald L. Rivest. *Introduction to Algorithms*. MIT Press, 1990.
6. Folk, Michael J., and Bill Zoellick. *File Structures*. 2nd Ed. Addison-Wesley, 1992.
7. Guibas L.J., and R. Sedgewick. "A dichromatic framework for balanced trees." *Proceedings of the 19th Annual Symposium on Foundations of Computer Science*, 1978.
8. Jones, Douglas W. "Application of Splay Trees to Data Compression." *Communications of the ACM*, Vol. 31 (1988), pp. 996-1007.
9. Kane, Thomas S. *The New Oxford Guide to Writing*. Oxford University Press, 1988.
10. King, Stephen. *On Writing*. Scribner, 2000.
11. Knuth, Donald E. *The Art of Computer Programming: Fundamental Algorithms*. 3rd Ed. Addison-Wesley, 1997.
12. ________. *The Art of Computer Programming: Seminumerical Algorithms*. 3rd Ed. Addison-Wesley, 1998.
13. ________. *The Art of Computer Programming: Sorting and Searching*. 2nd Ed. Addison-Wesley, 1998.
14. L'Ecuyer, Pierre. "Efficient and Portable Combined Random Number Generators." *Communications of the ACM*, Vol. 31 (1988), pp. 742-749, 774.

15. Nelson, Mark. *The Data Compression Book.* M&T Publishing, 1991.
16. Park, S.K., and K.W. Miller. "Random Number Generators: Good Ones are Hard to Find." *Communications of the ACM,* vol. 31 (1988), pp. 1192-1201.
17. Pham, Thuan Q. and Pankaj K. Garg. *Multithreaded Programming with Win32.* Prentice Hall, 1999.
18. Pugh, William. "Skip Lists: A Probabilistic Alternative to Balanced Trees." *Communications of the ACM,* Vol. 33 (1990), pp. 668-676.
19. Robbins, John. *Debugging Applications.* Microsoft Press, 2000.
20. Sedgewick, Robert. *Algorithms*. 2nd Ed. Addison-Wesley, 1988.
21. ________. *Algorithms in C.* 3rd Ed. Addison-Wesley, 1998.
22. Sleator, D.D., and R.E. Tarjan. "Self-adjusting binary search trees." *Journal of the ACM* (1985).
23. Thorpe, Danny. *Delphi Component Design.* Addison-Wesley Developers Press, 1996.
24. Wood, Derick. *Data Structures, Algorithms, and Performance.* Addison-Wesley, 1993.

Index

T

U

V

W

Z

About the CD

The companion CD-ROM is divided into the following three folders:

- BookSrc—contains all the source code discussed in the book
- Ezdsl—the author's freeware library EZDSL, which provide an object-oriented programming interface for classical data structures for Delphi
- TrialRun—several executables from TurboPower Software Company

For more information about EZDSL, see the ezdsl.doc file.

Warning: Opening the CD package makes this book nonreturnable.

CD/Source Code Usage License Agreement